52D CONGRESS, } SENATE. { EXTRACT FROM
2d Session. } { REPORT No. 1394.

WHOLESALE PRICES, WAGES,

AND

TRANSPORTATION.

REPORT

OF CHANGES IN

RAILWAY TRANSPORTATION RATES

ON

FREIGHT TRAFFIC THROUGHOUT THE UNITED STATES,

1852 to 1893.

PREPARED BY

McCAIN,

FOR THE SENATE COMMITTEE ON FINANCE.

WASHINGTON:
GOVERNMENT PRINTING OFFICE.
1893.

APPENDIX K.

REPORT UPON CHANGES IN RAILWAY TRANSPORTATION RATES ON FREIGHT TRAFFIC THROUGHOUT THE UNITED STATES, 1852 TO 1893.

CONTENTS.

LIST OF TABLES.

REPORT

UPON

CHANGES IN RAILWAY TRANSPORTATION RATES ON FREIGHT TRAFFIC THROUGHOUT THE UNITED STATES, 1852 TO 1893.

Hon. NELSON W. ALDRICH,
Chairman Subcommittee on Tariff (Finance Committee), United States Senate, Washington, D. C.:

DEAR SIR: I have the honor to present herewith a report upon the investigation of changes in freight rates, in compliance with the request to place your committee in possession of data showing to what extent railroad freight charges throughout the United States have changed since 1850.

An investigation of this character involves a wider range of inquiry than has probably previously been undertaken. The information sought by the committee is not known to have heretofore been collated to the extent now desired, either by the railroads or any of the numerous agencies from which statistics of the railways frequently emanate. The successful conclusion of the investigation, it will therefore be seen, has been largely if not wholly dependent upon the friendly coöperation of officials of the railways, from whom the schedules and records for the earlier dates were in the first place to be obtained.

It is therefore proper to express appreciation of the courtesies uniformly extended by these officials. Wherever the records had been preserved and were thought of service every facility was offered for their inspection, and valuable assistance rendered in the work of analyzing the rate schedules, many of which had become obsolete years before the present incumbents in office had entered the service.

From a preliminary examination of the field from which most of the records and material would have to be collected it was ascertained that it would be quite impossible to begin the investigation with a date as early as 1850. From personal inquiry at the principal offices of the railrords it was learned that in few cases were the rate schedules available for any considerable number of years. With some, a system had been adopted for the preservation of such records, but various occurrences, such as fire, bursting of steam pipes, removals, changes in official personnel of the roads, had caused their destruction or misplacement, and as no pressing necessity had arisen, their restoration had not been attempted. With other companies very complete records were found, but only in one or two cases for years prior to 1864. In a majority of instances rates prior to the year named were only to be obtained from the accounting records of the railroads, most of which have taken their place in the archives of the companies and could not now be reproduced without enormous labor to the roads, by whom the work would necessarily have to be performed. From 1864 to 1866 schedules were to be had in fragmentary form only and were not found to contain material sufficiently reliable to be of service.

In view of this condition it was seen that if the investigation was to be concluded within a reasonable period no extended research for material could be made for years prior to 1867, as this would require much time without the assurance of results to justify the labor.

The determination of the amount of data which would satisfactorily meet the requirements of a report of this character has not been the least of its troublesome features. In the several sections of the country are numerous railroads operating under the same general conditions and charging similar rates. To include the rates of all of such roads would result in much repetition and enlarge the report unnecessarily. The plan pursued has been to collect rates for as long a period as possible, for both competitive and local traffic of such rail and water carriers as will best represent the tendency of the changes in different sections. Articles of commercial prominence, such as grain, dressed beef, cotton, oil, coal, lumber, etc., are provided for by separate tables showing the rates between points where these articles comprise a large proportion of the traffic transported by the rail and water carriers. Territorial divisions of traffic associations and prominence of places have also largely guided in the selection of the rates. These, together with the somewhat elaborate exhibit of the operations and changes in freight classifications, as well as various data relating to mileage rates, it is believed will fully meet the purpose for which the investigation was undertaken.

Apropos of the general subject there have been included various data arranged to show the increase in tonnage movement by the carriers in different parts of the country. From such statements some idea may be formed of the revenue involved by the rate reductions and the consequent benefit to the shipping public.

The form of presentation chosen for the report will divide the data in four general headings, namely:

1. Development of Freight Classifications.
2. Changes in Competitive Rates.
3. Miscellaneous Data relating to Mileage Rates and Tonnage Movement.
4. Changes in Local Rates.

The numerous tables given are arranged to simplify the work of comparison, and are accompanied by such analysis and explanation as has been deemed necessary. From all of the forms of comparison presented it is clearly demonstrated that there has been a constant downward tendency in freight charges in all sections of the country.

Very respectfully submitted,

C. C. McCain.

THE DEVELOPMENT OF FREIGHT CLASSIFICATIONS.

The freight traffic of the railways of the United States is carried under two general classes of schedules, commonly known as Class Tariffs and Commodity Tariffs. The latter has reference to schedules applicable to such articles as grain, lumber, coal, live-stock, dressed beef, fertilizers, oil, etc., transported between sections of the country where these articles have attained a commercial and shipping importance which has made necessary specific rules for their transportation differing from those covering classified traffic, as well as a somewhat lower scale of rates than is applied to the latter.

Class tariffs are arranged to show the rates of the respective classes contained in the freight classifications. In the latter are found the great majority of articles carried by the railways, classified in accordance with the various elements that properly enter into the determination of freight charges; under these are also found the commodities above mentioned, and although exceptionally treated in certain sections as to rates, they are all amenable to some rule of the classification. The rate-making foundation for all commodities is seen to lie largely in the freight classification.

With the development of the railroad business of the country has followed the enlargment and extension of freight classifications. These publications are now current guides to the shipping public and have an enormous circulation. They are arranged in an enlarged and convenient manner, wherein may be found all commodities of commerce, described in every probable form of shipment, with a rate reference for each description, together with the rules and regulations under which each will be accepted for carriage. An effort will be here made to present the extent of the changes which have taken place in the principal classifications, and the advantages to the public resulting from the advancement in this branch of the railroad service.

Concerning the basis of constructing classifications, it may be said to have been early discovered that the charges for transportation of different articles of freight could not be apportioned among such articles with regard alone to the cost of carriage. This basis of determining the charges, it was found, would confine to narrow limits the movement of different articles whose bulk or weight was large in comparison to their value, while heavier articles with less bulk would be made to pay disproportionately low rates. "Under the system of apportioning the charges strictly to the cost some kinds of commerce which have been very useful to the country, and have a tendency to bring different sections into more intimate business and social relations, could never have amounted to any considerable magnitude, and in some cases could not have existed at all, for the simple reason that the value at the place of delivery would not equal the purchase price with the transportation added. The traffic would thus be precluded, because the charge for carriage would be greater than it could bear. On the other hand, the rates for the carriage of articles which, with small bulk or weight, concentrated great value would, on that system of making them, be absurdly low when compared to the value of the articles, and perhaps not less so when the comparison was with the value of the service in transporting them."

Accordingly it was found not to be unjust to distribute the entire cost of service among all articles carried, on a basis that gave greater consideration to the relative value of the service than to the cost. Such a method would be most beneficial to the country; it would enlarge commerce and extend communication, and would be better for the railroads because of the increased traffic which would be brought to them.

The value of the article, carried under this system, would be the most important element in determining what freight charge it should bear. Other considerations, however, equally important, must not be overlooked when the freight classification is to be made. The classifications as now constructed have for their foundation the following elements:

The competitive element, or the rates made necessary by competition.

The volume of the business; that is, the tonnage movement.

The direction in which the freight moves; that is, whether it moves in the direction in which most of the freight is transported or in the reverse direction in which empty cars are running.

The value of the article.

The bulk and weight.

The degree of risk attending transportation.

The facilities required for particular or special shipments.

The conditions attending transportation, such as furnishing special equipment, as in the case of private dressed-beef cars or cars specially adapted for freight of a perishable nature, or cars of large size for freight of extraordinary bulk.

Another condition which has also received consideration is the analogy which the new articles to be classified bear to other articles found in the classification.

The conditions under which railroad companies can afford to transport traffic have a large influence in determining the classification.

These are the general rules under which classifications are constructed, and while to a large extent controlling, the classifications are, notwithstanding, in a great measure a series of compromises, the participants of which are not alone the railroads, but also the shippers and representatives of business interests throughout the country, the latter being afforded ample opportunity to join with the railroads in the discussion as to the proper classification of articles of shipment affecting their interests.

While the pressure for reductions is very strong from certain localities, concessions are not now so readily granted, as the territory covered by the freight classifications is so large that great care in the assignment of articles to particular classes must be taken in order to avoid working an injury to any particular section. The commercial and transportation interests are regarded as identical, and the welfare of the whole territory and all interests affected must be considered. It is, however, occasionally observed that particular localities are to some extent preferentially served by the action of carriers who resist proposed changes in the classification for the reason that in their opinion they will operate to the prejudice of certain patrons. Thus exceptions to the classification are created by a road continuing to carry some article at one class, when in the opinion of a majority of the roads using the classification, the articles could well stand a higher rating. At this time fewer articles are rated independently of the classification than ever before in the history of the railroads.

The tendency of the character of classification is constantly toward uniformity, and this frequently in the face of strong opposition made by different carriers who have found it difficult to repel the pressure for special changes sought by patrons in the districts which they serve, and especially in the face of local influences which would seemingly benefit both the road and the shipper.

At this time there are practically but three freight classifications in use throughout the United States, namely, the Official classification, the Southern Railway and Steamship Association classification, and the Western classification. The application of these is as follows:

First. The Official classification is used almost exclusively throughout the territory east of Lake Michigan, Chicago, and the Mississippi River, and north of the Ohio and Potomac Rivers, to the Atlantic seaboard.

Second. The Southern Railway and Steamship Association classification is applied generally by roads south of the Ohio and east of the Mississippi River to the seaboard.

Third. The Western classification governs in the territory north and west of Chicago, west of a line drawn from Chicago to St. Louis, and west of the Mississippi River, St. Louis to New Orleans.

In each of the three divisions of territory described exceptions to these particular classifications are made to some extent by State commissions, and by individual roads for State or local traffic. Traffic carried between different points in the sections above described is usually taken at either one or the other of these leading classifications. For example, the classified traffic from the Atlantic seaboard to the Pacific coast is carried under the Western classification; traffic from Chicago to Atlanta, Ga., is carried under the Southern Railway and Steamship Association classification.

The territory throughout which the Official classification is shown to govern is the largest both in point of tonnage and communities served. At the date of the passage of the act to regulate commerce, one hundred and thirty-one railroad companies within the territory defined above as governed by the Official classification each had a separate classification. In addition to those classifications which had grown up mainly to foster local conditions, and were thought to be beneficial to the particular roads and shippers, there were five associations of railroad companies, each having a classification. These classifications were as follows:

First. The local classification of each railroad company.

Second. The through west-bound classification, generally known as the "Trunk line west-bound classification," applying upon through traffic originating at the seaboard cities and points east of the western termini of the trunk lines, and destined to Buffalo, Erie, Pittsburg, Parkersburg, etc., and to a number of competitive points, trade centers, or railroad junctions beyond.

Third. The East-bound classification, which alone applied to east-bound traffic originating in the territory east of Chicago and the Mississippi River, west of the western termini of the trunk lines and north of the Ohio River and destined to the western termini of the trunk lines and points east thereof.

Fourth. Traffic between competitive interior points in the Middle States, namely, New York, Pennsylvania, New Jersey, Delaware, Maryland, Virginia, and West Virginia, and between the several trunk lines and connecting roads was governed by the Joint Merchandise classification, which also applied to the local traffic on certain roads.

Fifth. The Middle and Western States classification applied to traffic between competitive interior points west of the western termini of the trunk lines east of the Mississippi River and north of the Ohio River.

When it became certain that the interstate-commerce act would become a law, early in 1887, the railroad companies decided at a meeting held for the purpose that it would be necessary to create and if possible adhere to a uniform classification. At this meeting there was appointed a special committee, composed of representatives of ten or twelve different roads, whose duty it was to go over the various classifications then in force and unite them into one classification, and the result of the work of this committee was the formation of Official classification No. 1.

Under the former arrangement the through or larger portion of the classified traffic was carried in two classifications; the West-bound classification was applied to traffic moving westward while an entirely separate classification was applied to traffic moving eastward. These two classifications, as well as the rates of the respective classes, were entirely dissimilar; the latter made provision for twelve or thirteen classes which embraced the heavier or bulk freight carried mainly in carload quantities from the western centers to the seaboard, while the former provided almost exclusively for package freight, usually transported in small or less than carload shipments, the rules and regulations applicable to each classification being in a few instances similar.

The conditions and the requirements upon which the present classification is based are of an entirely different character, as the new issue governs all traffic, through and local, between all stations of the roads within the territory described.

It may be interesting to learn the methods under which an article may receive its place in the classification. This will be here briefly explained for the Official classification, which is applied exclusively by carriers covering more tonnage than any of the other classifications in use.

The Official classification committee is composed of twelve general and assistant general freight agents, representing twelve of the principal lines in the territory using that classification. While the twelve men referred to are the official representatives of only twelve railroads the Official classification governs and is used by one hundred and fifty different railroads the total mileage of which is 65,000 miles. Over 50 per cent of the total tonnage of all roads in the United States is carried under the Official classification.

This classification committee was created for the purpose of defining the classes under which freight shall be transported by the various lines within the territory above described.

What is known as the "through" business of the Trunk Line Association and the Central Traffic Association is arranged for by a joint committee composed of members of the two associations named, and this joint committee appoints the classification committee, which latter committee has a permanent chairman. All applications bearing upon changes or additions in the classification may be submitted in writing at any time, either by the railroads or shippers, to the chairman of the classification committee, together with the various reasons in support of the application for such changes. The chairman acknowledges the receipt of every such application, following which an investigation is made as to the value, bulk, and various other features relating to the article for which a change is sought and which are usually considered when making a classification.

Upon the conclusion of the investigation the chairman renders a report to the classification committee for its consideration and action, with a recommendation for or against the granting of the application. The chairman may make temporary rulings regarding the classification of any article, but the final classification of all articles is only obtained by vote of the roads in joint committee.

Official classification No. 1 was issued April 1, 1887, and may be said to have been largely experimental, as it was hardly to be expected that the commerce of so large an area could at once be made to conform to the new conditions resulting from the consolidation of the widely different classifications formerly in use. Protests and applications for changes were at once received from shippers, as well as from many of the railroads, and a revision of the first issue was almost immediately begun, resulting in the publication of Official classification No. 2, on July 15, 1887. Applications from various interested parties, committees of shippers, and the railroads, were constantly before the classification committee, the greater portion of which received favorable consideration. The consequent revisions in the classifications have necessitated frequent issues of this publication, the last being No. 11 of January 2, 1893.

It is proposed to show by comparative statements what changes have taken place in the classification of many of the important articles of shipment resulting from a consolidation of different classifications as well as from direct reductions in the existing classifications, together with the resulting changes in the rates. Data for this purpose are given to some extent for each of the leading classifiacations now in use. The separate tables are provided with notes of explanation from which it will be possible to determine to what extent lower rates are due to changes in the classification alone.

The first of these tables is arranged to show for a large number of articles the classification and rates under the three important classifications employed between the Mississippi River and the seaboard prior to 1887, in comparison with the consolidated or Official classification as now governing throughout this territory. Changes in the rates under these comparisons result from three causes: First, a reduction in the classification; second, a reduction in the rate; third, the assignment of a carload classification to articles which were formerly provided for by a less than carload rate only and were charged the same rate when in carload quantities.

The first comparison made is that of the Joint Merchandise classification, which prior to 1887 applied between interior points in the Middle States. The points selected for the comparison are Philadelphia, Pa., to Elmira, N. Y. The present rates between these points are shown to be somewhat lower than in 1886, and the Official classification is now applied, which is on a very much lower scale. The table is arranged to show the class and rate under which articles were taken in 1886 compared with the class and rate now charged.

The effect of the change in the charge to the public resulting from the adoption of the new Official classification and the lowering of the rates in this territory is illustrated by the commodity of glassware N. O. S. (not otherwise specified). Under the Joint Merchandise classification glassware N. O. S., L. C. L. (less than car loads) was first class, rate 40 cents per 100 pounds. The same rate applied to shipments of carload quantities. Under the present Official classification glassware is classed as second class, rate 30 cents per 100 pounds; in less than carloads, and when in carloads, it is third class, rate 25 cents per 100 pounds. If there had been no change in the rate the lowering of the classification would have reduced the rate from first class, 40 cents, to second class, 32 cents; but the combined result of the lower classification and the lower rate produces a reduction of 10 cents per 100 pounds for quantities less than carloads, and 15 cents per 100 pounds for carload shipments.

The second comparison is that of the Middle and Western States classification, applying from Buffalo, Pittsburg, etc., to the Mississippi River, with the present Official, which embraces the same territory. The points and rates chosen for this comparison are those from Buffalo to East St. Louis; the rates of 1886 are given and those of 1893. There has been a material reduction in these rates, and a majority of the articles under the Official are found in lower classes than under the former or Middle and Western States classification. The combined results of these changes show important reductions in the charges to the public.

The third comparison is that of the present Official, which applies in both directions between New York and Chicago with the two former classifications as applied westward and eastward between the same points. In 1886 the rates between these points were on a distinct basis as between eastward and westward traffic, the eastward rates being considerably higher than those applied to westward business.

The eastward-bound traffic was divided into thirteen classes. By the adoption of the Official classification in 1887 the traffic was confined to six classes, and the rates in both directions were made alike. This effected very large reductions in the rates on traffic moving eastward formerly taken in the higher classes. The effect of this consolidation is illustrated by the article of liquid bluing, in glass. Less than carload shipments moving eastward, Chicago to New York, are now classified as second class, at a rate of 65 cents per 100 pounds, whereas formerly they were classified as second class at a rate of 85 cents per 100 pounds. Shipments in the same quantity moving westward were classified as first class with a rate of 75 cents, and are now taken at second class with a rate of 65 cents per 100 pounds. The same article in carload quantities prior to 1887 was carried from Chicago to New York at fourth class, 60 cents, and from New York to Chicago first class, 75 cents. At the present time carload shipments in both directions are taken at 30 cents per 100 pounds.

These tables should be studied carefully, as it will be seen, from the points for which comparisons are given, important sections of the country are represented, throughout which an enormous traffic is annually carried by the railroads. Reductions in the rates will appear for most of the articles given. In a few cases the rates for the less than carload shipments have been advanced, but it is noticed that in all of such instances reductions have been made on the same articles when carried in carload quantities.

COMPARISON OF CLASSIFICATION AND RATES.

TABLE 1—CLASSIFICATION AND RATES CHARGED ON IMPORTANT COMMODITIES BETWEEN PRINCIPAL POINTS UNDER THE SEVERAL FREIGHT CLASSIFICATIONS FORMERLY IN EFFECT AND WHICH HAVE BEEN MERGED WITH THE OFFICIAL CLASSIFICATION, AS COMPARED WITH THE CLASSIFICATION AND RATES CHARGED UNDER OFFICIAL CLASSIFICATION No. 11.

The names of the former classifications and points between which rates are stated are as follows, viz:

Classes (Rates in cents per 100 pounds.)

	1	2	3	4	5	6	A	B	C
Philadelphia, Pa., to Elmira, N. Y.—Joint Merchandise classification, 1886	40	32	23	18			15	14½	14
Official classification No. 11, 1893	35	30	25	18	15	13			

	1	2	3	4	5	6
Buffalo, N. Y., to East St. Louis, Ill.—Middle and Western States classification, 1886	65	50	38	26	21	18
Official classification No. 11, 1893	53½	47	34½	25	22	18

	1	2	3	4	5	6	7	8	9	10	11	12	13	Special.
Between New York, N. Y., and Chicago, Ill.—West-Bound Trunk-Line classification, 1886	75	65	45	35										25
East-Bound classification, 1886	100	85	70	60	50	45	40	35	30	25	25	30	30	
Official classification No. 11, 1893	75	65	50	35	30	25								

Joint Merchandise compared with Official No. 11. Between Philadelphia, Pa., and Elmira, N. Y.

Commodities.	Less than carloads. Class. Joint Merchandise, 1886.	Less than carloads. Class. Official No. 11, 1893.	Less than carloads. Rate. Joint Merchandise, 1886.	Less than carloads. Rate. Official No. 11, 1893.	Carloads. Class. Joint Merchandise, 1886.	Carloads. Class. Official No. 11, 1893.	Carloads. Rate. Joint Merchandise, 1883.	Carloads. Rate. Official No. 11, 1893.
Acid, in iron drums, O. R.	3	4	23	18	3	5	23	15
Ale, in wood	4	3	18	25	4	5	18	15
Alum, in barrels or casks	4	4	18	18	4	5	18	15
Ammonia, aqua, in iron drums	3	4	23	18	3	5	23	15
Anchors	4	4	18	18	4	5	18	15
Apples, green, in barrels	3	3	23	25	4	5	18	15
Apples, dried, in boxes	3	3	23	25	4	5	18	15
Argols, in barrels or casks	4	4	18	18	4	5	18	15
Arsenic, crude, in barrels or kegs	3	2	23	30	4	4	18	18
Asphaltum, in barrels or casks	4	4	18	18	A	6	15	13
Axes, boxed	2	4	32	18	2	5	32	15
Axle grease, in barrels or boxes	4	4	18	18	4	5	18	15
Axle grease, in buckets or cans	4	3	18	25	4	5	18	15
Babbit metal, in barrels or casks	....	4	....	18	...	5	....	15
Bacon, boxed	4	4	18	18	4	5	18	15
Bags or bagging, burlaps or gunny, in bales	4	3	18	25	4	4	18	18
Bags, paper	2	3	32	25	4	5	18	15
Baking-powder	3	3	23	25	3	4	23	18
Barb wire	4	4	18	18	4	5	18	15
Bark extract, tanner's, in barrels or casks	4	3	18	25	B.	5	14½	15
Barley, pearl, in barrels	2	5	22	15	4	6	18	13
Barrels, beer, empty	2	3	32	25	3	6	23	13
Barrels, flour	D1	1	80	35	1	1	40	35
Batting, cotton	1	1	40	35	1	1	40	35
Beans, dried, in bags or barrels	3	4	23	18	4	5	18	15
Bed springs, wire, coiled, in barrels or boxes	1	1	40	35	1	5	40	15
Belting, leather, rubber, or canvas	2	2	32	30	2	4	32	18
Binding twine, or cord, for harvesters, in bales	4	3	18	25	4	4	18	18
Bird seed, or bird food, in boxes	3	2	23	30	4	3	18	25
Blacking, shoe, in boxes	3	3	23	25	3	4	23	18
Blankets (not otherwise specified), in bales	1	1	40	35	1	1	40	35

Middle and Western States compared with Official No. 11. From Buffalo, N. Y., to East St. Louis, Ill.

Commodities.	Less than carloads. Class. Md. and West. States, 1886.	Less than carloads. Class. Official No. 11, 1893.	Less than carloads. Rate. Md. and West. States, 1886.	Less than carloads. Rate. Official No. 11, 1893.	Carloads. Class. Md. and West. States, 1886.	Carloads. Class. Official No. 11, 1893.	Carloads. Rate. Md. and West. States, 1886.	Carloads. Rate. Official No. 11, 1893.
Acid, in iron drums, O. R.	4	4	26	25	5	5	21	22
Ale, in wood	3	3	38	34½	5	5	21	22
Alum, in barrels or casks	4	4	26	25	5	5	21	22
Ammonia, aqua, in iron drums	4	4	26	25	5	5	21	22
Anchors	4	4	26	25	4	5	26	22
Apples, green, in barrels	3	3	38	34½	5	5	21	22
Apples, dried, in boxes	3	3	38	34½	5	5	21	22
Argols, in barrels or casks	4	4	26	25	4	5	26	22
Arsenic, crude, in barrels or kegs	3	2	38	47	3	4	38	25
Asphaltum, in barrels or casks	4	4	26	25	6	6	18	18
Axes, boxed	4	4	26	25	5	5	21	22
Axle grease, in barrels or boxes	4	4	26	25	5	5	21	22
Axle grease, in buckets or cans	3	3	38	34½	5	5	21	22
Babbit metal, in barrels or casks	....	4	....	25	....	5	....	22
Bacon, boxed	4	4	26	25	5	5	21	22
Bags or bagging, burlaps or gunny, in bales	3	3	38	34½	4	4	26	25
Bags, paper	4	3	26	34½	5	5	21	22
Baking-powder	2	3	50	34½	3	4	38	25
Barb wire	4	4	26	25	5	5	21	22
Bark extract, tanner's, in barrels or casks	3	3	38	34½	5	5	21	22
Barley, pearl, in barrels	5	5	21	22	6	6	18	18
Barrels, beer, empty	3	3	38	34½	6	6	18	18
Barrels, flour	1	1	65	53½	8	1	18	53½
Batting, cotton	1	1	65	53½	1	1	65	53½
Beans, dried, in bags or barrels	4	4	26	25	5	5	21	22
Bed springs, wire, coiled, in barrels or boxes	3	1	38	53½	3	5	38	22
Belting, leather, rubber, or canvas	3	2	38	47	3	4	38	25
Binding twine, or cord, for harvesters, in bales	4	3	26	34½	5	4	21	25
Bird seed, or bird food, in boxes	2	2	50	47	2	3	50	34½
Blacking, shoe, in boxes	3	3	38	34½	3	4	38	25
Blankets (not otherwise specified), in bales	1	1	65	53½	1	1	65	53½

East Bound and West Bound compared with Official No. 11. Between New York, N. Y., and Chicago, Ill.

Commodities.	Less than carloads. Class. East Bound, 1886.	Less than carloads. Class. West Bound, 1886.	Less than carloads. Class. Official No. 11, 1893.	Less than carloads. Rate. East Bound, 1886.	Less than carloads. Rate. West Bound, 1886.	Less than carloads. Rate. Official No. 11, 1893.	Carloads. Class. East Bound, 1886.	Carloads. Class. West Bound, 1886.	Carloads. Class. Official No. 11, 1893.	Carloads. Rate. East Bound, 1886.	Carloads. Rate. West Bound, 1886.	Carloads. Rate. Official No. 11, 1893.
Acid, in iron drums, O. R.	2	3	4	85	45	35	2	3	5	85	45	30
Ale, in wood	3	4	3	70	35	50	8	4	5	35	35	30
Alum, in barrels or casks	3	4	4	70	35	35	3	4	5	70	35	30
Ammonia, aqua, in iron drums	4	3	4	60	45	35	4	3	5	60	45	30
Anchors	6	4	4	45	35	35	6	4	5	45	35	30
Apples, green, in barrels	7	1	3	40	75	50	8	3	5	35	45	30
Apples, dried, in boxes	7	2	3	40	60	50	9	2	5	30	60	30
Argols, in barrels or casks	6	4	4	45	35	35	6	4	5	45	35	30
Arsenic, crude, in barrels or kegs	3	3	2	70	45	65	3	3	4	70	45	35
Asphaltum, in barrels or casks	6	4	4	45	35	35	10	4	6	25	35	25
Axes, boxed	6	3	4	45	45	35	6	3	5	45	45	30
Axle grease, in barrels or boxes	6	4	4	45	35	35	10	4	5	25	35	30
Axle grease, in buckets or cans	2	4	3	85	35	50	10	4	5	25	35	30
Babbit metal, in barrels or casks	6	3	4	45	45	35	8	3	5	35	45	30
Bacon, boxed	12	4	4	30	35	35	12	4	5	30	35	30
Bags or bagging, burlaps or gunny, in bales	4	4	3	60	35	50	6	4	4	45	35	35
Bags, paper	5	2	3	50	60	50	10	4	5	25	35	30
Baking-powder	6	4	3	45	35	50	8	4	4	35	35	35
Barb wire	10	4	4	25	35	35	10	4	5	25	35	30
Bark extract, tanner's, in barrels or casks	6	1	3	45	75	50	6	1	5	45	75	30
Barley, pearl, in barrels	12	4	5	30	35	30	13	4	6	30	35	25
Barrels, beer, empty	4	4	3	60	35	50	9	4	6	30	35	25
Barrels, flour	....	1	1	....	75	75	9	4	1	30	35	75
Batting, cotton	2	1	1	85	75	75	2	1	1	85	75	75
Beans, dried, in bags or barrels	9	4	4	30	35	35	10	4	5	25	35	30
Bed springs, wire, coiled, in barrels or boxes	6	1	1	45	75	75	10	1	5	25	75	30
Belting, leather, rubber, or canvas	2	2	2	85	60	65	2	2	4	85	60	35
Binding twine, or cord, for harvesters, in bales	4	2	3	60	60	50	4	4	4	60	35	35
Bird seed, or bird food, in boxes	3	2	2	70	60	65	5	2	3	50	60	50
Blacking, shoe, in boxes	3	4	3	70	35	50	3	4	4	70	35	35
Blankets (not otherwise specified), in bales	1	1	1	100	75	75	3	1	1	70	75	75

Blankets, shoddy, pressed in bales	1	2	40	30	1	2	40	30	1	2	65	47	1	2	65	47	1	1	2	100	75	65	3	1	2	70	75	65
Bleaching-powder	4	4	18	18	B	6	14½	13	4	4	26	25	5	6	21	18	6	(*)	4	45	25	35	6	(*)	6	45	25	26
Bluing, liquid, in barrels	2	3	32	25	2	4	32	18	2	3	50	34½	2	4	50	25	2	1	3	85	75	50	4	1	4	60	75	30
Bluing, liquid, in glass	1	2	40	30	1	4	40	18	2	2	50	47	2	4	50	25	2	1	2	85	75	65	4	1	4	60	75	30
Boiler flues, iron	3	4	23	18	A	5	15	15	4	4	26	25	5	5	21	22	4	3	4	60	45	35	6	3	5	45	45	35
Bolts, iron, in boxes	4	4	18	18	A	5	15	15	4	4	26	25	5	5	21	22	10	3	4	25	45	35	10	3	5	25	45	35
Bolts, iron, in kegs	4	4	18	18	A	5	15	15	4	4	26	25	5	5	21	22	10	4	4	25	35	35	10	4	5	25	35	30
Bonedust	4	4	18	18	C	6	14	13	4	4	26	25	6	6	18	18	6	4	4	45	35	35	6	4	6	45	35	25
Books, in boxes	1	1	40	35	1	2	40	30	1	1	65	53½	1	2	65	47	2	1	1	85	75	75	3	1	2	70	75	65
Boots and shoes, boxed	1	1	40	35	1	1	40	35	1	1	65	53½	1	1	65	53½	1	1	1	100	75	75	1	1	1	100	75	75
Borax, in barrels	4	3	18	25	4	4	18	18	3	3	38	34½	3	4	38	25	2	4	3	85	35	50	6	4	4	45	35	35
Bottles, O. R. B., in boxes, or barrels	3	2	3	30	4	5	18	15	3	2	38	34½	5	5	21	22	3	3	2	70	45	65	6	4	5	45	35	30
Boxes, paper	D 1	3 t 1	80	105	D 1	3 t 1	80	105	3 t 1	3 t 1	195	160½	3 t 1	3 t 1	195	160½	3 t 1	4 t 1	3 t 1	300	300	225	9	4 t 1	3 t 1	300	300	225
Boxes, paper, nested	D 1	D 1	80	70	D 1	D 1	80	70	3 t 1	D	195	160½	3 t 1	D 1	195	107	3 t 1	2 t 1	D 1	300	150	150	9	2 t 1	D 1	300	150	150
Brass, sheet	2	2	32	30	2	2	32	30	2	2	50	47	2	2	50	47	2	2	2	85	60	65	2	2	2	85	60	65
Brass fittings, boxed	2	3	32	25	2	3	32	25	3	3	38	34½	3	3	38	34½	2	2	3	85	60	50	2	2	3	85	60	50
Brass, scrap, in barrels or casks	4	3	18	25	4	4	18	18	4	3	26	25	4	4	26	25	4	3	3	60	45	50	8	3	4	35	45	35
Brick, common	4	5	18	15	C	6	14	13	4	5	26	25	6	6	18	18	6	4	5	45	35	30	10	4	6	25	35	20
Brooms, in boxes or crates	1	2	40	30	1	2	40	30	2	2	50	47	2	2	50	47	2	1	2	85	75	65	6	1	2	45	75	65
Brimstone, in barrels or hogsheads	4	4	18	18	4	6	18	13	4	4	26	25	4	6	26	18	6	4	4	45	35	35	6	4	6	45	35	20
Cabbages, in barrels	4	3	18	25	A	3	15	25	4	3	26	34½	5	3	21	34½	3	3	3	70	45	50	3	3	3	70	45	55
Cabbages, in crates	4	4	18	18	A	4	15	18	4	4	26	25	5	4	21	25	6	3	4	45	45	35	6	3	4	45	45	35
Cabbages	....	4	....	18	A	5	15	15	....	4	....	25	....	5	....	22	....	....	4	....	....	35	10	4	5	25	35	35
Candles, less than 25 boxes	2	4	32	18	2	5	32	15	4	4	26	25	4	5	26	22	4	2	4	60	60	35	4	2	5	60	60	35
Candles, more than 25 boxes	2	4	32	18	4	5	18	15	4	4	26	25	5	5	21	22	6	2	4	45	60	35	9	4	5	30	35	30
Canned vegetables	3	4	23	18	4	5	18	15	4	4	26	25	5	5	21	22	7	4	4	40	35	35	8	4	5	35	35	35
Canned fruit and fish	3	4	23	18	4	5	18	15	4	4	26	25	5	5	21	22	6	4	4	45	35	35	7	4	5	40	35	30
Carboys, empty, O. R.	1	3	40	25	4	5	18	15	1	3	65	34½	6	5	18	22	1	1	3	100	75	50	6	4	5	45	35	30
Cards, show chromo advertising	1	1	40	35	1	3	40	25	1	1	65	53½	1	3	65	34½	1	1	1	100	75	75	6	1	3	45	75	50
Carpeting	1	1	40	35	1	1	40	35	1	1	65	53½	1	1	65	53½	1	1	1	100	75	75	1	1	1	100	75	70
Carpeting, jute or hemp	1	2	40	30	1	2	40	30	1	2	65	47	1	2	65	47	1	2	2	100	60	65	1	2	2	100	60	60
Cartridges, metallic	2	2	32	30	2	4	32	18	....	2	....	47	....	4	....	25	4	2	2	60	60	65	6	2	4	45	60	30
Cement, building	4	5	18	15	C	6	14	13	5	5	21	22	(†)	6	....	18	8	(*)	5	35	25	30	10	(*)	6	25	25	20
Chains, iron, loose	2	4	32	18	A	5	15	15	3	4	38	25	5	5	21	22	2	2	4	85	60	35	2	2	5	85	60	30
Chain, cable	2	4	32	18	A	5	15	15	4	4	26	25	5	5	21	22	6	4	4	45	35	35	10	4	5	25	35	30
Charcoal, lump	4	3	18	25	B	6	14½	13	3	3	38	34½	6	6	18	18	....	3	3	....	45	50	10	4	6	25	35	25
Chinaware in boxes	1	1	40	35	1	1	40	35	1	1	65	53½	1	1	65	53½	1	1	1	100	75	75	1	1	1	100	75	75
Chinaware in barrels or casks	1	2	40	30	1	2	40	30	2	2	50	47	2	2	50	47	2	1	2	85	75	65	2	1	2	85	75	65
Chocolate	2	2	32	30	2	2	32	30	2	2	50	47	2	2	50	47	2	2	2	85	60	65	2	2	2	85	60	65
Cider in wood	4	3	18	25	A	5	15	15	4	3	26	25	5	5	21	22	6	4	3	45	35	50	10	4	5	25	35	30
Cigars in boxes, corded, sealed, and strapped	1	1	40	35	1	1	40	35	1	1	65	53½	1	1	65	53½	1	1	1	100	75	75	1	1	1	100	75	75
Clocks	1	1	40	35	1	1	40	35	1	1	65	53½	1	1	65	53½	1	1	1	100	75	75	1	1	1	100	75	75
Cloth, wire, in boxes or casks	2	3	32	25	2	5	32	15	1	3	65	53½	1	5	65	22	1	2	3	100	60	50	6	2	5	45	60	30
Cloth, wire, in rolls	3	3	23	25	3	5	23	15	1	3	65	53½	1	5	65	22	1	3	3	100	45	50	6	3	5	45	45	30
Clothing, boxed	1	1	40	35	1	1	40	35	1	1	65	53½	1	1	65	53½	1	1	1	100	75	75	1	1	1	100	75	75
Coçoa	2	2	32	30	2	2	32	30	2	2	50	47	2	2	50	47	2	2	2	85	60	65	2	2	2	85	60	65
Cocoanuts in bags	2	2	32	30	4	4	18	18	1	2	65	47	1	4	65	25	2	2	2	85	60	65	2	2	4	85	60	35
Coffee, ground or roasted	4	4	18	18	4	6	18	13	4	4	26	25	5	6	21	18	5	4	4	50	35	35	5	(*)	6	50	25	25
Coffee, green, in sacks	4	4	18	18	4	6	18	13	4	4	26	25	5	6	21	18	6	4	4	45	35	35	6	(*)	6	45	25	25

* Special.

† Special tariff.

Commodities.	Joint Merchandise compared with Official No. 11. Between Philadelphia, Pa., and Elmira, N. Y.							
	Less than carloads.				Carloads.			
	Class.		Rate.		Class.		Rate.	
	Joint Merchandise, 1886.	Official No. 11, 1893.	Joint Merchandise, 1886.	Official No. 11, 1893.	Joint Merchandise, 1886.	Official No. 11, 1893.	Joint Merchandise, 1886.	Official No. 11, 1893.
Cotton waste, pressed, in bales	4	4	18	18	4	4	18	18
Cotton waste, not pressed	1	1	40	35	1	1	40	35
Currants, dried, in boxes, kegs, or bags	3	3	23	25	3	4	23	18
Cutlery	2	2	32	30	2	2	32	30
Dates	3	2	23	30	4	4	18	18
Demijohns	D1	D1	80	70	4	D1	18	70
Dry goods as follows: calicoes, Canton flannel, canvas, corset jeans, cottonades, cotton warp, cotton yarn, crash, domestic checks, stripes, and cheviots, cotton duck, denims, twills, domestic, ginghams, glazed cambrics, etc., in bales or boxes	1	3	40	25	1	3	40	25
Dye woods in stock	3	3	23	25	3	3	23	25
Eggs, packed in barrels or boxes	2	2	32	30	4	2	18	30
Emery in barrels or casks	4	4	18	18	4	5	18	15
Emery in kegs	2	4	32	18	2	5	32	15
Emery wheels	1	2	40	30	1	4	40	18
Engines, stationary	3	2	23	30	4	5	18	15
Excelsior in bales	2	2	32	30	A	5	15	15
Extract of logwood in barrels	3	3	23	25	A	5	15	15
Extract of malt packed in boxes	1	1	40	35	1	3	40	25
Farina	4	4	18	18	4	5	18	15
Felt roofing	3	4	23	18	A	5	15	15
Fencing wire	....	3	....	25	....	5	....	15
Fertilizers, in barrels	4	4	18	18	C	6	14	13
Figs, in drums	1	1	40	35	1	1	40	35
Floor tiling	4	4	18	18	4	5	18	15
Flour, in barrels	4	5	18	15	A	6	15	13
Flour, in sacks	4	5	18	15	A	6	15	13
Gas fixtures	2	2	32	30	2	2	32	30
Gas pipe, iron	4	4	18	18	A	5	15	15

Commodities.	Middle and Western States compared with Official No. 11. From Buffalo, N. Y., to East St. Louis, Ill.							
	Less than carloads.				Carloads.			
	Class.		Rate.		Class.		Rate.	
	Md. and West. States, 1886.	Official No. 11, 1893.	Md. and West. States, 1886.	Official No. 11, 1893.	Md. and West. States, 1886.	Official No. 11, 1893.	Md. and West. States, 1886.	Official No. 11, 1893.
Cotton waste, pressed, in bales	3	4	38	25	3	4	38	25
Cotton waste, not pressed	1	1	65	53½	1	1	65	53½
Currants, dried, in boxes, kegs, or bags	3	3	38	34½	4	4	26	25
Cutlery	2	2	50	47	2	2	50	47
Dates	2	2	50	47	2	4	50	25
Demijohns	D1	D1	130	107	4	D1	26	107
Dry goods as follows: calicoes, Canton flannel, canvas, corset jeans, cottonades, cotton warp, cotton yarn, crash, domestic checks, stripes, and cheviots, cotton duck, denims, twills, domestic, ginghams, glazed cambrics, etc., in bales or boxes	1	3	65	34½	1	3	65	34½
Dye woods in stock	3	3	38	34½	3	3	38	34½
Eggs, packed in barrels or boxes	2	2	50	47	4	2	26	47
Emery in barrels or casks	2	4	50	25	2	5	50	22
Emery in kegs	2	4	50	25	2	5	50	22
Emery wheels	....	2	....	47	....	4	....	25
Engines, stationary	2	2	50	47	2	5	50	22
Excelsior in bales	2	2	50	47	6	5	18	22
Extract of logwood in barrels	2	3	50	34½	6	5	18	22
Extract of malt packed in boxes	2	1	50	53½	4	3	26	34½
Farina	5	4	21	25	6	5	18	22
Felt roofing	4	4	26	25	6	5	18	22
Fencing wire	....	3	....	34½	....	5	....	22
Fertilizers, in barrels	4	4	26	25	6	6	18	18
Figs, in drums	1	1	65	53½	1	1	65	53½
Floor tiling	4	4	26	25	5	5	21	22
Flour, in barrels	5	5	21	22	(*)	6	....	18
Flour, in sacks	5	5	21	22	(*)	6	....	18
Gas fixtures	2	2	50	47	2	2	50	47
Gas pipe, iron	4	4	26	25	5	5	21	22

Commodities.	East Bound and West Bound compared with Official No. 11. Between New York, N. Y., and Chicago, Ill.											
	Less than carloads.						Carloads.					
	Class.			Rate.			Class.			Rate.		
	East Bound, 1886.	West Bound, 1886.	Official No. 11, 1893.	East Bound, 1886.	West Bound, 1886.	Official No. 11, 1893.	East Bound, 1886.	West Bound, 1886.	Official No. 11, 1893.	East Bound, 1886.	West Bound, 1886.	Official No. 11, 1893.
Cotton waste, pressed, in bales	6	4	4	45	35	35	6	4	4	45	35	35
Cotton waste, not pressed	1	1	1	100	75	75	1	1	1	100	75	75
Currants, dried, in boxes, kegs, or bags	....	2	3	....	60	50	6	2	4	45	60	35
Cutlery	2	2	2	85	60	65	2	2	2	85	60	65
Dates	2	2	2	85	60	65	2	2	4	85	60	35
Demijohns	D1	2 t	D1	200	150	150	6	2 t 1	D1	45	150	150
Dry goods as follows: calicoes, Canton flannel, canvas, corset jeans, cottonades, cotton warp, cotton yarn, crash, domestic checks, stripes, and cheviots, cotton duck, denims, twills, domestic, ginghams, glazed cambrics, etc., in bales or boxes	1	1	3	100	75	50	1	1	3	100	75	50
Dye woods in stock	3	3	3	70	45	50	3	3	3	70	45	50
Eggs, packed in barrels or boxes	3	1	2	70	75	65	3	1	2	70	75	65
Emery in barrels or casks	4	4	4	60	35	35	....	....	5	....	....	30
Emery in kegs	4	2	4	60	60	35	4	2	5	60	60	30
Emery wheels	3	2	2	70	60	65	8	2	4	35	60	35
Engines, stationary	1	1	2	100	75	65	6	4	5	45	35	30
Excelsior in bales	2	2	2	85	60	65	9	4	5	30	35	30
Extract of logwood in barrels	2	2	3	85	60	50	2	2	5	85	60	30
Extract of malt packed in boxes	3	1	1	70	75	75	4	1	3	60	75	50
Farina	12	4	4	30	35	35	13	4	5	30	35	30
Felt roofing	6	4	4	45	35	35	9	4	5	50	35	30
Fencing wire	....	....	3	....	....	50	....	....	5	....	....	30
Fertilizers, in barrels	6	4	4	45	35	35	6	(*)	6	45	25	25
Figs, in drums	1	1	1	100	75	75	1	1	1	100	75	75
Floor tiling	6	4	4	45	35	35	6	4	5	45	35	30
Flour, in barrels	12	4	5	30	35	30	13	4	6	30	35	25
Flour, in sacks	12	2	5	30	60	30	13	2	6	30	60	25
Gas fixtures	2	2	2	85	60	65	2	2	2	85	60	65
Gas pipe, iron	10	4	4	25	35	35	10	4	5	25	35	30

Ginger	2	2	32	30	2	2	32	30	2	2	50	47	2	2	50	47	2	2	2	85	60	65	2	2	2	85	60	65
Ginsing, in sacks	1	1	40	35	1	1	40	35	1	1	65	53½	1	1	65	53½	1	1	1	100	75	75	1	1	1	100	75	75
Glass, window, over 80 united inches, O. R. B	1	3	40	25	1	5	40	15	4	3	26	34½	5	5	21	22	....	1	3	....	75	50	....	1	5	....	75	30
Glassware, N. O. S	1	2	40	30	1	3	40	25	3	2	38	47	3	3	38	34½	3	1	2	70	75	65	6	2	3	45	60	50
Glue, in barrels or casks	4	4	18	18	4	5	18	15	4	4	26	25	4	5	26	22	4	4	4	60	35	35	4	4	5	60	35	30
Glycerin, crude, in barrels or drums	3	3	23	25	3	4	23	18	4	3	26	34½	5	4	21	25	4	3	3	60	45	50	6	3	4	45	45	35
Grain, in barrels	4	5	18	15	A	6	15	13	....	5	....	22	....	6	....	18	12	4	5	30	35	30	13	4	6	30	35	25
Grain, in sacks	4	5	18	15	A	6	15	13	5	5	21	22	(*)	6	....	18	5	2	5	50	60	30	8	2	6	35	60	25
Graniteware, boxed	....	2	....	30	....	4	....	18	1	2	65	47	1	4	65	25	3	2	2	70	60	65	6	2	4	45	60	35
Grease, axle, in barrels or boxes	4	4	18	18	4	5	18	15	4	4	26	25	5	5	21	22	6	4	4	45	35	35	10	4	5	25	35	30
Grindstones, O. R	3	4	23	18	A	6	15	13	4	4	26	25	4	6	26	18	6	4	4	45	35	35	9	4	6	30	35	25
Grindstones, mounted, O. R	3	2	23	30	A	6	15	13	3	2	38	47	6	6	18	18	3	2	2	70	60	65	9	2	6	30	60	25
Grits, in barrels	3	5	23	15	3	6	23	13	5	5	21	22	(*)	6	....	18	12	4	5	30	35	30	13	4	6	30	35	25
Groceries, assorted, N. O. S	2	1	32	35	2	1	32	35	2	1	50	53½	2	1	50	53½	2	2	1	85	60	75	2	2	1	85	60	75
Guano, in barrels or bags	4	4	18	18	C	6	14½	13	4	4	26	25	6	6	18	18	6	4	4	45	35	35	10	4	6	25	35	25
Gum, chewing, in cases or barrels	....	2	....	30	....	2	....	25	1	2	65	47	1	2	65	47	2	1	2	85	75	65	2	1	2	85	75	65
Hair, in sacks	1	1	40	35	1	5	40	15	1	1	65	53½	1	5	65	22	1	1	1	100	75	75	1	1	5	100	75	30
Hair, in bales	3	3	23	25	3	5	23	15	1	3	65	34½	1	5	65	22	6	2	3	45	60	50	6	2	5	45	60	30
Hams, in bags	2	3	32	25	2	4	32	18	2	3	50	34½	5	4	21	25	12	2	3	30	60	50	12	2	4	30	60	35
Hay, in bales	1½t1	1	60	35	B	6	14½	13	1	1	65	53½	6	6	18	18	3	3	1	70	45	75	13	4	6	30	35	25
Hemp, covered	3	2	23	30	4	4	18	18	3	2	38	47	4	4	26	25	4	2	2	60	60	65	4	3	4	60	45	35
Hides, beef or calf, green, in bundles	4	4	18	18	A	5	15	15	4	4	26	25	5	5	21	22	6	4	4	45	35	35	12	4	5	30	35	30
Hinges, iron or steel, in boxes	....	4	....	18	....	5	....	15	4	4	26	25	5	5	21	22	6	3	4	45	45	35	6	3	5	45	45	30
Hoes, in boxes, barrels, or casks	2	4	32	18	4	4	18	18	4	4	26	25	5	4	21	25	6	2	4	45	60	35	6	4	4	45	35	35
Honey in cans, boxed	1	2	40	30	1	4	40	18	2	2	50	47	2	4	50	25	3	1	2	70	75	65	3	1	4	70	75	35
Hoofs and horns, in packages	4	4	18	18	C	5	14	15	4	4	26	25	6	5	18	22	6	3	4	45	45	35	9	4	5	30	35	30
Hops, in bales	2	2	32	30	3	3	23	25	3	2	38	47	3	3	38	34½	2	2	2	85	60	65	2	2	3	85	60	50
Horseshoes, in boxes or kegs	4	4	18	18	A	5	15	15	4	4	26	25	5	5	21	22	10	4	4	25	35	35	10	4	5	25	35	30
Hose, rubber, canvas, or leather, boxed	2	3	32	25	2	4	32	18	3	3	38	34½	3	4	38	25	....	2	3	....	60	50	....	2	4	....	60	35
Household goods, second-hand, O. R	1	1	40	35	2	2	32	30	1	1	65	53½	4	2	26	47	1	2t1	1	100	150	75	6	1	2	45	75	65
Hubs, in barrels or boxes	2	3	32	25	2	4	32	18	4	3	26	34½	5	4	21	25	....	2	3	....	60	50	....	2	4	....	60	35
Indigo	1	1	40	35	1	1	40	35	1	1	65	53½	1	1	65	53½	1	1	1	100	75	75	1	1	1	100	75	75
Ink, writing or printing, in boxes or barrels	2	2	32	30	2	3	32	25	3	2	38	47	3	3	38	34½	3	2	2	70	60	65	4	2	3	60	60	50
Ink, in glass or stone, boxed	1	1	40	30	1	3	40	25	2	1	50	53½	2	3	50	34½	3	1	1	70	75	75	4	1	3	60	75	50
Iron, castings, under 100 pounds each	2	4	32	18	A	5	15	15	1	4	65	25	3	5	38	22	2	1	4	85	75	35	10	3	5	25	45	30
Iron, nuts, bolts, washers, rivets, and staples, in boxes	4	4	18	18	A	5	15	15	4	4	26	25	5	5	21	22	10	3	4	25	45	35	10	3	5	25	45	30
Iron, car wheels	4	4	18	18	B	6	14½	13	4	4	26	25	5	6	21	18	10	4	4	25	35	35	10	4	6	25	35	25
Isinglass	1	1	40	35	1	1	40	35	2	1	50	53½	2	1	50	53½	2	1	1	85	75	75	2	1	1	85	75	75
Tacks, iron, boxed	2	4	32	18	2	4	32	18	4	4	26	25	4	4	26	25	....	2	4	....	60	35	....	2	4	....	60	35
Jute	3	3	23	25	4	4	18	18	....	3	....	34½	....	4	....	25	6	3	3	45	45	50	9	3	4	30	45	35
Jute butts	4	4	18	18	A	6	15	13	4	4	26	25	5	6	21	18	....	4	4	....	35	35	....	4	6	....	35	25
Ladders, step	1	1	40	35	1	5	40	15	1	1	65	53½	3	5	38	22	1	1	1	100	75	75	6	1	5	45	75	30
Lard, in barrels or boxes	4	4	18	18	4	5	18	15	4	4	26	25	5	5	21	22	12	4	4	30	35	35	12	4	5	30	35	30
Lead, black, in casks	4	4	18	18	A	5	15	15	4	4	26	25	5	5	21	22	3	3	4	70	45	35	3	4	5	70	35	30
Lampblack	1	1½	40	53	1	3	40	25	1	1½	65	80¼	5	3	21	34½	1½	1	1½	150	75	113	1½	1	3	150	75	50
Lead, white, in kegs or barrels	4	4	18	18	A	5	15	15	4	4	26	25	5	5	21	22	10	4	4	25	35	35	10	4	5	25	35	30
Leather, in rolls	2	3	32	25	4	4	18	18	3	3	38	34½	4	4	26	25	4	2	3	60	60	50	4	2	4	60	60	35
Leather, scrap, in bags or crates	3	3	23	25	3	5	23	18	....	3	....	34½	....	5	....	22	6	3	3	45	45	50	10	3	5	25	45	30

*Special.

Commodities.	Joint Merchandise compared with Official No. 11. Between Philadelphia, Pa., and Elmira, N. Y.								Middle and Western States compared with Official No. 11. From Buffalo, N. Y., to East St. Louis, Ill.								East Bound and West Bound compared with Official No. 11. Between New York, N. Y., and Chicago, Ill.											
	Less than carloads.				Carloads.				Less than carloads.				Carloads.				Less than carloads.						Carloads.					
	Class.		Rate.		Class.		Rate.		Class.		Rate.		Class.		Rate.		Class.			Rate.			Class.			Rate.		
	Joint Merchandise, 1886.	Official No. 11, 1893.	Joint Merchandise, 1886.	Official No. 11, 1893.	Joint Merchandise, 1886.	Official No. 11, 1893.	Joint Merchandise, 1886.	Official No. 11, 1893.	Md. and West. States, 1886.	Official No. 11, 1893.	Md. and West. States, 1886.	Official No. 11, 1893.	Md. and West. States, 1886.	Official No. 11, 1893.	Md. and West. States, 1886.	Official No. 11, 1893.	East Bound, 1886.	West Bound, 1886.	Official No. 11, 1893.	East Bound, 1886.	West Bound, 1886.	Official No. 11, 1893.	East Bound, 1886.	West Bound, 1886.	Official No. 11, 1893.	East Bound, 1886.	West Bound, 1886.	Official No. 11, 1893.
Lemons	1	2	40	30	2	3	32	25	1	2	65	47	3	3	38	34½	1	1	2	100	75	65	5	2	3	50	60	50
Licorice, root	2	2	32	30	A	4	15	18	3	2	38	47	3	4	38	25	2	2	2	85	60	65	2	2	4	85	60	35
Licorice, powdered, in barrels	....	2	....	30	....	4	....	18	3	2	38	47	3	4	38	25	5	2	2	50	60	65	5	2	4	50	60	35
Lime, in barrels	4	5	18	15	B	6	14½	13	5	5	21	22	(*)	6	....	18	8	4	5	35	35	30	10	4	6	25	35	25
Lime-water, in barrels	....	4	....	18	....	4	....	18	4	4	26	25	4	4	26	25	2	....	4	85	....	35	2	....	4	85	....	35
Logs	....	4	....	18	....	6	....	13	4	4	26	25	(*)	6	....	18	6	4	4	45	35	35	11	4	6	25	35	25
Lumber, sawed, not over 27 feet, pine and oak	4	4	18	18	B	6	14½	13	4	4	26	25	(*)	6	....	18	6	4	4	45	35	35	11	4	6	25	35	25
Lye, concentrated	4	4	18	18	4	5	18	15	4	4	26	25	5	5	21	22	6	4	4	45	35	35	9	4	5	30	35	30
Machines, sewing, K. D., boxed	1	1	40	35	4	3	18	25	3	1	38	53½	4	3	26	34½	2	2	1	85	60	75	2	2	3	85	60	50
Mahogany boards and planks	3	3	23	25	4	5	18	15	3	3	38	34½	4	5	26	22	3	3	3	70	45	50	3	4	5	70	35	30
Mahogany logs	4	4	18	18	4	5	18	15	4	4	26	25	4	5	26	22	6	4	4	45	35	35	6	4	5	45	35	30
Malt in barrels	4	5	18	15	A	6	15	13	....	5	....	22	....	6	....	18	12	4	5	30	35	30	13	4	6	30	35	25
Manganese	4	4	18	18	4	6	18	13	4	4	26	25	4	6	26	18	8	4	4	35	35	35	9	4	6	30	35	25
Manilla	4	3	18	25	4	4	18	18	3	3	38	34½	3	4	38	25	6	4	3	45	35	50	6	4	4	45	35	35
Marble slabs, unwrought, O. R.	....	4	....	18	....	5	....	15	4	4	26	25	5	5	21	22	6	4	4	45	35	35	6	4	5	45	35	30
Marble dust	4	4	18	18	B	6	14½	13	5	4	21	25	6	6	18	18	6	4	4	45	35	35	10	4	6	25	35	25
Mats, grass	1	....	40	....	1	....	40	....	3	....	38	....	4	....	26	....	1	2	....	100	60	....	1	2	....	100	60	....
Matting, hemp, jute, or pine fiber	....	2	....	30	....	4	....	18	2	2	50	47	4	4	26	25	1	1	2	100	75	65	1	1	4	100	75	35
Meal, in bulk	....	....	....	....	....	6	....	13	....	....	....	....	(*)	6	....	18	....	....	6	....	25	25	13	4	6	30	35	25
Meats, canned, boxed,	3	4	23	18	4	5	18	15	4	4	26	25	5	5	21	22	12	4	4	30	35	35	12	4	5	30	35	30
Meats, salted, boxed	4	4	18	18	4	5	18	15	4	4	26	25	5	5	21	22	12	4	4	30	35	35	12	4	5	30	35	30
Milk, condensed, in cans, boxed	3	3	23	25	3	4	23	18	3	3	38	34½	4	4	26	25	4	4	3	60	35	50	6	4	4	45	35	35
Millstones, in rough	4	4	18	18	A	5	15	15	4	4	26	25	5	5	21	22	6	4	4	45	35	35	6	4	5	45	35	30
Mineral water, in wood	3	4	23	18	4	5	18	15	4	4	26	25	5	5	21	22	6	3	4	45	45	35	9	4	5	30	35	30
Mineral pulp	4	4	18	18	C	5	14	15	....	4	....	25	....	5	....	22	....	....	4	....	35	35	....	4	5	....	35	30
Nails and spikes, in kegs	4	4	18	18	A	5	15	15	4	4	26	25	5	5	21	22	10	4	4	25	35	35	10	4	5	25	35	30
Nails, horseshoe, or finishing, in boxes	3	4	23	18	3	5	23	15	3	4	38	25	3	5	38	22	10	3	4	25	45	35	10	3	5	25	45	30
Nail rods	4	4	18	18	A	5	15	15	....	4	....	25	....	5	....	22	10	4	4	25	35	35	10	4	5	25	35	30
Naphthaline, dry, in barrels	1	3	40	25	4	5	18	15	....	3	....	34½	....	5	....	22	2	....	3	85	....	50	2	....	5	85	....	30
Nuts, hickory, in barrels	2	3	32	25	2	4	32	18	4	3	26	34½	4	4	26	25	6	2	3	45	60	50	6	2	4	45	60	35
Nuts, pecans, in barrels	2	3	32	25	2	4	32	18	3	3	38	34½	4	4	26	25	2	2	3	85	60	50	6	2	4	45	60	35

Oakum	2	2	32	30	2	4	32	18	2	2	50	47	2	4	50	25	2	2	2	85	60	65	2	2	4	85	60	35
Oil, petroleum, coal, kerosene, carbon, naphtha	3	....	23	....	4	....	18	....	3	....	38	....	(*)	....	....	....	3	2t1	....	70	150	....	3	4	....	70	35	....
Oranges	1	2	40	30	2	3	32	25	1	2	65	47	3	3	38	34½	1	1	2	100	75	65	5	2	3	50	60	50
Oysters, fresh, in cans	....	1½	....	53	....	1½	....	53	1	1½	65	80¼	1	1½	65	80¼	1	1½t1	1½	100	112½	113	1	1½	1½	100	112½	113
Packing, rubber	2	3	32	25	2	4	32	18	3	3	38	34½	3	4	38	25	2	3	3	85	45	50	2	3	4	85	45	35
Paints, asbestos, asphalt, chemical earth, iron, lead, metallic, mineral, ocher, paraffine, rubber, zinc, oxide, in oil, in barrels	4	3	18	25	A	5	15	15	3	3	38	34½	3	5	38	22	6	4	3	45	35	50	6	4	5	45	35	30
Paper bags	2	3	32	25	4	5	18	15	4	3	26	34½	5	5	21	22	5	4	3	50	35	50	10	4	5	25	35	30
Paper, wrapping, straw or manilla	2	3	32	25	4	5	18	15	4	3	26	34½	5	5	21	22	5	....	3	50	....	50	10	4	5	25	35	30
Paraffine wax	....	4	....	18	....	5	....	15	4	4	26	25	5	5	21	22	8	1	4	35	75	35	8	1	5	35	75	30
Pease, dried, in barrels or sacks	3	4	23	18	4	5	18	15	4	4	26	25	5	5	21	22	9	4	4	30	35	35	10	4	5	25	35	30
Pegs, shoe, in barrels	1	3	40	25	4	5	18	15	2	3	50	34½	2	5	50	22	4	2	3	60	60	50	9	2	5	30	60	30
Pickles, in barrels or casks	4	3	18	25	4	5	18	15	4	3	26	34½	5	5	21	22	6	4	3	45	35	50	9	4	5	30	35	30
Pipe, lead, on reels or in rolls, O. R	2	3	32	25	2	4	32	18	....	3	....	34½	....	4	....	25	6	1	3	45	75	50	7	1	6	40	75	35
Pitch, in barrels	4	4	18	18	A	6	15	13	4	4	26	25	6	6	18	18	6	4	4	45	35	35	10	4	6	25	35	25
Potash, muriate of, for fertilizing purposes	4	4	18	18	C	6	14	13	4	4	26	25	6	6	18	18	6	4	4	45	35	35	9	4	6	30	35	25
Presses, printing, boxed, O. R	1	2	40	30	1	5	40	15	3	2	38	47	3	5	38	22	3	2	2	70	60	65	3	2	5	70	60	30
Printed matter, in sheets, boxed	1	1	40	35	1	3	40	25	1	1	65	53½	1	3	65	34½	2	1	1	85	75	75	3	1	3	70	75	50
Printed matter, in bundles	....	1	....	35	....	3	....	25	....	1	....	53½	....	3	....	34½	1	1	1	100	75	75	1	1	3	100	75	50
Prunes, in boxes or kegs	3	3	23	25	4	4	18	18	2	3	50	34½	2	4	50	25	2	2	3	85	60	50	2	2	4	85	60	35
Prunes, in barrels or casks	3	3	23	25	4	4	18	18	3	3	38	34½	3	4	38	25	3	4	3	70	35	50	3	4	4	70	35	35
Pulp, mineral	4	4	18	18	C	5	14	15	....	4	....	25	....	5	....	22	....	3	4	....	45	35	....	4	5	....	35	30
Pulp, wood, wet	4	4	18	18	A	6	15	13	2	4	50	25	6	6	18	18	6	4	4	45	35	35	10	4	6	25	35	25
Pumice stone, in boxes, kegs, or bags	3	4	23	18	3	5	23	15	3	4	38	25	3	5	38	22	....	2	4	....	60	35	....	2	5	....	60	30
Pumice stone, in barrels or casks	3	4	23	18	3	5	23	15	3	4	38	25	3	5	38	22	3	4	4	70	35	35	3	4	5	70	35	30
Putty, in barrels	4	4	18	18	4	5	18	15	4	4	26	25	4	5	26	22	6	4	4	45	35	35	6	4	5	45	35	30
Radiators, steam	3	3	23	25	4	5	18	15	4	3	26	34½	5	5	21	22	6	3	3	45	45	50	9	4	5	30	35	30
Rags, in sacks	....	2	....	30	....	2	....	30	1	2	65	47	5	2	21	47	1	2	2	100	60	65	1	2	2	100	60	65
Rags, pressed, in bales	4	5	18	15	4	5	18	15	4	5	26	22	5	5	21	22	10	4	5	25	35	30	10	4	5	25	35	30
Raisins	2	3	32	25	3	4	23	18	2	3	50	34½	2	4	50	25	2	3	3	85	45	50	2	3	4	85	45	35
Rattan	1	1	40	35	1	3	40	25	1	1	65	53½	1	3	65	34½	1	1	1	100	75	75	1	1	3	100	75	50
Refrigerators	1	2	40	30	1	2	40	30	3	2	38	47	3	2	38	47	3	1	2	70	75	65	3	1	2	70	75	65
Rice	4	4	18	18	4	6	18	13	4	4	26	22	5	6	21	18	6	4	4	45	35	35	6	4	6	45	35	25
Roofing, felt	3	4	23	18	A	5	15	15	4	4	26	22	6	5	18	22	6	4	4	45	35	35	9	4	5	30	35	30
Roofing, paper	3	4	38	18	A	5	15	15	4	4	26	22	6	5	18	22	5	4	4	50	35	35	10	4	5	25	35	30
Rope, in coils	4	3	18	25	4	4	18	18	4	3	26	34½	5	4	21	25	6	4	3	45	35	50	6	4	4	45	35	35
Rope, wire	4	4	18	18	4	5	18	15	3	4	38	25	3	5	38	22	6	4	4	45	35	35	6	4	5	45	35	30
Rosin, in barrels	4	4	18	18	A	6	15	13	4	4	26	25	6	6	18	18	6	(*)	4	45	25	35	10	(*)	6	25	25	25
Rugs, woolen, hemp, or jute	1	1	40	35	1	4	40	18	1	1	65	53½	1	4	65	25	1	1	1	100	75	75	1	1	4	100	75	35
Sadirons, in boxes	4	4	18	18	A	5	15	15	4	4	26	25	5	5	21	22	6	2	4	45	60	35	6	2	5	45	60	30
Sadirons, in barrels	4	4	18	18	A	5	15	15	4	4	26	25	5	5	21	22	....	4	4	....	35	35	....	4	5	....	35	30
Salt, in boxes	....	4	....	18	....	4	....	18	4	4	26	25	4	4	26	25	6	2	4	45	60	35	6	2	4	45	60	35
Salt, in barrels	4	5	18	15	B	5	14½	15	5	5	21	22	(*)	5	....	22	6	(*)	5	45	25	30	6	(*)	5	45	25	30
Salts, Epsom or Glauber, in barrels	4	4	18	18	4	5	18	15	4	4	26	25	5	5	21	22	3	4	4	70	35	35	3	4	5	70	35	30
Sardines, in boxes	1	4	40	18	1	5	40	15	2	4	50	25	2	5	50	22	2	2	4	85	60	35	2	2	5	85	60	30
Sash weights, loose	4	3	18	25	A	5	15	15	3	3	38	34½	5	5	21	22	2	2	3	85	60	50	10	2	5	25	60	30
Sash weights, in bundles of 50 pounds	4	4	18	18	A	5	15	15	4	4	26	25	5	5	21	22	6	4	4	45	35	35	10	4	5	25	35	30
Scales and scale beams, not boxed	2	1	32	35	2	5	32	15	1	1	65	53½	4	5	26	22	1	1	1	100	75	75	1	1	5	100	75	30

* Special.

Commodities.	Joint Merchandise compared with Official No. 11. Between Philadelphia, Pa., and Elmira, N. Y.								Middle and Western States compared with Official No. 11. From Buffalo, N. Y., to East St. Louis, Ill.								East Bound and West Bound compared with Official No. 11. Between New York, N. Y., and Chicago, Ill.											
	Less than carloads.				Carloads.				Less than carloads.				Carloads.				Less than carloads.						Carloads.					
	Class.		Rate.		Class.		Rate.		Class.		Rate.		Class.		Rate.		Class.			Rate.			Class.			Rate.		
	Joint Merchandise, 1886.	Official No. 11, 1893.	Joint Merchandise, 1886.	Official No. 11, 1893.	Joint Merchandise, 1886.	Official No. 11, 1893.	Joint Merchandise, 1886.	Official No. 11, 1893.	Md. and West. States, 1886.	Official No. 11, 1893.	Md. and West. States, 1886.	Official No. 11, 1893.	Md. and West. States, 1886.	Official No. 11, 1893.	Md. and West. States, 1886.	Official No. 11, 1893.	East Bound, 1886.	West Bound, 1886.	Official No. 11, 1893.	East Bound, 1886.	West Bound, 1886.	Official No. 11, 1893.	East Bound, 1886.	West Bound, 1886.	Official No. 11, 1893.	East Bound, 1886.	West Bound, 1886.	Official No. 11, 1893.
Scythes, in boxes	2	3	32	25	2	3	32	25	1	3	65	34½	4	3	26	34½	3	2	3	70	60	50	3	2	3	70	60	50
Seeds, garden	1	2	40	30	1	5	40	15	3	2	38	47	4	5	26	22	3	1	2	70	75	65	6	4	5	45	35	30
Seeds, grass or orchard	3	3	23	25	4	5	18	15	3	3	38	34½	4	5	26	22	5	3	3	50	45	50	8	4	5	35	35	30
Shot, in kegs	3	4	23	18	3	5	23	15	4	4	26	25	5	5	21	22	6	4	4	45	35	35	8	4	5	35	35	30
Shovels or spades, in boxes	2	4	32	18	4	4	18	18	3	4	38	25	4	4	26	25	6	2	4	45	60	35	6	4	4	45	35	35
Slate roofing	4	4	18	18	B	6	14½	13	4	4	26	25	6	6	18	18	3	4	4	70	35	35	6	4	6	45	35	25
Slates, school, boxed	3	4	23	18	A	5	15	15	3	4	38	25	5	5	21	22	3	3	4	70	45	35	3	3	5	70	45	30
Slats, bed, in bundles	....	3	....	25	....	3	....	25	....	3	....	34½	....	3	....	34½	6	1	3	45	75	50	11	1	3	25	75	50
Soap, common, in boxes	4	4	18	18	4	6	18	13	4	4	26	25	5	6	21	18	7	4	4	40	35	35	9	4	6	30	35	25
Soda, sal	4	4	18	18	4	6	18	13	4	4	26	25	5	6	21	18	6	4	4	45	35	35	6	4	6	45	35	25
Spelter	3	4	23	18	4	6	18	13	4	4	26	25	6	6	18	18	6	4	4	45	35	35	10	4	6	25	35	25
Spikes, in kegs	4	4	18	18	A	5	15	15	4	4	26	25	5	5	21	22	10	4	4	25	35	35	10	4	5	25	35	30
Starch, in barrels or boxes	4	4	18	18	4	6	18	18	4	4	26	25	5	6	21	18	8	3	4	35	45	35	10	4	6	25	35	25
Stearine, in barrels	4	4	18	18	A	5	15	15	4	4	26	25	5	5	21	22	12	4	4	30	35	35	12	4	5	30	35	30
Strawboards, in bundles	2	3	32	25	A	5	15	15	4	3	26	34½	5	5	21	22	6	2	3	45	60	50	10	4	5	25	35	30
Sugar, maple	3	3	23	25	3	4	23	18	3	3	38	34½	3	4	38	25	6	2	3	45	60	50	6	4	4	45	35	35
Sugar, grape	....	4	....	18	....	6	....	13	4	4	26	25	5	6	21	18	....	2	4	....	60	35	....	4	6	....	35	25
Sugar, n. o. s	4	4	18	18	4	6	18	13	5	4	21	25	5	6	21	18	6	(*)	4	45	25	35	6	(*)	6	45	25	25
Sulphur, in barrels	4	4	18	18	4	4	18	18	4	4	26	25	4	4	26	25	6	4	4	45	35	35	6	4	4	45	35	35
Sirup, in cans, boxed	2	3	32	25	2	5	32	15	5	3	21	34½	5	5	21	22	6	2	3	45	60	50	6	2	5	45	60	30
Tacks, iron, in boxes	2	4	32	18	4	5	18	15	4	4	26	25	4	5	26	22	3	2	4	70	60	35	6	2	5	45	60	30
Tallow	4	4	18	18	A	5	15	15	4	4	26	25	5	5	21	22	12	4	4	30	35	35	12	4	5	30	35	30
Tapioca	1	3	40	25	1	5	40	15	2	3	50	34½	2	5	50	22	....	2	3	....	60	50	....	2	5	....	60	30
Tar, in barrels	4	4	18	18	A	6	15	13	4	4	26	25	6	6	18	18	6	4	4	45	35	35	10	4	6	25	35	25
Tea	1	1	40	35	1	1	40	35	1	1	65	53½	1	1	65	53½	1	1	1	100	75	75	3	1	1	70	75	75
Terra alba, in barrels	4	4	18	18	A	5	15	15	....	4	....	25	....	5	....	22	6	4	4	45	35	35	6	4	5	45	35	30
Toys, n. o. s., boxed	D1	1	80	35	D1	1	80	35	1	1	65	53½	1	1	65	53½	1	1½t1	1	100	112½	75	1	1½	1	100	112½	75
Tubing, iron	4	4	18	18	A	5	15	15	4	4	26	25	5	5	21	22	....	4	4	....	35	35	....	4	5	....	35	30
Umbrellas, in cases	1	1	40	35	1	1	40	35	1	1	65	53½	1	1	65	53½	1	1	1	100	75	75	1	1	1	100	75	75
Varnish, in cans, boxed	1	2	40	30	1	4	40	18	3	2	38	47	4	4	26	25	4	2	2	60	60	65	4	2	4	60	60	35
Vitriol, blue, in barrels	4	4	18	18	4	6	18	13	4	4	26	25	4	6	26	18	6	4	4	45	35	35	10	4	6	25	35	25

Vises, iron	2	4	32	18	2	5	32	15	4	4	26	25	5	5	21	22	6	2	4	45	60	35	6	2	5	45	60	30
Wadding	1	1	40	35	1	1	40	35	1	1	65	53½	1	1	65	53½	2	1	1	85	75	75	2	1	1	85	75	75
Washboards	2	2	32	30	4	5	18	15	3	2	38	47	5	5	21	22	3	2	2	70	60	65	9	4	5	30	35	30
Wheat, cracked	4	4	18	18	A	5	15	15	5	4	21	25	(*)	5	….	22	12	4	4	30	35	35	13	4	5	30	35	30
Wheelbarrows, iron or wood	1	3	40	25	4	5	18	15	1	3	65	34½	5	….	21	….	1½	1	3	150	75	50	9	4	5	30	35	30
Whiting	4	4	18	18	4	6	18	13	4	4	26	25	5	6	21	18	6	4	4	45	35	35	6	4	6	45	35	25
Wire screens	….	1	….	35	….	4	….	18	1	1	65	53½	1	4	65	25	1	2 t.1	1	100	150	75	6	2	4	45	150	35
Wire, copper	2	3	32	25	2	4	32	18	3	3	38	34½	3	4	38	25	2	2	3	85	60	50	2	2	4	85	60	35
Wire, binding	2	4	32	18	4	5	18	15	3	4	38	25	5	5	21	22	5	2	4	50	60	35	6	4	5	45	35	30
Wood pulp, wet	4	4	18	18	A	6	15	13	2	4	50	25	6	6	18	18	6	4	4	45	35	35	10	4	6	25	35	25

*Special.

The most satisfactory form of presenting the general results of the consolidation of the classifications which was made on April 1, 1887, is given by the following table, showing the number of articles covered by the former classifications which were superseded by the Official classifiication.

The table is arranged to show the total number of classifications or descriptions, and also the proportion receiving separately less than car load and car-load rates, together with the percentage of the number of descriptions in each classification.

TABLE 2—COMPARISON OF VARIOUS CLASSIFICATIONS FORMERLY IN USE IN THE TERRITORY NOW COVERED BY THE OFFICIAL CLASSIFICATION WITH OFFICIAL CLASSIFICATION NO. 11, EFFECTIVE JANUARY 2, 1893.

Name of classification.	Total number of classifications.		Classified as L. C. L. and C. L. quantity at same rating.		Classified as L. C. L. and C. L. quantity at lower rating.		Classified as C. L. with no rating for L. C. L.		Percentage of the number of classifications in each class to the total number in all classes. — Classes.																		Summary.	
	No.	Per cent.	No.	Per cent.	No.	Per cent.	No.	Per cent.	*1.	2.	3.	4.	5	6	.	8.	9.	10.	11.	12.	13.	A.	B.	C.	Special.	Total.	Total percentage above fourth class.	Total percentage in fourth class and lower.
Joint Merchandise	1,073	100.00	710	66.17	354	32.99	9	.84	33.15	17.52	9.53	26.28	....	....	....	....	....	....	....	....	....	7.64	3.78	2.10	....	100.00	60.20	39.80
Middle and West'n States	2,681	100.00	1,673	62.40	669	24.95	339	12.65	22.09	9.14	18.36	25.19	21.43	3.49	....	....	....	....	....	....	....	....	....	....	.30	100.00	49.59	50.41
West Bound	971	100.00	824	84.86	137	14.11	10	1.03	31.76	23.65	11.37	30.96	....	....	....	....	....	....	....	....	....	....	....	....	2.26	100.00	66.78	33.22
East Bound	2,037	100.00	1,210	59.40	529	25.97	298	14.63	19.36	10.21	12.39	5.81	3.39	22.14	.98	3.86	7.09	8.42	1.01	3.04	2.30	....	....	....	....	100.00	†51.16	‡48.84
Official No. 1	2,840	100.00	1,564	55.07	1,011	35.60	265	9.33	26.62	10.41	18.00	20.15	19.29	5.53	....	....	....	....	....	....	....	....	....	....	....	100.00	55.03	44.97
Official No. 11	5,634	100.00	2,121	37.65	3,105	55.11	408	7.24	22.54	11.96	18.71	18.63	23.46	4.70	....	....	....	....	....	....	....	....	....	....	....	100.00	53.21	46.79

* Percentage shown includes articles classified higher than 1 class as 4 t 1, D 1, etc.
† Percentage of number of articles in fifth class and higher.
‡ Percentage of number of articles in sixth and lower classes.

In explanation of the figures in the foregoing table it should be stated that the number of items shown represents the entire number of descriptions under which classified freight is shipped, and is much greater than the actual number of articles classified. The class under which any particular article may be shipped and the rate that may be obtained often varies, depending upon its relative size, the manner in which it is packed for shipment, and the degree of risk assumed by the carrier. For example, lead pipe is classified as follows:

	Class.
Lead pipe, on reels or in rolls, carriers risk, less than car loads	1
car load	4
Lead pipe, on reels or in rolls, owner's risk, less than car loads	3
car load	4
Lead pipe, not boxed, not otherwise specified, less than car loads	2
Lead pipe, in boxes or casks, less car load	4

This article is included in the total number of items given in the table as four descriptions, though in fact but one article is classified. The same rule is observed for each ot the classifications embraced in the table.

The largest increase in the classification is shown from a comparison of the old West Bound classification in effect prior to April, 1887, which applied from the seaboard to Chicago and other western competitive points. This provided for only 971 separate items. Of this number 824 or 84.86 per cent were classifications for shipments in quantities less than carloads, and which took the same rating when in carloads; 137 or 14.11 per cent were classifications for shipments in quantities less than carloads which had a separate lower rating when in carloads, and 10 or 1.3 per cent covered shipments in carloads only.

In the present Official classification there are 5,634 separate items, of which 2,121 or 37.65 per cent are for shipments in quantities less than carloads, which are given the same rating when in carloads; 3,105 or 55.11 per cent are for shipments in less than carload quantities, which have a separate lower rating when in carloads; and 408 or 7.24 per cent are for shipments in carload quantities only.

From these figures it is shown that the total number of items in the present Official classification exceeds by 4,663 the number in the former West Bound classification applying from the seaboard, and that the proportion classified as L. C. L., with the same rating for C. L., has decreased from 84.86 per cent in the old to 37.65 per cent in the new, while the proportion classified as L. C. L., with a lower rating when in carloads, has increased from 14.11 per cent in the old to 55.11 per cent in the new, and that 7.24 per cent of the present total number of items are for carload quantities only, as compared with 1.03 per cent in the former West Bound classification.

Of the total number of items in the old West Bound classification 66.78 per cent of the articles classified were classed above fourth-class, and 33.22 per cent were in fourth class or lower. These relations are shown to have greatly changed by the present Official classification, from which it is noticed that only 53.21 per cent of the articles classified are in classes higher than fourth class, and that 46.79 per cent are in fourth class or lower.

The number of articles for which no distinction was made as between the L. C. L. and C. L. rates were relatively more in the old classification than in the Official as now arranged, and conversely the number of articles which are classified lower when in C. L. than in L. C. L. quantities in the Official is relatively greater than the number similarly provided for in the old classification. Including the number of articles classified only in carload quantities with the articles classified both L.

C. L. and C. L., the total number of items in the former West Bound classification given a carload rating was 147 or 15.14 per cent, while in the present Official there are 3,513 or 62.35 per cent receiving a carload rating.

A similar comparison made with the Joint Merchandise classification, which governed shipments between the interior points in the Middle States, shows that there has been relatively a much greater increase in the articles which now may be taken at carload rates. The same may be said for the Middle and Western States classification, formerly applied westward from Buffalo and Pittsburg.

The former East Bound classification embraced a relatively larger tonnage taken at carload rates than either of the other old classifications mentioned, yet the application of the Official shows an increase of 2,686 items which may be now carried at carload rates between the points to which the East Bound classification formerly applied.

While the total number of items in the new classification is much greater than in the old classifications, it should be again explained that this numerical increase does not imply an addition to the traffic of new articles of commerce; it simply means that in many cases a commodity which under the old classifications was found in one class only, regardless of the manner in which it might be offered for shipment, is under the new classification placed in two or more different classes, according to the form in which it is received for transportation.

It is made apparent by a comparison of the percentages of classified items now receiving the carload rating, under the old and new classifications, that the public has been to a large degree benefited by the resulting lower rates thereon.

A further illustration of the extent of the enlargement of the classification now under consideration is found in the articles of furniture, agricultural implements, and machinery, as shown by the following table:

TABLE 3.—NUMBER OF DESCRIPTIONS.

	1867.			1876.			1887.			1893.		
	Total.	L. C. L.	C. L.	Total.	L. C. L.	C. L.	Total.	L. C. L.	C. L.	Total.	L. C. L.	C. L.
Furniture	8	8	......	20	20	2	84	65	19	193	147	46
Agricultural implements	4	4	......	5	5	2	114	89	25	180	128	52
Machinery	5	5	......	5	5	2	63	47	16	105	59	46

It would appear from the above figures that the carriers have now provided a classification and rating for every possible form of package in which these articles are offered for shipment, and that the number receiving a lower or carload rating has greatly increased.

Throughout all the tables presented a gradual downward tendency is observed for the entire classification. The extent of these changes is further shown by a comparison of the average rates on all traffic from New York to Chicago. Expressed on the basis of the number of descriptions carried in each class the average rate for all descriptions in the classification was, in 1886, 63.53 cents, and in 1893, 48.77 cents per 100 lbs. Thus the variation in the classification of 20.91 per cent from the higher to lower classes is equivalent to a reduction in the average rate of 14.75 cents per 100 lbs.

In the numerous publications which have appeared from time to time, intended to show the decline in rates, only passing comment has been bestowed upon changes in the rates resulting from changes in freight classifications. It is common to compare the rates for various classes between two points for different periods and to draw conclusions from the changes shown by such comparisons. When these comparisons omit reference to the changes made within the same period in the classification they are obviously incomplete. It is a part of the history of freight classifications that from the date of their adoption constant pressure is brought to bear upon carriers using them from all classes of shippers for a lower classification of the articles in which they have business interest. These demands have usually been met by the carriers, as is shown by the frequent revision and changes in the leading classifications. The changes which have taken place in the classifications since 1887 have been far-reaching in their benefits to the public by the consequent reduction in the freight charges. This has been especially noticeable throughout the section now governed by the Official classification, and the tables have been arranged to present as fully as possible the effect of these changes. Similar results for the other sections governed by a general classification will be shown by appropriate tables.

THE WESTERN CLASSIFICATION.

The Western classification governs the territory north and west of Chicago, west of a line drawn from Chicago to St. Louis, and west of the Mississippi River and St. Louis to New Orleans. Prior to 1887 there were many local classifications used throughout this territory, which it is understood have since been superseded and there are now few roads in the territory described not using the Western classification exclusively.

Traffic not covered by commodity rates to and from the Pacific coast was formerly carried under classifications different in name though similar to the Western. A comparison of these with the present Western would no doubt show important changes. As the greater portion of the traffic to and from the Pacific coast is carried at commodity rates, and a very full statement of the changes in these rates is given elsewhere, no comparison of the classifications applied to Pacific coast traffic will here be made. Seventy important Western roads, with a mileage of 90,000 miles, officially announce the adoption of the present Western classification.

The section served by this classification is seen to cover a vast area in which are located thousands of villages, towns, and cities, the transportation business of which is to a large extent affected by its operation. Excluding grain, coal, lumber, live stock, etc., which are principally carried at commodity rates, there yet remain many classes of merchandise, such as clothing, groceries, drugs, machinery, household effects, and innumerable other articles consumed in one form or another by the people, and which are covered by this classification.

Important changes have taken place resulting in lower freight charges to the public, the extent of which will be shown in the following table:

TABLE 4—COMPARISON OF THE VARIOUS CLASSIFICATIONS IN USE DURING THE PERIOD SINCE 1873 IN THE TERRITORY NOW COVERED BY THE WESTERN CLASSIFICATION NUMBER 15.

Year.	Total number of classifications.		Classified as L.C.L.; C.L. at same rating.		Classified as L.C.L. and C.L. quantities at lower rating.		Classified as C.L. and no rating for L.C.L.		Percentage of total number of classifications in each class.												Percentage in third class or higher.	Percentage lower than third class.
	No.	Per ct.	No.	Per ct.	No.	Per ct.	No.	Per ct.	*1	2	3	4	5	A	B	C	D	E	Special.	Total.		
1873	907	100.00	769	84.78	104	11.47	34	3.75	43.42	20.28	7.42	17.01	......	6.33	1.38	1.98	2.18	......	......	100.00	71.12	28.88
1878	897	100.00	757	84.39	133	14.83	7	0.78	38.93	18.45	12.52	19.80	......	2.91	3.79	1.46	2.14	......	......	100.00	69.90	30.10
1882	1,102	100.00	905	82.12	172	15.61	25	2.27	38.77	18.92	12.01	18.76	......	3.53	5.65	2.28	0.08	......	......	100.00	69.70	30.30
1886	1,593	100.00	939	58.95	591	37.10	63	3.95	31.91	14.33	12.91	16.35	7.37	7.97	2.88	1.97	1.56	......	2.75	100.00	59.15	40.85
1887	1,672	100.00	924	55.26	666	39.83	82	4.91	30.62	14.54	13.60	15.74	8.21	7.57	3.21	2.61	1.54	1.16	1.20	100.00	58.76	41.24
1893	3,658	100.00	1,642	44.89	1,731	47.32	285	7.79	28.39	12.69	12.82	16.92	10.65	9.22	3.16	2.19	1.91	0.93	1.12	100.00	53.90	46.10

NOTE.—1873, Chicago, Burlington and Quincy Railroad local freight classification, July 1, 1873.
1878, Chicago, Burlington and Quincy Railroad local freight classification, January 7, 1878.
1882, Chicago, Burlington and Quincy Railroad revised joint classification, January 1, 1882.
1886, Joint Western classification, February 1, 1886.
1887, Western classsification April 1, 1887.
1893, Western classification, January 1, 1893.

* Percentage shown includes articles classified higher than first-class as 4 times 1, D 1, etc.

The present Western classification contains 3,658 separate descriptions of articles. As compared with the classifications of previous years shown by the table, a large increase is observed. This increase is due to the addition of new articles, and principally from extending the classifications to provide for the different forms of shipment of articles already classified. By the arrangement adopted for the table it may be readily seen to what extent articles now receiving a carload rate have increased. For example, in 1882 only 17.88 per cent of the articles were given a carload rating. At the present time 47.32 per cent of the articles may be taken at lower rates when in carload quantities than when in less than carload quantities. There has also been a large increase in the number of articles which are carried in carload quantities only, making a total of 55.11 percent assigned a carload classification.

The tendency to reduction in the classification is also prominently shown by a comparison of the percentages of the articles carried in the separate classes. The summary of these percentages given in the last two columns shows that 46.10 per cent of the articles are now found in classes lower than third class, while in 1882 only 30 per cent of the articles were in such classes. The latter proportion is upon a total of only about a third of the number of articles now covered by the classification.

As further illustrative of the operations of the Western classification the following table is inserted, showing for a number of important articles the changes in the classification from Chicago to Missouri River points, together with the changes in the rates for the same commodities. From this table it may be readily seen to what extent reductions have been made, both in the classification and in the rates.

Similar reductions have taken place in the through and local rates of all railroads throughout the territory covered by this classification.

COMPARISON OF CLASSIFICATION AND RATES.

TABLE 5.—COMPARISON OF CLASSIFICATION AND RATES EFFECTIVE DURING THE YEARS 1878, 1887, AND 1893, IN TERRITORY GOVERNED BY WESTERN CLASSIFICATION. RATES USED ARE IN CENTS PER 100 POUNDS FROM CHICAGO, ILL., TO SOUTHWESTERN MISSOURI RIVER POINTS, VIZ: KANSAS CITY, MO.; ATCHISON, KANS., AND LEAVENWORTH, KANS.

[In cents per 100 lbs.]

	1	2	3	4	5	A	B	C	D	E
January, 1878	85	70	40	30	25	37½	30	20	.....	.....
April, 1887	90	75	50	35	30	32½	29½	23	23	16
January, 1893	75	60	42	30	25	30	25	20	17½	16

Commodities.	Less than carloads						Carloads.					
	Class.			Rate.			Class.			Rate.		
	1878	1887	1893	1878	1887	1893	1878	1887	1893	1878	1887	1893
Agricultural implements as follows:												
Cultivators, iron or wood, K. D., flat, in bundles	D1	1	1	170	90	75	D1	A	A	170	32½	30
Fanning mills, K. D., flat, in bundles	D1	1	1	170	90	75	D1	A	A	170	32½	30
Harvesting machines (self-binding harvesters, K. D.)	1	1	3	85	90	42	1	A	A	85	32½	30
Plows, n. o. s., K. D., boxed or crated	3	2	3	40	75	42	3	A	A	40	32½	30
Ale and porter in wood	3	3	3	40	50	42	4	3	5	30	50	25
Alum	3	3	3	40	50	42	3	3	4	40	50	30
Asbestus, in barrels or casks	4	4	4	30	35	30	4	5	5	30	30	25
Asphaltum	4	4	4	30	35	30	C	C	D	20	23	17½
Bags, burlap, gunny, or jute in bales	2	4	4	70	35	30	2	4	5	70	35	25
Baking powder, in tin boxes	2	3	3	70	50	42	2	4	4	70	35	30
Blacking, shoe, in boxes or kegs	2	2	2	70	75	60	2	2	4	70	75	30
Blue vitriol	2	2	4	70	75	30	2	4	5	70	35	25
Bluing	1	1	1	85	90	75	1	1	4	85	90	30
Borax	2	2	3	70	75	42	2	2	4	70	75	30
Brick, common, n. o. s	4	4	4	30	35	30	D	E	E	..	29½	16
Brimstone, in barrels and hogsheads	4	4	4	30	35	30	4	4	C	30	23	20
Canned fish (not sardines), fruits, meats, soups, and vegetables, n. o. s.	3	4	4	40	35	30	4	5	5	30	30	25
Chloride of lime	3	3	3	40	50	42	3	3	D	40	50	17½
Clay, common	4	4	4	30	35	30	4	E	E	30	16	16
Clothing, boxed	1	1	1	85	90	75	1	1	1	85	90	75
Coffee, green, in sacks	4	4	4	30	35	30	4	5	5	30	30	25
Crockery and earthenware, in hogsheads, casks, or crates	4	2	4	30	75	30	4	5	5	30	30	25
Dry goods, in boxes	1	1	1	85	90	75	1	1	1	85	90	75
Drugs and medicines	1	1	1	85	90	75	1	1	1	85	90	75
Eggs packed in barrels or boxes, prepaid	2	2	2	70	75	60	4	3	3	30	50	42
Farina	2	2	2	70	75	60	2	2	2	70	75	60
Felt for roofing	3	3	4	40	50	30	B	B	B	30	29½	25
Fertilizers, n. o. s	4	4	4	30	35	30	D	D	E	..	23	16
Fruit, dried or desiccated, n. o. s., in cans, boxes, barrels, or sacks released	2	3	3	70	50	42	2	4	4	70	35	30
Fruit, green, n. o. s	1	1	1	85	90	75	1	*3	3	85	46	42
Furniture, as follows:												
Bedsteads, n. o. s	2	2	2	70	75	60	2	A	A	70	32½	30
Chairs, common l. c. l., boxed	4	3	2	30	50	60	4	3	4	30	50	30
Mattresses	D1	1	1	170	90	75	1	1	1	85	90	75
Glass, window, common, not exceeding 86 inches	4	4	4	30	35	30	B	4	5	30	35	25
Glassware, n. o. s., in boxes, barrels, casks, or crates	3	1	2	40	90	60	3	3	4	40	50	30
Groceries, n. o. s	2	1	1	70	90	75	2	1	1	70	90	75
Hardware, n. o. s	2	2	2	70	75	60	2	2	2	70	75	60
Hides, green, in bundles	2	3	3	70	50	42	3	5	5	40	30	25
Hoops, hoop poles, C. L., loaded together	4	4	4	30	35	30	C	C	D	20	23	17½
Husks, in bales	1	2	3	85	75	42	D	D	C	.....	23	20
Ice, prepaid	1	1	1	85	90	75	D	E	E	.....	16	16
India-rubber goods	1	1	1	85	90	75	1	1	1	85	90	75
Iron chain, loose (except cable)	2	2	2	70	75	60	2	2	2	70	75	60
Iron horse and mule shoes	4	4	4	30	35	30	B	5	5	30	30	25
Iron nails and spikes, n. o. s., in kegs	4	4	4	30	35	30	B	5	5	30	30	25

*15 per cent less than 3.

COMPARISON OF CLASSIFICATION AND RATES.

TABLE 5.—COMPARISON OF CLASSIFICATION AND RATES EFFECTIVE DURING THE YEARS 1878, 1887, AND 1893, ETC.—Continued.

[In cents per 100 lbs.]

Commodities.	Less than carloads.						Carloads.					
	Class.			Rate.			Class.			Rate.		
	1878	1887	1893	1878	1887	1893	1878	1887	1893	1878	1887	1893
Jute and jute butts, in bales	3	3	3	40	50	42	B	B	B	30	29½	25
Lard, in barrels or tierces	4	4	4	30	35	30	4	5	5	30	30	25
Leather, in rolls or boxes	2	2	2	70	75	60	2	2	4	70	75	30
Licorice mass, in boxes	2	2	3	70	75	42	2	2	4	70	75	30
Lime	4	4	4	30	35	30	C	C	C	20	23	20
Lime water in barrels	2	2	3	70	75	42	2	2	D	70	75	17½
Looms	D1	D1	D1	170	180	150	D1	D1	A	170	180	30
Malt	4	4	4	30	35	30	B	B	C	30	29½	20
Manila, in bales	3	3	2	40	75	60	3	B	B	40	29½	25
Marble dust	4	4	4	30	35	30	C	C	D	20	23	17½
Matting, cocoa and hemp	2	2	2	70	75	60	2	2	2	70	75	60
Nuts, hickory, in barrels	2	2	2	70	75	60	2	3	A	70	50	30
Oakum, in bales	3	3	2	40	50	60	B	B	B	30	29½	25
Oilcloth, floor, in boxes or crates under 12 feet in length	3	3	2	40	50	60	3	3	3	40	50	42
Paints in oil, white lead, or zinc, chemical paraffin, rubber, rubber in cans, boxed, or in kegs or barrels	4	4	4	30	35	30	5	5	5	25	30	25
Paper, building or roofing	3	3	4	40	50	30	B	B	B	30	29½	25
Paraffin wax, in barrels or boxes	2	2	2	70	75	60	2	2	4	70	75	30
Paste, flour, in barrels	4	4	4	30	35	30	4	4	5	30	30	25
Pipe, sewer, o. r. b	2	2	3	70	75	42	C	C	E	20	23	16
Pipe, sewer, in crates or hogsheads	2	2	4	70	75	30	C	C	3	20	23	42
Pitch	4	4	4	30	35	30	D	C	D	.....	23	17½
Plaster, land, in sacks or barrels	4	4	4	30	35	30	D	E	C	.....	16	20
Potatoes	2	4	4	70	35	30	A	C	C	37½	23	20
Presses, cider	2	2	2	70	75	60	2	2	A	70	75	30
Printers' cases, in bundles	2	2	3	70	75	42	2	2	B	70	75	25
Pulp, wood	3	3	3	40	52	42	C	C	C	20	23	20
Pumps and tubina, wooden	3	3	3	40	50	42	A	A	B	37	32½	25
Raisins	2	2	2	70	75	60	3	3	3	40	50	42
Rice, in barrels	4	4	4	30	35	30	5	5	5	25	30	25
Rope, one-quarter inch or over	4	4	3	30	35	42	4	4	4	30	35	30
Saddlery, n. o. s., boxed	2	2	2	70	75	60	2	2	2	70	75	60
Sand, in bulk, c. l	4	4	4	30	35	30	D	E	E	.....	16	16
Sardines or shardines, domestic and imported, in boxes or kegs	2	2	2	70	75	60	2	2	5	70	75	25
Seeds, broom corn	1	3	3	85	50	42	4	5	A	30	30	30
Seeds, clover	2	3	3	70	50	42	4	5	A	30	30	30
Shot, in kegs, boxes, or gunnies	4	4	4	30	35	30	4	4	5	30	35	25
Slate, school	2	2	2	70	75	60	2	2	4	70	75	30
Slate, roofing	3	3	3	40	50	42	B	B	D	30	29½	17½
Soda, nitrate of	4	4	4	30	35	30	4	4	5	30	35	25
Soda, silicate of	4	4	4	30	35	30	4	5	5	30	30	25
Solder, in boxes	2	2	3	70	75	42	2	2	4	70	75	30
Starch, in boxes or barrels	3	3	3	40	50	42	4	4	5	30	35	25
Staves and heading	4	4	4	30	35	30	C	5	D	20	30	17½
Straw, baled and pressed	3	3	3	40	52	42	D	C	C	.....	23	20
Sugar, n. o. s., in boxes, barrels, or sacks	4	4	4	30	35	30	5	5	5	25	30	25
Sulphur, in sacks, barrels, or hogsheads	4	4	4	30	35	30	4	4	C.	30	35	20
Sirup, n. o. s., in barrels, kegs, or kits	4	4	4	30	35	30	5	5	5	25	30	25
Tallow	4	4	4	30	35	30	5	5	5	25	30	25
Tar, in barrels or cases	4	4	4	30	35	30	C	D	D	20	23	17½
Tile, drain, in crates or hogsheads	4	4	4	30	35	30	D	E	D	.....	16	17½
Tile, roofing	3	3	4	40	50	30	B	B	D	30	29½	17½
Tin, pig or slab	2	2	2	70	75	60	2	2	4	70	75	30
Tinware, nested in boxes, barrels, or crates	2	2	2	70	75	60	2	2	4	70	75	30
Wire cloth	2	2	2	70	75	60	2	4	4	70	35	30
Wood, roofing	1	3	4	85	50	30	1	5	5	85	30	25
Wool, in sacks	1	2	2	85	75	60	1	2	2	85	75	60
Wool, compressed in bales	3	3	3	40	50	42	3	3	3	40	50	42
Yeast cakes, powder, or crumbs	3	3	3	40	50	42	3	3	4	40	50	30
Zinc, pig or slabs	4	4	4	30	35	30	5	5	5	25	30	25

SOUTHERN RAILWAY AND STEAMSHIP ASSOCIATION CLASSIFICATION.

The classification of this association applies throughout the territory south of the Ohio and Potomac rivers, and east of the Mississippi River. In this classification, as well as in the previous ones mentioned, there have been extensive reductions by the increase in the number of descriptions of articles carried thereunder. A summary of the number of such descriptions is given below for several years:

TABLR 6.—COMPARISON OF VARIOUS CLASSIFICATIONS ADOPTED BY THE SOUTHERN RAILWAY AND STEAMSHIP ASSOCIATION AND IN EFFECT DURING THE YEARS NAMED.

Years.	Total number of classifications.		Classified as L. C. L. and C. L. quantities at same rating.		Classified as L. C. L. and C. L. quantities at lower rating.		Classified as C. L. with no rating for L. C. L.		Percentage of total number of classifications in each class. Classes.															Summary.	
	No.	Per cent.	No.	Per cent.	No.	Per cent.	No.	Per cent.	1	2	3	4	5	6	A	B	C	D	E	F	G	H	Special.	Total percentage third class and higher.	Total percentage lower than third class.
1876	893	100.00	840	94.07	47	5.26	6	0.67	32.62	16.91	12.34	15.11	14.26	3.30	1.06	.....	.....	.....	.....	.....	.....	.....	5.00	61.27	38.73
1880	983	100.00	829	84.33	117	11.90	37	3.77	26.18	12.55	14.55	15.00	19.45	6.64	0.55	0.45	0.09	1.18	0.18	0.18	0.18	0.09	2.73	53.28	46.72
1887	1,177	100.00	966	82.07	175	14.87	36	3.06	27.52	15.09	14.05	13.31	15.53	8.95	1.18	0.59	0.30	0.59	0.44	0.15	.....	0.08	2.22	56.66	43.34
1893	1,752	100.00	1,437	82.02	270	15.41	45	2.57	24.09	15.38	14.59	14.54	12.27	12.76	2.27	0.64	0.30	0.84	0.54	0.10	.....	0.05	1.63	54.06	45.94

From the foregoing it is shown that 82 per cent of the articles are now classified at less than carload quantities only, and that 17.98 per cent are assigned a carload rating. The latter proportion is observed to be relatively lower than for either of the other classifications for which data has been given. The rate reductions will be more fully illustrated by table following, which shows the changes between two important points in this section. The arrangement of the table permits of a comparison of changes in the classification and also of the rate changes.

COMPARISON OF CLASSIFICATION AND RATES.

TABLE 7.—COMPARISON OF CLASSIFICATION AND RATES EFFECTIVE DURING THE YEARS 1876, 1880, 1887, AND 1893, IN THE TERRITORY GOVERNED BY SOUTHERN RAILWAY AND STEAMSHIP ASSOCIATION. RATES USED ARE IN CENTS PER 100 POUNDS FROM LOUISVILLE, KY., TO ATLANTA, GA., AS FOLLOWS:

	1	2	3	4	5	6	A	B	C	D	E	F	G	H
1876	150	125	100	85	58	46	..	85	73	..	..	132	...	..
1880	119	104	89	76	61	46	28	47	43	38	52	81	138	71
1887	107	92	81	68	56	46	28	36	31	27	48	54	...	53
1893	107	92	81	68	56	46	28	35	28	24	48	48	...	53

Commodities.	Louisville, Ky., to Atlanta, Ga.							
	Class.				Rates in cents per 100 pounds.			
	1876	1880	1887	1893	1876	1880	1887	1893
Agricultural implements, C. L	A	......	5	6	......	......	56	46
Agricultural implements, L. C. L., as follows:								
Harrow teeth, packed	1½	......	4	6	225	......	68	46
Shellers, corn, packed	1	2	1	2	150	104	107	92
Spreaders, manure, K. D	......	......	2	3	......	......	92	81
Babbitt, metal, C. L	2	4	4	4	125	76	68	68
Barley, L. C. L	5	D	6	D	58	38	46	24
Barrels, half barrels, and kegs, except ale and beer, empty, C. L	A	4	4	6	......	76	68	46
Batting, cotton, N. O. S	D1	D1	D1	2	300	238	214	92
pressed in bales	D1	D1	D1	4	300	238	214	68
Bells, cast iron, L. C. L	2	2	2	3	125	104	92	81
C. L	2	2	2	5	125	104	92	56
Bluing liquid, in glass, packed	......	1	1	2	......	119	107	92
Blue, stone, in barrels or casks	4	5	5	6	85	61	56	46
Boilers, engines, or parts thereof, C. L	......	......	5	6	......	......	56	46
Boots, and in cases, C. L	1	1	1	2	150	119	107	92
Brimstone in barrels, L. C. L	4	5	3	5	85	61	81	56
Brooms, C. L	1	1	1	2	150	119	107	92
Burlaps	5	5	6	A	58	61	46	28
Canned goods, N. O. S., C. L	4	4	4	5	85	76	68	56
Cider, in wood, O. R. B. L., or spoiling	5	5	2	5	58	61	92	56
Coffee, green, in double sacks	5	6	6	6	58	46	46	46
Creameries, packed or wrapped	......	......	D1	3	......	......	214	81
Dry goods made wholly of cotton, viz: calicoes, canton flannels, cotton rope or twine, drills, etc., L. C. L	1	1	3	5	150	119	81	56
Drugs and medicine, N. O. S	1	1	1	1	150	119	107	107
Dry goods, same as above, C. L	1	1	4	5	150	119	68	56
Dye stuff, N. O. S., dry, in barrels	1	1	1	1	150	119	107	107
Excelsior, pressed in bales, C. L	3	3	4	6	100	89	68	46
Facings, coal and iron, in barrels, L. C. L	4	4	4	6	85	76	68	46
C. L	4	4	4	A	85	76	68	28
Felting	2	2	2	3	125	104	92	81
Fish, in cans, boxed, C. L	5	5	4	5	58	61	68	56
Fittings, iron pipe, in bundles, wired, L. C. L	......	......	D1	3	......	......	214	81
Foil, tin, in boxes	2	2	1	2	125	104	107	92
Freezers, ice cream	1	1	1	3	150	119	107	81
Fruit in cans, boxed, N. O. S. C. L	4	4	4	5	85	76	68	56
Fruit, green, N. O. S., prepaid, guaranteed	2	3	3	6	125	89	81	46
Fuse	1	1	D 1	1	150	119	214	107
Glassware, common, N. O. S. C. L	3	2	3	3	100	104	81	81
Glue, scrap	......	......	5	6	......	......	56	46
Grindstones, unmounted, C. L	5	5	6	A	58	61	46	28

TABLE 7.—COMPARISON OF CLASSIFICATION AND RATES EFFECTIVE DURING THE YEARS 1876, 1880, 1887, AND 1893, ETC.—Continued.

Commodities.	Louisville, Ky., to Atlanta, Ga.							
	Class.				Rates in cents per 100 pounds.			
	1876	1880	1887	1893	1876	1880	1887	1893
Groceries, N. O. S.	2	2	2	2	125	104	92	92
Handles, N. O. S., boxed or crated	5	5	4	4	58	61	68	68
Hardware, N. O. S., boxed	2	2	2	2	125	104	92	92
Hessians, in original bales	......	......	6	A	......	......	46	28
Hides, dry, in bales	3	3	3	4	100	89	81	68
compressed	4	4	4	5	85	76	68	56
green	4	4	4	5	85	76	68	56
salted	......	5	5	6	......	61	56	46
Hinges and nooks, in bbls. or casks	4	3	3	5	85	89	81	56
Iron roofing, N. O. S	2	6	3	6	125	46	81	46
Jellies, in cans, boxed, C. L	3	4	4	5	100	76	68	56
Logwood, extract, in bbls. or casks	2	2	2	5	125	104	92	56
Machinery, all kinds, C. L	4	5	5	6	85	61	56	46
Matches, C. L	1	1	1	3	150	119	107	81
Meal, oat, in boxes, L. C. L	......	......	2	4	......	......	92	68
C. L	......	......	2	C	......	......	92	28
Milk, condensed, boxed, C. L	4	4	4	5	85	76	68	56
Moss, pressed in bales, C. L	3	3	4	4	100	89	68	68
Pins, clothes, boxed, L. C. L	2	2	2	3	125	104	92	81
C. L	2	2	2	5	125	104	92	56
Plaster, calcined, C. L	......	......	6	A	......	......	46	28
Plaster of Paris, C. L	5	5	6	A	58	61	46	28
Plumbago (ship's option), in sacks, bbls. or box	......	5	5	6	......	61	56	46
Radiators, steam, packed, L. C. L	......	4	3	4	......	76	81	68
C. L	......	4	3	5	......	76	81	56
Rice, rough	5	5	5	D	58	61	56	24
Roots and herbs, value not over 6 cents per pound, L. C. L	......	3	4	5	......	89	68	56
Roots and herbs, value not over 6 cents per pound, C. L	......	3	4	6	......	89	68	46
Rope, N. O. S., L. C. L	4	3	3	4	85	89	81	68
C. L	4	3	3	6	85	89	81	46
bed cord, L. C. L	4	3	3	4	85	89	81	68
C. L	4	3	3	6	85	89	81	46
clothes line, L. C. L	2	3	3	4	125	89	81	68
C. L	2	3	3	6	125	89	81	46
wire	4	4	4	5	85	76	68	56
Saddlery, horse collars, bark or shuck	2	2	2	4	125	104	92	68
Seed, garden, C. L	1	2	2	4	150	104	92	68
millet, C. L	......	......	3	6	......	......	81	46
sorghum, C. L	......	......	2	6	......	......	92	46
Shot, in kegs, or doubled sacked	4	5	5	6	85	61	56	46
Slates, school, L. C. L	3	3	2	3	100	89	92	81
C. L	3	3	2	4	100	89	92	68
Starch, except corn starch	4	4	4	5	85	76	68	56
Sulphur, in barrels, L. C. L	4	4	3	5	85	76	81	56
Tallow, in barrels	4	5	B	B	85	61	36	35
Tacks, iron, in kegs	3	3	2	5	100	89	92	56
Tar, coal, in barrels, L. C. L	5	5	5	6	58	61	56	46
Tin plate, in boxes, O. R. wet rust and damage to tin or packing, C. L	3	5	5	6	100	61	56	46
Waters, mineral, in wood, C. L	5	4	5	5	58	76	56	56
Wheat, cracked, in barrels, C. L	......	......	5	6	......	......	56	46
boxes, L. C. L	......	......	2	5	......	......	92	56
C. L	......	......	2	5	......	......	92	56
Whiting, in barrels	4	5	5	6	85	61	56	46
Wool, mineral	......	......	1	2	......	......	107	92
Zinc, oxide	......	5	3	5	......	61	81	56

CHANGES IN COMPETITIVE RATES.

The through or competitive traffic of the United States is divided into several well-defined sections, the rate-making basis of each of which, as well as the competition, is distinctive in many features. Briefly described these sections are as follows:

(1) The territory north of the Ohio and Potomac rivers and east of Chicago and the Mississippi River.

(2) The territory south of the Ohio and Potomac rivers and east of the Mississippi River.

(3) The territory west of Chicago and the Mississippi River.

(4) Competitive traffic to and from Pacific coast.

In each of these sections the traffic is divided into several general descriptions, distinguishable by the character of the commodities, the direction of movement, and the operation of freight associations. For each the more important rates have been selected and such data given as will most fully present the tendency of the changes.

CHANGES IN RATES ON TRAFFIC FROM EASTERN SEABOARD CITIES TO WESTERN COMPETITIVE POINTS, VIA ALL-RAIL ROUTES.

Before proceeding to a study of the changes in the rates as shown by the tables for this traffic it is important that the methods under which the schedules are constructed should be first explained.

Freight tariffs covering the traffic from the eastern seaboard territory to western points are established under the rules and regulations of the associations known as the Trunk Line and Central Traffic Associations, the former embraces the important roads leading from the eastern seaboard to Buffalo, Erie, Salamanca, Pittsburg, Parkersburg, and Wheeling, which points are known as the western termini of the trunk lines, and are also the eastern termini of roads in the Central Traffic Association. Under agreements of several years standing it has been the custom of these roads, forming by connections through lines from the seaboard to the West, to determine through rates from New York to Chicago, and to adopt such rates as the standard or basis for the construction of tariffs from other eastern cities and points adjacent thereto, which are directly or indirectly in competition for western business.

The principal seaboard cities are, New York, Boston, Philadelphia and Baltimore, and adjacent to each of these are important industries commanding for the points at which they are located equal transportation rates and facilities with the larger cities. For twenty years or more the rates from Boston to Western competitive points have been the same as from New York. From Philadelphia and Baltimore the rates are "agreed differentials" less than New York, the Baltimore rates being also lower than Philadelphia rates.

The westward traffic from the seaboard is carried principally under classified tariffs. The number of classes and the rates for each as now in effect are shown in the following table:

TABLE 8.—WEST BOUND RATES, SEABOARD CITIES TO CHICAGO.

	Classes in cents per 100 pounds.					
	1	2	3	4	5	6
From New York to Chicago	75	65	50	35	30	25
From Boston to Chicago	75	65	50	35	30	25
From Philadelphia to Chicago	69	59	48	33	28	23
Philadelphia lower than New York	6	6	2	2	2	2
From Baltimore to Chicago	67	57	47	32	27	22
Baltimore lower than New York	8	8	3	3	3	3
Baltimore lower than Philadelphia	2	2	1	1	1	1

It is not known what differentials were allowed Philadelphia and Baltimore prior to 1875. It is found that the differences in 1875 were as follows:

TABLE 9.—WEST BOUND DIFFERENTIALS.

	Classes in cents per 100 pounds.				
	1	2	3	4	5
Philadelphia (lower than New York rates)	7	7	6	4	3
Baltimore (lower than New York rates)	10	9	8	6	5

In 1876 the system of determining the differentials was from time to time modified. Fixed differentials were again reëstablished in 1877. Those shown in connection with the table of rates above have been continuously in effect since that time and may, for the purposes of studying the rates herein presented, be considered as applicable to the entire period covered.

Under existing arrangements the roads leading from the East publish rates and issue through bills of lading to all western points located on the railroads within the territory west of Buffalo and Pittsburg, east of the Mississippi and north of the Ohio rivers. The agreed rates and distances from New York to Chicago are taken as the standard, or 100 per cent. Through rates to the principal western cities, towns, and junction points in the territory above described are computed at a percentage of the New York-Chicago rates, based generally on the relative mileage of such points to the Chicago mileage. For example, rates New York to Detroit, Mich., are computed at 78 per cent of the rate New York to Chicago. In the same manner rates New York to Indianaplis, Ind., are 93 per cent of the New York-Chicago rates; Cincinnati, O., 87 per cent; Erie, Penn., 60 per cent; Columbus, O., 77 per cent; Cleveland, O., 71 per cent; St. Louis, Mo., 116 per cent. Thus the New York-Chicago rates being at all times applied as the basis would, when changed, create relative changes in the rates to the other western points. In a similar manner the relation as to rates is maintained from the other eastern cities. When rates from New York to western points are changed like changes are made from Boston, Philadelphia, and Baltimore, and points receiving the same rates, the "differentials" as between the eastern cities being at all times maintained.

The general basis the construction of tariffs as here described from New York and other eastern cities to Chicago and other western points indicated, has been practically the same for years. With this explanation the tables presenting rates from New York may be accepted as indicating the changes from Boston, Philadelphia and Baltimore.

STANDARD AND DIFFERENTIAL ROUTES.

An important element in the arrangement of rate schedules is the distinction made in the class of railroads or routes, by which certain routes are under agreement allowed to charge lower rates than others to the same points of destination. This is another feature of the "differential" plan, and has within recent years been extensively applied in the territory now under consideration. From each of the eastern cities there are two classes of roads, which are commonly termed the "standard lines" and the "differential lines." The standard lines are those which are conceded to possess advantages over their competitors by reason of shorter all-rail distance, and superior facilities arising from old and well-established connections and freight organizations. The differential lines are those which, on account of the longer routes and inadequate facilities, or owing to their through routes being partly by water, or from other disadvantages, cannot command, at even rates with the more direct lines an amount of tonnage which under customary methods for determining such matters would be considered a fair proportion. With a view to equalizing these conditions, and securing the permanency of the tariffs, as well as to bring about a fair distribution of the traffic, the "differential lines" are accorded somewhat lower rates than the "standard lines." At this time there are ten different lines leading from New York competing for western business. The rates upon classified traffic, New York to Chicago, as now established by each of these lines are as follows:

TABLE 10.—WEST BOUND RATES, NEW YORK TO CHICAGO BY VARIOUS ROUTES.

	Classes (in cents per 100 pounds).					
	1.	2.	3.	4.	5.	6.
Standard lines:						
New York Central and Hudson River Railroad						
Pennsylvania Railroad	75	65	50	35	30	25
Baltimore and Ohio Railroad						
Differential lines:						
New York, Lake Erie and Western Railroad						
Lehigh Valley Railroad	70	61	47	33	29	24
West Shore Railroad						
Delaware, Lackawanna and Western Railroad						
New York, Ontario and Western Railroad	67	59	46	32	27	33
Chesapeake and Ohio Railway Route	65	57	44	31	26	22
Central Vermont Railroad Route	60	53	41	29	25	21

From other eastern cities similar arrangements exist, under which certain routes charge lower or differential rates.

The data presented by the tables following, covering all-rail rates, has been obtained from the older established companies whose records were found more complete in this respect; such companies are the standard lines under the system just described. Their rates are standard and are higher than those of the differential lines. This should be borne in mind when the tables are studied for the years subsequent to 1881, as since that time traffic of the different classes and commodities appearing in the tables was taken at lower rates when carried by any of the roads known as the differential lines. A statement covering the changes of each line, if such data were procurable, would present more fully the actual changes which have taken place. It does not, however, appear necessary to enlarge the report on this account, as under the methods described for constructing the rates the changes from New York may be accepted as representing the changes from all other eastern cities, both for the standard and differential lines.

TABLE 11.—RATES OF FREIGHT ON CLASSIFIED TRAFFIC VIA ALL-RAIL ROUTES, NEW YORK TO CHICAGO.

NOTE.—The rates shown are those of the standard lines under the freight classifications from time to time prevailing. Rates from Boston have been the same. Philadelphia and Baltimore were lower by amount of differentials. Certain routes charge lower rates.

Date.	Classes (rates in cents per 100 pounds).					
	1.	2.	3.	4.	5.	Sp'l or 6.
1862—Jan. 1	160	128	107	66	....	....
Apr. 7	149	117	85	50	....	....
Oct. 9	180	150	125	75	....	....
1863—May 14	160	117	94	55	....	....
Oct. 5	160	128	107	66	....	....
Nov. 23	180	150	124	85	....	....
1864—July 25	200	166	111	85	....	....
Sept. 20	215	180	120	96	....	....
1865—May 8	215	180	106	96	....	....
Oct. 16	215	180	90	82	....	....
1866—Feb. 5	215	170	82	82	....	....
Mar. 5	188	160	127	82	....	....
1867—Nov. 5	202	170	138	86	....	....
1868—June 4	188	160	127	82	....	....
Aug. 10	149	128	120	82	....	....
Sept. 7	188	160	127	82	....	....
Oct. 1	70	60	55	50	....	....
Dec. 7	202	170	138	86	....	....
1869—Feb. 1	188	160	127	82	55	....
Feb. 7	45	45	45	45	45	....
Mar. 15	160	160	127	82	55	....
July 1	188	160	127	82	55	....
Aug. 11	25	25	25	25	25	....
Aug. 23	38	38	38	38	38	....
Aug. 30	43	43	43	43	43	....
Sept. 22	40	40	40	40	40	....
Sept. 24	35	35	35	35	35	....
Oct. 4	50	50	50	50	50	....
Oct. 9	75	75	75	75	50	....
Nov. 1	140	125	100	80	50	....
Nov. 29	150	130	100	80	55	....
1870—Apr. 14	140	125	100	80	50	....
May 4	150	130	100	80	55	....
June 18	112	90	90	55	45	37
July 13	80	70	60	50	35	42
July 18	75	70	60	50	42	35
July 21	65	60	60	50	42	35
July 25	65	60	55	45	35	40
July 28	50	50	50	45	35	40
Aug. 12	50	50	50	50	40	....
Aug. 22	100	90	70	55	45	....
Sept. 8	125	110	85	65	50	....
Nov. 28	160	130	100	65	50	....
Dec. 26	180	150	120	80	60	....
1871—Feb. 20	150	130	100	70	55	....
Mar. 7	100	90	70	55	45	....
May 18	75	65	50	45	37	....
June 1	100	90	70	55	45	....
July 8	75	65	50	45	37	....
July 28	45	45	45	45	32	....
Aug. 16	40	40	40	40	28	....
Aug. 21	35	35	35	35	26	....
Sept. 1	30	30	30	30	24	....
Nov. 27	100	90	70	55	45	....
Dec. 15	125	110	85	65	50	....
1872—Aug. 1	75	70	60	45	35	....
Sept. 1	125	110	85	65	50	....
Sept. 2	100	90	70	55	45	....
1872—Oct. 14	125	110	85	65	50	....
1873—Apr. 14	100	90	75	60	45	....
June 11	75	70	60	45	35	....
Aug. 11	40	40	30	30	30	....
Aug. 13	27	27	18	18	17	....
Dec. 1	75	70	60	45	35	....
1874—Jan. 1	100	90	75	60	45	....
Aug. 3	75	70	60	45	35	....
1875—Jan. 20	100	90	75	60	45	....
Mar. 17	75	70	60	45	35	....
Apr. 6	60	55	50	40	30	....
May 18	40	40	35	35	25	....
Aug. 12	50	40	30	25	20	....
Nov. 15	75	70	60	45	35	....
Dec. 22	30	25	20	20	15	....
1876—Jan. 10	75	70	60	45	35	....
June 12	25	25	25	16	16	....
July 28	15	15	15	10	10	....
Dec. 18	50	45	40	30	25	....
1877—Mar. 12	75	70	60	45	35	....
Oct. 8	75	70	60	40	....	....
Oct. 22	100	90	75	45	....	....
Dec. 10	100	80	60	45	....	....
1878—Feb. 15	75	60	50	40	....	....
1881—Aug. 6	45	32	26	19	....	....
Nov. 14	60	50	40	28	....	....
1882—Jan. 24	45	32	26	19	....	....
July 1	60	50	40	30	25	....
Nov. 1	75	60	45	35	....	....
1883—June 22	75	60	45	35	25	....
1885—Jan. 26	50	40	30	25	18	....
Oct. 5	60	50	40	25	...	20
Nov. 18	75	60	45	35	....	25
1887—Apr. 1	75	65	50	35	30	25
1888—Jan. 9	75	65	50	38½	33	27½
Mar. 5	75	65	50	35	30	25
Nov. 12	50	40	35	30	25	20
Dec. 17*	75	65	50	35	30	25

* In effect January 1, 1893.

By this table is shown the changes in the rates of the several classes of freight from New York to Chicago from 1862 to the present time. The freight charges between the two most important shipping centers in the country are here presented for thirty years—a longer period than has ever previously appeared in one table.

Absence of knowledge of the circumstances under which the varying rates of the different years were established precludes the adoption of any form of analysis which could be applied to the whole period. The character of the rates of certain years might be easily traced to the events of those years notably affecting the transportation interests; 1864 and 1865 were years near the end of and just after the war. In 1877 the Trunk Line Association was formed, and in 1887 the Act to Regulate Commerce was passed. For these years higher rates are observed.

During the summer months the all rail lines are in competition with the lake-and-rail and canal and lake routes, to which competition has frequently been attributed the low all-rail rates; reductions by the latter at such times being necessary to retain a share of the business. While this may explain the changes in many of the years, it loses force when applied to such years as 1869–1875, and 1882, when the low rates were charged on dates on which the lake routes were closed.

In part only the foregoing may indicate the causes for changes in different years. Throughout the table may be recognized "war periods," which for the purpose of comparison it would be well to eliminate, if this could be correctly done, as only in this way may the changes in the normal rates of each class and commodity be shown. The rates of the table, however, represent figures at which an enormous traffic was carried, and although not in all cases appearing upon the published schedules they were obtained from reliable sources, are accurate, and should be permitted to remain in the tables for what they are worth.

It would be of interest to know the exact causes leading to the important fluctuations of each year, and it is to be regretted that the necessary information for this purpose is not at hand. For the present, at least, we shall have to be content with the reasons frequently advanced, viz, that when low rates prevailed the cause has been "active competition," or a "rate war," and when advanced they were simply "restored" to what was at the time considered the "normal basis."

While the extent of the variations are shown, the *tendency* of the changes may not readily be determined by the figures of Table 1, in the absence of knowledge as to what were the normal rates; the latter might be assumed to be highest rates or the rates prevailing for the longest period. While such a rule could well be applied to the rates of 1868, for example, when $2.02 first class per 100 pounds continued in effect for five months and was again restored after a period of lower rates, the same rule could not govern for 1869, during which there were thirteen changes and rates approaching the highest were in effect for an equal period.

The comparison which shall show the tendency of the changes must therefore be made upon a basis having the merits of equality. For this purpose the system of averages and percentages has been adopted, as shown by Tables 13 and 14.

While the presentation now made will be of interest, historically at least, it must be admitted that the tables furnish only a proximate basis for comparison, owing to the fact that in former years the methods of the carriers were such that the instances where the published tariff was charged were rather the exception than the rule. The devices for the secret lowering of rates to shippers commonly resorted to, in previous years were innumerable. The secret rates or reductions by rebates of one road were generally based upon the actual or assumed rates of a competitor, and while the rates of all ultimately fell to the same level and became the open rate, for a time at least, charges were made by some differing materially from any rates of record.

Before passing to Tables 13 and 14 it may be interesting to notice some of the extreme changes appearing in the preceding table. We find the highest and lowest rates as follows:

TABLE 12.—HIGHEST AND LOWEST WEST BOUND RATES.

	Cents per 100 pounds.	
	Highest.	Lowest.
Class 1	1864 and 1865....$2.15	$0.15 in 1876
Class 2	1864 and 1865.... 1.80	.15 in 1876
Class 3	1867............. 1.38	.15 in 1876
Class 4	1864 and 1865.... .96	.10 in 1876
Class 5	1870............. .60	.10 in 1876

For the years prior to 1868 changes do not appear to have been made as often as in years following. In October, 1868, a reduction from $1.88 to 70 cents was made, the latter rate continuing until December 7, or two months. At no time in the previous six years had the first-class rate been lower than $1.49, and for most of this time the normal rate had been nearer $2. The year 1869 was conspicuous for sharp fluctuations, with a rate at the beginning of the year of $2.02 first class, which was reduced on February 1 to $1.88, and again on the 17th of the same month to 45 cents. The latter was equivalent to a decline of 75 per cent on first class and about 50 per cent on fourth class. By this schedule it will be seen that the same rate was charged upon all classes. Here for the first time it is noticed that the principles of classification are entirely set aside.

In March the rates were advanced as abruptly as they declined, and in July $1.88 was again reached. In August a rate of 25 cents was established for all classes, the lowest rate from 1862 to 1876. This rate (August, 1869) was advanced on different dates during August, September, October, and November, until the $1.50 basis was reached. In 1870 important reductions were made, followed by advances to the $1.80 basis in December, which was again reduced to $1.50 in February, 1871. During the summer of 1871 rates were very low and again the classification was ignored. In December the $1.25 basis was resumed, and after reductions, again adopted in October, 1872, continuing until April, 1873, after which date no higher basis than $1 was reached. In August, September, October, November, and part of December, 1873, a 27-cent first-class and 17-cent fifth-class basis was charged, which were unusually low rates. The rates for 1874 and 1875 were comparatively better.

The rates of 1876 were far below the rates known to have been charged at any time within the periods covered by the table. In 1877 the 75-cent basis was restored, and in October of the same year the classification was reduced to four classes. In December the $1 basis was established, which lasted until February 15, 1878, when the 75-cent basis was again made effective. These rates continued in effect until August, 1881, three years and a half, an unusually long period. The rates of 1881 and 1882 were low; 1883 and 1884 the rates were higher and more steady; 1885 rates were low. From 1886 to the present time the class rates have been practically on the same basis. These comments relate principally to first class, and apply generally to all, although the class relations were not always maintained by the changes. At times there were only four classes and at others five or six. Lower rates usually followed the introduction of new classes.

TABLE 13.—AVERAGE RATES ON CLASSIFIED TRAFFIC, VIA ALL-RAIL ROUTES, NEW YORK TO CHICAGO.

Date.	Classes (rates in cents per 100 pounds).						Date.	Classes (rates in cents per 100 pounds).					
	1.	2.	3.	4.	5.	6 or spe'l.		1.	2.	3.	4.	5.	6 or spe'l.
1862	159	127	100	60	.....	......	1881	65	51	42	33	.....	......
1863	169	134	110	67	.....	......	1882	56	44	35	26	.....	......
1864	193	161	121	87	.....	......	1883	75	60	45	35	.....	......
1865	215	180	107	93	.....	......	1884	75	60	45	35	25	......
1866	193	163	120	82	.....	......	1885	56	45	34	27	.....	......
1867	190	162	129	83	.....	......	1886	75	60	45	35	.....	25
1868	170	144	119	78	.....	......	1887	75	64	49	35	.....	25
1869	132	122	100	72	.....	......	1888	73	63	49	35	30	25
1870	130	113	90	69	50	......	1889	75	65	50	35	30	25
1871	90	79	65	51	40	......	1890	75	65	50	35	30	25
1872	118	104	81	62	48	......	1891	75	65	50	35	30	25
1873	78	71	57	45	35	......	1892	75	65	50	35	30	25
1874	90	82	69	54	41	......							
1875	61	55	46	38	29	......							
1876	43	41	36	26	22	......							
1877	75	68	58	42	.....	......							
1878	78	62	51	41	.....	......							
1879	75	60	50	40	.....	......							
1880	75	60	50	40	.....	......							

This table gives the average rate of each class, New York to Chicago, for each year. These averages are obtained by multiplying the rates by the number of days each were in effect and dividing the sum of the multiples by the number of days in the year. This method is thought to be fairly accurate, and is undoubtedly the best available when it is impossible to obtain tonnage statistics showing the exact quantity of traffic carried at the separate rates. The next table will show the percentage or ratio of change in the yearly class averages given above. For this purpose the rates of 1867 are counted as 100, and the rates of the years following are expressed in percentages of the rates of 1867. Thus, in 1892 the first-class rate was 39.47 per cent of the rates of 1867; or, in other words, the same weight of freight may be now carried from New York to Chicago for 39 cents as was charged $1 in 1867.

TABLE 14.—PERCENTAGES OF THE YEARLY AVERAGE RATES ON CLASSIFIED TRAFFIC, NEW YORK TO CHICAGO.

Date.	Classes.					
	1.	2.	3.	4.	5.	6.
1867	100	100	100	100		
1868	89.47	88.89	92.25	93.98		
1869	69.47	75.31	77.52	86.75		
1870	68.42	69.75	69.77	83.13	100	
1871	47.37	48.77	50.39	61.45	80	
1872	62.11	64.20	62.79	74.70	96	
1873	41.05	43.83	44.19	54.22	70	
1874	47.37	50.62	53.49	65.06	82	
1875	32.11	33.95	35.66	45.78	58	
1876	22.63	25.31	27.91	31.33	44	
1877	39.47	41.98	41.96	50.60		
1878	41.05	38.27	39.53	49.40		
1879	39.47	37.04	38.76	48.19		
1880	39.47	37.04	38.76	48.19		
1881	34.21	31.48	32.56	39.76		
1882	29.47	27.16	27.13	31.33		
1883	39.47	37.04	34.88	42.17		
1884	39.47	37.04	34.88	42.17	50	
1885	29.47	27.78	26.36	32.53		
1886	39.47	37.04	34.88	42.17		
1887	39.47	39.51	37.98	42.17		
1888	38.42	38.89	37.98	42.17	60	
1889	39.47	40.12	38.76	42.17	60	
1890	39.47	40.12	38.76	42.17	60	
1891	39.47	40.12	38.76	42.17	60	
1892	39.47	40.12	38.76	42.17	60	

By this arrangement of the tables it may be seen at a glance what general changes have taken place. In many of the earlier years lower rates for some classes are noticed than have been charged since 1887. A study of the tables, however, will give prominence to the fact that the basis is now lower. In support of this conclusion it must be remembered that there is now a permanent fifth and sixth class, each of which has rates lower than was formerly charged for fourth class.

The yearly tonnage forwarded by the trunk lines from New York to and beyond the western termini of each shows a marked increase; the shipments for 1892 were 38 per cent higher than in 1886. The business for several years is shown in the table next given:

TABLE 15.—WEST BOUND TONNAGE.

	Tons.
1878	715,808
1879	803,770
1880	986,013
1881	1,198,097
1882	1,363,708
1883	997,645
1884	1,115,052
1885	1,194,350
1886	1,125,417
1887	1,314,254
1888	1,335,343
1889	1,219,769
1890	1,405,352
1891	1,465,094
1892	1,551,357

The proportions carried in the respective classes during these years were as follows:

TABLE 16.—PER CENT OF TONNAGE IN EACH CLASS.

Class.	1878.	1879.	1880.	1881.	1882.	1883.	1884.	1885.	1886.	1887.	1888.	1889.	1890.	1891.	1892.
1	30.4	31.3	26.4	25.1	23.1	29.5	25.6	24.8	23.3	18.9	19.3	22.2	21.0	19.4	19.9
2	6.9	7.2	6.7	6.4	6.2	8.0	7.6	7.1	7.9	7.5	7.2	6.9	6.4	5.7	5.4
3	4.8	5.0	4.4	5.1	4.2	4.9	4.1	4.2	5.2	8.1	10.4	12.8	12.3	11.4	11.3
4	57.9	48.7	50.1	53.7	58.9	42.8	32.9	29.3	20.9	14.1	13.5	13.0	12.7	11.1	10.4
5	0.0	6.5	10.6	9.7	7.6	14.8	29.8	34.6	42.7	16.1	9.2	7.8	10.0	9.1	9.6
6	0.0	0.0	0.0	0.0	0.0	0.0	0.0	0.0	.....	35.3	40.4	37.3	37.6	43.3	43.4
Special	0.0	1.3	1.8	0.0	0.0	0.0	0.0	0.0	.....	.....	.....	.....	.....	.....	.....
	100.0	100.0	100.0	100.0	100.0	100.0	100.0	100.0	100.0	100.0	100.0	100.0	100.0	100.0	100.0

The principal purpose served by the introduction of the latter table is to point out that about sixty per cent of the tonnage is now carried in the fourth, fifth, and sixth classes, the rates of which are 35, 30, and 25 cents per 100 pounds, respectively, New York to Chicago. Prior to 1886 no considerable number of articles were permanently assigned to fifth and sixth classes; they embraced usually a few commodities which had been assigned a special rate, which rate was seldom lower than 35 cents per 100 pounds, and often higher. It has been shown from an analysis of the freight classifications that 47 per cent of the descriptions in the classification now applying westward from the seaboard are found in the fourth and lower classes, and the tonnage of the same classes from New York is 60 per cent of the total traffic. The traffic represented by these figures now permanently receive lower rates than in 1886. Similar results would appear from an analysis of the rates and classification applying from other seaboard cities to the West.

The foregoing tables of rates, it will be noticed, refer to the yearly averages of the different classes. In order to ascertain the changes upon the entire traffic of all classes from New York, the following table has been compiled, by which is shown the monthly average rates for each year on the traffic from New York from 1878 to 1892, inclusive, and the yearly averages are given for the years 1886 to 1892, inclusive. These average rates, it should be explained, are arrived at on the assumption that all traffic from New York was destined to Chicago, and carried at the prevailing tariff rates for the years given. This rule is applied throughout the table, and when it is recalled that rates to all destinations east of the Mississippi River are made proportionate to the New York-Chicago rate, results sufficiently accurate are obtained to illustrate the charges for all traffic from the seaboard to western points other than Chicago, to which rates are made by the trunk lines.

Especial attention is directed to this table, as it contains rates representative of a traffic more extensive than is carried under any other set of competitive rates in the United States.

TABLE 17.—AVERAGE RATES PER HUNDRED POUNDS CHARGED TO CHICAGO, ILL., DURING EACH MONTH, 1878 TO 1892, INCLUSIVE, UPON FREIGHT FROM NEW YORK, N. Y., TO POINTS BEYOND TRUNK LINE TERMINI.

Month.	Year (average rate in cents per 100 pounds).														
	1878	1879	1880	1881	1882	1883	1884	1885	1886	1887	1888	1889	1890	1891	1892
January	64	53	47	49	23	47	45	40	43	40	45	45	43	43	41
February	60	55	49	51	26	49	47	30	45	40	47	45	43	45	42
March	55	55	51	51	26	49	47	30	45	38	47	43	40	41	43
April	53	55	51	49	26	47	45	30	45	45	40	43	40	39	42
May	51	53	47	49	26	47	43	30	43	40	43	45	43	40	41
June	51	53	47	47	26	45	43	23	40	43	40	43	43	40	39
July	51	53	49	49	38	45	45	23	43	43	40	47	45	42	41
August	53	55	53	30	38	47	47	26	43	40	43	45	43	43	42
September	53	55	53	26	38	47	45	23	43	40	40	43	43	42	42
October	53	49	51	26	43	45	45	32	40	40	43	45	45	42	42
November	51	47	51	26	49	45	45	38	38	40	33	43	43	41	42
December	51	45	49	26	47	43	45	45	40	43	33	43	43	42	41
Average yearly rate	53.7	51.9	49.9	37.5	29.4	47.7	44.6	30.1	42.6	41.0	41.0	43.7	42.9	41.4	41.5

Applying to a number of commodities the same plan for computation of averages and percentages as shown above by Tables 13 and 14 for classes, similar results as to the extent of the reductious are obtained. Tables 18 and 19 next following present the yearly average charges and percentages for a number of selected articles; reference to each will show the rates to be upon a much lower basis in the more recent years than formerly. It will also be noticed that the majority have now been assigned a separate car-load rating, where in previous years this distinction was not made and the the shipments in carload quantities were taken at higher rates. An extended analysis of the changes in each article appears unnecessary, as the tables fully present the reductions.

TABLE 18.—AVERAGE RATES ON VARIOUS COMMODITIES,

Year.	Commodities (rates in cents per 100 pounds).																	
	Dry goods.	Cotton piece goods.	Boots and shoes.	Furniture.		Stoves.		Coffee.		Soap.				Starch.		Tea.	Sugar.	
										Castile and fancy.		Common.						
				Less than carloads.	Carloads.	Less than carloads.	Carloads.	Less than carloads.	Carloads.	Less than carloads.	Carloads.	Less than carloads.	Carloads.	Less than carloads.	Carloads.		Less than carloads.	Carloads.
1867	190	190	190	190	190	190	190	162	162	162	162	129	129	162	162	190	83	83
1868	170	170	170	170	170	170	170	....	....	144	144	78	78	122	122	170	....	....
1869	132	132	132	132	132	132	132	....	....	122	122	72	72	100	100	132	....	....
1870	130	130	130	130	130	130	130	....	....	113	113	69	69	90	90	130	....	....
1871	90	90	90	90	90	90	90	40	40	79	79	51	51	65	65	90	40	40
1872	118	118	118	118	118	118	118	48	48	104	104	62	62	81	81	118	48	48
1873	78	78	78	78	78	78	78	35	35	71	71	45	45	57	57	78	35	35
1874	90	90	90	90	90	90	90	41	41	82	82	54	54	69	69	90	41	41
1875	61	61	61	61	61	61	61	28	28	55	55	38	38	46	46	61	28	28
1876	43	43	43	43	43	43	43	22	22	41	41	26	26	36	36	43	22	22
1877	75	75	75	75	75	75	63	35	35	68	68	42	42	52	52	75	35	35
1878	78	78	78	78	78	78	41	41	41	62	62	41	41	41	41	78	41	41
1879	75	75	75	75	75	75	40	40	40	60	60	40	40	40	40	75	40	40
1880	75	75	75	75	75	75	40	40	40	60	60	40	40	40	40	75	40	40
1881	65	65	65	65	65	65	33	33	33	51	51	33	33	33	33	65	33	33
1882	56	56	56	56	56	56	26	26	26	44	44	26	26	26	26	56	24	24
1883	75	75	75	75	75	75	35	35	35	60	60	35	35	35	35	75	30	30
1884	75	75	75	75	75	75	35	35	35	60	60	35	35	35	35	75	25	25
1885	56	56	56	56	56	56	27	27	27	45	45	27	27	27	27	56	20	20
1886	75	66	75	75	75	75	35	35	35	60	60	35	35	35	35	75	25	25
1887	75	50	75	75	67	56	31	35	27	64	64	35	31	35	27	75	33	25
1888	73	49	73	73	63	49	30	35	25	63	63	35	30	35	25	73	35	25
1889	75	50	75	75	65	50	30	35	25	65	65	35	30	35	25	75	35	25
1890	75	50	75	75	65	50	30	35	25	65	65	35	30	35	25	75	35	25
1891	75	50	75	75	65	35	26	35	25	49	44	35	26	35	25	75	35	25
1892 *	75	50	75	75	65	30	25	35	25	35	25	35	25	35	25	75	35	24

* Eight months, to August 31, inclusive.

VIA ALL-RAIL ROUTES, NEW YORK TO CHICAGO.

Commodities (rates in cents per 100 pounds).																						
Molasses.		Rice.				Crockery and earthenware.		Bagging		Leather		Lead.		Nails.			Agricultural implements		Machinery.		Beer.	
Less than carloads.	Carloads.	Less than carloads.	Carloads.	Groceries.	Drugs.	Less than carloads.	Carloads.	Less than carloads.	Carloads.	Less than carloads.	Carloads.	Less than carloads.	Carloads.	Less than carloads.	Carloads.	Hardware.	Less than carloads.	Carloads.	Less than carloads.	Carloads.	Less than carloads.	Carloads.
83	83	83	83	162	190	162	162	162	162	162	162	83	83	83	83	162	190	190	162	162	129	129
....	....	78	78	144	170	144	144	144	144	144	144	78	78	78	78	144	170	170	144	144	119	114
....	....	72	72	122	132	....	....	122	122	122	122	72	72	72	72	122	132	132	122	122	100	100
....	....	....	....	113	130	....	....	113	113	111	111	70	70	69	69	113	130	130	113	113	90	90
51	51	51	51	79	90	55	55	79	79	79	79	44	44	51	51	79	90	90	79	79	65	65
62	62	57	57	104	118	91	91	104	104	104	104	48	48	62	62	104	118	118	104	104	81	81
45	45	35	35	71	78	35	35	71	71	71	71	35	35	45	45	71	.....	62	71	71	57	57
54	54	41	41	82	90	41	41	82	82	82	82	41	41	54	54	82	.....	54	82	82	69	69
47	47	29	29	55	61	33	33	55	55	55	55	29	29	38	38	55	.....	38	55	55	46	46
26	26	22	22	41	43	22	22	41	41	41	41	22	22	26	26	41	.....	26	41	41	36	36
42	42	35	35	68	75	35	35	59	59	68	68	35	35	42	42	68	.....	41	68	59	52	52
41	41	41	41	62	78	41	41	41	41	62	62	41	41	41	41	62	.....	41	62	41	41	41
40	40	40	40	60	75	40	40	40	40	60	60	40	40	40	40	60	.....	40	60	40	40	40
40	40	40	40	60	75	40	40	40	40	60	60	40	40	40	40	60	.....	40	60	40	40	40
33	33	33	33	51	65	33	33	33	33	51	51	33	33	33	33	51	.....	33	51	33	33	33
24	24	26	26	44	56	26	26	26	26	44	44	26	26	26	26	44	.....	26	44	26	26	26
30	30	35	35	60	75	35	35	35	35	60	60	35	35	35	35	60	.....	36	60	35	35	35
25	25	35	35	60	75	35	35	35	35	60	60	35	35	35	35	60	.....	36	60	35	35	35
20	20	27	27	45	56	27	27	27	27	45	45	27	27	27	27	45	.....	27	45	27	27	27
25	25	35	35	60	75	35	35	35	35	60	60	35	35	35	35	60	.....	35	60	35	35	35
33	29	35	35	64	75	35	31	46	35	52	41	35	27	35	31	64	.....	31	41	31	46	31
35	30	35	25	63	73	35	30	49	35	49	35	35	25	35	30	63	49	30	35	30	49	30
35	30	35	25	65	75	35	30	50	35	50	35	35	25	35	30	65	50	30	35	30	50	30
35	30	35	25	65	75	35	30	50	35	50	35	35	25	35	30	65	50	30	35	30	50	30
35	30	35	25	65	75	35	30	50	35	50	35	35	25	31	26	65	50	30	35	34	50	30
35	30	35	25	65	75	35	30	50	35	50	35	35	25	30	25	65	50	30	35	35	50	30

TABLE 19.—PERCENTAGES OF THE YEARLY AVERAGE RATES ON VARIOUS

Year.	Commodities (rates in cents per 100 pounds).								
	Dry goods.	Cotton piece goods.	Boots and shoes.	Furniture.		Stoves.		Coffee.	
				Less than carloads.	Carloads.	Less than carloads.	Carloads.	Less than carloads.	Carloads.
1867	100.00	100.00	100.00	100.00	100.00	100.00	100.00	100.00	100.00
1868	89.47	89.47	89.47	89.47	89.47	89.47	89.47	....	....
1869	69.47	69.47	69.47	69.47	69.47	69.47	69.47	....	....
1870	68.42	68.42	68.42	68.42	68.42	68.42	68.42	....	....
1871	47.37	47.37	47.37	47.37	47.37	47.37	47.37	24.69	24.69
1872	62.11	62.11	62.11	62.11	62.11	62.11	62.11	29.63	29.63
1873	41.05	41.05	41.05	41.05	41.05	41.05	41.05	21.60	21.60
1874	47.37	47.37	47.37	47.37	47.37	47.37	47.37	25.31	25.31
1875	32.11	32.11	32.11	32.11	32.11	32.11	32.11	17.28	17.28
1876	22.63	22.63	22.63	22.63	22.63	22.63	22.63	13.58	13.58
1877	39.47	39.47	39.47	39.47	39.47	39.47	33.16	21.60	21.60
1878	41.05	41.05	41.05	41.05	41.05	41.05	21.58	25.31	25.31
1879	39.47	39.47	39.47	39.47	39.47	39.47	21.05	24.69	24.69
1880	39.47	39.47	39.47	39.47	39.47	39.47	21.05	24.69	24.69
1881	34.21	34.21	34.21	34.21	34.21	34.21	17.37	20.37	20.37
1882	29.47	29.47	29.47	29.47	29.47	29.47	13.68	16.05	16.05
1883	39.47	39.47	39.47	39.47	39.47	39.47	18.42	21.60	21.60
1884	39.47	39.47	39.47	39.47	39.47	39.47	18.42	21.60	21.60
1885	29.47	29.47	29.47	29.47	29.47	29.57	14.06	16.67	16.67
1886	39.47	34.74	39.47	39.47	39.47	39.47	18.42	21.60	21.60
1887	39.47	26.32	39.47	39.47	35.26	29.47	16.32	21.60	16.67
1888	38.42	25.79	38.42	38.42	33.16	25.79	15.79	21.60	15.43
1889	39.47	26.32	39.47	39.47	34.21	26.32	15.79	21.60	15.43
1890	39.47	26.32	39.47	39.47	34.21	26.32	15.79	21.60	15.43
1891	39.47	26.32	39.47	39.47	34.21	18.42	13.68	21.60	15.43
1892	39.47	26.32	39.47	39.47	34.21	15.79	13.16	21.60	15.43

Year.	Commodities (rates in cents per 100 pounds),									
	Rice.		Groceries.	Drugs.	Crockery and earthenware.		Bagging.		Leather.	
	Less than carloads.	Carloads.			Less than carloads.	Carloads.	Less than carloads.	Carloads.	Less than carloads.	Carloads.
1867	100.00	100.00	100.00	100.00	100.00	100.00	100.00	100.00	100.00	100.00
1868	93.98	93.98	88.89	89.47	88.89	88.89	88.89	88.89	88.89	88.89
1869	86.75	86.75	75.31	69.47	....	....	75.31	75.31	75.31	75.31
1870	....	....	69.75	68.42	....	....	69.75	69.75	68.52	68.52
1871	61.45	61.45	48.77	47.37	33.95	33.95	48.77	48.77	48.77	48.77
1872	68.67	68.67	64.20	62.11	56.17	56.17	64.20	64.20	64.20	64.20
1873	42.17	42.17	43.83	41.05	21.60	21.60	43.83	43.83	43.83	43.83
1874	49.40	49.40	50.62	47.37	25.31	25.31	50.62	50.62	50.62	50.62
1875	34.94	34.94	33.95	32.11	20.37	20.37	33.95	33.95	33.95	33.95
1876	26.51	26.51	25.31	22.63	13.58	13.58	25.31	25.31	25.31	25.31
1877	42.17	42.17	41.98	39.47	21.60	21.60	36.42	36.42	41.98	41.98
1878	49.40	49.40	38.27	41.05	35.31	35.31	35.31	35.31	38.27	38.27
1879	48.19	48.19	37.04	39.47	24.69	24.69	24.69	24.69	37.04	37.04
1880	48.19	48.19	37.04	39.47	24.69	24.69	24.69	24.69	37.04	37.04
1881	39.76	39.76	31.48	34.21	20.37	20.37	20.37	20.37	31.48	31.48
1882	31.33	31.33	27.16	29.47	16.05	16.05	16.05	16.05	27.16	27.16
1883	42.17	42.17	37.04	39.47	21.60	21.60	21.60	21.60	37.04	37.04
1884	42.17	42.17	37.04	39.47	21.60	21.60	21.60	21.60	37.04	37.04
1885	32.53	32.53	27.78	29.47	16.67	16.67	16.67	16.67	27.78	27.78
1886	42.17	42.17	37.04	39.47	21.60	21.60	21.60	21.60	37.04	37.04
1887	42.17	42.17	39.51	39.47	21.60	19.14	28.40	21.60	32.10	25.31
1888	42.17	30.12	38.89	38.42	21.60	18.52	30.25	21.60	30.25	21.60
1889	42.17	30.12	40.12	39.47	21.60	18.52	30.86	21.60	30.86	21.60
1890	42.17	30.12	40.12	39.47	21.60	18.52	30.86	21.60	30.86	21.60
1891	42.17	30.12	40.12	39.47	21.60	18.52	30.86	21.60	30.86	21.60
1892	42.17	30.12	40.12	39.47	21.60	18.52	30.86	21.60	30.86	21.60

COMMODITIES, VIA ALL-RAIL ROUTES, NEW YORK TO CHICAGO.

Commodities (rates in cents per 100 pounds).										
Soap.				Starch.		Tea.	Sugar.		Molasses.	
Castile and fancy.		Common.								
Less than car-loads.	Car-loads.	Less than car-loads.	Car-loads.	Less than car-loads.	Car-loads.		Less than car-loads.	Car-loads.	Less than car-loads.	Car-loads.
100.00	100.00	100.00	100.00	100.00	100.00	100.00	100.00	100.00	100.00	100.00
88.89	88.89	60.47	60.47	75.31	75.31	89.47	....	....	....	....
75.31	75.31	55.81	55.81	61.73	61.73	69.47	....	....	....	....
69.75	69.75	53.49	53.49	55.56	55.56	68.42	....	....	....	....
48.77	48.77	39.53	39.53	40.12	40.12	47.37	48.19	48.19	61.45	61.45
64.20	64.20	48.06	48.06	50.00	50.00	62.11	57.83	57.83	74.70	74.70
43.83	43.83	34.88	34.88	35.19	39.19	41.05	42.17	42.17	54.22	54.22
50.62	50.62	41.86	41.86	42.59	42.59	47.37	49.40	49.40	65.06	65.06
33.95	33.95	29.46	49.46	28.40	28.40	32.11	33.73	33.73	56.63	56.63
25.31	29.31	20.16	20.16	22.22	22.22	22.63	26.51	26.51	31.33	31.33
41.98	41.98	32.56	32.56	32.10	32.10	39.47	42.17	42.17	50.60	50.60
38.27	38.27	31.78	31.78	25.31	25.31	41.05	49.40	49.40	49.40	49.40
37.04	37.04	31.01	31.01	24.69	24.69	39.47	48.19	48.19	48.19	48.19
37.04	37.04	31.01	31.01	24.69	24.69	39.47	48.19	48.19	48.19	48.19
31.48	31.48	25.58	25.58	20.37	20.37	34.21	39.76	39.76	39.76	39.76
27.16	27.16	20.16	20.16	16.05	16.05	29.47	28.92	28.92	28.92	28.92
37.04	37.04	27.13	27.13	21.60	21.60	39.47	36.14	36.14	36.14	36.14
37.04	37.04	27.13	27.13	21.60	21.60	39.47	30.12	30.12	30.12	30.12
27.78	27.78	20.93	20.93	16.67	16.67	29.47	24.10	24.10	24.10	24.10
37.04	37.04	27.13	27.13	21.60	21.60	39.47	30.12	30.12	30.12	30.12
39.51	39.51	27.13	24.03	21.60	16.67	39.47	39.76	30.12	39.76	34.94
38.89	38.89	27.13	23.26	21.60	15.43	38.42	42.17	30.12	42.17	36.14
40.12	40.12	27.13	23.26	21.60	15.43	39.47	42.17	30.12	42.17	36.14
40.12	40.12	27.13	23.26	21.60	15.43	39.47	42.17	30.12	42.17	36.14
30.25	27.16	27.13	23.26	21.60	15.43	39.47	42.17	30.12	42.17	36.14
27.13	15.43	27.13	23.26	21.60	15.43	39.47	42.17	28.92	42.17	36.14

Commodities (rates in cents per 100 pounds).										
Lead.		Nails.		Hard-ware.	Agricultural implements.		Machinery.		Beer.	
Less than car-loads.	Car-loads.	Less than car-loads.	Car-loads.		Less than car-loads.	Car-loads.	Less than car-loads.	Car-loads.	Less than car-loads.	Car-loads.
100.00	100.00	100.00	100.00	100.00	100.00	100.00	100.00	100.00	100.00	100.00
93.98	98.98	93.98	93.98	88.89	89.47	89.47	88.89	88.89	92.25	92.25
86.75	86.75	86.75	86.75	75.31	69.47	69.47	75.31	75.31	77.52	77.52
84.34	84.34	83.13	83.13	69.75	68.42	68.42	69.75	69.75	69.77	69.77
53.01	53.01	61.45	61.45	48.77	47.37	47.37	48.77	48.77	50.39	50.39
57.83	57.83	74.70	74.70	64.20	62.11	62.11	64.20	64.20	62.79	62.79
42.17	42.17	54.22	54.22	43.83	....	32.63	43.83	43.83	44.19	44.19
49.40	49.40	65.06	65.06	50.62	....	28.42	50.62	50.62	53.49	53.49
34.94	34.94	45.78	45.78	33.95	....	20.00	33.95	33.95	35.66	35.66
26.51	26.51	31.33	31.33	25.31	....	13.68	25.31	25.31	27.91	27.91
42.17	42.17	50.60	50.60	41.98	....	21.58	41.98	36.42	40.31	40.31
49.40	49.40	49.40	49.40	38.27	....	21.58	38.27	25.31	31.78	31.78
48.19	48.19	48.19	48.19	37.04	....	21.05	37.04	24.69	31.01	31.01
48.19	48.19	48.19	48.19	37.04	....	21.05	37.04	24.69	31.01	31.01
39.76	39.76	39.76	39.76	31.48	....	17.37	31.48	20.37	25.58	25.58
31.33	31.33	31.33	31.33	27.16	....	13.68	27.16	16.05	20.16	20.16
42.17	42.17	42.17	42.17	37.04	....	18.95	37.04	21.60	27.13	27.13
42.17	42.17	42.17	42.17	37.04	....	18.95	37.04	21.60	27.13	27.13
32.53	32.53	32.53	32.53	27.78	....	14.06	27.78	16.67	20.93	20.93
42.17	42.17	42.17	42.17	37.04	....	18.42	37.04	21.60	27.13	27.13
42.17	32.53	42.17	37.35	39.51	....	16.32	25.31	19.14	35.66	24.03
42.17	30.12	42.17	36.14	38.89	25.79	15.79	21.60	18.52	37.98	23.26
42.17	30.12	42.17	36.14	40.12	26.32	15.79	21.60	18.52	38.76	23.26
42.17	30.12	42.17	36.14	40.12	26.32	15.79	21.60	18.52	38.76	23.26
42.17	30.12	37.35	31.33	40.12	26.32	15.79	21.60	20.99	38.76	23.26
42.17	30.12	36.14	30.12	40.12	26.32	15.79	21.60	21.60	38.76	23.26

Next following will be presented numerous tables showing changes in rates on important commodities from New York to a number of western competitive points. These points have been selected principally on account of their importance as commercial and distributing trade centers, and to which the greater portion of the westward traffic from the seaboard cities is carried.

The commodities given have been carefully selected and are intended to embrace (1) those representative of different commercial classes, (2) those of universal use, and (3) those which have been carried in practically the same form throughout the entire period covered. The shipping terms as now employed for many classified articles are quite unlike those of 1867, and the frequent changes in the nomenclature of the freight classifications have made it very difficult to trace the rating for many of the articles; but so far as has been possible the rates shown throughout the tables cover the same form of package, or represent the standard commercial package from time to time prevailing for these articles.

The dates appearing at the left hand in the tables indicate the dates on which a change was made in the rate itself of one or more articles, or a change in the classification of an article resulting in a change in the rate. The headlines are self-explanatory, columns being provided for less than carloads and carload rates for such articles as are carried in both forms. Where the figures are omitted and "special rate" inserted the records of the railroads failed to show the actual rate charged. In such cases the rate may be assumed to have been lower than the preceding rate shown. In the *parlance* of the railroads in former years the term "special rate" generally implied a *secret* rate, which was often omitted from the schedules and known only to the company and favored patrons.

TABLE 20.—RATES OF FREIGHT, ALL RAIL,

DISTANCE VIA SHORTEST ROUTE.—From New York, 912 miles;

[NOTE.—Where the rates are not specifically described as applying on less than

Date.	Dry goods.	Cotton piece goods.	Boots and shoes.	Furniture. Less than carloads.	Furniture. Carloads.	Stoves. Less than carloads.	Stoves. Carloads.	Coffee. Less than carloads.	Coffee. Carloads.	Soap. Castile and fancy. Less than carloads.	Soap. Castile and fancy. Carloads.	Soap. Common. Less than carloads.	Soap. Common. Carloads.	Starch. Less than carloads.	Starch. Carloads.	Tea.	Sugar. Less than carloads.	Sugar. Carloads.
	Commodities (rates in cents per 100 pounds).																	
1867—Jan. 1.....	188	188	188	188	188	188	188	160	160	160	160	127	127	160	160	188	82	82
Nov. 5.....	202	202	202	202	202	202	202	170	170	170	170	138	138	170	170	202	86	86
1868—Feb. 4.....	202	202	202	202	202	202	202	Special rate.		170	170	86	86	138	138	202	Special rate.	
June 4.....	188	188	188	188	188	188	188	..do....		160	160	82	82	127	127	188	..do....	
Aug. 10.....	149	149	149	149	149	149	149	..do....		128	128	82	82	120	120	149	..do....	
Sept. 7.....	188	188	188	188	188	188	188	160	160	160	160	82	82	127	127	188	..do....	
Oct. 1.....	70	70	70	70	70	70	70	Special rate.		60	60	50	50	55	55	70	..do....	
Dec. 7.....	202	202	202	202	202	202	202	..do....		170	170	86	86	138	138	202	..do....	
1869—Feb. 1.....	188	188	188	188	188	188	188	..do....		160	160	82	82	127	127	188	..do....	
Feb. 17.....	45	45	45	45	45	45	45	..do....		45	45	45	45	45	45	45	..do....	
Mar. 15.....	160	160	160	160	160	160	160	..do....		160	160	82	82	127	127	160	..do....	
Apr. 12.....	160	160	160	160	160	160	160	..do....		160	160	82	82	127	127	160	..do....	
July 1.....	188	188	188	188	188	188	188	..do....		160	160	82	82	127	127	188	..do....	
Aug. 11.....	25	25	25	25	25	25	25	..do....		25	25	25	25	25	25	25	..do....	
Aug. 23.....	38	38	38	38	38	38	38	..do....		38	38	38	38	38	38	38	..do....	
Aug. 30.....	43	43	43	43	43	43	43	..do....		43	43	43	43	43	43	43	..do....	
Sept. 22.....	40	40	40	40	40	40	40	..do....		40	40	40	40	40	40	40	..do....	
Sept. 24.....	35	35	35	35	35	35	35	..do....		35	35	35	35	35	35	35	..do....	
Oct. 4.....	50	50	50	50	50	50	50	..do....		50	50	50	50	50	50	50	..do....	
Oct. 9.....	75	75	75	75	75	75	75	..do....		75	75	75	75	75	75	75	..do....	
Nov. 1.....	140	140	140	140	140	140	140	..do....		125	125	80	80	100	100	140	..do....	
Nov. 29.....	150	150	150	150	150	150	150	..do....		130	130	80	80	100	100	150	..do....	
1870—Apr. 14.....	140	140	140	140	140	140	140	..do....		125	125	80	80	100	100	140	..do....	
May 4.....	150	150	150	150	150	150	150	..do....		130	130	80	80	100	100	150	38	38
May 7.....	150	150	150	150	150	150	150	..do....		130	130	80	80	100	100	150	38	38
June 18.....	112	112	112	112	112	112	112	..do....		90	90	55	55	90	90	112	38	38
July 13.....	80	80	80	80	80	80	80	..do....		70	70	50	50	60	60	80	Special rate.	
July 18.....	75	75	75	75	75	75	75	..do....		70	70	50	50	60	60	75	..do....	
July 21.....	65	65	65	65	65	65	65	..do....		60	60	50	50	60	60	65	..do....	
July 25.....	65	65	65	65	65	65	65	..do....		60	60	45	45	55	55	65	..do....	
July 28.....	50	50	50	50	50	50	50	..do....		50	50	45	45	50	50	50	..do....	
Aug. 12.....	50	50	50	50	50	50	50	..do....		50	50	50	50	50	50	50	..do....	
Aug. 22.....	100	100	100	100	100	100	100	..do....		90	90	55	55	70	70	100	..do....	
Sept. 8.....	125	125	125	125	125	125	125	..do....		110	110	65	65	85	85	125	..do....	
Nov. 28.....	160	160	160	160	160	160	160	..do....		130	130	65	65	100	100	160	..do....	
Dec. 26.....	180	180	180	180	180	180	180	60	60	150	150	80	80	120	120	180	60	60
1871—Feb. 20.....	150	150	150	150	150	150	150	55	55	130	130	70	70	100	100	150	55	55
Mar. 7.....	100	100	100	100	100	100	100	45	45	90	90	55	55	70	70	100	45	45
May 18.....	75	75	75	75	75	75	75	37	37	65	65	45	45	50	50	75	37	37
June 1.....	100	100	100	100	100	100	100	45	45	90	90	55	55	70	70	100	45	45
July 8.....	75	75	75	75	75	75	75	37	37	65	65	45	45	50	50	75	37	37
July 28.....	45	45	45	45	45	45	45	32	32	45	45	45	45	45	45	45	32	32
Aug. 16.....	40	40	40	40	40	40	40	28	28	40	40	40	40	40	40	40	28	28
Aug. 21.....	35	35	35	35	35	35	35	26	26	35	35	35	35	35	35	35	26	26
Sept. 1.....	30	30	30	30	30	30	30	24	24	30	30	30	30	30	30	30	24	24
Nov. 27.....	100	100	100	100	100	100	100	45	45	90	90	55	55	70	70	100	45	45
Dec. 15.....	125	125	125	125	125	125	125	50	50	110	110	65	65	85	85	125	50	50
1872—Aug. 1.....	75	75	75	75	75	75	75	35	35	70	70	45	45	60	60	75	35	35
Sept. 1.....	125	125	125	125	125	125	125	50	50	110	110	65	65	85	85	125	50	50
Sept. 2.....	100	100	100	100	100	100	100	45	45	90	90	55	55	70	70	100	45	45
Oct. 14.....	125	125	125	125	125	125	125	50	50	110	110	65	65	85	85	125	50	50
1873—Apr. 14.....	100	100	100	100	100	100	100	45	45	90	90	60	60	75	75	100	45	45
June 11.....	75	75	75	75	75	75	75	35	35	70	70	45	45	60	60	75	35	35
Aug. 11.....	40	40	40	40	40	40	40	30	30	40	40	30	30	30	30	40	30	30
Aug. 13.....	27	27	27	27	27	27	27	17	17	27	27	18	18	18	18	27	17	17
Dec. 1.....	75	75	75	75	75	75	75	35	35	70	70	45	45	60	60	75	35	35
1874—Jan. 1.....	100	100	100	100	100	100	100	45	45	90	90	60	60	75	75	100	45	45
Aug. 3.....	75	75	75	75	75	75	75	35	35	70	70	45	45	60	60	75	35	35
1875—Jan. 20.....	100	100	100	100	100	100	100	45	45	90	90	60	60	75	75	100	45	45

FROM NEW YORK, N. Y., TO CHICAGO, ILL.

Boston, 1,001 miles; Philadelphia, 822 miles; Baltimore, 801 miles.

carload or carload quantities, they apply on shipments regardless of quantity.]

Commodities (rates in cents per 100 pounds).																						
Molasses.		Rice.				Crockery and earthenware.		Bagging.		Leather.		Lead.		Nails.			Agricultural implements.		Machinery.		Beer.	
Less than carloads.	Carloads.	Less than carloads.	Carloads.	Groceries.	Drugs.	Less than carloads.	Carloads.	Less than carloads.	Carloads.	Less than carloads.	Carloads.	Less than carloads.	Carloads.	Less than carloads.	Carloads.	Hardware.	Less than carloads.	Carloads.	Less than carloads.	Carloads.	Less than carloads.	Carloads.
82	82	82	82	160	188	160	160	160	160	160	160	82	82	82	82	160	188	188	160	160	127	127
86	86	86	86	170	202	170	170	170	170	170	170	86	86	86	86	170	202	202	170	170	138	138
Special rate.		86	86	170	202	170	170	170	170	170	170	86	86	86	86	170	202	202	170	170	138	138
..do....		82	82	160	188	160	160	160	160	160	160	82	82	82	82	160	188	188	160	160	127	127
..do....		82	82	128	149	128	128	128	128	128	128	82	82	82	82	128	149	149	128	128	120	120
..do....		82	82	160	188	160	160	160	160	160	160	82	82	82	82	160	188	188	160	160	127	127
..do....		50	50	60	70	60	60	60	60	60	60	52	52	50	50	60	70	70	60	60	55	55
..do....		86	86	170	202	170	170	170	170	170	170	86	86	86	86	170	202	202	170	170	138	138
..do....		82	82	160	188	160	160	160	160	160	160	82	82	82	82	160	188	188	160	160	127	127
..do....		45	45	45	45	45	45	45	45	45	45	45	45	45	45	45	45	45	45	45	45	45
..do....		82	82	160	160	160	160	160	160	160	160	82	82	82	82	160	160	160	160	160	127	127
..do....		82	82	160	160	Special rate.		160	160	160	160	82	82	82	82	160	160	160	160	160	127	127
..do....		82	82	160	188	..do....		160	160	160	160	82	82	82	82	160	188	188	160	160	127	127
..do....		25	25	25	25	..do....		25	25	25	25	25	25	25	25	25	25	25	25	25	25	25
..do....		38	38	38	38	..do....		38	38	38	38	38	38	38	38	38	38	38	38	38	38	38
..do....		43	43	43	43	..do....		43	43	43	43	43	43	43	43	43	43	43	43	43	43	43
..do....		40	40	40	40	..do....		40	40	40	40	40	40	40	40	40	40	40	40	40	40	40
..do....		35	35	35	35	..do....		35	35	35	35	35	35	35	35	35	35	35	35	35	35	35
..do....		50	50	50	50	..do....		50	50	50	50	50	50	50	50	50	50	50	50	50	50	50
..do....		75	75	75	75	..do....		75	75	75	75	75	75	75	75	75	75	75	75	75	75	75
..do....		80	80	125	140	..do....		125	125	125	125	80	80	80	80	125	140	140	125	125	100	100
..do....		80	80	130	150	..do....		130	130	125	125	80	80	80	80	130	150	150	130	130	100	100
..do....		80	80	125	140	..do....		125	125	125	125	80	80	80	80	125	140	140	125	125	100	100
..do....		80	80	130	150	..do....		130	130	130	130	80	80	80	80	130	150	150	130	130	100	100
..do....		Special rate.		130	150	..do....		130	130	130	130	80	80	80	80	130	150	150	130	130	100	100
..do....		..do....		90	112	..do....		90	90	90	90	70	70	55	55	90	112	112	90	90	90	90
..do....		..do....		70	80	..do....		70	70	70	70	50	50	50	50	70	80	80	70	70	60	60
..do....		..do....		70	75	..do....		70	70	70	70	50	50	50	50	70	75	75	70	70	60	60
..do....		..do....		60	65	..do....		60	60	60	60	50	50	50	50	60	65	65	60	60	60	60
..do....		..do....		60	65	..do....		60	60	60	60	45	45	45	45	60	65	65	60	60	55	55
..do....		..do....		50	50	..do....		50	50	50	50	45	45	45	45	50	50	50	50	50	50	50
..do....		..do....		50	50	..do....		50	50	50	50	50	50	50	50	50	50	50	50	50	50	50
..do....		..do....		90	100	..do....		90	90	90	90	55	55	55	55	90	100	100	90	90	70	70
..do....		..do....		110	125	..do....		110	110	110	110	65	65	65	65	110	125	125	110	110	85	85
..do....		..do....		130	160	..do....		130	130	130	130	65	65	65	65	130	160	160	130	130	100	100
80	80	80	80	150	180	150	150	150	150	150	150	80	80	80	80	150	180	180	150	150	120	120
70	70	70	70	130	150	55	55	130	130	130	130	70	70	70	70	130	150	150	130	130	100	100
55	55	55	55	90	100	45	45	90	90	90	90	45	45	55	55	90	100	100	90	90	70	70
45	45	45	45	65	75	37	37	65	65	65	65	37	37	45	45	65	75	75	65	65	50	50
55	55	55	55	90	100	45	45	90	90	90	90	45	45	55	55	90	100	100	90	90	70	70
45	45	45	45	65	75	37	37	65	65	65	65	37	37	45	45	65	75	75	65	65	50	50
45	45	45	45	45	45	32	32	45	45	45	45	32	32	45	45	45	45	45	45	45	45	45
40	40	40	40	40	40	28	28	40	40	40	40	28	28	40	40	40	40	40	40	40	40	40
35	35	35	35	35	35	26	26	35	35	35	35	26	26	35	35	35	35	25	35	35	35	35
30	30	30	30	30	30	24	24	30	30	30	30	24	24	30	30	30	30	30	30	30	30	30
55	55	55	55	90	100	45	45	90	90	90	90	45	45	55	55	90	100	100	90	90	70	70
65	65	65	65	110	125	110	110	110	110	110	110	50	50	65	65	110	125	125	110	110	85	85
45	45	35	35	70	75	70	70	70	70	70	70	35	35	45	45	70	75	75	70	70	60	60
65	65	65	65	110	125	110	110	110	110	110	110	50	50	65	65	110	125	125	110	110	85	85
55	55	45	45	90	100	90	90	90	90	90	90	45	45	55	55	90	100	100	90	90	70	70
65	65	50	50	110	125	50	50	110	110	110	110	50	50	65	65	110	125	125	110	110	85	85
60	60	45	45	90	100	45	45	90	90	90	90	45	45	60	60	90	Spe'l rate.	60	90	90	75	75
45	45	35	35	70	75	35	35	70	70	70	70	35	35	45	45	70	.do .	45	70	70	60	60
30	30	30	30	40	40	30	30	40	40	40	40	30	30	30	30	40	.do .	30	40	40	30	30
18	18	17	17	27	27	17	17	27	27	27	27	17	17	18	18	27	.do .	18	27	27	18	18
45	45	35	35	70	75	35	35	70	70	70	70	35	35	45	45	70	.do .	45	70	70	60	60
60	60	45	45	90	100	45	45	90	90	90	90	45	45	60	60	90	.do .	60	90	90	75	75
45	45	35	35	70	75	35	35	70	70	70	70	35	35	45	45	70	.do .	45	70	90	60	60
60	60	45	45	90	100	45	45	90	90	90	90	45	45	60	60	90	.do .	60	90	90	75	75

TABLE 20.—RATES OF FREIGHT, ALL RAIL, FROM

DISTANCE VIA SHORTEST ROUTE.—From New York, 912 miles;

[NOTE.—Where the rates are not specifically described as applying on less than

Date.	Commodities (rates in cents per 100 pounds).																		
				Furniture.		Stoves.		Coffee.		Soap.				Starch.			Sugar.	
										Castile and fancy.		Common.						
	Dry goods.	Cotton piece goods.	Boots and shoes.	Less than carloads.	Carloads.	Less than carloads.	Carloads.	Less than carloads.	Carloads.	Less than carloads.	Carloads.	Less than carloads.	Carloads.	Less than carloads.	Carloads.	Tea.	Less than carloads.	Carloads.
1875—Feb. 23	100	100	100	100	100	100	100	30	30	90	90	60	60	75	75	100	30	30
Mar. 17	75	75	75	75	75	75	75	30	30	70	70	45	45	60	60	75	30	30
Apr. 6	60	60	60	60	60	60	60	30	30	55	55	40	40	50	50	60	30	30
May 18	40	40	40	40	40	40	40	25	25	40	40	35	35	35	35	40	25	25
Aug. 12	50	50	50	50	50	50	50	20	20	40	40	25	25	30	30	50	20	20
Nov. 15	75	75	75	75	75	75	75	35	35	70	70	45	45	60	60	75	35	35
Dec. 22	30	30	30	30	30	30	30	15	15	25	25	20	20	20	20	30	15	15
1876—Jan. 10	75	75	75	75	75	75	75	35	35	70	70	45	45	60	60	75	35	35
June 12	25	25	25	25	25	25	25	16	16	25	25	16	16	25	25	25	16	16
July 28	15	15	15	15	15	15	15	10	10	15	15	10	10	15	15	15	10	10
Dec. 18	50	50	50	50	50	50	50	25	25	45	45	30	30	40	40	50	25	25
1877—Mar. 12	75	75	75	75	75	75	75	35	35	70	70	45	45	60	60	75	35	35
Oct. 8	75	75	75	75	75	75	40	40	40	70	70	40	40	40	40	75	40	40
Oct. 22	100	100	100	100	100	100	45	45	45	90	90	45	45	45	45	100	45	45
Dec. 10	100	100	100	100	100	100	45	45	45	80	80	45	45	45	45	100	45	45
1878—Feb. 15	75	75	75	75	75	75	40	40	40	60	60	40	40	40	40	75	40	40
1881—Aug. 6	45	45	45	45	45	45	19	19	19	32	32	19	19	19	19	45	19	19
Nov. 14	60	60	60	60	60	60	28	28	28	50	50	28	28	28	28	60	28	28
1882—Jan. 24	45	45	45	45	45	45	19	19	19	32	32	19	19	19	19	45	19	19
July 1	60	60	60	60	60	60	30	30	30	50	50	30	30	30	30	60	25	25
Nov. 1	75	75	75	75	75	75	35	35	35	60	60	35	35	35	35	75	35	35
1883—June 22	75	75	75	75	75	75	35	35	35	60	60	35	35	35	35	75	25	25
1885—Jan. 26	50	50	50	50	50	50	25	25	25	40	40	25	25	25	25	50	18	18
Oct. 5	60	60	60	60	60	60	25	25	25	50	50	25	25	25	25	60	20	20
Nov. 18	75	75	75	75	75	75	35	35	35	60	60	35	35	35	35	75	25	25
1886—Aug. 26	75	75	75	75	75	75	35	35	35	60	60	35	35	35	35	75	25	25
1887—Apr. 1	75	50	75	75	65	50	30	35	25	65	65	35	30	35	25	75	35	25
1888—Jan. 9	75	50	75	75	65	50	33	38½	27½	65	65	38½	33	38½	27½	75	38½	27½
Mar. 5	75	50	75	75	65	50	30	35	25	65	65	35	30	35	25	75	35	25
Nov. 12	50	35	50	50	40	35	25	30	20	40	40	30	25	30	20	50	30	20
Dec. 17	75	50	75	75	65	50	30	35	25	65	65	35	30	35	25	75	35	25
1891—Apr. 9	75	50	75	75	65	30	25	35	25	65	65	35	25	35	25	75	35	25
June 20	75	50	75	75	65	30	25	35	25	35	25	35	25	35	25	75	35	25
1892—June 6	75	50	75	75	65	30	25	35	25	35	25	35	25	35	25	75	35	23

NEW YORK, N. Y. TO CHICAGO, ILL.—Continued.

Boston, 1,001 miles; Philadelphia, 822 miles; Baltimore, 801 miles.

carload or carload quantities, they apply on shipments regardless of quantity.]

Commodities (rates in cents per 100 pounds).																						
Molasses.		Rice.				Crockery and earthenware.		Bagging.		Leather.		Lead.		Nails.			Agricultural implements.		Machinery.		Beer.	
Less than carloads.	Carloads.	Less than carloads.	Carloads.	Groceries.	Drugs.	Less than carloads.	Carloads.	Less than carloads.	Carloads.	Less than carloads.	Carloads.	Less than carloads.	Carloads.	Less than carloads.	Carloads.	Hardware.	Less than carloads.	Carloads.	Less than carloads.	Carloads.	Less than carloads.	Carloads.
60	60	45	45	90	100	45	45	90	90	90	90	45	45	60	60	90	Sp'l rate.	60	90	90	75	75
60	60	35	35	70	75	35	35	70	70	70	70	35	35	45	45	70	.do .	45	70	70	60	60
60	60	30	30	55	60	30	30	55	55	55	55	30	30	40	40	55	.do .	40	55	55	50	50
60	60	25	25	40	40	40	40	40	40	40	40	25	25	35	35	40	.do .	35	40	40	35	35
25	25	20	20	40	50	20	20	40	40	40	40	20	20	25	25	40	.do .	25	40	40	30	30
45	45	35	35	70	75	35	35	70	70	70	70	35	35	45	45	70	.do .	45	70	70	60	60
20	20	15	15	25	30	15	15	25	25	25	25	15	15	20	20	25	.do	20	25	25	20	20
45	45	35	35	70	75	35	35	70	70	70	70	35	35	45	45	70	.do	45	70	70	60	60
16	16	16	16	25	25	16	16	25	25	25	25	16	16	16	16	25	.do .	16	25	25	25	23
10	10	10	10	15	15	10	10	15	15	15	15	10	10	10	10	15	.do .	10	15	15	15	15
30	30	25	25	45	50	25	25	45	45	45	45	25	25	30	30	45	.do .	25	45	45	40	40
45	45	35	35	70	75	35	35	70	70	70	70	35	35	45	45	70	.do .	45	70	70	60	60
40	40	40	40	70	75	40	40	40	40	70	70	40	40	40	40	70	.do .	40	70	40	40	40
45	45	45	45	90	100	45	45	45	45	90	90	45	45	45	45	90	.do .	45	90	45	45	45
45	45	45	45	80	100	45	45	45	45	80	80	45	45	45	45	80	.do .	45	80	45	45	45
40	40	40	40	60	75	40	40	40	40	60	60	40	40	40	40	60	.do .	40	60	40	40	40
19	19	19	19	32	45	19	19	19	19	32	32	19	19	19	19	32	.do .	19	32	19	19	19
28	28	28	28	50	60	28	28	28	28	50	50	28	28	28	28	50	.do .	28	50	28	28	28
19	19	19	19	32	45	19	19	19	19	32	32	19	19	19	16	32	.do .	19	32	19	19	19
25	25	30	30	50	60	30	30	30	30	50	50	30	30	30	30	50	.do	30	50	30	30	30
35	35	35	35	60	75	35	35	35	35	60	60	35	35	35	35	60	.do	35	60	35	35	35
25	25	35	35	60	75	35	35	35	35	60	60	35	35	35	35	60	.do .	36	60	35	35	35
18	18	25	25	40	50	25	25	35	25	40	40	25	25	25	25	40	.do	25	40	25	25	25
20	20	25	25	50	60	25	25	25	25	50	50	25	25	25	25	50	.do .	25	50	25	25	25
25	25	35	35	60	75	35.	35	35	35	60	60	35	35	35	35	60	.do .	35	60	35	35	35
25	25	35	35	60	75	35	35	35	35	60	60	35	35	35	35	60	do .	35	60	35	35	35
35	30	35	35	65	75	35	30	50	35	50	35	35	25	35	30	65	50	30	35	30	50	30
38½	33	38½	27½	65	75	38½	33	50	38½	50	38½	38½	27½	38½	33	65	50	33	38½	33	50	33
35	30	35	25	65	75	35	30	50	35	50	35	35	25	35	30	65	50	30	35	30	50	30
30	25	30	20	40	50	30	25	35	30	35	30	30	20	30	25	40	35	25	30	25	35	25
35	30	35	25	65	75	35	30	50	35	50	35	35	25	35	30	65	50	30	35	30	50	30
35	30	35	25	65	75	35	30	50	35	50	35	35	25	30	25	65	50	30	35	35	50	30
35	30	35	25	65	75	35	30	50	35	50	35	35	25	30	25	65	50	30	35	35	50	30
35	30	35	25	65	75	35	30	50	35	50	35	35	25	30	25	65	50	30	35	35	50	30

TABLE 21.—RATES OF FREIGHT, ALL RAIL, FROM

DISTANCE VIA SHORTEST ROUTE.—From New York, 997 miles;

[NOTE.—Where the rates shown are not specifically described as applying on less

Date.	Commodities (rates in cents per 100 pounds).																	
	Dry goods.	Cotton piece goods.	Boots and shoes.	Furniture.		Stoves.		Coffee.		Soaps. Castile and fancy.		Soaps. Common.		Starch.		Tea.	Sugar.	
				Less than carloads.	Carloads.	Less than carloads.	Carloads.	Less than carloads.	Carloads.	Less than carloads.	Carloads.	Less than carloads.	Carloads.	Less than carloads.	Carloads.		Less than carloads.	Carloads.
1867—Jan. 1	188	188	188	188	188	188	188	160	160	160	160	127	127	160	160	188	82	82
Nov. 5	202	202	202	202	202	202	202	170	170	170	170	138	138	160	160	202	86	86
1868—Feb. 4	202	202	202	202	202	202	202	Special rate.		170	170	86	86	138	138	202	Special rate.	
June 4	188	188	188	188	188	188	188	..do....		160	160	82	82	127	127	188	..do....	
Aug. 10	149	149	149	149	149	149	149	..do....		128	128	82	82	120	120	149	..do....	
Sept. 7	188	188	188	188	188	188	188	..do....		160	160	82	82	127	127	188	..do....	
Oct. 1	88	88	88	88	88	88	88	..do....		74	74	60	60	68	68	88	..do....	
Dec. 7	202	202	202	202	202	202	202	..do....		170	170	86	86	138	138	202	..do....	
1869—Feb. 1	188	188	188	188	188	188	188	..do....		160	160	82	82	127	127	188	..do....	
Mar. 15	160	160	160	160	160	160	160	..do....		160	160	82	82	127	127	160	..do....	
Apr. 12	160	160	160	160	160	160	160	..do....		160	160	82	82	127	127	160	..do....	
July 1	188	188	188	188	188	188	188	..do....		160	160	82	82	127	127	188	..do....	
Aug. 11	44	44	44	44	44	44	44	..do....		42	42	36	36	39	39	44	..do....	
Aug. 23	56	56	56	56	56	56	56	..do....		32	32	38	38	38	38	56	..do....	
Sept. 24	54	54	54	54	54	54	54	..do....		42	42	46	46	49	49	54	..do....	
Oct. 4	69	69	69	69	69	69	69	..do....		67	67	61	61	64	64	69	..do....	
Oct. 9	93	93	93	93	93	93	93	..do....		91	91	61	61	89	89	93	..do....	
Nov. 1	140	140	140	140	140	140	140	..do....		125	125	80	80	100	100	140	..do....	
Nov. 29	150	150	150	150	150	150	150	..do....		130	130	80	80	100	100	150	..do....	
1870—Apr. 14	140	140	140	140	140	140	140	..do....		125	125	80	80	100	100	140	38	38
May 7	150	150	150	150	150	150	150	..do....		130	130	80	80	100	100	150	38	38
June 18	112	112	112	112	112	112	112	..do....		90	90	55	55	70	70	112	38	38
July 13	80	80	80	80	80	80	80	..do....		70	70	50	50	60	60	80	Special rate.	
July 25	65	65	65	65	65	65	65	..do....		60	60	45	45	55	55	65	..do....	
Aug. 12	50	50	50	50	50	50	50	..do....		50	50	50	50	50	50	50	..do....	
Aug. 22	100	100	100	100	100	100	100	..do....		90	90	55	55	70	70	100	..do...	
Nov. 28	160	160	160	160	160	160	160	..do....		130	130	65	65	100	100	160	..do....	
Dec. 26	180	180	180	180	180	180	180	60	60	150	150	80	80	120	120	180	60	60
1871—Feb. 20	150	150	150	150	150	150	150	55	55	130	130	70	70	100	100	150	55	55
Mar. 13	100	100	100	100	100	100	100	45	45	90	90	90	90	70	70	100	45	45
May 18	75	75	75	75	75	75	75	37	37	65	65	45	45	50	50	75	37	37
June 1	100	100	100	100	100	100	100	45	45	90	90	55	55	70	70	100	45	45
July 8	75	75	75	75	75	75	75	37	37	65	65	45	45	50	50	75	37	37
July 28	42	42	42	42	42	42	42	26	26	42	42	31	31	36	36	42	26	26
Dec. 15	125	125	125	125	125	125	125	50	50	110	110	65	65	85	85	125	50	50
1872—Aug. 1	75	75	75	75	75	75	75	35	35	70	70	45	45	60	60	75	35	35
Sept. 1	125	125	125	125	125	125	125	50	50	110	110	65	65	85	85	125	50	50
Sept. 2	100	100	100	100	100	100	100	45	45	90	90	55	55	70	70	100	45	45
Oct. 14	125	125	125	125	125	125	125	50	50	110	110	65	65	85	85	125	50	50
1873—Apr. 14	100	100	100	100	100	100	100	45	45	90	90	60	60	75	75	100	45	45
June 11	75	75	75	75	75	75	75	35	35	70	70	45	45	60	60	75	35	35
Aug. 13	45	45	45	45	45	45	45	35	35	45	45	35	35	35	35	45	35	35
Aug. 21	40	40	40	40	40	40	40	30	30	40	40	30	30	30	30	40	30	30
Sept. 17	75	75	75	75	75	75	75	35	35	70	70	45	45	60	60	75	35	35
1874—Jan. 1	100	100	100	100	100	100	100	45	45	90	90	60	60	75	75	100	45	45
Aug. 3	75	75	75	75	75	75	75	35	35	70	70	45	45	60	60	75	35	35
1875—Jan. 20	100	100	100	100	100	100	100	45	45	90	90	60	60	75	75	100	45	45
Mar. 17	75	75	75	75	75	75	75	30	30	70	70	45	45	60	60	75	30	30
May 26	45	45	45	45	45	45	45	30	30	40	40	35	35	40	40	45	30	30
Aug. 12	50	50	50	50	50	50	50	20	20	40	40	25	25	30	30	50	20	20
Nov. 15	68	68	68	68	68	68	68	32	32	64	64	41	41	55	55	68	32	32
Dec. 22	22	22	22	22	22	22	22	11	11	19	19	16	16	15	15	22	11	11
1876—Jan. 10	75	75	75	75	75	75	75	20	20	70	70	25	25	60	60	75	20	20
June 12	25	25	25	25	25	25	25	16	16	25	25	16	16	25	25	25	16	16
1877—Jan. 1	50	50	50	50	50	50	50	25	25	45	45	30	30	40	40	50	25	25
Mar. 12	75	75	75	75	75	75	75	35	35	70	70	45	45	60	60	75	35	35
Oct. 8	75	75	75	75	75	75	40	40	40	70	70	40	40	40	40	75	40	40
Oct. 22	100	100	100	100	100	100	45	45	45	90	90	45	45	45	45	100	45	45
Dec. 10	100	100	100	100	100	100	45	45	45	80	80	45	45	45	45	100	45	45
1878—Feb. 15	75	75	75	75	75	75	40	40	40	60	60	40	40	40	40	75	40	40

NEW YORK, N. Y., TO MILWAUKEE, WIS.

Boston, 1,086 miles; Philadelphia, 907 miles; Baltimore, 886 miles.

than carload or carload quantities they apply on shipments regardless of quantity.]

Commodities (rates in cents per 100 pounds).																						
Molasses.		Rice.				Crockery and earthenware.		Bagging.		Leather.		Lead.		Nails.			Agricultural implements.		Machinery.		Beer.	
Less than carloads.	Carloads.	Less than carloads.	Carloads.	Groceries.	Drugs.	Less than carloads.	Carloads.	Less than carloads.	Carloads.	Less than carloads.	Carloads.	Less than carloads.	Carloads.	Less than carloads.	Carloads.	Hardware.	Less than carloads.	Carloads.	Less than carloads.	Carloads.	Less than carloads.	Carloads.
82	82	82	82	160	188	160	160	160	160	160	160	82	82	82	82	160	188	188	160	160	127	127
86	86	86	86	170	202	170	170	170	170	170	170	86	86	86	86	170	202	202	170	170	138	138
Special rate.		86	86	170	202	170	170	170	170	170	170	86	86	86	86	170	202	202	170	170	138	138
..do....		82	82	160	188	160	160	160	160	160	160	82	82	82	82	160	188	188	160	160	127	127
..do....		82	82	128	149	128	128	128	128	128	128	82	82	82	82	128	149	149	128	128	120	120
..do....		82	82	160	188	160	160	160	160	160	160	82	82	82	82	160	188	188	160	160	127	127
..do....		60	60	74	88	74	74	74	74	74	74	60	60	60	60	74	188	188	74	74	68	68
..do....		86	86	170	202	170	170	170	174	170	170	86	86	86	86	170	202	202	170	170	138	138
..do....		82	82	160	188	160	160	160	160	160	160	82	82	82	82	160	188	188	160	160	127	127
..do....		82	82	160	160	160	160	160	160	160	160	82	82	82	82	160	160	160	160	160	127	127
..do....		82	82	160	160	Special rate.		160	160	160	160	82	82	82	82	160	160	160	160	160	127	127
..do....		82	82	160	188	..do....		160	160	160	160	82	82	82	82	160	188	188	160	160	127	127
..do....		36	36	42	44	..do....		42	42	42	42	36	36	36	36	42	44	44	42	42	39	39
..do....		38	38	32	56	..do....		38	38	38	38	38	38	38	38	38	56	56	38	38	38	38
..do....		46	46	42	54	..do....		42	42	42	42	46	46	46	46	42	54	54	42	42	49	49
..do....		61	61	67	69	..do....		67	67	67	67	61	61	61	61	67	69	69	67	67	64	64
..do....		61	61	91	93	..do....		91	91	91	91	61	61	61	61	91	93	93	91	91	89	89
..do....		80	80	125	140	..do....		125	125	125	125	80	61	80	80	125	140	140	125	125	100	100
..do....		80	80	130	150	..do....		130	130	130	130	80	80	80	80	130	150	150	130	130	100	100
..do....		80	80	125	140	..do....		125	125	125	125	80	80	80	80	125	140	140	125	125	100	100
..do....		Special rate.		130	150	..do....		130	130	130	130	80	80	80	80	130	150	150	130	130	100	100
..do....		..do....		90	112	..do....		90	90	90	90	55	55	55	55	90	112	112	90	90	70	70
..do....		..do....		70	80	..do....		70	70	70	70	50	50	50	50	70	80	80	70	70	60	60
..do....		..do....		60	65	..do....		60	60	60	60	45	45	45	45	60	65	65	60	60	55	55
..do....		..do....		50	50	..do....		50	50	50	50	50	50	50	50	50	50	50	50	50	50	50
..do....		..do....		90	100	..do....		90	90	90	90	55	55	55	55	90	100	100	90	90	70	70
..do....		..do....		130	160	..do....		130	130	130	130	65	65	65	65	130	160	160	130	130	100	100
80	80	80	80	150	180	150	150	150	150	150	150	80	80	80	80	150	180	180	150	150	120	120
70	70	70	70	130	150	55	55	130	130	130	130	55	55	70	70	130	150	150	130	130	100	100
55	55	55	55	90	100	45	45	90	90	90	90	45	45	55	55	90	100	100	90	90	70	70
45	45	45	45	65	75	37	37	65	65	65	65	37	37	45	45	65	75	75	65	65	50	50
55	55	55	55	90	100	45	45	90	90	90	90	45	45	55	55	90	100	100	90	90	70	70
45	45	45	45	65	75	37	37	65	65	65	65	37	37	45	45	65	75	75	65	65	50	50
31	31	31	31	42	42	26	26	42	42	42	42	26	26	31	31	42	42	42	42	42	36	36
65	65	65	65	110	125	110	110	110	110	110	110	50	50	65	65	110	125	125	110	110	85	85
45	45	35	35	70	75	70	70	70	70	70	70	35	35	45	45	70	75	75	70	70	60	60
65	65	65	65	110	125	110	110	110	110	110	110	50	50	65	65	110	125	125	110	110	85	85
55	55	45	45	90	100	90	90	90	90	90	90	45	45	55	55	90	100	100	90	90	70	70
65	65	50	50	110	125	50	50	110	110	110	110	50	50	65	65	110	125	125	110	110	85	85
60	60	45	45	90	100	45	45	90	90	90	90	45	45	60	60	90	Sp'l rate	60	90	90	75	75
45	45	35	35	70	75	35	35	70	70	70	70	35	35	45	45	70	.do .	45	70	70	60	60
35	35	35	35	45	45	35	35	45	45	45	45	35	35	35	35	45	.do .	35	45	45	35	35
30	30	30	30	40	40	30	30	40	40	40	40	50	50	30	30	40	.do .	30	40	40	30	30
45	45	35	35	70	75	35	35	70	70	70	70	35	35	45	45	70	.do .	45	70	70	60	60
60	60	45	45	90	100	45	45	90	90	90	90	45	45	60	60	90	.do .	60	90	90	75	75
45	45	35	35	70	75	35	35	70	70	70	70	35	35	45	45	70	.do .	45	70	70	60	60
60	60	45	45	90	100	45	45	90	90	90	90	45	45	60	60	90	.do .	60	90	90	75	75
30	30	35	35	70	75	35	35	70	70	70	70	35	35	45	45	70	.do .	45	70	70	60	60
30	30	30	30	40	45	30	30	40	40	40	40	30	30	35	35	40	.do .	40	40	40	40	40
25	25	20	20	40	50	20	20	40	40	40	40	20	20	25	25	40	.do .	25	40	40	30	30
41	41	32	32	64	68	32	32	64	64	64	64	32	32	41	41	64	.do .	41	64	64	55	55
16	16	11	11	19	22	11	11	19	19	19	19	11	11	16	16	19	.do .	16	19	19	15	15
25	25	20	20	70	75	20	20	70	70	70	70	20	20	25	25	70	.do .	25	70	70	60	60
16	16	16	16	25	25	16	16	25	25	25	25	16	16	16	16	25	.do .	16	25	25	25	25
30	30	25	25	45	50	25	25	45	45	45	45	25	25	30	30	45	.do .	30	45	45	40	40
45	45	35	35	70	75	35	35	70	70	70	70	35	35	45	45	70	.do .	45	70	70	60	60
40	40	40	40	70	75	40	40	40	40	70	70	40	40	40	40	70	.do .	40	70	70	40	40
45	45	45	45	90	100	45	45	45	45	90	90	45	45	45	45	90	.do .	45	90	45	45	45
45	45	45	45	80	100	45	45	45	45	80	80	45	45	45	45	80	.do .	45	80	45	45	45
40	40	40	40	60	75	40	40	40	40	60	60	40	40	40	40	60	.do .	40	60	40	40	40

TABLE 21.—RATES OF FREIGHT, ALL RAIL, FROM NEW

DISTANCE VIA SHORTEST ROUTE.—From New York, 997 miles; Boston,

[NOTE.—Where the rates shown are not specifically described as applying on less

Date.	Commodities (rates in cents per 100 pounds.)																	
				Furniture.		Stoves.		Coffee.		Soap.				Starch.			Sugar.	
										Castile and fancy.		Common.						
	Dry goods.	Cotton piece goods.	Boots and shoes.	Less than carloads.	Carloads.	Less than carloads.	Carloads.	Less than carloads.	Carloads.	Less than carloads.	Carloads.	Less than carloads.	Carloads.	Less than carloads.	Carloads.	Tea.	Less than carloads.	Carloads.
1881—Aug. 6	45	45	45	45	45	45	19	19	19	32	32	19	19	19	19	45	19	19
Nov. 14	60	60	60	60	60	60	28	28	28	50	50	28	28	28	28	60	28	28
1882—Jan. 24	45	45	45	45	45	45	19	19	19	32	32	19	19	19	19	45	19	19
July 1	60	60	60	60	60	60	30	30	30	50	50	30	30	30	30	60	25	25
Nov. 1	75	75	75	75	75	75	35	35	35	60	60	35	35	35	35	75	35	35
1883—June 22	75	75	75	75	75	75	35	35	35	60	60	35	35	35	35	75	25	25
1885—Jan. 26	50	50	50	50	50	50	25	25	25	40	40	25	25	25	25	50	18	18
Oct. 5	60	60	60	60	60	60	25	25	25	50	50	25	25	25	25	60	20	20
Nov. 18	75	75	75	75	75	75	35	35	35	60	60	35	35	35	35	75	25	25
1886—Aug. 26	75	50	75	75	75	75	35	35	35	60	60	35	35	35	35	75	25	25
1887—Apr. 1	75	50	75	75	65	50	30	25	25	65	65	35	30	35	25	75	35	25
1888—Jan. 9	75	50	75	75	65	50	33	38½	27½	65	65	38½	33	38½	27½	75	38½	27½
Mar. 5	75	50	75	75	65	50	30	35	25	65	65	35	30	35	25	75	35	25
Nov. 12	50	35	50	50	40	35	25	30	20	40	40	30	25	30	20	50	30	20
Dec. 17	75	50	75	75	65	50	30	35	25	65	65	35	30	35	25	75	35	25
1889—Feb. 18	75	50	75	75	65	50	30	35	25	65	65	35	30	35	25	75	35	25
1891—Apr. 9	75	50	75	75	60	30	25	35	25	65	65	35	30	35	25	75	35	25
1892—June 6	75	50	75	75	60	30	25	35	25	35	25	35	25	35	25	75	35	23

YORK, N. Y., TO MILWAUKEE, WIS.—Continued.

1,086 miles; Philadelphia, 907 miles; Baltimore, 886 miles—Continued.

than carload or carload quantities they apply on shipments regardless of quantity.]

Commodities (rates in cents per 100 pounds).

Molasses.		Rice.		Groceries.	Drugs.	Crockery and earthenware.		Bagging.		Leather.		Lead.		Nails.		Hardware.	Agricultural implements.		Machinery.		Beer.	
Less than carloads.	Carloads.	Less than carloads.	Carloads.			Less than carloads.	Carloads.	Less than carloads.	Carloads.	Less than carloads.	Carloads.	Less than carloads.	Carloads.	Less than carloads.	Carloads.		Less than carloads.	Carloads.	Less than carloads.	Carloads.	Less than carloads.	Carloads.
19	19	19	19	32	45	19	19	19	19	32	32	19	19	19	19	32	Sp'l rate.	19	32	19	19	19
28	28	28	28	50	60	28	28	28	28	50	50	28	28	28	28	50	.do .	28	50	28	28	28
19	19	19	19	32	45	19	19	19	19	32	32	19	19	19	19	32	.do .	19	32	19	19	19
25	25	30	30	50	60	30	30	30	30	50	50	30	30	30	30	50	.do .	30	50	30	30	30
35	35	35	35	60	75	35	35	35	35	60	60	35	35	35	35	60	.do .	35	60	35	35	35
25	25	35	35	60	75	35	35	35	35	60	60	35	35	35	35	60	.do .	35	60	35	35	35
18	18	25	25	40	50	25	25	25	25	40	40	25	25	25	25	40	.do .	25	40	25	25	25
20	20	25	25	50	60	25	25	25	25	50	50	25	25	25	25	50	.do .	25	50	25	25	25
25	25	25	25	60	75	35	35	35	35	60	60	35	35	35	35	60	.do .	35	60	35	35	35
25	25	35	35	60	75	35	35	35	35	60	60	35	35	35	35	60	.do .	35	60	35	35	35
35	30	35	35	65	75	35	30	50	35	50	35	35	25	35	30	65	50	30	35	30	50	30
38½	33	38½	27½	65	75	38½	33	50	38½	38½	27½	38½	27½	38½	33	65	50	27½	38½	33	50	33
35	30	35	25	65	75	35	30	50	35	50	35	35	25	35	30	65	50	30	35	30	50	30
30	25	30	20	40	50	30	25	35	30	35	30	30	20	30	25	40	35	25	30	25	35	25
30	25	35	25	65	75	35	30	50	35	50	35	35	25	35	30	65	50	30	35	30	50	30
35	30	35	25	65	75	35	30	50	35	50	35	35	25	35	30	65	50	30	35	30	50	30
35	30	35	25	65	75	35	30	50	35	50	35	35	25	30	25	65	50	30	35	30	50	30
35	30	35	25	65	75	35	30	50	35	50	35	35	25	30	25	65	50	30	35	30	50	30

TABLE 22.—RATES OF FREIGHT, ALL RAIL, FROM

DISTANCE VIA SHORTEST ROUTE.—From New York, 998 miles;

[NOTE.—Where the rates shown are not specifically described as applying on less

Date.	Commodities (rates in cents per 100 pounds).																	
				Furniture.		Stoves.		Coffee.		Soap.				Starch.			Sugar.	
										Castile and fancy.		Common.						
	Dry goods.	Cotton piece goods.	Boots and shoes.	Less than carloads.	Carloads.	Less than carloads.	Carloads.	Less than carloads.	Carloads.	Less than carloads.	Carloads.	Less than carloads.	Carloads.	Less than carloads.	Carloads.	Tea.	Less than carloads.	Carloads.
1867—Jan. 1	205	205	205	205	205	205	205	176	176	176	176	139	139	176	176	205	99	90
May 15	217	217	217	217	217	217	217	185	185	185	185	148	148	185	185	217	94	94
Nov. 5	235	235	235	235	235	235	235	198	198	198	198	161	161	198	198	235	99	99
1868—Feb. 4	235	235	235	235	235	235	235	Special rate.		198	198	99	99	161	161	235	Special rate.	
June 4	217	217	217	217	217	217	217	..do....		185	185	94	94	148	148	217	..do....	
Aug. 10	173	173	173	173	173	173	173	..do....		148	148	94	94	138	138	173	..do....	
Sept. 7	217	217	217	217	217	217	217	..do....		185	185	94	94	148	148	217	..do....	
Oct. 1	110	110	110	110	110	110	110	..do....		94	94	73	73	84	84	110	..do....	
Oct. 22	59	59	59	59	59	59	59	..do....		59	59	59	59	59	59	59	..do....	
Dec. 7	235	235	235	235	235	235	235	..do....		198	198	99	99	161	161	235	..do....	
1869—Feb. 1	217	217	217	217	217	217	217	..do....		185	185	94	94	148	148	217	..do....	
Feb. 17	57	57	57	57	57	57	57	..do....		57	57	57	57	57	57	57	..do....	
Mar. 15	185	185	185	185	185	185	185	..do....		185	185	94	94	148	148	185	..do....	
Apr. 12	185	185	185	185	185	185	185	..do....		185	185	94	94	148	148	185	..do....	
July 1	217	217	217	217	217	217	217	..do....		185	185	94	94	148	148	217	..do....	
Aug. 11	35	35	35	35	35	35	35	..do....		35	35	35	35	35	35	35	..do....	
Sept. 22	45	45	45	45	45	45	45	..do....		45	45	45	45	45	45	45	..do....	
Oct. 4	60	60	60	60	60	60	60	..do....		60	60	60	60	60	60	60	..do....	
Oct. 9	87	87	87	87	87	87	87	..do....		87	87	60	60	87	87	87	..do....	
Nov. 1	163	163	163	163	163	163	163	..do....		146	146	94	94	117	117	163	..do....	
Nov. 29	176	176	176	176	176	176	176	..do....		151	151	94	94	117	117	176	..do....	
1870—Apr. 14	176	176	176	176	176	176	176	..do....		151	151	94	94	117	117	176	45	45
May 7	176	176	176	176	176	176	176	..do....		151	151	94	94	117	117	176	45	45
June 18	124	124	124	124	124	124	124	..do....		99	99	63	63	80	80	124	45	45
July 13	92	92	92	92	92	92	92	..do....		80	80	55	55	68	68	92	45	45
July 21	80	80	80	80	80	80	80	..do....		70	70	55	55	63	63	80	45	45
July 25	75	75	75	75	75	75	75	..do....		65	65	48	48	60	60	75	45	45
July 28	55	55	55	55	55	55	55	..do....		55	55	48	48	55	55	55	45	45
Aug. 12	57	57	57	57	57	57	57	..do....		57	57	57	57	57	57	57	45	45
Aug. 22	110	110	110	110	110	110	110	..do....		99	99	63	63	80	80	110	45	45
Sept. 8	145	145	145	145	145	145	145	..do....		129	129	76	76	99	99	145	45	45
Nov. 28	178	178	178	178	178	178	178	..do....		144	144	72	72	113	113	178	45	45
Dec. 26	202	202	202	202	202	202	292	67	67	168	168	89	89	134	134	202	67	67
1871—Feb. 20	168	168	168	168	168	168	168	62	62	144	144	79	79	113	113	168	62	62
Mar. 7	110	110	110	110	110	110	110	48	48	99	99	63	63	80	80	110	48	48
Mar. 13	113	113	113	113	113	113	113	51	51	101	101	62	62	79	79	113	51	51
May 18	84	84	84	84	84	84	84	41	41	72	72	50	50	57	57	84	41	41
June 1	113	113	113	113	113	113	113	51	51	101	101	62	62	79	79	113	51	51
July 8	84	84	84	84	84	84	84	41	41	72	72	50	50	57	57	84	41	41
July 28	53	53	53	53	53	53	53	37	37	53	53	50	50	53	53	53	37	37
Aug. 16	45	45	45	45	45	45	45	32	32	45	45	45	45	45	45	45	32	32
Aug. 22	40	40	40	40	40	40	40	29	29	40	40	40	40	40	40	40	29	29
Sept. 1	35	35	35	35	35	35	35	27	27	35	35	35	35	35	35	35	27	27
Nov. 27	113	113	113	113	113	113	113	51	51	101	101	62	62	62	62	113	51	51
Dec. 15	140	140	140	140	140	140	140	56	56	123	123	73	73	95	95	140	56	56
1872—April 27	140	140	140	140	140	140	140	56	56	123	123	73	73	95	95	140	56	56
Aug. 1	84	84	84	84	84	84	84	39	39	78	78	50	50	67	67	84	39	39
Sept. 1	140	140	140	140	140	140	140	56	56	123	123	73	73	95	95	140	56	56
Sept. 2	112	112	112	112	112	112	112	50	50	101	101	62	62	78	78	112	50	50
Oct. 14	140	140	140	140	140	140	140	56	56	123	123	73	73	95	95	140	56	56
1873—April 14	112	112	112	112	112	112	112	50	50	101	101	67	67	84	84	112	50	50
June 11	84	84	84	84	84	84	84	39	39	78	78	50	50	67	67	84	39	39
Aug. 11	45	45	45	45	45	45	45	34	34	45	45	34	34	34	34	45	34	34
Sept. 17	84	84	84	84	84	84	84	39	39	78	78	50	50	67	67	84	39	39
1874—Jan. 1	112	112	112	112	112	112	112	50	50	101	101	67	67	84	84	112	50	50
Aug. 3	84	84	84	84	84	84	84	39	39	78	78	50	50	67	67	84	39	39
1875—Jan. 20	112	112	112	112	112	112	112	50	50	101	101	67	67	84	84	112	50	50
Mar. 17	112	112	112	112	112	112	112	34	34	101	101	67	67	84	84	112	34	34
April 1	105	105	105	105	105	105	105	48	48	95	95	62	62	81	81	105	48	48
April 6	112	112	112	112	112	112	112	50	50	101	101	67	67	84	84	112	50	50
Aug. 12	80	80	80	80	80	80	80	30	30	60	60	37	37	46	46	80	30	30
Dec. 22	55	55	55	55	55	55	55	32	32	45	45	32	32	32	36	55	32	32

NEW YORK, N. Y., TO PEORIA, ILL.

Boston, 1,164 miles; Philadelphia, 908 miles; Baltimore, 887 miles.

than carload or carload quantities they apply on shipments regardless of quantity.]

Commodities (rates in cents per 100 pounds).

Molasses.		Rice.				Crockery and earthenware.		Bagging.		Leather.		Lead.		Nails.			Agricultural implements.		Machinery.		Beer.	
Less than carloads.	Carloads.	Less than carloads.	Carloads.	Groceries.	Drugs.	Less than carloads.	Carloads.	Less than carloads.	Carloads.	Less than carloads.	Carloads.	Less than carloads.	Carloads.	Less than carloads.	Carloads.	Hardware.	Less than carloads.	Carloads.	Less than carloads.	Carloads.	Less than carloads.	Carloads.
90	90	90	90	176	205	176	176	176	176	176	176	90	90	90	90	176	205	205	176	176	139	139
94	94	94	94	185	217	185	185	185	185	185	185	94	94	94	94	185	217	217	185	185	148	148
99	99	99	99	198	235	198	198	198	198	198	198	99	99	99	99	198	235	235	198	198	161	161
Special rate.		99	99	198	235	198	198	198	198	198	198	99	99	99	99	198	235	235	198	198	161	161
..do....		94	94	185	217	185	185	185	185	185	185	94	94	94	94	185	217	217	185	185	148	148
..do....		94	94	148	173	148	148	148	148	148	148	94	94	94	94	148	173	173	148	148	138	138
..do....		94	94	185	217	185	185	185	185	185	185	94	94	94	94	185	217	217	185	185	148	148
..do....		73	73	94	110	94	94	94	94	94	94	73	73	73	73	94	110	110	94	94	84	84
..do....		59	59	59	59	59	59	59	59	59	59	59	59	59	59	59	59	59	59	59	59	59
..do....		99	99	198	235	198	198	198	198	198	198	99	99	99	99	198	235	235	198	198	161	161
..do....		94	94	185	217	185	185	185	185	185	185	94	94	94	94	185	217	217	185	185	148	148
..do....		57	57	57	57	57	57	57	57	57	57	57	57	57	57	57	57	57	57	57	57	57
..do....		94	94	185	185	185	185	185	185	185	185	94	94	94	94	185	185	185	185	185	148	148
..do....		94	94	185	185	Special rate.		185	185	185	185	94	94	94	94	185	185	185	185	185	148	148
..do....		94	94	185	217	..do....		185	185	185	185	94	94	94	94	185	217	217	185	185	148	148
..do....		35	35	35	35	..do....		35	35	35	35	35	35	35	35	35	35	35	35	35	35	35
..do....		45	45	45	45	..do....		45	45	45	45	45	45	45	45	45	45	45	45	45	45	45
..do....		60	60	60	60	..do....		60	60	60	60	60	60	60	60	60	60	60	60	60	60	60
..do....		60	60	87	87	..do....		87	87	87	87	60	60	60	60	87	87	87	87	87	87	87
..do....		94	94	146	163	..do....		146	146	146	146	94	94	94	94	146	163	163	146	146	117	117
..do....		94	94	151	176	..do....		151	151	151	151	94	94	94	94	151	176	176	151	151	117	117
..do....		94	94	151	176	..do....		151	151	151	151	94	94	94	94	151	176	176	151	151	117	117
..do....		Special rate.		151	176	..do....		151	151	151	151	94	94	94	94	151	176	176	151	151	117	117
..do....		..do....		99	124	..do....		99	99	99	99	63	63	63	63	99	124	124	99	99	80	80
..do....		..do....		80	92	..do....		80	80	80	80	55	55	55	55	80	92	92	80	80	68	68
..do....		..do....		70	80	..do....		70	70	70	70	55	55	55	55	70	80	80	70	70	63	63
..do....		..do....		65	75	..do....		65	65	65	65	48	48	48	48	65	75	75	65	65	60	60
..do....		..do....		55	55	..do....		55	55	55	55	48	48	48	48	55	55	55	55	55	55	55
..do....		..do....		57	57	..do....		57	57	57	57	57	57	57	57	57	57	57	57	57	57	57
..do....		..do....		99	110	..do....		99	99	99	99	63	63	63	63	99	110	110	99	99	80	80
..do....		..do....		129	145	..do....		129	129	129	129	76	76	76	76	129	145	145	129	129	99	99
..do....		..do....		144	178	..do....		144	144	144	144	72	72	72	72	144	178	178	144	144	113	113
89	89	89	89	168	202	168	168	168	168	168	168	89	89	89	89	168	202	202	168	168	134	134
79	79	79	79	144	168	62	62	144	144	144	144	62	62	79	79	144	168	168	144	144	113	113
63	63	63	63	99	110	48	48	99	99	99	99	48	48	63	63	99	110	110	99	99	80	80
62	62	62	62	101	113	51	51	101	101	101	101	51	51	62	62	101	113	113	101	101	79	79
50	50	50	50	72	84	41	41	72	72	72	72	41	41	50	50	72	84	84	72	72	57	57
62	62	62	62	101	113	51	51	101	101	101	101	51	51	62	62	101	113	113	101	101	79	79
50	50	50	50	72	84	41	41	72	72	72	72	41	41	50	50	72	84	84	72	72	57	57
50	50	50	50	53	53	37	37	53	53	53	53	37	37	50	50	53	53	53	53	53	53	53
45	45	45	45	45	45	32	32	45	45	45	45	32	32	45	45	45	45	45	45	45	45	45
40	40	40	40	40	40	29	29	40	40	40	40	29	29	40	40	40	40	40	40	40	40	40
35	35	35	35	35	35	27	27	35	35	35	35	27	27	35	35	35	35	35	35	35	35	35
62	62	62	62	101	113	51	51	101	101	101	101	51	51	62	62	101	113	113	101	101	79	79
73	73	73	73	123	140	123	123	123	123	123	123	56	56	73	73	123	140	140	123	123	95	95
73	73	56	56	123	140	123	123	123	123	123	123	56	56	73	73	123	140	140	123	123	95	95
50	50	39	39	78	84	78	78	78	78	78	78	39	39	50	50	78	84	84	78	78	67	67
73	73	73	73	123	140	56	56	123	123	123	123	56	56	73	73	123	140	140	123	123	95	95
62	62	50	50	101	112	101	101	101	101	101	101	50	50	62	62	101	112	112	101	101	78	78
73	73	56	56	123	140	56	56	123	123	123	123	56	56	73	73	123	140	140	123	123	95	95
67	67	50	50	101	112	50	50	101	101	101	101	50	50	67	67	101	Sp'l rate.	67	101	101	84	84
50	50	39	39	78	84	39	39	78	78	78	78	39	39	50	50	78	.do .	50	78	78	67	67
34	34	34	34	45	45	34	34	45	45	45	45	34	34	34	34	45	.do .	34	45	45	34	34
50	50	39	39	78	84	39	39	78	78	78	78	39	39	50	50	78	.do .	50	78	78	67	67
67	67	50	50	101	112	50	50	101	101	101	101	50	50	67	67	101	.do .	67	101	101	84	84
50	50	39	39	78	84	39	39	78	78	78	78	39	39	50	50	78	.do .	50	78	78	67	67
67	67	50	50	101	112	50	50	101	101	101	101	50	50	67	67	101	.do .	67	101	101	84	84
34	34	50	50	101	112	50	50	101	101	101	101	50	50	67	67	101	.do .	67	101	101	84	84
62	62	48	48	95	105	48	48	95	95	95	95	48	48	62	62	95	.do .	62	95	95	81	81
67	67	50	50	101	112	50	50	101	101	101	101	50	50	67	67	101	.do .	67	101	101	84	84
37	37	30	30	60	80	30	30	60	60	60	60	30	30	37	37	60	.do .	37	60	60	46	46
32	32	32	32	45	55	32	32	45	45	45	45	32	32	32	32	45	.do .	32	45	45	36	36

TABLE 22.—RATES OF FREIGHT, ALL RAIL, FROM

DISTANCE VIA SHORTEST ROUTE.—From New York, 998 miles;

[NOTE.—Where the rates shown are not specifically described as applying on less

Date.	Commodities (rates in cents per 100 pounds).																	
				Furniture.		Stoves.		Coffee.		Soap.				Starch.			Sugar.	
										Castile and fancy.		Common.						
	Dry goods.	Cotton piece goods.	Boots and shoes.	Less than carloads.	Carloads.	Less than carloads.	Carloads.	Less than carloads.	Carloads.	Less than carloads.	Carloads.	Less than carloads.	Carloads.	Less than carloads.	Carloads.	Tea.	Less than carloads.	Carloads.
1876—Jan. 10	84	84	84	84	84	84	84	39	39	78	78	50	50	67	97	84	39	39
June 12	28	28	28	28	28	28	28	18	18	28	28	28	28	28	28	28	28	28
July 28	17	17	17	17	17	17	17	12	12	17	17	12	12	17	17	17	12	12
Dec. 18	56	56	56	56	56	56	56	28	28	50	50	45	45	45	45	56	28	28
1877—Mar. 12	84	84	84	84	84	84	84	39	39	78	78	50	50	67	67	84	39	39
Oct. 8	84	84	84	84	84	84	45	45	45	78	78	45	45	45	45	84	45	45
Oct. 22	112	112	112	112	112	112	50	50	50	101	101	50	50	50	50	112	50	50
Dec. 30	112	112	112	112	112	112	50	50	50	90	90	50	50	50	50	112	50	50
1878—Feb. 15	84	84	84	84	84	84	45	45	45	67	67	45	45	45	45	84	45	45
1881—Aug. 6	50	50	50	50	50	50	21	21	21	36	36	21	21	21	21	50	21	21
1882—July 1	67	67	67	67	67	67	34	34	34	56	56	34	34	34	34	67	28	28
Nov. 1	84	84	84	84	84	84	39	39	39	67	67	39	39	39	39	84	39	39
1883—June 22	84	84	84	84	84	84	39	39	39	67	67	39	39	39	39	84	28	28
1885—Jan. 26	56	56	56	56	56	56	28	28	28	45	45	28	28	28	28	56	20	20
Oct. 5	67	67	67	67	67	67	28	28	28	56	56	28	28	28	28	67	22	22
Nov. 18	84	84	84	84	84	84	39	39	39	67	67	39	39	39	39	84	28	28
1886—Mar. 10	83	83	83	83	83	83	39	39	39	66	66	39	39	39	39	83	28	28
Aug. 26	83	50	83	83	83	83	39	39	39	66	66	39	39	39	39	83	28	28
1887—Apr. 1	83	55	83	83	72	55	33	39	28	72	72	39	33	39	28	83	39	28
1888—Jan. 9	83	55	83	83	72	55	36	42	30	72	72	42	36	42	30	83	42	30
Mar. 5	83	55	83	83	72	55	33	39	28	72	72	39	33	39	28	83	39	28
Nov. 12	55	39	55	55	44	39	28	33	22	44	44	33	28	33	22	55	33	22
Dec. 17	83	55	83	83	72	55	33	39	28	72	72	39	33	39	28	83	39	28
1891—Apr. 9	83	55	83	83	72	33	28	39	28	72	72	39	33	39	28	83	39	28
1892—June 6	83	55	83	83	72	33	28	39	28	39	28	39	28	39	28	83	39	25

NEW YORK, N. Y., TO PEORIA, ILL.—Continued.

Boston, 1,164 miles; Philadelphia, 908 miles; Baltimore, 887 miles.

than carload or carload quantities they apply on shipments regardless of quantity.]

Commodities (rates in cents per 100 pounds).

Molasses.		Rice.				Crockery and earthenware.		Bagging.		Leather.		Lead.		Nails.			Agricultural implements.		Machinery.		Beer.	
Less than carloads.	Carloads.	Less than carloads.	Carloads.	Groceries.	Drugs.	Less than carloads.	Carloads.	Less than carloads.	Carloads.	Less than carloads.	Carloads.	Less than carloads.	Carloads.	Less than carloads.	Carloads.	Hardware.	Less than carloads.	Carloads.	Less than carloads.	Carloads.	Less than carloads.	Carloads.
50	50	39	39	78	84	39	39	78	78	78	78	39	39	50	50	78	Sp'l rate,	50	78	78	67	67
28	28	28	28	28	28	18	18	28	28	28	28	18	18	28	28	28	.do .	18	28	28	28	28
12	12	12	12	17	17	12	12	17	17	17	17	12	12	12	12	17	.do .	12	17	17	17	17
34	34	28	28	50	56	28	28	50	50	50	50	28	28	34	34	50	.do .	34	50	50	45	45
50	50	39	39	78	84	39	39	78	78	78	78	39	39	50	50	78	.do .	50	78	78	67	67
45	45	45	45	78	84	45	45	45	45	78	78	45	45	45	45	78	.do .	45	78	45	45	45
50	50	50	50	101	112	50	50	50	50	101	101	50	50	50	50	101	.do .	50	101	50	50	50
50	50	50	50	90	112	50	50	50	50	90	90	50	50	50	50	90	.do .	50	90	50	50	50
45	45	45	45	67	84	45	45	45	45	67	67	45	45	45	45	67	.do .	45	67	45	45	45
21	21	21	21	36	50	21	21	21	21	36	36	21	21	21	21	36	.do .	21	36	21	21	21
28	28	34	34	56	67	34	34	34	34	56	56	34	34	34	34	56	.do .	34	56	34	34	34
39	39	39	39	67	84	39	39	39	39	67	67	39	39	39	39	67	.do .	39	67	39	39	39
28	28	39	39	67	84	39	39	39	39	67	67	39	39	39	39	67	.do .	39	67	39	39	39
20	20	28	28	45	56	28	28	28	28	45	45	28	28	28	28	45	.do .	28	45	28	28	28
22	22	28	28	56	67	28	28	28	28	56	56	28	28	28	28	56	.do .	28	56	28	28	28
28	28	39	39	67	84	39	39	39	39	67	67	39	39	39	39	67	.do .	39	67	39	39	39
28	28	39	39	66	83	39	39	39	39	66	66	39	39	39	39	66	.do .	39	66	39	39	39
28	28	39	39	66	83	39	39	39	39	66	66	39	39	39	39	66	.do .	39	66	39	39	39
39	33	39	28	72	83	39	33	55	39	55	39	39	28	39	33	72	55	33	39	33	55	33
42	36	42	30	72	83	42	36	55	42	55	42	42	30	42	36	72	55	36	42	36	55	36
39	33	39	28	72	83	39	33	55	39	55	39	39	28	39	33	72	55	33	39	33	55	33
33	28	33	22	44	55	33	28	39	33	39	33	33	22	33	28	44	39	28	33	28	39	28
39	33	39	28	72	83	39	33	55	39	55	39	39	28	39	33	72	55	33	39	33	55	33
39	33	39	28	72	83	39	33	55	39	55	39	39	28	33	28	72	55	33	39	33	55	33
39	33	39	28	72	83	39	33	55	39	55	39	39	28	33	28	72	55	33	39	33	55	33

TABLE 23.—RATES OF FREIGHT, ALL RAIL FROM

DISTANCE VIA SHORTEST ROUTE.—From New York, 1,065 miles;

[Note.—Where the rates shown are not specifically described as applying on less

Date.		Commodities (rates in cents per 100 pounds).																		
		Dry goods.	Cotton piece goods.	Boots and shoes.	Furniture.		Stoves.		Coffee.		Soaps.				Starch.		Tea.	Sugar.	
											Castile and fancy.		Common.						
					Less than carload.	Carloads.	Less than carload.	Carloads.	Less than carload.	Carloads.	Less than carload.	Carloads.	Less than carload.	Carloads.	Less than carload.	Carloads.		Less than carload.	Carloads.
1867—Jan.	1.....	242	242	242	242	242	242	242	190	190	190	190	140	140	190	190	242	100	100
Nov.	5.....	262	262	262	262	262	262	262	221	221	221	221	181	181	221	221	262	114	114
1868—Feb.	4.....	262	262	262	262	262	262	262	Special rate.		221	221	114	114	181	181	262	Special rate.	
June	4.....	242	242	242	242	262	262	262	..do....		207	207	108	108	168	168	242	..do....	
Aug.	10.....	194	194	194	194	194	194	194	..do....		168	168	108	108	157	157	194	..do....	
Sept.	7.....	242	242	242	242	262	262	262	..do....		207	207	108	108	168	168	242	..do....	
Dec.	7.....	262	262	262	262	262	262	262	..do....		221	221	114	114	181	181	262	..do....	
1869—Feb.	1.....	242	242	242	242	242	242	242	..do....		207	207	108	108	168	168	242	..do....	
Feb.	4.....	230	230	230	230	230	230	230	..do....		197	197	103	103	157	157	230	..do....	
Mar.	15.....	97	197	197	197	197	197	197	..do....		197	197	103	103	157	157	197	..do....	
May	12.....	197	197	197	197	197	197	197	..do....		197	197	103	103	157	158	197	..do....	
July	1.....	230	230	230	230	230	230	230	..do....		197	197	103	103	157	157	230	..do....	
Aug.	11.....	35	35	35	35	35	35	35	..do....		35	25	35	35	35	35	35	..do....	
Aug.	23.....	56	56	56	56	56	56	56	..do....		56	56	56	56	56	56	56	..do....	
Aug.	30.....	58	58	58	58	58	58	58	..do....		58	58	58	58	58	58	58	..do....	
Sept.	22.....	53	53	53	53	53	53	53	..do....		53	53	53	53	53	53	53	..do....	
Sept.	24.....	50	50	50	50	50	50	50	..do....		50	50	50	50	50	50	50	..do....	
Oct.	4.....	70	70	70	70	70	70	70	..do....		70	70	70	70	70	70	70	..do....	
Oct.	9.....	100	100	100	100	100	100	100	..do....		100	100	70	70	100	100	100	..do....	
Nov.	1.....	178	178	178	178	178	178	178	..do....		159	159	104	104	129	129	178	..do....	
Nov.	29.....	191	191	191	191	191	191	191	..do....		166	166	104	104	129	129	191	..do....	
1870—Apr.	14.....	191	191	191	191	191	191	191	..do....		166	166	104	104	129	129	191	50	50
May	7.....	191	191	191	191	191	191	191	..do....		166	166	104	104	129	129	191	50	50
July	13.....	100	100	100	100	100	100	100	..do....		90	90	65	65	75	75	100	50	50
July	18.....	90	90	90	90	90	90	90	..do....		85	85	65	65	75	75	90	50	50
July	21.....	80	80	80	80	80	80	80	..do....		75	75	65	65	70	70	80	50	50
Aug.	22.....	125	125	125	125	125	125	125	..do....		113	113	74	74	93	93	125	50	50
Sept.	8.....	165	165	165	165	165	165	165	..do....		145	145	89	89	113	113	165	50	50
Nov.	28.....	200	200	200	200	200	200	200	..do....		163	163	84	84	129	129	200	50	50
Dec.	26.....	226	226	226	226	226	226	226	79	79	189	189	103	103	151	151	226	79	79
1871—Feb.	20.....	189	189	189	189	189	189	189	73	73	163	163	92	92	129	129	189	73	73
Mar.	7.....	125	125	125	125	125	125	125	54	54	113	113	74	74	93	93	125	54	54
1871—Mar.	13.....	129	129	129	129	129	129	129	62	62	116	116	73	73	92	92	129	62	62
May	18.....	97	97	97	97	97	97	97	51	51	84	84	60	60	68	68	97	51	51
June	1.....	129	129	129	129	129	129	129	62	62	116	116	73	73	92	92	129	62	62
July	8.....	97	97	97	97	97	97	97	51	51	84	84	60	60	68	68	97	51	51
	28.....	60	60	60	60	60	60	60	45	45	60	60	60	60	60	60	60	45	45
Aug.	16.....	50	50	50	50	50	50	50	35	35	50	50	50	50	50	50	50	35	35
	22.....	45	45	45	45	45	45	45	35	35	45	45	45	45	45	44	45	35	35
Sept.	1.....	40	40	40	40	40	40	40	32	32	40	40	40	40	40	40	40	32	32
Nov.	27.....	129	129	129	129	129	129	129	62	62	116	116	73	73	92	92	129	62	62
Dec.	15.....	158	158	158	158	158	158	158	67	67	140	140	85	85	110	110	158	67	67
1872—Apr.	27.....	158	158	158	158	158	158	158	67	67	140	140	85	85	110	110	158	67	67
Aug.	1.....	97	97	97	97	97	97	97	49	49	91	91	61	61	79	79	97	49	49
Sept.	1.....	158	158	158	158	158	158	158	67	67	140	140	85	85	110	110	158	67	67
	2.....	128	128	128	128	128	128	128	61	61	116	116	73	73	91	91	128	61	61
Oct.	14.....	158	158	158	158	158	158	158	67	67	140	140	85	85	110	110	158	67	67
1873—Apr.	14.....	128	128	128	128	128	128	128	61	61	116	116	79	79	97	97	128	61	61
June	11.....	97	97	97	97	97	97	97	49	49	91	91	61	61	79	79	97	49	49
Aug.	11.....	55	55	55	55	55	55	55	43	43	55	55	43	43	43	43	55	43	43
Sept.	17.....	97	97	97	97	97	97	97	49	49	91	91	61	61	79	79	97	49	49
1874—Jan.	1.....	128	128	128	128	128	128	128	61	61	116	116	79	79	97	97	128	61	61
Aug.	3.....	97	97	97	97	97	97	97	35	35	91	91	61	61	79	79	97	35	35
1875—Jan.	20.....	128	128	128	128	128	128	128	61	61	116	116	79	79	97	97	128	61	61
Feb.	23.....	128	128	128	128	128	128	128	43	43	116	116	79	79	97	97	128	43	43
Mar.	17.....	97	97	97	97	97	97	97	24	24	91	91	61	61	79	79	97	24	24
Apr.	6.....	60	60	60	60	60	60	60	30	30	55	55	40	40	50	50	60	30	30
May	26.....	70	70	70	70	70	70	70	36	36	70	70	50	50	50	50	70	36	36
	29.....	43	43	43	43	43	43	43	31	31	43	43	36	36	39	39	43	31	31
Aug.	12.....	67	67	67	67	67	67	67	31	31	55	55	36	36	43	43	67	31	31
Dec.	22.....	43	43	43	43	43	43	43	25	25	36	36	31	31	31	31	43	25	25
1876—July	28.....	25	25	25	25	25	25	25	19	19	25	25	19	19	25	25	25	19	19

New York, N. Y., to St. Louis Mo.

Boston, 1,186 miles; Philadelphia, 975 miles; Baltimore, 934 miles.

than carload or carload quantities they apply on shipments regardless of quantity.

Commodities (rates in cents in 100 pounds).

Molasses.		Rice.		Groceries.	Drugs.	Crockery and earthenware.		Bagging		Leather.		Lead.		Nails.		Hardware.	Agricultural implements.		Machinery.		Beer.	
Less than carload.	Carloads.	Less than carload.	Carloads.			Less than carload.	Carloads.	Less than carload.	Carloads.	Less than carload.	Carloads.	Less than carload.	Carloads.	Less than carload.	Carloads.		Less than carload.	Carloads.	Less than carload.	Carloads.	Less than carload.	Carloads.
100	100	100	100	190	242	190	190	190	190	190	190	100	100	100	100	190	242	242	190	190	140	140
114	114	114	114	221	262	221	221	221	221	221	221	114	114	114	114	221	262	262	221	221	181	181
Special rate.		114	114	221	262	221	221	221	221	221	221	114	114	114	114	221	262	262	221	221	181	181
..do....		108	108	207	242	207	207	207	207	207	207	108	108	108	108	207	242	242	207	207	168	168
..do....		108	108	168	194	168	168	168	168	168	168	108	108	108	108	168	194	194	168	168	157	158
..do....		108	108	207	242	207	207	207	207	207	207	108	108	108	108	207	242	242	207	207	168	168
..do....		114	114	221	262	221	221	221	221	221	221	114	114	114	114	221	262	262	221	221	181	181
..do....		108	108	207	242	207	207	207	207	207	207	108	108	108	108	207	242	242	207	207	168	168
..do....		103	103	197	230	197	197	197	197	197	197	108	103	103	108	197	230	230	197	197	157	157
..do....		103	103	197	197	197	197	197	197	197	197	103	103	103	108	197	197	197	197	197	157	157
..do....		103	103	197	197	Special rate.		197	197	197	197	103	103	103	103	197	197	197	197	197	157	157
..do....		103	103	197	230	..do....		197	197	197	197	103	103	103	103	197	230	230	197	197	157	157
..do....		35	35	35	35	..do....		35	35	35	35	35	35	35	35	35	35	35	35	35	35	35
..do....		56	56	56	56	..do....		56	56	56	56	56	56	56	56	56	56	56	56	56	56	56
..do....		58	58	58	58	..do....		58	58	58	58	58	58	58	58	58	58	58	58	58	58	58
..do....		53	53	53	53	..do....		53	53	53	53	53	53	53	53	53	53	5	53	53	53	53
..do....		50	50	50	50	..do....		50	50	50	50	50	50	50	50	50	50	50	50	50	50	50
..do....		70	70	70	70	..do....		70	70	70	70	70	70	70	70	70	70	70	70	70	70	70
..do....		70	70	100	100	..do....		100	100	100	100	70	70	70	70	100	100	100	100	100	100	100
..do....		104	104	159	178	..do....		159	159	159	159	104	104	104	104	159	178	178	159	159	129	129
..do....		104	104	166	191	..do....		166	166	166	166	104	104	104	104	166	191	191	166	166	129	129
..do....		104	104	166	191	..do....		166	166	166	166	104	104	104	104	166	191	191	166	166	129	129
..do....		Special rate.		166	191	..do....		166	166	166	166	104	104	104	104	166	191	191	166	166	129	129
..do....		..do....		90	100	..do....		90	90	90	90	75	75	65	65	90	100	100	90	90	75	75
..do....		..do....		85	90	..do....		85	85	85	85	75	75	65	65	85	90	90	85	85	75	75
..do....		..do....		75	80	..do....		75	75	75	75	65	65	65	65	75	80	80	75	75	70	70
..do....		..do....		113	125	..do....		113	113	113	113	74	74	74	74	113	125	125	113	113	93	93
..do....		..do....		145	165	..do....		145	145	145	145	89	89	89	89	145	165	165	145	145	113	113
..do....		..do....		163	200	..do....		163	163	163	163	84	84	84	84	163	200	200	163	163	129	129
103	103	103	103	189	226	189	189	189	189	189	189	103	103	103	103	189	226	226	189	189	151	151
92	92	92	92	163	189	73	73	163	163	163	163	73	73	92	92	163	189	189	163	163	129	129
74	74	74	74	113	125	54	54	113	113	113	113	54	54	74	74	113	125	125	113	113	93	93
73	73	73	73	116	129	62	62	116	116	116	116	62	62	73	73	116	129	129	116	116	92	92
60	60	60	60	84	97	51	51	84	84	84	84	51	51	60	60	84	97	97	84	84	68	68
73	73	73	73	116	129	62	62	116	116	116	116	62	62	73	73	116	129	129	116	116	92	92
60	60	60	60	84	97	51	51	84	84	84	84	51	51	60	60	84	97	97	84	84	68	68
60	60	60	60	60	60	45	45	60	60	60	60	45	45	60	60	60	60	60	60	60	60	60
50	50	50	50	50	50	35	35	50	50	50	50	35	35	50	50	50	50	50	50	50	50	50
45	45	45	45	45	45	35	35	45	45	45	45	35	35	45	45	45	45	45	45	45	45	45
40	40	40	40	40	40	32	32	40	40	40	40	32	22	40	40	40	40	40	40	40	40	40
73	73	73	73	116	129	62	62	116	116	116	116	62	62	73	73	116	129	129	116	116	92	92
85	85	85	85	140	158	140	140	140	140	140	140	67	67	85	85	140	158	158	140	140	110	110
85	85	67	67	140	158	140	140	140	140	140	140	67	67	85	85	140	158	158	140	140	110	110
61	61	49	49	91	97	91	91	91	91	91	91	49	49	61	61	91	97	97	91	91	79	79
85	85	85	85	140	158	140	140	140	140	140	140	67	57	85	85	140	158	158	140	140	110	110
73	73	61	61	116	128	116	116	116	116	116	116	61	61	73	73	116	128	128	116	116	91	91
85	85	67	67	140	158	67	67	140	140	140	140	67	67	85	85	140	158	158	140	140	110	110
79	79	61	61	116	128	61	61	116	116	116	116	61	61	79	79	116	Spc'l rate.	79	116	116	97	97
61	61	49	49	91	97	49	49	91	91	91	91	49	49	61	61	91	.do .	61	91	91	79	79
43	43	43	43	55	55	43	43	55	55	55	55	43	43	43	43	55	.do .	43	55	55	43	43
61	61	49	49	91	97	49	49	91	91	91	91	49	49	61	61	91	.do .	61	91	91	79	79
79	79	61	61	116	128	61	61	116	116	116	116	61	61	79	79	116	.do .	79	116	116	97	97
61	61	35	35	91	97	35	35	91	91	91	94	35	35	61	61	91	.do .	61	91	91	79	79
79	79	61	61	116	128	61	61	116	116	116	116	61	61	79	79	116	.do .	79	116	116	97	97
79	79	61	61	116	128	61	61	116	116	116	116	61	61	79	79	116	.do .	79	116	116	97	97
24	24	49	49	91	97	49	49	91	19	91	91	49	49	61	61	91	.do .	61	91	91	79	79
40	40	30	30	55	60	30	30	55	55	55	55	30	30	40	40	55	.do .	40	55	55	50	50
50	50	36	36	70	70	36	36	70	70	70	70	36	36	50	50	70	.do .	50	70	70	50	50
36	36	31	31	43	43	31	31	43	43	43	43	31	31	36	36	43	.do .	36	43	43	39	39
36	36	31	31	55	67	31	31	55	55	55	55	31	31	36	36	55	.do .	36	55	55	43	43
31	31	25	25	36	43	25	25	36	36	36	36	25	25	31	31	36	.do .	31	36	36	31	31
19	19	19	19	25	25	19	19	25	25	25	25	19	19	19	19	25	.do .	19	25	25	25	25

TABLE 23.—RATES OF FREIGHT, ALL RAIL, FROM

DISTANCE VIA SHORTEST ROUTE.—From New York, 1,065 miles;

[NOTE.—Where the rates shown are not specifically described as applying on less

Date.	Commodities (rates in cents per 100 pounds).																		
				Furniture.		Stoves.		Coffee.		Soaps.				Starch.			Sugar.	
										Castile and fancy.		Common.						
	Dry goods.	Cotton piece goods.	Boots and shoes.	Less than carloads.	Carloads.	Less than carloads.	Carloads.	Less than carloads.	Carloads.	Less than carloads.	Carloads.	Less than carloads.	Carloads.	Less than carloads.	Carloads.	Tea.	Less than carloads.	Carloads.
1876—Dec. 18.....	67	67	67	67	67	67	67	36	36	61	61	43	43	55	55	67	36	36
1877—Mar. 12.....	97	97	97	97	97	97	97	49	49	91	91	61	61	79	79	97	49	49
Oct. 8.....	97	97	97	97	97	97	55	55	55	91	91	55	55	55	55	97	55	55
Oct. 22.....	128	128	128	128	128	128	61	61	61	116	116	61	61	61	61	128	61	61
Dec. 10.....	127	127	127	127	127	127	60	60	60	102	102	60	60	60	60	127	60	60
1878—Feb. 15.....	96	96	96	96	96	96	54	54	54	78	78	54	54	54	54	96	54	54
1879—Sept. 15.....	94	94	94	94	94	94	53	53	53	76	76	53	53	53	53	94	53	53
1881—Aug. 6.....	59	59	59	59	59	59	28	28	28	43	43	28	28	28	28	59	28	28
Nov. 14.....	76	76	76	76	76	76	38	38	38	65	65	38	38	38	38	76	38	38
1882—July 1.....	76	76	76	76	76	76	41	41	41	65	65	41	41	41	41	76	35	35
Nov. 1.....	94	94	94	94	94	94	47	47	47	76	76	47	47	47	47	94	47	47
1883—June 22.....	94	94	94	94	94	94	47	47	47	76	76	47	47	47	47	94	35	35
1885—Jan. 26.....	65	65	65	65	65	65	35	35	35	53	53	35	35	35	35	65	26	26
Oct. 5.....	76	76	76	76	76	76	35	35	35	65	65	35	35	35	35	76	29	29
Nov. 18.....	94	94	94	94	94	94	47	47	47	76	76	47	47	47	47	94	35	35
1886—Mar. 10.....	92	92	92	92	92	92	46	46	46	75	75	46	46	46	46	92	34	34
Aug. 26.....	92	63	92	92	92	92	46	46	46	75	75	46	46	46	46	92	34	34
1887—Apr. 1.....	92	63	92	92	92	75	46	46	34	75	75	41	35	41	29	92	34	34
1888—Aug. 15.....	87	58	87	87	75	58	38	41	29	75	75	41	35	41	29	87	41	29
1891—Apr. 9.....	87	58	87	87	75	35	29	41	29	75	75	41	35	41	29	87	41	29
1892—June 6.....	87	58	87	87	75	35	29	41	29	41	29	41	29	41	29	87	41	27

NEW YORK, N. Y., TO ST. LOUIS, MO.—Continued.

Boston, 1,186 miles; Philadelphia, 975 miles; Baltimore, 934 miles.

than carload or carload quantities they apply on shipments regardless of quantity.]

Commodities (rates in cents per 100 pounds).																						
Molasses.		Rice.				Crockery and earthenware.		Bagging.		Leather.		Lead.		Nails.			Agricultural implements.		Machinery.		Beer.	
Less than carloads.	Carloads.	Less than carloads.	Carloads.	Groceries.	Drugs.	Less than carloads.	Carloads.	Less than carloads.	Carloads.	Less than carloads.	Carloads.	Less than carloads.	Carloads.	Less than carloads.	Carloads.	Hardware.	Less than carloads.	Carloads.	Less than carloads.	Carloads.	Less than carloads.	Carloads.
43	43	36	36	61	67	36	36	61	61	61	61	36	36	43	43	61	Sp'l rate.	43	61	61	55	55
61	61	49	49	91	97	49	49	91	91	91	91	49	49	61	61	91	.do.	61	91	91	79	79
55	55	55	55	91	97	55	55	55	55	91	91	55	55	55	55	91	.do.	55	91	55	55	55
61	61	61	61	116	128	61	61	61	61	116	116	61	61	61	61	116	.do.	61	116	61	61	61
60	60	60	60	102	127	60	60	60	60	102	102	60	60	60	60	102	.do.	60	102	60	60	60
54	54	54	54	78	96	54	55	54	54	78	78	54	54	54	54	78	.do.	54	78	54	54	54
53	53	53	53	76	94	53	53	53	53	76	76	53	53	53	53	76	.do.	53	76	53	53	53
28	28	28	28	43	59	28	28	28	28	43	43	28	28	28	28	43	.do.	28	43	28	28	28
38	38	38	38	65	76	38	38	38	38	65	65	38	38	38	38	65	.do.	38	65	38	38	38
35	35	41	41	65	76	41	41	41	41	65	65	41	41	41	41	65	.do.	41	65	41	41	41
47	47	47	47	76	94	47	47	47	47	76	76	47	47	47	47	76	.do.	47	76	47	47	47
35	35	47	47	76	94	47	47	47	47	76	76	47	47	47	47	76	.do.	47	76	47	47	47
26	26	35	35	53	65	35	35	35	35	53	53	35	35	35	35	53	do.	35	53	35	35	35
29	29	35	35	65	76	35	35	35	35	65	65	35	35	35	35	65	.do.	35	65	35	35	35
35	35	47	47	76	94	47	47	47	47	76	76	47	47	47	47	76	.do.	47	76	47	47	47
34	34	46	46	75	92	46	46	46	46	75	75	46	46	46	46	75	92	46	75	46	46	46
34	34	46	46	75	92	46	46	46	46	75	75	46	46	46	46	75	92	46	75	46	46	46
34	34	46	34	75	92	46	46	46	46	75	46	46	46	46	46	75	75	46	46	46	46	46
41	35	41	29	75	87	41	35	58	41	58	41	41	29	41	35	75	58	35	41	35	51	35
41	35	41	29	75	87	41	35	58	41	58	41	41	29	35	29	75	58	35	41	35	51	35
41	35	41	29	75	87	41	35	58	41	58	41	41	29	35	29	75	58	35	41	35	51	35

TABLE 24.—RATES OF FREIGHT, ALL RAIL,

DISTANCE VIA SHORTEST ROUTE.—From New York, 1,100 miles;

[NOTE.—Where the rates shown are not specifically described as applying on less

Date.		Commodities. (Rates in cents per 100 pounds.)																
					Furniture.		Stoves.		Coffee.		Soaps.				Starch.			Sugar.	
											Castile and fancy.		Common.						
		Dry goods.	Cotton piece goods.	Boots and shoes.	Less than carloads.	Carloads.	Less than carloads.	Carloads.	Less than carloads.	Carloads.	Less than carloads.	Carloads.	Less than carloads.	Carloads.	Less than carloads.	Carloads.	Tea.	Less than carloads.	Carloads.
1867—Jan.	1	250	250	250	250	250	250	250	195	195	195	195	142	142	195	195	250	100	100
Nov.	5	273	273	273	273	273	273	273	229	229	229	229	185	185	229	229	273	114	114
1868—Feb.	4	273	273	273	273	273	273	273	Special rate.		229	229	114	114	185	185	273	Special rate.	
June	4	250	250	250	250	250	250	250	..do....		214	214	108	108	171	171	250	..do....	
Aug.	10	200	200	200	200	200	200	200	..do....		171	171	108	108	160	160	200	..do....	
Sept.	7	250	250	250	250	250	250	250	..do....		214	214	108	108	171	171	250	..do....	
Oct.	1	95	95	95	95	95	95	95	..do....		85	85	70	70	75	75	95	..do....	
Dec.	7	273	273	273	273	273	273	273	..do....		229	229	114	114	185	185	273	..do....	
1869—Feb.	1	250	250	250	250	250	250	250	..do....		214	214	108	108	171	171	250	..do....	
	17	87	87	87	87	87	87	87	..do....		87	87	87	87	87	87	87	..do....	
Mar.	15	214	214	214	214	214	214	214	..do....		214	214	108	108	171	171	214	..do....	
Apr.	12	214	214	214	214	214	214	214	..do....		214	214	108	108	171	171	214	..do....	
July	1	250	250	250	250	250	250	250	..do....		214	214	108	108	171	171	250	..do....	
Aug.	11	42	42	42	42	42	42	42	..do....		42	42	42	42	42	42	42	..do....	
Oct.	9	100	100	100	100	100	100	100	..do....		100	100	70	70	100	100	100	..do....	
	13	168	168	168	168	168	168	168	..do....		134	134	88	88	102	102	168	..do....	
Nov.	1	188	188	188	188	188	188	188	..do....		168	168	108	108	134	134	188	..do....	
	29	202	202	202	202	202	202	202	..do....		174	174	108	108	134	134	202	..do....	
1870—Apr.	14	202	202	202	202	202	202	202	..do....		174	174	108	108	134	134	202	50	50
May	7	202	202	202	202	202	202	202	..do....		174	174	108	108	134	134	202	50	50
June	18	142	142	142	142	142	142	142	..do....		114	114	72	72	92	92	142	50	50
Aug.	12	64	64	64	64	64	64	64	..do....		64	64	64	64	64	64	64	Special rate.	
	22	126	126	126	126	126	126	126	..do....		114	114	72	72	92	92	126	..do....	
Sept.	8	168	168	168	168	168	168	168	..do....		148	148	88	88	114	114	168	..do....	
Nov.	28	204	204	204	204	204	204	204	..do....		164	164	82	82	129	129	204	..do....	
Dec.	26	231	231	231	231	231	231	231	76	76	192	192	102	102	153	153	231	76	76
1871—Feb.	20	192	192	192	192	192	192	192	70	70	164	164	90	90	129	129	192	70	70
Mar.	7	126	126	126	126	126	126	126	56	56	114	114	72	72	92	92	126	56	56
	13	129	129	129	129	129	129	129	59	59	115	115	70	70	90	90	129	59	56
May	18	96	96	96	96	96	96	96	47	47	82	82	57	57	65	65	96	47	47
June	1	129	129	129	129	129	129	129	59	59	115	115	70	70	90	90	129	59	59
July	8	96	96	96	96	96	96	96	47	47	82	82	57	57	65	65	96	47	47
July	26	76	76	76	76	76	76	76	41	41	70	70	51	51	59	59	76	41	41
	28	65	65	65	65	65	65	65	45	45	65	65	57	57	65	65	65	45	45
Aug.	16	51	51	51	51	51	51	51	36	36	51	51	51	51	51	51	51	36	36
	22	45	45	45	45	45	45	45	35	35	45	45	45	45	45	45	45	35	35
Sept.	1	40	40	40	40	40	40	40	34	34	40	40	40	40	40	40	40	34	34
Nov.	27	129	129	129	129	129	129	129	59	59	115	115	70	70	90	90	129	59	59
Dec.	15	160	160	160	160	160	160	160	64	64	141	141	83	83	109	109	160	64	64
1872—Apr.	27	160	160	160	160	160	160	160	64	64	141	141	83	83	109	109	160	64	64
Aug.	1	96	96	96	96	96	96	96	45	45	90	90	58	58	77	77	96	45	45
Sept.	1	160	160	160	160	160	160	160	64	64	141	141	83	83	109	109	160	64	64
	2	128	128	128	128	128	128	128	58	58	115	115	70	70	90	90	128	58	58
Oct.	14	160	160	160	160	160	160	160	64	64	141	141	83	83	109	109	160	64	64
1873—Apr.	14	128	128	128	128	128	128	128	58	58	115	115	77	77	96	96	128	58	58
July	22	96	96	96	96	96	96	96	45	45	90	90	58	58	77	77	96	45	45
Aug.	12	64	64	64	64	64	64	64	38	38	64	64	38	38	51	51	64	38	38
Sept.	3	51	51	51	51	51	51	51	38	38	51	51	38	38	38	38	51	38	38
	17	96	96	96	96	96	96	96	45	45	90	90	58	58	77	77	96	45	45
1874—Jan.	1	128	128	128	128	128	128	128	58	58	115	115	77	77	96	96	128	58	58
Aug.	3	96	96	96	96	94	96	96	45	45	90	90	58	58	77	77	96	45	45
1875—Jan.	20	128	128	128	128	128	128	128	58	58	115	115	77	77	96	96	128	58	58
Mar.	17	96	96	96	96	96	96	96	38	38	90	90	58	58	77	77	96	38	38
June	1	70	70	70	70	70	70	70	36	36	70	70	50	05	50	50	70	36	36
Aug.	12	64	64	64	64	64	64	64	26	26	51	51	32	32	38	38	64	26	26
Nov.	15	96	96	96	96	96	96	96	45	45	90	90	58	58	77	77	96	45	45
Dec.	22	38	38	38	38	38	38	38	19	19	32	32	26	26	26	26	38	19	19
1876—Jan.	10	96	96	96	96	96	96	96	45	45	90	90	58	58	77	77	96	45	45
June	2	96	96	96	96	96	96	96	26	26	90	90	58	58	77	77	96	26	26
	12	32	32	32	32	32	32	32	21	21	32	32	21	21	32	32	32	21	21
Dec.	18	64	64	64	64	64	64	64	32	32	58	58	38	38	51	51	64	32	32

FROM NEW YORK, N. Y., TO CAIRO, ILL.

Boston, 1,221 miles; Philadelphia, 1,010 miles; Baltimore, 943 miles.

thancarload or carload quantities they apply on shipments regardless of quantity.]

Commodities. (Rates in cents per 100 pounds.)																						
Molasses.		Rice.				Crockery and earthenware.		Bagging.		Leather.		Lead.		Nails.			Agricultural implements.		Machinery.		Beer.	
Less than carloads.	Carloads.	Less than carloads.	Carloads.	Groceries.	Drugs.	Less than carloads.	Carloads.	Less than carloads.	Carloads.	Less than carloads.	Carloads.	Less than carloads.	Carloads.	Less than carloads.	Carloads.	Hardware.	Less than carloads.	Carloads.	Less than carloads.	Carloads.	Less than carloads.	Carloads.
100	100	100	100	195	250	195	195	195	195	195	195	100	100	100	100	195	250	250	195	195	142	142
114	114	114	114	229	273	229	229	229	229	229	229	114	114	114	114	229	273	273	229	229	185	185
Special rate.		114	114	229	273	229	229	229	229	229	229	114	114	114	114	229	273	273	229	229	185	185
..do....		108	108	214	250	214	214	214	214	214	214	108	108	108	108	214	250	250	214	214	171	171
..do....		108	108	171	200	171	171	171	171	171	171	108	108	108	108	171	200	200	171	171	160	160
..do....		108	108	214	250	214	214	214	214	214	214	108	108	108	108	214	250	250	214	214	171	171
..do....		70	70	85	95	85	85	85	85	85	85	70	70	70	70	85	95	95	85	85	78	78
..do....		114	114	229	273	229	229	229	229	229	229	114	114	114	114	229	273	273	229	229	185	185
..do....		108	108	214	250	214	214	214	214	214	214	108	108	108	108	214	250	250	214	214	171	171
..do....		87	87	87	87	87	87	87	87	87	87	87	87	87	87	87	87	87	87	87	87	87
..do....		108	108	214	214	214	214	214	214	214	214	108	108	108	108	214	214	214	214	214	171	171
..do....		108	108	214	214	Special rate.		214	214	214	214	108	108	108	108	214	214	214	214	214	171	171
..do....		108	108	214	250	..do....		214	214	214	214	214	214	108	108	214	250	250	214	214	171	171
..do....		42	42	42	42	..do....		42	42	42	42	42	42	42	42	42	42	42	42	42	42	42
..do....		70	70	100	100	..do....		100	100	100	100	70	70	70	70	100	100	100	100	100	100	100
..do....		88	88	134	168	..do....		134	134	134	134	88	88	88	88	134	168	168	134	134	102	102
..do....		108	108	168	188	..do....		168	168	168	168	108	108	108	108	168	188	188	168	168	134	134
..do....		108	108	174	202	..do....		174	174	174	174	108	108	108	108	174	202	202	174	174	134	134
..do....		108	108	174	202	..do....		174	174	174	174	108	108	108	108	174	202	202	174	174	134	134
..do....		Special rate.		174	202	..do....		174	174	174	174	108	108	108	108	174	202	202	174	174	134	134
..do....		..do....		114	142	..do....		114	114	114	114	72	72	72	72	114	142	142	114	114	92	92
..do....		..do....		64	64	..do....		64	64	64	64	64	64	64	64	64	64	64	64	64	64	64
..do....		..do....		114	126	..do....		114	114	114	114	72	72	72	72	114	126	126	114	114	92	92
..do....		..do....		148	168	..do....		148	148	148	148	88	88	88	88	148	168	168	148	148	114	114
..do....		..do....		164	204	..do....		164	164	164	164	82	82	82	82	164	204	204	164	164	129	129
102	102	102	102	192	231	192	192	192	192	192	192	102	102	102	102	192	231	231	192	192	153	153
90	90	90	90	164	192	70	70	164	164	164	164	70	70	90	90	164	192	192	164	164	129	129
72	72	72	72	114	126	56	56	114	114	114	114	56	56	72	72	114	126	126	114	114	92	92
70	70	70	70	115	129	59	59	115	115	115	115	59	59	70	70	115	129	129	115	115	90	90
57	57	57	57	82	96	47	47	82	82	82	82	47	47	57	57	82	96	96	82	82	65	65
70	70	70	70	115	129	59	59	115	115	115	115	59	59	70	70	115	129	129	115	115	90	90
57	57	57	57	82	96	47	47	82	82	82	82	47	47	57	57	82	96	96	82	82	65	65
51	51	51	51	70	76	41	41	70	70	70	70	41	41	51	51	70	76	76	70	70	59	59
57	57	57	57	65	65	45	45	65	65	65	65	45	45	57	57	65	65	45	65	65	65	65
51	51	51	51	51	51	36	36	51	51	51	51	36	36	51	51	51	51	51	51	51	51	51
45	45	45	45	45	45	35	35	45	45	45	45	35	35	45	45	45	45	45	45	45	45	45
40	40	40	40	40	40	34	34	40	40	40	40	34	34	40	40	40	40	40	40	40	40	40
70	70	70	70	115	129	59	59	115	115	115	115	59	59	70	70	115	129	129	115	115	90	90
83	83	83	83	141	160	141	141	141	141	141	141	64	64	83	83	141	160	160	141	141	109	199
83	83	64	64	141	160	141	141	141	141	141	141	64	64	83	83	141	160	160	141	141	109	109
58	58	45	45	90	96	90	90	90	90	90	90	45	45	58	58	90	96	96	90	90	77	77
83	83	83	83	141	160	141	141	141	141	141	141	64	64	83	83	141	160	160	141	141	109	109
70	70	58	58	115	128	115	115	115	115	115	115	58	58	70	70	115	128	128	115	115	90	90
83	83	64	64	141	160	64	64	141	141	141	141	64	64	83	83	141	160	160	141	141	109	109
77	77	58	58	115	128	58	58	115	115	115	115	58	58	77	77	115	Sp'l rate.	77	115	115	96	96
58	58	45	45	90	96	45	45	90	90	90	90	45	45	58	58	90	.do.	58	90	90	77	77
38	38	38	38	64	64	38	38	64	64	64	64	38	38	38	38	64	.do.	38	64	64	51	51
38	38	38	38	51	51	38	38	51	51	51	51	38	28	38	38	51	.do.	38	51	51	38	38
58	58	45	45	90	96	45	45	90	90	90	90	45	45	58	58	90	.do.	58	90	90	77	77
77	77	58	58	115	128	58	58	115	115	115	115	58	58	77	77	115	.do.	77	115	115	96	96
58	58	45	45	90	96	45	45	90	90	90	90	45	45	58	58	90	.do.	58	90	90	77	77
77	77	58	58	115	128	58	58	115	115	115	115	58	58	77	77	115	.do.	77	115	115	96	96
38	38	45	45	90	96	45	45	90	90	90	90	45	45	58	58	90	.do.	58	90	90	77	77
50	50	36	36	70	70	36	36	70	70	70	70	36	36	50	50	70	.do.	50	70	70	50	50
32	32	26	26	51	64	26	26	51	51	51	51	26	26	32	32	51	.do.	32	51	51	38	38
58	58	45	45	90	90	45	45	90	90	90	90	45	45	58	58	90	.do.	58	90	90	77	77
26	26	19	19	32	38	19	19	32	32	32	32	19	19	26	26	32	.do.	26	32	32	26	26
58	58	45	45	90	96	45	45	90	90	90	90	45	45	58	58	90	.do.	58	90	90	77	77
32	32	26	26	90	96	26	26	90	90	90	90	26	26	32	32	90	.do.	32	90	90	77	77
21	21	21	21	32	32	21	21	32	32	32	32	21	21	21	21	32	.do.	21	32	32	32	32
38	38	32	32	58	64	32	32	58	58	58	58	32	32	38	38	58	.do.	38	58	58	51	51

TABLE 24.—RATES OF FREIGHT, ALL RAIL, FROM

DISTANCE VIA SHORTEST ROUTE.—From New York, 1,100 miles;

[NOTE.—Where the rates shown are not specifically described as applying on less

Date.	Commodities (rates in cents per 100 pounds.)																	
	Dry goods.	Cotton piece goods.	Boots and shoes.	Furniture.		Stoves.		Coffee.		Soap.				Starch.		Tea.	Sugar.	
										Castile and fancy.		Common.						
				Less than carloads.	Carloads.	Less than carloads.	Carloads.	Less than carloads.	Carloads.	Less than carloads.	Carloads.	Less than carloads.	Carloads.	Less than carloads.	Carloads.		Less than carloads.	Carloads.
1877—Mar. 12	96	96	96	96	96	96	96	45	45	90	90	58	58	77	77	96	45	45
Oct. 8	96	96	96	96	96	96	51	51	51	90	90	51	51	51	51	96	51	51
22	128	128	128	128	128	128	58	58	58	115	115	58	58	58	58	128	58	58
Dec. 19	128	128	128	128	128	128	58	58	58	102	102	58	58	58	58	128	58	58
1878—Feb. 15	96	96	96	96	96	96	51	51	51	77	77	51	51	51	51	96	51	51
1881—Aug. 6	58	58	58	58	58	58	25	25	25	41	41	25	25	25	25	58	25	25
Nov. 14	77	77	77	77	77	77	36	36	36	64	64	36	36	36	36	77	36	36
1882—Jan. 24	58	58	58	58	58	58	25	25	25	41	41	25	25	25	25	58	25	25
July 1	77	77	77	77	77	77	38	38	38	64	64	38	38	38	38	77	32	32
Nov. 1	96	96	96	96	96	96	45	45	45	77	77	45	45	45	45	96	45	45
1883—June 22	96	96	96	96	96	96	45	45	45	77	77	45	45	45	45	96	32	32
1885—Jan. 26	64	64	64	64	64	64	32	32	32	51	51	32	32	32	32	64	23	23
June 1	51	51	51	51	51	51	23	23	23	38	38	23	23	23	23	51	19	19
Oct. 5	77	77	77	77	77	77	32	32	32	64	64	32	32	32	32	77	26	26
Nov. 18	96	96	96	96	96	96	45	45	45	77	77	45	45	45	45	96	32	32
1886—Mar. 10	90	90	90	90	90	90	42	42	42	72	72	42	42	42	42	90	30	30
Aug. 26	90	60	90	90	90	90	42	42	42	72	72	42	42	42	42	90	30	30
1887—Apr. 1	90	60	90	90	78	60	36	42	30	78	78	42	36	42	30	90	42	30
1888—Jan. 9	90	60	90	90	78	60	40	46	33	78	78	46	40	46	33	90	46	33
Mar. 5	90	60	90	90	78	60	36	42	30	78	78	42	36	42	30	90	42	30
Nov. 12	60	42	60	60	48	42	30	36	24	48	48	36	30	36	24	60	36	24
Dec. 17	90	60	90	90	78	60	36	42	30	78	78	42	36	42	30	90	42	30
1891—Apr. 9	90	60	90	90	78	36	30	42	30	78	78	42	36	42	30	90	42	30
1892—Mar. 16	90	60	90	90	78	36	30	42	30	42	30	42	30	42	30	90	42	25
May 2	90	60	90	90	78	36	30	42	30	42	30	42	30	42	30	90	42	30
June 6	90	60	90	90	78	36	30	42	30	42	30	42	30	42	30	90	42	28

NEW YORK, N. Y., TO CAIRO, ILL.—Continued.

Boston, 1,221 miles; Philadelphia, 1,010 miles; Baltimore, 943 miles.

than carload or carload quantities they apply on shipments regardless of quantity.]

Molasses. Less than carloads.	Molasses. Carloads.	Rice. Less than carloads.	Rice. Carloads.	Groceries.	Drugs.	Crockery and earthenware. Less than carloads.	Crockery and earthenware. Carloads.	Bagging. Less than carloads.	Bagging. Carloads.	Leather. Less than carloads.	Leather. Carloads.	Lead. Less than carloads.	Lead. Carloads.	Nails. Less than carloads.	Nails. Carloads.	Hardware.	Agricultural implements. Less than carloads.	Agricultural implements. Carloads.	Machinery. Less than carloads.	Machinery. Carloads.	Beer. Less than carloads.	Beer. Carloads.
Commodities (rates in cents per 100 pounds.)																						
58	58	45	45	90	96	45	45	90	90	90	90	45	45	58	58	90	Sp'l rate.	58	90	90	77	77
51	51	51	51	90	96	51	51	51	51	90	90	51	51	51	51	90	.do.	51	90	51	51	51
58	58	58	58	115	128	58	58	58	58	115	115	58	58	58	58	115	.do.	58	115	58	58	58
58	58	58	58	102	128	58	58	58	58	102	102	58	58	58	58	102	.do.	58	102	58	58	58
51	51	51	51	77	96	51	51	51	51	77	77	51	51	51	51	77	.do.	51	77	51	51	51
25	25	25	25	41	58	25	25	25	25	41	41	25	25	25	25	41	.do.	25	41	25	25	25
36	36	36	36	64	77	36	36	36	36	64	64	36	36	36	36	64	.do.	36	64	36	36	36
25	25	25	25	41	58	25	25	25	25	41	41	25	25	25	25	41	.do.	25	41	25	25	25
32	32	38	38	64	77	38	38	38	38	64	64	38	38	38	38	64	.do.	38	64	38	38	38
45	45	45	45	77	96	45	45	45	45	77	77	45	45	45	45	77	.do.	45	77	45	45	45
32	32	45	45	77	96	45	45	45	45	77	77	45	45	45	45	77	.do.	45	77	45	45	45
23	23	32	32	51	64	32	32	32	32	51	51	32	32	32	32	51	.do.	32	51	32	32	32
19	19	23	23	38	51	23	23	23	23	38	38	23	23	23	23	38	.do.	23	38	23	23	23
26	26	32	32	64	77	32	32	32	32	64	64	32	32	32	32	64	.do.	32	64	32	32	32
32	32	45	45	77	96	45	45	45	45	77	77	45	45	45	45	77	.do.	45	77	45	45	45
30	30	42	42	72	90	42	42	42	42	72	72	42	42	42	42	72	.do.	42	72	42	42	42
30	30	42	42	72	90	42	42	42	42	72	72	42	42	42	42	72	.do.	42	72	42	42	42
42	36	42	42	78	90	42	36	60	42	60	42	42	30	42	36	78	60	36	42	36	60	36
46	40	46	33	78	90	46	40	60	46	60	46	46	33	46	40	78	60	40	46	40	60	40
42	36	42	30	78	90	42	36	60	42	60	42	42	30	42	36	78	60	36	42	36	60	36
36	30	36	24	48	60	36	30	42	36	42	36	36	24	36	30	48	42	30	36	30	42	30
42	36	42	30	78	90	42	36	60	42	60	42	42	30	42	36	78	60	36	42	36	60	36
42	36	42	30	78	90	42	36	60	42	60	42	42	30	36	30	78	60	36	42	36	60	36
42	36	42	30	78	90	42	36	60	42	60	42	42	30	36	30	78	60	36	42	36	60	36
42	36	42	30	78	90	42	36	60	42	60	42	42	30	36	30	78	60	36	42	36	60	36
42	36	42	30	78	90	42	36	60	42	50	42	42	30	36	30	78	60	36	42	36	60	36

TABLE 25.—RATES OF FREIGHT, ALL RAIL, FROM

DISTANCE VIA SHORTEST ROUTE—From New York, 1,158 miles;

[NOTE.—Where the rates shown are not specifically described as applying on less

Date.	Commodities, rates in cents per 100 pounds.																		
	Dry goods.	Cotton piece goods.	Boots and shoes.	Furniture.		Stoves.		Coffee.		Soaps.				Starch.		Tea.	Sugar.	
										Castile and fancy.		Common.						
				Less than carloads.	Carloads.	Less than carloads.	Carloads.	Less than carloads.	Carloads.	Less than carloads.	Carloads.	Less than carloads.	Carloads.	Less than carloads.	Carloads.		Less than carloads.	Carloads.
1867—Jan. 1	270	270	270	270	270	270	270	235	235	235	235	175	175	235	235	270	125	125
May 15	256	256	256	256	256	256	256	222	222	222	222	175	175	222	222	256	125	125
1868—Feb. 4	256	256	256	256	256	256	256	Special rate.		222	222	125	125	175	175	256	Special rate.	
Aug. 10	234	234	234	234	234	234	234	..do....		200	200	125	125	175	175	234	..do....	
27	215	215	215	215	215	215	215	..do....		190	190	113	113	160	160	215	..do....	
Oct. 1	127	127	127	127	127	127	127	..do....		113	113	86	86	103	103	127	..do....	
Dec. 7	215	215	215	215	215	215	215	..do....		190	190	113	113	160	160	215	..do....	
1869—Feb. 17	87	87	87	87	87	87	87	..do....		85	85	74	74	80	80	87	..do....	
Mar. 15	190	190	190	190	190	190	190	..do....		190	190	113	113	160	160	190	..do....	
May 12	190	190	190	190	190	190	190	..do....		190	190	81	81	93	93	190	..do....	
Aug. 2	107	107	107	107	107	107	107	..do....		190	190	81	81	93	93	107	..do....	
3	88	88	88	88	88	88	87	..do....		87	87	76	76	83	83	88	..do....	
11	69	69	69	69	69	69	69	..do....		68	68	57	57	63	63	69	..do....	
30	102	102	102	102	102	102	102	..do....		93	93	80	80	85	85	102	..do....	
Sept. 22	95	95	95	95	95	95	95	..do....		86	86	73	73	78	78	95	..do....	
24	92	92	92	92	92	92	92	..do....		83	83	70	70	75	75	92	..do....	
Nov. 1	209	209	209	209	209	209	209	..do....		183	183	121	121	148	148	209	..do....	
1870—May 7	209	209	209	209	209	209	209	..do....		183	183	121	121	148	148	209	..do....	
July 15	148	148	148	148	148	148	148	..do....		130	130	90	90	108	108	148	..do....	
21	145	145	145	145	145	145	145	..do....		130	130	94	94	114	114	145	..do....	
25	142	142	142	142	142	142	142	..do....		124	124	87	87	108	108	142	..do....	
28	125	125	125	125	125	125	125	..do....		115	115	87	87	104	104	125	..do....	
Aug. 12	125	125	125	125	125	125	125	..do....		115	115	94	94	104	104	125	..do....	
24	166	166	166	166	166	166	166	..do....		148	148	95	95	120	120	166	..do....	
Sept. 8	198	198	198	198	198	198	198	..do....		176	176	109	109	139	139	198	..do....	
Nov. 28	229	229	229	229	229	229	229	..do....		191	191	105	105	153	153	229	..do....	
Dec. 26	229	229	229	229	229	229	229	92	92	191	191	105	105	153	153	229	92	92
1871—Feb. 20	207	207	207	207	207	207	207	83	83	182	182	111	111	148	148	207	83	83
Mar. 7	166	166	166	166	166	166	166	75	75	148	148	95	95	120	120	166	75	75
13	168	168	168	168	168	168	168	78	78	151	151	95	95	121	121	168	78	78
29	154	154	154	154	154	154	154	74	74	139	139	87	87	110	110	154	74	74
Apr. 29	115	115	115	115	115	115	115	56	56	104	104	65	65	83	83	115	56	56
May 18	115	115	115	115	115	115	115	56	56	104	104	65	65	83	83	115	56	56
July 26	95	95	95	95	95	95	95	53	53	90	90	62	62	77	77	95	53	53
28	86	86	86	86	86	86	86	57	57	82	82	69	69	77	77	86	57	57
Aug. 16	84	84	84	84	84	84	84	51	51	80	80	69	69	75	75	84	51	51
17	70	70	70	70	70	70	70	51	51	70	70	69	69	70	70	70	51	51
21	100	100	100	100	100	100	100	60	60	90	90	75	75	80	80	100	60	60
Nov. 27	115	115	115	115	115	115	115	56	56	104	104	65	65	83	83	115	56	56
Dec. 15	193	193	193	193	193	193	193	82	82	172	172	105	105	135	135	193	82	82
1872—Apr. 27	192	192	192	192	192	192	192	82	82	171	171	105	105	134	134	192	82	82
Aug. 1	130	130	130	130	130	130	130	63	63	125	125	79	79	79	79	130	63	63
15	135	135	135	135	135	135	135	63	63	125	125	79	79	105	105	135	63	63
16	114	114	114	114	114	114	114	57	57	107	107	72	72	94	94	114	57	57
Sept. 1	192	192	192	192	192	192	192	82	82	171	171	105	105	134	134	192	82	82
9	162	162	162	162	162	162	162	74	74	146	146	89	89	115	115	162	74	74
Oct. 14	188	188	188	188	188	188	188	79	79	167	167	100	100	131	131	188	79	79
1873—Apr. 14	162	162	162	162	162	162	162	74	74	146	146	95	95	120	120	162	74	74
June 11	136	136	136	136	136	136	136	63	63	125	125	79	79	105	105	136	63	63
July 22	135	135	135	135	135	135	135	63	63	125	125	79	79	105	105	135	63	63
Aug. 12	98	98	98	98	98	98	98	58	58	93	93	63	63	73	73	98	58	58
Sept. 17	135	135	135	135	135	135	135	63	63	125	125	79	79	105	105	135	63	63
1874—Jan. 1	162	162	162	162	162	162	162	74	74	146	146	95	95	120	120	162	74	74
Feb. 17	131	131	131	131	131	131	131	67	67	118	118	84	84	102	102	131	67	67
Aug. 3	115	115	115	115	115	115	115	57	57	108	108	72	72	94	94	115	57	57
1875—Jan. 20	131	131	131	131	131	131	131	67	67	118	118	84	84	102	102	131	67	67
Mar. 17	115	115	115	115	115	115	115	50	50	108	108	72	72	94	94	115	50	50
Sept. 9	94	94	94	94	94	94	94	41	41	78	78	51	51	63	63	94	41	41
Nov. 15	120	120	120	120	120	120	120	57	57	110	110	72	72	95	95	120	57	57
Dec. 22	73	73	73	73	73	73	73	36	36	63	63	45	45	52	52	73	36	36
1876—Jan. 10	120	120	120	120	120	120	120	57	57	110	110	72	72	95	95	120	57	57

NEW YORK, N. Y., TO MEMPHIS, TENN.

Boston, 1,371 miles; Philadelphia, 1,068 miles; Baltimore, 972 miles.

than carload or carload quantities they apply on shipments regardless of quantity.]

Commodities, rates in cents per 100 pounds.

Molasses.		Rice.				Crockery and earthen ware.		Bagging.		Leather.		Lead.		Nails.			Agricultural implements.		Machinery.		Beer.	
Less than carloads.	Carloads.	Less than carloads.	Carloads.	Groceries.	Drugs.	Less than carloads.	Carloads.	Less than carloads.	Carloads.	Less than carloads.	Carloads.	Less than carloads.	Carloads.	Less than carloads.	Carloads.	Hardware.	Less than carloads.	Carloads.	Less than carloads.	Carloads.	Less than carloads.	Carloads.
125	125	125	125	225	270	235	235	235	235	235	235	125	125	125	125	235	270	270	235	235	175	175
125	125	125	125	222	256	222	222	222	222	222	222	125	125	125	125	222	256	256	222	222	175	175
Special rate.		125	125	222	256	222	222	222	222	222	222	125	125	125	125	222	256	256	222	222	175.	175
..do....		125	125	200	234	200	200	200	200	200	200	125	125	125	125	200	234	234	200	200	175	175
..do....		113	113	190	215	190	190	190	190	190	190	113	113	113	113	190	215	215	190	190	160	160
..do....		86	86	113	127	113	113	113	113	113	113	86	86	86	86	113	127	127	113	113	103	103
..do....		113	113	190	215	190	190	190	190	190	190	113	113	113	113	190	215	215	190	190	160	160
..do....		74	74	85	87	85	85	85	85	85	85	74	74	74	74	85	87	87	85	85	80	80
..do....		113	113	190	190	190	190	190	190	190	190	113	113	113	113	190	190	190	190	190	160	160
..do....		113	113	190	190	Special rate.		190	190	190	190	113	113	113	113	190	190	190	190	190	160	160
..do....		81	81	100	107	..do....		100	100	100	100	81	81	81	81	100	107	107	100	100	93	93
..do....		76	76	87	88	..do....		87	87	87	87	76	76	76	76	87	88	88	87	87	83	83
..do....		57	57	68	69	..do....		68	68	68	68	57	57	57	57	68	69	69	68	68	63	63
..do....		80	80	93	102	..do....		93	93	93	93	80	80	80	80	93	102	102	93	93	85	85
..do....		73	73	86	95	..do....		86	86	86	86	73	73	73	73	86	95	95	86	86	78	78
..do....		70	70	83	92	..do....		83	83	83	83	70	70	70	70	83	92	92	83	83	75	75
..do....		121	121	183	209	..do....		183	183	183	183.	121	121	121	121	183	209	209	183	183	148	148
..do....		Special rate.		183	209	..do....		183	183	183	183	121	121	121	121	183	209	209	183	183	148	148
..do....		..do....		130	148	..do....		130	130	130	130	90	90	90	90	130	148	148	130	130	108	108
..do....		..do....		130	145	..do....		130	130	130	130	94	94	94	94	130	145	145	130	130	114	114
..do....		..do....		124	142	..do....		124	124	124	124	87	87	87	87	124	142	142	124	124	108	108
..do....		..do....		115	125	..do....		115	115	115	115	87	87	87	87	115	125	125	115	115	104	104
..do....		..do....		115	125	..do....		115	115	115	115	94	94	94	94	115	125	125	115	115	104	104
..do....		..do....		148	166	..do....		148	148	148	148	95	95	95	95	148	166	166	148	148	120	120
..do....		..do....		176	198	..do....		176	176	176	176	109	109	109	109	176	198	198	176	176	139	139
..do....		..do....		191	229	..do....		191	191	191	191	105	105	105	105	191	229	229	191	191	153	153
105	105	105	105	191	229	191	191	191	191	191	191	105	105	105	105	191	229	229	191	191	153	153
111	111	111	111	182	207	83	83	182	182	182	182	83	83	111	111	182	207	207	182	182	148	148
95	95	95	95	148	166	75	75	148	148	148	148	75	75	95	95	148	166	166	148	148	120	120
95	95	95	95	151	168	78	78	151	151	151	151	78	78	95	95	151	168	168	151	151	121	121
87	87	87	87	139	154	74	74	139	139	139	139	74	74	87	87	139	154	154	139	139	110	110
65	65	65	65	104	115	56	56	104	104	104	104	56	56	65	65	104	115	115	104	104	83	83
65	65	65	65	104	115	56	56	104	104	104	104	56	56	65	65	104	115	115	104	104	83	83
62	62	62	62	90	95	53	53	90	90	90	90	53	53	62	62	90	95	95	90	90	77	77
69	69	69	69	82	86	57	57	82	82	82	82	57	57	69	69	82	86	86	82	82	77	77
69	69	69	69	80	84	51	51	80	80	80	80	51	51	69	69	80	84	84	80	80	75	75
69	69	69	69	70	70	51	51	70	70	70	70	51	51	69	69	70	70	70	70	70	70	70
75	75	75	75	90	100	60	60	90	90	90	90	60	60	75	75	90	100	100	90	90	80	80
65	65	65	65	104	115	56	56	104	104	104	104	56	56	65	65	104	115	115	104	104	83	83
105	105	105	105	172	193	172	172	172	172	172	172	82	82	105	105	172	193	193	172	172	135	135
105	105	82	82	171	192	171	171	171	171	171	171	82	82	105	105	171	192	192	171	171	134	134
79	79	63	63	125	130	125	125	125	125	125	125	63	63	79	79	125	130	130	125	125	79	79
79	79	63	63	125	135	125	125	125	125	125	125	63	63	79	79	125	135	135	125	125	105	105
72	72	57	57	107	114	107	107	107	107	107	107	57	57	72	72	107	114	114	107	107	94	94
105	105	82	82	171	192	171	171	171	171	171	171	82	82	105	105	171	192	192	171	171	134	134
89	89	74	74	146	162	146	146	146	146	146	146	74	74	89	89	146	162	162	146	146	115	115
100	100	79	79	167	188	167	167	167	167	167	167	79	79	100	100	167	188	188	167	167	131	131
95	95	74	74	146	162	74	74	146	146	146	146	74	74	95	95	146	Sp'l rate.	95	146	146	120	170
79	79	63	63	125	136	63	63	125	125	125	125	63	63	79	79	125	.do .	79	125	125	105	105
79	79	63	63	125	135	63	63	125	125	125	125	63	63	79	79	125	.do .	79	125	125	105	105
63	63	58	58	93	98	58	58	93	93	93	93	58	58	63	63	93	.do .	63	93	93	73	73
79	79	63	63	125	135	63	63	125	125	125	125	63	63	79	79	125	.do .	79	125	125	105	105
95	95	74	84	146	162	74	74	146	146	146	146	74	74	95	95	146	.do .	95	146	146	120	120
84	84	67	67	118	131	67	67	118	118	118	118	67	67	84	84	118	.do .	84	118	118	102	102
72	72	57	57	108	115	57	57	108	108	108	108	57	57	72	72	108	.do .	72	108	108	94	94
84	84	67	67	118	131	67	67	118	118	118	118	67	67	84	84	118	.do .	84	118	118	102	102
72	72	57	57	108	115	57	57	108	108	108	108	57	57	72	72	108	.do .	72	108	108	94	94
51	51	41	41	78	94	41	41	78	78	78	78	41	41	51	51	78	.do .	51	78	78	63	63
72	72	57	57	110	120	57	57	110	110	110	110	57	57	72	72	110	.do .	72	110	110	95	95
45	45	36	36	63	73	36	36	63	63	63	63	36	36	45	45	63	.do .	45	63	63	52	52
72	72	57	57	110	120	57	57	110	110	110	110	57	57	72	72	110	.do .	72	110	110	95	95

TABLE 25.—RATES OF FREIGHT, ALL RAIL, FROM

DISTANCE VIA SHORTEST ROUTE.—From New York, 1,158 miles;

[NOTE.—Where the rates shown are not specifically described as applying on less

Date.	Commodities (rates in cents per 100 pounds).																	
	Dry goods.	Cotton piece goods.	Boots and shoes.	Furniture.		Stoves.		Coffee.		Soap.				Starch.		Tea.	Sugar.	
										Castile and fancy.		Common.						
				Less than carloads.	Carloads.	Less than carloads.	Carloads.	Less than carloads.	Carloads.	Less than carloads.	Carloads.	Less than carloads.	Carloads.	Less than carloads.	Carloads.		Less than carloads.	Carloads.
1876—June 2.....	120	120	120	120	120	120	120	41	41	110	110	72	72	95	95	120	41	41
12.....	68	68	68	68	68	68	68	37	37	63	63	41	41	58	58	68	37	37
Dec. 18.....	94	94	94	94	94	94	94	47	47	84	84	56	56	73	73	94	47	47
1877—Mar. 12.....	145	145	145	145	145	145	145	61	61	130	130	74	74	110	110	145	74	74
Sept. 10.....	114	114	114	114	114	114	114	56	56	107	107	71	71	93	93	114	56	56
Oct. 8.....	114	114	114	114	114	114	65	65	65	107	107	65	65	65	65	114	65	65
22.....	116	116	116	116	116	116	67	67	67	109	109	67	67	67	67	116	67	67
1878—Feb. 15.....	114	114	114	114	114	114	65	65	65	97	97	65	65	65	65	114	65	65
Mar. 4.....	114	114	114	114	114	114	63	63	63	93	93	63	63	63	63	114	63	63
1880—Feb. 12.....	107	107	107	107	107	107	49	49	49	87	87	49	49	49	49	107	49	49
1881—Aug, 6.....	75	75	75	75	75	75	35	35	35	50	50	35	35	35	35	75	35	35
Nov. 14.....	83	83	83	83	83	83	41	41	41	63	63	41	41	41	41	83	41	41
1882—Jan. 22	100	100	100	100	100	100	45	45	45	80	80	45	45	45	45	100	45	45
June 28.....	99	99	99	99	99	99	53	53	53	82	82	53	53	53	53	99	44	44
July 1.....	116	116	116	116	116	116	57	57	57	99	99	57	57	57	57	116	52	52
Sept. 1.....	99	99	99	99	99	99	53	53	53	82	82	53	53	53	53	99	44	44
Nov. 1.....	114	114	114	114	114	114	58	58	58	93	93	58	58	58	58	114	58	58
1883—June 22.....	114	114	114	114	114	114	58	58	58	93	93	58	58	58	88	114	48	48
1884—Jan. 1.....	114	114	114	114	114	114	58	58	58	93	93	58	58	58	58	114	44	44
1885—Jan. 1.....	112	112	112	112	112	112	56	56	56	91	91	56	56	56	56	112	42	42
26.....	40	40	40	40	40	40	25	25	25	35	35	25	25	25	25	40	20	20
June 1.....	80	80	80	80	80	80	42	42	42	65	65	42	42	42	42	80	39	39
Oct. 5.....	102	70	102	102	102	102	50	50	50	86	86	50	50	50	50	102	44	44
1887—Apr. 1....	102	70	102	102	86	70	44	50	44	86	86	86	50	50	50	102	50	44
1890—Apr. 1.....	100	65	100	100	85	65	38	45	35	85	85	45	38	45	35	100	45	35
Nov. 1.....	100	65	100	100	85	65	38	45	35	85	85	45	38	45	35	100	45	35
1891—Apr. 9.....	100	65	100	100	85	38	35	45	35	85	85	45	35	45	35	100	45	35
June 20.....	100	65	100	100	85	38	35	45	35	45	35	45	35	45	35	100	45	35

NEW YORK, N. Y., TO MEMPHIS, TENN.—Continued.

Boston, 1,371 miles; Philadelphia, 1,068 miles; Baltimore, 972 miles.

than carload or carload quantities they apply on shipments regardless of quantity.]

Commodities (rates in cents per 100 pounds).																									
Molasses.		Rice.				Crockery and earthenware.		Bagging.		Leather.		Lead.		Nails.			Agricultural implements.		Machinery.		Beer.	
Less than carloads.	Carloads.	Less than carloads.	Carloads.	Groceries.	Drugs.	Less than carloads.	Carloads.	Less than carloads.	Carloads.	Less than carloads.	Carloads.	Less than carloads.	Carloads.	Less than carloads.	Carloads.	Hardware.	Less than carloads.	Carloads.	Less than carloads.	Carloads.	Less than carloads.	Carloads.
51	51	41	41	110	120	41	41	110	110	110	110	41	41	51	51	110	Sp'l rate.	51	110	110	95	95
41	41	37	37	63	68	37	37	63	63	63	63	37	37	41	41	63	.do .	41	63	63	58	58
56	56	47	47	84	94	47	47	84	84	84	84	47	47	56	56	84	.do .	56	84	84	73	73
61	61	61	61	130	145	61	61	130	130	130	130	61	61	74	74	130	.do .	74	130	130	110	110
71	71	56	56	107	114	56	56	107	107	107	107	56	56	71	71	107	.do .	71	107	107	93	93
65	65	65	65	107	114	65	65	65	65	107	107	65	65	65	65	107	.do .	65	107	65	65	65
67	67	67	67	109	116	67	67	67	67	109	109	67	67	67	67	109	.do .	67	109	67	67	67
65	65	65	65	97	114	65	65	65	65	97	97	65	65	65	65	97	.do .	65	97	65	65	65
63	63	63	63	93	114	63	63	63	63	93	93	63	63	63	63	93	.do .	63	93	63	63	63
49	49	49	49	87	107	49	49	49	49	87	87	49	49	49	49	87	.do .	49	87	49	49	49
35	35	35	35	50	75	35	35	35	35	50	50	35	35	35	35	50	.do .	35	50	35	35	35
41	41	41	41	63	83	41	41	41	41	63	63	41	41	41	41	63	.do .	41	63	41	41	41
45	45	45	45	80	100	45	45	45	45	80	80	45	45	45	45	80	.do .	45	80	45	45	45
44	44	53	53	82	99	53	53	53	53	82	82	53	53	53	53	82	.do .	53	82	53	53	53
52	52	57	57	99	116	57	57	57	57	99	99	57	57	57	57	99	.do .	57	99	57	57	57
44	44	53	53	82	99	53	53	44	44	82	82	53	53	53	53	82	.do .	53	82	53	53	53
58	58	58	58	93	114	58	58	58	58	93	93	58	58	58	58	93	.do .	58	93	58	58	58
48	48	58	58	93	114	58	58	58	58	93	93	58	58	58	58	93	.do .	58	93	58	58	58
44	44	58	58	93	114	58	58	58	58	93	93	58	58	58	58	93	.do .	58	93	58	58	58
42	42	56	56	91	112	56	56	56	56	91	91	56	56	56	56	91	.do .	56	91	56	56	56
20	20	25	25	35	40	25	25	25	25	35	35	25	25	25	25	35	.do .	25	35	25	25	25
39	39	42	42	65	80	42	42	42	42	65	65	42	42	42	42	65	.do .	42	65	42	42	42
44	44	50	50	86	102	50	50	50	50	86	86	50	50	50	50	86	.do .	50	86	50	50	50
50	44	50	44	86	102	50	44	70	50	70	50	50	44	50	44	86	.do .	44	50	44	70	44
45	35	45	35	85	100	45	38	65	45	65	45	45	35	45	38	85	65	38	45	38	65	38
45	38	45	35	85	100	45	38	65	45	65	45	45	35	45	38	85	65	38	45	38	65	38
45	38	45	35	85	100	45	38	65	45	65	45	45	35	38	35	85	65	38	45	38	65	38
45	38	45	35	85	100	45	38	65	45	65	45	45	35	38	35	85	65	38	45	38	65	38

TABLE 26.—RATES OF FREIGHT, ALL RAIL, FROM

DISTANCE VIA SHORTEST ROUTE.—From New York, 999 miles;

[NOTE.—Where the rates shown are not specifically described as applying on less

Date.	Commodities (rates in cents per 100 pounds).																	
	Dry goods.	Cotton piece goods.	Boots and shoes.	Furniture.		Stoves.		Coffee.		Soaps.				Starch.		Tea.	Sugar.	
										Castile and fancy.		Common.						
				Less than carloads.	Carloads.	Less than carloads.	Carloads.	Less than carloads.	Carloads.	Less than carloads.	Carloads.	Less than carloads.	Carloads.	Less than carloads.	Carloads.		Less than carloads.	Carloads.
1867—Jan. 1	255	255	255	255	255	255	255	215	215	215	215	170	170	215	215	255	118	118
May 15	262	262	262	262	262	262	262	223	223	223	223	177	177	223	223	262	122	122
Nov. 5	280	280	280	280	280	280	280	234	234	234	234	189	189	234	234	280	126	126
1868—Feb. 4	280	280	280	280	280	280	280	Special rate.		223	223	126	126	189	189	280	Special rate.	
June 4	262	262	262	262	262	262	262	..do....		223	223	122	122	177	177	262	..do....	
Aug. 10	205	205	205	205	205	205	205	..do....		176	176	100	100	140	140	205	..do....	
Oct. 1	108	108	108	108	108	108	108	..do....		96	96	75	75	87	87	108	..do....	
Dec. 7	205	205	205	205	205	205	205	..do....		176	176	100	100	140	140	205	..do....	
1869—Feb. 17	70	70	70	70	70	70	70	..do....		69	69	65	65	67	67	70	..do....	
Mar. 15	176	176	176	176	176	176	176	..do....		176	176	100	100	140	140	176	..do....	
Aug. 2	88	88	88	88	88	88	88	..do....		83	83	75	75	77	77	88	..do....	
Aug. 3	70	70	70	70	70	70	70	..do....		69	69	65	65	67	67	70	..do....	
Aug. 11	53	53	53	53	53	53	53	..do....		51	51	48	48	49	49	53	..do....	
Aug. 23	80	80	80	80	80	80	80	..do....		75	75	68	68	71	71	80	..do....	
Sept. 22	73	73	73	73	73	73	73	..do....		68	68	61	61	64	64	73	..do....	
Sept. 24	70	70	70	70	70	70	70	..do....		65	65	58	58	61	61	70	..do....	
Nov. 1	187	187	187	187	187	187	187	..do....		165	165	109	109	134	134	187	..do....	
1870—May 7	187	187	187	187	187	187	187	..do....		165	165	109	109	134	134	187	..do....	
July 15	123	123	123	123	123	123	123	..do....		107	107	75	75	89	89	123	..do....	
July 21	120	120	120	120	120	120	120	..do....		108	108	79	79	94	94	120	..do....	
July 25	117	117	117	117	117	117	117	..do....		102	102	72	72	88	88	117	..do....	
July 28	100	100	100	100	100	100	100	..do....		93	93	72	72	84	84	100	..do....	
Aug. 12	100	100	100	100	100	100	100	..do....		93	93	79	79	84	84	100	..do....	
Aug. 24	141	141	141	141	141	141	141	..do....		125	125	80	80	101	101	141	..do....	
Sept. 8	173	173	173	173	173	173	173	..do....		153	153	94	94	120	120	173	..do....	
Nov. 28	204	204	204	204	204	204	204	..do....		168	168	90	90	134	134	204	..do....	
Dec. 26	204	204	204	204	204	204	204	81	81	168	168	90	90	134	134	204	81	81
1871—Feb. 20	182	182	182	182	182	182	182	72	72	159	159	96	96	129	129	182	72	72
Mar. 7	141	141	141	141	141	141	141	64	64	125	125	80	80	101	101	141	64	64
Mar. 27	143	143	143	143	143	143	143	67	67	128	128	80	80	102	102	143	67	67
Mar. 29	135	135	135	135	135	135	135	66	66	122	122	66	66	97	97	135	66	66
Apr. 29	115	115	115	115	115	115	115	56	56	104	104	65	65	83	83	115	56	56
July 26	95	95	95	95	95	95	95	53	53	90	90	62	62	77	77	95	53	53
July 28	74	74	74	74	74	74	74	51	51	72	72	63	63	69	69	74	51	51
Aug. 16	72	72	72	72	72	72	72	45	45	70	70	63	63	67	67	72	45	45
Aug. 17	70	70	70	70	70	70	70	45	45	70	70	63	63	67	67	70	45	45
Aug. 21	85	85	85	85	85	85	85	53	53	175	175	65	65	70	70	85	53	53
Nov. 27	115	115	115	115	115	115	115	56	56	104	104	65	65	83	83	115	56	56
Dec. 15	168	168	168	168	168	168	168	72	72	149	149	91	91	117	117	168	72	72
1872—Apr. 27	167	167	167	167	167	167	167	72	72	148	148	91	91	116	116	167	72	72
Aug. 1	110	110	110	110	110	110	110	53	53	102	102	68	68	88	88	110	53	53
Aug. 16	101	101	101	101	101	101	101	50	50	95	95	64	64	83	83	101	50	50
Sept. 1	167	167	167	167	167	167	167	72	72	148	148	91	91	116	116	167	72	72
Sept. 9	137	137	137	137	137	137	137	64	64	123	123	78	78	98	98	137	64	64
Oct. 14	163	163	163	163	163	163	163	69	69	144	144	89	89	114	114	163	69	69
1873—Apr. 14	137	137	137	137	137	137	137	64	64	123	123	84	84	103	103	137	64	64
June 11	110	110	110	110	110	110	110	53	53	102	102	68	68	88	88	110	53	53
Aug. 12	73	73	73	73	73	73	73	48	48	70	70	52	52	56	56	73	48	48
Sept. 17	110	110	110	110	110	110	110	53	53	102	102	68	68	88	88	110	53	53
1874—Jan. 1	137	137	137	137	137	137	137	64	64	123	123	84	84	103	103	137	64	64
Feb. 17	115	115	115	115	115	115	115	75	75	105	105	75	75	90	90	115	60	60
Aug. 3	101	101	101	101	101	101	101	50	50	95	95	64	64	83	83	101	50	50
1875—Jan. 20	115	115	115	115	115	115	115	75	75	105	105	75	75	90	90	115	60	60
Mar. 17	101	101	101	101	101	101	101	44	44	95	95	64	64	83	83	101	44	44
June 15	59	59	59	59	59	59	59	53	53	59	59	53	53	53	53	59	41	41
Sept. 9	67	67	67	67	67	67	67	34	34	63	63	42	42	50	50	67	34	34
Nov. 15	103	103	103	103	103	103	103	50	50	95	95	63	63	82	82	103	50	50
Dec. 22	56	56	56	56	56	56	56	29	29	48	48	36	36	39	39	56	29	29
Dec. 24	115	115	115	115	115	115	115	60	60	105	105	75	75	90	90	115	60	60
1876—Jan. 10	103	103	103	103	103	103	103	50	50	95	95	63	63	82	82	103	50	50
June 2	103	103	103	103	103	103	103	34	34	95	95	42	42	82	82	103	34	34
June 12	51	51	51	51	51	51	51	30	30	48	48	32	32	45	45	51	30	30
Dec. 18	77	77	77	77	77	77	77	40	40	69	69	47	47	60	60	77	40	40
1877—Mar. 12	125	125	125	125	125	125	125	55	55	115	115	69	69	100	100	125	55	55

NEW YORK, N. Y., TO NASHVILLE, TENN.

Boston, 1,202 miles; Philadelphia, 909 miles; Baltimore, 813 miles.

than carload or carload quantities they apply on shipments regardless of quantity.]

Commodities (rates in cents per 100 pounds).

Molasses.		Rice.				Crockery and earthenware.		Bagging.		Leather.		Lead.		Nails.			Agricultural implements.		Machinery.		Beer.	
Less than carloads.	Carloads.	Less than carloads.	Carloads.	Groceries.	Drugs.	Less than carloads.	Carloads.	Less than carloads.	Carloads.	Less than carloads.	Carloads.	Less than carloads.	Carloads.	Less than carloads.	Carloads.	Hardware.	Less than carloads.	Carloads.	Less than carloads.	Carloads.	Less than carloads.	Carloads.
118	118	118	118	215	255	215	215	215	215	215	215	118	118	118	118	215	255	255	215	215	170	170
122	122	122	122	223	262	223	223	223	223	223	223	122	122	122	122	223	262	262	223	223	177	177
126	126	126	126	234	280	234	234	234	234	234	234	126	126	126	126	234	280	280	234	234	189	189
Special rate.		126	126	234	280	234	234	234	234	234	234	126	126	126	126	234	280	280	234	234	189	189
..do....		122	122	223	262	223	223	223	223	223	223	122	122	122	122	223	262	262	223	223	177	177
..do....		100	100	176	205	176	176	176	176	176	176	100	100	100	100	176	205	205	176	176	140	140
..do....		75	75	96	108	96	96	96	96	96	96	75	75	75	75	96	108	108	96	96	87	87
..do....		100	100	176	205	176	176	176	176	176	176	100	100	100	100	176	205	205	176	176	140	140
..do....		65	65	69	70	69	69	69	69	69	69	65	65	65	65	69	70	70	69	69	67	67
..do....		100	100	176	176	Special rate.		176	176	176	176	100	100	100	100	176	176	176	176	176	140	140
..do....		75	75	83	88	..do....		83	83	83	83	75	75	75	75	83	88	88	83	83	77	77
..do....		65	65	69	70	..do....		69	69	69	69	65	65	65	65	69	70	70	69	69	67	67
..do....		48	48	51	53	..do....		51	51	51	51	48	48	48	48	51	53	53	51	51	49	49
..do....		68	68	75	80	..do....		75	75	75	75	68	68	68	68	75	80	80	75	75	71	71
..do....		61	61	68	73	..do....		68	68	68	68	61	61	61	61	68	73	73	68	68	64	64
..do....		58	58	65	70	..do....		65	65	65	65	58	58	58	58	65	70	70	65	65	61	61
..do....		109	109	165	187	..do....		165	165	165	165	109	109	109	109	165	187	187	165	165	134	134
..do....		Special rate.		165	187	..do....		165	165	165	165	109	109	109	109	165	187	187	165	165	134	134
..do....		..do....		107	123	..do....		107	107	107	107	75	75	75	75	107	123	123	107	107	89	89
..do....		..do....		108	120	..do....		108	108	108	108	79	79	79	79	108	120	120	108	108	94	94
..do....		..do....		102	117	..do....		102	102	102	102	72	72	72	72	102	117	117	102	102	88	88
..do....		..do....		93	100	..do....		93	93	93	93	72	72	72	72	93	100	100	93	93	84	84
..do....		..do....		93	100	..do....		93	93	93	93	79	79	79	79	93	100	100	93	93	84	84
..do....		..do....		125	141	..do....		125	125	125	125	80	80	80	80	125	141	141	125	125	101	101
..do....		..do....		153	173	..do....		153	153	153	153	94	94	94	94	153	173	173	153	153	120	120
..do....		..do....		168	204	..do....		168	168	168	168	90	90	90	90	168	204	204	168	168	134	134
90	90	90	90	168	204	168	168	168	168	168	168	90	90	90	90	168	204	204	168	168	134	134
96	96	96	96	159	182	72	72	159	159	159	159	72	72	96	96	159	182	182	159	159	129	129
80	80	80	80	125	141	64	64	125	125	125	125	64	64	80	80	125	141	141	125	125	101	101
80	80	80	80	128	143	67	67	128	128	128	128	67	67	80	80	128	143	143	128.	128	102	102
66	66	66	66	122	135	66	66	122	122	122	122	66	66	66	66	122	135	135	122	122	97	97
65	65	65	65	104	115	56	56	104	104	104	104	56	56	65	65	104	115	115	104	104	83	83
62	62	62	62	90	95	53	53	90	90	90	90	53	53	62	62	90	95	95	90	90	77	79
63	63	63	63	72	74	51	51	72	72	72	72	51	51	63	63	72	74	74	72	72	69	69
63	63	63	63	70	72	45	45	70	70	70	70	45	45	63	63	70	72	72	70	70	67	67
63	63	63	63	70	70	45	45	70	70	70	70	45	45	63	63	70	70	70	70	70	67	67
65	65	65	65	175	85	53	53	75	75	75	75	53	53	65	65	75	85	85	75	75	70	70
65	65	65	65	104	115	56	56	104	104	104	104	56	56	65	65	104	115	115	104	104	83	83
91	91	91	91	149	168	149	149	149	149	149	149	72	72	91	91	149	168	168	149	149	117	117
91	91	91	91	148	167	148	148	148	148	148	148	72	72	91	91	148	167	167	148	148	116	116
68	68	53	53	102	110	102	102	102	102	102	102	53	53	68	68	102	110	110	102	102	88	88
64	64	50	50	95	101	95	95	95	95	95	95	50	50	64	64	95	101	101	95	95	83	83
91	91	91	91	148	167	148	148	148	148	148	148	72	72	91	91	148	167	167	148	148	116	116
78	78	64	64	123	137	123	123	123	123	123	123	64	64	78	78	123	137	137	123	123	98	98
89	89	69	69	144	163	69	69	144	144	144	144	69	69	89	89	144	163	163	144	144	114	114
84	84	64	64	123	137	64	64	123	123	123	123	64	64	84	84	123	Sp'l rate.	84	123	123	103	103
68	68	53	53	102	110	53	53	102	103	102	102	53	53	68	68	102	.do .	68	102	102	88	88
52	52	48	48	70	73	48	48	70	70	70	70	48	48	52	52	70	.do .	52	70	70	56	56
68	68	53	53	102	110	53	53	102	102	102	102	53	53	68	68	102	.do .	68	102	102	88	88
84	84	64	64	123	137	64	64	123	123	123	123	64	64	84	84	123	.do .	84	123	123	103	103
75	75	60	60	105	115	60	60	105	105	105	105	60	60	75	75	105	.do .	75	105	105	90	90
64	64	50	50	95	101	50	50	95	95	95	95	50	50	64	64	95	.do .	64	95	95	83	83
75	75	60	60	105	115	60	60	105	105	105	105	60	60	75	75	105	.do .	75	105	105	90	90
64	64	50	50	95	101	50	50	95	95	95	95	50	50	64	64	95	.do .	64	95	95	83	83
53	53	41	41	59	59	41	41	59	59	59	59	41	41	53	53	59	.do .	53	59	59	53	53
42	42	34	34	63	67	34	34	63	63	63	63	34	34	42	42	63	.do .	42	63	63	50	50
63	63	50	50	95	103	50	50	95	95	95	95	50	50	63	63	95	.do .	63	95	95	82	82
36	36	29	29	48	56	29	29	48	48	48	48	29	29	36	36	48	.do .	36	48	48	39	39
75	75	60	60	105	115	60	60	105	105	105	105	60	60	75	75	105	.do .	75	105	105	90	90
63	63	50	50	95	103	50	50	95	95	95	95	50	50	63	63	95	.do .	63	95	95	82	82
42	42	34	34	95	103	34	34	95	95	95	95	34	34	42	42	95	.do .	42	95	95	82	82
32	32	30	30	48	51	30	30	48	48	48	48	30	30	32	32	48	.do .	32	48	48	45	45
47	47	40	40	69	77	40	40	69	69	69	69	40	40	47	47	69	.do .	47	69	69	60	60
69	69	55	55	115	125	55	55	115	115	115	115	55	55	69	69	115	.do .	69	115	115	100	110

TABLE 26.—RATES OF FREIGHT, ALL RAIL, FROM

DISTANCE VIA SHORTEST ROUTE.—From New York, 999 miles;

[NOTE.—Where the rates shown are not specifically described as applying on less

Date.		Commodities (rates in cents per 100 pounds).																	
					Furniture.		Stoves.		Coffee.		Soap. Castile and fancy.		Soap. Common.		Starch.			Sugar.	
		Dry goods.	Cotton piece gooods.	Boots and shoes.	Less than carloads.	Carloads.	Less than carloads.	Carloads.	Less than carloads.	Carloads.	Less than carloads.	Carloads.	Less than carloads.	Carloads.	Less than carloads.	Carloads.	Tea.	Less than carloads.	Carloads.
1877—Sept.	10	100	100	100	100	100	100	100	49	49	94	94	63	63	82	82	100	49	49
Oct.	8	125	125	125	125	125	125	57	57	57	115	115	57	57	57	57	125	57	57
Oct.	22	113	113	113	113	113	113	55	55	55	102	102	55	55	55	55	113	55	55
1878—Feb.	15	100	100	100	100	100	100	57	57	57	84	84	57	57	57	57	100	57	57
Mar.	4	100	100	100	100	100	100	55	55	55	82	82	55	55	55	55	100	55	55
1880—Feb.	12	93	93	93	93	93	93	53	53	53	76	76	53	53	53	53	93	53	53
1881—Aug.	6	65	65	65	65	65	65	30	30	30	50	50	30	30	30	30	65	30	30
Nov.	14	69	69	69	69	69	69	33	33	33	52	52	33	33	33	33	69	33	33
1882—Jan.	22	83	83	83	83	83	83	37	37	37	64	64	37	37	37	37	83	37	37
June	28	94	94	94	94	94	94	49	49	49	78	78	49	49	49	49	94	49	49
July	1	99	99	99	99	99	99	49	49	49	78	78	49	49	49	49	99	49	49
Nov.	1	109	109	109	109	109	109	51	54	54	89	89	54	51	54	54	109	54	54
1883—June	22	109	109	109	109	109	109	54	54	54	89	89	54	54	54	54	109	44	44
1885—Jan.	1	107	107	107	107	107	107	52	52	52	87	87	52	52	52	52	107	42	42
Jan.	26	40	40	40	40	40	40	25	25	25	35	35	25	25	25	25	40	20	20
June	1	75	75	75	75	75	75	37	37	37	60	60	37	37	37	37	75	34	34
Oct.	5	97	65	97	97	97	95	47	45	45	81	81	45	45	45	45	97	39	39
1890—Apr.	21	91	60	91	91	78	60	36	42	31	78	78	42	36	42	31	91	42	31
1891—Apr.	9	91	60	91	91	78	36	31	42	31	78	78	42	31	42	31	91	42	31
June	20	91	60	91	91	78	36	31	42	31	42	31	42	31	42	31	91	42	31

NEW YORK, N. Y., TO NASHVILLE, TENN.—Continued.

Boston, 1,202 miles; Philadelphia, 909 miles; Baltimore, 813 miles.

than carload or carload quantities they apply on shipments regardless of quantity.]

Commodities (rates in cents per 100 pounds).																								
Molasses.		Rice.				Crockery and earthenware.		Bagging.		Leather		Lead.		Nails.			Agricultural implements.		Machinery.		Beer.	
Less than carloads.	Carloads.	Less than carloads.	Carloads.	Groceries.	Drugs.	Less than carloads.	Carloads.	Less than carloads.	Carloads.	Less than carloads.	Carloads.	Less than carloads.	Carloads.	Less than carloads.	Carloads.	Hardware.	Less than carloads.	Carloads.	Less than carloads.	Carloads.	Less than carloads.	Carloads.
63	63	49	49	94	100	49	49	94	94	94	94	49	49	63	63	94	Sp'l rate.	63	94	94	82	52
57	57	57	57	115	125	57	57	57	57	115	115	57	57	57	57	115	.do .	57	115	57	57	57
55	55	55	55	102	113	55	55	55	55	102	102	55	55	55	55	102	.do .	55	102	55	55	55
57	57	57	57	84	100	57	57	57	57	84	81	57	57	57	57	84	.do .	57	84	57	57	57
55	55	55	55	82	100	55	55	55	55	82	82	55	55	55	55	82	.do .	55	82	55	55	53
53	53	53	53	76	93	53	53	53	53	76	76	53	53	53	53	76	.do .	53	76	53	53	53
30	30	30	30	50	65	30	30	30	30	50	50	30	30	30	30	50	.do .	30	50	30	30	30
33	33	33	33	52	69	33	33	33	33	52	52	33	33	33	33	52	.do .	33	52	33	33	33
37	37	37	37	64	83	37	37	37	37	64	64	37	37	37	37	64	.do .	37	64	37	37	37
49	49	49	49	78	94	49	49	49	49	78	78	49	49	49	49	78	.do .	49	78	49	49	49
49	49	49	49	78	99	49	49	49	49	78	78	49	49	49	49	78	.do .	49	78	49	49	49
54	54	54	54	89	109	54	54	54	54	89	89	54	54	54	54	89	.do .	54	89	54	54	54
44	44	54	54	89	109	54	54	54	54	89	89	54	54	54	54	89	.do .	54	89	54	54	54
42	42	52	52	87	107	52	52	52	52	87	87	52	52	52	52	87	.do .	52	87	52	52	52
20	20	25	25	35	40	25	25	25	25	35	35	25	25	25	25	35	.do .	25	35	25	25	25
34	34	37	37	60	75	37	37	37	37	60	60	37	37	37	37	60	.do .	37	60	37	37	37
39	39	45	45	81	97	45	45	45	45	81	81	45	45	45	45	81	.do .	45	81	45	45	45
42	36	42	31	78	91	42	36	60	42	.60	42	42	31	42	36	78	60	36	42	36	60	36
42	36	42	31	78	91	42	36	60	42	60	42	42	31	36	31	78	60	36	42	36	60	36
42	36	42	31	78	91	42	36	60	42	60	42	42	31	36	31	78	60	36	42	36	60	36

TABLE 27.—RATES OF FREIGHT, ALL RAIL, FROM

DISTANCE VIA SHORTEST ROUTE.—From New York, 867 miles;

[NOTE.—Where the rates shown are not specifically described as applying on less

Date.	Commodities (rates in cents per 100 pounds).																		
	Dry goods.	Cotton piece goods.	Boots and shoes.	Furniture.		Stoves.		Coffee.		Soap. Castile and fancy.		Soap. Common.		Starch.		Tea.	Sugar.	
				Less than carloads.	Carloads.	Less than carloads.	Carloads.	Less than carloads.	Carloads.	Less than carloads.	Carloads.	Less than carloads.	Carloads.	Less than carloads.	Carloads.		Less than carloads.	Carloads.
1867—Jan. 1.....	200	200	200	200	200	200	200	170	170	170	170	135	135	170	170	200	88	88
May 15.....	212	212	212	212	212	212	212	183	183	183	183	147	147	183	183	212	97	97
Nov. 5.....	230	230	230	230	230	230	230	194	194	194	194	159	159	194	194	230	101	101
1868—Feb. 4.....	230	230	230	230	230	230	230	Special rate.		194	194	101	101	159	159	230	Special rate.	
June 4.....	212	212	212	212	212	212	212	..do....		183	183	97	97	147	147	212	..do....	
Aug. 10.....	172	172	172	172	172	172	172	..do....		148	148	97	97	139	139	172	..do....	
Sept. 7.....	212	212	212	212	212	212	212	..do....		183	183	97	97	147	147	212	..do....	
Oct. 1.....	75	75	75	75	75	75	75	..do....		68	68	60	60	65	65	75	..do....	
Dec. 7.....	230	230	230	230	230	230	230	..do....		194	194	101	101	159	159	230	..do....	
1869—Feb. 1.....	212	212	212	212	212	212	212	..do....		183	183	97	97	147	147	212	..do....	
Feb. 17.....	55	55	55	55	55	55	55	..do....		55	55	55	55	55	55	55	..do....	
Mar. 15.....	183	183	183	183	183	183	183	..do....		183	183	97	47	147	147	183	..do....	
Apr. 12.....	183	183	183	183	183	183	183	..do....		183	183	97	97	147	147	183	..do....	
May 12.....	55	55	55	55	55	55	55	..do....		55	55	55	55	55	55	55	..do....	
July 1.....	212	212	212	212	212	212	212	..do....		183	183	97	97	147	147	212	..do....	
Aug. 2.....	55	55	55	55	55	55	55	..do....		55	55	55	55	55	55	55	..do....	
Aug. 11.....	37	37	37	37	37	37	37	..do....		37	37	37	37	37	37	37	..do....	
Aug. 23.....	50	50	50	50	50	50	50	..do....		50	50	50	50	50	50	50	..do....	
Aug. 30.....	55	55	55	55	55	55	55	..do....		55	55	55	55	55	55	55	..do....	
Sept. 22.....	48	48	48	48	48	48	48	..do....		48	48	48	48	48	48	48	..do....	
Sept. 24.....	45	45	45	45	45	45	45	..do....		45	45	45	45	45	45	45	..do....	
Oct. 4.....	63	63	63	63	63	63	63	..do....		63	63	63	63	63	63	63	..do....	
Oct. 9.....	90	90	90	90	90	90	90	..do....		90	90	63	63	63	63	90	..do....	
Oct. 13.....	145	145	145	145	145	145	145	..do....		118	118	80	80	90	90	145	..do....	
Nov. 1.....	162	162	162	162	162	162	162	..do....		145	145	96	96	118	118	162	..do....	
Nov. 29.....	173	173	173	173	173	173	173	..do....		150	150	96	96	118	118	173	..do....	
1870—Mar. 7.....	173	173	173	173	173	173	173	..do....		150	150	96	96	118	118	173	..do....	
Apr. 14.....	173	173	173	173	173	173	173	..do....		150	150	96	96	118	118	173	50	50
May 7.....	173	173	173	173	173	173	173	..do....		150	150	96	96	118	118	173	50	50
June 18.....	123	123	123	123	123	123	123	..do....		106	106	64	64	82	82	123	50	50
July 13.....	94	94	94	94	94	94	94	..do....		82	82	59	59	62	62	94	50	50
July 18.....	90	90	90	90	90	90	90	..do....		82	82	59	59	69	69	90	50	50
July 21.....	80	80	80	80	80	80	80	..do....		75	75	59	59	69	69	80	50	50
July 25.....	77	77	77	77	77	77	77	..do....		69	69	52	52	63	63	77	50	50
July 28.....	60	60	60	60	00	60	60	..do....		60	60	52	52	69	69	60	50	50
Aug. 12.....	60	60	60	60	60	60	60	..do....		60	60	59	59	69	69	60	Special rate.	
Aug. 22.....	112	112	112	112	112	112	112	..do....		100	100	64	64	81	81	112	..do....	
Sept. 8.....	144	144	144	144	144	144	144	..do....		128	128	78	78	100	100	144	..do....	
Nov. 28.....	175	175	175	175	175	175	175	..do....		143	143	74	74	114	114	175	..do....	
Dec. 26.....	198	198	198	198	198	198	198	69	69	166	166	90	90	133	133	198	69	69
1871—Feb. 20.....	166	166	166	166	166	166	166	64	64	143	143	81	81	114	114	166	64	64
Mar. 7.....	112	112	112	112	112	112	112	52	52	160	160	64	64	82	82	112	52	52
Mar. 13.....	114	114	114	114	114	114	114	55	55	103	103	64	64	82	82	114	55	55
May 18.....	86	86	86	86	86	86	86	45	45	75	75	53	53	60	60	86	45	45
June 1.....	114	114	114	114	114	114	114	55	55	64	64	64	64	82	82	114	55	55
July 8.....	86	86	86	86	86	86	86	45	45	75	75	53	53	60	60	86	45	45
July 26.....	70	70	70	70	70	70	70	40	40	65	65	48	48	56	56	70	40	40
July 28.....	56	56	56	56	56	56	56	43	43	56	56	53	53	56	56	56	43	43
Aug. 16.....	45	45	45	45	45	45	45	35	35	45	45	45	45	45	45	45	35	35
Aug. 22.....	38	38	38	38	38	38	38	27	27	38	38	38	38	38	38	38	27	27
Nov. 27.....	114	114	114	114	114	114	114	55	55	103	103	64	64	82	82	114	55	55
Dec. 15.....	139	139	139	139	139	139	139	59	59	123	123	75	75	97	97	139	59	59
1872—Apr. 11.....	139	139	139	139	139	139	139	59	59	123	123	75	75	97	97	139	59	59
July 11.....	139	139	139	139	139	139	139	60	60	123	123	76	76	97	97	139	60	60
Aug. 1.....	86	86	86	86	86	86	86	44	44	81	81	55	55	71	71	86	44	44
Sept. 1.....	139	139	139	139	139	139	139	60	60	123	123	76	76	97	97	139	60	60
Sept. 2.....	113	113	113	113	113	113	113	55	55	102	102	65	65	81	81	113	55	55
Oct. 14.....	139	139	139	139	139	139	139	60	60	123	123	76	76	97	97	139	60	60
1873—Apr. 14.....	113	113	113	113	113	113	113	55	55	102	102	71	71	86	86	113	55	55
June 11.....	86	86	86	86	86	86	86	44	44	81	81	55	55	71	71	86	44	44

NEW YORK, N. Y., TO LOUISVILLE, KY.

Boston, 1,017 miles; Philadelphia, 777 miles; Baltimore, 703 miles.

than carload or carload quantities they apply on shipments regardless of quantity.]

Commodities (rates in cents per 100 pounds).

Molasses.		Rice.				Crockery and earthenware.		Bagging.		Leather.		Lead.		Nails.			Agricultural implements.		Machinery.		Beer.	
Less than carloads.	Carloads.	Less than carloads.	Carloads.	Groceries.	Drugs.	Less than carloads.	Carloads.	Less than carloads.	Carloads.	Less than carloads.	Carloads.	Less than carloads.	Carloads.	Less than carloads.	Carloads.	Hardware.	Less than carloads.	Carloads.	Less than carloads.	Carloads.	Less than carloads.	Carloads.
88	88	88	88	170	200	170	170	170	170	170	170	88	88	88	88	170	200	200	170	170	135	135
97	97	97	97	183	212	183	183	183	183	183	183	97	97	97	97	183	212	212	183	183	147	147
101	101	101	101	194	230	194	194	194	194	194	194	101	101	101	101	194	230	230	194	194	159	159
Special rate.		101	101	194	230	194	194	194	194	194	194	101	101	101	101	194	230	230	194	194	159	159
..do....		97	97	183	212	183	183	183	183	183	183	97	97	97	97	183	212	212	183	183	147	147
..do....		97	97	148	172	148	148	148	148	148	148	97	97	97	97	148	172	172	148	148	139	139
..do....		97	97	183	212	183	183	183	183	183	183	97	97	97	97	183	212	212	183	183	147	147
..do....		60	60	68	75	68	68	68	68	68	68	60	60	60	60	68	75	75	68	68	65	65
..do....		101	101	194	230	194	194	194	194	194	194	101	101	101	101	194	230	230	194	194	159	159
..do....		97	97	183	212	183	183	183	183	183	183	97	97	97	97	183	212	212	183	183	147	147
..do....		55	55	55	55	55	55	55	55	55	55	55	55	55	55	55	55	55	55	55	55	55
..do....		97	97	183	183	183	183	183	183	183	183	97	97	97	97	183	183	183	183	183	147	147
..do....		97	97	183	183	Special rate.		183	183	183	183	97	97	97	97	183	183	183	183	183	147	147
..do....		55	55	55	55	..do....		55	55	55	55	55	55	55	55	55	55	55	55	55	55	55
..do....		97	97	183	212	..do....		183	183	183	183	97	97	97	97	183	212	212	212	212	147	147
..do....		55	55	55	55	..do....		55	55	55	55	55	55	55	55	55	55	55	55	55	55	55
..do....		37	37	37	37	..do....		37	37	37	37	37	37	37	37	37	37	37	37	37	37	37
..do....		50	50	50	50	..do....		50	50	50	50	50	50	50	50	50	50	50	50	50	50	50
..do....		55	55	55	55	..do....		55	55	55	55	55	55	55	55	55	55	55	55	55	55	55
..do....		48	48	48	48	..do....		48	48	48	48	48	48	48	48	48	48	48	48	48	48	48
..do....		45	45	45	45	..do....		45	45	45	45	45	45	45	45	45	45	45	45	45	45	45
..do....		63	63	63	63	..do....		63	63	63	63	63	63	63	63	63	63	93	63	63	63	63
..do....		63	63	90	90	..do....		90	90	90	90	63	63	63	63	90	90	90	90	90	90	90
..do....		80	80	118	145	..do....		118	118	118	118	80	80	80	80	118	145	145	118	118	90	90
..do....		96	96	145	162	..do....		145	145	145	145	96	96	96	96	145	162	162	145	145	118	118
..do....		96	96	150	173	..do....		150	150	150	150	96	96	96	96	150	173	173	150	150	118	118
..do....		Special rate.		150	173	..do....		150	150	150	150	96	96	96	96	150	173	173	150	150	118	118
..do....		96	96	150	173	..do....		150	150	150	150	96	96	96	96	150	173	173	150	150	118	118
..do....		Special rate.		150	173	..do....		150	150	150	150	96	96	96	96	150	173	173	150	150	118	118
..do....		..do....		106	123	..do....		106	106	106	106	64	64	64	64	106	123	123	106	106	82	82
..do....		..do....		82	94	..do....		82	82	82	82	59	59	59	59	82	94	94	82	82	62	62
..do....		..do....		82	90	..do....		82	82	82	82	59	59	59	59	82	90	09	82	82	69	69
..do....		..do....		75	80	..do....		75	75	75	75	59	59	59	59	75	80	80	75	75	69	69
..do....		..do....		69	77	..do....		69	69	69	69	52	52	52	52	69	77	77	69	69	63	63
..do....		..do....		60	60	..do....		60	60	60	60	52	52	52	52	60	60	60	60	60	69	69
..do....		..do....		60	60	..do....		60	60	60	60	59	59	59	59	60	60	60	60	60	69	69
..do....		..do....		100	112	..do....		100	100	100	100	64	64	64	64	100	112	112	100	100	81	81
..do....		..do....		128	144	..do....		128	128	128	128	78	78	78	78	128	144	144	128	128	100	100
..do....		..do....		143	175	..do....		143	143	143	143	74	74	74	74	143	175	175	143	143	114	114
90	90	90	90	166	198	166	166	166	166	166	166	90	90	90	90	166	198	198	166	166	133	133
81	81	81	81	143	166	64	64	143	143	143	143	64	64	81	81	143	166	166	143	143	114	114
64	64	64	64	100	112	52	52	100	100	100	100	52	52	64	64	100	112	112	100	100	82	82
64	64	64	64	103	114	55	55	103	103	103	103	55	55	64	64	103	114	114	103	103	82	82
53	53	53	53	75	86	45	45	75	75	75	75	45	45	53	53	75	86	86	75	75	60	60
64	64	64	64	64	114	55	55	103	103	103	103	55	55	64	64	103	114	114	103	103	82	82
53	53	53	53	75	86	45	45	75	75	75	75	45	45	53	53	75	86	86	75	75	60	60
48	48	48	48	65	70	40	40	65	65	65	65	40	40	48	48	65	70	70	65	65	56	56
53	53	53	53	56	56	43	43	56	56	56	56	43	43	53	53	56	56	56	56	56	56	56
45	45	45	45	45	45	35	35	45	45	45	45	35	35	45	45	45	45	45	45	45	45	45
38	38	38	38	38	38	27	27	38	38	38	38	27	27	38	38	38	38	38	38	38	38	38
64	64	64	64	103	114	55	55	103	103	103	103	55	55	64	64	103	114	114	103	103	82	82
75	75	75	75	123	139	123	123	123	123	123	123	59	59	75	75	123	139	139	123	123	97	97
75	75	59	59	123	139	123	123	123	123	123	123	59	59	75	75	123	139	139	123	123	97	97
75	75	60	60	123	139	123	123	123	123	123	123	60	60	76	76	123	139	139	123	123	97	97
55	55	44	44	81	81	81	81	81	81	81	81	44	44	55	55	81	86	86	81	81	71	71
76	76	76	76	123	139	123	123	123	123	123	123	60	60	76	76	123	139	139	123	123	97	97
65	65	55	55	102	113	102	102	102	102	102	102	55	55	65	65	102	113	113	102	102	81	81
76	76	60	60	123	139	60	60	123	123	123	123	60	60	76	76	123	139	139	123	123	97	97
71	71	55	55	102	113	55	55	102	102	102	102	55	55	71	71	102	Sp'l rate.	71	102	102	86	86
55	55	44	44	81	86	44	44	81	81	81	81	44	44	55	55	81	.do .	55	81	81	71	71

TABLE 27.—RATES OF FREIGHT, ALL RAIL, FROM

DISTANCE VIA SHORTEST ROUTE.—From New York, 867 miles;

[NOTE.—Where the rates shown are not specifically described as applying on less

Date.	Commodities (rates in cents per 100 pounds).																	
	Dry goods.	Cotton piece goods.	Boots and shoes.	Furniture.		Stoves.		Coffee.		Soap.				Starch.		Tea.	Sugar.	
										Castile and fancy.		Common.						
				Less than carloads.	Carloads.	Less than carloads.	Carloads.	Less than carloads.	Carloads.	Less than carloads.	Carloads.	Less than carloads.	Carloads.	Less than carloads.	Carloads.		Less than carloads.	Carloads.
1873—Aug. 11.....	49	49	49	49	49	49	49	39	39	49	49	39	39	39	39	49	39	39
Aug. 16.....	48	48	48	48	48	48	48	38	38	48	48	38	38	38	38	48	38	38
Aug. 26.....	49	49	49	49	49	49	49	39	39	49	49	39	39	39	39	49	39	39
Sept. 17.....	86	86	86	86	86	86	86	44	44	81	81	55	55	71	71	86	44	44
1874—Jan. 1.....	113	113	113	113	113	113	113	55	55	102	102	71	71	86	86	113	55	55
Aug. 3.....	86	86	86	86	86	86	86	44	44	81	81	55	55	71	71	86	44	44
1875—Jan. 20.....	113	113	113	113	113	113	113	55	55	102	102	71	71	86	86	113	55	55
Feb. 23.....	113	113	113	113	113	113	113	39	39	102	102	71	71	86	86	113	39	39
Mar. 17.....	86	86	86	86	86	86	86	44	44	81	81	55	55	71	71	86	44	44
Apr. 6.....	71	71	71	71	71	71	71	39	39	65	65	49	49	60	60	71	39	39
Apr. 23.....	50	50	50	50	50	50	50	35	35	50	50	45	45	45	45	50	35	35
May 18.....	50	50	50	50	50	50	50	35	35	50	50	45	45	45	45	50	35	35
May 29.....	38	38	38	38	38	38	38	27	27	38	38	33	33	35	35	38	27	27
Aug. 12.....	60	60	60	60	60	60	60	28	28	49	49	34	34	39	39	60	28	28
Nov. 15.....	86	86	86	86	86	86	86	44	44	81	81	55	55	71	71	86	44	44
Dec. 22.....	39	39	39	39	39	39	39	23	23	34	34	28	28	28	28	39	23	23
1876—Jan. 10.....	86	86	86	86	86	86	86	44	44	81	81	55	55	71	71	86	44	44
June 2.....	86	86	86	86	86	86	86	28	28	81	81	34	34	71	71	86	28	28
June 12.....	34	34	34	34	34	34	34	24	24	34	34	24	24	34	34	34	24	24
July 28.....	23	23	23	23	23	23	23	18	18	23	23	18	18	23	23	23	18	18
Aug. 7.....	34	34	34	34	34	34	34	24	24	34	34	24	24	34	34	34	24	24
Dec. 18.....	60	60	60	60	60	60	60	34	34	55	55	39	39	49	49	60	34	34
1877—Mar. 12.....	86	86	86	86	86	86	86	44	44	81	81	55	55	71	71	86	44	44
Oct. 8.....	86	86	86	86	86	86	49	40	49	81	81	49	49	49	49	86	49	49
Oct. 22.....	113	113	113	113	113	113	55	55	55	102	102	55	55	55	55	113	55	55
Dec. 10.....	113	113	113	113	113	113	55	55	55	92	92	55	55	55	55	113	55	55
1878—Feb. 10.....	86	86	86	86	86	86	49	49	49	71	71	49	49	49	49	86	49	49
1880—July 1.....	83	83	83	83	83	83	46	46	46	68	68	46	46	46	46	83	46	46
1881—Aug 6.....	52	52	52	52	52	52	24	24	24	38	38	24	24	24	24	52	24	24
Nov. 14.....	68	68	68	68	68	68	34	34	34	57	57	34	34	34	34	68	34	34
1882—Jan. 24.....	52	52	52	52	52	52	24	24	24	38	38	24	24	24	24	52	24	24
July 1.....	68	68	68	68	68	68	36	36	36	57	57	36	36	36	36	68	31	31
Nov. 1.....	83	83	83	83	83	83	41	41	41	68	68	41	41	41	41	83	41	41
1883—June 22.....	83	83	83	83	83	83	41	41	41	68	68	41	41	41	41	83	31	31
1885—Jan. 1.....	82	82	82	82	82	82	40	40	40	67	67	40	40	40	40	82	30	30
Jan. 26.....	56	56	56	56	56	56	30	30	30	45	45	30	30	30	30	56	22	22
June 1.....	45	45	45	45	45	45	22	22	22	35	35	22	22	22	22	45	19	19
Oct. 5.....	67	67	67	67	67	67	30	30	30	56	56	30	30	30	30	67	24	24
Nov. 18.....	82	82	82	82	82	82	40	40	40	67	67	40	40	40	40	82	30	30
1886—Mar. 10.....	75	75	75	75	75	75	37	37	37	61	61	37	37	37	37	75	27	27
Aug. 26.....	75	51	75	75	65	50	30	35	25	65	65	30	30	30	30	75	35	25
1887—Apr. 1.....	75	51	75	75	65	50	30	35	25	65	65	35	30	35	25	75	35	25
June 13.....	75	50	75	75	65	50	30	30	25	65	65	35	30	35	25	75	35	25
1888—Jan. 9.....	75	50	75	75	65	50	33	38½	27½	65	65	38½	33	38½	27½	75	38½	27½
Mar. 5.....	75	50	75	75	65	50	30	35	25	65	65	35	30	35	25	75	35	25
Nov. 12....	50	35	50	50	40	35	25	30	20	40	40	30	25	30	20	50	30	20
Dec. 17.....	75	50	75	75	65	50	30	35	25	65	65	35	30	35	25	75	35	25
1891—Apr. 9.....	75	50	75	75	65	30	25	35	25	65	65	35	25	35	25	75	35	25
1892—Mar. 16.....	75	50	75	75	65	30	25	35	25	35	25	35	25	35	25	75	35	21
May 2.....	75	50	75	75	65	30	25	35	25	35	25	35	25	35	25	75	35	25

NEW YORK, N. Y., TO LOUISVILLE, KY.—Continued.

Boston, 1,017 miles; Philadelphia, 777 miles; Baltimore, 703 miles.

than carload or carload quantities they apply on shipments regardless of quantity.]

Commodities (rates in cents per 100 pounds).

Molasses.		Rice.				Crockery and earthenware.		Bagging.		Leather.		Lead.		Nails.			Agricultural implements.		Machinery.		Beer.	
Less than carloads.	Carloads.	Less than carloads.	Carloads.	Groceries.	Drugs.	Less than carloads.	Carloads.	Less than carloads.	Carloads.	Less than carloads.	Carloads.	Less than carloads.	Carloads.	Less than carloads.	Carloads.	Hardware.	Less than carloads.	Carloads.	Less than carloads.	Carloads.	Less than carloads.	Carloads.
39	39	39	39	49	49	39	39	49	49	49	49	39	39	39	39	49	Sp'l rate.	39	49	49	39	39
38	38	38	38	48	48	38	38	48	48	48	48	38	38	38	38	48	.do .	38	48	48	38	38
39	39	39	39	49	49	39	39	49	49	49	49	39	39	39	39	49	.do .	39	49	49	39	39
55	55	44	44	81	86	44	44	81	81	81	81	44	44	55	55	81	.do .	55	81	81	71	71
71	71	55	55	102	113	55	55	102	102	102	102	55	55	71	71	102	.do .	71	102	102	86	86
55	55	44	44	81	86	44	44	81	81	81	81	44	44	55	55	81	.do .	55	81	81	71	71
71	71	55	55	102	113	55	55	102	102	102	102	55	55	71	71	102	.do .	71	102	102	86	86
71	71	55	55	102	113	55	55	102	102	102	102	55	55	71	71	102	.do .	71	102	102	86	86
55	55	44	44	81	86	44	44	81	81	81	81	44	44	55	55	81	.do .	55	81	81	71	71
49	49	39	39	65	71	39	39	65	65	65	65	39	39	49	49	65	.do .	49	65	65	60	60
45	45	35	35	50	50	35	35	50	50	50	50	35	35	45	45	50	.do .	45	50	50	45	45
45	45	40	40	50	50	40	40	50	50	50	50	40	40	45	45	50	.do .	45	50	50	45	45
33	33	27	27	38	38	27	27	38	38	38	38	27	27	33	33	38	.do .	33	38	38	35	35
34	34	28	28	49	60	28	28	49	49	49	49	28	28	34	34	49	.do .	34	49	49	39	39
55	55	44	44	81	86	44	44	81	81	81	81	44	44	55	55	81	.do .	55	81	81	71	71
28	28	23	23	34	39	23	23	34	34	34	34	23	23	28	28	34	.do .	28	34	34	28	28
55	55	44	44	81	86	44	44	81	81	81	81	44	44	55	55	81	.do .	55	81	81	71	71
34	34	28	28	81	86	28	28	81	81	81	81	28	28	34	34	81	.do .	34	81	81	71	71
24	24	24	24	34	34	24	24	34	34	34	34	24	24	24	24	34	.do .	24	34	34	34	34
18	18	18	18	23	23	18	18	23	23	23	23	18	18	18	18	23	.do .	18	23	23	23	23
24	24	24	24	34	34	24	24	34	34	34	34	24	24	24	24	34	.do .	24	34	34	34	34
39	39	34	34	55	60	34	34	55	55	55	55	34	34	39	39	55	.do .	39	55	55	49	49
55	55	44	44	81	86	44	44	81	81	81	81	44	44	55	55	81	.do .	55	81	81	71	71
49	49	49	49	81	86	49	49	49	49	81	81	49	49	49	49	81	.do .	49	81	49	49	49
55	55	55	55	102	113	55	55	55	55	102	102	55	55	55	55	102	.do .	55	102	55	55	55
51	51	55	55	92	113	55	55	55	55	92	92	55	55	55	55	92	.do .	55	92	55	55	55
49	49	49	49	71	86	49	49	49	49	71	71	49	49	49	49	71	.do .	49	71	49	49	49
46	46	46	46	68	83	46	46	46	46	68	68	46	46	46	46	68	.do .	46	68	46	46	46
24	24	24	24	38	52	24	24	24	24	38	38	24	24	24	24	38	.do .	24	38	24	24	24
34	34	34	34	57	68	34	34	34	34	57	57	34	34	34	34	57	.do .	34	57	34	34	34
24	24	24	24	38	52	24	24	24	24	38	38	24	24	24	24	38	.do .	24	38	24	24	24
31	31	36	36	57	68	36	36	36	36	57	57	36	36	36	36	57	.do .	36	57	36	36	36
41	41	41	41	68	83	41	41	41	41	68	68	41	41	41	41	68	.do .	41	68	41	41	41
31	31	41	41	68	83	41	41	41	41	68	68	41	41	41	41	68	.do .	41	68	41	41	41
30	30	40	40	67	82	40	40	40	40	67	67	40	40	40	40	67	.do .	40	82	40	40	40
22	22	30	30	45	56	30	30	30	30	45	45	30	30	30	30	45	.do .	30	45	30	30	30
19	19	22	22	35	45	22	22	22	22	35	35	22	22	22	22	35	.do .	22	35	22	22	22
24	24	30	30	56	67	30	30	30	30	56	56	30	30	30	30	56	.do .	30	56	30	30	30
30	30	40	40	67	82	40	40	40	40	67	67	40	40	40	40	67	.do .	40	67	40	40	40
27	27	37	37	61	75	37	37	37	37	61	61	37	37	37	37	61	.do .	37	61	37	37	37
35	30	35	25	65	75	35	30	50	35	50	35	35	25	35	30	65	50	30	35	30	50	30
35	30	35	25	65	75	35	30	50	35	50	35	35	25	35	30	65	50	30	35	30	50	30
35	30	35	35	65	75	35	30	50	35	50	35	35	25	35	30	65	50	30	35	30	50	30
38½	33	38½	27½	65	75	38	33	50	38½	50	38½	38½	27½	38½	33	65	50	33	38½	33	50	33
35	30	35	35	65	75	35	30	50	35	50	35	35	25	35	30	65	50	30	35	30	50	30
30	25	30	20	40	50	30	25	30	35	35	30	30	20	30	25	40	35	25	30	25	35	25
35	30	35	25	65	75	35	30	50	35	50	35	35	25	35	30	65	50	30	35	30	50	30
35	30	35	25	65	75	35	30	50	35	50	35	35	25	30	25	65	50	30	35	30	50	30
35	30	35	25	65	75	35	30	50	35	50	35	35	25	30	25	65	50	30	35	30	50	30
35	30	35	25	65	75	35	30	50	35	50	35	35	25	30	25	65	50	30	35	30	50	30

TABLE 28.—RATES OF FREIGHT, ALL RAIL, FROM

DISTANCE, VIA SHORTEST ROUTE.—From New York, 757 miles;

[NOTE.—Where the rates shown are not specifically described as applying on less

Date.	Commodities (rates in cents per 100 pounds).																	
	Dry goods.	Cotton piece goods.	Boots and shoes.	Furniture.		Stoves.		Coffee.		Soap.				Starch.		Tea.	Sugar.	
										Castile and fancy.		Common.						
				Less than carloads.	Carloads.	Less than carloads.	Carloads.	Less than carloads.	Carloads.	Less than carloads.	Carloads.	Less than carloads.	Carloads.	Less than carloads.	Carloads.		Less than carloads.	Carloads.
1867—Jan. 1.....	176	176	176	176	176	176	176	150	150	150	150	120	120	150	150	176	76	76
Nov. 5.....	190	190	190	130	190	190	190	160	160	160	160	130	130	160	160	190	80	80
1868—Feb. 4.....	190	190	190	190	190	190	190	Special rate.		160	160	80	80	130	130	190	Special rate.	
June 4.....	176	176	176	176	176	176	176	..do....		150	150	76	76	120	120	176	..do....	
Aug. 10.....	140	140	140	140	140	140	140	..do....		120	120	76	76	112	112	140	..do....	
Sept. 7.....	176	176	176	176	176	176	176	..do....		150	150	76	76	120	120	176	..do....	
Oct. 1.....	60	60	60	60	60	60	60	..do....		56	56	45	45	50	50	60	..do....	
Dec. 7.....	190	190	190	190	190	190	190	..do....		160	160	80	80	130	130	190	..do....	
1869—Feb. 1.....	176	176	176	176	176	176	176	..do....		150	150	76	76	120	120	176	..do....	
Feb. 17.....	40	40	40	40	40	40	40	..do....		40	40	40	40	40	40	40	..do....	
Mar. 15.....	150	150	150	150	150	150	150	..do....		150	150	76	76	120	120	150	..do....	
Apr. 15.....	150	150	150	150	150	150	150	..do....		150	150	76	26	120	120	150	..do....	
May 12.....	40	40	40	40	40	40	40	..do....		40	40	40	40	40	40	40	..do....	
July 1.....	176	176	176	176	176	176	176	..do....		150	150	76	76	120	120	176	..do....	
Aug. 2.....	40	40	40	40	40	40	40	..do....		40	40	40	40	40	40	40	..do....	
Aug. 11.....	25	25	25	25	25	25	25	..do....		25	25	25	25	25	25	25	..do....	
Aug. 23.....	35	35	35	35	35	35	35	..do....		35	35	35	35	35	35	35	..do....	
Aug. 30.....	40	40	40	40	40	40	40	..do....		40	40	40	40	40	40	40	..do....	
Sept. 22.....	35	35	35	35	35	35	35	..do....		35	35	35	35	35	35	35	..do....	
Oct. 4.....	48	48	48	48	48	48	48	..do....		48	48	48	48	48	48	48	..do....	
Oct. 9.....	70	70	70	70	70	70	70	..do....		70	70	48	48	70	70	70	..do....	
Oct. 13.....	118	118	118	118	118	118	118	..do....		95	95	62	62	70	70	118	..do....	
Nov. 1.....	132	132	132	132	132	132	132	..do....		118	118	76	76	94	94	132	..do....	
Nov. 29.....	142	142	142	142	142	142	142	..do....		122	122	76	76	94	94	142	..do....	
1870—Apr. 14.....	142	142	142	142	142	142	142	..do....		122	122	76	76	94	94	142	36	36
May 7.....	142	142	142	142	142	142	142	..do....		122	122	76	76	94	94	142	36	36
June 18.....	100	100	100	100	100	100	100	..do....		80	80	50	50	65	65	100	36	36
July 13.....	74	74	74	74	74	74	74	..do....		65	65	45	45	55	55	74	36	36
July 18.....	70	70	70	70	70	70	70	..do....		65	65	45	45	55	55	70	36	36
July 21.....	65	65	65	65	65	65	65	..do....		60	60	45	45	55	55	65	36	36
July 25.....	60	60	60	60	60	60	60	..do....		54	54	40	40	50	50	60	36	36
July 28.....	45	45	45	45	45	45	45	..do....		45	45	40	40	45	45	45	36	36
Aug. 12.....	45	45	45	45	45	45	45	...do...		45	45	45	45	45	45	45	Special rate.	
Aug. 22.....	90	90	90	90	90	90	90	...do...		80	80	50	50	65	65	90	..do....	
Sept. 8.....	118	118	118	118	118	118	118	...do...		104	104	62	62	80	80	118	..do....	
Nov. 28.....	146	146	146	146	146	146	146	...do...		118	118	59	59	93	93	146	..do....	
Dec. 26.....	166	166	166	166	166	166	166	55	55	138	138	73	73	110	110	166	55	55
1871—Feb. 20.....	138	138	138	138	138	138	138	51	51	118	118	65	65	95	95	138	51	51
Mar. 7.....	90	90	90	90	90	90	90	40	40	80	80	50	50	65	65	90	40	40
Mar. 13.....	93	93	93	93	93	93	93	42	42	83	83	51	51	65	65	93	42	42
May 18.....	69	69	69	69	69	69	69	34	34	59	59	41	41	46	46	69	34	34
June 18.....	93	93	93	93	93	93	93	42	42	83	83	51	51	65	65	93	42	42
July 8.....	69	69	69	69	69	69	69	34	34	59	59	41	41	46	46	69	34	34
July 26.....	55	55	55	55	55	55	55	30	30	51	51	37	37	42	42	55	30	30
July 28.....	40	40	40	40	40	40	40	30	30	40	40	40	40	40	40	40	30	30
Aug. 16.....	35	35	35	35	35	35	35	25	25	35	35	35	35	35	35	35	25	25
Aug. 22.....	32	32	32	32	32	32	32	24	24	32	32	32	32	32	32	32	24	24
Sept. 1.....	28	28	28	28	28	28	28	23	23	28	28	28	28	28	28	28	23	23
Sept. 8.....	28	28	28	28	28	28	28	22	22	28	28	28	28	28	28	28	22	22
Nov. 27.....	93	93	93	93	93	93	93	42	42	83	83	51	51	65	65	93	42	42
Dec. 15.....	115	115	115	115	115	115	115	46	46	101	101	60	60	78	78	115	46	46
1872—Apr. 27.....	115	115	115	115	115	115	115	46	46	101	101	60	60	78	78	115	46	46
Aug. 1.....	70	70	70	70	70	70	70	32	32	64	64	41	41	55	55	70	32	32
Sept. 1.....	115	115	115	115	115	115	115	46	46	101	104	60	60	78	78	115	46	46
Sept. 2.....	92	92	92	92	92	92	92	41	41	83	83	51	51	64	64	92	41	41
Oct. 14.....	115	115	115	115	115	115	115	46	46	101	101	60	60	78	78	115	46	46
1873—Apr. 14.....	92	92	92	92	92	92	92	41	41	83	83	55	55	70	70	92	41	41
June 11.....	70	70	70	70	70	70	70	32	32	64	64	41	41	55	55	70	32	32
Aug. 11.....	37	37	37	37	37	37	37	28	28	37	37	28	28	28	28	37	28	28
Aug. 12.....	40	40	40	40	40	40	40	30	30	40	40	30	30	30	30	40	30	30

NEW YORK, N. Y., TO CINCINNATI, OHIO.

Boston, 907 miles; Philadelphia, 667 miles; Baltimore, 593 miles.

than carload or carload quantities they apply on shipments regardless of quantity.]

Commodities (rates in cents per 100 pounds).																							
Molasses.		Rice.				Crockery and earthenware.		Bagging.		Leather.		Lead.		Nails.			Agricultural implements.		Machinery.		Beer.		
Less than carloads.	Carloads.	Less than carloads.	Carloads.	Groceries.	Drugs.	Less than carloads.	Carloads.	Less than carloads.	Carloads.	Less than carloads.	Carloads.	Less than carloads.	Carloads.	Less than carloads.	Carloads.	Hardware.	Less than carloads.	Carloads.	Less than carloads.	Carloads.	Less than carloads.	Carloads.	
76	76	76	76	150	176	150	150	150	150	150	150	76	76	76	76	150	176	176	150	150	120	120	
80	76	80	80	160	190	160	160	160	160	160	160	80	80	80	80	160	190	190	160	160	130	130	
Special rate.		80	80	160	190	160	160	160	160	160	160	80	80	80	80	160	190	190	160	160	130	130	
..do....		76	76	150	176	150	150	150	150	150	150	76	76	76	76	150	176	176	150	150	120	120	
..do....		76	76	120	140	120	120	120	120	120	120	76	76	76	76	120	140	140	120	120	112	112	
..do....		76	76	150	176	150	150	150	150	150	150	76	76	76	76	150	176	176	150	150	120	120	
..do....		45	45	56	60	56	56	56	56	56	56	45	45	45	45	56	60	60	56	56	50	50	
..do....		80	80	160	190	160	160	160	160	160	160	80	80	80	80	160	190	190	160	160	130	130	
..do....		76	76	150	176	150	150	150	150	150	150	76	76	76	76	150	176	176	150	150	120	120	
..do....		40	40	40	40	40	40	40	40	40	40	40	40	40	40	40	40	40	40	40	40	40	
..do....		76	76	150	150	150	150	150	150	150	150	76	76	76	76	150	150	150	150	150	120	120	
..do....		76	76	150	150	Special rate.		150	150	150	150	76	76	76	76	150	150	150	150	150	120	120	
..do....		40	40	40	40	..do....		40	40	40	40	40	40	40	40	40	40	40	40	40	40	40	
..do....		76	76	150	176	..do....		150	150	150	150	76	76	76	76	150	176	176	150	150	120	120	
..do....		40	40	40	40	..do....		40	40	40	40	40	40	40	40	40	40	40	40	40	40	40	
..do....		25	25	25	25	..do....		25	25	25	25	25	25	25	25	25	25	25	25	25	25	25	
..do....		35	35	35	35	..do....		35	35	35	35	35	35	35	35	35	35	35	35	35	35	35	
..do....		40	40	40	40	..do....		40	40	40	40	40	40	40	40	40	40	40	40	40	40	40	
..do....		35	35	35	35	..do....		35	35	35	35	35	35	35	35	35	35	35	35	35	35	35	
..do....		48	48	48	48	..do....		48	48	48	48	48	48	48	48	48	48	48	48	48	48	48	
..do....		48	48	70	70	..do....		70	70	70	70	48	48	48	48	70	70	70	70	70	70	70	
..do....		62	62	95	118	..do....		95	95	95	95	62	62	62	62	95	118	118	95	95	70	70	
..do....		76	76	118	132	..do....		118	118	118	118	76	76	76	76	118	132	132	118	118	94	94	
..do....		76	76	122	142	..do....		122	122	122	122	76	76	76	76	122	142	142	122	122	94	94	
..do....		76	76	122	142	..do....		122	122	122	122	76	76	76	76	122	142	142	122	122	94	94	
..do....		Special rate.		122	142	..do....		122	122	122	122	76	76	76	76	122	142	142	122	122	94	94	
..do....		..do....		80	100	..do....		80	80	80	80	50	50	50	50	80	100	100	80	80	65	65	
..do....		..do....		65	74	..do....		65	65	65	65	45	45	45	45	65	74	74	65	65	55	55	
..do....		..do....		65	70	..do....		65	65	65	65	45	45	45	45	65	70	70	65	65	55	55	
..do....		..do....		60	65	..do....		60	60	60	60	45	45	45	45	60	65	65	60	60	55	55	
..do....		..do....		54	60	..do....		54	54	54	54	40	40	40	40	54	60	60	54	54	50	50	
..do....		..do....		45	45	..do....		45	45	45	45	40	40	40	40	45	45	45	45	45	45	45	
..do....		..do....		45	45	..do....		45	45	45	45	45	45	45	45	45	45	45	45	45	45	45	
..do....		..do....		80	90	..do....		80	80	80	80	50	50	50	50	80	90	90	80	80	65	65	
..do....		..do....		104	118	..do....		104	104	104	104	62	62	62	62	104	118	118	104	104	80	80	
..do....		..do....		118	146	..do....		118	118	118	118	59	59	59	59	118	146	166	118	118	93	93	
73	73	73	73	138	166	138	138	138	138	138	138	73	73	73	73	138	166	166	138	138	110	110	
65	65	65	65	118	138	51	51	118	118	118	118	51	51	65	65	118	138	138	118	118	93	93	
50	50	50	50	80	90	40	40	80	80	80	80	40	40	50	50	80	90	90	80	80	65	65	
51	51	51	51	83	93	42	42	83	83	83	83	42	42	51	51	83	93	93	83	83	65	65	
41	41	41	41	59	69	34	34	59	59	59	59	34	34	41	41	59	69	69	59	59	46	46	
51	51	51	51	83	93	42	42	83	83	83	83	42	42	51	51	83	93	93	83	83	65	65	
41	41	41	41	59	69	34	34	59	59	59	59	34	34	41	41	59	69	69	59	59	46	46	
37	37	37	37	51	55	30	30	51	51	51	51	30	30	37	37	51	55	55	51	51	42	42	
40	40	40	40	40	40	30	30	40	40	40	40	30	30	40	40	40	40	40	40	40	40	40	
35	35	35	35	35	35	25	25	35	35	35	35	25	25	35	35	35	35	35	35	35	35	35	
32	32	32	32	32	32	24	24	32	32	32	32	24	24	32	32	32	32	32	32	32	32	32	
28	28	28	28	28	28	23	23	28	28	28	28	23	23	28	28	28	28	28	28	28	28	28	
28	28	28	28	28	28	22	22	28	28	28	28	22	22	28	28	28	28	28	28	28	28	28	
51	51	51	51	83	93	42	42	83	83	83	83	42	42	51	51	83	93	93	83	83	65	65	
60	60	60	60	101	115	101	101	101	101	101	101	46	46	60	60	101	115	115	101	151	78	78	
60	60	46	46	101	115	101	101	101	101	101	101	46	46	60	60	101	115	115	101	101	78	78	
41	41	32	32	64	70	64	64	64	64	64	64	32	32	41	41	64	70	70	64	64	55	55	
60	60	60	60	101	115	101	101	101	101	101	101	46	46	60	60	101	115	115	101	101	78	78	
51	51	41	41	83	92	83	83	83	83	83	83	41	41	51	51	83	92	92	83	83	64	64	
60	60	46	46	101	115	46	46	101	101	101	101	46	46	60	60	101	115	115	101	101	78	78	
55	55	41	41	83	92	41	41	83	83	83	83	41	41	55	55	83	Sp'l rate.	55	83	83	70	70	
41	41	32	32	64	70	32	32	64	64	64	64	32	32	41	41	64	.do .	41	64	64	55	55	
28	28	28	28	37	37	28	28	37	37	37	37	28	28	28	28	37	.do .	28	37	37	28	28	
30	30	30	30	40	40	30	30	40	40	40	40	30	30	30	30	40	.do .	30	40	40	30	30	

TABLE 28.—RATES OF FREIGHT, ALL RAIL, FROM

DISTANCE, VIA SHORTEST ROUTE.—From New York, 757 miles;

[NOTE.—Where the rates shown are not specifically described as applying on less

Date.	Commodities (rates in cents per 100 pounds).																		
	Dry goods.	Cotton piece goods.	Boots and shoes.	Furniture.		Stoves.		Coffee.		Soap.				Starch.		Tea.	Sugar.	
										Castile and fancy.		Common.						
				Less than carloads.	Carloads.	Less than carloads.	Carloads.	Less than carloads.	Carloads.	Less than carloads.	Carloads.	Less than carloads.	Carloads.	Less than carloads.	Carloads.		Less than carloads.	Carloads.
1873—Aug. 16	37	37	37	37	37	37	37	28	28	37	37	28	28	28	28	37	28	28
Sept. 17	70	70	70	70	70	70	70	32	32	64	64	41	41	55	55	70	32	32
1874—Jan. 1	92	92	92	92	92	92	92	41	41	83	83	55	55	70	70	92	41	41
Aug. 3	70	70	70	70	70	70	70	32	32	64	64	41	41	55	55	70	32	32
1875—Jan. 20	92	92	92	92	92	92	92	41	41	83	83	55	55	70	70	92	41	41
Feb. 23	92	92	92	92	92	92	92	41	28	83	83	55	55	70	70	92	41	28
Mar. 17	70	70	70	70	70	70	70	28	28	64	64	41	41	55	55	70	28	28
Apr. 6	55	55	55	55	55	55	55	28	28	51	51	37	37	46	46	55	28	28
Apr. 23	40	40	40	40	40	40	40	25	25	40	40	35	35	35	35	40	25	25
May 18	40	40	40	40	40	40	40	25	25	40	40	35	35	35	35	40	25	25
May 29	28	28	28	28	28	28	28	19	19	28	28	23	23	25	25	28	19	19
Aug. 12	46	46	46	46	46	46	46	19	19	37	37	23	23	28	28	46	19	19
Nov. 15	70	70	70	70	70	70	70	32	32	64	64	41	41	55	55	70	32	32
Dec. 22	30	30	30	30	30	30	30	15	15	25	25	20	20	20	20	30	15	15
1876—Jan. 10	70	70	70	70	70	70	70	32	32	64	64	41	41	55	55	70	32	32
June 2	70	70	70	70	70	70	70	20	20	64	64	25	25	55	55	70	20	20
June 12	25	25	25	25	25	25	25	16	16	25	25	16	16	25	25	25	16	16
July 28	15	15	15	15	15	15	15	10	10	15	15	10	10	15	15	15	10	10
Aug. 7	25	25	25	25	25	25	25	16	16	25	25	16	16	25	25	25	16	16
Dec. 18	46	46	46	46	46	46	46	23	23	41	41	28	28	37	37	46	23	23
1877—Mar. 12	70	70	70	70	70	70	70	32	32	64	64	41	41	55	55	70	32	32
Oct. 8	70	70	70	70	70	70	37	37	37	64	64	37	37	37	37	70	37	37
Oct. 22	92	92	92	92	92	92	41	41	41	83	83	41	41	41	41	92	41	41
Dec. 10	92	92	92	92	92	92	41	41	41	73	73	41	41	41	41	92	41	41
1878—Feb. 15	70	70	70	70	70	70	37	37	37	55	55	37	37	37	37	70	37	37
1881—Aug. 6	41	41	41	41	41	41	18	18	18	29	29	18	18	18	18	41	18	18
Nov. 14	55	55	55	55	55	55	26	26	26	46	46	26	26	26	26	55	26	26
1882—Jan. 24	41	41	41	41	41	41	18	18	18	32	32	18	18	18	18	41	18	18
June 22	70	70	70	70	70	70	32	32	32	55	55	32	32	32	32	70	23	23
July 1	55	55	55	55	55	55	28	28	28	46	46	28	28	28	28	55	23	23
Nov. 1	70	70	70	70	70	70	32	32	32	55	55	32	32	32	32	70	32	32
1883—June 22	70	70	70	70	70	70	32	32	32	55	55	32	32	32	32	70	23	23
1885—Jan. 26	46	46	46	46	46	46	23	23	23	37	37	23	23	23	23	46	17	17
June 1	37	37	37	37	37	37	17	17	17	28	28	17	17	17	17	37	14	14
Oct. 5	55	55	55	55	55	55	23	23	23	46	46	23	23	23	23	55	18	18
Nov. 18	70	70	70	70	70	70	32	32	32	55	55	32	32	32	32	70	23	23
1886—Mar. 10	65	65	65	65	65	65	30	30	30	52	52	30	30	30	30	65	22	22
Aug. 26	65	44	65	65	65	65	30	30	30	52	52	30	30	30	30	65	22	22
1887—Apr. 1	65	44	65	65	57	44	26	30	22	57	57	30	26	30	22	65	30	22
1888—Jan. 9	65	44	65	65	57	44	29	33	24	57	57	33	29	33	24	65	33	24
Mar. 5	65	44	65	65	57	44	26	30	22	57	57	30	26	30	22	65	30	22
Nov. 12	44	30	44	44	35	30	22	26	17	35	35	26	22	26	17	44	26	17
Dec. 17	65	44	65	65	57	44	26	30	22	57	57	30	26	30	22	65	30	22
1891—Apr. 9	65	44	65	65	57	26	22	30	22	57	57	30	22	30	22	65	30	22
1892—Mar. 6	65	44	65	65	57	26	22	30	22	30	22	30	22	30	22	65	30	18
May 2	65	44	65	65	57	26	22	30	22	30	22	30	22	30	22	65	30	22
June 6	65	44	65	65	57	26	22	30	22	30	22	30	22	30	22	65	30	20

NEW YORK, N. Y., TO CINCINNATI, OHIO—Continued.

Boston, 907 miles; Philadelphia, 667 miles; Baltimore, 593 miles.

than carload or carload quantities they apply on shipments regardless of quantity.]

Commodities (rates in cents per 100 pounds).																						
Molasses.		Rice.				Crockery and earthenware.		Bagging.		Leather.		Lead.		Nails.			Agricultural implements.		Machinery.		Beer.	
Less than carloads.	Carloads.	Less than carloads.	Carloads.	Groceries.	Drugs.	Less than carloads.	Carloads.	Less than carloads.	Carloads.	Less than carloads.	Carloads.	Less than carloads.	Carloads.	Less than carloads.	Carloads.	Hardware.	Less than carloads.	Carloads.	Less than carloads.	Carloads.	Less than carloads.	Carloads.
28	28	28	28	37	37	28	28	37	37	37	37	28	28	28	28	37	Sp'l rate.	28	37	37	28	28
41	41	32	32	64	70	32	32	64	64	64	64	32	32	41	41	64	.do .	41	64	64	55	55
55	55	41	41	83	92	41	41	83	83	83	83	41	41	55	55	83	.do .	55	83	83	70	70
41	41	32	32	64	70	32	32	64	64	64	64	32	32	41	41	64	.do .	41	64	64	55	55
55	55	41	41	83	92	41	41	83	83	83	83	41	41	55	55	83	.do .	55	83	83	70	70
55	55	41	41	83	92	41	41	83	83	83	83	41	41	55	55	83	.do .	55	83	83	70	70
28	28	32	32	64	70	32	32	64	64	64	64	32	32	41	41	64	.do .	41	64	64	55	55
37	37	28	28	51	55	28	28	51	51	51	51	28	28	37	37	51	.do .	37	51	51	46	46
35	35	25	25	40	40	25	25	40	40	40	40	25	25	35	35	40	.do .	35	40	40	35	35
35	35	30	30	40	40	30	30	40	40	40	40	30	30	35	35	40	.do .	35	40	40	35	35
23	23	19	19	28	28	19	19	28	28	28	28	19	19	23	23	28	.do .	23	28	28	25	25
23	23	19	19	37	46	19	19	37	37	37	37	19	19	23	23	37	.do .	23	37	37	28	28
41	41	32	32	64	70	32	32	64	64	64	64	32	32	41	41	64	.do .	41	64	64	55	55
20	20	15	15	25	30	15	15	25	25	25	25	15	15	20	20	25	.do .	20	25	25	20	20
41	41	32	32	64	70	32	32	64	64	64	64	32	32	41	41	64	.do .	41	64	64	55	55
25	25	20	20	64	70	20	20	64	64	64	64	20	20	25	25	64	.do .	25	64	64	55	55
16	16	16	16	25	25	16	16	25	25	25	25	16	16	16	16	25	.do .	16	25	25	25	25
10	10	10	10	15	15	10	10	15	15	15	15	10	10	10	10	15	.do .	10	15	15	15	15
16	16	16	16	25	25	16	16	25	25	25	25	16	16	16	16	25	.do .	16	25	25	25	25
28	28	23	23	41	46	23	23	41	41	41	41	23	23	28	28	41	.do .	28	41	41	37	37
41	41	32	32	64	70	32	32	64	64	64	64	32	32	41	41	64	.do .	41	64	64	55	55
37	37	37	37	64	70	37	37	37	37	64	64	37	37	37	37	64	.do .	37	64	37	37	37
41	41	41	41	83	92	41	41	41	41	83	83	41	41	41	41	83	.do .	41	83	41	41	41
41	41	41	41	73	92	41	41	41	41	73	73	41	41	41	41	73	.do .	41	73	41	41	41
37	37	37	37	55	70	37	37	37	37	55	55	37	37	37	37	55	.do .	37	55	37	37	37
18	18	18	18	29	41	18	18	18	18	29	29	18	18	18	18	29	.do .	18	29	18	18	18
26	26	26	26	46	55	26	26	26	26	46	46	26	26	26	26	46	.do .	26	46	26	26	26
18	18	18	18	32	41	18	18	18	18	32	32	18	18	18	18	32	.do .	18	32	18	18	18
23	23	32	32	55	70	32	32	32	32	55	55	32	32	32	32	55	.do .	32	55	32	32	32
23	23	28	28	46	55	28	28	28	28	46	46	28	28	28	28	46	.do .	28	46	28	28	28
32	32	32	32	55	70	32	32	32	32	55	55	32	32	32	32	55	.do .	32	55	32	32	32
23	23	32	32	55	70	32	32	32	32	55	55	32	32	32	32	55	.do .	32	55	32	32	32
17	17	23	23	37	46	23	23	23	23	37	37	23	23	23	23	37	.do .	23	37	23	23	23
14	14	17	17	28	37	17	17	17	17	28	28	17	17	17	17	28	.do .	17	28	17	17	17
18	18	23	23	46	55	23	23	23	23	46	46	23	23	23	23	46	.do .	23	46	23	23	23
23	23	32	32	55	70	32	32	32	32	55	55	32	32	32	32	55	.do .	32	55	32	32	32
22	22	30	30	52	65	30	30	30	30	52	52	30	30	30	26	52	.do .	30	52	30	30	30
22	22	30	30	52	65	30	30	30	30	52	52	30	30	30	26	52	.do .	30	52	30	30	30
30	26	30	30	57	65	30	26	44	30	44	30	30	22	30	26	57	44	26	30	26	44	26
33	29	33	24	57	65	33	29	44	33	44	33	33	24	33	29	57	44	29	33	29	44	29
30	26	30	22	57	65	30	26	44	30	44	30	30	22	30	26	57	44	26	30	26	44	26
26	22	26	17	35	44	26	22	30	26	30	26	26	17	26	22	35	30	22	26	22	30	22
30	26	30	22	57	65	30	26	44	30	44	30	30	22	30	26	57	44	26	30	26	44	26
30	26	30	22	57	65	30	26	44	30	44	30	30	22	26	22	57	44	26	30	26	44	26
30	26	30	22	57	65	30	26	44	30	44	30	30	22	26	22	57	44	26	30	26	44	26
30	26	30	22	57	65	30	26	44	30	44	30	30	22	26	22	57	44	26	30	26	44	26
30	26	30	22	57	65	30	26	44	30	44	30	30	22	26	22	57	44	26	30	26	44	26

TABLE 29.—RATES OF FREIGHT, ALL RAIL, FROM

DISTANCE VIA SHORTEST ROUTE.—From New York, 825 miles;

[NOTE.—Where the rates shown are not specifically described as applying on less

Date.	Dry goods.	Cotton piece goods.	Boots and shoes.	Furniture. Less than carloads.	Furniture. Carloads.	Stoves. Less than carloads.	Stoves. Carloads.	Coffee. Less than carloads.	Coffee. Carloads.	Soaps. Castile and fancy. Less than carloads.	Soaps. Castile and fancy. Carloads.	Soaps. Common. Less than carloads.	Soaps. Common. Carloads.	Starch. Less than carloads.	Starch. Carloads.	Tea.	Sugar. Less than carloads.	Sugar. Carloads.
1867—Jan. 1	183	183	183	183	183	183	183	156	156	156	156	124	124	156	156	183	79	79
Nov. 5	199	199	199	199	199	199	199	166	166	166	166	135	135	166	166	199	83	83
1868—Feb. 4	199	199	199	199	199	199	199	Special		166	166	83	83	135	135	199	Special	
June 4	183	183	183	183	183	183	183	..do....		156	156	70	70	124	124	183	..do....	
Aug. 10	146	146	146	146	146	146	146	..do....		125	125	79	79	117	117	146	..do....	
Sept. 7	183	183	183	183	183	183	183	..do....		156	156	79	79	124	124	183	..do....	
Oct. 1	65	65	65	65	65	65	65	..do....		58	58	48	48	53	53	65	..do....	
Dec. 7	199	199	199	199	199	199	199	..do....		166	166	83	83	135	135	199	..do....	
1869—Feb. 1	183	183	183	183	183	183	183	..do....		156	156	79	79	124	124	183	..do....	
Feb. 17	45	45	45	45	45	45	45	..do....		45	45	45	45	45	45	45	..do....	
Mar. 15	156	156	156	156	156	156	156	..do....		156	156	79	79	124	124	156	..do....	
April 12	156	156	156	156	156	156	156	..do....		156	156	79	79	124	124	156	..do....	
July 1	183	183	183	183	183	183	183	..do....		156	156	79	79	124	124	183	..do....	
Aug. 2	45	45	45	45	45	45	45	..do....		45	45	45	45	45	45	45	..do....	
Aug. 11	30	30	30	30	30	30	30	..do....		30	30	30	30	30	30	30	..do....	
Aug. 23	38	38	38	38	38	38	38	..do....		38	38	38	38	38	38	38	..do....	
Aug. 30	42	42	42	42	42	42	42	..do....		42	42	42	42	42	42	42	..do....	
Sept. 22	37	37	37	37	37	37	37	..do....		37	37	37	37	37	37	37	..do....	
Oct. 4	50	50	50	50	50	50	50	..do....		50	50	50	50	50	50	50	..do....	
Oct. 9	73	73	73	73	73	73	73	..do....		73	73	50	50	73	73	73	..do....	
Oct. 13	122	122	122	122	122	122	122	..do....		98	98	64	64	74	74	122	..do....	
Nov. 1	137	137	137	137	137	137	137	..do....		123	123	79	79	98	98	137	..do....	
Nov. 29	148	148	148	148	148	148	148	..do....		127	127	79	79	98	98	148	..do....	
1870—April 14	148	148	148	148	148	148	148	..do....		127	127	79	79	98	98	148	38	38
May 7	148	148	148	148	148	148	148	..do....		127	127	79	79	98	98	148	38	38
June 18	104	104	104	104	104	104	104	..do....		83	83	53	53	67	67	104	38	38
July 13	78	78	78	78	78	78	78	..do....		67	67	47	47	57	57	78	38	38
July 18	74	74	74	74	74	74	74	..do....		67	67	47	47	57	57	74	38	38
July 21	70	70	70	70	70	70	70	..do....		65	65	47	47	57	57	70	38	38
July 25	63	63	63	63	63	63	63	..do....		56	56	42	42	52	52	63	38	38
July 28	47	47	47	47	47	47	47	..do....		47	47	42	42	47	47	47	38	38
Aug. 12	47	47	47	47	47	47	47	..do....		47	47	47	47	47	47	47	Special	
1870—Aug. 22	92	92	92	92	92	92	92	..do....		83	83	53	53	67	67	92	..do....	
Sept. 8	122	122	122	122	122	122	122	..do....		108	108	64	64	83	83	122	..do....	
Nov. 28	151	151	151	151	151	151	151	..do....		122	122	61	61	96	96	151	..do....	
Dec. 26	171	171	171	171	171	171	171	56	56	142	142	75	75	113	113	171	56	56
1871—Feb. 20	142	142	142	142	142	142	142	52	52	124	122	67	67	96	96	142	52	52
Mar. 7	92	92	92	92	92	92	92	42	42	83	83	53	53	67	67	92	42	42
Mar. 13	96	96	96	96	96	96	96	44	44	85	85	52	52	67	67	96	44	44
May 18	71	71	71	71	71	71	71	35	35	61	61	42	42	48	48	71	35	35
June 1	96	96	96	96	96	96	96	44	44	85	85	52	52	67	67	96	44	44
July 8	71	71	71	71	71	71	71	35	35	61	61	42	42	48	48	71	35	35
July 26	57	57	57	57	57	57	57	30	30	52	52	38	38	43	43	57	30	30
July 28	45	45	45	45	45	45	45	32	32	45	45	42	42	45	45	45	32	32
Aug. 16	38	38	38	38	38	38	38	27	27	38	38	38	38	38	38	38	27	27
Aug. 22	33	33	33	33	33	33	33	25	25	33	33	33	33	33	33	33	25	25
Sept. 1	29	29	29	29	29	29	29	24	24	29	29	29	29	29	29	29	24	24
Nov. 27	96	96	96	96	96	96	96	44	44	85	85	52	52	67	67	96	44	44
Dec. 15	118	118	118	118	118	118	118	47	47	104	104	62	62	80	80	118	47	47
1872—April 27	118	118	118	118	118	118	118	47	47	104	104	62	62	80	80	118	47	47
Aug. 1	71	71	71	71	71	71	71	33	33	66	66	43	43	57	57	71	33	33
Sept. 1	118	118	118	118	118	118	118	47	47	104	104	62	62	80	80	118	47	47
Sept. 2	95	95	95	95	95	95	95	43	43	85	85	52	52	66	66	95	43	43
Oct. 14	118	118	118	118	118	118	118	47	47	104	104	62	62	80	80	118	47	47
1873—April 14	95	95	95	95	95	95	95	43	43	85	85	57	57	71	71	95	43	43
June 11	71	71	71	71	71	71	71	33	33	66	66	43	43	57	57	71	33	33
Aug. 11	38	38	38	38	38	38	38	28	28	38	38	28	28	28	28	38	28	28
Aug. 12	40	40	40	40	40	40	40	30	30	40	40	30	30	30	30	40	30	30
Aug. 21	38	38	38	38	38	38	38	28	28	38	38	28	28	28	28	38	28	28
Sept. 17	71	71	71	71	71	71	71	33	33	66	66	43	43	57	57	71	33	33
1874—Jan. 1	95	95	95	95	95	95	95	43	43	85	85	57	57	71	71	95	43	43
Aug. 3	71	71	71	71	71	71	71	33	33	66	66	43	43	57	57	71	33	33
1875—Jan. 20	95	95	95	95	95	95	95	43	43	85	85	57	57	71	71	95	43	43
Feb. 23	95	95	95	95	95	95	95	43	28	85	85	57	57	71	71	95	43	28

Commodities (rates in cents per 100 pounds).

NEW YORK, N. Y., TO INDIANAPOLIS, IND.

Boston, 946 miles; Philadelphia, 735 miles; Baltimore, 708 miles.

than carload or carload quantities they apply on shipments regardless of quantity.]

(Commodities (rates in cents per 100 pounds.)																						
Molasses.		Rice.				Crockery and earthenware.		Bagging.		Leather		Lead.		Nails.			Agricultural implement.		Machinery.		Beer.	
Less than carloads.	Carloads.	Less than carloads.	Carloads.	Groceries.	Drugs.	Less than carloads.	Carloads.	Less than carloads.	Carloads.	Less than carloads.	Carloads.	Less than carloads.	Carloads.	Less than carloads.	Carloads.	Hardware.	Less than carloads.	Carloads.	Less than carloads.	Carloads.	Less than carloads.	Carloads.
79	79	79	79	156	183	156	156	156	156	156	156	79	79	79	79	156	183	183	156	156	124	124
83	83	83	83	166	199	166	166	166	166	166	165	83	83	83	83	166	199	199	166	166	135	135
Special		83	83	166	199	166	166	166	166	166	166	83	83	83	83	166	199	199	166	166	135	135
..do....		79	79	156	183	156	156	156	156	156	156	79	79	79	79	156	183	183	156	156	124	124
..do....		79	79	125	146	125	125	125	125	125	125	79	79	79	79	125	146	146	125	125	117	117
..do....		79	79	156	183	156	156	156	156	156	156	79	79	79	79	156	183	183	156	156	124	124
..do....		48	48	58	65	58	58	58	58	58	58	48	48	48	48	58	65	65	58	58	53	53
..do....		83	83	166	199	166	166	166	166	166	166	83	83	83	83	166	199	199	166	166	135	135
..do....		79	79	156	183	156	156	156	156	156	156	79	79	79	79	156	183	183	156	156	124	124
..do....		45	45	45	45	45	45	45	45	45	45	45	45	45	45	45	45	45	45	45	45	45
..do....		79	79	156	156	156	156	156	156	156	156	79	79	79	79	156	156	156	156	156	124	124
..do....		79	79	156	156	Special		156	156	156	156	79	79	79	79	156	156	156	156	156	124	124
..do....		79	79	156	183	..do....		156	156	156	156	79	79	79	79	156	183	156	156	156	124	124
..do....		45	45	45	45	..do....		45	45	45	45	45	45	45	45	45	45	45	45	45	45	45
..do....		30	30	30	30	..do....		30	30	30	30	30	30	30	30	30	30	30	30	30	30	30
..do....		38	38	38	38	..do....		38	38	38	38	38	38	38	38	38	38	38	38	38	38	38
..do....		42	42	42	42	..do....		42	42	42	42	42	42	42	42	42	42	42	42	42	42	42
..do....		37	37	37	37	..do....		37	37	37	37	37	37	37	37	37	37	37	37	37	37	37
..do....		50	50	50	50	..do....		50	50	50	50	50	50	50	50	50	50	50	50	50	50	50
..do....		50	50	73	73	..do....		73	73	73	73	50	50	50	50	73	73	73	73	73	73	73
..do....		64	64	98	122	..do....		98	98	98	98	64	64	64	64	98	122	122	98	98	74	74
..do....		79	79	123	137	..do....		123	123	123	123	79	79	79	79	123	137	137	123	123	98	98
..do....		79	79	127	148	..do....		127	127	127	127	79	70	79	79	127	148	148	127	127	98	98
..do....		79	79	127	148	..do....		127	127	127	127	79	79	79	79	127	148	148	127	127	98	98
..do....		Special		127	148	..do....		127	127	127	127	79	79	79	79	127	148	148	127	127	98	98
..do....		..do....		83	104	..do....		83	83	83	83	53	53	53	53	83	104	104	83	83	67	67
..do....		..do....		67	78	..do....		67	67	67	67	47	47	47	47	67	78	78	67	67	57	57
..do....		..do....		67	74	..do....		67	67	67	67	47	47	47	47	67	71	74	67	67	57	57
..do....		..do....		65	70	..do....		65	65	65	65	47	47	47	47	65	70	70	65	65	57	57
..do....		..do....		56	63	..do....		56	56	56	56	42	42	42	42	56	63	63	56	56	52	52
..do....		..do....		47	47	..do....		47	47	47	47	42	42	42	42	47	47	47	47	47	47	47
..do....		..do....		47	47	..do....		47	47	47	47	47	47	47	47	47	47	47	47	47	47	47
..do....		..do....		83	92	..do....		83	83	83	83	53	53	53	53	83	92	92	83	83	67	67
..do....		..do....		108	122	..do....		108	108	108	108	64	64	64	64	108	122	122	108	108	83	83
..do....		..do....		122	151	..do....		122	122	122	122	61	61	61	61	122	151	151	122	122	96	96
75	75	75	75	142	171	142	142	142	142	142	142	75	75	75	75	142	171	171	142	142	113	113
67	67	67	67	122	142	52	52	122	122	122	122	52	52	67	67	122	142	142	122	122	96	96
53	53	53	53	83	92	42	42	83	83	83	83	42	42	53	53	83	92	92	83	83	67	67
52	52	52	52	85	96	44	44	85	85	85	85	44	44	52	52	85	96	96	85	85	67	67
42	42	42	42	61	71	35	35	61	61	61	61	35	35	42	42	61	71	71	61	61	48	48
52	52	52	52	85	96	44	44	85	85	85	85	44	44	52	52	85	96	96	85	85	67	67
42	42	42	42	61	71	35	35	61	61	61	61	35	35	42	42	61	71	71	61	61	48	48
38	38	38	38	52	57	30	30	52	52	52	52	30	30	38	38	52	57	57	52	52	43	43
42	42	42	42	45	45	32	32	45	45	45	45	32	32	42	42	45	45	45	45	45	45	45
38	38	38	38	38	38	27	27	38	38	38	38	27	27	38	38	38	38	38	38	38	38	38
33	33	33	33	33	33	25	25	33	33	33	33	25	25	33	33	33	33	33	33	33	33	38
29	29	29	29	29	29	24	24	29	29	29	29	24	24	29	29	29	29	29	29	29	29	29
52	52	52	52	85	96	44	44	85	85	85	85	44	44	52	52	85	96	96	85	85	67	67
62	62	62	62	104	118	104	104	104	104	104	104	47	47	62	62	104	118	118	104	104	80	80
62	62	47	47	104	118	104	104	104	104	104	104	47	47	62	62	104	118	118	104	104	80	80
43	43	33	33	66	71	66	66	66	66	66	66	33	33	43	43	66	71	71	66	66	57	57
62	62	47	47	104	118	104	104	104	104	104	104	47	47	62	62	104	118	118	104	104	80	80
52	52	43	43	85	95	85	85	85	85	85	85	43	43	52	52	85	95	95	85	85	66	66
62	62	47	47	104	118	47	47	104	104	104	104	47	47	62	62	104	118	118	104	104	80	80
57	57	43	43	85	95	43	43	85	85	85	85	43	43	57	57	85	Sp'l	57	85	85	71	71
43	43	33	33	66	71	33	33	66	66	66	66	33	33	43	43	66	.do .	43	66	66	57	57
28	28	28	28	38	38	28	28	38	38	38	38	28	28	28	28	38	.do .	28	38	38	28	28
30	30	30	30	40	40	30	30	40	40	40	40	30	30	30	30	30	.do .	30	40	40	30	30
28	28	28	28	38	38	28	28	38	38	38	38	28	28	28	28	38	.do .	28	38	38	28	28
43	43	33	33	66	71	33	33	66	66	66	66	33	33	43	43	66	.do .	43	66	66	57	57
57	57	43	43	85	95	43	43	85	85	85	85	43	43	57	57	85	.do .	57	85	85	71	71
43	43	33	33	66	71	33	33	66	66	66	66	33	33	43	43	66	.do .	43	66	66	57	57
57	57	43	43	85	95	43	43	85	85	85	85	43	43	57	57	85	.do .	57	85	85	71	71
57	57	43	43	85	95	43	43	85	85	85	85	43	43	57	57	85	.do .	57	85	85	71	71

TABLE 29.—RATES OF FREIGHT, ALL RAIL, FROM

DISTANCE VIA SHORTEST ROUTE.—From New York, 825 miles;

[NOTE.—Where the rates showed are not specifically described as applying on less

Date.	Commodities (rates in cents per 100 pounds.)																	
				Furniture.		Stoves.		Coffee.		Soap.				Starch.			Sugar.	
										Castile and fancy.		Common.						
	Dry goods	Cotton piece goods.	Boots and shoes.	Less than carloads.	Carloads.	Less than carloads.	Carloads.	Less than carloads.	Carloads.	Less than carloads.	Carloads.	Less than carloads.	Carloads.	Less than carloads.	Carload.	Tea.	Less than carloads.	Carloads.
1875—Mar. 17.....	71	71	71	71	71	71	71	28	28	66	66	43	43	57	57	71	28	28
Apr. 6.....	57	57	57	57	57	57	57	28	28	52	52	38	38	47	47	57	28	28
May 18.....	51	51	51	51	51	51	51	25	25	47	47	34	34	42	42	51	25	25
May 29.....	28	28	28	28	28	28	28	19	19	28	28	24	24	26	26	28	19	19
Aug. 12.....	47	47	47	47	47	47	47	19	19	38	38	24	24	28	28	47	19	19
Nov. 15.....	71	71	71	71	71	71	71	33	33	66	66	43	43	57	57	71	33	33
Dec. 22.....	30	30	30	30	30	30	30	15	15	25	25	20	20	20	20	30	15	15
1876—Jan. 10.....	71	71	71	71	71	71	71	33	33	66	66	43	43	57	57	71	33	33
June 2.....	71	71	71	71	71	71	71	20	20	66	66	25	25	57	57	71	20	20
June 12.....	25	25	15	25	25	25	25	16	16	25	25	16	16	25	25	25	16	16
July 28.....	15	15	15	15	15	15	15	10	10	15	15	10	10	15	15	15	10	10
Aug. 7.....	25	25	25	25	25	25	25	16	16	25	25	16	16	25	25	25	16	16
Dec. 18.....	47	47	47	47	47	47	47	24	24	43	43	28	28	38	38	47	24	24
1877—Mar. 12.....	71	71	71	71	71	71	71	33	33	66	66	43	43	57	57	71	33	33
Oct. 8.....	71	71	71	71	71	71	38	38	38	66	66	38	38	38	38	71	38	38
Oct. 22.....	95	95	95	95	95	95	43	43	43	85	85	43	43	43	43	95	43	43
Dec. 10.....	95	95	95	95	95	95	43	43	43	76	76	43	43	43	43	95	43	43
1878—Feb. 15.....	71	71	71	71	71	71	38	38	38	57	57	38	38	38	38	71	38	38
1881—Aug. 6.....	43	43	43	43	43	43	18	18	18	30	30	18	18	18	18	43	18	18
Nov. 14.....	57	57	57	57	57	57	27	27	27	47	47	27	27	27	27	57	27	27
1882—Jan. 24.....	43	43	43	43	43	43	18	18	18	32	32	18	18	18	18	43	18	18
July 1.....	57	57	57	57	57	57	28	28	28	47	47	28	28	28	28	57	24	24
Nov. 1....	71	71	71	71	71	71	33	33	33	57	57	33	33	33	33	71	33	33
1883—June 22.....	71	71	71	71	71	71	33	33	33	57	57	33	33	33	33	71	24	24
1885—Jan. 26.....	47	47	47	47	47	47	24	24	24	38	38	24	24	24	24	47	17	17
June 1.....	38	38	38	38	38	38	17	17	17	28	28	17	17	17	17	38	14	14
Oct. 5.....	57	57	57	57	57	57	24	24	24	47	47	24	24	24	24	57	19	19
Nov. 18.....	71	71	71	71	71	71	33	33	33	57	57	33	33	33	33	71	24	24
1886—Mar. 10.....	70	70	70	70	70	70	33	33	33	56	56	33	33	33	33	70	23	23
Aug. 26.....	70	47	70	70	70	70	33	33	33	56	56	33	33	33	33	70	23	23
1887—Apr. 1.....	70	47	70	70	60	47	28	33	23	60	60	33	28	33	23	70	33	23
1888—Jan. 9.....	70	47	70	70	60	47	31	36	26	60	60	36	31	36	31	70	36	26
Mar. 5.....	70	47	70	70	60	47	28	33	23	60	60	33	28	33	23	70	33	23
Nov. 12.....	47	33	47	47	37	33	23	28	19	37	37	28	23	28	19	47	28	19
Dec. 17.....	70	47	70	70	60	47	28	33	23	60	60	33	28	33	23	70	33	23
1891—Apr. 9.....	70	47	70	70	60	28	23	33	23	60	60	33	23	33	23	70	33	23
1892—Mar. 16.....	70	47	70	70	60	28	23	33	23	33	23	33	23	33	23	70	33	20
May 2.....	70	47	70	70	60	28	23	33	23	33	23	33	23	33	23	70	33	23
June 6.....	70	47	70	70	60	28	23	33	23	33	23	33	23	33	23	70	33	21

NEW YORK, N. Y., TO INDIANAPOLIS, IND.—Continued.

Boston, 946 miles; Philadelphia, 735 miles; Baltimore, 708 miles.

than carload or carload quanties they apply on shipments regardless of quantity.]

Commodities (rates in cents per 100 pounds).																						
Molasses.		Rice.				Crockery and earthenware.		Bagging.		Leather		Lead.		Nails.			Agricultural implements		Machinery.		Beer.	
Less than carloads.	Carloads.	Less than carloads.	Carloads.	Groceries.	Drugs.	Less than carloads.	Carloads.	Less than carload.	Carloads.	Less than carloads.	Carloads.	Less than carloads.	Carloads.	Less than carloads.	Carloads.	Hardware.	Less than carloads.	Carloads.	Less than carloads.	Carloads.	Less than carloads.	Carloads.
28	28	33	33	66	71	33	33	66	66	66	66	33	33	43	43	66	Sp'l	43	66	66	57	57
38	38	28	28	52	57	28	28	52	52	52	52	28	28	38	38	52	.do .	38	52	52	47	47
34	34	27	27	47	51	27	27	47	47	47	27	27	27	34	34	47	.do .	34	47	47	42	42
24	24	19	19	28	28	19	19	28	28	28	28	19	19	24	24	28	.do .	24	28	28	26	26
24	24	19	19	38	47	19	19	38	38	38	38	19	19	24	24	38	.do .	24	38	38	28	28
43	43	33	33	66	71	33	33	66	66	66	66	33	33	43	43	66	.do .	43	66	66	57	57
20	20	15	15	25	30	15	15	25	25	25	25	15	15	20	20	25	.do .	20	25	25	20	20
43	43	33	33	66	71	33	33	66	66	66	66	33	33	43	43	66	.do .	43	66	66	57	57
25	25	20	20	66	71	20	20	66	66	66	66	20	20	25	25	66	.do .	25	66	66	57	57
16	16	16	16	25	25	16	16	25	25	25	25	16	16	16	16	25	.do .	16	25	25	25	25
10	10	10	10	15	15	10	10	15	15	15	13	10	10	10	10	15	.do .	10	15	15	15	25
16	16	16	16	25	25	16	16	25	25	25	25	16	16	16	16	25	.do .	16	25	25	25	25
28	28	24	24	43	47	24	24	43	43	43	43	24	24	28	28	43	.do .	28	43	43	38	38
43	43	33	33	66	71	33	33	66	66	66	66	33	33	43	43	66	.do .	43	66	66	57	57
38	38	38	38	66	71	38	38	38	38	66	66	38	38	38	*38	66	.do .	38	66	38	58	38
43	43	43	43	85	95	43	43	43	43	85	85	43	43	43	43	85	.do .	43	85	43	43	43
43	43	43	43	76	95	43	43	43	43	76	76	43	43	43	43	76	.do .	43	76	43	43	43
38	38	38	38	57	71	38	38	38	38	57	57	38	38	38	38	57	.do .	38	57	38	38	38
18	18	18	18	30	43	18	18	18	18	30	30	18	18	18	18	30	.do .	18	30	18	18	18
27	27	27	27	47	57	27	27	27	27	47	47	27	27	27	27	47	.do .	27	47	27	27	27
18	18	18	18	32	43	18	18	18	18	32	32	18	18	18	18	32	.do .	18	32	18	18	18
28	28	28	28	47	57	28	28	28	28	47	47	28	28	28	28	47	.do .	28	47	28	28	28
33	33	33	33	57	71	33	33	33	33	57	57	33	33	33	33	57	.do .	33	57	33	33	33
24	24	33	33	57	71	33	33	33	33	57	57	33	33	33	33	57	.do .	33	57	33	33	33
17	17	24	24	38	47	24	24	24	24	38	38	24	24	24	24	38	.do .	24	38	24	24	24
14	14	17	17	28	38	17	17	17	17	28	28	17	17	17	17	28	.do .	17	28	17	17	17
19	19	24	24	47	57	24	24	24	24	47	47	24	24	24	24	47	.do .	24	47	24	24	24
24	24	33	33	57	71	33	33	33	33	57	57	33	33	33	33	57	.do .	33	57	33	33	33
23	23	33	33	56	70	33	33	33	33	56	56	33	33	33	33	56	.do .	33	56	33	33	33
23	23	33	33	56	70	33	33	33	33	56	56	33	33	33	33	56	.do .	33	56	33	33	33
33	28	33	33	60	70	33	28	47	33	47	33	33	23	33	28	60	47	28	33	28	47	28
36	31	36	26	60	70	36	31	47	36	47	36	36	31	36	31	60	47	31	36	31	47	31
33	28	33	23	60	70	33	28	47	33	47	33	33	23	33	28	60	47	28	33	28	47	28
28	23	28	19	37	47	28	23	33	28	33	28	28	19	28	23	37	33	23	28	23	33	23
33	23	33	23	60	70	33	28	47	33	47	33	33	23	33	28	60	47	28	33	28	47	28
33	28	33	23	60	70	33	28	47	33	47	33	33	23	28	23	60	47	28	33	28	47	28
33	28	33	23	60	70	33	28	47	33	47	33	33	23	28	23	60	47	28	33	28	47	28
33	28	33	23	60	70	33	28	47	33	47	33	33	23	28	23	60	47	28	33	28	47	28
33	28	33	23	60	70	33	28	47	33	47	33	33	23	28	23	60	47	28	33	28	47	28

TABLE 30.—RATES OF FREIGHT, ALL RAIL, FROM

DISTANCE VIA SHORTEST ROUTE.—From New York, 637 miles;

[NOTE.—Where the rates shown are not specifically described as applying on less

Date.		Commodities (rates in cents per 100 pounds).																	
					Furniture.		Stoves.		Coffee.		Soaps.				Starch.			Sugar.	
											Castile and fancy.		Common.						
		Dry Goods.	Cotton piece goods.	Boots and shoes.	Less than carloads.	Carloads.	Less than carloads.	Carloads.	Less than carloads.	Carloads.	Less than carloads.	Carloads.	Less than carloads.	Carloads.	Less than carloads.	Carloads.	Tea.	Less than carloads.	Carloads.
1867—Jan.	1.....	153	153	153	153	153	153	153	131	131	131	131	104	104	131	131	153	67	67
Nov.	1.....	166	166	166	166	166	166	166	140	140	140	140	114	114	140	140	166	70	70
1868—Feb.	4.....	166	166	166	166	166	166	166	Special rate.		140	140	70	70	114	114	166	Special rate.	
June	4.....	153	153	153	153	153	153	153	..do....		131	131	67	67	104	104	153	..do....	
Aug.	10.....	123	123	123	123	123	123	123	..do....		105	105	67	67	98	98	123	..do....	
Sep.	7.....	153	153	153	153	153	153	153	..do....		131	131	67	67	104	104	153	..do....	
Oct.	1.....	60	60	60	60	60	60	60	..do....		56	56	45	45	50	50	60	..do....	
Dec.	7.....	166	166	166	166	166	166	166	..do....		140	140	70	70	114	114	166	..do....	
1869—Feb.	1.....	153	153	153	153	153	153	153	..do....		131	131	67	67	104	104	153	..do....	
	17.....	38	38	38	38	38	38	38	..do....		38	38	38	38	38	38	38	..do....	
Mar.	15	131	131	131	131	131	131	131	..do....		131	131	67	67	104	104	131	..do....	
May	12.....	131	131	131	131	131	131	131	..do....		131	131	67	67	104	104	131	..do....	
July	1.....	153	153	153	153	153	153	153	..do....		131	131	67	67	104	104	153	..do....	
Aug.	11.....	26	26	26	26	26	26	26	..do....		26	26	26	26	26	26	26	..do....	
	23.....	32	32	32	32	32	32	32	..do....		32	32	32	32	32	32	32	..do....	
	30.....	35	35	35	35	35	35	35	..do....		35	35	35	35	35	35	35	..do....	
Sept.	22.....	32	32	32	32	32	32	32	..do....		32	32	32	32	32	32	32	..do....	
	24.....	30	30	30	30	30	30	30	..do....		30	30	30	30	30	30	30	..do....	
Oct.	4.....	42	42	42	42	42	42	42	..do....		42	42	42	42	42	42	42	..do....	
	9.....	61	61	61	61	61	61	61	..do....		61	61	41	41	61	61	61	..do....	
	13.....	103	103	103	103	103	103	103	..do....		82	82	52	52	62	62	103	..do....	
Nov.	1.....	115	115	115	115	115	115	115	..do....		103	103	67	67	82	82	115	..do....	
	29.....	124	124	124	124	124	124	124	..do....		107	107	67	67	82	82	124	..do....	
1870—Apr.	14.....	124	124	124	124	124	124	124	..do....		107	107	67	67	82	82	124	32	32
May	7.....	124	124	124	124	124	124	124	..do....		107	107	67	67	82	82	124	32	32
June	18.....	87	87	87	87	87	87	87	..do....		70	70	44	44	56	56	87	32	32
July	13.....	65	65	65	65	65	65	65	..do....		56	56	39	39	48	48	65	32	32
	21.....	60	60	60	60	60	60	60	..do....		55	55	39	39	48	48	60	32	32
	25.....	53	53	53	53	53	53	53	..do....		46	46	35	35	43	43	53	32	32
	28.....	40	40	40	40	40	40	40	..do....		40	40	35	35	40	40	40	32	32
Aug.	12.....	40	40	40	40	40	40	40	..do....		40	40	35	35	40	40	40	Special rate.	
	22.....	77	....	77	77	77	77	77	..do....		70	70	44	44	56	56	77	..do....	
Sept.	8.....	103	103	103	103	103	103	103	..do....		91	91	54	54	70	70	103	..do ...	
Nov.	28.....	127	127	127	127	127	127	127	..do....		103	103	51	51	81	81	127	..do....	
Dec.	26.....	144	144	144	144	144	144	144	48	48	120	120	63	63	95	95	144	48	48
1871—Feb.	20.....	120	120	120	120	120	120	120	44	44	103	103	56	56	81	81	120	44	44
Mar.	7.....	77	77	77	77	77	77	77	35	35	70	70	44	44	56	56	77	35	35
	13.....	81	81	81	81	81	81	81	37	37	72	72	44	44	56	56	81	37	37
May	18.....	60	60	60	60	60	60	60	29	29	51	51	35	35	40	40	60	29	29
June	1.....	81	81	81	81	81	81	81	37	37	72	72	44	44	56	56	81	37	37
July	8.....	60	60	60	60	60	60	60	29	29	51	51	51	51	40	40	60	29	29
	26.....	48	48	48	48	48	48	48	26	26	44	44	32	32	37	37	48	26	26
	28.....	40	40	40	40	40	40	40	29	29	40	40	35	35	40	40	40	29	29
Aug.	16.....	32	32	32	32	32	32	32	23	23	32	32	32	32	32	32	32	23	23
	22.....	28	28	28	28	28	28	28	21	21	28	28	28	28	28	28	28	21	21
Sept.	1.....	23	23	28	23	23	23	23	20	20	23	23	23	23	23	23	23	20	20
Nov.	27.....	81	81	81	81	81	81	81	37	37	72	72	44	44	56	56	81	37	37
Dec.	15.....	100	100	100	100	100	100	100	40	40	88	88	52	52	68	68	100	40	40
1872—Apr.	27.....	100	100	100	100	100	100	100	40	40	88	88	52	52	68	68	100	40	40
Aug.	1.....	60	60	60	60	60	60	60	28	28	56	56	36	36	48	48	60	28	28
Sept.	1.....	100	100	100	100	100	100	100	40	40	88	88	52	52	68	68	100	40	40
	2.....	80	80	80	80	80	80	80	36	36	72	72	44	44	56	56	80	36	36
Oct.	14.....	100	100	100	100	100	100	100	40	40	88	88	52	52	68	68	100	40	40
1873—Apr.	14.....	80	80	80	80	80	80	80	36	36	72	72	48	48	60	60	80	36	36
June	11.....	60	60	60	60	60	60	60	28	28	56	56	36	36	48	48	60	28	28
Aug.	11.....	32	32	32	32	32	32	32	24	24	32	32	24	24	24	24	32	24	24
	12.....	40	40	40	40	40	40	40	30	30	40	40	30	30	30	30	40	30	30
	21.....	32	32	32	32	32	32	32	24	24	32	32	24	24	24	24	32	24	24
Sept.	17.....	60	60	60	60	60	60	60	28	28	56	56	36	36	48	48	60	28	28
1874—Jan.	1.....	80	80	80	80	80	80	80	36	36	72	72	48	48	60	60	80	36	36
Aug.	3.....	60	60	60	60	60	60	60	28	28	56	56	36	36	48	48	60	28	28

NEW YORK, N. Y., TO COLUMBUS, OHIO.

Boston, 801 miles; Philadelphia, 547 miles; Baltimore, 526 miles.

than carload or carload quantities they apply on shipments regardless of quantity.]

Commodities (rates in cents per 100 pounds).																						
Molasses.		Rice.				Crockery and earthenware.		Bagging.		Leather.		Lead.		Nails.			Agricultural implements.		Machinery.		Beer.	
Less than carloads.	Carloads.	Less than carloads.	Carloads.	Groceries.	Drugs.	Less than carloads.	Carloads.	Less than carloads.	Carloads.	Less than carloads.	Carloads.	Less than carloads.	Carloads.	Less than carloads.	Carloads.	Hardware.	Less than carloads.	Carloads.	Less than carloads.	Carloads.	Less than carloads.	Carloads.
67	67	67	67	131	153	131	131	131	131	131	131	67	67	67	67	131	153	153	131	131	104	104
70	70	70	70	140	166	140	140	140	140	140	140	70	70	70	70	140	166	166	140	140	114	114
Special rate.		70	70	140	166	140	140	140	140	140	140	70	70	70	70	140	166	166	140	140	114	114
..do....		67	67	131	153	131	131	131	131	131	131	67	67	67	67	131	153	153	131	131	104	104
..do....		67	67	105	123	105	105	105	105	105	105	67	67	67	67	105	123	123	105	105	98	98
..do....		67	67	131	153	131	131	131	131	131	131	67	67	67	67	131	153	153	131	131	104	104
..do....		45	45	56	60	56	56	56	56	56	56	45	45	45	45	56	60	60	56	56	50	50
..do....		70	70	140	166	140	140	140	140	140	140	70	70	70	70	140	166	166	140	140	114	114
..do....		67	67	131	153	131	131	131	131	131	131	67	67	67	67	131	153	153	131	131	104	104
..do....		38	38	38	38	38	38	38	38	38	38	38	38	38	38	38	38	38	38	38	38	38
..do....		67	67	131	131	131	131	131	131	131	131	67	67	67	67	131	131	131	131	131	104	104
..do....		67	67	131	131	Special rate.		131	131	131	131	67	67	67	67	131	131	131	131	131	104	104
..do....		67	67	131	153	..do....		136	131	131	131	67	67	67	67	131	153	153	131	131	104	104
..do....		26	26	26	26	..do....		26	26	26	26	26	26	26	26	26	26	26	26	26	26	26
..do....		32	32	32	32	..do....		32	32	32	32	32	32	32	32	32	32	32	32	32	32	32
..do....		35	35	35	35	..do....		35	35	35	35	35	35	35	35	35	35	35	35	35	35	35
..do....		32	32	32	32	..do....		32	32	32	32	32	32	32	32	32	32	32	32	32	32	32
..do....		30	30	30	30	..do....		30	30	30	30	30	30	30	30	30	30	30	30	30	30	30
..do....		42	42	42	42	..do....		42	42	42	42	42	42	42	42	42	42	42	42	42	42	42
..do....		42	42	61	61	..do....		61	61	61	61	42	42	42	42	61	61	61	61	61	61	61
..do....		52	52	82	103	..do....		82	82	82	82	52	52	52	52	82	103	103	82	82	62	62
..do....		67	67	103	115	..do....		103	103	103	103	67	67	67	67	103	115	115	103	103	82	82
..do....		67	67	107	124	..do....		107	107	107	107	67	67	67	67	107	124	124	107	107	82	82
..do....		67	67	107	124	..do....		107	107	107	107	67	67	67	67	107	124	124	107	107	82	82
..do....		Special rate.		107	124	..do....		107	107	107	107	67	67	67	67	107	124	124	107	107	82	82
..do....		..do....		70	87	..do....		70	70	70	70	44	44	44	44	70	87	87	70	70	56	56
..do....		..do....		56	65	..do....		56	56	56	56	39	39	39	39	56	65	65	56	56	48	48
..do....		..do....		55	60	..do....		55	55	55	55	39	39	39	39	55	60	60	55	55	48	48
..do....		..do....		46	53	..do....		46	46	46	46	35	35	35	35	46	53	53	46	46	43	43
..do....		..do....		40	40	..do....		40	40	40	40	35	35	35	35	40	40	40	40	40	40	40
..do....		..do....		40	40	..do....		40	40	40	40	40	40	40	40	40	40	40	40	40	40	40
..do....		..do....		70	77	..do....		70	70	70	70	44	44	44	44	70	77	77	70	70	56	56
..do....		..do....		91	103	..do....		91	91	91	91	54	54	54	54	91	103	103	91	91	70	70
..do....		..do....		103	127	..do....		103	103	103	103	51	51	51	51	103	127	127	103	103	81	81
63	63	63	63	120	144	120	120	120	120	120	120	63	63	63	63	120	144	144	120	120	95	95
56	56	56	56	103	120	103	103	103	103	103	103	44	44	56	56	103	120	120	103	103	81	81
44	44	44	44	70	77	70	70	70	70	70	70	35	35	44	44	70	77	77	70	70	56	56
44	44	44	44	72	81	72	72	72	72	72	72	37	37	44	44	72	81	81	72	72	56	56
35	35	35	35	51	60	29	29	51	51	51	51	29	29	35	35	51	60	60	51	51	40	40
44	44	44	44	72	81	37	37	72	72	72	72	37	37	44	44	72	81	81	72	72	56	56
51	51	51	51	51	60	29	29	51	51	51	29	29	29	51	51	51	60	60	51	51	40	40
32	32	32	32	44	48	26	26	44	44	44	44	26	26	32	32	44	48	48	44	44	37	37
35	35	35	35	40	40	29	29	40	40	40	40	29	29	35	35	40	40	40	40	40	40	40
32	32	32	32	32	32	23	23	32	32	32	32	23	23	32	32	32	32	32	32	32	32	32
28	28	28	28	28	28	21	21	28	28	28	28	21	21	28	28	28	28	28	28	28	28	28
23	23	23	23	23	23	20	20	23	23	23	23	20	20	23	23	23	23	23	23	23	23	23
44	44	44	44	72	81	37	37	72	72	72	72	37	37	44	44	72	81	81	72	72	56	56
52	52	52	52	88	100	88	88	88	88	88	88	40	40	52	52	88	100	100	88	88	68	68
52	52	40	40	88	100	88	88	88	88	88	88	40	40	52	52	88	100	100	88	88	68	68
36	36	28	28	56	60	56	56	56	56	56	56	28	28	36	36	56	60	60	56	56	48	48
52	52	40	40	88	100	88	88	88	88	88	88	40	40	52	52	88	100	100	88	88	68	68
44	44	36	36	72	80	72	72	72	72	72	72	36	36	44	44	72	80	80	72	72	56	56
52	52	40	40	88	100	40	40	88	88	88	88	40	40	52	52	88	100	100	88	88	68	68
48	48	36	36	72	80	36	36	72	72	72	72	36	36	48	48	72	Sp'l rate.	48	72	72	60	60
36	36	28	28	56	60	28	28	56	56	56	56	28	28	36	36	56	.do .	36	56	56	48	48
24	24	24	24	32	32	24	24	32	32	32	32	24	24	24	24	32	.do .	24	32	32	24	24
30	30	30	30	40	40	30	30	40	40	40	40	30	30	30	30	40	.do .	30	40	40	30	30
24	24	24	24	32	32	24	24	32	32	32	32	24	24	24	24	32	.do .	24	32	32	24	24
36	36	28	28	56	60	28	28	56	56	56	56	28	28	36	36	56	.do .	36	56	56	48	48
48	48	36	36	72	80	36	36	72	72	72	72	36	36	48	48	72	.do .	48	72	72	60	60
36	36	28	28	56	60	28	28	56	56	56	56	28	28	36	36	56	.do .	36	56	56	48	48

TABLE 30.—RATES OF FREIGHT, ALL RAIL, FROM

DISTANCE VIA SHORTEST ROUTE.—From New York, 637 miles;

[NOTE.—Where the rates shown are not specficially described as applying on less

Date.		Commodities (rates in cents per 100 pounds.)																		
		Dry goods.	Cotton piece goods.	Boots and shoes.	Furniture.		Stoves.		Coffee.		Soaps. Castile and fancy.		Soaps. Common.		Starch.		Tea.	Sugar.	
					Less than carloads.	Carloads.	Less than carloads.	Carloads.	Less than carloads.	Carloads.	Less than carloads.	Carloads.	Less than carloads.	Carloads.	Less than carloads.	Carloads.		Less than carloads.	Carloads.
1875—Jan.	20	80	80	80	80	80	80	80	36	36	72	72	48	48	60	60	80	36	36
Feb.	23	80	80	80	80	80	80	80	24	24	72	72	48	48	60	60	80	24	24
Mar.	17	60	60	60	60	60	60	60	24	24	56	56	36	36	48	48	60	24	24
Apr.	6	48	48	48	48	48	48	48	24	24	44	44	32	32	40	40	48	24	24
May	18	43	43	43	43	43	43	43	22	22	40	40	29	29	36	36	43	22	22
	29	27	27	27	27	27	27	27	18	18	27	27	20	20	25	25	27	18	18
Aug.	12	40	40	40	40	40	40	40	16	16	32	32	20	20	25	25	40	16	16
Nov.	15	60	60	60	60	60	60	60	28	28	56	56	36	36	48	48	60	28	28
Dec.	22	30	30	30	30	30	30	30	15	15	25	25	20	20	20	20	30	15	15
1876—Jan.	10	60	60	60	60	60	60	60	28	28	56	56	36	36	48	48	60	28	28
June	2	60	60	60	60	60	60	60	20	20	56	56	25	25	48	48	60	20	20
	12	25	25	25	25	25	25	25	16	16	25	25	16	16	25	25	25	16	16
July	28	15	15	15	15	15	15	15	10	10	15	15	15	15	15	15	15	10	10
Aug.	7	25	25	25	25	25	25	25	16	16	25	25	16	16	25	25	25	16	16
Dec.	18	40	40	40	40	40	40	40	20	20	36	36	25	25	32	32	40	20	20
1877—Mar.	12	60	60	60	60	60	60	60	28	28	56	56	36	36	48	48	60	28	28
Oct.	8	60	60	60	60	60	60	32	32	32	56	56	32	32	32	32	60	32	32
	22	80	80	80	80	80	80	36	36	36	72	72	36	36	36	36	80	36	36
Dec.	10	80	80	80	80	80	80	36	36	36	64	64	36	36	36	36	80	36	36
1878—Feb.	15	60	60	60	60	60	60	32	32	32	48	48	32	32	32	32	60	32	32
1881—Aug.	6	36	36	36	36	36	36	15	15	15	26	26	15	15	15	15	36	15	15
Nov.	14	48	48	48	48	48	48	22	22	22	40	40	22	22	22	22	48	22	22
1882—Jan.	24	39	39	39	39	39	39	18	18	18	32	32	18	18	18	18	39	18	18
July	1	48	48	48	48	48	48	24	24	24	40	40	24	24	24	24	48	20	20
Nov.	1	60	60	60	60	60	60	28	28	28	48	48	28	28	28	28	60	28	28
1883—June	22	60	60	60	60	60	60	28	28	28	48	48	28	28	28	28	60	20	20
1885—Jan.	26	40	40	40	40	40	40	20	20	20	32	32	20	20	20	20	40	14	14
June	1	32	32	32	32	32	32	14	14	14	24	24	14	14	14	14	32	12	12
Oct.	5	48	48	48	48	48	48	20	20	20	40	40	20	20	20	20	48	16	16
Nov.	18	60	60	60	60	60	60	28	28	28	48	48	28	28	28	28	60	20	20
1886—Mar.	10	58	58	58	58	58	58	27	27	27	46	46	27	27	27	27	58	19	19
Aug.	26	58	39	58	58	58	58	27	27	27	46	46	27	27	27	27	58	19	19
1887—Apr.	1	58	39	58	58	58	39	23	27	19	50	50	27	23	27	19	58	27	19
June	13	59	39	59	59	51	39	23	27	23	51	51	27	23	27	20	59	27	20
1888—Jan.	9	59	39	59	59	51	39	26	30	21	51	51	30	26	30	21	59	30	21
Mar.	5	59	39	59	59	51	39	23	27	20	51	51	27	23	27	20	59	27	20
Nov.	12	39	27	39	39	31	27	20	23	16	31	31	23	20	23	16	39	23	16
Dec.	17	59	39	59	59	51	39	23	27	20	51	51	27	23	27	20	59	27	20
1891—Apr.	9	59	39	59	59	51	23	20	27	20	27	20	27	20	27	20	59	27	20
1892—Mar.	16	59	39	59	59	51	23	20	27	20	27	20	27	20	27	20	59	27	16
May	2	59	39	59	59	51	23	20	27	20	27	20	27	20	27	20	59	27	20
June	6	59	39	59	59	51	23	20	27	20	27	20	27	20	27	20	59	27	18

NEW YORK, N. Y., TO COLUMBUS, OHIO—Continued.

Boston, 801 miles; Philadelphia, 547 miles; Baltimore, 526 miles.

than carload or carload quantities they apply on shipments regardless of quantity.]

Commodities (rates in cents 100 pounds.)																									
Molasses.		Rice.				Crockery and earthenware.		Bagging.		Leather		Lead.		Nails.			Agricultural implements		Machinery.		Beer.	
Less than carloads.	Carloads.	Less than carloads.	Carloads.	Groceries.	Drugs.	Less than carloads.	Carloads.	Less than carloads.	Carloads.	Less than carloads.	Carloads.	Less than carloads.	Csrloads.	Less than carloads.	Carloads.	Hardware.	Less than carloads.	Carloads.	Less than carloads.	Carloads.	Less than carloads.	Carloads.
48	48	36	36	72	80	36	36	72	72	72	72	36	36	48	48	72	Sp'l rate.	48	72	72	60	60
48	48	36	36	72	80	36	36	72	72	72	72	36	36	48	48	72	.do.	48	72	72	60	60
24	24	28	28	56	60	28	28	56	56	56	56	28	28	36	36	56	.do.	36	56	56	48	48
32	32	24	24	44	48	24	24	44	44	44	44	24	24	32	32	44	.do.	32	44	44	40	40
29	29	23	23	40	43	23	23	40	40	40	40	23	23	29	29	40	.do.	29	40	40	36	36
28	28	18	18	27	27	18	18	27	27	27	27	18	18	20	20	27	.do.	20	27	27	25	25
20	20	16	16	32	40	16	16	32	32	32	32	16	16	20	20	32	.do.	20	32	32	25	25
36	36	28	28	56	60	28	28	56	56	56	56	28	28	36	36	56	.do.	36	56	56	48	48
20	20	15	15	25	30	15	15	25	25	25	25	15	15	20	20	25	.do.	20	25	25	20	20
36	36	28	28	56	60	28	28	56	56	56	56	28	28	36	36	56	.do.	36	56	56	48	48
25	25	20	20	56	60	20	20	56	56	56	56	20	20	25	25	56	.do.	25	56	56	48	48
16	16	16	16	25	25	16	16	25	25	25	25	16	16	16	16	25	.do.	16	25	25	25	25
10	10	10	10	15	15	10	10	15	15	15	15	10	10	10	10	15	.do.	10	15	15	15	15
16	16	16	16	25	25	16	16	25	25	25	25	16	16	16	16	25	.do.	16	25	25	25	25
25	25	20	20	36	40	20	20	36	36	36	36	20	20	25	25	36	.do.	25	36	36	32	32
36	36	28	28	56	60	28	28	56	56	56	56	28	28	36	36	56	.do.	36	56	56	48	48
32	32	32	32	56	60	32	32	32	32	56	56	32	32	32	32	56	.do.	32	56	32	32	32
36	36	36	36	72	80	36	36	36	36	72	72	36	36	36	36	72	.do.	36	72	36	36	36
36	36	36	36	64	80	36	36	36	36	64	64	36	36	36	36	64	.do.	36	64	36	36	36
32	32	32	32	48	60	32	32	32	32	48	48	32	32	32	32	48	.do.	32	48	32	32	32
15	15	15	15	26	36	15	15	15	15	26	26	15	15	15	15	26	.do.	15	26	15	15	15
22	22	22	22	40	48	22	22	22	22	40	40	22	22	22	22	40	.do.	22	40	22	22	22
18	18	18	18	32	39	18	18	18	18	32	32	18	18	18	18	32	.do.	18	32	18	18	18
20	20	24	24	40	48	24	24	24	24	40	40	24	24	24	24	40	.do.	24	40	24	24	24
28	28	28	28	48	60	28	28	28	28	48	48	28	28	28	28	48	.do.	28	48	28	28	28
20	20	28	28	48	60	28	28	28	28	48	48	28	28	28	28	48	.do.	28	48	28	28	28
14	14	20	20	32	40	20	20	20	20	32	32	20	20	20	20	32	.do.	20	32	20	20	20
12	12	14	14	24	32	14	14	14	14	24	24	14	14	14	14	24	do	14	24	14	14	14
16	16	20	20	40	48	20	20	20	20	40	40	20	20	20	20	40	.do.	20	40	20	20	20
20	20	28	28	48	60	28	28	28	28	48	48	28	28	28	28	48	.do.	28	48	28	28	28
19	19	27	27	46	58	27	27	27	27	46	46	27	27	27	27	46	.do.	27	46	27	27	27
19	19	27	27	46	58	27	27	27	27	46	46	27	27	27	27	46	.do.	27	46	27	27	27
27	23	27	27	50	58	27	23	39	27	39	27	27	19	27	23	50	39	23	27	23	39	23
27	23	27	27	51	59	27	23	39	27	39	27	27	20	27	23	51	39	23	27	23	39	23
30	26	30	21	51	59	30	26	39	30	39	30	30	21	30	26	51	39	26	30	26	39	26
27	23	27	20	51	59	27	23	39	27	39	27	27	20	27	23	51	39	23	27	23	39	23
23	20	23	16	31	39	23	20	27	23	27	23	23	16	23	20	31	27	20	23	20	27	20
27	23	27	20	51	59	27	23	39	27	39	27	27	20	27	23	51	39	23	27	23	39	23
27	23	27	20	51	59	27	23	39	27	39	27	27	20	23	20	51	39	23	27	23	39	23
27	23	27	20	51	59	27	23	39	27	39	27	27	20	23	20	51	39	23	27	23	39	23.
27	23	27	20	51	59	27	23	39	27	39	27	27	20	23	20	51	39	23	27	23	39	23
27	23	27	20	51	59	27	23	39	27	39	27	27	20	23	20	51	39	23	27	23	39	23

TABLE 31.—RATES OF FREIGHT, ALL RAIL, FROM

DISTANCE VIA SHORTEST ROUTE.—From New York, 639 miles;

[NOTE.—Where the rates shown are not specifically described as applying on less

Date.	Commodities (rates in cents per 100 pounds).																		
				Furniture.		Stoves.		Coffee.		Soaps.				Starch.			Sugar.	
										Castile and fancy.		Common.						
	Dry goods.	Cotton piece goods.	Boots and shoes.	Less than carloads.	Carloads.	Less than carloads.	Carloads.	Less than carloads.	Carloads.	Less than carloads.	Carloads.	Less than carloads.	Carloads.	Less than carloads.	Carloads.	Tea.	Less than carlo.ds.	Carloads.
1867—Jan. 1.....	134	134	134	134	134	134	134	114	114	114	114	92	92	114	114	134	58	58
May 15....	134	134	134	134	134	134	134	114	114	114	114	91	91	114	114	134	59	59
Nov. 5.....	144	144	144	144	144	144	144	121	121	121	121	99	99	121	121	144	64	64
1868—Feb. 4.....	144	144	144	144	144	144	144	Special rate.		121	121	64	64	99	99	144	Special rate.	
June 4.....	134	134	134	134	134	134	134	..do....		114	114	59	59	91	91	134	..do....	
Aug. 10.....	106	106	106	106	106	106	106	..do....		91	91	59	59	86	86	106	..do....	
Sept. 7.....	134	134	134	134	134	134	134	..do....		114	114	59	59	91	91	134	..do....	
Dec. 7.....	150	150	150	150	150	150	150	..do....		121	121	60	60	99	99	150	..do....	
1869—Feb. 1.....	134	134	134	134	134	134	134	..do....		114	114	59	59	59	59	134	..do....	
Feb. 17.....	57	57	57	57	57	57	57	..do....		57	57	57	57	57	57	57	..do....	
Mar. 15.....	114	114	114	114	114	114	114	..do....		114	114	59	59	91	91	114	..do....	
Apr. 12.....	114	114	114	114	114	114	114	..do....		114	114	59	59	91	91	114	..do....	
July 1.....	134	134	134	134	134	134	134	..do....		114	114	59	59	91	91	134	..do....	
Aug. 23.....	28	28	28	28	28	28	28	..do....		28	28	28	28	28	28	28	..do....	
Oct. 9.....	53	53	53	53	53	53	53	..do....		53	53	53	53	53	53	53	..do....	
Oct. 13.....	90	90	90	90	90	90	90	..do....		72	72	47	47	54	54	90	..do....	
Nov. 1.....	100	100	100	100	100	100	100	..do....		90	90	58	58	72	72	100	..do....	
Nov. 29.....	108	108	108	108	108	108	108	..do....		93	93	58	58	72	72	108	..do....	
1870—Apr. 14.....	108	108	108	108	108	108	108	..do....		93	93	58	58	72	72	108	30	30
May 4.....	113	113	113	113	113	113	113	..do....		98	98	58	58	79	79	113	30	30
May 7.....	113	113	113	113	113	113	113	..do....		98	98	58	58	79	79	113	30	30
June 18.....	84	84	84	84	84	84	84	..do....		68	68	43	43	54	54	84	30	30
July 25.....	46	46	46	46	46	46	46	..do....		42	42	31	31	39	39	46	30	30
July 28.....	35	35	35	35	35	35	35	..do....		35	35	31	31	35	35	35	30	30
Aug. 12.....	36	36	36	36	36	36	36	..do....		36	36	36	36	36	36	36	Special rate.	
Aug. 22.....	72	72	72	72	72	72	72	..do....		68	68	43	43	54	54	72	..do....	
Sept. 8.....	90	90	90	90	90	90	90	..do....		79	79	47	47	54	54	90	..do....	
Nov. 28.....	112	112	112	112	112	112	112	..do....		91	91	45	45	71	71	112	..do....	
Dec. 26.....	127	127	127	127	127	127	127	42	42	106	106	56	56	84	84	127	42	42
1871—Feb. 15.....	88	88	88	88	88	88	88	35	35	78	78	46	46	60	60	88	35	35
Feb. 20.....	106	106	106	106	106	106	106	39	39	91	91	50	50	70	70	106	39	39
Mar. 13.....	71	71	71	71	71	71	71	32	32	64	64	39	39	50	50	71	32	32
May 18.....	53	53	53	53	53	53	53	26	26	45	45	26	26	36	36	53	26	26
June 1.....	71	71	71	71	71	71	71	32	32	64	64	39	39	50	50	71	32	32
July 8.....	53	53	53	53	53	53	53	26	26	45	45	31	31	36	36	53	26	26
July 26.....	42	42	42	42	42	42	42	23	23	39	39	28	28	32	32	42	23	23
July 29.....	52	52	52	52	52	52	52	30	30	44	44	35	35	39	39	52	30	30
Aug. 16.....	31	31	31	31	31	31	31	21	21	31	31	21	21	31	31	31	21	21
Aug. 22.....	25	25	25	25	25	25	25	19	19	25	25	25	25	25	25	25	19	19
Sept. 2.....	21	21	21	21	21	21	21	17	17	21	21	21	21	21	21	21	17	17
Sept. 5.....	52	52	52	52	52	52	52	30	30	44	44	35	35	39	39	52	30	30
Nov. 27.....	71	71	71	71	71	71	71	32	32	64	64	39	39	50	50	71	32	32
Dec. 15.....	88	88	88	88	88	88	88	35	35	78	78	46	46	60	60	88	35	35
1872—Apr. 27.....	88	88	88	88	88	88	88	35	35	78	78	46	46	60	60	88	35	35
Aug. 1.....	53	53	53	53	53	53	53	25	25	49	49	39	39	42	42	53	25	25
Sept. 1......	88	88	88	88	88	88	88	35	35	78	78	46	46	60	60	88	35	35
Sept. 2.....	70	70	70	70	70	70	70	32	32	63	63	39	39	49	49	70	32	32
Oct. 14....	88	88	88	88	88	88	88	35	35	78	78	46	46	60	60	88	35	35
1873—Apr. 15.....	70	70	70	70	70	70	70	32	32	63	63	42	42	53	53	70	32	32
July 22.....	53	53	53	53	53	53	53	25	25	49	49	32	32	42	42	53	25	25
Aug. 12.....	50	50	50	50	50	50	50	30	30	40	40	30	30	30	30	50	30	30
Aug. 13.....	29	29	29	29	29	29	29	22	22	29	29	22	22	22	22	29	22	22
Sept. 17.....	53	53	53	53	53	53	53	25	25	49	49	32	32	42	42	53	25	25
1874—Jan. 1.....	70	70	70	70	70	70	70	32	32	63	63	42	42	53	53	70	32	32
Aug. 3.....	53	53	53	53	53	53	53	25	25	49	49	32	32	42	42	53	25	25
1875—Jan. 20.....	70	70	70	70	70	70	70	32	32	63	-63	42	42	53	53	70	32	32
Mar. 17.....	53	53	53	53	53	53	53	21	21	49	49	32	32	42	42	53	21	21
Aug. 12.....	40	40	40	40	40	40	40	15	15	30	30	20	20	25	25	40	15	15
Nov. 15.....	53	53	53	53	53	53	53	25	25	49	49	32	32	42	42	53	25	25
Dec. 22.....	30	30	30	30	30	30	30	15	15	25	25	20	20	20	20	30	15	15

NEW YORK, N. Y., TO DETROIT, MICH.

Boston, 710 miles; Philadelphia, 648 miles; Baltimore, 628 miles.

than carload or carload quantities they apply on shipments regardless of quantity.]

Commodities (rates in cents per 100 pounds).																						
Molasses.		Rice.				Crockery and earthenware.		Bagging.		Leather.		Lead.		Nails.			Agricultural implements.		Machinery.		Beer.	
Less than carloads.	Carloads.	Less than carloads.	Carloads.	Groceries.	Drugs.	Less than carloads.	Carloads.	Less than carloads.	Carloads.	Less than carloads.	Carloads.	Less than carloads.	Carloads.	Less than carloads.	Carloads.	Hardware.	Less than carloads.	Carloads.	Less than carloads.	Carloads.	Less than carloads.	Carloads.
58	58	58	58	114	134	114	114	114	114	114	114	58	58	58	58	114	134	134	114	114	92	92
59	59	59	59	114	134	114	114	114	114	114	114	59	59	59	59	114	134	134	114	114	91	91
64	64	64	64	121	144	121	121	121	121	121	121	64	64	64	64	121	144	144	121	121	99	99
Special rate.		64	64	121	144	121	121	121	121	121	121	64	64	64	64	121	144	144	121	121	99	99
..do....		59	59	114	134	114	114	114	114	114	114	59	59	59	59	114	134	134	114	114	91	91
..do....		59	59	91	106	91	91	91	91	91	91	59	59	59	59	91	106	106	91	91	86	86
..do....		59	59	114	134	114	114	114	114	91	91	59	59	59	59	114	134	134	114	114	91	91
..do....		60	60	121	150	121	121	121	121	99	99	60	60	60	60	121	150	150	121	121	99	99
..do....		59	59	114	134	114	114	114	114	91	91	59	59	59	59	114	134	134	114	114	59	59
..do....		57	57	57	57	57	57	57	57	57	57	57	57	57	57	57	57	57	57	57	57	57
..do....		59	59	114	114	114	114	114	114	91	91	59	59	59	59	114	114	114	114	114	91	91
..do....		59	59	114	114	Special rate.		114	114	91	91	59	59	59	59	114	114	114	114	114	91	91
..do....		59	59	114	134	..do....		114	114	114	114	59	59	59	59	114	134	134	114	114	91	91
..do....		28	28	28	28	..do....		28	28	28	28	28	28	28	28	28	28	28	28	28	28	28
..do....		37	37	53	53	..do....		53	53	53	53	37	37	37	37	53	53	53	53	53	53	53
..do....		47	47	72	90	..do....		72	72	72	72	47	47	47	47	72	90	90	72	72	54	54
..do....		58	58	90	100	..do....		90	90	90	90	58	58	58	58	90	100	100	90	90	72	72
..do....		58	58	93	108	..do....		93	93	93	93	58	58	58	58	93	108	108	93	93	72	72
..do....		58	58	93	108	..do....		93	93	93	93	58	58	58	58	93	108	108	93	93	72	72
..do....		58	58	98	113	..do....		98	98	98	98	58	58	58	58	98	113	113	98	98	79	79
..do....		Special rate.		98	113	..do....		98	98	98	98	58	58	58	58	98	113	113	98	98	79	79
..do....		..do....		68	84	..do....		68	68	68	68	43	43	43	43	68	84	84	68	68	54	54
..do....		..do....		42	46	..do....		42	42	42	42	31	31	31	31	42	46	46	42	42	39	39
..do....		..do....		35	35	..do....		35	35	35	35	31	31	31	31	35	35	35	35	35	35	35
..do....		..do....		36	36	..do....		36	36	36	36	36	36	36	36	36	36	36	36	36	36	36
..do....		..do....		68	72	..do....		68	68	68	68	43	43	43	43	68	72	72	68	68	54	54
..do....		..do....		79	90	..do....		79	79	79	79	47	47	47	47	79	90	90	79	79	61	61
..do....		..do....		91	112	..do....		91	91	91	91	45	45	45	45	91	112	112	91	91	71	71
56	56	56	56	106	127	106	106	106	106	106	106	56	56	56	56	106	127	127	106	106	84	84
46	46	46	46	78	88	35	35	78	78	78	78	35	35	46	46	78	88	88	78	78	60	60
50	50	50	50	91	106	39	39	91	91	91	91	39	39	50	50	91	106	106	91	91	71	71
39	39	39	39	64	71	32	32	64	64	64	64	32	32	39	39	64	71	71	64	64	50	50
31	31	31	31	45	53	26	26	45	45	45	45	26	26	31	31	45	53	53	45	45	36	36
39	39	39	39	64	71	32	32	64	64	64	64	32	32	39	39	64	71	71	64	64	50	50
31	31	31	31	45	53	26	26	45	45	45	45	26	26	31	31	45	53	53	45	45	36	36
28	28	28	28	39	42	23	23	39	39	39	39	23	23	28	28	39	42	42	39	39	32	32
35	35	35	35	44	52	30	30	44	44	44	44	30	30	35	35	44	52	52	44	44	39	39
31	31	31	31	31	31	21	21	31	31	31	31	21	21	31	31	31	31	31	31	31	31	31
25	25	25	25	25	25	19	19	25	25	25	25	19	19	25	25	25	25	25	25	25	25	25
21	21	21	21	21	21	17	17	21	21	21	21	17	17	21	21	21	21	21	21	21	21	21
35	35	35	35	44	52	30	30	44	44	44	44	30	30	35	35	44	52	52	44	44	39	39
39	39	39	39	64	71	32	32	64	64	64	64	32	32	39	39	64	71	71	64	64	50	50
46	46	46	46	78	88	78	78	78	78	78	78	35	35	46	46	78	88	88	78	78	60	60
46	46	35	35	78	88	78	78	78	78	78	78	35	35	46	46	78	88	88	78	78	60	60
32	32	25	25	49	53	49	49	49	49	49	49	25	25	32	32	49	53	53	49	49	42	42
46	46	46	46	78	88	78	78	78	78	78	78	35	35	46	46	78	88	88	78	78	60	60
39	39	32	32	63	70	63	63	63	63	63	63	32	32	39	39	63	70	70	63	63	49	49
46	46	35	35	78	88	35	35	78	78	78	78	35	35	46	46	78	88	88	78	78	60	60
42	42	32	32	63	70	32	32	63	63	63	63	32	32	42	42	63	Spe'l rate.	42	63	63	53	53
32	32	25	25	49	53	25	25	49	49	49	49	25	25	32	32	49	.do .	32	49	49	42	42
30	30	30	30	40	50	30	30	40	40	40	40	40	30	30	30	40	.do .	30	40	40	30	30
22	22	22	22	29	29	22	22	29	29	29	29	22	22	22	22	29	.do .	22	29	29	22	22
32	32	25	25	49	53	25	25	49	49	49	49	25	25	32	32	49	.do .	32	49	49	42	42
42	42	32	32	63	70	32	32	63	63	63	63	32	32	42	42	63	.do .	42	63	63	53	53
32	32	25	25	49	53	25	25	49	49	49	49	25	25	32	32	49	.do .	32	49	49	42	42
42	42	32	32	63	70	32	32	63	63	63	63	32	32	42	42	63	.do .	42	63	63	53	53
32	32	25	25	49	53	25	25	49	49	49	49	25	25	32	32	49	.do .	32	49	49	42	42
20	20	15	15	30	40	15	15	30	30	30	30	15	15	20	20	30	.do .	20	30	30	25	25
32	32	25	25	49	53	25	25	49	49	49	49	25	25	32	32	49	.do .	32	49	49	42	42
20	20	15	15	25	30	15	15	25	25	25	25	15	15	20	20	25	.do .	30	25	25	20	20

TABLE 31.—RATES OF FREIGHT, ALL RAIL, FROM

DISTANCE VIA SHORTEST ROUTE.—From New York, 639 miles;

[NOTE.—Where the rates shown are not specifically described as applying on less

Date.	Commodities (rates in cents per 100 pounds.)																		
	Dry goods.	Cotton piece goods.	Boots and shoes.	Furniture.		Stoves.		Coffee.		Soaps.				Starch.		Tea.	Sugar.	
										Castile and fancy.		Common.						
				Less than carloads.	Carloads.	Less than carloads.	Carloads.	Less than carloads.	Carloads.	Less than carloads.	Carloads.	Less than carloads.	Carloads.	Less than carloads.	Carloads.		Less than carloads.	Carloads.
1876—Jan. 10	53	53	53	53	53	53	53	25	25	49	49	32	32	42	42	53	25	25
June 12	25	25	25	25	25	25	25	16	16	25	25	16	16	25	25	25	16	16
Dec. 18	40	40	40	40	40	40	40	20	20	35	35	25	25	30	30	40	20	20
1877—Mar. 12	53	53	53	53	53	53	53	25	25	49	49	32	32	42	42	53	25	25
1877—Oct. 8	53	53	53	53	53	53	28	28	28	49	49	28	28	28	28	53	28	28
Oct. 22	70	70	70	70	70	70	32	32	32	63	63	32	32	32	32	70	32	32
Dec. 10	70	70	70	70	70	70	32	32	32	56	56	32	32	32	32	70	32	32
1878—Feb. 14	53	53	53	53	53	53	28	28	28	42	42	28	28	28	28	53	28	28
1881—Aug. 6	32	32	32	32	32	32	14	14	14	22	22	14	14	14	14	32	14	14
Nov. 14	42	42	42	42	42	42	20	20	20	35	35	20	20	20	20	42	20	20
1882—July 1	42	42	42	42	42	42	21	21	21	35	35	21	21	21	21	42	18	18
Nov. 1	53	53	53	53	53	53	25	25	25	42	42	25	25	25	25	53	25	25
1883—June 22	53	53	53	53	53	53	25	25	25	42	42	25	25	25	25	53	18	18
1885—Jan. 26	35	35	35	35	35	35	18	18	18	28	28	18	18	18	18	35	13	13
June 1	28	28	28	28	28	28	13	13	13	21	21	13	13	13	13	28	11	11
Oct. 5	42	28	42	42	42	42	18	18	18	35	35	18	18	18	18	42	14	14
Nov. 18	53	32	53	53	53	53	25	25	25	42	42	25	25	25	25	53	18	18
1886—Mar. 10	59	35	59	59	59	59	37	27	27	47	47	27	27	27	27	59	20	20
Aug. 26	59	39	59	59	59	59	27	27	27	47	47	27	27	27	27	59	20	20
1887—Apr. 1	59	39	59	59	51	39	23	27	20	51	51	27	23	27	20	59	27	20
1888—Jan. 9	59	39	59	59	51	39	26	30	21	51	51	30	26	30	21	59	30	21
Mar. 5	59	39	59	59	51	39	23	27	20	51	51	27	23	27	20	59	27	20
Aug. 15	59	39	59	59	51	59	23	27	20	51	51	27	23	27	20	59	27	20
Nov. 12	39	27	39	39	31	27	20	23	16	31	31	23	20	23	16	39	23	16
Dec. 17	59	39	59	59	51	39	23	27	20	51	51	27	23	27	20	59	27	20
1889—Feb. 18	59	39	59	59	51	59	23	27	20	51	51	27	23	27	20	59	27	20
1891—Apr. 9	59	39	59	59	51	23	20	27	20	51	51	27	20	27	20	59	27	20
1892—Mar. 16	59	39	59	59	51	23	20	27	20	27	20	27	20	27	20	59	27	16
May 2	59	39	59	59	51	23	20	27	20	27	20	27	20	27	20	59	27	20
June 6	59	39	59	59	51	23	20	27	20	27	20	27	20	27	20	59	27	18

NEW YORK, N. Y., TO DETROIT, MICH.—Continued.

Boston, 710 miles; Philadelphia, 618 miles; Baltimore, 628 miles.

than carload or carload quantities they apply on shipments regardless of quantities.]

Commodities (rate in cents per 100 pounds).																						
Molasses.		Rice.				Crockery and earthenware.		Bagging.		Leather.		Lead.		Nails.			Agricultural implements.		Machinery.		Beer.	
Less than carloads.	Carloads.	Less than carloads.	Carloads.	Groceries.	Drugs.	Less than carloads.	Carloads.	Less than carloads.	Carloads.	Less than carloads.	Carloads.	Less than carloads.	Carloads.	Less than carloads.	Carloads.	Hardware.	Less than carloads.	Carloads.	Less than carloads.	Carloads.	Less than carloads.	Carloads.
32	32	25	25	49	53	25	25	49	49	49	49	25	25	32	32	49	Spe'l rate.	32	49	49	42	42
16	16	16	16	25	25	16	16	25	25	25	25	16	16	16	16	25	.do .	16	25	25	25	25
25	25	20	20	35	40	20	20	35	35	35	35	20	20	25	25	35	.do .	25	35	35	30	30
32	32	25	25	49	53	25	25	49	49	49	49	25	25	32	32	49	.do .	32	49	49	42	42
28	28	28	28	49	53	28	28	28	28	49	49	28	28	28	28	49	.do .	28	49	28	28	28
32	32	32	32	63	70	32	32	32	32	63	63	32	32	32	32	63	.do .	32	63	32	32	32
32	32	32	32	56	70	32	32	32	32	56	56	32	32	32	32	56	.do .	32	56	32	32	32
28	28	28	28	42	53	28	28	28	28	42	42	28	28	28	28	42	.do .	28	42	28	28	28
14	14	14	14	22	32	14	14	14	14	22	22	14	14	14	14	22	.do .	14	22	14	14	14
20	20	20	20	35	42	20	20	20	20	35	35	20	20	20	20	35	.do .	20	35	20	20	20
18	18	21	21	35	42	21	21	21	21	35	35	21	21	21	21	35	.do .	21	35	21	21	21
25	25	25	20	42	53	25	25	25	25	42	42	25	25	25	25	42	.do .	25	42	25	25	25
18	18	25	25	42	53	25	25	25	25	42	42	25	25	25	25	42	do .	25	42	25	25	25
13	13	18	18	28	35	18	18	18	18	28	28	18	18	18	18	28	.do .	18	28	18	18	18
11	11	13	13	21	28	13	13	13	13	21	21	13	13	13	13	21	.do .	13	21	13	13	13
14	14	18	18	35	42	18	18	18	18	35	35	18	18	18	18	35	.do .	18	35	18	18	18
18	18	25	25	42	53	25	25	25	25	42	42	25	25	25	25	42	.do .	25	42	25	25	25
20	20	27	27	47	59	27	27	27	27	47	47	27	27	27	27	47	.do .	27	47	27	27	27
20	20	27	27	47	59	27	27	27	27	47	47	27	27	27	27	47	.do .	27	47	27	27	27
27	23	27	27	51	59	27	23	39	27	39	27	27	20	27	23	51	39	23	27	23	39	23
30	26	30	21	51	59	30	26	39	30	39	30	30	21	30	26	51	39	26	30	26	39	26
27	23	27	20	51	59	27	23	39	27	39	27	27	20	27	23	51	39	23	27	23	39	23
27	23	27	20	51	59	27	23	39	27	39	27	27	20	27	23	51	39	23	27	23	39	23
23	20	23	16	31	39	23	20	27	23	27	23	23	16	23	20	31	27	20	23	20	27	20
27	23	27	20	51	59	27	23	38	27	39	27	27	20	27	23	51	39	23	27	23	39	23
27	23	27	20	51	59	27	23	39	27	39	27	27	20	27	23	51	39	23	27	23	29	23
27	23	27	20	51	59	27	23	39	27	39	27	27	20	23	20	51	39	23	27	23	39	23
27	23	27	20	51	59	27	23	39	27	39	27	27	20	23	20	51	39	23	27	23	39	23
27	23	27	20	51	59	27	23	39	27	39	27	27	20	23	20	51	39	23	27	23	39	23
27	23	27	20	51	59	27	23	39	27	39	27	27	20	23	20	51	39	23	27	23	39	23

TABLE 32.—RATES OF FREIGHT, ALL RAIL, FROM

DISTANCE VIA SHORTEST ROUTE.—From New York, 592 miles;

[NOTE.—Where the rates shown are not specially described as applying to less

Date.	Commodities (rates in cents per 100 pounds).																	
	Dry goods.	Cotton piece goods.	Boots and shoes.	Furniture.		Stoves.		Coffee.		Soap.				Starch.		Tea.	Sugar.	
										Castile or fancy.		Common.						
				Less than carloads.	Carloads.	Less than carloads.	Carloads.	Less than carloads.	Carloads.	Less than carloads.	Carloads.	Less than carloads.	Carloads.	Less than carloads.	Carloads.		Less than carloads.	Carloads.
1867—Jan. 1	126	126	126	126	126	126	126	107	107	107	107	86	86	107	107	126	54	54
Nov. 5	136	136	136	136	136	136	136	114	114	114	114	93	93	114	114	136	57	57
1868—Feb. 4	136	136	136	136	136	136	136	Special rate.		114	114	57	57	93	93	136	Special rate.	
June 4	126	126	126	126	126	126	126	do.		107	107	54	54	86	86	126	do.	
Aug. 10	100	100	100	100	100	100	100	do.		86	86	54	54	80	80	100	do.	
Sept. 7	126	126	126	126	126	126	126	do.		107	107	54	54	86	86	126	do.	
Oct. 1	60	60	60	60	60	60	60	do.		56	56	45	45	50	50	60	do.	
Dec. 7	136	136	136	136	136	136	136	do.		114	114	57	57	93	93	136	do.	
1869—Feb. 1	126	126	126	126	126	126	126	do.		107	107	54	54	86	86	126	do.	
17	35	35	35	35	35	35	35	do.		35	35	35	35	35	35	35	do.	
Mch. 15	107	107	107	107	107	107	107	do.		107	107	54	54	86	86	107	do.	
May 12	107	107	107	107	107	107	107	do.		107	107	54	54	86	86	107	do.	
July 1	126	126	126	126	126	126	126	do.		107	107	54	54	86	86	126	do.	
Aug. 11	20	20	20	20	20	20	20	do.		20	20	20	20	20	20	20	do.	
23	25	25	25	25	25	25	25	do.		25	25	25	25	25	25	25	do.	
30	29	29	29	29	29	29	29	do.		29	29	29	29	29	29	29	do.	
Sept. 22	25	25	25	25	25	25	25	do.		25	25	25	25	25	25	25	do.	
24	22	22	22	22	22	22	22	do.		22	22	22	22	22	22	22	do.	
Oct. 4	34	34	34	34	34	34	34	do.		34	34	34	34	34	34	34	do.	
9	50	50	50	50	50	50	50	do.		50	50	34	34	34	34	50	do.	
13	84	84	84	84	84	84	84	do.		67	67	44	44	51	51	84	do.	
Nov. 1	94	94	94	94	94	94	94	do.		84	84	54	54	67	67	94	do.	
29	101	101	101	101	101	101	101	do.		87	87	54	54	67	67	101	do.	
1870—Mch. 7	101	101	101	101	101	101	101	do.		87	87	54	54	67	67	101	do.	
Apr. 19	101	101	101	101	101	101	101	do.		87	87	54	54	67	67	101	31	31
May 4	112	112	112	112	112	112	112	do.		96	96	62	62	76	76	112	Special rate.	
June 18	71	71	71	71	71	71	71	do.		57	57	36	36	46	46	71	do.	
July 25	43	43	43	43	43	43	43	do.		38	38	28	28	35	35	43	do.	
28	32	32	32	32	32	32	32	do.		32	32	28	28	32	32	32	do.	
Aug. 12	32	32	32	32	32	32	32	do.		32	32	32	32	32	32	32	do.	
22	63	63	63	63	63	63	63	do.		57	57	36	36	46	46	63	do.	
24	73	73	73	73	73	73	73	do.		65	65	42	42	52	52	73	do.	
1870—Sept. 8	84	84	84	84	84	84	84	do.		74	74	44	44	57	57	84	do.	
Nov. 28	104	104	104	104	104	104	104	do.		84	84	42	42	66	66	104	do.	
Dec. 26	118	118	118	118	118	118	118	39	39	98	98	52	52	78	78	118	39	39
1871—Feb. 20	98	98	98	98	98	98	98	36	36	84	84	46	46	66	66	98	36	36
Mch. 7	63	63	63	63	63	63	63	28	28	57	57	36	36	46	46	63	28	28
13	73	73	73	73	73	73	73	33	33	65	65	40	40	50	50	73	33	33
May 18	49	49	49	49	49	49	49	24	24	42	42	29	29	33	33	49	24	24
June 1	73	73	73	73	73	73	73	33	33	65	65	40	40	50	50	73	33	33
July 8	54	54	54	54	54	54	54	29	29	47	47	34	34	38	38	54	29	29
26	39	39	39	39	39	39	39	21	21	36	36	26	26	30	30	39	21	21
28	40	40	40	40	40	40	40	30	30	40	40	35	35	39	39	40	30	30
29	40	40	40	40	40	40	40	29	29	40	40	34	34	38	38	40	29	29
Aug. 16	29	29	29	29	29	29	29	20	20	29	29	29	29	29	29	29	20	20
22	23	23	23	23	23	23	23	17	17	23	23	23	23	23	23	23	17	17
Sept. 5	40	40	40	40	40	40	40	30	30	40	40	35	35	39	39	40	30	30
6	23	23	23	23	23	23	23	20	20	23	23	23	23	23	23	23	20	20
11	20	20	20	20	20	20	20	16	16	20	20	20	20	20	20	20	16	16
Nov. 27	73	73	73	73	73	73	73	33	33	65	65	40	40	50	50	73	33	33
Dec. 15	82	82	82	82	82	82	82	33	33	72	72	43	43	56	56	82	33	33
1872—Aug. 1	49	49	49	49	49	49	49	23	23	46	46	30	30	39	39	49	23	23
Sept. 1	82	82	82	82	82	82	82	33	33	72	72	43	43	56	56	82	33	33
2	65	65	65	65	65	65	65	30	30	59	59	36	36	46	46	65	30	30
Oct. 14	82	82	82	82	82	82	82	33	33	72	72	43	43	56	56	82	33	33
1873—Apr. 14	65	65	65	65	65	65	65	30	30	59	59	39	39	49	49	65	30	30
June 1	49	49	49	49	49	49	49	23	23	46	46	30	30	39	39	49	23	23
11	26	26	26	26	26	26	26	20	20	26	26	20	20	20	20	26	20	20
12	40	40	40	40	40	40	40	23	23	40	40	30	30	30	30	40	23	23

NEW YORK, N. Y., TO CLEVELAND, OHIO.

Boston, 663 miles; Philadelphia, 541 miles; Baltimore, 521 miles.

than carload or carload quantities they apply on shipments regardless of quantity.]

Commodities (rates in cents per 100 pounds).																						
Molasses.		Rice.				Crockery and earthenware.		Bagging.		Leather.		Lead.		Nails.			Agricultural implements.		Machinery.		Beer.	
Less than carloads.	Carloads.	Less than carloads.	Carloads.	Groceries.	Drugs.	Less than carloads.	Carloads.	Less than carloads.	Carloads.	Less than carloads.	Carloads.	Less than carloads.	Carloads.	Less than carloads.	Carloads.	Hardware.	Less than carloads.	Carloads.	Less than carloads.	Carloads.	Less than carloads.	Carloads.
54	54	54	54	107	126	107	107	107	107	107	107	54	54	54	54	107	126	126	107	107	86	86
57	57	57	57	114	136	114	114	114	114	114	114	57	57	57	57	114	136	136	114	114	93	93
Special rate.		57	57	114	136	114	114	114	114	114	114	57	57	57	57	114	136	136	114	114	93	93
..do....		54	54	107	126	107	107	107	107	107	107	54	54	54	54	107	126	126	107	107	86	86
..do....		54	54	86	100	86	86	86	86	86	86	54	54	54	54	86	100	100	86	86	80	80
..do....		54	54	107	126	107	107	107	107	107	107	54	54	54	54	107	126	126	107	107	86	86
..do...		45	45	56	60	56	56	56	56	56	56	45	45	45	45	56	60	60	56	56	50	50
..do....		57	57	114	113	114	114	114	114	114	114	57	57	57	57	114	136	136	114	114	93	93
..do....		54	54	107	126	107	107	107	107	107	107	54	54	54	54	107	126	126	107	107	86	86
..do....		35	35	35	35	35	35	35	35	35	35	35	35	35	35	35	35	35	35	35	35	35
..do....		54	54	107	107	ı07	107	107	107	107	107	54	54	54	54	107	107	107	107	107	86	86
..do....		54	54	107	107	Special rate.		107	107	107	107	54	54	54	54	107	107	107	107	107	86	86
..do....		54	54	107	126	..do....		107	107	107	107	54	54	54	54	107	126	126	107	107	86	86
..do....		20	20	20	20	..do....		20	20	20	20	20	20	20	20	20	20	20	20	20	20	20
..do....		25	25	25	25	..do....		25	25	25	25	25	25	25	25	25	25	25	25	25	25	25
..do....		29	29	29	29	..do....		29	29	29	29	29	29	29	29	29	29	29	29	29	29	29
..do....		25	25	25	25	..do....		25	25	25	25	25	25	25	25	25	25	25	25	25	25	25
..do....		22	22	22	22	..do....		22	22	22	22	22	22	22	22	22	22	22	22	22	22	22
..do....		34	34	34	34	..do....		34	34	34	34	34	34	34	34	34	34	34	34	34	34	34
..do....		34	34	50	50	..do....		50	50	50	50	34	34	34	34	50	50	50	50	50	50	50
..do....		44	44	67	84	..do....		67	67	67	67	44	44	44	44	67	84	84	67	67	51	51
..do....		54	54	84	94	..do....		84	84	84	84	54	54	54	54	84	94	94	84	84	67	67
..do....		54	54	87	101	..do....		87	87	87	87	54	54	54	54	87	101	101	87	87	67	67
..do....		Special rate.		87	101	..do....		87	87	87	87	54	54	54	54	87	101	101	87	87	67	67
..do....		..do....		87	101	..do....		87	87	87	87	54	54	54	54	87	101	101	87	87	67	67
.do....		62	62	96	112	..do...		96	96	96	96	62	62	62	62	96	112	112	ς6	96	76	76
..do....		Special rate.		57	71	..do....		57	57	57	57	36	36	36	36	57	71	71	57	57	46	46
..do....		..do....		38	43	..do....		38	38	38	38	28	28	28	28	38	43	43	38	38	35	35
..do....		..do....		32	32	..do....		32	32	32	32	28	28	28	28	32	32	32	32	32	32	32
..do....		..do....		32	32	..do....		32	32	32	32	32	32	32	32	32	32	32	32	32	32	32
..do....		..do....		57	63	..do....		57	57	57	57	36	36	36	36	57	63	63	57	57	46	46
..do....		..do....		65	73	..do....		65	65	65	65	42	42	42	42	65	73	73	65	65	52	52
..do....		..do....		74	84	..do....		74	74	74	74	44	44	44	44	74	84	84	74	74	57	57
..do....		..do....		84	104	..do....		84	84	84	84	42	42	42	42	84	104	104	84	84	66	66
52	52	52	52	98	118	98	98	98	98	98	98	52	52	52	52	98	118	118	98	98	78	78
46	46	46	46	84	98	36	36	84	84	84	84	36	36	46	46	84	98	98	84	84	66	66
36	36	36	36	57	63	28	28	57	57	57	57	28	28	36	36	57	63	63	57	57	46	46
40	40	40	40	65	73	33	33	65	65	65	65	33	33	40	40	65	73	73	65	65	50	50
29	29	29	29	42	49	24	24	42	42	42	42	24	24	29	29	42	49	49	42	42	33	33
40	40	40	40	65	73	33	33	65	65	65	65	33	33	40	40	65	73	73	65	65	50	50
34	34	34	34	47	54	29	29	47	47	47	47	29	29	34	34	47	54	54	47	47	38	38
26	26	26	26	36	39	21	21	36	36	36	36	21	21	26	26	36	39	39	36	36	30	30
35	35	35	35	40	40	30	30	40	40	40	40	30	30	35	35	40	40	40	40	40	39	39
34	34	34	34	40	40	29	29	40	40	40	40	29	29	34	34	40	40	40	40	40	38	38
29	29	29	29	29	29	20	20	29	29	29	29	20	20	29	29	29	29	29	29	29	29	29
23	23	23	23	23	23	17	17	23	23	23	23	17	17	23	23	23	23	23	23	23	23	23
35	35	35	35	40	40	30	30	40	40	40	40	30	30	35	35	40	40	40	40	40	39	39
23	23	23	23	23	23	20	20	23	23	23	23	20	20	23	23	23	23	23	23	23	23	23
20	20	20	20	20	20	16	16	20	20	20	20	16	16	20	20	20	20	20	20	20	20	20
40	40	40	40	65	73	33	33	65	65	65	65	33	33	40	40	65	73	73	65	65	50	50
43	43	33	33	72	82	72	72	72	72	72	72	33	33	43	43	72	82	82	72	72	56	56
30	30	23	23	46	49	46	46	46	46	46	46	23	23	30	30	46	49	49	46	46	39	39
43	43	33	33	72	82	72	72	72	72	72	72	33	33	43	43	72	82	82	72	72	56	56
36	36	30	30	59	65	59	59	59	59	59	59	30	30	36	36	59	65	65	59	59	46	46
43	43	33	33	72	82	33	33	72	72	72	72	33	33	43	43	72	82	82	72	72	56	56
39	39	30	30	59	65	30	30	59	59	59	59	30	30	39	39	59	39	Sp'l rate	59	59	49	49
30	30	23	23	46	49	23	23	46	46	46	46	23	23	30	30	46	30	.do	46	46	49	49
20	20	20	20	26	26	20	20	26	26	26	26	20	20	20	30	26	20	.do	26	26	20	20
30	30	23	23	40	40	23	23	40	40	40	40	23	23	30	30	40	30	.do	40	40	30	30

TABLE 32.—RATES OF FREIGHT, ALL RAIL, FROM

DISTANCE VIA SHORTEST ROUTE.—From New York, 592 miles;

[NOTE.—Where the rates shown are not specifically described as applying on less

Date.		Dry goods.	Cotton piece goods.	Boots and shoes.	Furniture. Less than carloads.	Furniture. Carloads.	Stoves. Less than carloads.	Stoves. Carloads.	Coffee. Less than carloads.	Coffee. Carloads.	Soaps. Castile and fancy. Less than carloads.	Soaps. Castile and fancy. Carloads.	Soaps. Common. Less than carloads.	Soaps. Common. Carloads.	Starch. Less than carloads.	Starch. Carloads.	Tea.	Sugar. Less than carloads.	Sugar. Carloads.
1873—June	13.....	29	29	29	29	29	29	29	22	22	29	29	22	22	22	22	29	22	22
	16.....	35	35	35	35	35	35	35	23	23	35	35	26	26	26	26	35	23	23
Sept.	17.....	49	49	49	49	49	49	49	23	23	46	46	30	30	39	39	49	23	23
1874—Jan.	1.....	65	65	65	65	65	65	65	30	30	59	59	39	39	49	49	65	30	30
Aug.	3.....	49	49	49	49	49	49	49	23	23	35	35	30	30	26	26	49	23	23
1875—Jan.	20.....	65	65	65	65	65	65	65	30	30	59	59	39	39	49	49	65	30	30
Mar.	17.....	49	49	49	49	49	49	49	20	20	35	35	30	30	26	26	49	20	20
May	26.....	35	35	35	35	35	35	35	18	18	32	32	23	23	30	30	35	18	18
	29.....	25	25	25	25	25	25	25	15	15	25	25	18	18	20	20	25	15	15
Aug.	12.....	40	40	40	40	40	40	40	15	15	30	30	20	20	25	25	40	15	15
Nov.	15.....	49	49	49	49	49	49	49	23	23	46	46	30	30	39	39	49	23	23
Dec.	22.....	30	30	30	30	30	30	30	15	15	25	25	20	20	20	20	30	15	15
1876—Jan.	10.....	49	49	49	49	49	49	49	23	23	46	46	30	30	39	39	49	23	23
June	12.....	25	25	25	25	25	25	25	16	16	25	25	16	16	25	25	25	16	16
July	28.....	15	15	15	15	15	15	15	10	10	15	15	10	10	15	15	15	10	10
1877—Mar.	12.....	49	49	49	49	49	49	49	23	23	46	46	30	30	39	39	49	23	23
Oct.	8.....	49	49	49	49	49	49	26	26	26	46	46	26	26	26	26	49	26	26
	22.....	65	65	65	65	65	65	30	30	30	59	59	30	30	30	30	65	30	30
Dec.	10.....	65	65	65	05	65	65	30	30	30	52	52	30	30	30	30	65	30	30
1878—Feb.	14.....	49	49	49	49	49	49	26	26	26	39	39	26	26	26	26	49	26	26
1881—Aug.	6.....	30	30	30	30	30	30	13	13	13	21	21	13	13	13	13	30	13	13
Nov.	14.....	39	39	39	39	39	39	19	19	19	33	33	19	19	19	19	39	19	19
1882—Jan.	24.....	39	39	39	39	29	39	18	18	18	32	32	18	18	18	18	39	18	18
July	1.....	39	39	39	39	39	39	20	20	20	33	33	20	20	20	20	39	17	17
Nov.	1.....	49	49	49	49	49	49	23	23	23	39	39	23	23	23	23	49	23	23
1883—June	22.....	49	49	49	49	49	49	23	23	23	39	39	23	23	23	23	49	17	17
Jan.	26.....	33	33	33	33	33	33	17	17	17	26	26	17	17	17	17	33	12	12
June	1.....	26	26	26	26	26	26	12	12	12	20	20	12	12	12	12	26	10	10
Oct.	5.....	39	26	39	39	39	39	17	17	17	33	33	17	17	17	17	39	13	13
Nov.	18.....	49	30	49	49	49	49	23	23	23	39	39	23	23	23	23	49	17	17
1886—Mar.	10.....	53	32	53	53	53	53	25	25	25	43	43	25	25	25	25	53	18	18
Aug.	26.....	53	36	53	53	53	53	25	25	25	43	43	25	25	25	25	53	18	18
1887—Apr.	1.....	53	36	53	53	46	36	21	25	18	46	46	25	21	25	18	53	25	18
1888—Jan.	9.....	53	36	53	53	46	36	23	27	20	46	46	27	23	27	20	53	27	20
Aug.	15.....	53	36	53	53	46	53	21	25	18	46	46	25	21	25	18	53	25	18
Nov.	12.....	36	25	36	36	28	25	18	21	14	25	25	21	18	21	14	36	21	14
Dec.	17.....	53	36	53	53	46	36	21	25	18	46	46	25	21	25	18	53	25	18
1891—Apr.	9.....	53	36	53	53	46	21	18	25	18	46	46	25	21	25	18	53	25	18
1892—Mar.	16.....	53	36	53	53	46	21	18	25	18	25	18	25	18	25	18	53	25	15
May	2.....	53	36	53	53	46	21	18	25	18	25	18	25	18	25	18	53	25	18
June	6.....	53	36	53	53	46	21	18	25	18	25	18	25	18	25	18	53	25	16

Commodities (rates in cents per 100 pounds).

NEW YORK, N. Y., TO CLEVELAND, OHIO—Continued.

Boston, 663 miles; Philadephia, 541 miles; Baltimore, 521 miles.

than carload or carload quantities they apply on shipments regardless of quantity.]

Commodities (rates in cents per 100 pounds).																						
Molasses.		Rice.				Crockery and earthenware.		Bagging.		Leather.		Lead.		Nails.			Agricultural implements.		Machinery.		Beer.	
Less than carloads.	Carloads.	Less than carloads.	Carloads.	Groceries.	Drugs.	Less than carloads.	Carloads.	Less than carloads.	Carloads.	Less than carloads.	Carloads.	Less than carloads.	Carloads.	Less than carloads.	Carloads.	Hardware.	Less than carloads.	Carloads.	Less than carloads.	Carloads.	Less than carloads.	Carloads.
22	22	22	22	29	29	22	22	29	29	29	29	22	22	22	22	29	22	Sp'l rate	29	29	22	22
26	26	23	23	35	35	23	23	35	35	35	25	23	23	26	26	35	26	.do	35	35	26	26
30	30	23	23	46	49	23	23	46	46	46	46	23	23	30	30	46	30	.do	46	46	39	39
39	39	30	30	59	65	30	30	59	59	59	59	30	30	39	39	59	39	.do	59	59	49	49
30	30	23	23	35	35	23	23	35	35	35	35	23	23	30	30	35	30	.do	35	35	26	26
39	39	30	30	59	65	30	30	59	59	59	59	30	30	39	39	59	.do .	39	59	59	49	94
30	30	23	23	35	49	23	23	35	35	35	35	23	23	30	30	35	.do .	30	35	35	26	26
23	23	18	18	32	35	18	18	32	32	32	32	18	18	23	23	32	.do .	23	32	32	30	30
18	18	15	15	25	25	15	15	25	25	25	25	15	15	18	18	25	.do .	18	25	25	20	20
20	20	15	15	30	40	15	15	30	30	30	30	15	15	20	20	30	.do .	20	30	30	25	25
30	30	23	23	46	49	23	23	46	46	46	46	23	23	30	30	46	.do .	30	46	46	39	39
20	20	15	15	25	30	15	15	25	25	25	25	15	15	20	20	25	.do .	20	25	25	20	20
30	30	23	23	46	49	23	23	46	46	46	46	23	23	30	30	46	.do .	30	46	46	39	39
16	16	16	16	25	25	16	16	25	25	25	25	16	16	16	16	25	.do .	16	25	25	25	25
10	10	10	10	15	15	10	10	15	15	15	15	10	10	10	10	15	.do .	10	15	15	15	15
30	30	23	23	46	49	23	23	46	46	46	46	23	23	30	30	46	.do .	30	46	46	39	39
26	26	26	26	46	49	26	26	26	26	46	46	26	26	26	26	46	.do .	26	46	26	26	26
30	30	30	30	59	65	30	30	30	30	59	59	30	30	30	30	59	.do .	30	59	30	30	30
30	30	30	30	52	65	30	30	30	30	52	52	30	30	30	30	52	.po .	30	52	30	30	30
26	26	26	26	39	49	26	26	26	26	39	39	26	26	26	26	39	.do .	26	39	26	26	26
13	13	13	13	21	30	13	13	13	13	21	21	13	13	13	13	21	.do .	13	21	13	13	13
19	19	19	19	33	39	19	19	19	19	33	33	19	19	19	19	33	.do .	19	33	19	19	19
18	18	18	18	32	39	18	18	18	18	32	32	18	18	18	18	32	.do .	18	32	18	18	18
17	17	20	20	33	39	20	20	20	20	33	33	20	20	20	20	33	.do .	20	33	20	20	20
23	23	23	23	39	49	23	23	23	23	39	39	23	23	23	23	39	.do .	23	39	23	23	23
17	17	23	23	39	49	23	23	23	23	39	39	23	23	23	23	39	.do .	23	39	23	23	23
12	12	17	17	26	33	17	17	17	17	26	26	17	17	17	17	26	.do .	17	26	17	17	17
10	10	12	12	20	26	12	12	12	12	20	20	12	12	12	12	20	.do .	12	20	12	12	12
13	13	17	17	33	39	17	17	17	17	33	33	17	17	17	17	33	.do .	17	33	17	17	17
17	17	23	23	39	49	23	23	23	23	39	39	23	23	23	23	39	.do	23	39	23	23	23
18	18	25	25	43	53	25	25	25	25	43	43	25	25	25	25	43	.do .	25	43	25	25	25
18	18	25	25	43	53	25	25	25	25	43	43	25	25	25	25	43	.do .	25	43	25	25	25
25	21	25	25	46	53	25	21	36	25	36	25	25	18	25	21	46	36	21	25	21	36	21
27	23	27	27	46	53	27	23	36	27	36	27	27	20	27	23	46	36	23	27	23	36	23
25	21	25	18	46	53	21	18	36	25	36	25	25	18	25	21	46	36	21	25	21	36	21
21	18	21	14	25	36	21	18	25	21	21	14	21	14	21	18	25	25	18	21	18	25	18
25	21	25	18	46	53	25	21	36	25	36	25	25	18	25	21	46	36	21	25	21	36	21
25	21	25	18	46	53	21	18	36	25	36	25	25	18	21	18	46	36	21	25	21	36	21
25	21	25	18	46	53	21	18	36	25	36	25	25	18	21	18	46	36	21	25	21	36	21
25	21	25	18	46	53	21	18	36	25	36	25	25	18	21	18	46	36	21	25	21	36	21
25	21	25	18	46	53	21	18	36	35	36	25	25	18	21	18	46	36	21	25	21	36	21

TABLE 33.—RATES OF FREIGHT, ALL RAIL,

DISTANCE VIA SHORTEST ROUTE.—From New York, 497 miles;

[NOTE.—Where the rates shown are not specifically described as applying on less than

Date.	Commodities (rates in cents per 100 pounds).																	
	Dry goods.	Cotton piece goods.	Boots and shoes.	Furniture.		Stoves.		Coffee.		Soaps.				Starch.		Tea.	Sugar.	
										Castile and fancy.		Common.						
				Less than carloads.	Carloads.	Less than carloads.	Carloads.	Less than carloads.	Carloads.	Less than carloads.	Carload.	Less than carload.	Carloads.	Less than carloads.	Carloads.		Less than carloads.	Carloads.
1867—May 15	113	113	113	113	113	113	113	95	95	95	95	75	75	95	95	113	50	50
Nov. 5	120	120	120	120	120	120	120	100	100	100	100	80	80	100	100	120	52	52
1868—Feb. 4	120	120	120	120	120	120	120	Special rate.		100	100	52	52	80	80	120	Special rate.	
June 4	113	113	113	113	113	113	113	..do....		95	95	50	50	75	75	113	..do....	
Aug. 10	95	95	95	95	95	95	95	..do....		80	80	50	50	71	71	95	..do....	
Sept. 7	113	113	113	113	113	113	113	..do....		95	95	50	50	75	75	113	..do....	
Dec. 7	120	120	120	120	120	120	120	..do....		100	100	52	52	80	80	120	..do....	
1869—Feb. 1	113	113	113	113	113	113	113	..do....		95	95	50	50	75	75	113	..do....	
Mar. 15	100	100	100	100	100	100	100	..do....		95	95	50	50	75	75	100	..do....	
Mar. 29	95	95	95	95	95	95	95	..do....		95	95	50	50	75	75	95	..do....	
April 12	95	95	95	95	95	95	95	..do....		95	95	50	50	75	75	95	..do....	
July 1	108	108	108	108	108	108	108	..do....		95	95	50	50	75	75	108	..do....	
Aug. 11	35	35	35	35	35	35	35	..do....		35	35	35	35	35	35	35	..do....	
Aug. 30	30	30	30	30	30	30	30	..do....		30	30	30	30	30	30	30	..do....	
Sept. 24	25	25	25	25	25	25	25	..do....		25	25	25	25	25	25	25	..do....	
Oct. 4	50	50	50	50	50	50	50	..do....		45	45	35	35	40	40	50	..do....	
Oct. 13	80	80	80	80	80	80	80	..do....		63	63	41	41	48	48	80	..do....	
Nov. 1	83	83	83	83	83	83	83	..do....		74	74	48	48	59	59	83	..do....	
Nov. 29	89	89	89	89	89	89	89	..do....		76	76	48	48	59	59	89	..do....	
1870—May 7	89	89	89	89	89	89	89	..do....		76	76	48	48	59	59	89	..do....	
June 22	71	71	71	71	71	71	71	..do....		57	57	36	36	46	46	71	..do....	
July 7	75	75	75	75	75	75	75	..do....		60	60	38	38	50	50	75	..do....	
July 25	38	38	38	38	38	38	38	..do....		34	34	25	25	31	31	38	..do....	
July 28	32	32	32	32	32	32	32	..do....		32	32	25	25	31	31	32	..do....	
Aug. 12	32	32	32	32	32	32	32	..do....		32	32	32	32	32	32	32	..do....	
Aug. 23	55	55	55	55	55	55	55	..do....		50	50	32	32	40	40	55	..do....	
Sept. 8	74	74	74	74	74	74	74	..do....		65	65	40	40	50	50	74	..do....	
Nov. 28	90	90	90	90	90	90	90	..do....		71	71	36	36	56	56	90	..do....	
Dec. 26	106	106	106	106	106	106	106	35	35	88	88	46	46	70	70	106	35	35
1871—Feb. 20	88	88	88	88	88	88	88	32	32	75	75	41	41	58	58	88	32	32
Mar. 13	59	59	59	59	59	59	59	26	26	52	52	32	32	41	41	59	26	26
May 18	45	45	45	45	45	45	45	22	22	40	40	27	27	32	32	45	22	22
June 1	59	59	59	59	59	59	59	26	26	52	52	32	32	41	41	59	26	26
July 8	45	45	45	45	45	45	45	22	22	40	40	27	27	32	32	45	22	22
Aug. 16	29	29	29	29	29	29	29	20	20	29	29	29	29	29	29	29	20	20
Aug. 18	27	27	27	27	27	27	27	17	17	27	27	27	27	27	27	27	17	17
Aug. 22	23	23	23	23	23	23	23	17	17	23	23	23	23	23	23	23	17	17
Nov. 29	59	59	59	59	59	59	59	26	26	52	52	32	32	41	41	59	26	26
Dec. 15	82	82	82	82	82	82	82	33	33	72	72	43	43	56	56	82	33	33
1872—Apr. 27	82	82	82	82	82	82	82	33	33	72	72	43	43	56	56	82	33	33
Aug. 1	49	49	49	49	49	49	49	23	23	46	46	30	30	39	39	49	23	23
Sept. 1	82	82	82	82	82	82	82	33	33	72	72	43	33	56	56	82	33	33
Sept. 2	55	55	55	55	55	55	55	25	25	50	50	31	31	39	39	55	25	25
Oct. 14	82	82	82	82	82	82	82	33	33	72	72	43	43	56	56	82	33	33
1873—Apr. 14	65	65	65	65	65	65	65	25	25	55	55	35	35	45	45	65	25	25
June 11	49	49	49	49	49	49	49	23	23	46	46	30	30	39	39	49	23	23
July 22	49	49	49	49	49	49	49	20	20	40	40	30	30	35	35	49	20	20
Aug. 11	22	22	22	22	22	22	22	17	17	22	22	17	17	17	17	22	17	17
Aug. 12	40	40	40	40	40	40	40	30	30	40	40	30	30	30	30	40	30	30
Aug. 13	35	35	35	35	35	35	35	18	18	35	35	26	26	28	28	35	18	18
Aug. 16	35	35	35	35	35	35	35	23	23	35	35	26	26	26	26	35	23	23
Aug. 21	29	29	29	29	29	29	29	22	22	29	29	22	22	22	22	29	22	22
Sept. 17	45	45	45	45	45	45	45	20	20	40	40	30	30	35	35	45	20	20
1874—Jan. 1	60	60	60	60	60	60	60	25	25	50	50	30	30	40	40	60	25	25
Aug. 3	45	45	45	45	45	45	45	20	20	40	40	30	30	35	35	45	20	20
1875—Jan. 20	60	60	60	60	60	60	60	25	25	50	50	30	30	40	40	60	25	25
Mar. 17	45	45	45	45	45	45	45	20	20	40	40	30	30	35	35	45	20	20
Dec. 22	30	30	30	30	30	30	30	15	15	25	25	20	20	20	20	30	15	15
1876—Jan. 10	45	45	45	45	45	45	45	23	23	46	46	30	30	35	35	45	20	20
June 12	25	25	25	25	25	25	25	16	16	25	25	16	16	25	25	25	16	16
July 28	15	15	15	15	15	15	15	10	10	15	15	10	10	15	15	15	10	10

FROM NEW YORK, N. Y., TO ERIE, PA.

Boston, 568 miles; Philadelphia, 446 miles; Baltimore, 425 miles.

carload or carload quantities they apply on shipments regardless of quantity.]

Commodities (rates in cents per 100 pounds).																						
Molasses.		Rice.				Crockery and earthenware.		Bagging.		Leather.		Lead.		Nails.			Agricultural implements.		Machinery.		Beer.	
Less than carloads.	Carloads.	Less than carloads.	Carloads.	Groceries.	Drugs.	Less than carloads.	Carloads.	Less than carloads.	Carloads.	Less than carloads.	Carloads.	Less than carloads.	Carloads.	Less than carloads.	Carloads.	Hardware.	Less than carloads.	Carloads.	Less than carloads.	Carloads.	Less than carloads.	Carloads.
50	50	50	50	95	113	95	95	95	95	95	95	50	50	50	50	95	113	113	113	113	75	75
52	52	52	52	100	120	100	100	100	100	100	100	52	52	52	52	100	120	120	120	120	80	80
Special rate.		52	52	100	120	100	100	100	100	100	100	52	52	52	52	100	120	120	120	120	80	80
..do....		50	50	95	113	95	95	95	95	95	95	50	50	50	50	95	113	113	113	113	75	75
..do....		50	50	80	95	80	80	80	80	80	80	50	50	50	50	80	95	95	95	95	71	71
..do....		50	50	95	113	95	95	95	95	95	95	50	50	50	50	95	113	113	113	113	75	75
..do....		52	52	100	120	100	100	100	100	100	100	52	52	52	52	100	120	120	120	120	80	80
..do....		50	50	95	113	95	95	95	95	95	95	50	50	50	50	95	113	113	113	113	75	75
..do....		50	50	95	100	95	95	95	95	95	95	50	50	50	50	95	100	100	100	100	75	75
..do....		50	50	95	95	95	95	95	95	55	95	50	50	50	50	95	95	95	95	95	75	75
..do....		50	50	95	95	Special rate.		95	95	95	95	50	50.	50	50	95	95	95	95	95	75	75
..do....		50	50	95	108	..do....		95	95	95	95	50	50	50	50	95	108	108	95	95	75	75
..do....		35	35	35	35	..do....		35	35	35	35	35	35	35	35	35	35	35	35	35	35	35
..do....		30	30	30	30	..do....		30	30	30	30	30	30	30	30	30	30	30	30	30	30	30
..do....		25	25	25	25	..do....		25	25	25	25	25	25	25	25	25	25	25	25	25	25	25
..do....		35	35	45	50	..do....		45	45	45	45	35	35	35	35	45	50	50	45	45	40	40
..do....		41	41	63	80	..do....		63	63	63	63	41	41	41	41	63	80	80	63	63	48	48
..do....		48	48	74	83	..do....		74	74	74	74	48	48	48	48	74	83	83	74	74	59	59
..do....		48	48	76	89	..do....		76	76	76	76	48	48	48	48	76	89	89	76	76	59	59
..do....		Special rate.		76	89	..do....		76	76	76	76	48	48	48	48	76	89	89	76	76	59	59
..do....		..do....		57	71	..do....		57	57	57	57	36	36	36	36	57	71	71	57	57	46	46
..do....		..do....		60	75	..do....		60	60	60	60	38	38	38	38	60	75	75	60	60	50	50
..do....		..do....		34	38	..do....		34	34	34	34	25	25	25	25	34	38	38	34	34	31	31
..do....		..do....		32	32	..do....		32	32	32	32	25	25	25	25	32	32	32	32	32	31	31
..do....		..do....		32	32	..do....		32	32	32	32	32	32	32	32	32	32	32	32	32	32	32
..do....		..do....		50	55	..do....		50	50	50	50	31	31	31	32	50	55	55	50	50	40	40
..do....		..do....		65	74	..do....		65	65	65	65	40	40	40	40	65	74	74	65	65	50	50
..do....		..do....		71	90	..do....		71	71	71	71	36	36	36	36	71	90	90	71	71	56	56
46	46	46	46	88	106	88	88	88	88	88	88	46	46	46	46	88	106	106	88	88	70	70
41	41	41	41	75	88	32	32	75	75	75	75	32	32	41	41	75	88	88	75	75	58	58
32	32	32	32	52	59	26	26	52	52	52	52	26	26	32	32	52	59	59	52	52	41	41
27	27	27	27	40	45	22	22	40	40	40	40	22	22	27	27	40	45	45	40	40	32	32
32	32	32	32	52	59	26	26	52	52	52	52	26	26	32	32	52	59	59	52	52	41	41
27	27	27	27	40	45	22	22	40	40	40	40	22	22	27	27	40	45	45	40	40	32	32
29	29	29	29	29	29	20	20	29	29	29	29	20	20	29	29	29	29	29	29	20	29	29
27	27	27	27	27	27	17	17	27	27	27	27	17	17	27	27	27	27	27	27	27	27	27
23	23	23	23	23	23	17	17	23	23	23	23	17	17	23	23	23	23	23	23	23	23	23
32	32	32	32	52	59	26	26	52	52	52	52	26	26	32	32	52	59	59	52	52	41	41
43	43	43	43	72	82	72	72	72	72	72	72	33	33	43	43	72	82	82	72	72	56	56
43	43	33	33	72	82	72	72	72	72	72	72	33	33	43	43	72	82	82	72	72	56	56
30	30	23	23	46	49	46	46	46	46	46	46	23	23	30	30	46	49	49	46	46	39	39
43	43	43	43	72	82	72	72	72	72	72	72	33	33	43	43	72	82	82	72	72	56	56
31	31	25	25	50	55	50	50	50	50	50	50	25	25	31	31	50	55	55	50	50	39	39
43	43	33	33	72	82	33	33	72	72	72	72	33	33	43	43	72	82	82	72	72	56	56
35	35	25	25	55	65	25	25	55	55	55	55	25	25	35	35	55	Spe'l rate.	35	55	55	45	45
30	30	23	23	46	49	23	23	46	46	46	46	23	23	30	30	46	.do .	30	46	46	39	39
30	30	20	20	40	49	20	20	40	40	40	40	20	20	30	30	40	.do .	30	40	40	35	35
17	17	17	17	22	22	17	17	22	22	22	22	17	17	17	17	22	.do .	17	22	22	17	17
30	30	30	30	40	40	30	30	40	40	40	40	30	30	30	30	40	.do .	30	40	40	30	30
26	26	18	18	35	35	18	18	35	35	35	35	18	18	26	26	35	.do .	26	35	35	28	28
26	26	23	23	35	35	23	23	35	35	35	35	23	23	26	26	35	.do .	23	35	35	26	26
22	22	22	22	29	29	22	22	29	29	29	29	22	22	22	22	29	.do .	22	29	29	22	22
30	30	20	20	40	45	20	20	40	40	40	40	20	20	30	30	40	.do .	30	40	40	35	35
30	30	25	25	50	60	25	25	50	50	50	50	25	25	30	30	50	.do .	30	50	50	40	40
30	30	20	20	40	45	20	20	40	40	40	40	20	20	30	30	40	.do .	30	40	40	35	35
30	30	25	25	50	60	25	25	50	50	50	50	25	25	30	30	50	.do .	30	50	50	40	40
30	30	20	20	40	45	20	20	40	40	40	40	20	20	30	30	40	.do .	30	40	40	35	35
20	20	15	15	25	30	15	15	25	25	25	25	15	15	20	20	25	.do .	20	25	25	20	20
30	30	20	20	46	45	23	23	46	46	46	46	20	20	30	30	46	.do .	30	46	46	35	35
16	16	16	16	25	25	16	16	25	25	25	25	16	16	16	16	25	.do .	16	25	25	25	25
10	10	10	10	15	15	10	10	15	15	15	15	10	10	10	10	15	.do .	10	15	15	15	51

TABLE 33.—RATES OF FREIGHT, ALL RAIL, FROM

DISTANCE VIA SHORTEST ROUTE.—From New York, 497 miles;

[NOTE.—Where the rates shown are not specifically described as applying on less

Date.	Dry goods.	Cotton piece goods.	Boots and shoes.	Furniture. Less than carloads.	Furniture. Carloads.	Stoves. Less than carloads.	Stoves. Carloads.	Coffee. Less than carloads.	Coffee. Carloads.	Soaps. Castile and fancy. Less than carloads.	Soaps. Castile and fancy. Carloads.	Soaps. Common. Less than carloads.	Soaps. Common. Carloads.	Starch. Less than carloads.	Starch. Carloads.	Tea.	Sugar. Less than carloads.	Sugar. Carloads.
	Commodities (rates in cents per 100 pounds).																	
1877—Oct. 8.....	40	40	40	40	40	40	24	24	24	35	35	24	24	24	24	40	24	24
Oct. 22.....	60	60	60	60	60	60	26	26	26	50	50	26	26	26	26	60	26	26
Dec. 10.....	60	60	60	60	60	60	26	26	26	44	44	26	26	26	26	60	26	26
Dec. 18.....	40	40	40	40	40	40	20	20	20	35	35	25	25	35	30	40	20	20
1878—Feb. 14.....	43	43	43	43	43	43	23	23	23	35	35	23	23	23	23	43	23	23
1882—Jan. 24.....	30	30	30	30	30	30	13	13	13	21	21	13	13	13	13	30	13	13
Apr. 24.....	19	19	19	19	19	19	10	10	10	16	16	10	10	10	10	19	10	10
July 1.....	35	35	35	35	35	35	17	17	17	30	30	17	17	17	17	35	13	13
Nov. 1.....	43	43	43	43	43	43	20	20	20	35	35	20	20	20	20	43	20	20
1883—June 22.....	43	43	43	43	43	43	20	20	20	35	35	20	20	20	20	43	15	15
1887—Apr. 1.....	45	30	45	45	39	30	18	21	15	39	39	23	20	23	16½	45	21	15
1888—Jan. 9.....	45	30	45	45	39	30	20	23	16½	39	39	23	20	23	16½	45	23	16½
Mar. 5.....	45	30	45	45	39	30	18	21	15	39	39	21	18	21	15	45	21	15
Nov. 12.....	30	21	30	30	24	21	15	18	12	24	24	18	15	18	12	30	18	12
Dec. 17.....	45	30	45	45	39	30	18	21	15	39	39	21	18	21	15	45	21	15
1889—Feb. 18.....	45	30	45	45	39	45	18	21	15	39	39	21	18	21	15	45	21	15
1891—Apr. 9.....	45	30	45	45	39	18	15	21	15	39	39	21	18	21	15	45	21	15
1892—Mar. 16.....	45	30	45	45	39	18	15	21	15	21	18	21	18	21	18	45	21	13
May 2.....	45	30	45	45	39	18	15	21	15	21	15	21	15	21	15	45	21	15

NEW YORK, N. Y., TO ERIE, PA.—Continued.

Boston, 568 miles; Philadelphia, 446 miles; Baltimore, 425 miles.

than carload or carload quantities they apply on shipments regardless of quantity.]

Commodities (rates in cents per 100 pounds).																								
Molasses.		Rice.				Crockery and earthenware.		Bagging.		Leather		Lead.		Nails.			Agricultural implements.		Machinery.		Beer.	
Less than carloads.	Carloads.	Less than carloads.	Carloads.	Groceries.	Drugs.	Less than carloads.	Carloads.	Less than carloads.	Carloads.	Less than carloads.	Carloads.	Less than carloads.	Carloads.	Less than carloads.	Carloads.	Hardware.	Less than carloads.	Carloads.	Less than carloads.	Carloads.	Less than carloads.	Carloads.
24	24	24	24	35	40	24	24	21	24	40	40	24	24	24	24	35	Spe'l rate.	24	40	24	24	24
26	26	26	26	50	60	26	26	26	26	50	50	26	26	26	26	50	.do .	26	50	26	26	36
26	26	26	26	44	60	26	26	26	26	44	44	26	26	26	26	44	.do .	26	44	26	26	26
25	25	20	20	35	40	20	20	35	35	35	35	20	20	25	25	35	.do .	25	35	20	30	30
23	23	23	23	35	43	23	23	23	23	35	35	23	23	23	23	35	.do .	23	35	23	23	23
13	13	13	13	21	30	13	13	13	13	21	21	13	13	13	13	21	.do .	13	21	13	13	13
10	10	10	10	16	19	10	10	10	10	16	16	10	10	10	10	16	.do .	10	16	10	10	10
13	13	17	17	30	35	17	17	17	17	30	30	17	17	17	17	30	.do .	17	30	17	17	17
20	20	20	20	35	43	20	20	20	20	35	35	20	20	20	20	35	.do .	20	35	20	20	20
15	15	20	20	35	43	20	20	20	20	35	35	20	20	20	20	35	.do .	20	35	20	20	20
21	18	21	21	39	45	21	18	30	21	30	21	21	15	21	18	39	30	18	21	18	30	18
23	20	23	16½	39	45	23	20	30	23	30	23	23	16½	23	20	39	23	20	23	20	30	20
21	18	21	15	39	45	21	18	30	21	30	21	21	15	21	18	39	30	18	21	18	30	18
18	15	18	12	24	30	18	15	21	18	21	18	18	12	18	15	24	21	15	18	15	21	15
21	18	21	15	39	45	21	18	30	21	30	21	21	15	21	18	39	30	18	21	18	30	18
21	18	21	15	39	45	21	18	30	21	30	21	21	15	21	18	39	30	18	21	18	30	18
21	18	21	15	39	45	21	18	30	21	30	21	21	15	18	15	39	30	18	21	18	30	18
21	18	21	15	39	45	21	18	30	21	30	21	21	15	18	15	39	45	18	21	18	30	18
21	18	21	15	39	45	21	18	30	21	30	21	21	15	18	15	39	45	18	21	18	30	18

TABLE 34.—RATES OF FREIGHT, ALL RAIL, FROM

DISTANCE VIA SHORTEST ROUTE.—From New York, 409 miles;

[NOTE.—Where the rates shown are not specifically described as applying on less

Date.		Commodities (rates in cents per 100 pounds.)																
					Furniture.		Stoves.		Coffee.		Soap.				Starch.			Sugar.	
											Castile and fancy.		Common.						
		Dry goods.	Cotton piece goods.	Boots and shoes.	Less than carloads.	Carloads.	Less than carloads.	Carloads.	Less than carloads.	Carloads.	Less than carloads.	Carloads.	Less than carloads.	Carloads.	Less than carloads.	Carloads.	Tea.	Less than carloads.	Carloads.
1867—May	15	88	88	88	88	88	88	88	75	75	75	75	50	50	75	75	88	33	33
Nov.	5	95	95	95	95	95	95	95	80	80	80	80	65	65	80	80	95	40	40
Dec.	23	110	110	110	110	110	110	110	95	95	95	95	75	75	95	95	110	55	55
1868—Feb.	4	110	110	110	110	110	110	110	Special rate.		95	95	55	55	75	75	110	Special rate.	
Mar.	24	95	95	95	95	95	95	95	..do....		80	80	40	40	65	65	95	..do....	
May	8	95	95	95	95	95	95	95	..do....		80	80	35	35	65	65	95	..do....	
June	23	87	87	87	87	87	87	87	..do....		71	71	35	35	58	58	87	..do....	
Dec.	8	110	110	110	110	110	110	110	..do....		95	95	55	55	75	75	110	..do....	
1869—Mar.	1	95	95	95	95	95	95	95	..do....		80	80	40	40	65	65	95	..do....	
Apr.	12	95	95	95	95	95	95	95	..do....		80	80	40	40	65	65	95	..do....	
Apr.	16	87	87	87	87	87	87	87	..do....		71	71	35	35	58	58	87	..do....	
Sept.	24	50	50	50	50	50	50	50	..do....		40	40	20	20	30	30	50	..do....	
Oct.	4	60	60	60	60	60	60	60	..do....		50	50	30	30	40	40	60	..do....	
Nov.	18	66	66	66	66	66	66	66	..do....		59	59	38	38	47	47	66	..do....	
Dec.	7	110	110	110	110	110	110	110	..do....		95	95	55	55	75	75	110	..do....	
1870—Mar.	7	110	110	110	110	110	110	110	..do....		95	95	55	55	75	75	110	..do....	
Apr.	1	87	87	87	87	87	87	87	..do....		71	71	35	35	71	71	87	..do....	
July	7	60	60	60	60	60	60	60	..do....		50	50	30	30	40	40	60	..do....	
Nov.	28	80	80	80	80	80	80	80	..do....		65	65	32½	32½	50	50	80	..do....	
Dec.	26	90	90	90	90	90	90	90	30	30	72	72	40	40	60	60	90	30	30
1871—Feb.	20	90	90	90	90	90	90	90	30	30	72	72	40	40	60	60	90	30	30
May	18	70	70	70	70	70	70	70	25	25	60	60	35	35	50	50	70	25	25
Dec.	2	90	90	90	90	90	90	90	30	30	72	72	40	40	60	60	90	30	30
Dec.	8	85	85	85	85	85	85	85	....	....	65	65	40	40	60	60	85	....	....
Dec.	15	82	82	82	82	82	82	82	30	30	72	72	43	43	56	56	82	30	30
1872—Apr.	27	70	70	70	70	70	70	70	25	25	60	60	35	35	50	50	70	25	25
Aug.	1	55	55	55	55	55	55	55	25	25	45	45	35	35	40	40	55	25	25
Sept.	1	85	85	85	85	85	85	85	....	....	65	65	40	40	60	60	85	....	....
Sept.	2	70	70	70	70	70	70	70	25	25	60	60	35	35	50	50	70	25	25
Oct.	14	85	85	85	85	85	85	85	30	30	65	65	40	40	60	60	85	30	30
1873—Jan.	14	75	75	75	75	75	75	75	30	30	60	60	40	40	50	50	75	30	30
Apr.	14	65	65	65	65	65	65	65	25	25	55	55	35	35	45	45	65	25	25
July	22	50	50	50	50	50	50	50	20	20	40	40	30	30	35	35	50	20	20
Aug.	13	22	22	22	22	22	22	22	17	17	22	22	17	17	17	17	22	17	17
1874—Jan.	1	60	60	60	60	60	60	60	25	25	50	50	30	30	40	40	60	25	25
Aug.	1	45	45	45	45	45	45	45	20	20	40	40	30	30	35	35	45	20	20
Dec.	24	85	85	85	85	85	85	85	....	....	65	65	40	40	60	60	85	....	....
1875—Jan.	20	60	60	60	60	60	60	60	25	25	50	50	30	30	40	40	60	25	25
Mar.	17	45	45	45	45	45	45	45	20	20	40	40	30	30	35	35	45	20	20
Dec.	22	30	30	30	30	30	30	30	15	15	25	25	20	20	20	20	30	15	15
1876—Jan.	10	45	45	45	45	45	45	45	20	20	40	40	30	30	35	35	45	20	20
June	12	25	25	25	25	25	25	25	16	16	25	25	16	16	25	25	25	16	16
July	28	15	15	15	15	15	15	15	10	10	15	15	10	10	15	15	15	10	10
Aug.	7	25	25	25	25	25	25	25	16	16	25	25	16	16	25	25	25	16	16
Dec.	18	40	40	40	40	40	40	40	20	20	35	35	25	25	30	30	40	20	20
1877—Mar.	12	45	45	45	45	45	45	45	20	20	40	40	30	30	35	35	45	20	20
Oct.	8	45	45	45	45	45	45	24	24	24	40	40	24	24	24	24	45	24	24
Oct.	22	60	60	60	60	60	60	26	26	26	50	50	26	26	26	26	60	26	26
Dec.	10	60	60	60	60	60	60	26	26	26	44	44	26	26	26	26	60	26	26
1878—Feb.	14	43	43	43	43	43	43	23	23	23	35	35	23	23	23	23	43	23	23
Mar.	28	43	43	43	43	43	43	23	23	23	35	35	23	23	23	23	43	23	23
1880—Jan.	1	43	43	43	43	43	43	23	23	23	35	35	23	23	23	23	43	23	23
1881—Aug.	6	30	30	30	30	30	30	13	13	13	21	21	13	13	13	13	30	13	13
1882—Jan.	24	39	39	39	39	39	39	18	18	18	32	32	18	18	18	18	39	18	18
July	1	35	35	35	35	35	35	17	17	17	30	30	17	17	17	17	35	13	13
Nov.	1	43	43	43	43	43	43	20	20	20	35	35	17	17	17	17	43	20	20
1883—June	22	43	43	43	43	43	43	20	20	20	35	35	20	20	20	20	43	15	15
1887—Apr.	1	39	28	39	39	33	28	16	19	13	33	33	19	16	19	13	39	19	13
1888—Jan.	9	39	28	39	39	33	28	17	20	14	33	33	20	17	20	14	39	20	14
Mar.	5	39	28	39	39	33	28	16	19	13	33	33	19	16	19	13	39	19	13
1891—June	20	39	28	39	39	33	28	16	19	13	19	13	19	13	19	13	39	19	13

NEW YORK, N. Y., TO BUFFALO, N. Y.

Boston, 480 miles; Philadelphia, 418 miles; Baltimore, 398 miles.

than carload or carload quantities they apply on shipments regardless of quantity.]

Commodities (rates in cents).																						
Molasses.		Rice.				Crockery and earthenware.		Bagging.		Leather.		Lead.		Nails.			Agricultural implements.		Machinery.		Beer.	
Less than carloads.	Carloads.	Less than carloads.	Carloads.	Groceries.	Drugs.	Less than carloads.	Carloads.	Less than carloads.	Carloads.	Less than carloads.	Carloads.	Less than carloads.	Carloads.	Less than carloads.	Carloads.	Hardware.	Less than carloads.	Carloads.	Less than carloads.	Carloads.	Less than carloads.	Carloads.
33	33	33	33	75	88	75	75	75	75	75	75	33	33	33	33	75	88	88	75	75	50	50
40	40	40	40	80	95	80	80	80	80	80	80	40	40	40	40	80	95	95	80	80	65	65
55	55	55	55	95	110	95	95	95	95	95	95	55	55	55	55	95	110	110	95	95	75	75
Special rate.		55	55	95	110	95	95	95	95	95	95	55	55	55	55	95	110	110	95	95	75	75
..do....		40	40	80	95	80	80	80	80	80	80	40	40	40	40	80	95	95	80	80	65	65
..do....		35	35	80	95	80	80	80	80	80	80	35	35	35	35	80	95	95	80	80	65	65
..do....		35	35	71	87	71	71	71	71	71	71	35	35	35	35	71	87	87	71	71	58	58
..do....		55	55	95	110	95	95	95	95	95	95	55	55	55	55	95	110	110	95	95	75	75
..do....		40	40	80	95	80	80	80	80	80	80	40	40	40	40	80	95	95	80	80	65	65
..do....		40	40	80	95	Special rate.		80	80	80	80	40	40	40	40	80	95	95	80	80	65	65
..do....		35	35	71	87	..do....		71	71	71	71	35	35	35	35	71	87	87	71	71	58	58
..do....		Special rate.		40	50	..do....		40	40	40	40	20	20	20	20	40	50	50	40	40	30	30
..do....		..do....		50	60	..do....		50	50	50	50	30	30	30	30	50	60	60	50	50	40	40
..do....		..do....		59	66	..do....		59	59	59	59	38	38	38	38	59	66	66	59	59	47	47
..do....		55	55	95	110	..do....		95	95	95	95	55	55	55	55	95	110	110	95	95	75	75
..do....		Special rate.		95	110	..do....		95	95	95	95	55	55	55	55	95	110	110	95	95	75	75
..do....		..do....		71	87	..do....		71	71	71	71	35	35	35	35	71	87	87	71	71	71	71
..do....		..do....		50	60	..do....		50	50	50	50	30	30	30	30	50	60	60	50	50	40	40
..do....		..do....		65	80	..do....		65	65	65	65	32½	32½	32½	32½	65	80	80	80	80	50	50
40	40	40	40	72	90	72	72	72	72	72	72	40	40	40	40	72	90	90	90	90	60	60
40	40	40	40	72	90	30	30	72	72	72	72	30	30	40	40	72	90	90	90	90	60	60
35	35	35	35	60	70	25	25	60	60	60	60	25	25	35	35	60	70	70	70	70	50	50
40	40	40	40	72	90	30	30	72	72	72	72	30	30	40	40	72	90	90	90	90	60	60
....	....	40	40	65	85	....	....	65	65	65	65	....	....	40	40	65	85	85	65	65	60	60
43	43	43	43	72	82	72	72	72	72	72	72	30	30	43	43	72	82	82	72	72	56	56
35	35	30	30	60	70	60	60	60	60	60	60	25	25	35	35	60	70	70	60	60	50	50
35	35	25	25	45	55	45	45	45	45	45	45	25	25	35	35	45	55	55	45	45	40	40
40	40	40	40	65	85	65	65	65	65	65	65	32½	32½	40	40	65	85	85	65	65	60	60
35	35	25	25	60	70	60	60	60	60	60	60	25	25	35	35	60	70	70	60	60	50	50
40	40	30	30	65	85	30	30	65	65	65	65	30	30	40	40	65	85	85	65	65	60	60
40	40	30	30	60	75	30	30	60	60	60	60	30	30	40	40	60	75	75	60	60	50	50
35	35	25	25	55	65	25	25	55	55	55	55	25	25	35	35	55	Sp'l rate	35	55	55	45	45
30	30	20	20	40	50	20	20	40	40	40	40	20	20	30	30	40	.do.	30	40	40	35	35
17	17	17	17	22	22	17	17	22	22	22	22	17	17	17	17	22	.do.	17	22	22	17	17
30	30	25	25	50	60	25	25	50	50	50	50	25	25	30	30	50	.do.	30	50	50	40	40
30	30	20	20	40	45	20	20	40	40	40	40	20	20	30	30	40	.do.	30	40	40	35	35
40	40	....	....	65	85	....	....	65	65	65	65	....	....	40	40	65	.do.	40	65	65	60	60
30	30	25	25	50	60	25	25	50	50	50	50	25	25	30	30	50	.do.	30	50	50	40	40
30	30	20	20	40	45	20	20	40	40	40	40	20	20	30	30	40	.do.	30	40	40	35	35
20	20	15	15	25	30	15	15	25	25	25	25	15	15	20	20	25	.do.	20	25	25	20	20
30	30	20	20	40	45	20	20	40	40	40	40	20	20	30	30	40	.do.	30	40	40	35	35
16	16	16	16	25	25	16	16	25	25	25	25	16	16	16	16	25	.do.	16	25	25	25	25
10	10	10	10	15	15	10	10	15	15	15	15	10	10	10	10	15	.do.	10	15	15	15	15
16	16	16	16	25	25	16	16	25	25	25	25	16	16	16	16	25	.do.	16	25	25	25	25
25	25	20	20	35	40	20	20	35	35	35	35	20	20	25	25	35	.do.	25	35	35	30	30
30	30	20	20	40	45	20	20	40	40	40	40	20	20	30	30	40	.do.	30	40	40	35	35
24	24	24	24	40	45	24	24	24	24	40	40	24	24	24	24	40	.do.	24	40	24	24	24
26	26	26	26	50	60	26	26	26	26	50	50	26	26	26	26	50	.do.	26	50	26	26	26
26	26	26	26	44	60	26	26	26	26	44	44	26	26	26	26	44	.do.	26	44	26	26	26
23	23	23	23	35	43	23	23	23	23	35	35	23	23	23	23	35	.do.	25	35	23	23	23
23	23	23	23	35	43	23	23	23	23	35	35	23	23	23	23	35	.do.	23	43	23	23	23
23	23	23	23	35	43	23	23	23	23	35	35	23	23	23	23	35	.do.	23	35	23	23	23
13	13	13	13	21	30	13	13	13	13	21	21	13	13	13	13	21	.do.	13	21	13	13	13
18	18	18	18	32	39	18	18	18	18	32	32	18	18	18	18	32	.do.	18	32	18	18	18
13	13	17	17	30	35	17	17	17	17	30	30	17	17	17	17	30	.do.	17	30	17	17	17
20	20	20	20	35	43	20	20	20	20	35	35	20	20	20	20	35	.do.	20	35	20	20	20
15	15	20	20	35	43	20	20	20	20	35	35	20	20	20	20	35	.do.	20	35	20	20	20
19	16	19	19	33	39	19	16	28	19	28	19	19	13	19	16	33	28	16	19	16	28	16
20	17	20	14	33	39	20	17	28	20	28	20	20	14	20	17	33	28	17	20	17	28	17
19	16	19	13	33	39	19	16	28	19	28	19	19	13	19	16	33	28	16	19	16	28	16
19	16	19	13	33	39	19	16	28	19	28	19	19	13	19	16	33	28	16	19	16	28	16

TABLE 35.—RATES OF FREIGHT, ALL RAIL,

DISTANCE VIA SHORTEST ROUTE.—From New York, 359 miles;

[NOTE.—Where the rates shown are not specifically described as applying on less

Date.	Commodities (rates in cents per 100 pounds).																	
	Dry goods.	Cotton piece goods.	Boots and shoes.	Furniture.		Stoves.		Coffee.		Soap.				Starch.		Tea.	Sugar.	
										Castile and fancy.		Common.						
				Less than carloads.	Carloads.	Less than carloads.	Carloads.	Less than carloads.	Carloads.	Less than carloads.	Carloads.	Less than carloads.	Carloads.	Less than carloads.	Carloads.		Less than carloads.	Carloads.
1867—May 15	84	84	84	84	84	84	84	71	71	71	71	46	46	71	71	84	32	32
Nov. 5	90	90	90	90	90	90	90	75	75	75	75	60	60	75	75	90	36	36
Dec. 23	105	105	105	105	105	105	105	90	90	90	90	70	70	90	90	105	53	53
1868—Feb. 4	105	105	105	105	105	105	105	Special rate.		90	90	53	53	70	70	105	Special rate.	
Mar. 23	85	85	85	85	85	85	85	..do....		70	70	36	36	58	58	85	..do....	
May 8	85	85	85	85	85	85	85	..do....		70	70	30	30	58	58	85	..do....	
May 15	77	77	77	77	77	77	77	..do....		66	66	30	30	55	55	77	..do....	
1869—Mar. 1	85	85	85	85	85	85	85	..do....		70	70	36	36	58	58	85	..do....	
Apr. 15	77	77	77	77	77	77	77	..do....		66	66	30	30	55	55	77	..do....	
Dec. 7	105	105	105	105	105	105	105	..do....		90	90	53	53	70	70	105	..do....	
1870—Mar. 7	105	105	105	105	105	105	105	..do....		90	90	53	53	70	70	105	..do....	
Apr. 1	77	77	77	77	77	77	77	..do....		66	66	30	30	55	55	77	..do....	
Nov. 28	77	77	77	77	77	77	77	....	....	62	62	30	30	48	48	77	....	....
Dec. 26	85	85	85	85	85	85	85	30	30	67	67	40	40	55	55	85	30	30
1871—Feb. 20	85	85	85	85	85	85	85	30	30	67	67	40	40	55	55	85	30	30
Mar. 13	81	81	81	81	81	81	81	30	30	68	68	34	34	58	58	81	30	30
May 18	60	60	60	60	60	60	60	25	25	50	50	30	30	40	40	60	25	25
Dec. 2	85	85	85	85	85	85	85	30	30	67	67	40	40	55	55	85	30	30
Dec. 8	77	77	77	77	77	77	77	....	....	62	62	37	37	55	55	77	....	....
Dec. 15	77	77	77	77	77	77	77	30	30	62	62	37	37	55	55	77	30	30
1872—Apr. 5	77	77	77	77	77	77	77	....	....	62	62	34	34	55	55	77	....	....
Apr. 27	77	77	77	77	77	77	77	30	30	62	62	37	37	55	55	77	30	30
Sept. 2	77	77	77	77	77	77	77	30	30	62	62	34	34	55	55	77	30	30
Oct. 14	77	77	77	77	77	77	77	30	30	62	62	34	34	55	55	77	30	30
1873—Jan. 14	70	70	70	70	70	70	70	27	27	55	55	35	35	45	45	70	27	27
Apr. 14	60	60	60	60	60	60	60	22	22	50	50	30	30	40	40	60	22	22
Aug. 8	50	50	50	50	50	50	50	20	20	40	40	30	30	35	35	50	20	20
Dec. 6	45	45	45	45	45	45	45	20	20	40	40	30	30	35	35	45	20	20
1874—Jan. 1	55	55	55	55	55	55	55	22	22	45	45	30	30	35	35	55	22	22
Aug. 1	45	45	45	45	45	45	45	20	20	40	40	30	30	35	35	45	20	20
Dec. 24	77	77	77	77	77	77	77	....	....	62	62	37	37	55	55	77	....	....
1875—Jan. 20	55	55	55	55	55	55	55	22	22	45	45	30	30	40	40	55	22	22
Mar. 17	45	45	45	45	45	45	45	20	20	40	40	30	30	35	35	45	20	20
Dec. 2	77	77	77	77	77	77	77	....	....	62	62	37	37	55	55	77	....	....
Dec. 22	30	30	30	30	30	30	30	15	15	25	25	20	20	20	20	30	15	15
1876—Jan. 10	45	45	45	45	45	45	45	20	20	40	40	30	30	35	35	45	20	20
Apr. 3	45	45	45	45	45	45	45	20	20	40	40	30	30	35	35	45	20	20
June 12	45	45	45	45	45	45	45	20	20	40	40	30	30	35	35	45	20	20
1877—Oct. 8	45	45	45	45	45	45	22	22	22	40	40	22	22	22	22	45	22	22
Oct. 22	55	55	55	55	55	55	24	24	24	45	45	24	24	24	24	55	24	24
Dec. 10	55	55	55	55	55	55	24	24	24	40	40	24	24	24	24	55	24	24
1878—Feb. 14	40	40	40	40	40	40	20	20	20	30	30	20	20	20	20	40	20	20
1881—Aug. 6	30	30	30	30	30	30	13	13	13	21	21	13	13	13	13	30	13	13
1882—Jan. 24	39	39	39	39	39	39	18	18	18	32	32	18	18	18	18	39	18	18
July 1	35	35	35	35	35	35	17	17	17	30	30	17	17	17	17	35	13	13
1892—Feb. 1	39	39	39	39	33	28	16	19	13	19	13	19	13	19	13	39	19	13

FROM NEW YORK, N. Y., TO ROCHESTER, N. Y.

Boston, 412 miles; Philadelphia, 375 miles; Baltimore, 354 miles.

than carload or carload quantities they apply on shipments regardless of quantity.]

Commodities (rates in cents per 100 pounds).																						
Molasses.		Rice.				Crockery and earthenware.		Bagging.		Leather.		Lead.		Nails.			Agricultural implements.		Machinery.		Beer.	
Less than carloads.	Carloads.	Less than carloads.	Carloads.	Groceries.	Drugs.	Less than carloads.	Carloads.	Less than carloads.	Carloads.	Less than carloads.	Carloads.	Less than carloads.	Carloads.	Less than carloads.	Carloads.	Hardware.	Less than carloads.	Carloads.	Less than carloads.	Carloads.	Less than carloads.	Carloads.
32	32	32	32	71	84	71	71	71	71	71	71	32	32	32	32	71	84	84	71	71	46	46
36	36	36	36	75	90	75	75	75	75	75	75	36	36	36	36	75	90	90	75	75	60	60
53	53	53	53	90	105	90	90	90	90	90	90	53	53	53	53	90	105	105	90	90	70	70
Special rate.		53	53	90	105	90	90	90	90	90	90	53	53	53	53	90	105	105	90	90	70	70
..do....		36	36	70	85	70	70	70	70	70	70	36	36	36	36	70	85	85	70	70	58	58
..do....		30	30	70	85	70	70	70	70	70	70	30	30	30	30	70	85	85	70	70	58	58
..do....		30	30	66	77	66	66	66	66	66	66	30	30	30	30	66	77	77	66	66	55	55
..do....		36	36	70	85	Special rate.		70	70	70	70	36	36	36	36	70	85	85	70	70	58	58
..do....		30	30	66	77	..do....		66	66	66	66	30	30	30	30	66	77	77	66	66	55	55
..do....		53	53	90	105	..do....		90	90	90	90	53	53	53	53	90	105	105	90	90	70	70
..do....		Special rate.		90	105	62	62	90	90	90	90	53	53	53	53	90	105	105	90	90	70	70
..do....		..do....		66	77	..do....		66	66	66	66	30	30	30	30	66	77	77	66	66	55	55
30	30	30	30	62	77	..do....		62	62	62	62	30	30	30	30	62	77	77	62	62	48	48
30	40	40	40	67	85	67	67	67	67	67	67	40	40	40	40	67	85	85	67	67	55	55
40	40	40	40	67	85	30	30	67	67	67	67	30	30	40	40	67	85	85	67	67	55	55
34	34	34	34	68	81	30	30	68	68	68	68	30	30	34	34	68	81	81	68	68	58	58
30	30	30	30	50	60	25	25	50	50	50	50	25	25	30	30	50	60	60	50	50	40	40
40	40	40	40	67	85	30	30	67	67	67	67	30	30	40	40	67	85	85	67	67	55	55
37	37	37	37	62	77	....	....	62	62	62	62	....	....	37	37	62	77	77	62	62	55	55
37	37	37	37	62	77	62	62	62	62	62	62	30	30	37	37	62	77	77	62	62	55	55
34	34	34	34	62	77	....	....	62	62	62	62	....	....	34	34	62	77	77	62	62	55	55
37	37	30	30	62	77	62	62	62	62	62	62	30	30	37	37	62	77	77	62	62	55	55
34	34	30	30	62	77	62	62	62	62	62	62	30	30	34	34	62	77	77	62	62	55	55
34	34	30	30	62	77	30	30	62	62	62	62	30	30	34	34	62	77	77	62	62	55	55
35	35	27	27	55	70	27	27	55	55	55	55	27	27	35	35	55	70	70	55	55	45	45
30	30	22	22	50	60	22	27	50	50	50	50	22	22	30	30	50	Spe'l rate.	30	50	50	40	40
30	30	20	20	40	50	20	20	40	40	40	40	20	20	30	30	40	.do.	30	40	40	35	35
30	30	20	20	40	45	20	20	40	40	40	40	20	20	30	30	40	.do.	30	40	40	35	35
22	22	22	22	45	55	22	22	45	45	45	45	22	22	30	30	45	.do.	30	45	45	40	40
20	20	20	20	40	45	20	20	40	40	40	40	20	20	30	30	40	.do.	30	40	40	35	35
37	37	....	....	62	77	....	....	62	62	62	62	....	....	37	37	62	.do.	37	62	62	55	55
30	30	22	22	45	55	22	22	45	45	45	45	22	22	30	30	45	.do.	30	45	45	40	40
30	30	20	20	40	45	20	20	40	40	40	40	20	20	30	30	40	.do.	30	40	40	35	35
37	37	....	....	62	77	....	....	62	62	62	62	....	....	37	37	62	.dc.	37	62	62	55	55
20	20	15	55	25	30	15	15	25	25	25	25	15	15	20	20	25	.do.	20	25	25	20	20
30	30	20	20	40	45	20	20	40	40	40	40	20	20	30	30	40	.do.	30	40	40	35	35
30	30	20	20	40	45	20	20	40	40	40	40	30	30	30	30	40	do.	30	40	40	35	35
30	30	20	20	40	45	20	20	40	40	40	40	20	20	30	30	40	.do.	30	40	40	35	35
22	22	22	22	40	45	22	22	22	22	40	40	22	22	22	22	40	.do.	22	40	22	22	22
24	24	24	24	45	55	24	24	24	24	45	45	24	24	24	24	45	.do.	24	45	24	24	24
24	24	24	24	40	55	24	24	24	24	40	40	24	24	24	24	40	.do.	24	40	24	24	24
20	20	20	20	30	40	20	20	20	20	30	30	20	20	20	20	30	.do.	20	30	20	20	20
13	13	13	13	21	30	13	13	13	13	21	21	13	13	13	13	21	.do.	13	21	13	13	13
18	18	18	18	32	39	18	18	18	18	32	32	18	18	18	18	32	.do.	18	32	18	18	18
13	13	17	17	30	35	17	17	17	17	30	30	17	17	17	17	30	.do.	17	30	17	17	17
19	16	19	13	33	39	19	16	28	19	28	19	19	13	19	16	33	28	16	19	16	28	16

TABLE 36.—RATES OF FREIGHT, ALL RAIL, FROM

DISTANCE VIA SHORTEST ROUTE.—From New York, 444 miles;

[NOTE.—Where the rates shown are not specifically described as applying on less

Date.	Commodities (rates in cents per 100 pounds).																		
	Dry goods.	Cotton piece goods.	Boots and shoes.	Furniture.		Stoves.		Coffee.		Soaps.				Starch.		Tea.	Sugar.	
										Castile and fancy.		Common.						
				Less than carloads.	Carloads.	Less than carloads.	Carloads.	Less than carloads.	Carloads.	Less than carloads.	Carloads.	Less than carloads.	Carloads.	Less than carloads.	Carloads.		Less than carloads.	Carloads.
1868—Oct. 2	55	55	55	55	55	55	55	Special rate.		53	53	33	33	46	46	55	Special rate.	
Oct. 3	33	33	33	33	33	33	33	..do....		33	33	33	33	33	33	33	..do....	
Nov. 2	71	71	71	71	71	71	71	..do....		56	56	33	33	46	46	71	..do....	
Dec. 1	86	86	86	86	86	86	86	..do....		71	71	33	33	56	56	86	..do....	
1869—May 12	86	86	86	86	86	86	86	..do....		71	71	33	33	56	56	86	..do....	
Nov. 29	71	71	71	71	71	71	71	..do....		56	56	36	36	46	46	71	..do....	
1870—May 7	71	71	71	71	71	71	71	..do....		56	56	36	36	46	46	71	..do....	
July 13	52	52	52	52	52	52	52	..do....		45	45	31	31	35	35	52	23	23
July 28	38	38	38	38	38	38	38	..do....		38	38	28	28	35	35	38	22	22
Aug. 11	32	32	32	32	32	32	32	..do....		32	32	28	28	32	32	32	22	22
Aug. 15	32	32	32	32	32	32	32	..do....		32	32	30	30	32	32	32	Special rate.	
Aug. 22	60	60	60	60	60	60	60	..do....		50	50	31	31	40	40	60	..do....	
Aug. 24	59	59	59	59	59	59	59	..do....		50	50	31	31	40	40	59	..do....	
Sept. 8	71	71	71	71	71	71	71	..do....		56	56	36	36	46	46	71	..do....	
Nov. 29	71	71	71	71	71	71	71	..do....		56	56	33	33	46	46	71	..do....	
Dec. 1	86	86	86	86	86	86	86	..do....		71	71	33	33	56	56	86	..do....	
Dec. 26	86	86	86	86	86	86	86	33	33	71	71	33	33	56	56	86	33	33
1871—Jan. 1	86	86	86	86	86	86	86	33	33	71	71	36	36	56	56	86	33	33
Feb. 20	86	86	86	86	86	86	86	30	30	71	71	36	36	56	56	86	30	30
Mar. 13	59	59	59	59	59	59	59	26	26	52	52	32	32	41	41	59	26	26
Apr. 21	55	55	55	55	55	55	55	25	25	50	50	30	30	40	40	55	25	25
May 18	45	45	45	45	45	45	45	22	22	40	40	27	27	32	32	45	22	22
June 1	59	59	59	59	59	59	59	25	25	52	52	32	32	41	41	59	25	25
June 15	45	45	45	45	45	45	45	22	22	40	40	26	26	32	32	45	22	22
July 28	38	38	38	38	38	38	38	22	22	38	38	26	26	32	32	38	22	22
Aug. 7	32	32	32	32	32	32	32	22	22	32	32	26	26	32	32	32	22	22
Aug. 16	29	29	29	29	29	29	29	20	20	29	29	26	26	29	29	29	20	20
Aug. 22	23	23	23	23	23	23	23	17	17	23	23	23	23	23	23	23	17	17
Sept. 5	20	20	20	20	20	20	20	16	16	20	20	20	20	20	20	20	16	16
Dec. 1	54	54	54	54	54	54	54	28	28	48	48	30	30	38	38	54	28	28
Dec. 15	54	54	54	54	54	54	54	28	28	48	48	30	30	38	38	54	28	28
1872—Jan. 1	54	54	54	54	54	54	54	23	23	48	48	30	30	38	38	54	23	23
1872—Apr. 27	54	54	54	54	54	54	54	23	23	48	48	30	30	38	38	54	23	23
Aug. 1	45	45	45	45	45	45	45	20	20	43	43	25	25	37	37	45	20	20
Aug. 6	43	43	43	43	43	43	43	19	19	39	39	25	25	33	33	43	19	19
Sept. 2	53	53	53	53	53	53	53	23	23	48	48	30	30	37	37	53	23	23
Oct. 14	53	53	53	53	53	53	53	23	23	48	48	30	30	37	37	53	23	23
Oct. 15	66	66	66	66	66	66	66	25	25	51	51	31	31	41	41	66	25	25
Oct. 19	45	45	45	45	45	45	45	23	23	40	40	27	27	32	32	45	23	23
Oct. 29	66	66	66	66	66	66	66	25	25	51	51	31	31	41	41	66	25	25
1873—Apr. 14	55	55	55	55	55	55	55	20	20	51	51	27	27	41	41	55	20	20
June 26	50	50	50	50	50	50	50	20	20	40	40	27	27	35	35	50	20	20
July 22	45	45	45	45	45	45	45	20	20	40	40	27	27	35	35	45	20	20
Aug. 2	44	44	44	44	44	44	44	18	18	36	36	26	26	31	31	44	18	18
Aug. 11	38	38	38	38	38	38	38	18	18	36	36	26	26	28	28	38	18	18
Aug. 13	35	35	35	35	35	35	35	18	18	35	35	26	26	28	28	35	18	18
Aug. 16	33	33	33	33	33	33	33	18	18	33	33	25	25	25	25	33	18	18
Aug. 20	29	29	29	29	29	29	29	18	18	29	29	22	22	22	22	29	18	18
Sept. 17	45	45	45	45	45	45	45	20	20	40	40	27	27	35	35	45	20	20
Sept. 18	40	40	40	40	40	40	40	18	18	35	35	27	27	30	30	40	18	18
Sept. 22	40	40	40	40	40	40	40	18	18	35	35	27	27	30	30	40	18	18
1874—Apr. 20	50	50	50	50	50	50	50	20	20	40	40	25	25	35	35	50	20	20
July 31	40	40	40	40	40	40	40	18	18	35	35	25	25	30	30	40	18	18
1875—Jan. 19	53	53	53	53	53	53	53	23	23	44	44	28	28	35	35	53	23	23
Feb. 17	53	53	53	53	53	53	53	20	20	44	44	28	28	35	35	53	20	20
Mar. 16	40	40	40	40	40	40	40	18	18	35	35	25	25	30	30	40	18	18
June 21	23	23	23	23	23	23	23	16	16	23	23	16	16	19	19	23	16	16
Aug. 12	35	35	35	35	35	35	35	14	14	25	25	18	18	22	22	35	14	14
Aug. 13	35	35	35	35	35	35	35	15	15	25	25	20	20	23	23	35	15	15
Nov. 15	36	36	36	36	36	36	36	16	16	32	32	24	24	28	28	36	16	16
Dec. 22	27	27	27	27	27	27	27	14	14	23	23	18	18	18	18	27	14	14

PHILADELPHIA, PA., TO PITTSBURG, PA.

Boston, 657 miles; Philadelphia, 354 miles; Baltimore, 333 miles.

than carload or carload quantities they apply on shipments regardless of quantity.]

Commodities (rates in cents per 100 pounds).																						
Molasses.		Rice.				Crockery and earthenware.		Bagging.		Leather.		Lead.		Nails.			Agricultural implements.		Machinery.		Beer.	
Less than carloads.	Carloads.	Less than carloads.	Carloads.	Groceries.	Drugs.	Less than carloads.	Carloads.	Less than carloads.	Carloads.	Less than carloads.	Carloads.	Less than carloads.	Carloads.	Less than carloads.	Carloads.	Hardware.	Less than carloads.	Carloads.	Less than carloads.	Carloads.	Less than carloads.	Carloads.
Special rate.		33	33	53	55	53	53	53	53	53	53	33	33	33	33	53	55	55	53	53	46	46
..do....	....	....	33	33	33	33	33	33	33	33	33	33	33	33	33	33	33	33	33	33	33
..do....	....	....	56	71	56	56	56	56	56	56	33	33	33	33	56	71	71	56	56	46	46
..do....	....	....	71	86	71	71	71	71	71	71	33	33	33	33	71	86	86	71	71	56	56
..do....	....	....	71	86	Special rate.		71	71	71	71	33	33	33	33	71	86	86	71	71	56	56
..do....	36	36	56	71	..do....		56	56	56	56	36	36	36	36	56	71	71	56	56	46	46
..do....	Special rate.		56	71	..do....		56	56	56	56	36	36	36	36	56	71	71	56	56	46	46
..do....	..do....		45	52	..do....		45	45	45	45	31	31	31	31	45	52	52	45	45	35	35
..do....	..do....		38	38	..do....		38	38	38	38	28	28	28	28	38	38	38	38	38	25	35
..do....	..do....		32	32	..do....		32	32	32	32	28	28	28	28	32	32	32	32	32	32	32
..do....	..do....		32	32	..do....		32	32	32	32	30	30	30	30	32	32	32	32	32	32	32
..do....	..do....		50	60	..do....		50	50	50	50	31	31	31	31	50	60	60	50	50	40	40
..do....	..do....		50	59	..do....		50	50	50	50	31	31	31	31	50	59	59	50	50	40	40
..do....	..do....		56	71	..do....		56	56	56	56	36	36	36	36	56	71	71	56	56	46	46
..do....	..do....		56	71	..do....		56	56	56	56	33	33	33	33	56	71	71	56	56	46	46
..do....	..do....		71	86	..do....		71	71	71	71	33	33	33	33	71	86	86	71	71	56	56
33	33	33	33	71	86	71	71	71	71	71	71	33	33	33	33	71	86	86	71	71	56	56
36	36	36	36	71	86	71	71	71	71	71	71	36	36	36	36	71	86	86	71	71	56	56
36	36	36	36	71	86	30	30	71	71	71	71	30	30	36	36	71	86	86	71	71	56	56
32	32	32	32	52	59	26	26	52	52	52	52	26	26	32	32	52	59	59	52	52	41	41
30	30	30	30	50	55	25	25	50	50	50	50	25	25	30	30	50	55	55	50	50	40	40
27	27	27	27	40	45	22	22	40	40	40	40	22	22	27	27	40	45	45	40	40	32	32
32	32	32	32	52	59	25	25	52	52	52	52	25	25	32	32	52	59	59	52	52	41	41
26	26	26	26	40	45	22	22	40	40	40	40	22	22	26	26	40	45	45	40	40	32	32
26	26	26	26	38	38	22	22	38	38	38	38	22	22	26	26	38	38	38	38	38	32	32
26	26	26	26	32	32	22	22	32	32	32	32	22	22	26	26	32	32	32	32	32	32	32
26	26	26	26	29	29	20	20	29	29	29	29	20	20	26	26	29	29	29	29	29	29	29
23	23	23	23	23	23	17	17	23	23	23	23	17	17	23	23	23	23	23	23	23	23	23
20	20	20	20	20	20	16	16	20	20	20	20	16	16	20	20	20	20	20	20	20	20	20
30	30	30	30	48	54	28	28	48	48	48	48	28	28	30	30	48	54	54	48	48	38	38
30	30	30	30	48	54	48	48	48	48	48	48	28	28	30	30	48	54	54	48	48	38	38
30	30	30	30	48	54	48	48	48	48	48	48	23	23	30	30	48	54	54	48	48	38	38
30	30	23	23	48	54	48	48	48	48	48	48	23	23	30	30	48	54	54	48	48	38	38
25	25	20	20	43	45	43	43	43	43	43	43	20	20	25	25	43	45	45	43	43	37	37
25	25	19	19	39	43	39	39	39	39	39	39	19	19	25	25	39	43	43	39	39	33	33
30	30	23	23	48	53	48	48	48	48	48	48	23	23	30	30	48	53	53	48	48	37	37
30	30	23	23	48	53	23	23	48	48	48	48	23	23	30	30	48	53	53	48	48	37	37
31	31	25	25	51	66	25	25	51	51	51	51	25	25	31	31	51	66	66	51	51	41	41
27	27	23	23	40	45	23	23	40	40	40	40	23	23	27	27	40	45	45	40	40	32	32
31	31	25	25	51	66	25	25	51	51	51	51	25	25	31	31	51	66	66	51	51	41	41
27	27	20	20	51	55	20	20	51	51	51	51	20	20	27	27	51	Spc'l rate.	27	51	51	41	41
27	27	20	20	40	50	20	20	40	40	40	40	20	20	27	27	40	.do .	27	40	40	35	35
27	27	20	20	40	45	20	20	40	40	40	40	20	20	27	27	40	.do .	27	40	40	35	35
26	26	18	18	36	44	18	18	36	36	36	36	18	18	26	26	36	.do .	26	36	36	31	31
26	26	18	18	36	38	18	18	36	36	36	36	18	18	26	26	36	.do .	26	36	36	28	28
26	26	18	18	35	35	18	18	35	35	35	35	18	18	26	26	35	.do .	26	35	35	28	28
25	25	18	18	33	33	18	18	33	33	33	33	18	18	25	25	33	.do .	25	33	33	25	25
22	22	18	18	29	29	18	18	29	29	29	29	18	18	22	22	29	.do .	22	29	29	22	22
27	27	20	20	40	45	20	20	40	40	40	40	20	20	27	27	40	.do .	27	40	40	35	35
27	27	18	18	35	40	18	18	35	35	35	35	18	18	27	27	35	.do .	27	35	35	30	30
25	25	18	18	35	40	18	18	35	35	35	35	18	18	25	25	35	.do .	25	35	35	30	30
25	25	20	20	40	50	20	20	40	40	40	40	20	20	25	25	40	.do .	25	40	40	35	35
25	25	18	18	35	40	18	18	35	35	35	35	18	18	25	25	35	.do .	25	35	35	30	30
28	28	23	23	44	53	23	23	44	44	44	44	23	23	28	28	44	.do .	28	44	44	35	35
25	25	20	20	44	53	20	20	44	44	44	44	20	20	25	25	44	.do .	25	44	44	35	35
25	25	18	18	35	40	18	18	35	35	35	35	18	18	25	25	35	.do .	25	35	35	30	30
16	16	16	16	23	23	16	16	23	23	23	23	16	16	16	16	23	.do .	16	23	23	19	19
18	18	14	14	25	35	14	14	25	25	25	25	14	14	18	18	25	.do .	18	25	25	22	22
20	20	15	15	25	35	15	15	25	25	25	25	15	15	20	20	25	.do .	20	25	25	23	23
24	24	16	16	32	32	16	16	32	32	32	32	16	16	24	24	32	.do .	24	32	32	28	28
18	18	14	14	23	23	14	14	23	23	23	23	14	14	18	18	23	.do .	18	23	23	18	18

TABLE 36.—RATES OF FREIGHT, ALL RAIL, FROM

DISTANCE VIA SHORTEST ROUTE.—From New York, 444 miles;

[NOTE.—Where the rates shown are not specifically described as applying on less

Date.	Commodities (rates in cents per 100 pounds).																	
				Furniture.		Stoves.		Coffee.		Soaps.				Starch.			Sugar.	
										Castile and fancy.		Common.						
	Dry goods.	Cotton piece goods.	Boots and shoes.	Less than carloads.	Carloads.	Less than carloads.	Carloads.	Less than carloads.	Carloads.	Less than carloads.	Carloads.	Less than carloads.	Carloads.	Less than carloads.	Carloads.	Tea.	Less than carloads.	Carloads.
1876—Jan. 10	36	36	36	36	36	36	36	16	16	32	32	24	24	38	38	36	16	16
June 3	36	36	36	36	36	36	36	16	16	32	32	20	20	28	28	36	16	16
June 12	22	22	22	22	22	22	22	14	14	22	22	14	14	22	22	22	14	14
Dec. 18	36	36	36	36	36	36	36	18	18	32	32	23	23	27	27	36	18	18
1877—Mar. 12	41	41	41	41	41	41	41	18	18	36	36	27	27	32	32	41	18	18
Apr. 7	42	42	42	42	42	42	42	19	19	39	39	27	27	34	34	42	19	19
Oct. 8	42	42	42	42	42	42	22	22	22	39	39	22	22	22	22	42	22	22
22	54	54	54	54	54	54	24	24	24	44	44	24	24	24	24	54	24	24
Dec. 10	54	54	54	54	54	54	24	24	24	38	38	24	24	24	24	54	24	24
1878—Feb. 15	37	37	37	37	37	37	21	21	21	29	29	21	21	21	21	37	21	21
1879—Jan. 1	37	37	37	37	37	37	21	21	21	29	29	21	21	21	21	37	21	21
1880—Jan. 1	37	37	37	37	37	37	21	21	21	29	29	21	21	21	21	37	21	21
1881—Aug. 6	30	30	30	30	30	30	13	13	13	21	21	13	13	13	13	30	13	13
Nov. 12	37	37	37	37	37	37	17	17	17	30	30	17	17	17	17	37	17	17
1882—Jan. 24	37	37	37	37	37	37	17	17	17	30	30	17	17	17	17	37	17	17
June 28	33	33	33	33	33	33	16	16	16	28	28	16	16	16	16	33	16	16
July 1	33	33	33	33	33	33	16	16	16	28	28	16	16	16	16	33	12	12
Nov. 1	37	37	37	37	37	37	18	18	18	29	29	18	18	18	18	37	18	18
1883—June 23	37	37	37	37	37	37	18	18	18	29	29	18	18	18	18	37	13	13
1884—Jan. 1	37	37	37	37	37	37	18	18	18	29	29	18	18	18	18	37	13	13
1885—Jan. 26	21	21	21	21	21	21	13	13	13	16	16	13	13	13	13	21	10	10
June 1	20	20	20	20	20	20	11	11	11	16	16	11	11	11	11	20	9	9
Oct. 1	29	29	29	29	29	29	13	13	13	24	24	13	13	13	13	29	10	10
Nov. 18	37	37	37	37	37	37	18	18	18	29	29	18	18	18	18	37	13	13
1886—Jan. 21	37	37	37	37	37	37	18	18	18	29	29	18	18	18	18	37	13	13
1887—Apr. 1	39	39	39	39	33	28	16	19	13	33	33	19	16	16	13	39	19	13
July 15	39	39	39	39	33	28	16	19	13	33	33	19	16	16	13	39	19	13
1888—Jan. 9	39	39	39	39	33	28	18	21	14½	33	33	21	18	21	14½	39	21	14½
Mar. 5	39	39	39	39	33	28	16	19	13	33	33	19	16	19	13	39	19	13
Nov. 14	24	24	24	24	19	19	13	16	10	19	19	16	13	16	10	24	16	10
Dec. 17	39	39	39	39	33	28	16	19	13	33	33	19	16	19	13	39	19	13
1891—Apr. 9	39	39	39	39	33	16	13	19	13	33	33	19	13	19	13	39	19	13
June 20	39	39	39	39	33	16	13	19	13	19	13	19	13	19	13	39	19	13

PHILADELPHIA, PA., TO PITTSBURG, PA.—Continued.

Boston, 657 miles; Philadelphia, 354 miles; Baltimore, 333 miles.

than carload or carload quantities they apply on shipments regardless of quantity.]

Commodities (rates in cents per 100 pounds).																						
Molasses.		Rice.				Crockery and earthenware.		Bagging.		Leather.		Lead.		Nails.			Agricultural implements.		Machinery.		Beer.	
Less than carloads.	Carloads.	Less than carloads.	Carloads.	Groceries.	Drugs.	Less than carloads.	Carloads.	Less than carloads.	Carloads.	Less then carloads.	Carloads.	Less than carloads.	Carloads.	Less than carloads.	Carloads.	Hardware.	Less than carloads.	Carloads.	Less than carloads.	Carloads.	Less than carloads.	Carloads.
24	24	16	16	32	32	16	16	32	32	32	32	16	16	24	24	32	Sp'l rate.	24	32	32	28	28
20	20	16	16	32	32	16	16	32	32	32	32	16	16	20	20	32	.do .	20	32	32	28	28
14	14	14	14	22	22	14	14	22	22	22	22	14	14	14	14	22	.do .	14	22	22	22	22
23	23	18	18	32	32	18	18	32	32	32	32	18	18	23	23	32	.do .	23	32	32	27	27
27	27	18	18	36	36	18	18	36	36	36	36	18	18	27	27	36	.do .	27	36	36	32	32
27	27	19	19	39	39	19	19	39	39	39	39	19	19	27	27	39	.do .	27	39	39	34	34
22	22	22	22	39	39	22	22	22	22	39	39	22	22	22	22	....	.do .	22	39	22	22	22
24	24	24	24	44	44	24	24	24	24	44	44	24	24	24	24	44	.do .	24	44	24	24	24
24	24	24	24	38	38	24	24	24	24	38	38	24	24	24	24	38	.do .	24	38	24	24	24
21	21	21	21	29	29	21	21	21	21	29	29	21	21	21	21	29	.do .	21	29	21	21	21
21	21	21	21	29	29	21	21	21	21	29	29	21	21	21	21	29	.do .	21	29	21	21	21
21	21	21	21	29	29	21	21	21	21	29	29	21	21	21	21	29	.do .	21	29	21	21	21
13	13	13	13	21	21	13	13	13	13	21	21	13	13	13	13	21	.do .	13	21	13	13	13
17	17	17	17	30	30	17	17	17	17	30	30	17	17	17	17	30	.do .	17	30	17	17	17
17	17	17	17	30	30	17	17	17	17	30	30	17	17	17	17	30	.do .	17	30	17	17	17
16	16	16	16	28	28	16	16	16	16	28	28	16	16	16	16	28	.do .	16	28	16	16	16
12	12	16	16	28	28	16	16	16	16	28	28	16	16	16	16	28	.do .	16	28	16	16	16
18	18	18	18	29	29	18	18	18	18	29	29	18	18	18	18	29	.do .	18	29	18	18	18
18	18	18	18	29	29	18	18	18	18	29	29	18	18	18	18	29	.do .	18	29	18	18	18
18	18	18	18	29	29	18	18	18	18	29	29	18	18	18	18	29	.do .	18	29	18	18	18
13	13	13	13	16	16	13	13	13	13	16	16	13	13	13	13	16	.do .	13	16	13	13	13
11	11	11	11	16	16	11	11	11	11	16	16	11	11	11	11	16	.do .	11	16	11	11	11
13	13	13	13	24	24	13	13	13	13	24	24	13	13	13	13	24	.do .	13	24	13	13	13
18	18	18	18	29	29	18	18	18	18	29	29	18	18	18	18	29	.do .	18	29	18	18	18
18	18	18	18	29	29	18	18	18	18	29	29	18	18	18	18	29	.do .	18	29	18	18	18
19	16	19	19	33	33	19	16	28	19	28	19	19	13	19	16	33	28	16	19	16	28	16
19	16	19	13	33	33	19	16	28	19	28	19	19	13	19	16	33	28	16	19	16	28	16
21	18	21	14½	33	33	21	18	28	21	28	21	21	14½	21	18	33	28	18	21	18	28	18
19	16	19	13	33	33	19	16	28	19	28	19	19	13	19	16	33	28	16	19	16	28	16
16	13	16	10	19	19	16	13	19	16	19	16	16	10	16	13	19	19	13	16	13	19	13
19	16	19	13	33	33	19	16	28	19	28	19	19	13	19	16	33	28	16	19	16	28	16
19	16	19	13	33	33	19	16	28	19	28	19	19	16	13	16	33	28	16	19	16	28	16
19	16	19	13	33	33	19	16	28	19	28	19	19	16	13	16	33	28	16	19	16	28	16

RATES FROM THE SEABOARD VIA RAIL AND LAKE ROUTES.

The season of navigation upon the Great Lakes usually extends from April 1 to November 30 of each year. During this period from 17 to 20 per cent of the traffic from the seaboard to points beyond the western termini of the trunk lines is transported by the routes operating via the lakes. Such traffic is carried by the rail lines to Ogdensburg and Buffalo, N. Y., and Erie, Pa., thence via the lakes to Toledo, Detroit, Milwaukee, Chicago, and Duluth; at the latter points connection is again made with rail carriers, thus forming through routes to all principal competitive points in the West, Southwest, and Northwest.

Under long existing arrangements the rates via the rail-and-lake routes have been lower than those of the all-rail routes. The basis upon which these relations were established is not known for the entire period under consideration. Inferior facilities and longer time have been the principal disadvantages of the lake routes, in recognition of which the differential system of rates has been applied. With these rates, as in the case of the all-rail rates, New York to Chicago are the standard points on which tariffs are constructed. The differences existing in the all-rail and lake-and-rail rates between New York and Chicago represent the difference between the rates of these respective routes from other seaboard points to the West generally. These differences for several years have been as follows:

TABLE 37.—WEST BOUND RAIL AND LAKE RATES, NEW YORK TO CHICAGO.

Year.		Classes (in cents per 100 pounds).					
		1.	2.	3.	4.	5.	6.
1867	All rail	202	170	138	86	......	.....
	Lake route	118	100	85	57	......	.....
1868	All rail	188	160	127	82	......	.....
	Lake route	126	106	91	60	......	.....
1872	All rail	125	110	85	65	50	.....
	Lake route	87	77	60	46	35	.....
1893	All rail	75	65	50	35	30	25
	Lake route	54	47	37	27	23	20

The classes, it will be seen, correspond to those of the Official classification, and classified traffic via the lake routes has been taken for the years indicated under the classifications applying from the seaboard which were superseded by the Official.

The foregoing shows very large reductions, especially in the rates of the lower classes; articles formerly taken at fourth and fifth classes, at the rates of 45 and 35 cents, respectively, are now found in the three lower classes, namely, fourth, fifth, and sixth, at rates of 27, 23, and 20 cents per 100 pounds. It should also be remembered that the changes and reductions in the freight classifications have also operated to reduce the rates carried via the lake routes. The successive changes since 1867, so far as it has been possible to obtain them, are shown in tables to follow. Many of the articles covered by the classes have been and are still, from time to time, carried at commodity rates independently of the classification. In such instances the rates are invariably lower than the rates these articles would receive under the classifications.

TABLE 38.—FREIGHT RATES CHARGED FOR THE TRANSPORTATION OF CLASSIFIED TRAFFIC FROM NEW YORK TO CHICAGO, VIA LAKE AND RAIL LINES, FROM MAY 6, 1867, GOVERNED BY OFFICIAL CLASSIFICATION.

	Classes (in cents per 100 pounds).						
	1.	2.	3.	4.	5.	6.	Special.
1867—May 6	118	100	85	57	......	......	......
Nov. 5	127	106	87	58	......	......	......
1868—Apr. 8	126	106	91	60	......	......	......
June 4	117	100	86	57	......	......	......
June 9	117	100	85	57	......	......	......
Aug. 10	94	80	76	57	......	......	......
Sept. 1	117	100	85	57	......	......	38
1869—Apr. 16	100	100	85	57	......	......	38
July 1	117	100	85	57	......	......	38
Nov. 1	100	90	70	57	......	......	35
1870—Apr. 11	106	91	70	57	......	......	38
1872—Apr. 27	87	77	60	46	......	......	35
Aug. 1	51	48	40	31	......	......	24
Oct. 14	87	77	60	46	......	......	35
Oct. 25	87	77	60	45	......	......	35
1873—Apr. 14	70	63	53	42	......	......	32
1877—Oct. 22	70	63	53	31	......	......	......
1878—May 20	51	41	34	27	......	......	......
Oct. 24	54	44	37	30	......	......	......
1879—Apr. 28	54	44	37	30	......	......	......
1880—Apr. 2	54	44	37	30	......	......	......
1881—May 2	54	44	37	30	......	......	......
1882—July 1	44	37	30	23	20	......	......
Nov. 1	54	44	34	27	......	......	......
1883—Apr. 25	54	44	34	27	......	......	......
June 22	54	44	34	27	......	......	20
1884—Apr. 21	54	44	34	27	......	......	20
1885—Apr. 27	37	30	23	20	15	......	......
June 1	30	23	20	15	13	......	......
Oct. 5	44	37	30	20	17	......	......
Nov. 18	54	44	34	27	20	......	......
1886—Apr. 12	54	44	34	27	20	......	......
1887—Apr. 5	54	47	37	27	23	20	......
1888—Apr. 6	54	47	37	27	23	20	......
May 14	44	39	31	23	19	16	......
Oct. 13	51	45	35	24	20	17	......
1889—Apr. 8	54	47	37	27	23	20	......
1890—Apr. 7	54	47	37	27	23	20	......
1891—Apr. 15	54	47	37	27	23	20	......
1892—Apr. 18	54	47	37	27	23	20	......

By the standard lines the same rates apply from Boston and adjacent territory. From Philadelphia and Baltimore somewhat lower rates are made, and certain routes from New York and Boston are allowed differential rates, which are lower than the lowest rates of the standard lake routes. By such differential lines the rates are upon an extremely low basis, as will be seen by reference to the following rates of a differential line from Boston to Chicago:

TABLE 39.—RATES VIA DIFFERENTIAL LINE.

Class.	Cents per 100 pounds.					
	1887.	1888.	1889.	1890.	1891.	1892.
1	44	27	44	44	36	41
2	39	24	39	39	31	36
3	31	19	31	31	24	29
4	23	15	23	23	18	21
5	19	14	20	20	15	19
6	16	15	18	18	15	17
Boots and shoes	......	30	......	......	25	30
Dry goods	......	30	......	......	22	25
Binder's twine	......	17½	15	......	13	15
Caustic soda and soda ash	......	13	13	13	12	14
Sugar	......	13	......	13	13	16
Canned goods	......	......	......	......	12	......
Jute butts	......	......	......	......	......	15
Flax	......	......	......	......	......	15

The foregoing are representative of the very low basis that would be charged to other Western points the rates to which are made relatively higher than the Chicago rates.

RATES VIA THE CANAL AND LAKE ROUTES.

Another through route largely patronized by the public is that from New York via the Erie Canal to Buffalo, thence via the lake lines to Toledo, Detroit, Chicago, Milwaukee, and the West. The scale of rates in effect during the last season by this route to Chicago was as follows:

TABLE 40.—LAKE-CANAL RATES NEW YORK TO CHICAGO, 1892.

Classes.	Cents per 100 pounds.
1	30
2	25
3	20
4	18
5	16
6	14

From Boston certain carriers operate through lines, connecting with the Erie Canal at points in eastern New York State, thence to Buffalo via canal, in connection with lake lines to the West. By this line the rates of the past season from Boston to Chicago were:

TABLE 41.—LAKE AND CANAL RATES FROM BOSTON.

Classes.	Cents per 100 pounds.
1	40
2	35
3	29
4	21
5	18
6	17

The traffic seeking these routes is mainly composed of heavy or bulky articles, usually found in the lower classes of the classification or carried at commodity rates. There is no data at this time available to show the decline of the rates by these routes.

Nearly all of the points covered by the foregoing statements of commodity rates may be reached by the lake and rail and canal routes, which are open to the public, during the summer months of each year and at a scale of charges much lower than the rates of the all-rail routes as given in the tables referred to.

CLASSIFED RATES VIA ALL-RAIL ROUTES CHICAGO TO NEW YORK.

It has been shown with respect to westward rates from the seaboard that New York and Chicago are taken as the standard points or basis upon which rates to other Western points are computed. The same general plan is observed with regard to the rates eastward from Chicago and other Western points to the Atlantic seaboard. The present rates by the standard routes from Chicago to the various Eastern cities are as follows:

TABLE 42.—EAST BOUND RATES—ALL-RAIL.

Chicago to—	Classes (in cents per 100 pounds).					
	1.	2.	3.	4.	5.	6.
Boston	82	71	55	39	33	27
New York	75	65	50	35	30	25
Philadelphia	73	63	48	33	28	23
Baltimore	72	62	47	32	27	22

The Chesapeake and Ohio route, owing to its longer distance, charges somewhat lower rates.

With the tables presenting the westward rates from New York to Chicago it was fully explained how the charges to other western points are made by the percentage basis, and also that when the rates New York to Chicago are changed, similar changes are made from the seabord to western points generally. The same plan is applied when making rates from Chicago and other western points to the seaboard cities and points in the vicinity thereof, the rates to which are made with regard to the seaboard rates. When a change is made in the Chicago rates, all other points are similarly affected. Therefore a statement of the changes in the rates from Chicago to New York will serve to illustrate the changes which have taken place from other western points to the seaboard cities. Such a table here follows, showing the class rates from 1871 up to the present time.

During the period covered there have been several changes in the character of the classification which applied to these rates. Prior to 1880 it is shown that the traffic was confined to 4 classes; from 1880 to 1887 the traffic was distributed among eleven or twelve classes, and subsequent to 1887 the classification governing provided for six classes only. Since 1887 the rates for all classes are shown to be on a considerably lower basis than prior to that year. This result was brought about by the adjustment at that time, by which the rates, both eastward and westward, were made alike, and further by the adoption of the Official classification for eastward traffic.

It is again mentioned that similar reductions were made from all points north of the Ohio, east of the Mississippi, and west of Buffalo and Pittsburg, to the principal seaboard points, and, further, that traffic originating west of the territory indicated has also received the benefit of these lower rates.

TABLE 43.—FREIGHT RATES CHARGED FOR THE TRASPORTATION OF CLASSIFIED TRAFFIC FROM CHICAGO, ILL., TO NEW YORK, N. Y., FROM OCTOBER 22, 1871.

Date.	Rates in cents per 100 pounds.											
	1.	2.	3.	4.	5.	6.	7.	8.	9.	10.	11.	12.
1871—Oct. 22	160	125	85	65	....	....	....	....	....	....	....	....
1872—Mar. 26	160	125	85	60	....	....	....	....	....	....	....	....
May 1	160	125	85	50	....	....	....	....	....	....	....	....
Aug. 26	160	125	85	45	....	....	....	....	....	....	....	....
Sept. 2	160	125	85	50	....	....	....	....	....	....	....	....
Sept. 9	160	125	85	60	....	....	....	....	....	....	....	....
Sept. 16	160	125	85	60	....	....	....	....	....	....	....	....
Oct. 14	160	125	85	65	....	....	....	....	....	....	....	....
1873—Apr. 14	160	125	85	60	....	....	....	....	....	....	....	....
Apr. 29	160	125	85	50	....	....	....	....	....	....	....	....
May 20	160	125	85	45	....	....	....	....	....	....	....	....
Sept. 5	160	125	85	50	....	....	....	....	....	....	....	....
Sept. 15	160	125	85	55	....	....	....	....	....	....	....	....
Dec. 8	160	125	85	60	....	....	....	....	....	....	....	....
1874—Feb. 3	160	125	85	55	....	....	....	....	....	....	....	....
Feb. 16	160	125	85	50	....	....	....	....	....	....	....	....
Mar. 9	160	125	85	45	....	....	....	....	....	....	....	....
Mar. 18	160	125	85	40	....	....	....	....	....	....	....	....
Apr. 20	150	110	70	40	....	....	....	....	....	....	....	....
Apr. 27	150	110	80	40	....	....	....	....	....	....	....	....
May 6	150	110	80	45	....	....	....	....	....	....	....	....
Oct. 1	150	110	80	40	....	....	....	....	....	....	....	....
Nov. 24	150	110	85	45	....	....	....	....	....	....	....	....
Dec. 1	150	110	85	45	....	....	....	....	....	....	....	....
Dec. 11	150	110	85	40	....	....	....	....	....	....	....	....
1875—Oct. 1	150	110	85	35	....	....	....	....	....	....	....	....
Oct. 11	150	110	85	40	....	....	....	....	....	....	....	....
Oct. 12	150	110	85	40	....	....	....	....	....	....	....	....
Dec. 1	150	110	85	45	....	....	....	....	....	....	....	....
Dec. 20	150	110	85	50	....	....	....	....	....	....	....	....
1876—Oct. 1	150	110	85	40	....	....	....	....	....	....	....	....
Mar. 1	150	110	85	50	....	....	....	....	....	....	....	....
Mar. 10	150	110	85	45	....	....	....	....	....	....	....	....
Apr. 1	150	110	85	45	....	....	....	....	....	....	....	....
Apr. 17	150	110	85	40	....	....	....	....	....	....	....	....
Dec. 18	150	110	85	35	....	....	....	....	....	....	....	....
1877—Jan. 1	150	110	85	40	....	....	....	....	....	....	....	....
Jan. 15	150	110	85	45	....	....	....	....	....	....	....	....
Feb. 12	150	110	85	40	....	....	....	....	....	....	....	....
Apr. 9	150	110	85	35	....	....	....	....	....	....	....	....
Apr. 30	150	110	85	40	....	....	....	....	....	....	....	....
July 2	150	110	85	35	....	....	....	....	....	....	....	....
Oct. 17	150	110	85	40	....	....	....	....	....	....	....	....
1878—Feb. 11	150	110	85	30	....	....	....	....	....	....	....	....
Apr. 1	120	90	70	30	....	....	....	....	....	....	....	....
May 17	120	90	70	25	....	....	....	....	....	....	....	....
Aug. 5	120	90	70	30	....	....	....	....	....	....	....	....
Sept. 2	120	90	70	35	....	....	....	....	....	....	....	....
Nov. 25	120	90	70	40	....	....	....	....	....	....	....	....
1879—Mar. 24	120	90	70	25	....	....	....	....	....	....	....	....
June 9	120	90	70	20	....	....	....	....	....	....	....	....
June 23	120	90	70	25	....	....	....	....	....	....	....	....
Aug. 4	120	90	70	30	....	....	....	....	....	....	....	....
Aug. 25	90	70	50	35	....	....	....	....	....	....	....	....
Oct. 1	120	90	70	35	....	....	....	....	....	....	....	....
Oct. 13	120	90	70	40	....	....	....	....	....	....	....	....
Nov. 10	120	90	70	45	....	....	....	....	....	....	....	....
1880—Mar. 8 (new classification)	....	....	....	....	....	....	....	....	....	....	....	....
Mar. 8	120	90	70	60	50	45	45	35	35	33	50	....
Apr. 1	120	90	70	60	50	45	45	35	35	30	50	....
Apr. 14	120	90	70	60	50	45	35	30	35	30	40	....
Nov. 1	120	90	70	60	50	45	35	30	35	35	40	....
Nov. 22	120	90	70	60	50	45	40	35	35	35	45	....
1881—Mar. 7	120	90	70	60	50	45	40	35	45	35	45	....
Apr. 1	120	90	70	60	50	45	35	30	40	30	45	....
Apr. 11	120	90	70	60	50	45	35	25	40	30	45	....
Apr. 18	120	90	70	60	50	45	35	30	40	30	45	....
May 9	100	85	70	60	50	45	35	30	40	30	45	....
June 8	100	85	70	60	50	45	30	25	35	30	45	....
June 15	100	85	70	60	50	45	25	20	30	30	45	....
1882—Jan. 23	100	85	70	60	50	45	25	20	30	35	45	....
Mar. 13	100	85	70	60	50	45	30	25	35	30	45	....
Nov. 1	100	85	70	60	50	45	30	25	35	35	45	....
Dec. 1	100	85	70	60	50	45	35	30	40	35	45	....
1883—Apr. 1	100	85	70	60	50	45	35	30	40	30	45	....
Apr. 19	100	85	70	60	50	45	35	25	40	30	45	....
Apr. 23	100	85	70	60	50	45	30	25	35	30	45	....
Nov. 1	100	85	70	60	50	45	30	25	35	35	45	....
Nov. 26	100	85	70	60	50	45	35	30	40	35	45	....
1884—Jan. 5	100	85	70	60	50	45	25	20	30	35	45	....

TABLE 43.—FREIGHT RATES CHARGED FOR THE TRANSPORTATION OF CLASSIFIED TRAFFIC FROM CHICAGO, ILL., ETC.—Continued.

Date.	Rates in cents per 100 pounds.											
	1.	2.	3.	4.	5.	6.	7.	8.	9.	10.	11.	12.
1884—Jan. 14	100	85	70	60	50	45	35	30	40	35	45	....
Mar. 14	100	85	70	60	50	45	25	20	30	35	45	....
Mar. 21	100	85	70	60	50	45	20	15	25	35	45	....
Apr. 1	100	85	70	60	50	45	20	15	25	30	45	....
June 24	100	85	70	60	50	45	25	25	30	30	45	....
July 21	100	85	70	60	50	45	30	25	35	30	45	....
Nov. 1	100	85	70	60	50	45	30	25	35	35	....	....
Dec. 15	100	85	70	60	50	45	30	25	35	32	....	....
1885—Apr. 6	100	85	70	60	50	45	40	35	30	25	30	25
Nov. 1	100	85	70	60	50	45	40	35	30	25	35	25
Nov. 23	100	85	70	60	50	45	40	35	30	25	35	30
Dec. 21	100	85	70	60	50	45	40	35	30	25	35	30
1886—Jan. 15	100	85	70	60	50	45	40	35	30	25	30	30
Apr. 1	100	85	70	60	50	45	40	35	30	25	25	30
Nov. 1	100	85	70	60	50	45	40	35	30	25	30	30
Dec. 20	100	85	70	60	50	45	40	35	30	25	30	35
Dec. 27	100	85	70	60	50	45	40	35	35	30	30	35
1887—Apr. 1 (new Official classification)	....	....	....	....	....	....	....	....	....	....	....	....
Apr. 1	75	65	50	35	30	25	....	....	....	....	....	....
1888—Jan. 9	75	65	50	38½	33	27½	....	....	....	....	....	....
Mar. 5	75	65	50	35	30	25	....	....	....	....	....	....
Nov. 12	50	40	35	30	25	20	....	....	....	....	....	....
Dec. 17	75	65	50	35	30	25	....	....	....	....	....	....
1892—May 9	75	65	50	35	30	20	....	....	....	....	....	....
June 13	75	65	50	35	30	25	....	....	....	....	....	....

Data have been collected showing the tonnage movement of the classified traffic via the all-rail routes Chicago to New York taken under these rates, which is shown to have largely increased. A statement of such tonnage is below given, from which may be seen the volume of traffic affected by these rates. The statement covers only traffic originating at or passing through Chicago, and does not embrace the numerous other points east of the Mississippi River; the rates from which, as before explained, have been correspondingly reduced.

TABLE 44.—EAST BOUND TONNAGE.

	Tons.
1880	2, 340, 346
1881	2, 871, 100
1882	2, 106, 877
1883	2, 257, 703
1884	2, 839, 449
1885	3, 187, 023
1886	1, 872, 388
1887	2, 210, 043
1888	2, 366, 889
1889	2, 462, 664
1890	3, 066, 460
1891	2, 556, 624
1892	2, 421, 206

NOTE.—The foregoing does not include tonnage of livestock and dressed meats, for which see Table 54.

GRAIN RATES, ALL RAIL, CHICAGO TO NEW YORK.

The following table presents the changes which have taken place in the grain rates by the all-rail routes from Chicago to New York from 1864. The methods previously mentioned as to the manner of constructing rates from points other than Chicago to the seaboard apply also to this table, and the rates there shown may be accepted as representing the changes which have taken place from all competitive points east of the Mississippi River to the seaboard:

GRAIN RATES ALL RAIL, CHICAGO TO NEW YORK.

TABLE 45.—RATES IN CENTS PER 100 POUNDS CHARGED UPON GRAIN, ALL RAIL, FROM CHICAGO, ILL., TO NEW YORK, N. Y., FROM MARCH 28, 1864.

Date.	Rate.	Date.	Rate.	Date.	Rate.	Date.	Rate.
1864—Mar. 28...	100	1867—Sept. 2...	75	1875—Dec. 1...	45	1884—Mar. 21...	15
Apr. 4...	90	Sept. 23...	85	1876—Mar. 7...	40	June 24...	20
Apr. 12...	80	1868—Sept. 1...	60	Apr. 13...	35	July 21...	25
Apr. 14...	75	Sept. 7...	65	Apr. 26...	22½	1885—Mar. 10...	20
July 11...	80	Sept. 14..	70	May 5...	20	Nov. 23...	25
July 22...	85	Dec. 7...	75	Dec. 18...	30	1886—Dec. 20...	30
July 28...	80	1869—Jan. 25...	70	1877—Jan. 2...	35	1887—Mar. 23...	25
Sept. 7...	90	Mar. 11...	50	Apr. 2...	30	1888—Jan. 8.....	27½
Sept. 10...	95	1870—Jan. 22...	55	Sept. 4...	35	Mar. 8.....	25
Nov. 12...	100	Mar. 4...	50	Oct. 17...	40	Oct. 10...	20
Nov. 16...	115	Mar. 22...	45	1878—Mar. 11...	30	Dec. 15...	25
Nov. 28...	125	May 23...	40	Apr. 1...	25	1889—July 13...	20
Dec. 13...	138	Aug. 29...	45	May 17...	20	Aug. 1:	
Dec. 24...	160	Aug. 31...	50	Aug. 5...	25	Wheat..	25
1865—Apr. 22...	100	Oct. 31...	55	Aug. 17...	30	Corn....	20
May 15...	70	Nov. 22...	60	Nov. 25...	35	1890—May 12:	
Sept. 6...	62½	1871—Mar. 4...	50	1879—Mar. 24...	20	Oats....	22
Sept. 11...	70	Apr. 7...	45	June 9...	15	May 26:	
Sept. 27...	77½	June 26...	40	June 23...	22	Oats....	20
Oct. 10...	85	July 10...	45	Aug. 4 .	25	June 9;	
Oct. 17...	95	Aug. 11...	50	Aug. 25...	30	Grain,	
Oct. 27...	105	Sept. 21...	55	Oct. 13...	35	except	
Nov. 2...	115	Oct. 2...	60	Nov. 10...	40	corn,	
Nov. 7...	120	Oct. 25...	65	1880—Mar. 1...	35	and oats	22½
Nov. 9...	130	1872—Mar. 25...	60	Apr. 14...	30	1891—Nov. 24:	
1866—Jan. 9...	80	May 1...	50	Nov. 22...	35	Grain,	
Feb. 26...	70	Aug. 26...	45	1881—Apr. 1...	30	except	
May 11...	55	Sept. 2...	50	Apr. 11...	25	corn...	22½
June 7...	60	Sept. 9...	55	Apr. 18...	30	Dec. 29...	25
July 5...	65	Sept. 16...	60	June 8...	25	1892—May 9...	20
Sept. 18...	75	Oct. 14...	65	June 15...	15-20	June 13...	22½
Sept. 27...	85	1873—Apr. 14...	16	Sept. 26...	12½-20	Oct. 10...	25
Oct. 10...	90	May 20...	45	Oct. 10...	12½-15		
Oct. 15...	100	Sept. 5...	50	Nov. 1...	20		
Nov. 5...	105	Nov. 20...	55	Dec. 9...	12½-20		
Dec. 8...	90	Dec. 8...	60	1882—Mar. 13...	25		
1867—Feb. 7...	80	1874—Feb. 3...	55	Dec. 1...	30		
Mar. 4...	70	Apr. 15...	40	1883—Apr. 19...	25		
Mar. 22...	60	May 6...	45	Nov. 26...	30		
Apr. 15...	50	Dec. 11...	40	1884—Jan. 5...	20		
June 8...	75	1875—Oct. 1...	30	Jan. 14...	30		
June 21...	70	Oct. 12...	40	Mar. 14...	20		

GRAIN RATES VIA LAKE-AND-RAIL AND LAKE-AND-CANAL ROUTES, CHICAGO TO THE SEABOARD.

Through routes are formed by the lake lines running to Buffalo and there connecting with the rail carriers, and also with the Erie Canal. Via each of these routes a large traffic is carried, destined to the seaboard. The principal shipments are wheat, corn, and other grains. Large reductions have been made in the rates by these routes. Here following is given a statement showing the changes in the rates on wheat and corn from Chicago to New York from 1877, when forwarded by routes operating via the lakes to Buffalo and thence via rail. A second table shows rates for a similar period on like commodities from Chicago to New York when taken by lake to Buffalo and thence via the canal.

These two tables are compiled from the reports of the Chicago Board of Trade, and are understood to cover the quotations of the prevailing rates for the period covered.

A third table, compiled from the tariffs of the Western Transit Company, a lake line operating from Chicago to Buffalo, which publishes through rates to the seaborad, shows changes in the rates on various grain articles from 1887. A comparison of the wheat rates for the seasons of 1887 and 1892 shows the former to have been 14 cents, while for the latter year it was 8 cents.

The fourth table following shows the average rates charged on wheat and corn when carried by canal from Buffalo to New York, for each month during the season of navigation, for the years 1856 and 1857 and from 1862, and also shows the highest rate during each year charged on wheat and the average for the season for the same commodity. The average season rate on wheat for the first year given upon the table is shown as 14.4 cents per bushel, while that for 1892 was 3.4 cents.

The rates from St. Louis to the seaboard are computed at 116 per cent of the rates from Chicago to New York. For the purpose of equalizing the rates via the various routes crossing the Mississippi River, it is agreed by the lines interested that the rates from St. Louis shall be applied at the other river crossings on such traffic as may originate at points west of the Mississippi River. Under this arrangement the rates upon such traffic to New York from Dubuque, Clinton, Rock Island, East Burlington, East Hannibal, and the other river crossings, are the same as from St. Louis. When changes occurred in the rates from Chicago, similar changes were made necessary from other western points on and east of the Mississippi River which are governed by the percentage basis. The rates upon grain and other traffic passing eastward via the Mississippi River points named would be correspondingly changed.

While a more extended reference might be made to the influences which operate to reduce the grain rates by the various routes from Chicago, this appears unnecessary, as the tables present a very full history of the reductions which have taken place.

TABLE 46.—FREIGHT RATES CHARGED FOR THE TRANSPORTATION OF WHEAT
THE OPENING OF THE SEASON

In effect during—	Rates in cents per bushel.														
	Wheat.														
	1877.	1878.	1879.	1880.	1881.	1882.	1883.	1884.	1885.	1886.	*1887	1888.	1889.	1890.	1891,
Apr.—First week	.....	12	.....	.....	.....	.....	11¾	.....	.....	.....	.....	.....	.....	.....	8½
Second week	.....	12	.....	.....	.....	12½	12	.....	.....	.....	.....	.....	9¼	9¾	8½
Third week	.....	11	.....	17	.....	12½	12	.....	.....	.....	.....	.....	8½	9	8½
Fourth week	.....	10	.....	17	.....	10	12	12	.....	.....	.....	10¾	8½	8¾	8½
Fifth week	.....	.....	.....	.....	.....	10½	.....	.....	.....	12	.....	.....	.....	.....	.....
May —First week	13	11	12¼	16	15	10	11⅝	12	.....	12	.....	10½	8½	8¼	8½
Second week	13	10¾	12	15½	15	10	10¾	11	9⅖	12	.....	10½	8¼	8¼	8½
Third week	13	10	11¾	15	14¾	9½	10	10	9 3/20	12	.....	10¼	8¼	8¼	8½
Fourth week	12½	9	11½	12½	13¾	9½	10	10	8½	12	.....	10¼	8¼	8¼	8½
Fifth week	.....	.....	11¼	15	.....	.....	.....	10	8	.....	.....	.....	.....	8¼	7½
June—First week	13	8½	11	15¼	11	9	10	10	7½	12	.....	10¼	8¼	8¼	7½
Second week	13	9	10¾	16	10½	9	10	10	7⅗	12	.....	10¼	8¼	8¼	7½
Third week	13	9	10¼	16	11	9	10¼	10	7⅖	12	.....	10¼	8¼	8½	7½
Fourth week	13	9	9¾	16	9¾	9½	10	10	7½	12	.....	10¼	8¼	8½	7½
Fifth week	13	9	.....	.....	.....	.....	10¼	.....	.....	.....	.....	10¼	8¼	.....	.....
July —First week	13	9	9	16	9¼	9¾	10	10	7½	12	.....	10¼	8¼	8¾	7½
Second week	12	7½	8½	16	9	8½	9¾	10	8½	12	.....	10¼	8	8¾	7½
Third week	12	7½	9	13½	8½	8½	9¾	10	10⅗	12	.....	10½	8¾	8½	7½
Fourth week	12	7½	9½	13½	7½	8½	10¾	9	10⅖	12	.....	10½	8	8½	7½
Fifth week	.....	.....	.....	12	7	8½	.....	.....	9¾	.....	.....	.....	.....	.....	.....
Aug. —First week	12	7½	10	13	6¼	10	11	9	10⅖	12	.....	11	8	8½	8
Second week	12	7¾	11	14½	6¾	10	11¾	9	9¾	12	.....	11	8	8½	8½
Third week	12½	8	11	13	7½	9½	11¼	10	9 13/20	12	.....	11½	8¼	8½	9½
Fourth week	12½	9¼	11	12	8	9½	12	10	9¾	12	.....	11¾	8½	8½	9½
Fifth week	.....	11½	12	.....	.....	.....	.....	10	.....	.....	.....	.....	9	8½	9½
Sept.—First week	13	12	12	14½	8½	9½	12¼	12	7½	12	.....	11¾	9	8½	9½
Second week	13	12½	12	12	8½	9½	12¾	11½	7½	12	.....	11¾	9	8½	9½
Third week	14	13	13	12	8½	10	12½	10	7½	12	.....	12	9	8½	9½
Fourth week	16	14	14	12	7½	10	12¼	9	7¼	12	.....	12	9	8½	9½
Fifth week	16	.....	.....	.....	.....	10¼	11½	.....	.....	.....	.....	12	.....	.....	.....
Oct. —First week	16	14	15	12	6¼	10¼	12¼	9	7¼	12	.....	11½	9	8½	9½
Second week	18	14½	15	12½	6	10	11¼	9	7½	12	.....	11½	9½	8½	9½
Third week	18	14½	15	14	9½	10¼	11	9	8½	12	.....	11	9½	8½	8
Fourth week	18	14	15½	14	9½	10¾	11½	10	10⅖	12	.....	11	9½	8½	8
Fifth week	.....	.....	.....	14	9½	.....	.....	.....	10¾	.....	.....	.....	.....	.....	8
Nov. —First week	18	14	17¾	14	9¾	11	11¾	11	10¾	12	.....	11½	10½	8½	8½
Second week	17	13½	19	14	9¾	10¾	11¾	9	11¼	12	.....	11½	10½	8½	9
Third week	17	13¼	20	17	9¾	11	11¼	9	11¼	12	.....	11½	9½	8½	9½
Fourth week	18	13½	19	17	.....	10¼	11¾	9	12¼	12	.....	11	8¾	8½	10
Fifth week	.....	14½	18½	.....	.....	.....	.....	9	.....	.....	.....	.....	.....	8½	.....
Dec. —First week	18½	.....	.....	.....	.....	10¼	.....	.....	.....	.....	.....	.....	.....	.....	10

*No rates.

AND CORN FROM CHICAGO TO NEW YORK VIA LAKE AND RAIL ROUTES FROM OF NAVIGATION IN 1877.

Rates in cents per bushel.														
Corn.														
1877.	1878.	1879.	1880.	1881.	1882.	1883.	1884.	1885.	1886.	*1887.	1888.	1889.	1890.	1891.
......	11¼	......	......	......	......	11½	......	......	......	......	......	......	......	7¼
......	11½	......	......	......	11¼	11½	......	......	......	......	......	8¾	8½	7¼
......	10¼	......	15	......	11¼	11½	......	......	......	......	......	8	8	7¼
......	10	......	15	......	9½	11	11	......	......	......	10	8	7¾	7¼
......	......	......	......	......	10	......	......	......	11⅕	......	......	......	......	......
13	10	9	15	14	9½	10½	11	......	11⅕	......	9¾	8	7¼	7¼
13	10	8¾	14	14	9½	10	9	8⅖	11⅕	......	9¾	7¾	7¼	7¼
13	10	10¾	12½	13¼	9	9¼	9	8 3/20	11⅕	......	9½	7¾	7¼	7¼
11	8½	10½	11¼	12¾	9	9¼	9	7 13/20	11⅕	......	9½	7¾	7¼	7¼
......	......	10	14	......	......	......	9	7	......	......	......	......	7¼	6¼
12	8¾	10	13½	9¾	9	9¼	9	6 3/20	11⅕	......	9½	7¾	7	6¼
12	8¼	9¾	13½	11½	9	9¼	8½	6⅘	11⅕	......	9½	7¾	7	6¼
12	8¼	9¼	14½	10	9	9½	8½	6⅖	11⅕	......	9½	7¾	7¼	6¼
12	8	8¾	14½	8½	9¼	9¼	8½	6½	11⅕	......	9½	7¾	7¼	6¼
12	8	......	......	......	......	9½	......	......	......	......	9½	7¾	......	......
12	8	8¼	15	8¼	9¼	9¼	8½	6½	11⅕	......	9½	7¾	7½	6¼
11	7	8	15	7¾	8½	9	8½	7⅖	11⅕	......	9½	7½	7½	6½
11	7	8	13	7	8½	9	8½	9⅗	11⅕	......	10	7½	7¼	6½
11	7	8½	13	6½	8	10	7	9⅗	11⅕	......	10	7¼	7¼	6½
......	......	......	12	5¾	8½	......	......	8¾	......	......	......	......	......	......
11	7	9	12½	5¾	10	10¼	7	9⅗	11⅕	......	10½	7¼	7¼	7
11	7¼	10	14	5¾	10	10¾	8	8¾	11⅕	......	10½	7¼	7¼	7¼
11½	7½	10	14	6½	9½	10½	9	8 13/20	11⅕	......	10¾	7½	7¼	8½
11½	8½	10	11	7¾	9½	11½	9	8¾	11⅕	......	11	7¾	7¼	8½
......	11	11	......	......	......	......	9	......	......	......	......	8¼	7¼	8½
12	11	11	14	7½	9½	11¼	11	6½	11⅕	......	11	8¼	7¼	8½
12	11½	11	11¼	7½	9	11¾	10	6½	11⅕	......	11	8¼	7¼	8½
13	12	12	11¼	7½	9½	11½	9	6½	11⅕	......	11¼	8¼	7¼	8½
15	13	18	11¼	6¼	9½	11¼	8	6¼	11⅕	......	11¼	8¼	7¼	8½
15	......	......	......	......	9¾	10¾	......	......	......	......	11¼	......	......	......
16	13	14	11	5½	9¾	11	7⅘	6¼	11⅕	......	10¾	8¼	7¼	8½
16	13½	14	11⅓	5	9⅜	10½	8	6½	11⅕	......	10¾	8½	7¼	8½
16	13½	14	12	8¼	9¾	10¼	8	7½	11⅕	......	10¼	8½	7¼	7
16	13	14½	13	8½	10¼	10¾	8¼	9⅖	11⅕	......	10¼	8½	7¼	7
......	......	......	13	8¼	......	......	......	9¾	......	......	......	......	......	7
16	13	16¾	13	8½	10¼	10½	10	9¾	11⅕	......	10¾	9½	7¼	8
16	12¾	18	13	8½	10¼	10¾	8½	10¼	11⅕	......	10¾	9½	7¼	8½
16	12½	18	14	9	10	10½	8½	10¼	11⅕	......	10¾	8½	7¼	9
16	12½	17	16½	......	10	10¾	8½	11¼	11⅕	......	10¼	7¾	7¼	9½
......	13½	17½	......	......	......	......	8½	......	......	......	......	......	7¼	......
16	......	......	......	......	10	......	......	......	......	......	......	......	......	9½

*No rates.

TABLE 47.— FREIGHT RATES CHARGED FOR THE TRANSPORTATION OF WHEAT THE OPENING OF THE SEASON

	Rates in cents per bushel.													
	Wheat.													
	1878.	1879.	1880.	1881.	1882.	1883.	1884.	1885.	1886.	1887.	1888.	1889.	1890.	1891.
Apr.—First week	9 1/2	....	....	....	....	....	....	....	....	....	....	....	8 3/8	....
Second week	9 1/2	....	13 3/4	....	....	....	....	....	....	....	....	....	7 5/8	....
Third week	9 1/2	....	12 3/4	....	9	....	....	....	....	....	....	....	7 1/8	....
Fourth week	9 1/2	....	10 3/4	....	9	....	....	....	....	....	....	....	6 7/8	....
Fifth week	....	....	....	....	8 3/4	....	....	....	....	10 1/4	....	....	....	....
May—First week	9 1/2	....	9 1/2	....	8 1/4	....	7 5/8	....	....	10 1/4	....	7 3/8	6 3/4	5 1/2
Second week	9 3/4	8 1/2	10 1/4	13	8	10	6 1/2	....	9 1/10	9 1/4	5 5/8	7 1/8	6 3/4	5
Third week	8	7 1/2	10 3/4	10 1/2	8	7 1/4	6 3/4	5	9 1/10	8 5/8	....	7 1/8	6 3/4	4 3/4
Fourth week	7 3/4	7	11 1/2	9 3/4	7 3/4	7 1/4	....	....	8 3/10	8 5/8	....	6 7/8	6 3/8	4 3/8
Fifth week	....	6 1/2	12 1/4	....	....	....	....	....	8 3/10	....	....	....	6 7/8	5 1/8
June—First week	8 1/4	6 1/4	13	9 3/4	7	7 1/4	....	....	6 3/10	8 5/8	....	7 1/8	6 5/8	4 7/8
Second week	8 1/4	6 1/2	14 3/4	9 3/4	7 1/4	7 1/4	....	....	6 1/10	10 1/4	....	7 1/8	6 7/8	4 7/8
Third week	7 3/4	6 3/4	14 1/4	9	8	7 5/8	6 5/8	....	7 1/10	11	....	6 7/8	6 7/8	5
Fourth week	7 1/8	6 3/8	14	7 1/2	7	7	6 3/8	....	7 1/10	10 1/4	....	6 5/8	7 1/8	5 1/8
Fifth week	6 3/4	....	....	....	....	7 1/4	....	....	....	....	....	6 5/8	....	....
July—First week	6 3/4	7 1/2	12 3/4	8 1/4	6 1/2	6 3/4	....	....	7 1/4	9 1/2	....	6 5/8	7	5 1/4
Second week	6 3/4	7 1/2	12 3/4	8	6 3/4	6 3/4	....	....	7 1/4	8 1/2	....	6 5/8	6 3/4	4 7/8
Third week	6 3/4	8	10 1/2	7 1/2	7	6 3/4	....	....	8	7 3/4	....	7 1/8	6 3/4	5 7/8
Fourth week	7	9	10 1/4	7 1/4	7	7 1/4	6 5/8	3 7/8	8	7 7/8	6	6 7/8	6 5/8	....
Fifth week	....	....	11	6 1/4	7 1/2	....	....	....	8 1/5	....	....	....	....	....
Aug.—First week	7	9 1/2	11 3/4	6 1/4	9	7 3/4	6 1/4	....	9	8 1/4	7 1/8	6 7/8	6	6 3/8
Second week	8	11	11 3/4	6 3/4	8	8 1/2	6 1/2	....	9	8 1/8	....	7 1/4	6 1/8	7 5/8
Third week	8	11 1/4	11 3/4	7 1/4	7 3/4	9	6 7/8	....	10	7 5/8	8 1/4	7 3/8	6 3/8	7 3/8
Fourth week	11 1/4	11 3/4	11 3/4	7 1/2	8	9	7 1/8	4 3/4	12	8 3/4	....	7 7/8	6 3/8	7 1/8
Fifth week	12 1/2	12 1/4	....	....	....	....	6 1/2	....	....	....	....	8 1/4	6 3/8	7 3/8
Sept.—First week	13 1/4	12 1/2	10 1/2	8 3/4	7 3/4	10 1/2	7 3/4	....	11 1/4	8 7/8	....	8 1/8	6 5/8	7 7/8
Second week	13 1/2	13	11 1/8	8 1/4	8	11 1/2	....	3 1/2	11	8 1/2	8 1/4	8 3/4	6 7/8	8 3/8
Third week	14	14	11 1/8	8 1/2	8 1/2	11 1/4	....	....	11	8 5/8	....	8 3/4	6 7/8	8 3/8
Fourth week	13 1/4	14 1/2	11 1/8	7 1/4	9	11 1/4	7 1/4	....	10 1/5	9	....	8 7/8	6 3/4	8 3/8
Fifth week	....	....	....	....	9	11	....	....	....	....	....	....	....	....
Oct.—First week	13 1/4	15 1/4	11 1/4	6	9 1/4	11	....	....	11	9	....	8 3/4	7	8 1/2
Second week	14	15 1/4	12 1/4	6 3/4	9 3/4	10	....	....	10 1/2	9 1/4	....	8 7/8	6 7/8	7 1/4
Third week	13	17 1/2	14	8 1/4	10 1/2	9 1/4	....	....	10 1/2	10 1/4	....	9	7 3/8	7 1/4
Fourth week	11 3/4	18	14 3/8	8 1/2	10 1/4	9 1/2	....	5 1/4	9 1/10	10 1/4	....	8 7/8	6 7/8	7 5/8
Fifth week	....	....	16 1/4	8 3/4	....	....	....	....	9 3/5	....	....	....	....	7 5/8
Nov.—First week	12 1/4	19 1/4	17	8	9 3/4	9 1/2	....	....	9 1/10	10 3/8	....	8 7/8	6 7/8	7 7/8
Second week	11 3/4	19	16	....	10	9 3/4	....	....	10 1/10	10 1/4	....	8 1/8	6 5/8	8 3/4
Third week	12 3/4	21	15 1/8	....	10 1/4	....	....	....	....	12	....	8	5 5/8	9 3/8
Fourth week	....	....	....	....	....	....	....	....	....	....	....	9 1/8	5 7/8	....
Fifth week	....	....	....	....	....	....	....	....	....	....	....	....	6 7/8	....
Dec.—First week	....	....	....	....	....	....	....	....	....	....	....	....	....	....

AND CORN FROM CHICAGO TO NEW YORK, VIA LAKE AND CANAL ROUTES FROM
OF NAVIGATION OF 1878.

Rates in cents per bushel.													
Corn.													
1878.	1879.	1880.	1881.	1882.	1883.	1884.	1885.	1886.	1887.	1888.	1889.	1890.	1891.
8												8	
9		12¾										7	
8½		11¾		8¼								6⅜	
8¼		9¾		8¼								6¼	
				7¾					9½				
8½		8¾		7½		6⅝			9⅞		6¾	6	4¾
9	7½	9½	11¾	7¼	9¼	5⅞		8¾	8⅝	6⅜	6⅝	6	4⅜
7	6½	9½	9¾	7¼	6½	5⅞		9¼	8⅛	5⅛	6½	6	4
6¾	6	10½	8¾	6¾	6½			8	8	6¾	6¼	5¾	3⅞
	6	11¼						8				6¼	4½
7¼	5½	12	8¾	6½	6½			6	8½	5⅝	6½	6	4⅜
7¼	6	13¾	8¾	6½	6½			5¾	9⅝	9	6½	6¼	4½
6¾	6	13¼	8	7¼	6¼	6		6¾	10¼	8½	6¼	6¼	4½
6	5⅞	13¼	6¾	6¼	6¼	5⅝	3½	6¾	9¾	4⅜	6	6½	4⅛
6					6½						6		
5⅞	6¼	11¾	7¼	5¾	6			6 1/10	8¾	5	6	6¼	4¾
5⅞	6	11¾	6½	6	6			6 1/10	8	4¾	6	6	4⅜
6	7	9¾	6½	6¼	6			6⅕	7⅛	5⅛	6½	6	4¾
6	8¼	9¼	6¼	6⅜	6½	5⅞	3⅝	6⅕	7⅛		6¼	5⅞	
		10	5¾	6⅝				7⅖					
6¼	8½	10¾	5¼	8¼	7¼	6		7⅕	7¾		6¼	5⅜	6
7	10¼	10⅝	5¾	7½	7¾	5¾		7⅕	7⅜		6¾	5⅜	7
7	10½	10½	6½	7¼	8¼	6		8⅕	7¼		6¾	5⅝	6⅞
10¼	11	10¾	6½	7	8¼	6¼	4⅛	10⅕	8¼		7¼	5⅝	6⅝
11¼	11½					6¾	4¾				7⅝	5⅝	6¾
12¼	11¾	10	8¼	7	9¾	7	4¼	10	8⅜		7⅝	5⅞	7
12½	12	10	7¼	7½	10⅛		4	9⅘	8	7⅝	8	6⅛	7¾
13	12½	10	8	8	10¾			9⅗	8½		8	6	7¾
11¾	13	9¾	6¼	8¼	10¾	6¼		10⅓	8½	7⅝	8⅛	6	7¾
				8¼	10¼					7½			
11¾	14	10⅛	5¼	8½	10¼			10¾	8½		8	6¼	7¾
13	13¾	11¼	5¼	9	9¼			10¼	8¾	6¾	8⅛	5⅞	6⅞
12	16⅝	12¾	7¼	9¾	8½			10¼	9¾	6½	8⅛	5½	6⅝
10½	16¾	13½	7¾	9½	8¾			8⅘	9¾	6¾	8½	6⅛	7
		14¾	7¾					9 3/10					7
10½	18¼	15¾	7	9½	9		5½	8⅕	9⅝	7½	8⅛	6½	7¼
11	18¼	14¾		9	9			9⅕	9¾		7¼	5¾	8⅜
11¾	19	14¼		9¼					11½		7⅛	4⅝	8¾
											7½	5⅜	
												6⅜	

TABLE 48—FREIGHT RATES IN CENTS PER BUSHEL AND THEIR EQUIVALENTS IN CENTS PER 100 POUNDS CHARGED FOR THE TRANSPORTATION OF GRAIN FROM CHICAGO TO NEW YORK, VIA LAKE TO BUFFALO, N. Y., AND THENCE VIA RAIL, DURING THE PERIOD COVERED BY THE RECORDS OF THE INTERSTATE COMMERCE COMMISSION.

Date.	Commodities (rates in cents).											
	Wheat.		Corn.		Rye.		Flaxseed.		Barley.		Oats.	
	Per bushel.	Per 100 pounds.	Per bushel.	Per 100 pounds.	Per bushel.	Per 100 pounds.	Per bushel.	Per 100 pounds.	Per bushel.	Per 100 pounds.	Per bushel.	Per 100 pounds.
1887—Apr. 18..	14.125	23.542	13.125	23.438	13.125	23.438	13.125	23.438	11.5	23.958	8.5	26.563
Apr. 28..	13.125	21.875	12.125	21.652	12.125	21.652	12.125	21.652	10.5	21.875	8	25
Apr. 30..	12	20	11.2	20	11.2	20	11.2	20	10	20.833	8	25
Oct. 7..	12.75	21.25	12	21.429	12	21.429	12	21.429	11	22.917	8.5	26.563
Oct. 25..	13.5	22.5	12.5	22.321	12.5	22.321	12.5	22.321	11.5	23.958	9	28.125
Oct. 31..	13.75	22.917	12.75	22.768	12.75	22.768	12.75	22.768	11.75	24.479	9.25	28.906
Nov. 4..	13.5	22.5	12.5	22.321	12.5	22.321	12.5	22.321	11.5	23.958	9	28.125
Nov. 7..	12.25	20.417	11.5	20.536	11.5	20.536	11.5	20.536	10.5	21.875	8	25
Nov. 19..	12.75	21.25	12	21.429	12	21.429	12	21.429	11	22.917	8.5	26.563
1888—Apr. 20..	10.75	17.917	10	17.857	10	17.857	10	17.857	9	18.75	6.75	21.094
May 5..	10.5	17.5	9.75	17.411	9.75	17.411	9.75	17.411	8.75	18.229	6.5	20.313
May 17..	10.25	17.083	9.5	16.964	9.5	16.964	9.5	16.964	8.5	17.708	6.5	20.313
Aug. 1..	11	18.333	10.5	18.75	10.5	18.75	10.5	18.75	9.5	19.792	7.25	22.656
Aug. 14..	11.5	19.167	10.75	19.196	10.75	19.196	10.75	19.196	9.75	20.313	7.5	23.438
Aug. 22..	11.75	19.583	11	19.643	11	19.643	11	19.643	10	20.833	7.75	24.219
Sept. 10..	12	20	11.25	20.089	11.25	20.089	11.25	20.089	10.25	21.354	8.25	25.781
Oct. 5..	11.5	19.167	10.75	19.196	10.75	19.196	10.75	19.196	9.75	20.313	7.75	24.219
Oct. 20..	11	18.333	10.25	18.304	10.25	18.304	10.25	18.304	9.25	19.271	7.25	22.656
Nov. 1..	11.5	19.167	10.75	19.196	10.75	19.196	10.75	19.196	9.75	20.313	7.75	24.219
Nov. 22..	11	18.333	10.25	18.304	10.25	18.304	10.25	18.304	9.25	19.271	7.25	22.656
1889—Apr. 8..	9.25	15.417	8.75	15.625	8.75	15.625	9.25	16.518	8.75	18.229	6.25	19.531
Apr. 17..	8.5	14.167	8	14.286	8	14.286	8.5	15.179	8	16.667	5.5	17.188
May 13..	8.25	13.75	7.75	13.839	7.75	13.839	8.25	14.732	7.75	16.146	5.25	16.406
July 12..	8	13.333	7.5	13.395	7.5	13.393	8	14.286	7.5	15.625	5.25	16.406
July 22..	8.75	14.583	7.5	13.393	7.5	13.393	8.75	15.625	7.5	15.625	5.5	17.188
July 29..	8	13.333	7.25	12.946	7.25	12.946	8	14.286	7.25	15.104	5.25	16.406
Aug. 16..	8.25	13.75	7.5	13.393	7.5	13.393	8.25	14.732	7.5	15.625	5.5	17.188
Aug. 20..	8.5	14.167	7.75	13.839	7.75	13.839	8.5	15.179	7.75	16.146	5.5	17.188
Aug. 28..	9	15	8.25	14.732	8.25	14.732	9	16.071	8.25	17.188	6	18.75
Sept. 17..	9	15	8.25	14.732	8.25	14.732	9	16.071	8.25	17.188	6.375	19.922
Oct. 7..	9.5	15.833	8.5	15.179	8.5	15.179	9.5	16.964	8.5	17.708	6.5	20.313
Nov. 4..	10.5	17.5	9.5	16.964	9.5	16.964	10.5	18.75	9.5	19.792	7.5	23.438
Nov. 8..	9.5	15.833	8.5	15.179	8.5	15,179	9.5	16.964	8.5	17.708	6.5	20.313
Nov. 15..	8.75	14,583	7.75	13.839	7.75	13.839	8.75	15.625	7.75	16.146	6.5	20.313
1890—Apr. 10..	9.75	16.25	8.5	15.179	9	16.071	9.75	17.411	9	18.75	6.5	20.313
Apr. 15..	9	15	8	14.286	8.5	15.179	9	16.071	8.5	17.708	6	18.75
Apr. 19..	8.75	14.583	7.75	13.839	8.25	14.732	8.75	15.625	8.25	17.188	5.75	17.969
Apr. 28..	8.25	13.75	7.25	12.946	7.75	13.839	8.25	14.732	7.75	16.146	5.25	16.406
May 12..	8.25	13.75	7.25	12.946	7.75	13.839	8.25	14.732	7.75	16.146	5.25	16.406
June 2..	8.25	13.75	7	12.5	7.75	13.8[illegible]9	8.25	14.732	7.75	16.146	5.25	16.406
June 20..	8.5	14.167	7.25	12.946	8	14.286	8.5	15.179	8	16.667	5.5	17.188
July 5..	8.75	14.583	7.5	13.393	8.25	14.732	8.75	15.625	8.25	17.188	5.75	17.969
July 16..	8.5	14.167	7.25	12.946	8	14.286	8.5	15.179	8	16.667	5.25	16.406
Aug. 18..	8.5	14.167	7.25	12.946	8	14.286	8.5	15.179	8	16.667	5.25	16.406
1891—May 26..	7.5	12.5	6.25	11.161	6.25	11.161	7.5	13.393	6.25	13.021	4.5	14.063
July 25..	8	13.333	7	12.5	7	12.5	8	14.286	7	14.583	4.75	14.844
Aug. 7..	8.5	14.167	7.25	12.946	8	14.286	8.5	15.179	8	16.667	5.25	16.406
Aug. 11..	9	15	7.5	13.393	8	14.286	8.5	15.179	8	16.667	5.25	16.406
Aug. 12..	10	16.666	8.75	15.625	8.75	15.625	10	17.857	8.75	18.229	6.5	20.313
Aug. 14..	9.5	15.833	8.5	15.179	8.5	15.179	9.5	16.964	8.5	17.708	6.5	20.313
Oct. 10..	9	15	8	14.286	8	14.286	9	16.071	8	16.667	6	18.75
Oct. 14..	8	13.333	7	12.5	7	12.5	8	14.286	7	14.583	5.5	17.188
Nov. 6..	8.5	14.167	8	14.286	8	14.286	8.5	15.179	8	16.667	6	18.75
Nov. 12..	9	15	8.5	15.179	8.5	15.179	9	16.071	8.5	17.708	6	18.75
Nov. 16..	9.5	15.833	9	16.071	9	16.071	9.5	16.964	9	18.75	6	18.75
Nov. 20..	10	16.666	9.5	16.964	9.5	16.964	10	17.857	9.5	19.792	6.25	19.531
1892—Apr. 13..	8	13.333	7.5	13.393	7.5	13.393	8	14.286	7.5	15.625	5.5	17.188
May 9..	7	11.666	6.75	12.054	6.75	12.054	7	12.5	6.75	14.063	5	15.625
Sept. 24..	7.5	12.5	7	12.5	7	12.5	7	12.5	7	14.583	5	15.625
Oct. 10..	8	13.333	7.5	13.393	7.5	13.393	8	14.286	7.5	15.625	5.5	17.188

LAKE EQUIPMENT.

The following table is presented to show the increase in the number and capacity of boats operating on the Great Lakes. The table is arranged to show the character of each vessel and its tonnage capacity, comparison being made for the years 1886 and 1890. The principal fact brought out by this table is that steel propellers of greater capacity are rapidly taking the places of sailing vessels:

TABLE 49.—COMPARISON OF NUMBER AND NET TONNAGE OF ALL CLASSES OF BOATS COMPRISING THE FLOATING EQUIPMENT OF THE GREAT LAKES AND THE NUMBER AND TONNAGE OF EACH CLASS DURING 1886 AND 1890.

[Compiled from reports of Eleventh Census.]

Classification.	Vessels.				Net tonnage capacity.			
	Number.		Percentage.		Tons.		Percentage.	
	1886.	1890.	Increase.	Decrease.	1886.	1890.	Increase.	Decrease.
Total	1,997	2,055	2.9	....	634,652	826,360	30.2	....
A—Structure:								
Side-wheel steamers	43	42	....	2.3	14,150	16,949	19.8	....
Propellers under 1,000 tons	335	431	25.7	....	177,402	154,232	....	13.1
Propellers between 1,000 and 1,500 tons	72	122	69.4	....	86,728	151,611	74.8	....
Propellers over 1,500 tons	21	110	423.8	....	34,868	188,390	440.3	....
Tugs	466	448	....	3.9	11,737	12,520	6.7	....
Schooners	730	557	....	23.7	183,792	158,620	....	13.7
Barges	330	325	....	1.5	125,975	144,038	14.3	....
B—Material:								
Steel	6	68	1,033.3	....	6,459	99,457	1,439.8	....
Iron	35	39	11.4	....	22,714	24,673	8.6	....
Composite	2	13	550.0	....	63	13,554	21,414.3	....
Wood	1,954	1,935	....	1.0	605,416	688,676	13.8	....
C—Motive power:								
Steam vessels	937	1,153	23.1	....	324,885	523,702	61.2	....
Sailing vessels	1,060	902	....	14.9	309,769	302,658	....	2.3

TABLE 50.—RATES CHARGED FOR THE TRANSPORTATION OF WHEAT AND CORN FROM BUFFALO TO NEW YORK, VIA ERIE CANAL, DURING THE YEARS 1856 AND 1857.

Date.	Rates (in cents per bushel).		Date.	Rates (in cents per bushel).		Date.	Rates (in cents per bushel).	
	Wheat.	Corn.		Wheat.	Corn.		Wheat.	Corn.
1856—May 13	18	15	1856—Sept. 16	20	16	1857—July 15	13	9½
May 20	19	15½	Sept. 23	21	16½	July 22	15	11
May 27	22	17½	Sept. 30	22½	18	July 29	14	11
June 3	22	17½	Oct. 7	22½	18	Aug. 5	14	10½
June 10	16½	13	Oct. 14	23	18	Aug. 12	14	10½
June 17	17	13	Oct. 21	23	18	Aug. 19	14	10½
June 24	18	14	Oct. 28	23	18	Aug. 26	13½	9
July 1	18	14	Nov. 4	23	18	Sept. 2	13	9½
July 8	18	14	Nov. 11	21	16	Sept. 9	15	12
July 15	18	14	1857—May 13	17½	14½	Sept. 16	15	11
July 22	18	14	May 20	17½	14½	Sept. 23	15	12
July 29	17½	14	May 27	17	12½	Sept. 30	14	11
Aug. 5	19	15	June 3	17½	13½	Oct. 4	18	12½
Aug. 12	18	14	June 10	17	11½	Oct. 7	15	11
Aug. 19	17	13	June 17	15	11	Oct. 11	16	....
Aug. 26	16	12	June 24	13	10¼	Oct. 14	16	12
Sept. 2	17	13	July 1	12½	9½	Oct. 21	18	16
Sept. 9	19	15	July 8	12½	10	Oct. 28	16	13

TABLE 51.—THE AVERAGE RATES CHARGED FOR THE TRANSPORTATION OF WHEAT AND CORN VIA CANAL FROM BUFFALO TO NEW YORK, DURING EACH MONTH OF THE SEASON OF NAVIGATION, FROM 1862, AND ALSO THE HIGHEST AND AVERAGE RATE ON WHEAT DURING EACH SEASON.

Years.	Rates (in cents per bushel).															
	May.		June.		July.		August.		September.		October.		November.		Highest Wheat.	Season average, Wheat.
	Wheat.	Corn.	Wheat.	Corn.	Wheat.	Corn.	Wheat.	Corn.	Wheat.	Corn.	Wheat.	Corn.	Wheat.	Corn.		
1862	13.5	11.5	12.8	10.8	14.2	12.2	15.1	13.1	17.2	15.1	18.3	16.1	19.6	17.3	24½	14.4
1863	14.6	12.6	14.3	12.3	14.6	12.6	13.9	11.9	14.0	12.0	16.4	14.4	19.6	17.6	25	15.3
1864	16.8	14.8	18.1	16.2	19.0	16.9	21.3	18.8	18.4	16.3	18.7	16.2	18.9	16.4	22	18.7
1865	14.7	12.7	13.6	11.6	14.4	12.4	14.5	12.5	15.6	13.6	21.7	19.2	23.1	20.3	26	16.8
1866	13.6	11.6	16.6	14.3	17.8	14.8	15.7	13.3	17.5	14.6	17.7	14.8	19.6	16.3	23	16.9
1867	12.3	10.3	13.2	11.2	13.8	11.8	13.7	11.7	16.3	13.4	21.1	18.1	19.1	16.3	25	15.6
1868	14.5	11.8	13.5	11.0	13.7	11.2	14.1	11.6	16.2	13.6	18.0	15.3	19.2	16.2	24	15.6
1869	13.9	11.6	13.7	11.7	12.5	10.5	14.0	12.0	16	13.7	21.5	18.4	21.7	19.0	24	16.2
1870	11.5	10.7	10.8	9.6	10.9	9.5	9.4	9.2	10.8	10.0	13.3	11.9	11.9	11.5	16	11.2
1871	11.6	10.6	10.2	9.2	11.1	10.1	11.7	10.7	13.6	12.6	13.9	12.9	16.0	14.5	17	12.6
1872	12.8	11.8	12.1	11.0	11.5	10.5	12.0	11.0	12.5	11.3	14.2	12.6	15.0	13.9	18	13
1873	11.8	10.6	10.6	9.6	10.2	9.2	10.6	9.6	11.8	10.0	12.7	11.3	12.3	10.6	14	11.4
1874	11.8	10.8	11.3	10.3	9.5	8.6	9.0	8.0	9.5	8.6	9.5	8.5	9.7	8.7	12	10
1875	7.4	6.6	6.9	6.3	7.5	6.9	8.1	7.4	7.0	6.5	8.2	7.4	10.5	9.1	11	7.9
1876	6.7	5.8	6.2	5.4	5.9	5.4	5.8	5.3	6.2	5.6	8.3	7.5	7.6	5.5	10	6.6
1877	5.8	5.0	5.0	4.9	5.4	4.7	7.0	6.4	7.7	6.7	10.9	9.2	10.0	8.7	12	7.4
1878	5.8	5.2	4.7	4.1	4.3	3.8	5.2	4.6	8.0	7.1	8.0	7.0	5.8	5.2	8.5	6
1879	4.7	4.2	4.1	3.6	5.2	4.7	6.5	5.9	8.1	7.4	8.0	7.9	10.2	8.8	12	6.8
1880	6.9	5.5	6.9	6.4	6.0	5.4	5.9	5.4	5.9	5.[illegible]	6.7	6.0	8.8	7.5	9	6.5
1881	5.3	4.8	4.7	4.2	4.3	3.8	4.0	3.5	4.8	4.3	5.0	4.5	5.0	4.6	7	4.6
1882	4.9	4.5	4.3	3.9	4.4	4.0	5.4	4.9	5.8	5.3	6.8	6.2	6.1	5.5	8	5.4
1883	5.0	4.5	4.3	3.9	3.9	3.6	4.6	4.3	6.3	5.9	5.5	5.0	4.6	4.1	6.5	4.9
1884	3.8	3.4	3.4	3.1	3.6	3.2	4.2	3.8	4.7	4.2	5.0	4.4	4.7	4.2	5.5	4.2
1885	4.2	3.8	3.1	2.9	3.0	2.8	3.7	3.3	3.5	3.2	4.2	3.9	5.0	4.5	6	3.8
1886	5.7	5.1	3.8	3.4	4.0	3.6	5.4	4.8	6.0	5.5	5.5	5.0	4.8	4.5	6.5	5
1887	5.1	4.6	4.5	4.1	3.8	3.4	4.0	3.6	4.5	4.1	4.8	4.4	5.8	5.3	7	4.6
1888	3.4	3.1	2.5	2.3	2.5	2.3	4.1	3.8	3.9	3.6	3.7	3.4	3.5	3.2	4.5	3.4
1889	4.0	3.6	3.8	3.4	4.0	3.6	4.4	3.9	5.0	4.5	5.0	4.5	5.0	4.4	5	4.8
1890	3.9	3.5	3.8	3.4	3.6	3.2	3.8	3.4	3.9	3.5	4.0	3.6	3.5	3.1	4.2	3.8
1891	2.8	2.5	2.9	2.6	2.8	2.5	3.8	3.5	4.2	3.8	4.6	4.2	4.0	3.6	4¾	3.5
1892	2.7	2.4	2.2	2.0	2.4	2.2	3.0	2.6	3.8	3.4	4.7	4.4	4.6	4.3	6	3.4

LIVE STOCK AND DRESSED MEATS TRAFFIC FROM CHICAGO.

Practically all the live stock and dressed meat traffic forwarded to the Atlantic seaboard may be said to originate at Chicago, so far as the purposes of the rates now to be referred to are concerned. The basis upon which the rates covering this traffic are constructed is similar to that explained for the previous tables covering what is called the "dead freight" traffic; the rates from other Western points east of the Mississippi River to the seaboard are made with regard to the rates from Chicago. In former years it was not invariably the custom to preserve the relation between such points; the roads from St. Louis and other Western points would make such rates as the interests of the business might require without regard to the rates from Chicago. St. Louis has been an important shipping point for traffic of this character, and it has been generally the custom to maintain the rate from St. Louis to the seaboard on these articles 5 cents higher than from Chicago. The present rates from Chicago to the Eastern cities are as follows:

TABLE 52.—EAST BOUND LIVE STOCK AND DRESSED MEATS RATES.

	Rates (in cents per 100 pounds) from Chicago to—			
	Boston.	Philadelphia.	Baltimore.	New York.
Cattle	28	26	25	28
Hogs	30	28	27	30
Sheep	30	28	27	30
Horses and mules	60	58	57	60
Dressed beef	45	43	42	45
Dressed hogs, refrigerator cars	45	43	42	45
Dressed hogs, common cars	45	43	42	45

Here following is given a statement showing the rates on live stock and dressed meats from Chicago to New York, from 1872 to the present time. The differences shown in the above table for points other than New York may, for the purposes of comparison, be accepted as applying throughout the period covered by this table; and it may be also understood that the changes from Chicago were followed by similar changes from other points east of the Mississippi River from which this traffic is forwarded.

TABLE 53.—FREIGHT RATES CHARGED FOR THE TRANSPORTATION OF LIVE STOCK AND DRESSED MEATS FROM CHICAGO TO NEW YORK VIA ALL RAIL LINES FROM MARCH 26, 1872.

Date.	Rates (in cents per 100 pounds.)						
	Cattle.	Hogs.	Sheep.	Horses and mules.	Dressed beef.	Dressed hogs, refrigerator cars.	Dressed hogs, common cars.
1872—Mar. 26	....	....	....	....	90	....	....
Nov. 20	....	....	....	....	95	....	....
1874—Dec. 1	....	....	....	....	85	....	....
1875—Nov. 2	....	....	....	....	70	....	....
1876—Nov. 18	....	....	....	....	65	....	....
1877—Apr. 30	....	....	....	....	85	....	....
Sept. 4	....	....	....	....	70	....	....
Oct. 22	....	....	....	....	75	....	....
1878—Sept. 2	....	....	....	....	90	....	....
1879—June 9	35	35	60	60	67½	....	....
June 26	35	35	60	60	56	....	....
Aug. 4	50	40	60	60	80	....	....
Aug. 25	50	45	60	60	80	....	....
Oct. 13	50	50	60	60	80	....	....
Nov. 10	55	55	65	65	88	....	....
1880—Mar. 1	55	50	65	65	88	....	....
Apr. 14	55	40	65	65	88	....	....
Sept. 20	55	35	65	65	88	....	....
Nov. 1	55	40	65	65	88	....	....
1881—Mar. 14	50	40	60	60	80	....	....
Apr. 1	50	35	60	60	80	....	....
May 9	25	35	60	60	40	....	....
June 8	25	30	60	60	40	....	....
June 15	25	25	60	60	40	....	....
1882—Mar. 13	25	30	60	60	40	....	....
Apr. 17	40	30	50	60	64	....	....
Dec. 1	40	35	50	60	64	....	....
1883—Apr. 23	40	30	50	60	64	....	....
Nov. 26	40	35	50	60	64	....	....
1884—Jan. 5	40	25	50	60	64	....	....
Jan. 14	40	35	50	60	64	....	....
Mar. 14	40	25	50	60	64	....	....
Mar. 21	40	20	50	60	64	....	....
May 5	30	20	40	60	48	....	....
June 24	30	25	40	60	48	....	....
July 21	30	30	40	60	48	....	....
Sept. 1	20	30	40	60	32	....	....
Dec. 8	40	30	50	60	70	....	....
1885—Mar. 23	40	25	50	60	70	....	....

TABLE 53.—FREIGHT RATES CHARGED FOR THE TRANSPORTATION OF LIVE STOCK AND DRESSED MEATS FROM CHICAGO TO NEW YORK, ETC.—Continued.

Date.	Rates (in cents per 100 pounds.)						
	Cattle.	Hogs.	Sheep.	Horses and mules.	Dressed beef.	Dressed hogs, refrigerator cars.	Dressed hogs, common cars.
1885—May 3	30	25	40	60	52½	....	....
July 1	25	20	40	60	43½	....	....
July 13	25	25	40	60	43½	....	....
Nov. 23	25	30	40	60	43½	....	....
1886—Jan. 1	25	30	25	60	43	43½	35
Mar. 1	35	30	45	60	65	55	50
Dec. 20	35	35	45	60	65	55	50
1887—Apr. 22	35	35	40	60	65	65	60
June 4	35	30	40	60	65	65	60
Nov. 21	31½	30	36	60	58½	58½	54
Nov. 23	28½	30	32½	60	52½	52½	48½
Nov. 24	25½	30	29	60	47	47	43
Nov. 25	23	30	26	60	42½	42½	39
Nov. 26	20½	30	23½	60	38½	38½	35
Nov. 28	18½	30	21	60	34½	34½	31½
Nov. 29	16½	30	19	60	31	31	28½
Dec. 26	35	30	40	60	65	65	60
1888—May 14	25	30	25	60	65	65	60
June 18	16½	25	25	60	65	65	60
June 25	16½	25	25	60	40	40	40
June 26	16½	25	25	60	35	35	35
June 29	16½	25	25	60	30½	30½	30½
July 2	14½	25	25	60	26½	26½	26½
July 3	12½	25	25	60	23	23	23
July 5	11	20	25	60	20	20	20
July 6	9½	20	25	60	17½	17½	17½
July 7	8½	20	25	60	15½	15½	15½
July 9	7½	20	25	60	13½	13½	13½
July 10	6½	20	25	60	12	12	12
July 11	5½	20	25	60	10½	10½	10½
July 12	5½	20	25	60	9	9	9
July 13	5½	20	25	60	8	8	8
July 14	5½	18	25	60	7	7	7
Aug. 3	5½	18	25	60	22½	22½	22½
Aug. 20	14½	18	25	60	25	25	25
Aug. 25	10	18	25	60	25	25	25
Sept. 24	15	18	25	60	35	35	35
Oct. 15	15	25	25	60	35	35	35
Oct. 22	15	30	25	60	35	35	35
Nov. 7	15	25	25	60	35	35	35
Dec. 17	22½	30	30	60	50	50	45
1889—May 1	26	30	30	60	45	45	45
1890—May 26	26	25	30	60	45	45	45
June 16	22½	25	30	60	42	42	42
June 20	22½	25	30	60	39	39	39
June 26	21	25	30	60	36	36	36
June 30	19½	25	30	60	33	33	33
July 3	18	25	30	60	30	30	30
July 11	18	23	30	60	30	30	30
Nov. 24	26	30	30	60	45	45	45
1891—Apr. 20	28	30	30	60	45	45	45
1892—June 16	28	25	30	60	45	45	45
Oct. 10	28	30	30	60	45	45	45

From the above it is shown that following each period of reduction the rates were again advanced to a figure considered by the railroads as the normal rate. In 1882, 1883, and 1884 the normal rates were not higher than 40, 30, 50, 60, and 64 cents per 100 pounds on the respective commodities. The rates established in March, 1886, namely, 35, 30, 45, 60, and 65, were apparently deemed the maximum rates which could then be obtained. This basis continued until November, 1887, when the rates rapidly declined, and were again restored, in December, to the preceding basis. In May, 1888, certain reductions were made, which were followed in June and July by frequent and greater declines, when the following lowest open rates found were reached, namely, 5½, 18, 25, 60, and 7. Slight advances were made on different dates until December 17, when the following basis was adopted, 22½, 30, 30, 60, and 50. Further adjustment occurred on May 1, 1889, when the rates were changed to 26, 30, 30, 60, 45. These rates continued until June 16, 1890, over a year, without change, but the rates were again several times reduced until July 3, when the low basis of 18, 25, 30, 50, 30 was reached. Advances were made in November of the same year, and again in April, 1891, when the following rates were established, namely, 28, 30, 30, 60, 45, which have continued in effect up to the present time.

The changes in the cattle rates show that the normal or standard rates have been considerably reduced. The normal rate in 1885 was 40 cents, 1886 35 cents, and in 1891 and 1892 28 cents. No higher rate than 28 cents on cattle from Chicago to New York has been charged since May, 1888. Similar results are shown for the dressed beef rates; in 1885 the normal rate was 70 cents; 1886, 65 cents. This latter rate prevailed a part of 1887 and 1888, but the restoration which took place after the numerous reductions in 1888 gave the rate of 50 cents to dressed beef, which on May 1, 1889, was reduced to 45 cents. Further reductions were made in 1890, and the 45 cent rate was restored in the latter part of the same year, since which time it has not been higher.

The highest rates now applied to this traffic, when peace prevails between the competitive carriers, are on a much lower basis than were charged under similar conditions in former years.

The tonnage of live stock and dressed beef carried from Chicago and points west thereof to the Eastern cities and the Atlantic seaboard at the above rates is shown in the following table, covering from 1880 to and including 1892. From this table it is possible to estimate the enormous saving in revenue to the public by the reductions in the rates for this traffic.

TABLE 54—LIVE STOCK AND DRESSED MEATS TONNAGE FROM CHICAGO.

Year.	Tons.
1880	649,464
1881	720,923
1882	775,406
1883	847,793
1884	788,111
1885	848,020
1886	912,352
1887	1,047,273
1888	1,194,224
1889	1,498,226
1890	1,639,495
1891	1,569,396
1892	1,582,254

OIL RATES.

Here below is given a table showing the changes in the rates on crude petroleum and its products from the points in the oil region as indicated by the table to the seaboard points named, from 1877 to 1888.

TABLE 55.—FREIGHT RATES CHARGED FOR THE TRANSPORTATION OF CRUDE PETROLEUM AND ITS PRODUCTS FROM THE OIL REGIONS TO PHILADELPHIA, PA., BALTIMORE, MD., AND COMMUNIPAW, N. J., FROM DECEMBER 1, 1877.

Date.	Rates (in cents, per barrel).							
	Refinery products.				Crude.			
	From Pittsburg, Pa., Oil City, Pa., and Olean, N. Y., to—				From Olean, N. Y., Clarendon, Kane, and Warren, Pa, to—		From Pittsburg and Oil City districts to—	
	Philadelphia, Pa., and Baltimore, Md.		Communipaw, N. J.		Baltimore, Md., and Philadelphia, Pa.	Communipaw, N. J.	Baltimore, Md., and Philadelphia, Pa.	Communipaw, N. J.
	In tanks.	In barrels.	In tanks.	In barrels.				
1877—Dec. 1	175	175	190	190	100	115	125	140
1879—Jan. 23	45	45	50	50	......	......	......	......
May 9	......	......	......	......	70	85	......	......
June 2	......	......	......	......	......	......	95	110
June 23	......	......	......	......	25	30	50	55
1880—April 1	50	50	63	63	50	60	75	85
May 15	69½	69½	82½	82½	65	75	90	100
June 7	38	38	51	51	41	60	41	51
Aug. 10	50	50	60	60	50	50	50	60
Sept. 27	......	......	......	......	33	33	48	48
1881—Oct. 1	43	43	48	48	......	......	......	......
1884—Feb. 1	45	45	52	52	40	45	50	55
1888—Sept. 13	45	58	52	66	......	......	......	......

COAL RATES.

Here following are given three statements showing the rates on anthracite and bituminous coal from the principal regions on the Lehigh Valley and Pennsylvania railroads. The first table shows anthracite coal rates to tide-water and the successive changes therein from 1877 to the present time. The second table covers rates from the same regions westward to Buffalo for the same period. The third covers the changes in the bituminous coal rates from collieries in the Clearfield region on the Pennsylvania railroad to Jersey City, Philadelphia, and Baltimore.

TABLE 56.—THE AVERAGE FREIGHT RATES PER TON OF 2,240 POUNDS CHARGED FOR THE TRANSPORTATION OF ANTHRACITE COAL FROM COLLIERIES ON THE LEHIGH VALLEY RAILROAD IN THE LEHIGH, MAHANOY, AND WYOMING REGIONS, TO PERTH AMBOY, FROM JUNE 7, 1875.

Date.	From Lehigh and Mahanoy regions.			From Wyoming region.		
	Prepared sizes.	Pea and buckwheat.	Culm.	Prepared sizes.	Pea and buckwheat.	Culm.
1875—June 7	$2.56	.....	.....	$2.86	.....	.....
July 1	2.54	.....	.....	2.84	.....	.....
Aug. 1	2.56	.....	.....	2.86	.....	.....
Sept. 1	2.58	.....	.....	2.88	.....	.....
Oct. 1	2.60	.....	.....	2.90	.....	.....
1876—Feb. 1	2.41	.....	.....	2.71	.....	.....
Mar. 1	2.30	.....	.....	2.60	.....	.....
May 1	2.32	.....	.....	2.62	.....	.....
June 1	2.34	.....	.....	2.64	.....	.....
July 1	2.36	.....	.....	2.66	.....	.....
Aug. 1	2.42	.....	.....	2.72	.....	.....
Sept. 1	1.59	.....	.....	1.89	.....	.....
Nov. 1	1.62	.....	.....	1.92	.....	.....
1877—Apr. 1	1.36	.....	.....	1.57	.....	.....
Sept. 1	1.49	.....	.....	1.70	.....	.....
Sept. 24	1.59	.....	.....	1.80	.....	.....
Oct. 29	1.49	.....	.....	1.70	.....	.....
1878—Feb. 1	1.62	.....	.....	1.83	.....	.....
Mar. 25	1.67	.....	.....	1.88	.....	.....
June 3	1.72	.....	.....	1.93	.....	.....
June 26	1.75	.....	.....	1.96	.....	.....
1879—Jan. 13	1.62	.....	.....	1.83	.....	.....
Feb. 17	1.49	.....	.....	1.70	.....	.....
Mar. 1	1.36	.....	.....	1.57	.....	.....
Mar. 19	1.25	.....	.....	1.46	.....	.....
Apr. 1	1.10	.....	.....	1.31	.....	.....
Apr. 14	1.00	.....	.....	1.21	.....	.....
Nov. 1	1.15	.....	.....	1.36	.....	.....
Nov. 10	1.25	.....	.....	1.46	.....	.....
Nov. 24	1.40	.....	.....	1.61	.....	.....
1880—Jan. 4	$1.40	.....	.....	$1.61	.....	.....
Mar. 1	1.60	.....	.....	1.81	.....	.....
Apr. 5	1.75	.....	.....	1.96	.....	.....
Sept. 13	1.90	.....	.....	2.11	.....	.....
1882—May 29	1.75	.....	.....	1.96	.....	.....
July 10	1.90	.....	.....	2.11	.....	.....
1884—Apr. 1	1.77	$1.57	$1.57	1.86	$1.66	$1.66
1885—Feb. 2	1.57	1.37	1.37	1.66	1.46	1.46
Aug. 27	1.37	1.17	1.17	1.46	1.26	1.26
1886—Oct. 1	1.47	1.27	1.27	1.56	1.36	1.36
1887 Apr. 4	1.56	1.41	1.41	1.67	1.52	1.52
Nov. 21	1.81	1.66	1.66	1.92	1.77	1.77
Dec. 12	1.90	1.75	1.75	2.00	1.85	1.85
1888—Mar. 12	1.70	1.55	1.55	1.80	1.65	1.65
Apr. 2	1.70	1.45	1.45	1.80	1.55	1.55
May 1	1.70	1.40	1.20	1.80	1.50	1.30
Sept. 1	1.80	1.40	1.20	1.90	1.50	1.30
1889—Apr. 15*	1.70	1.40	1.20	1.75	1.45	1.25
1892—Sept. 12	1.85	1.55	1.35	1.85	1.55	1.35

* On and after this date buckwheat takes the same rate as culm.

TABLE 57—AVERAGE FREIGHT RATES, PER TON OF 2,240 POUNDS, CHARGED FOR THE TRANSPORTATION OF ANTHRACITE COAL FROM COLLIERIES ON THE LEHIGH VALLEY RAILROAD, IN THE WYOMING AND LEHIGH REGIONS, TO BUFFALO, N. Y., FROM AUGUST 1, 1875.

Date.	From Wyoming region.		From Lehigh region.	
	Coal cars.	Box cars.	Coal cars.	Box cars.
1875—Aug. 1	$4.09			
Sept. 1	4.12			
1876—May 1	3.80			
June 1	3.72			
Sept. 1	2.83			
Oct. 1	2.97			
Oct. 27	3.22			
1877—Jan. 1	3.26			
May 1	2.61			
May 21	2.43			
June 1	2.38			
Aug. 6	2.61			
Aug. 20	3.41			
Oct. 15	2.97			
Oct. 22	2.74			
1878—Feb. 1	2.90			
May 1	2.53			
July 1	2.69			
Sept. 2	2.85	$2.85		
1879—Apr. 1	2.00	1.85		
Oct. 20	2.16	1.85		
May 1	2.34	2.05		
Dec. 1	2.58	2.38		
1880—Apr. 1	2.77	2.47		
May 3	2.77	2.47		$3.02
June 1	2.87	2.57		3.07
Aug. 2	2.96	2.66		3.13
Dec. 1	3.12	2.82		3.29
1881—Jan. 1	3.26	2.96		3.58
Apr. 25	2.93	2.63		3.25
July 1	3.01	2.71		3.13
Oct. 1	3.15	2.85		3.27
1882—Apr. 17	2.84	2.54		2.96
June 1	2.78	2.48	$3.35	3.05
1882—July 10	$2.92	$2.62	$3.49	$3.19
Sept. 4	3.00	2.70	3.57	3.27
Nov. 1	3.11	2.81	3.68	3.38
1883—Apr. 23	2.74	2.44	3.06	2.76
July 2	2.87	2.57	3.19	2.89
Sept. 1	2.93	2.63	3.25	2.95
1884—May 1	2.62	2.32	2.94	2.64
Aug. 1	2.71	2.41	3.03	2.73
1885—May 1	2.35	2.15	2.74	2.62
Nov. 2	2.50	2.30	2.97	2.77
1886—May 1	2.20	2.00	2.57	2.47
Aug. 2	2.30	2.00	2.77	2.47
Nov. 15	2.30	2.15	2.72	2.62
1887—Apr. 4	2.25	2.25	2.72	2.72
Apr. 21	2.00	2.00	2.32	2.32
Nov. 7	2.25	2.25	2.25	2.25
1888—Apr. 16	2.00	2.00	2.00	2.00
May 1	2.00	2.00	2.00	2.00
Sept. 1	2.25	2.25	2.25	2.25
1889—Apr. 15	2.00	2.00	2.00	2.00
1892—May 2	2.25	2.25	2.25	2.25
Sept. 12	2.50	2.50	2.50	2.50
Sept. 19	2.50	2.50	2.70	2.70

TABLE 58—AVERAGE FREIGHT RATES CHARGED DURING EACH YEAR FROM 1873 FOR THE TRANSPORTATION OF BITUMINOUS COAL FROM COLLIERIES IN THE CLEARFIELD REGION, ON PENNSYLVANIA RAILROAD, TO JERSEY CITY, PHILADELPHIA, AND BALTIMORE.

Year.	Jersey City.	Philadelphia.	Baltimore.
1873	$4.05	$3.55	$3.55
1874	4.05	3.55	3.55
1875	3.80	3.55	3.55
1876	3.55	3.55	3.55
1877	3.55	3.25	3.25
1878	3.55	2.25	3.25
1879	3.55	2.50	2.50
1880	3.75	2.50	2.50
1881	3.33	2.50	2.50
1882	3.33	2.50	2.50
1883	$3.33	$2.50	$2.25
1884	2.93	2.20	2.20
1885	2.45	2.00	2.00
1886	2.45	2.00	2.00
1887	2.25	2.10	2.00
1888	2.25	2.10	2.00
1889	2.25	2.00	2.00
1890	2.25	2.00	2.00
1891	2.25	2.00	2.00
1892	2.25	2.00	2.00

Rates shown for years 1873 to 1886, inclusive, are for net ton; subsequent rates are for gross tons.

RATES ON CLASSIFIED TRAFFIC AND COMMODITIES BETWEEN VARIOUS WESTERN POINTS.

Here following will be given a series of tables showing the changes in rates between principal competitive localities west of Chicago and the Mississippi River. The points selected are the termini of the principal competitive routes in the section indicated. The rates between such points are the standard, or basis upon which the charges to numerous other places are established, and should be accepted not alone as showing the changes between the points given by the tables, but as also representing the reductions which have taken place in a large area of country tributary to the carriers operating between the points embraced in the tables. Traffic coming to or destined beyond these termini has also been to a large extent affected by these changes:

RATES ON CLASSIFIED TRAFFIC AND COMMODITIES FROM CHICAGO TO ST. PAUL, MINN.

The two tables following show the rates from Chicago to St. Paul. The first embraces the class rates from 1883 to the present time; the second covers the rates on the various commodities, some of which are shown for as early as 1871. The class rates are governed by the Western classification, in connection with which it should be remembered that the classification has been greatly reduced. The table of commodities is compiled based upon the rates of the commodoties and the classification, and embraces for such articles both the changes which may have taken place in the rates and in the classification.

TABLE 59.—FREIGHT RATES CHARGED FOR THE TRANSPORTATION OF CLASSIFIED TRAFFIC FROM CHICAGO TO ST. PAUL, FROM NOVEMBER 1, 1883.

[Governed by Western classification.]

Date.	Classes (rates in cents per 100 pounds).									
	1.	2.	3.	4.	5.	A.	B.	C.	D.	E.
1883—Nov. 1	75	60	40	30	25	25	20	17½	15	......
Nov. 21	75	60	40	30	25	25	20	17½	15	......
1884—Apr. 1	60	45	35	25	20	25	20	17½	15	......
1885—Apr. 13	50	40	30	20	15	20	17½	15	12½	......
Nov. 16	60	45	35	22½	17½	22½	20	17½	15	......
1886—July 20	40	30	20	15	10	17½	15	12½	10	......
Nov. 1	72	60	40	28	24	26	23	18	18	......
1887—Apr. 1	80	70	48	33	28	30	26	23	20	......
June 16	75	60	45	30	20	25	20	16	13	12
Aug. 1	50	40	30	20	12½	17½	15	13	10	8
Sept. 1	50	40	30	20	12½	17½	15	13	10	8
Nov. 15	50	40	30	20	12½	17½	15	13	10	8
1888—June 4	60	50	35	25	17	18	16	14	12	10
July 19	60	50	35	25	17	17½	15	14	12	10
Oct. 10	60	50	40	25	20	25	20	17	14	13
1889—July 8	60	50	40	25	20	25	20	17	14	13
Sept. 25	40	35	22	17	12½	17	13	10	10	10
Nov. 20	60	50	40	25	20	25	20	17	14	13
1890—Feb. 17	40	35	22	17	12½	17	15	12	10	10
Aug. 1	50	40	30	20	15	20	15	12½	11	10
Nov. 17	60	50	40	25	18	25	18	15	13	12
1891—Jan. 1	**60**	**50**	**40**	**25**	**20**	**25**	**20**	**17**	**14**	**13**

TABLE 60.—RATES OF FREIGHT, ALL RAIL, FROM

[NOTE.—Where the rates shown are not specifically described as applying on less than

Date.	Commodities (rates in cents per 100 pounds).													
	Dry goods.	Cotton piece goods.	Boots and shoes.	Oil in barrels.	Hard coal.	Stoves.		Coffee.		Tea.	Sugar.		Molasses.	
						Less than carloads.	Carloads.	Less than carloads.	Carloads.		Less than carloads.	Carloads.	Less than carloads.	Carloads.
1871—Jan. 9	130	....	130	70	35	....	....	....	70	....	....	70	....	....
Mar. 25	85	....	85	35	35	....	....	....	35	....	....	35	....	....
Aug. 10	70	....	70	25	25	....	....	....	25	....	....	25	....	....
Oct. 16	100	....	100	50	30	....	....	....	50	....	....	50	....	....
Dec. 1	130	....	130	70	35	....	....	....	70	....	....	70	....	....
1872—Apr. 22	75	....	75	30	30	....	....	....	30	....	....	30	....	....
Aug. 15	75	....	75	30	25	....	....	....	30	....	....	30	....	....
1873—Nov. 17	100	....	100	50	30	....	....	....	50	....	....	50	....	....
1874—Apr. 7	80	....	80	35	30	....	....	....	35	....	....	35	....	....
May 21	80	....	80	35	30	....	....	....	35	....	....	35	....	....
Aug. 10	80	....	80	35	22½	....	....	....	35	....	....	35	....	....
Sept. 1	80	....	80	35	30	....	....	....	35	....	....	35	....	....
Nov. 23	100	....	100	55	22½	....	....	....	55	....	....	55	....	....
1879—Jan. 2	90	....	90	80	20	....	....	....	45	....	....	45	....	....
Mar. 30	60	....	60	60	15	....	....	....	25	....	....	25	....	....
Nov. 3	75	....	75	90	20	....	....	....	35	....	....	35	....	....
1880—Mar. 22	60	....	60	60	20	....	....	....	25	....	....	25	....	....
1881—Jan. 24	75	....	75	90	20	....	....	....	35	....	....	35	....	....
Apr. 11	60	....	60	70	20	....	....	....	25	....	....	25	....	....
Nov. 15	60	....	60	60	15	....	....	....	25	....	....	25	....	....
1882—Feb. 2	75	....	75	25	20	....	....	....	35	....	....	35	....	....
Feb. 20	60	....	60	20	15	....	....	....	25	....	....	25	....	....
1883—Nov. 1	75	75	75	....	....	40	25	30	25	75	30	25	30	25
1884—Mar. 1	75	75	75	....	....	40	25	30	25	75	30	25	30	25
Apr. 1	60	60	60	....	....	35	20	25	20	60	25	20	25	20
1885—Apr. 3	50	50	50	....	....	30	15	20	15	50	20	15	20	15
Nov. 16	60	60	60	....	....	35	17½	22½	17½	60	22½	17½	17½	17½
1886—July 1	60	60	60	....	....	35	17½	22½	17½	60	22½	17½	17½	17½
July 20	40	40	40	....	....	20	10	15	10	40	15	10	15	10
Nov. 1	72	72	72	....	....	40	24	28	24	72	28	24	28	24
1887—Apr. 1	80	80	80	....	....	48	28	33	28	80	33	28	33	28
June 6	75	75	75	....	....	45	20	30	20	75	30	20	30	20
Aug. 1	50	50	50	....	....	30	12½	20	12½	50	20	12½	20	12½
Nov. 15	50	30	50	12½	10	30	12½	20	12½	50	20	12½	20	12½
1888—June 4	60	35	60	17	10	35	17	25	17	60	25	17	25	17
July 19	60	35	60	17	10	35	17	25	17	60	25	17	25	17
Sept. 4	60	....	60	17	10	....	....	....	17	....	....	17	....	....
Oct. 10	60	35	60	20	12½	40	20	25	20	62	25	20	25	20
Nov. 20	60	....	60	17	12½	....	....	....	20	....	....	20	....	....
1889—Jan. 10	60	35	60	25	12½	40	20	25	20	60	25	20	25	20
Apr. 1	60	60	60	....	....	40	20	25	20	60	25	20	25	20
July 5	60	....	60	25	12½	....	....	....	10	....	....	10	....	....
Sept. 5	60	....	60	12½	12½	....	....	....	20	....	....	12½	....	....
Sept. 25	40	40	40	12½	12½	22	19	17	12½	40	17	12½	17	12½
Nov. 20	60	60	60	12½	12½	40	20	25	20	60	25	20	25	20
1890—Feb. 17	40	40	40	12½	12½	22	10	17	12½	40	17	12½	17	12½
Aug. 1	50	50	50	12½	12½	30	10	20	15	50	20	15	20	15
Nov. 17	60	60	60	12½	12½	30	10	25	18	60	25	18	25	18
1891—Jan. 1	60	....	60	10	12½	....	....	....	20	....	....	20	....	....
Jan. 22	60	....	60	12½	12½	....	....	....	20	....	....	20	....	....
1892—June 10	60	....	60	15	12½	....	....	....	20	....	....	20	....	....

CHICAGO, ILL., TO ST. PAUL, MINN.

carload or carload quantities they apply on shipments regardless of quantity.]

Commodities (rates in cents per 100 pounds).																				
Rice.				Crockery and earthenware.		Bagging.		Leather.		Lead.		Nails.					Machinery.		Beer.	
Less than carloads.	Carloads.	Groceries.	Drugs.	Less than carloads.	Carloads.	Less than carloads.	Carloads.	Less than carloads.	Carloads.	Less than carloads.	Carloads.	Less than carloads.	Carloads.	Hardware.	Lumber.	Salt.	Less than carloads.	Carloads.	Less than carloads.	Carloads.
																*60				
															30	*60				
															30	*60				
															30	*60				
															20	*50				
															20	*30				
															20					
																12½				
															20					
															17½	12½				
															20					
															17½	12½				
30	25	75	75	30	25	30	30	60	60	30	17½	30	25	60			60	25		
30	25	75	75	30	20	30	30	60	60	30	25	30	25	60			60	25	40	24
25	20	60	60	25	20	25	25	45	45	25	20	25	20	45			45	25	35	20
20	15	50	50	20	17½	20	20	40	40	20	15	20	15	50			40	20	30	16
22½	17½	60	60	22½	20	22½	22½	45	45	22½	17½	22½	17½	45			45	22½	35	18
22½	17½	60	60	22½	22½	22½	22½	45	45	22½	17½	22½	17½	45			45	22½	35	18
15	10	40	40	15	15	15	15	30	30	15	10	15	10	30			30	17½	20	12
28	24	72	72	28	28	28	28	60	60	28	24	28	25	60			60	26	40	22½
33	28	80	80	33	33	33	33	70	70	33	28	33	28	70			70	30	48	26½
30	20	75	75	30	20	30	30	60	60	30	20	30	20	60			60	25	45	24
20	12½	50	50	20	12½	20	20	40	40	20	12½	20	12½	40			40	17½	30	16
20	12½	50	50	20	12½	20	20	40	40	20	12½	20	12½	40	12½	10	40	17½	30	16
25	17	60	60	25	17	25	25	50	50	25	17	25	17	60	12½	12	50	18	35	20
25	17	60	60	25	17	25	25	50	50	25	17	25	17	60	12½	12	50	17½	35	20
															14					
25	20	60	60	25	20	25	25	50	50	25	20	25	20	50	14	14	50	25	40	20
															14	14				
25	20	60	60	50	20	25	25	50	50	25	20	25	20	50	14	14	50	25	40	20
25	20	60	60	25	20	25	20	50	25	25	20	25	20	50			50	25	40	20
															14	14				
															14	14				
17	12½	40	40	17	12½	17	12½	35	17	17	12½	17	9	35	14	8⅓	35	17	22	12½
25	20	60	60	25	20	25	20	50	25	25	20	25	20	50	14	14	50	25	40	20
17	12½	40	40	17	12½	17	12	35	17	17	12½	17	12½	35	14	8¾	35	17	22	12½
20	15	50	50	20	15	40	15	40	20	20	15	20	10	40	14	12½	40	20	30	15
25	18	60	60	25	18	25	18	50	25	25	18	25	18	50	14	12½	50	25	40	18
															14	12½				
															14	12½				
															14	12½				

* Rate in cents per barrel.

RATES ON CLASSIFIED TRAFFIC, ST. PAUL, MINN., TO CHICAGO.

The following table shows the changes which have taken place in rates of freight carried in the classes from St. Paul, Minn., to Chicago, from 1883 up to the present time.

With this table, as well as the others referred to, the changes which have been pointed out for the Western classification are to be also here considered, in order that the correct result of the reductions which have taken place may be fully understood.

TABLE 61.—FREIGHT RATES CHARGED FOR THE TRANSPORTATION OF CLASSIFIED TRAFFIC AND GRAIN FROM ST. PAUL TO CHICAGO FROM NOVEMBER 1, 1883.

[Governed by Western classification.]

Date.	Class (rates in cents per 100 pounds.)												
	1.	2.	3.	4.	5.	A.	B.	C.	D.	E.	Wheat and its products.	Corn and grain.	Rye and barley.
1883—Nov. 1	75	60	40	30	25	25	20	17½	15	.....	20	20	20
1884—Apr. 1	60	45	35	25	20	25	20	17½	15	.....	20	17½	17½
1885—Apr. 13	50	40	30	20	15	20	17½	15	12½	.....	17½	15	15
Nov. 16	60	45	35	22½	17½	22½	20	17½	15	....	17½	15	15
1886—July 20	45	35	25	20	15	20	17½	15	12½	.....	......	......	......
Nov. 1	72	60	48	28	24	26	23	18	18	.....	......	12½	12½
1887—Apr. 1	80	70	48	33	28	30	26	23	20	.....	......	18	18
June 16	75	60	45	30	20	25	20	16	13	12	......	......	......
Aug. 1	50	40	30	20	12½	17½	15	13	10	8	......	......	......
Sept. 1	50	40	30	20	12½	17½	15	13	10	8	12½	12½	12½
June 4	60	50	35	25	17	18	16	14	12	10	12½	12½	12½
July 19	60	50	35	25	17	17½	15	14	12	10	12½	12½	12½
Oct. 10	60	50	40	25	20	25	20	17	14	13	12½	12½	12½
1890—Nov. 17	60	50	40	25	18	25	18	15	13	12	12½	12½	12½
1891—Jan. 1	60	50	40	25	20	25	20	17	14	13	12½	12½	12½

RATES FROM CHICAGO TO MISSOURI RIVER POINTS.

Rates from Chicago to Missouri River points, such as Kansas City and St. Joseph, Mo., and Atchinson and Leavenworth, Kans,, are used as a basis for constructing the rates from Chicago to points in Kansas, Nebraska, Colorado, and Utah. They are therefore important rates, at which a large traffic is carried, and when changed similarly affect rates to the western points indicated. A table is here given showing the changes in rates from Chicago to the Missouri River from 1877 to date.

The traffic taken between these points is governed by the Western classification, which, it has elsewhere been shown, has by its expansion reduced the classification on a large proportion of articles carried thereunder. Accordingly the traffic taken at the classified rates here given has received the benefit of the changes in the classification, and this fact should be kept in mind when the rates of this table are under consideration.

Data have also been collected showing the actual changes in the rates of a number of articles between Chicago and Kansas City, and are given in the second table following. This table covers a period of nearly thirty years, and the rates of 1892 are shown to be in many instances less than a third of those of 1864. Some remarkable reductions are observed, notably the rates on stoves.

TABLE 62.—FREIGHT RATES CHARGED FOR THE TRANSPORTATION OF CLASSIFIED TRAFFIC FROM CHICAGO TO KANSAS CITY MO.; ATCHISON, KANS.; LEAVENWORTH, KANS., AND ST. JOSEPH, MO., FROM JANUARY 1, 1877.

[Governed by Western classification.]

Date.	Classes (rates in cents per 100 pounds).									
	1.	2.	3.	4.	5.	A.	B.	C.	D.	E.
1877—Jan. 1	85	70	40	30	25	37½	30	20	......	.....
1882—Aug. 1	90	75	50	32	28	37½	32	23	......	.....
Nov. 1	90	75	50	32	28	37½	32	23	23	.....
1884—June 2	90	75	50	35	30	32½	29½	23	23	.....
1887—April 1	90	75	50	35	30	32½	29½	23	20	16
Aug. 1	90	75	50	35	30	32½	29½	23	20	16
Dec. 20	75	60	40	30	25	30	25	20	17½	16
1888—Jan. 9	75	60	40	30	25	30	25	15	15	15
Mar. 26	75	60	40	30	25	30	25	20	17½	16
1890—Feb. 22	60	50	35	25	18	25	20	15	14	13
Aug. 1	70	58	42	28	21	28	23	18	16	15
1891—Jan. 1	75	60	42	30	25	30	25	20	17½	16

TABLE 63—RATES OF FREIGHT, ALL-RAIL, FROM

[NOTE.—Where the rates shown are not specifically described as applying on less than carload

Date.	Commodities (rates in cents per 100 pounds).											
	Dry goods.	Cotton piece goods.	Boots and shoes.	Stoves.		Coffee.		Tea.	Sugar.		Molasses.	
				Less than carloads.	Carloads.	Less than carloads.	Carloads.		Less than carloads.	Carloads.	Less than carloads.	Carloads.
1864—Feb. 12	154	154	154	154	154	94	94	131	94	94	94	94
1865—Mar. 27	170	170	170	170	170	103	103	152	103	103	103	103
1869—Oct. 25	120	120	120	120	65	65	65	85	65	65	65	65
1870—Mar. 24	100	100	100	100	50	50	50	70	50	50	50	50
1871—Nov. 1	100	100	100	45	45	45	45	70	45	45	45	45
1874—Apr. 20	90	90	90	75	*8500	60	35	90	40	35	40	35
1875—Mar. 1	100	100	100	60	45	60	45	100	45	40	45	40
1876—Jan. 19	85	85	85	45	25	45	25	85	30	25	30	25
Feb. 1	90	90	90	50	40	50	35	90	40	35	40	35
1877—Jan. 29	85	85	85	45	25	30	25	85	30	25	30	25
Nov. 1	85	85	85	45	25	30	30	85	30	30	30	30
1878—Jan. 28	85	85	85	45	25	30	30	85	30	30	30	30
Mar. 25	85	85	85	45	25	30	25	85	30	25	30	25
1882—Aug. 1	90	90	90	50	28	32	28	90	32	28	32	28
Nov. 1	90	90	90	50	28	22	28	90	32	28	32	28
1883—Jan. 1	90	90	90	50	28	32	28	90	32	28	32	28
Apr. 16	90	90	90	50	28	32	28	90	32	28	32	28
1884—June 2	90	90	90	50	30	35	30	90	35	30	35	30
1885—Nov. 23	90	90	90	50	30	33½	30	90	33½	30	33½	30
1887—Aug. 1	90	90	90	50	30	33½	30	90	33½	30	33½	30
Dec. 20	75	55	75	40	25	28½	25	75	28½	25	28½	25
1888—Jan. 9	75	45	75	40	25	28½	25	75	28½	25	28½	25
Mar. 26	75	55	75	40	25	28½	25	75	28½	25	28½	25
Apr. 2	75	45	75	40	25	28½	25	75	28½	25	28½	25
1889—Jan. 10	75	45	75	40	25	28½	25	75	28½	25	28½	25
Apr. 1	75	45	75	40	25	28½	25	75	28½	25	28½	25
1890—Feb. 22	60	40	60	35	18	23½	18	60	23½	18	23½	18
Aug. 1	70	47	70	42	21	28	21	70	28	21	28	21
1891—Jan. 1	75	47	75	42	25	30	25	75	30	25	30	25
1892—Sept. 1	75	47	75	42	25	30	25	75	30	25	30	25

* Per carload.

CHICAGO, ILL., TO KANSAS CITY, MO.

or carload quantities, they apply on shipments regardless of quantity.]

Commodities (rates in cents per 100 pounds).																		
Rice.				Gunny, jute, and burlaps.		Leather.		Soap, common.		Nails.			Agricultural implements.		Machinery.		Beer.	
Less than carloads.	Carloads.	Groceries.	Drugs.	Less than carloads.	Carloads.	Less than carloads.	Carloads.	Less than carloads.	Carloads.	Less than carloads.	Carloads.	Hardware.	Less than carloads.	Carloads.	Less than carloads.	Carloads.	Less than carloads.	Carloads.
94	94	131	131	131	131	131	131	94	94	112	112	112	Special		131	131	....	....
103	103	152	152	152	152	152	152	103	103	119	119	119	...do.....		152	152	.....	....
65	65	65	120	105	105	85	85	65	65	65	65	85	120	.....	120	Sp'l	.....	....
50	50	50	100	70	70	70	70	50	50	50	50	90	100	.do .	70	*$110	50	50
45	45	45	100	70	70	70	70	45	45	45	45	70	100	*$100	70	*$100	50	50
40	35	75	90	40	40	75	75	40	35	40	*$85	60	90	*$85	90	*$85	40	40
45	40	75	100	45	45	75	75	45	40	45	40	60	100	*$90	100	*$90	60	45
40	35	70	90	40	40	50	50	40	35	40	35	50	90	*$80	90	*$80	50	40
30	25	70	85	30	30	70	70	30	25	30	25	45	85	*$75	85	*$75	45	30
30	25	85	85	30	30	70	70	30	25	30	25	45	.....	37½	70	37½	45	30
30	30	85	85	30	30	70	70	30	30	30	30	45	.....	37½	70	37½	30	30
30	30	85	85	30	30	70	70	30	30	30	30	45	.....	37½	70	37½	45	30
30	25	85	85	30	30	70	70	30	25	30	25	45	.....	37½	70	37½	45	30
32	28	90	90	32	32	75	75	32	28	32	23	50	.....	37½	75	37½	50	30
32	28	90	90	32	32	75	75	32	28	32	25	75	.....	37½	75	37½	50	25
32	28	90	90	32	32	75	75	32	28	32	28	75	.....	37½	75	37½	50	25
32	28	90	90	32	32	75	75	32	28	32	28	75	.....	37½	75	37½	50	25. 6
35	30	90	90	35	35	75	75	35	30	35	30	75	.....	32½	75	32½	50	28
33½	30	90	90	35	35	75	75	35	30	35	30	75	.....	32½	75	32½	50	28
33½	30	90	90	35	35	75	75	35	30	35	25	75	.....	32½	75	32½	50	28
28½	25	75	75	30	30	60	60	30	25	30	25	60	.....	30	60	30	40	24
28½	25	75	75	30	30	60	60	30	25	30	25	60	.....	30	60	30	40	24
28½	25	75	75	30	30	60	60	30	25	30	25	60	.....	30	60	30	40	24
28½	25	75	75	30	30	60	60	30	25	30	25	60	.....	30	60	30	40	24
28½	25	75	75	30	30	60	60	30	25	30	25	60	.....	30	60	30	40	25
28½	25	75	75	30	25	60	30	30	25	30	25	60	.....	30	60	30	40	25
23½	18	60	60	25	18	50	25	25	18	25	18	50	.....	25	50	25	35	18
28	21	70	70	28	21	58	28	28	21	28	21	58	.....	28	58	28	42	21
30	25	75	75	30	25	60	30	30	25	30	25	60	.....	30	60	30	42	25
30	25	75	75	30	25	60	30	30	25	30	25	60	.....	30	60	30	42	25

* Per carload.

RATES FROM ST. LOUIS TO MISSOURI RIVER POINTS.

Two tables following are given, the first table showing the rates on various classes from St. Louis to Missouri River points, and the second table showing the rates on a number of commodities between the same points. These tables are governed by the Western classification:

TABLE 64.—WEST-BOUND RATES, ST. LOUIS TO MISSOURI RIVER POINTS, VIZ, KANSAS CITY, ST. JOSEPH, ATCHISON, AND LEAVENWORTH.

Date.	Classes (in cents per 100 pounds).									
	1.	2.	3.	4.	5.	A.	B.	C.	D.	E.
1877—Jan. 1	65	50	35	25	20	25	20	15	.....	.....
1882—Aug. 1	70	55	40	27	23	25	22	18	.....	.....
Nov. 1	70	55	40	27	23	25	22	18	18	.....
1884—June 2	70	55	40	30	25	25	22	18	18	.....
1887—Apr. 1	70	55	40	30	25	25	22	18	15	12
Aug. 1	70	55	40	30	25	25	22	18	15	11
Dec. 20	55	40	30	25	20	22½	17½	15	12½	11
1888—Jan. 9	55	40	30	25	20	22½	17½	10	10	10
Mar. 26	55	40	30	25	20	22½	17½	15	12½	11
1890—Feb. 22	40	30	25	20	13	17½	12½	10	9	8
Mar. 3	50	38	32	23	16	20½	15½	13	11	10
1891—Jan. 1	55	40	32	25	20	22½	17½	15	12½	11

TABLE 65.—RATES OF FREIGHT, ALL RAIL, FROM

[NOTE.—Where the rates shown are not specifically described as applying on less than

Date.	Commodities (rates in cents per 100 pounds).												
	Dry goods.	Cotton piece goods.	Boots and shoes.	Stoves.		Coffee.		Tea.	Sugar.		Molasses.	
				Less than carloads.	Carloads.	Less than carloads.	Carloads.		Less than carloads.	Carloads.	Less than carloads.	Carloads.
1883—Jan. 1	70	70	70	40	23	27	23	70	27	23	27	23
Apr. 16	70	70	70	40	23	27	23	70	27	23	27	23
1884—Mar. 1	70	70	70	40	23	27	23	70	27	23	27	23
June 2	70	70	70	40	25	30	25	70	30	25	30	25
1885—Nov. 23	70	70	70	40	25	28½	25	70	28½	25	28½	25
1886—July 1	70	70	70	40	25	28½	25	70	28½	25	28½	25
1887—Apr. 1	70	70	70	40	25	28½	25	70	28½	25	28½	25
Aug. 1	70	70	70	40	25	28½	25	70	28½	25	28½	25
Dec. 20	55	40	55	30	20	23½	20	55	23½	20	23½	20
1888—Jan. 9	55	30	55	30	20	23½	20	55	23½	20	23½	20
Mar. 26	55	40	55	30	20	23½	20	55	23½	20	23½	20
Apr. 2	55	30	55	30	20	23½	20	55	23½	20	23½	20
1889—Jan. 10	55	30	55	30	20	23½	20	55	23½	20	23½	20
Apr. 1	55	30	55	30	20	23½	20	55	23½	20	23½	20
1890—Feb. 22	40	25	40	25	13	18½	13	40	18½	13	18½	13
Aug. 1	50	32	50	32	16	23	16	50	23	16	23	16
1891—Jan. 1	55	32	55	32	20	23	20	55	25	20	25	20

St. Louis, Mo., to Kansas City, Mo.

carload or carload quantities they apply on shipments regardless of quantity.]

Commodities (rates in cents per 100 pounds).																		
Rice.				Crockery and earthen ware.		Bagging.		Leather.		Lead.		Nails.			Machinery.		Beer.	
Less than carloads.	Carloads.	Groceries.	Drugs.	Less than carloads.	Carloads.	Less than carloads.	Carloads.	Less than carloads.	Carloads.	Less than carloads.	Carloads.	Less than carloads.	Carloads.	Hardware.	Less than carloads.	Carloads.	Less than carloads.	Carloads.
27	23	70	70	27	23	27	27	55	55	27	18	27	23	55	55	25	.....	....
27	23	70	70	27	23	27	27	55	55	27	23	27	23	55	55	25	40	21½
27	23	70	70	27	22	27	27	55	55	27	23	27	23	55	55	25	40	21½
30	25	70	70	30	22	30	30	55	55	30	25	30	25	55	55	25	40	24
28½	25	70	70	30	22	30	30	55	55	30	25	30	25	55	55	25	40	24
28½	25	70	70	30	30	30	30	55	55	30	25	30	25	55	55	25	40	24
28½	25	70	70	30	25	30	30	55	55	30	12½	30	25	55	55	25	40	24
28½	25	70	70	30	25	30	30	55	55	30	12½	30	20	55	55	25	40	24
23½	20	55	55	25	20	25	25	40	40	25	12½	25	20	40	40	22½	30	20
23½	20	55	55	25	20	25	25	40	40	25	12½	25	20	40	40	22½	30	20
23½	20	55	55	25	20	25	25	40	40	25	12½	25	20	40	40	22½	30	20
23½	20	55	55	25	20	25	25	40	40	25	12½	25	20	40	40	22½	30	20
23½	20	55	55	40	20	25	25	40	40	25	12½	25	20	40	40	22½	30	20
23½	20	55	55	25	20	25	20	40	25	25	12½	25	20	40	40	22½	30	20
18½	13	40	40	20	13	20	13	30	20	20	12½	20	13	30	30	17½	25	13
23	16	50	50	23	16	23	16	38	23	23	12½	23	16	38	38	20½	32	16
25	20	55	55	25	20	25	20	40	25	25	12½	25	20	40	40	22½	32	20

RATES FROM ST. LOUIS, MO., TO ST. PAUL, MINN.

The following table presents the rates from 1883 to 1890, inclusive, on the traffic above indicated. Important reductions are shown to have taken place in the rates of each class. It will also be recalled that the Western classification, which governs this traffic, has been greatly reduced.

A second table covering the same points is given, which shows for an equal period the changes in the various important commodities.

TABLE 66.—FREIGHT RATES CHARGED FOR THE TRANSPORTATION OF CLASSIFIED TRAFFIC AND GRAIN FROM ST. LOUIS, MO., TO ST. PAUL, MINN., VIA ALL-RAIL LINES, FROM NOVEMBER 1, 1883.

[Governed by Western classification.]

Date.	Rates (in cents per 100 pounds).											
	1.	2.	3.	4.	5.	A.	B.	C.	D.	E.	Wheat.	Other grain.
1883—Nov. 1	75	60	40	30	25	25	20	17½	15	......	20	20
1884—Apr. 1	60	45	35	25	20	25	20	17½	15	......	20	17½
1885—Apr. 13	50	40	30	20	15	20	17½	15	12½	......	17½	15
Nov. 16	60	45	35	22½	17½	22½	20	17½	15	......	17½	15
1886—July 20	40	30	20	15	10	17½	15	12½	10	......	15	15
Nov. 1	72	60	40	28	24	26	23	18	18	......	17½	17½
1887—Apr. 1	84	73½	50½	34½	29½	31½	27½	24	21	......	17½	19
June 16	79	63	47	31½	21	26	21	17	13½	12½	17½	19
Aug. 1	52½	42	31½	21	13	18	16	14	10½	8½	17½	19
Sept. 1	52½	42	31½	21	13	18	16	14	10½	8½	13	13
1888—June 4	63	52½	37	26	18	19	17	15	13	10½	13	13
July 19	63	52½	37	26	18	18½	16	15	13	10½	13	13
Oct. 10	63	52½	42	26	21	26	21	18	15	13½	13	13
Nov. 10	63	52½	42	26	21	26	21	18	15	13½	15	15
1889—Sept. 25	52	45½	28½	22	15	22	15	13	13	12	15	15
Sept. 26	63	52½	42	26	21	26	21	18	15	13½	15	15
Oct. 19	52	45½	28½	22	15	22	15	13	13	12	15	15
Nov. 1	55	45	30	25	15	22½	17½	15	13	12	15	15
Nov. 20	63	52½	42	26	21	26	21	18	15	13½	15	15
1890—Feb. 17	42	31½	23	18	13	18	16	12½	10½	10½	15	15
Aug. 1	52½	42	31½	21	16	21	16	13	11½	10½	15	15
Nov. 17	63	52½	42	26	19	26	19	16	13½	12½	15	15

TABLE 67.—RATES OF FREIGHT, ALL RAIL,

[NOTE.—Where the rates shown are not specifically described as applying on less

Date.	Commodities (rates in cents per 100 pounds).												
	Dry goods.	Cotton piece goods.	Boots and shoes.	Stoves.		Coffee.		Tea.	Sugar.		Molasses.	
				Less than carloads.	Carloads.	Less than carloads.	Carloads.		Less than carloads.	Carloads.	Less than carloads.	Carloads.
1883—Nov. 1	75	75	75	40	25	30	25	75	30	25	30	25
1884—Mar. 1	75	75	75	40	25	30	25	75	30	25	30	25
Apr. 1	60	60	60	35	20	25	20	60	25	20	25	20
1885—Apr. 13	50	50	50	30	15	20	15	50	20	15	20	15
Nov. 16	60	60	60	35	17½	22½	17½	60	22½	17½	22½	17½
1886—July 1	60	60	60	35	17½	22½	17½	60	22½	17½	22½	17½
July 20	40	40	40	20	10	15	10	40	15	10	15	10
Nov. 1	72	72	72	40	24	28	24	72	28	24	28	24
1887—Apr. 1	84	31½	84	50½	29½	34½	29½	84	34½	29½	34½	29½
June 16	79	31½	79	47	31½	31½	21	79	31½	21	31½	21
Aug. 1	52½	31½	52½	31½	13	21	13	52½	21	13	21	13
1888—June 4	63	35	63	37	18	26	18	63	26	18	26	18
July 19	63	35	63	37	18	26	18	63	26	18	26	18
Oct. 10	63	37	63	42	21	26	21	63	26	21	26	21
1889—Jan. 10	63	63	63	42	21	26	21	63	26	21	26	21
Apr. 1	63	63	63	42	21	26	21	63	26	21	26	21
Sept. 25	52	52	52	28½	15	22	15	52	22	15	22	15
Sept. 26	63	63	63	42	21	26	21	63	26	21	26	21
Oct. 19	52	52	52	28½	15	22	15	52	22	15	22	15
Nov. 1	55	55	55	30	15	25	15	55	25	15	25	15
Nov. 20	63	63	63	42	21	26	21	63	26	21	26	21
1890—Feb. 17	42	42	42	23	13	18	13	42	18	13	18	13
Aug. 1	52½	52½	52½	31½	16	21	16	52½	21	16	21	16
Nov. 17	63	63	63	42	19	26	19	63	26	19	26	19

FROM ST. LOUIS, MO., TO ST. PAUL, MINN.

than carload or carload quantities they apply on shipments regardless of quantity.]

Commodities (rates in cents per 100 pounds).																		
Rice.		Groceries.	Drugs.	Crockery and earthenware.		Bagging.		Leather.		Lead.		Nails.		Hardware.	Machinery.		Beer.	
Less than carloads.	Carloads.			Less than carloads.	Carloads.	Less than carloads.	Carloads.	Less than carloads.	Carloads.	Less than carloads.	Carloads.	Less than carloads.	Carloads.		Less than carloads.	Carloads.	Less than carloads.	Carloads.
30	25	75	75	30	25	30	30	60	60	30	17½	30	25	60	60	25	.....	....
30	25	75	75	30	20	30	30	60	60	30	25	30	25	60	60	25	40	24
25	20	60	60	25	20	25	25	45	45	25	20	25	20	45	45	25	35	20
20	15	50	50	20	17½	20	20	40	40	20	15	20	15	40	40	20	30	16
22½	17½	60	60	22½	20	22½	22½	45	45	22½	17½	22½	17½	45	45	22½	35	18
22½	17½	60	60	22½	22½	22½	22½	45	45	22½	17½	22½	17½	45	45	22½	35	18
15	10	40	40	15	15	15	15	30	30	15	10	15	10	30	30	17½	20	12
28	24	72	72	28	28	28	28	60	60	28	24	28	24	60	60	26	40	22½
34½	29½	84	84	34½	29½	34½	34½	73½	73½	34½	29½	34½	29½	73½	73½	31½	50½	27½
31½	21	79	79	31½	21	31½	31½	63	63	31½	21	31½	21	63	63	26	47	25½
21	13	52½	52½	21	13	21	21	42	42	21	13	21	13	42	42	18	31½	16¾
26	18	63	63	26	18	26	26	52½	52½	26	18	26	18	52½	52½	19	37	20¾
26	18	63	63	26	18	26	26	52½	52½	26	18	26	18	52½	52½	18½	37	20¼
26	21	63	63	26	21	26	26	52½	52½	26	21	26	21	52½	52½	26	42	20¾
26	21	63	63	52½	21	26	26	52½	52½	26	21	26	21	52½	52½	26	42	21
26	21	63	63	26	21	26	21	52½	26	26	21	26	21	52½	52½	26	42	21
22	15	52	52	22	15	22	15	45½	22	22	15	22	15	45½	45½	22	28½	15
26	21	63	63	26	21	26	21	52½	26	26	21	26	21	52½	52½	26	42	21
22	15	52	52	22	15	22	15	45½	22	22	15	22	15	45½	45½	22	28½	15
25	15	55	55	25	15	25	15	45	25	25	15	25	15	45	45	22½	30	15
26	21	63	63	26	21	26	21	52½	26	26	21	26	21	52½	52½	26	42	21
18	13	42	42	18	13	18	13	31½	18	18	13	18	13	31½	31½	18	23	13
21	16	.....	52½	21	16	21	16	42	21	21	16	21	16	42	42	21	31½	16
26	19	.....	63	26	19	26	19	52½	26	26	19	26	19	52½	52½	26	42	19

RATES FROM ST. PAUL, MINN., TO ST. LOUIS, MO.

The following table gives the class rates from 1883 to the present time between St. Paul and St. Louis. The Western classification governs the rates shown in this table.

TABLE 68.—FREIGHT RATES CHARGED FOR THE TRANSPORTATION OF CLASSIFIED TRAFFIC AND GRAIN FROM ST. PAUL, MINN., TO ST. LOUIS, MO., VIA RAIL LINES, FROM NOVEMBER, 1, 1883.

[Governed by Western classification.]

Date.	Rates (in cents per 100 pounds).											
	1	2	3	4	5	A	B	C	D	E	Wheat.	Other grain.
1883—Nov. 1	75	60	40	30	25	25	20	17½	15	......	20	20
1884—Apr. 1	60	45	35	25	20	25	20	17½	15	......	20	17½
1885—Apr. 13	50	40	30	20	15	20	17½	15	12½	......	17½	15
Nov. 1	60	45	35	22½	17½	22½	20	17½	15	......	17½	15
1886—July 20	45	35	25	20	15	20	17½	15	12½	......	17½	15
Nov. 1	72	60	40	28	24	26	23	18	18	......	17½	12½
1887—Apr. 1	84	73½	50½	34½	29½	31½	27½	24	21	......	17½	12½
June 16	79	63	47	31½	21	26	21	17	13½	12½	17½	12½
Aug. 1	52½	42	31½	21	13	18	16	14	10½	8½	17½	12½
Sept. 1	52½	42	31½	21	13	18	16	14	10½	8½	13	13
1888—June 4	63	52½	37	26	18	19	17	15	13	10½	13	13
July 19	63	52½	37	26	18	18½	16	15	13	10½	13	13
Oct. 10	63	52½	42	26	21	26	21	18	15	13½	13	13
Nov. 10	63	52½	42	26	21	26	21	18	15	13½	15	15
1889—Jan. 1	63	52½	42	26	21	26	21	18	15	13½	16	16
1890—Aug. 1	63	52½	42	26	21	26	21	18	15	13½	16	16
Nov. 17	63	52½	42	26	19	26	19	16	13½	12½	16	16
1891—Jan. 1	63	52½	42	26	21	26	21	18	15	13½	16	*16
1893—Jan. 22	63	52½	42	26	21	26	21	18	15	13½	16	17

* Barley, 17 cents since February 3, 1891.

Table 69 here following shows the yearly average rates per bushel on wheat, flour, and barley, via Mississippi River steamers, from St. Paul to St. Louis since 1856:

TABLE 69.—AVERAGE FREIGHT RATES CHARGED FOR THE TRANSPORTATION OF WHEAT, FLOUR, AND BARLEY, FROM ST. PAUL TO ST. LOUIS VIA MISSISSIPPI RIVER STEAMERS DURING EACH YEAR FROM 1856.

[Compiled from Reports of St. Louis Merchants' Exchange.]

Year.	Commodity. (Rates in cents per bushel.)			Year.	Commodity. (Rates in cents per bushel.)			Year.	Commodity. (Rates in cents per bushel.)		
	Wheat.	Flour.	Barley.		Wheat.	Flour.	Barley.		Wheat.	Flour.	Barley.
1856	18	60	14	1869	20	68	15	1888	9	30	7.2
1857	14	50	12	1870	18	60	15	1889	9	30	7.2
1858	14	50	11	1871	15	50	12	1890	6	20	4.8
1859	15	50	12	1872	15	50	12	1891	6	20	4.8
1860	16	52	12	1879	12	40	9.6	1892	7½	25	6
1861	15	50	12	1880	10.8	36	8.6				
1862	18	60	14	1881	10.8	36	8.6				
1863	19	62	14	1882	10.2	35	8.4				
1864	25	75	19	1883	10.2	35	8.4				
1865	24	73	19	1884	10.2	35	8.4				
1866	23	72	18	1885	10.2	35	8.4				
1867	21	70	16	1886	9	30	7.2				
1868	20	68	15	1887	9	30	7.2				

Data for the years 1873 to 1878, inclusive, not at hand.

RATES FROM MISSOURI RIVER POINTS TO CHICAGO.

The first table following shows the rates from principal Missouri River points to Chicago, from 1877 to the present time, both for classes and several important commodities. The class rates were governed by various classifications, all of which have been superseded by the Western classification.

The second table shows changes between the same points on some of the articles that are included in the first table, but in addition gives the changes in rates on packing-house products, and covers for all of the articles earlier dates than those given in the first table.

TABLE 70.—RATES OF FREIGHT CHARGED FOR THE TRANSPORTATION OF CLASSIFIED TRAFFIC AND IMPORTANT COMMODITIES FROM ATCHISON, KANS., ST. JOSEPH, MO., KANSAS CITY, MO., AND LEAVENWORTH, KANS., TO CHICAGO, ILL., FROM JANUARY 2, 1877.

Date.	Rates (in cents per 100 pounds).													Rates per car.		
	1.	2.	3	4.	5.	6.	7.	8.	9.	10.	Wheat.	Rye and barley.	Corn and oats.	Cattle.	Hogs.	Sheep.
1877—Jan. 2	75	60	45	30	...	...	...	...	...	...	30	22½	22½	$67.50	$67.50	$50.00
May 1	75	60	45	30	...	...	...	...	...	...	30	25	25	70.00	70.00	50.00
July 12	75	60	45	30	...	...	...	...	...	...	28	21	21	67.50	67.50	50.00
Aug. 20	75	60	45	30	...	...	...	...	...	...	30	25	25	67.50	67.50	50.00
Nov. 1	75	60	45	30	...	...	...	...	...	...	30	25	25	67.50	67.50	45.00
1878—Jan. 12	75	60	45	25	...	...	...	...	...	...	30	20	20	67.50	67.50	45.00
Jan. 14	75	60	45	25	...	...	...	...	...	...	25	20	20	67.50	67.50	45.00
July 25	75	60	45	25	...	...	...	...	...	...	25	20	20	67.50	57.50	45.00
Nov. 18	75	60	45	31	...	...	...	...	...	...	25	20	20	67.50	57.50	45.00
Nov. 27	75	60	45	31	...	...	...	...	...	...	25	20	20	67.50	57.50	45.00
1879—Feb. 1	75	60	45	31	...	...	...	...	...	...	25	20	20	67.50	57.50	45.00
Feb. 10	75	60	45	26	...	...	...	...	...	...	25	20	20	67.50	57.50	45.00
Mar. 1	75	60	45	25	...	...	...	...	...	...	25	20	20	67.50	47.50	45.00
Nov. 1	75	60	45	26½	...	...	...	...	...	...	28	23	23	67.50	47.50	45.00
1880—Feb. 2	75	60	45	27	...	...	...	...	...	...	26½	21½	21½	67.50	47.50	45.00
Mar. 1	75	60	45	27	...	...	...	...	...	...	25½	20½	20½	67.50	47.50	45.00
Apr. 5 (new classification)	75	60	45	27	27	27	27	20½	25½	25½	25½	20½	20½	67.50	47.50	45.00
Apr. 14	75	60	45	27	27	27	25½	20	25½	25½	25	20	20	67.50	47.50	45.00
Apr. 21	75	60	45	27	27	27	25½	20	25½	25½	18	14	14	67.50	47.50	45.00
Apr. 24	75	60	45	27	27	27	25½	20	25½	25½	15	12	12	67.50	47.50	45.00
Sept, 29	75	60	45	27	27	27	25½	20	25½	25½	27½	22½	22½	67.50	47.00	45.00
Oct. 27	75	60	45	27	27	27	25½	20	25½	25½	25	20	20	67.50	47.50	45.00
Nov. 1	75	60	45	27	27	27	25½	20	25	25½	27½	22½	22½	67.50	47.50	45.00
Nov. 6	75	60	45	27	27	27	26½	20	25	25½	25	20	20	67.50	47.50	45.00
Nov. 22	75	60	45	27	27	27	26½	20	26½	25½	25½	20½	20½	67.50	47.50	45.00
1881—Jan. 1	75	60	45	27	27	27	26½	20½	25½	25½	25½	20½	20½	67.50	47.50	45.00
Mar. 8	75	60	45	27	27	27	26½	20½	27	25½	25½	20½	20½	67.50	47.50	45.00
Apr. 1	75	60	45	27	27	27	25½	20	26½	25	25	20	20	67.50	47.50	45.00
July 23	75	60	45	27	27	27	25	20	26	25	25	20	20	67.50	47.50	45.00
Nov. 7	75	60	45	27	27	27	25	20	26	25	25	20	20	60.00	47.50	45.00
1882—Jan. 2	75	60	45	27	27	27	25	20	26	25	25	20	20	60.00	45.00	45.00
Feb. 1	75	60	45	27	27	27	25	20	25	25	20	18	18	60.00	45.00	45.00
Mar. 13	75	60	45	27	27	27	25	19	25½	25	21	16½	16½	60.00	47.50	45.00
Apr. 1	75	60	45	27	27	27	25	20	25½	25	25	20	20	65.00	50.00	45.00
Aug. 1	75	60	45	27	27	27	25	20	25½	25	27½	22½	22½	65.00	50.00	45.00
Oct. 16	75	60	45	30	27	27	25	20	25½	25	25	20	20	65.00	50.00	45.00
Dec. 1	75	60	45	30	27	27	25½	20	26½	25½	25	20	20	65.00	50.00	45.00
1883—Jan. 1	75	60	45	30	27	27	25½	20	26½	25½	25	20	20	65.00	42.50	45.00

TABLE 70.—RATES OF FREIGHT CHARGED FOR THE TRANSPORTATION OF CLASSIFIED TRAFFIC AND IMPORTANT COMMODITIES, ETC.—Continued.

	Rates (in cents per 100 pounds).													Rates per car.		
	1.	2.	3.	4.	5.	6.	A.	B.	C.	D.	Wheat.	Rye and barley.	Corn and oats.	Cattle.	Hogs.	Sheep.
1883—May 5 (new classification)	90	75	50	32	28	25	37½	32	23	23	25	20	20	$65.00	$42.50	$45.00
Nov. 12	90	75	50	32	28	25	37½	32	23	23	25	20	20	65.00	45.00	45.00
Dec. 17	90	75	50	32	28	25	37½	32	23	23	25	20	20	65.00	45.00	45.00
1884—Jan. 15	90	75	50	32	28	25½	37½	32	23	23	25	20	20	65.00	42.50	45.00
Mar. 15	90	75	50	32	28	25	37½	32	23	23	25	20	20	65.00	42.50	45.00
June 2	90	75	50	35	30	25	32½	29½	23	23	25	20	20	65.00	42.50	45.00
June 16	90	75	50	35	30	25	32½	29½	23	23	25	20	20	65.00	42.50	40.00
1886—Aug. 23	90	75	50	35	30	22½	32½	29½	23	23	25	20	20	65.00	42.50	40.00
1887—Jan. 1	90	75	50	35	30	25	32½	29½	23	23	25	20	20	65.00	42.50	40.00

	Rates (in cents per 100 pounds).													Rates per car.		
	1.	2.	3.	4.	5.	A.	B.	C.	D.	E.	Wheat.	Rye and barley.	Corn and oats.	Cattle.	Hogs.	Sheep.
1887—Apr. 1 (new classification)	90	75	50	35	30	32½	29½	23	20	16	25	20	20	$65.00	$55.00	$45.00
Aug. 1	90	75	50	35	30	32½	29½	23	20	16	22½	20	20	65.00	45.00	45.00
Dec. 20	75	60	40	30	25	30	25	20	17½	16	22½	20	20	60.00	45.00	45.00
1888—Jan 9	75	60	40	30	25	30	25	15	15	15	22½	20	20	60.00	45.00	45.00
Mar. 26	75	60	40	30	25	30	25	20	17½	16	22½	20	20	60.00	45.00	45.00
Oct. 1	75	60	40	30	25	30	25	20	17½	16	22½	20	20	60.00	40.00	40.00
Oct. 25	75	60	40	30	25	30	25	20	17½	16	22½	20	20	*27½	*25	*27½
1889—July 16	75	60	40	30	25	30	25	20	17½	16	22½	20	20	*22	*25	*22
Dec. 21	75	60	40	30	25	30	25	20	17½	16	22½	20	20	*18	*25	*22
1890—Jan. 25	75	60	40	30	25	30	25	20	17½	16	22½	20	20	*12½	*25	*22
Aug. 25	75	60	40	30	25	30	25	20	17½	16	22½	20	20	*22	*25	*25
Oct. 1	75	60	40	30	25	30	25	20	17½	16	20	20	17	*22	*25	*25
1891—Jan. 1	75	60	42	30	25	30	25	20	17½	16	20	20	17	*23½	*22	*25
Jan. 15	75	60	42	30	25	30	25	20	17½	16	23	20	(†)	*23½	*22	*25

* In cents per 100 pounds.

† Corn 19 cents, oats 20 cents.

TABLE 71.—FREIGHT RATES CHARGED FOR THE TRANSPORTATION OF IMPORTANT COMMODITIES FROM KANSAS CITY, MO., TO CHICAGO, ILL., FROM MAY 25, 1869.

Date.	Live hogs per car.	In cents per 100 pounds.			Date.	Live hogs per car.	In cents per 100 pounds.		
		Packing-house products.	Wheat.	Other grain.			Packing-house products.	Wheat.	Other grain.
1869—May 25	....	......	44	34	1887—Feb. 1	$42.50	25	25	20
1871—July 1	....	......	40	35	Feb. 15	42.50	25	25	20
Nov. 1	$94.00	......	30	30	Apr. 1	55.00	25	25	20
1874—Apr. 20	70.00	......	30	30	Aug. 1	45.00	25	22½	20
1879—Jan. 17	57.50	31	25	20	Dec. 20	45.00	20	22½	20
Feb. 1	57.50	31	25	20	1888—Jan. 9	45.00	20	22½	20
Mar. 1	47.50	25	25	20	Feb. 8	45.00	13	22½	10
Sept. 15	47.50	25	25	20	Feb. 9	35.00	12½	22½	10
Oct. 16	47.50	26½	25	20	Feb. 16	30.00	13	22½	10
Oct. 22	47.50	26½	25	20	Feb. 27	30.00	11	22½	10
Nov. 10	47.50	26½	28	23	Mar. 1	30.00	10	22½	10
1880—Apr. 17	47.50	25½	25	20	Mar. 26	45.00	20	22½	20
Apr. 21	47.50	25½	25	20	May 11	45.00	20	22½	20
Apr. 24	47.50	25½	25	20	June 29	40.00	20	22½	20
Nov. 8	47.50	26½	25	20	Oct. 1	40.00	20	22½	20
1881—Apr. 1	47.50	25½	25	20	Oct. 15	37.50	20	22½	20
July 23	47.50	25	25	20	1889—Apr. 1	37.50	20	22½	20
Dec. 20	47.50	25	25	20	May 25	37.50	20	22½	20
1882—Feb. 1	45.00	25	20	18.2	July 19	37.50	18	22½	20
Feb. 6	45.00	25	20	18.2	Nov. 1	33.00	18	22½	20
Mar. 13	47.50	25	21	16.1	1890—Mar. 3	33.00	18	22½	20
Apr. 1	50.00	25	25	20	Apr. 22	33.00	12	22½	20
Nov. 27	50.00	25	25	20	Aug. 25	37.50	18	22½	20
Dec. 1	50.00	27	25	20	Oct. 1	37.50	18	20	*20
1883—Jan. 1	42.50	27	25	20	1891—Jan. 1	33.00	22	20	*20
May 15	42.50	25	25	20	Jan. 15	33.00	22	23	†20
June 11	42.50	25	25	20					
Dec. 17	45.00	25	25	20					
1884—Jan. 15	42.50	25	25	20					
1885—Jan. 1	42.50	25	25	20					
1886—Jan. 1	42.50	25	25	20					
Aug. 23	42.50	22½	25	20					
Aug. 26	42.50	22½	25	20					
1887—Jan. 1	42.50	22½	25	20					
Jan. 10	42.50	25	25	20					

* Corn and oats, 17 cents. † Corn, 19 cents.

RATES FROM MISSOURI RIVER POINTS TO ST. LOUIS, MO.

The following table shows the rates from the principal Missouri River points, such as Atchison, Kansas City, St. Joseph, and Leavenworth, to St. Louis, for classified traffic, the principal grain articles, and cattle, hogs, and sheep, the period covered being from 1877 to the present time. The freight classification governing these rates has changed at various times, and such changes have resulted in a lower classification of the articles taken under the class rates in this table. For the articles specially mentioned it may be seen exactly what changes have taken place.

The second table, although partially covering rates shown in the first, embraces also the rates for packing-house products, and shows the changes since January 17, 1879.

TABLE 72.—FREIGHT RATES CHARGED FOR THE TRANSPORTATION OF CLASSIFIED TRAFFIC AND VARIOUS COMMODITIES FROM ATCHISON, KANS., KANSAS CITY, MO., ST. JOSEPH, MO., AND LEAVENWORTH, KANS., TO ST. LOUIS, MO., VIA RAIL LINES, FROM JANUARY 2, 1877.

[Governed by Western classification.]

Date.	Rates (in cents per 100 pounds).													Rates per car.		
	1.	2.	3.	4.	5.	6.	7.	8.	9.	10.	Wheat.	Corn and oats.	Rye and barley.	Cattle.	Hogs.	Sheep.
1877—Jan. 2	60	45	30	25	....	....	....	....	....	....	25	17½	17½	$50.00	$50.00	$37.50
May 1	60	45	30	25	....	....	....	....	....	....	25	18	18	50.00	50.00	37.50
June 1	60	45	30	25	....	....	....	....	....	....	25	18½	18½	50.00	50.00	37.50
July 12	60	45	30	25	....	....	....	....	....	....	23	16	16	50.00	50.00	37.50
Aug. 20	60	45	30	25	....	....	....	....	....	....	25	20	20	50.00	50.00	37.50
Sept. 7	60	45	30	25	....	....	....	....	....	....	24	19	19	50.00	50.00	37.50
Oct. 19	60	45	30	24	....	....	....	....	....	....	24	19	19	50.00	50.00	37.50
Nov. 1	60	45	30	24	....	....	....	....	....	....	24	19	19	50.00	50.00	33.00
1878—Jan. 12	60	45	30	20	....	....	....	....	....	....	24	16	16	50.00	50.00	33.00
Jan. 14	60	45	30	20	....	....	....	....	....	....	20	16	16	50.00	50.00	33.00
May 6	60	45	30	20	....	....	....	....	....	....	20	15	15	50.00	50.00	33.00
July 25	60	45	30	20	....	....	....	....	....	....	20	15	15	50.00	40.00	30.00
Nov. 18	60	45	30	25	....	....	....	....	....	....	20	15	15	50.00	40.00	30.00
Nov. 27	60	45	30	25	....	....	....	....	....	....	20	15	15	45.00	30.00	30.00
1879—Feb. 1	60	45	30	25	....	....	....	....	....	....	20	15	15	50.00	40.00	30.00
Feb. 10	60	45	30	20	....	....	....	....	....	....	20	15	15	50.00	40.00	30.00
1880—Apr. 5 (new classification)	60	45	30	20	20	20	20	15	22	20	20	15	15	50.00	40.00	30.00
Apr. 21	60	45	30	20	20	20	20	15	20	20	13	9	9	50.00	40.00	30.00
Apr. 24	60	45	30	20	20	20	20	15	20	20	10	7	7	50.00	40.00	30.00
Sept. 29	60	45	30	20	20	20	20	15	20	20	18	13	13	50.00	40.00	30.00
Oct. 27	60	45	30	20	20	20	20	15	20	20	20	15	15	50.00	40.00	30.00
Nov. 6	60	45	30	20	19	20	20	15	20	20	20	15	15	50.00	40.00	30.00
1881—Nov. 7	60	45	30	20	19	20	20	15	20	20	20	15	15	45.00	40.00	30.00
1882—Jan. 2	60	45	30	20	19	20	20	15	20	20	20	15	15	45.00	30.00	30.00
Feb. 1	60	45	30	20	19	20	20	15	20	20	17	15	15	45.00	30.00	30.00
Mar. 13	60	45	30	20	19	20	20	15	20	20	17	12½	12½	45.00	40.00	30.00
Apr. 1	60	45	30	20	19	20	20	15	20	20	20	15	15	47.50	40.00	30.00
Aug. 1	60	45	30	20	19	20	20	15	20	20	22½	17½	17½	47.50	40.00	30.00
Oct. 16	60	45	30	23	19	20	20	15	20	20	20	15	15	47.50	40.00	30.00
1883—Jan. 1	60	45	30	23	19	20	20	15	20	20	20	15	15	47.50	30.00	30.00

Date.	Rates (in cents per 100 pounds).													Rates per car.		
	1.	2.	3.	4.	5.	6.	A.	B.	C.	D.	Wheat.	Corn and oats.	Rye and barley.	Cattle.	Hogs.	Sheep.
1883—May 15 (new classification)	70	55	40	27	23	20	25	22	18	18	20	15	15	$47.50	$30.00	$30.00
Nov. 12	70	55	40	27	23	20	25	22	18	18	20	15	15	47.50	32.50	30.00
Dec. 17	70	55	40	27	23	20	25	22	18	18	20	15	15	47.50	30.00	30.00
1884—June 2	70	55	40	30	25	20	25	22	18	18	20	15	15	47.50	30.00	30.00
June 16	70	55	40	30	25	20	25	22	18	18	20	15	15	47.50	30.00	25.00
1886—Aug. 23	70	55	40	30	25	20	25	22	18	18	20	15	15	47.50	30.00	25.00
1887—Jan. 1	70	55	40	30	25	20	25	22	18	18	20	15	15	47.50	30.00	25.00

TABLE 72.—FREIGHT RATES CHARGED FOR THE TRANSPORTATION OF CLASSIFIED TRAFFIC AND VARIOUS COMMODITIES, ETC.—Continued.

Date.	Rate (in cents per 100 pounds).													Rates per car.		
	1.	2.	3.	4.	5.	A.	B.	C.	D.	E.	Wheat.	Corn and oats.	Rye and barley.	Cattle.	Hogs.	Sheep.
1887—Apr. 5 (new classification)	70	55	40	30	25	25	22	18	15	12	20	15	15	$47.50	$35.00	30.00
Aug. 1	70	55	40	30	25	25	22	18	15	12	17½	15	15	47.50	30.00	30.00
Dec. 20	55	40	30	25	20	22½	17½	15	12½	11	17½	15	15	42.50	30.00	30.00
1888—Jan. 9	55	40	30	25	20	22½	17½	10	10	10	17½	15	15	42.50	30.00	30.00
Mar. 26	55	40	30	25	20	22½	17½	15	12½	11	17½	15	15	42.50	30.00	30.00
Oct. 1	55	40	30	25	20	22½	17½	15	12½	11	17½	15	15	42.50	25.00	25.00
Oct. 25	55	40	30	25	20	22½	17½	15	12½	11	17½	15	15	*18¾	*15	*20
1889—July 19	55	40	30	25	20	22½	17½	15	12½	11	17½	15	15	*13¼	*21½	*14½
Dec. 21	55	40	30	25	20	22½	17½	15	12½	11	17½	15	15	*9¼	*21½	*14½
1890—Jan. 30	55	40	30	25	20	22½	17½	15	12½	11	17½	15	15	*7½	*21½	*14½
Aug. 25	55	40	30	25	20	22½	17½	15	12½	11	17½	15	15	*18½	*21½	*21½
Oct. 1	55	40	30	25	20	22½	17½	15	12½	11	15	12	15	*18½	*21½	*21½
1891—Jan. 15	55	40	30	25	20	22½	17½	15	12½	11	18	†14	15	*18½	*21½	*21½
1892—Aug. 1	55	40	30	25	20	22½	17½	15	12½	11	18	†14	15	*14¾	*15	*17½

* Cents per 100 pounds. † Oats, 15 cents.

TABLE 73.—FREIGHT RATES CHARGED FOR THE TRANSPORTATION OF GRAIN AND MEAT PRODUCTS FROM KANSAS CITY, MO., TO ST. LOUIS, MO., FROM JANUARY 17, 1879.

Date.	Packing-house products.	Wheat.	Other grain.	Date.	Packing-house products.	Wheat.	Other grain.	Date.	Packing-house products.	Wheat.	Other grain.
	Cents per 100 pounds.				Cents per 100 pounds.				Cents per 100 pounds.		
1879—Jan. 17	25	25	15	1883—June 11	20	20	15	1888—June 29	15	17½	15
Feb. 1	25	25	15	Dec. 17	20	20	15	Oct. 1	15	17½	15
Mar. 1	20	20	15	1884—Jan. 15	20	20	15	Oct. 15	15	17½	15
Sept. 15	20	20	15	1885—Jan. 1	20	20	15	1889—Apr. 1	15	17½	15
Oct. 16	20	20	15	1886—Jan. 1	20	20	15	May 25	15	17½	15
Oct. 22	20	20	15	Aug. 23	17½	20	15	July 19	13	17½	15
Nov. 10	20	20	15	Aug. 26	17½	20	15	Nov. 1	13	17½	15
1880—Apr. 17	20	20	15	1887—Jan. 1	17½	20	15	1890—Mar. 3	13	17½	15
Apr. 21	20	20	15	Jan. 10	20	20	15	Apr. 23	7	17½	15
Apr. 24	20	20	15	Feb. 1	20	20	15	Aug. 25	13	17½	15
Nov. 8	20	20	15	Feb. 15	20	20	15	Oct. 1	13	15	*15
1881—Apr. 1	20	20	15	Apr. 1	20	20	15	1891—Jan. 1	15	15	*15
July 23	20	20	15	Aug. 1	20	17½	15	Jan. 15	15	18	†15
Dec. 20	20	20	15	Dec. 20	15	17½	15				
1882—Feb. 1	20	17	15	1888—Jan. 9	15	17½	15				
Feb. 6	20	17	15	Feb. 8	9	17½	5				
Mar. 13	20	17	12½	Feb. 11	7½	17½	5				
Apr. 1	20	20	15	Feb. 16	6	17½	5				
Nov. 27	20	20	15	Feb. 27	6	17½	5				
Dec. 1	20	20	15	Mar. 1	6	17½	5				
1883—Jan. 1	20	20	15	Mar. 26	15	17½	15				
May 15	20	20	15	May 11	15	17½	15				

* Corn and oats, 12 cents. † Corn, 14 cents.

GRAIN RATES FROM KANSAS AND NEBRASKA POINTS.

Below are given two tables showing changes in rates on wheat, corn, and other grain from Kansas and Nebraska points to Chicago. The first table begins with 1883, and shows the successive changes up to the present time from Nebraska points. In the second table will be found similar data from Kansas points, beginning with 1886.

An effort has been made to collect data which would show the changes in the through rates from Kansas and Nebraska to the seaboard. Owing to the fact that the rates from these localities to the seaboard are not published as through rates, it has been found impossible to compile these rates for a period sufficiently long to serve for the purposes of comparison. In explanation of the manner in which the through rates are determined it may be said that rates are published by the Western roads from Kansas and Nebraska to Chicago and to the Mississippi River. The rates to the Mississippi River are usually 5 cents per 100 pounds less than the rates to Chicago. The through rates to the Eastern seaboard are generally made on the combination of the rates east and west of the Mississippi River. It has been explained that the rates eastward from the Mississippi River to the seaboard are constructed upon a percentage basis of the Chicago rate; at present this percentage is 116. In order to ascertain the rates from the Mississippi River the tables showing the grain rates via all-rail from Chicago may be extended to apply from the Mississippi River by increasing them 16 per cent. By this process it is shown that a rate of 25 cents per 100 pounds all-rail from Chicago to New York is equivalent to 29 cents per 100 pounds from the Mississippi River to New York. The rates from Kansas and Nebraska to the Mississippi River, as above mentioned, may be obtained by deducting 5 cents from the Chicago rate. For example, the rate on corn from Lincoln, Nebr., to Chicago is at present 20 cents per 100 pounds; accordingly the rate to the Mississippi River would be 15 cents per 100 pounds. Combining the rates thus obtained east and west of the Mississippi River it is shown that the through rate from Lincoln, Nebr., to New York on corn would be 15 cents plus 29 cents, or 44 cents. This plan of computing the through rate would apply to traffic passing as through shipments from Western points to the seaboard for equal periods, and may be followed, if rates are to be obtained for even dates, in the table showing the eastward rates from Chicago (see Table 45, p. 118) and in the tables here given.

Traffic of this character may be taken to Chicago, and thence forwarded East via the lakes. In such cases it would be almost impossible to compute the through rate; there would always be doubt as to the proper charge eastward from Chicago. The method suggested will assist in arriving at through rates to the seaboard if such rates are desired for the all-rail routes.

TABLE 74.—FREIGHT RATES CHARGED FOR THE TRANSPORTATION OF WHEAT AND CORN FROM POINTS IN NEBRASKA NAMED TO CHICAGO, FROM JANUARY 1, 1883, TO THE PRESENT TIME.

Date.	Rates, in cents per 100 pounds.																	
	Wheat.									Corn.								
	Gilmore, Nebr.	Elkhorn, Nebr.	Lincoln, Nebr.	Beatrice, Nebr.	Fremont, Nebr.	Columbus, Nebr.	Cedar Rapids, Nebr.	Central City, Nebr.	Ord, Nebr.	Gilmore, Nebr.	Elkhorn, Nebr.	Lincoln, Nebr.	Beatrice, Nebr.	Fremont, Nebr.	Columbus, Nebr.	Cedar Rapids, Nebr.	Central City, Nebr.	Ord, Nebr.
1883—Jan. 1	35	....	....	....	....	....	....	....	....	30	....	....	....	....	....	....	....	....
Feb. 1	35	....	....	....	38	....	....	....	....	30	....	....	....	33	....	....	....	....
Feb. 20	35	37	35	....	38	....	....	....	....	30	32	30	....	33	....	....	....	....
Apr. 16	35	37	35	....	38	40	....	....	....	30	32	30	....	33	35	....	....	....
1884—Jan. 10	35	37	35	....	38	40	....	43	....	30	32	30	....	33	33	38	....	....
1885—July 13	35	37	35	....	38	40	45	43	....	30	32	30	....	33	33	40	....	....
Sept. 10	35	35	35	37	35	38	45	43	....	30	30	30	32	30	33	40	38	....
1886—Aug. 16	35	35	35	37	33	38	45	43	....	30	30	30	32	28	33	40	38	....
Aug. 19	35	35	35	37	33	38	45	43	43	30	30	30	32	28	33	40	38	38
Nov. 1	35	35	35	37	35	38	42	43	43	30	30	30	32	30	33	37	38	38
1887—Apr. 5	35	35	35	37	35	38	42	43	40	30	30	30	32	30	33	37	38	35
Apr. 7	27	27	31	31	30	34	38	39	40	22	22	26	27	25	29	33	34	35
June 6	27	27	28	30	28	29	30	30	33	22	22	23	25	23	24	25	25	28
Nov. 1	25	25	27	28	27	29	30	30	33	20	20	22	23	22	24	25	25	28
1890—June 16	25	25	27	28	27	29	31	30	33	20	20	22	23	22	24	26	25	28
July 17	25	25	25	26	25	26½	28½	27½	30	20	20	20	21	20	21½	23	22½	25
Oct. 24	20	21	22	22	22	24½	27	26	30	17	18	19	19	19	21½	23½	22	25
1891—Jan. 15	23	25	25	26	25	27	29	28	30	19	20	20	21	20	22	24	23	25

NOTE.—Between March 7 and 26, 1888, all through rates on grain were withdrawn, and rates were made on a combination of locals.

TABLE 75.—FREIGHT RATES CHARGED FOR THE TRANSPORTATION OF WHEAT, CORN, AND OATS FROM POINTS IN KANSAS AND NEBRASKA TO CHICAGO, ILL., FROM 1886 TO THE PRESENT TIME.

To Chicago, Ill., from—	Rates, in cents per 100 pounds.																					
	Wheat.							Corn.								Oats.						
	1886.	1887.	1888.	1889.	1890, prior to Oct. 20.	Oct. 20, 1890.	Jan. 15, 1891.	1886.	1887.	1888.	1889.	1890, prior to Feb. 20.	Feb. 20, 1890.	Oct. 20, 1890.	Jan. 15, 1891.	1886.	1887.	1888.	1889.	1890, prior to Feb. 20.	Feb. 20, 1890.	Jan. 15, 1891.
Abiline, Kans	...	38½	30	30	30	25	28	...	33	25	25	25	22½	21	23	...	33	25	25	25	21	23
Argonia, Kans	47½	44	35	35	35	28	33	36	33	30	30	30	25	24	28	36	33	30	30	30	24	28
Augusta, Kans	45	38½	31	31	31	26	30	34	32½	26	26	26	23½	22	25	34	32½	26	26	26	22	25
Belle Plaine, Kans	46½	39½	33	33	33	27	32	35	34	28	28	28	25	23	27	35	34	28	28	28	23	27
Beloit, Kans	...	...	30	30	30	25	28	...	...	25	25	25	22½	21	23	...	...	25	25	25	21	23
Benedict, Kans	...	32	31	31	31	26	27	...	26	26	26	26	23½	22	23	...	26	26	26	26	22	23
Burlington, Kans	37	37	30	30	30	25	28	30	30	25	25	25	22½	21	23	30	30	25	25	25	21	23
Chanute, Kans	34	34	31	30	30	25	27	27	27	26	25	25	22½	21	23	27	27	26	25	25	21	23
Cherokee, Kans	32½	31	28½	28½	28½	25	27	25	25	25	25	25	22½	21	23	25	25	25	25	25	21	23
Cherryvale, Kans	34	34	31	31	31	25	27	29	28	26	26	26	23½	22	23	29	28	26	26	26	22	23
Clearwater, Kans	...	39½	33	33	33	26	31	...	34	28	28	28	25	22	26	...	34	28	28	28	22	26
Coffeeville, Kans	38	35	32	32	32	26	27	31	28	27	27	27	24½	23	23	31	28	27	27	27	23	23
Colby, Kans	...	...	34	33	33	30	30	...	...	29	28	28	25	25	25	...	...	29	28	28	25	25
Colony, Kans	...	35	30	30	30	25	27	...	28	25	25	25	22½	21	23	...	28	25	25	25	21	23
Columbus, Kans	32½	32	30	30	30	25	27	25	26	26	26	26	23½	21	23	25	26	26	26	26	21	23
Concordia, Kans	...	...	30	30	30	25	28	...	...	25	25	25	22½	21	23	...	...	25	25	25	21	23
Dodge City, Kans	52	45	37	37	37	30	34	45	37	32	32	32	25	25	27	45	37	32	32	32	25	27
Eldorado, Kans	43	38	31	31	31	26	30	34	32½	26	26	26	23½	22	25	34	32½	26	26	26	22	25
Elk City, Kans	41	35	32	32	32	27	29	31	28	27	27	27	24½	23	24	31	28	27	27	27	23	24
Emporia, Kans	41	35	30	30	30	25	28	32	31	25	25	25	22½	21	23	32	31	25	25	25	21	23
Eureka, Kans	43	35	31	31	31	26	30	34	31	26	26	26	23½	22	25	34	31	26	26	26	22	25
Fairbury, Nebr	40	35	29	29	29	23	27	32	30	24	24	24	21½	20	22	32	30	24	24	24	20	24
Fort Scott, Kans	30	29	27	27	27	25	25	25	23	23½	23½	23½	21	21	23	25	23	23½	23½	23½	21	23
Fredonia, Kans	...	32	31	31	31	26	29	...	26	26	26	26	23½	22	24	...	26	26	26	26	22	24
Garnett, Kans	32	32	29½	29½	29½	25	27	26	26	25	25	25	22½	21	23	26	26	25	25	25	21	23
Girard, Kans	31	31	28½	28½	28½	25	27	25	25	25	25	25	22½	21	23	25	25	25	25	25	21	23
Great Bend, Kans	45½	41½	32	32	32	27	31	34	34	27	27	27	24½	23	26	34	34	27	27	27	23	26
Hiawatha, Kans	35	27	25	25	25	20	23	28	22	20	20	20	20	17	19	28	22	20	20	20	17	19
Humboldt, Kans	35	35	31	30	30	25	27	28	28	26	25	25	22½	21	23	28	28	26	25	25	21	23
Hutchinson, Kans	45	40½	31	31	31	26	30	34	34	26	26	26	23½	22	25	34	34	26	26	26	22	25
Independence, Kans	37	34	31½	31½	31½	26	27	30	28	27	27	27	24½	22	23	30	28	27	27	27	22	23
Iola, Kans	34	34	31	30	30	25	27	27	27	26	25	25	22½	21	23	27	27	26	25	25	21	23
Kingman, Kans	47½	40	33	33	33	28	32	36	34	28	28	28	25	24	27	36	34	28	28	28	24	27
Kinsley, Kans	49	42½	37	37	27	30	33	40	35	32	32	32	25	25	27	40	35	32	32	32	25	27
Larned, Kans	47	42½	34½	34½	34½	30	32	37	35	29½	29½	29½	25	25	27	37	35	29½	29½	29½	25	27
Lenora, Kans	...	...	32	32	32	29	30	...	...	27	27	27	24½	24	25	...	...	27	27	27	24	25
Lyons, Kans	45½	40½	31	31	31	26	30	34	34	26	26	26	23½	22	25	34	34	26	26	26	22	25
McPherson, Kans	45	40½	31	31	31	26	30	34	34	26	26	26	23½	22	25	34	34	26	26	26	22	25
Mankato, Kans	...	...	30	30	30	25	28	...	...	25	25	25	22½	21	23	...	...	25	25	25	21	23
Manhattan, Kans	...	36½	29	29	29	23	27	...	31	24	24	24	21½	20	22	...	31	24	24	24	20	22
Marysville, Kans	27	35	29	28	28	22	26	32	30	24	23	23	20½	19	21	32	30	24	23	23	19	21
Mound Valley, Kans	...	34	31	31	31	25	27	...	28	26	26	26	23½	22	23	...	28	26	26	26	22	23
Neosho Falls, Kans	...	35	31	30	30	25	27	...	28	26	25	25	22½	21	23	...	28	26	25	25	21	23
Niota, Kans	...	36	32	32	32	27	30	...	28	27	27	27	24½	23	26	...	28	27	27	27	23	26
Norwich, Kans	...	40	33	33	33	28	32	...	34	28	28	28	25	24	27	...	34	28	28	28	24	27
Osage City, Kans	...	34½	29	29	29	23	27	...	30	24	24	24	21½	20	22	...	30	24	24	24	20	22
Ottawa, Kans	33½	32	28½	28½	28½	23	27	27	26	24	24	24	21½	20	22	27	26	24	24	24	20	22
Paola, Kans	35	30	27	27	27	23	25	24	24	24	23½	23½	21	20	22	24	24	24	23½	23½	20	22
Parsons, Kans	32½	32	30	30	30	25	27	25	26	25½	25	25	22½	21	23	25	26	25½	25	25	21	23
Pittsburg, Kans	32½	31	28½	28½	28½	25	27	25	25	25	25	25	22½	21	23	25	25	25	25	25	21	23
Pleasanton, Kans	...	32	29½	27	27	25	25	...	26	25	23½	23½	21	21	23	...	26	25	23½	23½	21	23
Pratt, Kans	...	43	36	36	36	29½	32	...	34	31	31	31	25	25	27	...	34	31	31	31	25	27
Sabetha, Kans	35	30	25	25	25	20	24	28	25	20	20	20	20	17	20	28	25	20	20	20	17	21
Salina, Kans	...	...	30	30	30	25	29	...	...	25	25	25	22½	21	24	...	...	25	25	25	21	25
Severy, Kans	44	36	31	31	31	26	30	34	31	26	26	26	23½	22	25	34	31	26	26	26	22	25
Scott City, Kans	...	46½	34	34	34	30	31	...	40	29	29	29	25	25	26	...	40	29	29	29	25	26
Seneca, Kans	37	32	27	27	27	21	25	30	27	22	22	22	20	18	21	30	27	22	22	22	18	22
Topeka, Kans	...	31½	29	29	29	23	27	...	28	24	24	24	21½	20	22	...	28	24	24	24	20	24
Walnut, Kans	32½	31	28½	29½	29½	25	27	25	24	25	25	25	22½	21	23	25	24	25	25	25	21	23
Weir City, Kans	32½	31	28½	28½	28½	25	27	25	25	25	25	25	22½	21	23	25	25	25	25	25	21	23
Wichita, Kans	45	39½	31	31	31	26	30	34	34	26	26	26	23½	22	25	34	34	26	26	26	22	25
Winfield, Kans	47	39½	32	32	32	27	32	35	34	27	27	27	24½	23	27	35	34	27	27	27	23	27

RATES ON GRAIN AND OTHER ARTICLES TRANSPORTED VIA THE MISSISSIPPI RIVER ROUTES.

Several tables are here presented showing the rates on grain, flour, pork, meats, and hay, carried by the river lines from St. Louis to the important river points south, to and including New Orleans.

A statement is also given showing the tonnage of grain carried from St. Louis to New Orleans via the Mississippi River boats from 1870 to 1892, inclusive.

TABLE 76.—AVERAGE FREIGHT RATES CHARGED DURING VARIOUS YEARS FOR THE TRANSPORTATION OF GRAIN IN SACKS, VIA STEAMERS, AND WHEAT, CORN, AND RYE, VIA BARGES FROM ST. LOUIS, MO., TO NEW ORLEANS, LA.

[Compiled from reports of St. Louis Merchants' Exchange.]

Year.	Rate in cents.			
	Grain in sacks (per 100 pounds).	Per bushel.		
		Wheat, in bulk.	Corn and rye.	
			High water.	Low water.
1866	....	....	12 2/3	15 3/5
1867	....	....	15 1/3	20 1/2
1868	....	....	8 7/10	13 3/4
1869	....	....	8 2/5	11 1/5
1870	....	....	10 3/5	15 7/10
1871	....	....	7 1/2	18 1/5
1872	....	....	11	21 3/5
1873	....	....	7	11
1874	....	....	5 1/2	9
1875	....	....	5 3/5	11 1/2
1876	....	....	5 3/8	12 3/5
1877	21	8 1/2	8	9
1878	17 1/2	7 1/4	5	9
1879	18	7 3/4	5	11
1880	19	8 1/4	7	9 1/2
1881	20	6	4	8
1882	20	6 5/12	5 1/2	7
1883	17 3/4	5 1/2	5	7
1884	14	6 5/8	5	7
1885	15	6 2/5	5	7
1886	16	6 1/2	5	7
1887	18 1/4	6	5	7
1888	15	6 1/2	5	7 1/2
1889	17.93	5.95	5	7
1890	15.66	6.58	5	7
1891	16.28	6.88	5	7 1/2
1892	16.87	6.50	5	7

TABLE 77.—SHOWING THE HIGHEST AND LOWEST FREIGHT RATES AND THAT CONTINUING FOR THE LONGEST PERIOD DURING EACH YEAR, CHARGED FOR THE TRANPORTATION OF FLOUR, PORK, GRAIN, MEATS, AND HAY, FROM ST. LOUIS, MO., TO MEMPHIS, TENN., VICKSBURG, MISS., AND NEW ORLEANS, LA., VIA MISSISSIPPI RIVER STEAMERS, FROM 1866.

[Compiled from reports of St. Louis Merchants' Exchange.]

	Rates in cents.														
	Flour (per barrel).			Pork (per barrel).			Sack grain (per 100 pounds).			Meats (per 100 pounds).			Hay (per 100 pounds).		
	Memphis, Tenn.	Vicksburg, Miss.	New Orleans, La.	Memphis, Tenn.	Vicksburg, Miss.	New Orleans, La.	Memphis, Tenn.	Vicksburg, Miss.	New Orleans, La.	Memphis, Tenn.	Vicksburg, Miss.	New Orleans, La.	Memphis, Tenn.	Vicksburg, Miss.	New Orleans, La.
1866—Highest	60	.....	150	125	.....	200	.....	.....	.....	.....	.....	.....	.....	.....	.....
Lowest	50	.....	40	75	.....	60	.....	.....	.....	.....	.....	.....	.....	.....	.....
Longest period	50	.....	70	75	.....	100	.....	.....	.....	.....	.....	.....	.....	.....	.....
1867—Highest	.....	.....	150	.....	.....	250	.....	.....	.....	.....	.....	.....	.....	.....	.....
Lowest	.....	.....	40	.....	.....	60	.....	.....	.....	.....	.....	.....	.....	.....	.....
Longest period	.....	.....	100	.....	.....	150	.....	.....	.....	.....	.....	.....	.....	.....	.....
1868—Highest	.....	.....	100	.....	.....	175	.....	.....	.....	.....	.....	.....	.....	.....	.....
Lowest	.....	.....	20	.....	.....	40	.....	.....	.....	.....	.....	.....	.....	.....	.....
Longest period	.....	.....	40	.....	.....	65	.....	.....	.....	.....	.....	.....	.....	.....	.....
1869—Highest	60	.....	75	100	.....	125	.....	.....	.....	.....	.....	.....	.....	.....	.....
Lowest	30	.....	30	50	.....	50	.....	.....	.....	.....	.....	.....	.....	.....	.....
Longest period	30	.....	45	50	.....	70	.....	.....	.....	.....	.....	.....	.....	.....	.....
1870—Highest	75	.....	125	125	.....	125	.....	.....	.....	.....	.....	.....	.....	.....	.....
Lowest	10	.....	35	40	.....	50	.....	.....	.....	.....	.....	.....	.....	.....	.....
Longest period	50	.....	50	75	.....	90	.....	.....	.....	.....	.....	.....	.....	.....	.....
1871—Highest	80	120	125	140	175	190	.....	.....	.....	.....	.....	.....	50	65	100
Lowest	25	30	25	40	45	40	.....	.....	.....	.....	.....	.....	25	25	25
Longest period	30	40	25	50	75	40	.....	.....	.....	.....	.....	.....	25	40	25
1872—Highest	75	110	125	110	175	190	.....	.....	.....	.....	.....	.....	45	75	75
Lowest	25	30	30	40	45	45	.....	.....	.....	.....	.....	.....	25	30	30
Longest period	30	40	40	50	65	60	.....	.....	.....	.....	.....	.....	40	40	35
1873—Highest	.....	.....	100	.....	.....	150	.....	.....	.....	.....	.....	.....	.....	.....	60
Lowest	.....	.....	25	.....	.....	37½	.....	.....	.....	.....	.....	.....	.....	.....	22½
Longest period	.....	.....	100	.....	.....	150	.....	.....	.....	.....	.....	.....	.....	.....	60
1874—Highest	.....	.....	70	.....	.....	105	.....	.....	.....	.....	.....	.....	.....	.....	40
Lowest	.....	.....	15	.....	.....	37½	.....	.....	.....	.....	.....	.....	.....	.....	17½
Longest period	.....	.....	35	.....	.....	50	.....	.....	.....	.....	.....	.....	.....	.....	20
1875—Highest	80	80	75	120	125	108	.....	.....	.....	.....	.....	.....	40	40	40
Lowest	20	20	20	30	30	30	.....	.....	.....	.....	.....	.....	15	15	15
Longest period	25	40	40	60	75	60	.....	.....	.....	.....	.....	.....	20	25	25
1876—Highest	80	90	80	115	132	132	.....	.....	.....	40	45	40	43	48	45
Lowest	20	25	20	30	37½	30	.....	.....	.....	12½	12½	10	15	15	15
Longest period	25	35	35	37½	50	50	.....	.....	.....	17½	17½	17½	22½	22½	22½
1877—Highest	50	60	60	70	90	90	25	35	35	25	35	35	30	35	35
Lowest	25	40	30	37½	60	52½	12½	20	15	12½	20	15	17½	25	20
Longest period	30	40	40	45	60	60	15	20	20	15	20	20	20	25	25
1878—Highest	100	100	70	150	150	75	50	50	35	50	50	35	30	35	30
Lowest	15	20	20	30	30	30	7½	10	10	7½	10	10	15	15	15
Longest period	15	20	20	30	30	30	7½	10	10	7½	10	10	15	15	15
1879—Highest	45	70	60	60	105	90	20	35	30	20	35	30	25	40	35
Lowest	20	25	20	30	45	30	10	15	10	10	15	10	15	20	15
Longest period	25	35	25	37½	52½	37½	12½	17½	12½	12½	17½	12½	17½	22½	17½
1880—Highest	45	60	50	60	90	75	51	30	25	20	30	25	25	35	30
Lowest	25	40	30	30	60	45	12½	20	15	15	20	15	17½	25	20
Longest period	40	40	30	60	60	45	20	20	15	20	20	15	25	25	20
1881—Highest	45	60	50	67½	90	75	22½	30	25	22½	30	25	27½	35	32½
Lowest	30	40	30	45	60	45	15	20	15	15	20	15	20	25	20
Longest period	30	60	45	45	90	67½	15	30	22½	17½	30	22½	20	35	27½
1882—Highest	35	60	50	52½	90	75	17½	30	25	17½	.....	.....	22½	35	30
Lowest	25	40	40	45	60	60	12½	20	20	15	.....	.....	17½	25	25
Longest period	25	40	40	45	60	60	12½	20	20	15	.....	.....	17½	25	25
1883—Highest	35	50	45	52½	75	67½	17½	25	22½	17½	25	22½	22½	30	27½
Lowest	25	40	25	37½	60	37½	12½	20	12½	12½	20	12½	17½	25	17½
Longest period	25	40	50	37½	75	60	12½	25	20	12½	25	20	17½	30	25
1884—Highest	30	45	45	35	67½	52½	15	22½	17½	15	22½	17½	20	27½	22½
Lowest	25	40	40	25	60	37½	13	20	12½	13	20	12½	17½	25	17½
Longest period	25	40	40	25	60	37½	13	20	12½	13	20	12½	18	25	17½
1885—Highest	30	45	35	45	67½	52½	15	22½	17½	15	22½	17½	17½	27½	22½
Lowest	30	45	30	45	67½	45	15	22½	15	15	22½	15	17½	27½	20
Longest period	30	45	35	45	67½	52½	15	22½	17½	15	22½	17½	17½	27½	22½
1886—Highest	30	40	35	45	60	52½	15	20	17½	15	20	17½	17½	25	22½
Lowest	20	35	30	30	52½	45	10	17½	15	10	17½	15	13	20	20
Longest period	**24**	**35**	**35**	**36**	**52½**	**52½**	**12**	**17½**	**17½**	**12**	**17½**	**17½**	**13**	**20**	**22½**

TABLE 77.—SHOWING THE HIGHEST AND LOWEST FREIGHT RATES, ETC.—Continued.

[Complied from reports of St. Louis Merchants' Exchange.]

	Rates in cents.														
	Flour (per barrel.)			Pork (per barrel.)			Sack grain (per 100 pounds.)			Meats (per 100 pounds.)			Hay (per 100 pounds.		
	Memphis, Tenn.	Vicksburg, Miss.	New Orleans, La.	Memphis, Tenn.	Vicksburg, Miss.	New Orleans, La.	Memphis, Tenn.	Vicksburg, Miss.	New Orleans, La.	Memphis, Tenn.	Vicksburg, Miss.	New Orleans, La.	Memphis, Tenn.	Vicksburg, Miss.	New Orleans, La.
1887—Highest	40	40	40	60	60	60	20	20	20	20	20	20	25	25	22½
Lowest	20	35	35	30	52½	45	10	17½	15	10	17½	15	13	20	20
Longest period	20	40	35	30	60	52½	10	20	17½	10	20	17½	13	22½	22½
1888—Highest	30	40	35	45	60	52½	15	20	17½	15	20	17½	17	20	20
Lowest	20	35	25	30	52½	37½	10	17½	12½	10	17½	12½	13	20	17½
Longest period	20	35	35	30	52½	37½	10	17½	12½	10	17½	12½	13	20	20
1889—Highest	35	50	40	52½	75	60	17½	25	20	17½	25	20	22½	25	20
Lowest	20	40	35	37½	60	52½	10	17½	17½	10	20	17½	13	20	20
Longest period	25	40	35	37½	60	52½	11	17½	17½	12½	20	17½	13	20	20
1890—Highest	25	40	35	37½	60	52½	12½	17½	17½	12½	17½	17½	15	20	20
Lowest	20	30	30	30	45	45	10	15	15	10	15	15	12½	17½	17½
Longest period	20	40	30	30	52½	45	10	17½	15	10	17½	15	12½	20	17½
1891—Highest	40	50	40	60	75	60	20	25	20	20	25	20	22½	27½	22½
Lowest	20	35	30	30	52½	45	10	17½	15	10	17½	15	12½	20	17½
Longest period	20	35	30	30	52½	45	10	17½	15	10	17½	15	12½	20	17½
1892—Highest	40	50	40	60	75	60	20	25	20	20	25	20	22½	34	22½
Lowest	20	35	30	30	52½	45	10	17½	15	10	17½	15	12	20	17½
Longest period	20	35	35	30	52½	52½	10	17½	17½	10	17½	17½	12	20	20

TABLE 78.—STATEMENT SHOWING THE NUMBER OF BUSHELS OF THE DIFFERENT VARIETIES OF BULK GRAIN AND THE TOTAL OF ALL GRAIN SHIPPED FROM ST. LOUIS TO NEW ORLEANS VIA MISSISSIPPI RIVER BOATS DURING EACH YEAR FROM 1870.

[Compiled from reports of St. Louis Merchants' Exchange.]

Year.	Wheat.	Corn.	Rye.	Oats.	Total.
	Bushels.	*Bushels.*	*Bushels.*	*Bushels.*	*Bushels.*
1870	66, 000	....	....	....	66, 000
1871	....	309, 077	....	3, 000	312, 077
1872	....	1, 711, 039	....	....	1, 711, 039
1873	....	1, 373, 969	....	....	1, 373, 969
1874	365, 252	1, 047, 794	....	10, 000	1, 423, 046
1875	135, 961	172, 617	....	....	308, 578
1876	37, 142	1, 737, 237	....	....	1, 774, 379
1877	351, 453	3, 578, 057	171, 843	....	4, 101, 353
1878	1, 876, 639	2, 857, 056	609, 041	108, 867	5, 451, 603
1879	2, 390, 897	3, 585, 589	157, 424	30, 928	6, 164, 838
1880	5, 913, 272	9, 804, 392	45, 000	....	15, 762, 664
1881	4, 197, 981	8, 640, 720	22, 423	132, 823	12, 993, 947
1882	5, 637, 391	2, 529, 712	15, 994	150, 320	8, 333, 417
1883	1, 435, 043	9, 029, 509	205, 430	389, 826	11, 059, 508
1884	1, 318, 688	4, 496, 785	344, 864	487, 221	6, 647, 556
1885	50, 000	8, 180, 039	36, 093	401, 787	8, 667, 919
1886	743, 439	7, 501, 730	....	598, 755	8, 834, 924
1887	3, 973, 737	7, 365, 340	....	217, 722	11, 556, 799
1888	1, 247, 952	5, 844, 042	....	160, 584	7, 252, 578
1889	1, 651, 950	12, 398, 955	17, 432	89, 707	14, 158, 046
1890	1, 409, 440	8, 717, 849	....	89, 960	10, 217, 244
1891	6, 940, 215	1, 482, 731	45, 600	....	8, 468, 546
1892	5, 149, 708	3, 228, 645	....	36, 857	8, 415, 211

RATES ON CLASSIFIED TRAFFIC AND COMMODITIES BETWEEN VARIOUS SOUTHERN POINTS.

An effort has been made to procure the changes between such points in the territory south of the Ohio River as will represent the principal competitive traffic. The Southern Railway and Steamship Association classification applies throughout this section. This classification is so arranged that the lower or lettered classes embrace only one commodity, the tables are accordingly worded to show these articles separately and the changes which have taken place in the rates of each.

TABLE 79.—FREIGHT RATES CHARGED FOR THE TRANSPORTATION OF CLASSIFIED TRAFFIC AND IMPORTANT COMMODITIES VIA ALL-RAIL, ST. LOUIS, MO., TO CHATTANOOGA, TENN., FROM JANUARY 15, 1879.

Date.	Rates (in cents per 100 pounds).												Rates (in cents per barrel.)	
	1.	2.	3.	4.	5.	6.	Bagging and cotton ties.	Lard, meats, bacon, pork, and packed and loose meats (carloads).	Flour in sacks.	Grain.	Ale and beer in wood.	Whisky in wood.	Flour in barrels.	Beef and pork in barrels.
1879—Jan. 15	95	83	72	46	41	39	32	42	41	38	42	......	76	115
Apr. 1	95	83	72	46	41	39	37	42	41	38	42	46	76	115
Sept. 19	98	86	75	56	48	42	41	37	35	31	41	56	61	131
Nov. 15	98	86	75	56	48	42	46	42	40	36	41	56	71	146
1880—Apr. 8	101	87	74	60	51	40	36	44	41	37	50	61	75	160
Sept. 1	107	94	80	69	56	45	30	44	41	37	48	65	77	132
1881—May 5	107	94	80	69	56	45	36	44	41	37	48	65	77	132
Sept. 1	90	80	70	61	52	44	37	40	35	33	52	61	68	129
Oct. 1	87	78	70	61	52	43	26	38	34	32	50	59	65	117
Nov. 25	87	78	70	61	52	43	36	43	39	37	55	64	75	133
1882—Jan. 1	87	78	70	61	52	43	36	43	39	37	50	59	75	133
Apr. 12	102	90	75	60	52	43	31	38	34	30	42	50	61	109
July 10	102	90	75	60	32	43	31	33	29	25	42	50	51	99
1883—May 1	119	102	84	66	55	44	31	42	22	30	48	55	61	126
June 15	119	102	84	66	55	44	31	42	32	30	48	55	61	122
1884—Feb. 17	111	94	81	66	54	43	27	35	30½	27	44	53	57	103
Mar. 3	112	95	82	66	54	43	27	35	30½	27	44	53	57	103
Apr. 10	95	88	81	63	52	43	27	24	29½	24	42	48	51	99
1885—Feb. 18	104	88	77	62	52	43	27	34	28½	24	42	48	51	84
July 15	104	88	77	62	52	43	27	34	29	24	42	48	52	84
1887—July 15	106	90	79	64	54	45	29	36	32	26	44	50	56	*36
1888—Jan. 23	104	88	77	62	52	43	27	34	30	24	42	48	52	*34
Sept. 30	104	88	77	62	52	43	27	34	30	24	42	47	52	*34
1889—Oct. 14	104	88	77	62	52	40	27	34	30	24	42	43	52	*34
Mar. 1	104	88	77	61	52	40	27	34	32	26	42	43	56	*34
1891—Mar. 31	104	88	77	61	52	40	27	34	30	24	42	43	52	*34

*Cents per 100 pounds.

TABLE 80.—FREIGHT RATES CHARGED FOR THE TRANSPORTATION OF CLASSIFIED TRAFFIC AND IMPORTANT COMMODITIES VIA ALL-RAIL, ST. LOUIS, MO., TO ATLANTA, GA., FROM SEPTEMBER 19, 1879.

Date.	Rates (in cents per 100 pounds).												Rates (in cents per barrel).	
	1.	2.	3.	4.	5.	6.	Bagging and cotton ties.	Lard, meats, bacon, pork, and packed and loose meats (carloads).	Flour in sacks.	Grain.	Ale and beer in wood.	Whisky in wood.	Flour in barrels.	Beef and pork in barrels.
1879—Sept. 19	133	115	97	79	66	52	49	53	54	49	58	......	98	185
Nov. 15	133	115	97	79	66	52	54	58	59	54	58	79	107	200
1880—Apr. 8	133	115	97	79	66	52	47	58	53	48	65	80	97	196
Sept. 1	140	123	105	90	72	54	33	55	51	45	61	84	96	163
1881—Sept. 1	118	105	92	80	68	57	47	51	45	42	67	81	87	162
Oct. 1	115	103	92	80	68	56	34	48	43	40	64	75	83	148
Nov. 25	115	103	92	80	68	56	40	53	48	45	69	80	93	164
1882—Jan. 1	115	103	92	80	68	56	40	53	48	45	64	75	93	164
Apr. 12	130	115	97	79	68	56	41	51	46	42	61	66	84	153
July 10	130	115	97	79	68	56	39	44	39	35	59	66	70	132
Sept. 1	153	132	110	87	72	57	39	57	42	40	63	73	80	171
1883—May 1	153	132	110	87	72	57	39	50	42	40	63	73	80	150
June 15	153	132	110	87	72	57	39	50	42	40	63	73	80	146
July 15	153	132	110	87	72	57	39	48	40	38	61	71	76	140
1884—Feb. 17	145	124	107	87	71	56	35	46	39½	36	58	70	75	136
Mar. 3	146	125	108	87	71	56	35	46	39½	36	58	70	75	136
Apr. 10	135	115	101	82	68	56	35	44	38½	32	56	63	67	130
1885—Feb. 18	135	115	101	82	68	56	35	44	37½	32	56	63	67	108
July 15	135	115	101	82	68	56	35	44	38	32	56	63	68	108
1887—July 15	137	117	103	84	70	58	37	46	40	34	58	65	72	*46
1888—Jan. 23	135	115	101	82	68	56	35	44	38	32	56	63	68	*44
1891—Oct. 15	135	115	101	82	68	56	35	43	35	29	56	63	62	43

* Cents per 100 pounds.

TABLE 81.—FREIGHT RATES CHARGED FOR THE TRANSPORTATION OF CLASSIFIED TRAFFIC AND IMPORTANT COMMODITIES VIA ALL-RAIL, ST. LOUIS, MO., to CHARLESTON, S. C., AND SAVANNAH, GA., FROM JANUARY 15, 1879.

Date.	Rate (in cents per 100 pounds).												Rates (in cents per barrel).	
	1.	2.	3.	4.	5.	6.	Bagging and cotton ties.	Lard, meats, bacon, pork, and packed and loose meats (carloads).	Flour in sacks.	Grain.	Ale and beer in wood.	Whisky in wood.	Flour in barrels.	Beef and pork in barrels.
1879—Jan. 15	207	167	135	84	83	72	64	64	62	56	64	......	112	220
Apr. 1	162	127	100	63	61	52	59	62	60	54	62	73	108	210
Sept. 19	165	130	103	73	59	50	57	60	60	55	65	70	104	206
Nov. 15	165	130	103	73	59	50	67	70	70	65	65	70	124	236
1880—Feb. 1	165	130	103	73	59	50	62	65	65	60	60	70	114	220
Apr. 8	165	125	100	85	70	60	63	65	60	55	70	70	104	223
Sept. 1	165	125	100	85	70	60	53	55	52	50	70	75	94	183
1881—Apr. 15	165	125	100	85	70	60	61	58	47	47	73	78	88	199
May 5	165	125	100	85	70	60	61	58	52	52	73	78	98	199
Sept. 1	145	120	100	85	70	60	49	53	47	44	70	83	91	169
Nov. 25	131	108	90	77	63	53	46	46	42	42	67	71	82	150
1882—Apr. 20	130	115	97	79	68	56	50	45	41	37	51	51	74	126
July 10	130	115	97	79	68	56	50	40	36	32	51	51	64	120
Sept. 1	130	110	97	84	71	57	50	49	44	42	64	84	84	147
1883—May 1	130	110	97	84	71	57	50	42	37	36	51	51	70	126
June 15	130	110	97	84	71	57	46	42	37	36	51	51	70	122
1884—Feb. 17	122	102	94	84	70	56	42	40	36½	30	48	50	69	118
Mar. 3	123	103	95	84	70	56	42	40	36½	30	48	69	69	118
Apr. 10	123	103	95	84	70	56	42	40	36½	30	48	50	63	118
1885—Feb. 18	123	103	95	84	70	56	42	40	35½	30	48	63	63	99
July 15	123	103	95	84	70	56	42	40	35½	30	48	50	63	99
Nov. 2	123	103	95	84	70	56	42	40	36	30	48	50	64	99
1887—July 15	125	105	97	86	72	58	44	42	38	32	50	52	68	*42
1888—Jan. 23	123	103	95	84	70	56	42	40	36	30	48	50	64	*40
Sept. 30	123	103	95	84	70	56	42	40	31	25	48	50	54	*40
1889—Oct. 14	123	103	95	84	70	56	42	43	37	31	48	50	66	*43
1890—Mar. 1	123	103	95	84	70	56	42	43	39	33	48	50	70	*43
1891—Oct. 15	123	103	95	84	70	56	42	43	34	28	48	50	60	*43

* Cents per 100 pounds.

TABLE 82.—FREIGHT RATES CHARGED FOR THE TRANSPORTATION OF CLASSIFIED TRAFFIC AND IMPORTANT COMMODITIES VIA ALL-RAIL, ST. LOUIS, MO., TO JACKSONVILLE, FLA., FROM JANUARY 15, 1879.

Date.	Rates (in cents per 100 pounds).												Rates (in cents per barrel).	
	1.	2.	3.	4.	5.	6.	Bagging and cotton ties.	Lard, meats, bacon, pork, and packed and loose meats (carloads).	Flour in sacks.	Grain.	Ale and beer in wood.	Whisky in wood.	Flour in barrels.	Beef and pork in barrels.
1879—Jan. 15	238	192	154	96	95	87	72	75	72	65	75	......	130	257
Jan. 15	213	167	129	81	80	72	57	65	62	55	65	......	110	225
Apr. 1	193	152	119	75	73	67	67	73	70	63	73	......	126	247
Sept. 19	165	130	103	73	59	50	47	50	50	45	55	60	84	174
Nov. 15	165	130	103	73	59	50	57	60	60	55	55	60	104	204
1880—Apr. 8	165	125	100	85	70	60	58	60	55	50	65	70	94	237
Sept. 1	165	125	100	85	70	60	53	60	57	55	78	78	105	212
1881—May 5	175	134	108	92	76	65	66	63	57	57	78	83	108	215
Sept. 1	155	129	108	92	76	65	54	58	62	49	75	88	101	185
Nov. 25	141	117	98	84	69	58	51	51	47	47	72	76	92	166
1882—Apr. 20	140	124	105	86	74	61	55	50	46	42	56	56	84	142
July 10	140	124	105	86	74	61	55	50	46	42	56	56	84	150
Sept. 1	140	119	105	91	77	62	55	54	49	47	69	68	94	162
1883—May 1	140	119	105	91	77	62	55	47	42	41	56	56	80	141
1884—Jan. 15	140	119	105	91	77	62	51	47	42	41	56	56	80	137
Feb. 17	132	111	102	91	76	61	47	45	41½	35	53	55	79	133
Mar. 3	133	112	103	91	76	61	47	45	41½	35	53	55	79	133
Apr. 10	123	103	95	84	70	56	42	40	36½	30	48	50	63	118
1885—Feb. 18	123	103	95	84	70	56	42	40	35½	30	48	50	63	99
July 15	125	103	95	84	70	56	42	40	36	30	48	50	64	99
1887—July 15	123	105	97	86	72	58	44	42	38	32	50	52	68	*42
1888—Jan. 23	123	103	95	84	70	56	42	40	36	30	48	50	64	*40
1889—Oct. 14	123	103	95	84	70	56	42	43	37	31	48	50	66	*43
1890—Mar. 1	123	103	95	84	70	56	42	43	39	33	48	50	70	*43
1891—Oct. 15	123	103	95	84	70	56	42	43	34	28	48	50	60	*43

* Cents per 100 pounds.

TABLE 83.—REIGHT RATES CHARGED FOR THE TRANSPORTATION OF CLASSIFIED TRAFFIC AND IMPORTANT COMMODITIES VIA ALL-RAIL, CHICAGO, ILL., TO CHATTANOOGA, TENN., FROM APRIL 1, 1879.

Date.	Rates (in cents per 100 pounds).												Rates (in cents per barrel).	
	1.	2.	3.	4.	5.	6.	Bagging and cotton ties.	Lard, meats, bacon, pork, and packed and loose meats (carloads).	Flour in sacks.	Grain.	Ale and beer in wood.	Whisky in wood.	Flour in barrels.	Beef and pork in barrels.
1879—Apr. 1	115	100	86	58	51	48	46	50	48	45	50	58	90	137
Sept. 19	115	100	86	65	55	48	45	42	39	35	46	65	70	141
Nov. 15	115	100	86	65	55	48	50	47	44	40	46	65	80	156
1880—Apr. 8	118	101	85	69	58	46	40	49	45	41	55	70	83	172
Sept. 1	124	108	91	78	63	51	34	49	45	41	53	74	86	142
1881—May 5	124	108	91	78	63	51	42	49	45	41	53	74	86	142
Oct. 1	101	91	80	69	59	48	30	42	37	34	57	67	72	125
Nov. 25	101	91	80	69	59	48	42	47	42	39	62	72	82	141
1882—Jan. 1	101	91	80	69	59	48	42	47	42	39	57	67	82	141
Apr. 12	117	100	83	66	56	47	35	42	38	34	46	54	69	121
July 10	117	100	83	66	56	47	35	37	33	29	46	54	59	111
1883—May 3	134	112	92	72	59	48	35	46	36	34	52	59	69	138
June 15	134	112	92	72	59	48	35	46	36	34	52	59	69	134
1884—Feb. 17	134	112	92	72	59	48	35	41	35	32	51	58	64	119
Apr. 10	126	105	87	68	57	48	35	40	34	29	49	53	58	115
1885—Feb. 18	126	105	87	68	55	46	33	40	34	29	49	53	58	102
1886—Mar. 1	126	105	87	68	55	46	33	40	34	29	49	53	58	*40
1888—Jan. 23	116	99	82	65	55	45	32	38	34	29	47	53	58	*38
Sept. 30	116	99	82	65	55	45	32	38	34	29	47	52	58	*38
1889—Oct. 14	116	99	82	65	55	42	32	38	34	29	47	48	58	*38
1890—Mar. 1	116	99	82	64	55	42	32	38	35	31	47	48	62	*38
1891—Mar. 31	116	99	82	64	55	42	32	38	33	29	47	48	58	*38

* Cents per 100 pounds.

TABLE 84.—FREIGHT RATES CHARGED FOR THE TRANSPORTATION OF CLASSIFIED TRAFFIC AND IMPORTANT COMMODITIES VIA ALL-RAIL, CHICAGO, ILL., TO ATLANTA, GA., FROM SEPTEMBER 19, 1879.

Date.	Rates (in cents per 100 pounds).												Rates (in cents per barrel.)	
	1.	2.	3.	4.	5.	6.	Bagging and cotton ties.	Lard, meats, bacon, pork, and packed and loose meats (carloads).	Flour in sacks.	Grain.	Ale and beer in wood.	Whisky in wood.	Flour in barrels.	Beef and pork in barrels.
1879—Sept. 19	150	129	108	88	73	58	53	58	58	53	63	88	106	195
Nov. 15	150	129	108	88	73	58	58	63	63	58	63	......	116	210
Sept 8	150	129	108	88	73	58	51	63	57	52	70	......	105	208
1880—Sept. 1	155	135	116	99	79	60	36	61	56	49	68	......	105	179
1881—May 5	155	135	116	99	79	60	43	61	56	49	68	92	105	179
Oct. 1	129	116	102	88	75	61	38	52	46	42	71	83	90	156
Nov. 25	129	116	102	88	75	61	43	57	51	47	76	88	100	172
1882—Jan. 1	129	116	102	88	75	61	43	57	51	47	71	83	100	172
Apr. 12	145	125	105	85	72	60	45	55	50	46	65	72	92	165
July 10	145	125	105	85	72	60	43	48	43	39	63	70	78	144
Sept. 1	168	142	118	93	76	61	43	61	46	44	67	88	88	183
1883—May 1	168	142	118	93	76	61	43	54	46	44	67	77	88	162
June 15	168	142	118	93	76	61	43	54	46	44	67	77	88	158
July 15	168	142	118	93	76	61	43	52	44	42	65	75	84	152
1884—Feb. 17	168	142	118	93	76	61	43	52	44	41	65	75	82	152
Apr. 10	157	132	111	88	73	61	43	50	43	37	63	68	74	146
1885—Feb. 18	157	132	111	88	71	59	41	50	43	37	63	68	74	126
1886—Mar. 1	157	132	111	88	71	59	41	50	43	37	63	68	74	*50
1888—Jan. 15	147	126	106	85	71	58	40	48	42	37	61	68	74	*48
1889—Oct. 14	147	126	106	85	71	58	40	50	44	39	63	70	78	*50
1890—Mar. 1	147	126	106	85	71	58	40	48	41	37	61	68	74	*48
1891—Oct, 15	147	126	106	85	71	58	40	47	38	34	61	68	68	*47

* Cents per 100 pounds.

TABLE 85.—FREIGHT RATES CHARGED FOR THE TRANSPORTATION OF CLASSIFIED TRAFFIC AND IMPORTANT COMMODITIES VIA ALL-RAIL, CHICAGO, ILL., TO CHARLESTON S. C., AND SAVANNAH, GA., FROM APRIL 1, 1879.

Date.	Rates (in cents per 100 pounds).												Rates (in cents per barrel).	
	1.	2.	3.	4.	5.	6.	Bagging and cotton ties.	Lard, meats, bacon, pork, and packed and loose meats (carloads).	Flour in sacks.	Grain.	Ale and beer in wood.	Whisky in wood.	Flour in barrels.	Beef and pork in barrels.
1879—Apr. 1	162	127	100	63	61	52	59	62	60	54	62	73	108	210
Sept. 19	162	127	100	70	56	47	54	57	57	52	52	67	99	194
Nov. 15	162	127	100	63	61	52	64	67	67	62	62	67	119	224
1880—Feb. 1	162	127	100	70	56	47	59	62	62	57	57	62	109	208
Apr. 8	162	127	97	82	67	57	60	62	57	52	67	72	99	211
Sept. 1	162	122	97	82	67	57	50	52	49	47	67	72	89	171
1881—Apr. 15	162	122	97	82	67	57	58	55	44	44	70	75	83	187
May 5	162	122	97	82	67	57	58	55	49	49	70	75	93	187
Oct. 1	142	117	97	82	67	57	46	50	44	41	67	80	86	157
Nov. 25	142	117	97	82	67	57	47	47	42	42	70	75	84	150
1882—Apr. 20	145	125	105	85	72	60	54	49	45	41	55	55	82	138
July 10	145	125	105	85	72	60	54	44	40	36	55	72	72	132
Sept. 1	145	120	105	90	75	61	54	53	48	46	68	68	92	159
1883—May 1	145	120	105	90	75	61	54	46	41	40	55	78	78	138
June 15	145	120	105	90	75	61	54	46	41	40	55	55	78	134
1884—Feb. 17	145	120	105	90	75	61	50	46	35	40	55	55	76	134
Mar. 3	145	120	105	90	75	61	50	46	41	35	55	55	76	134
Apr. 10	145	120	105	90	75	61	50	46	41	35	55	55	70	134
1885—Feb. 18	145	120	105	90	73	59	48	46	41	35	55	55	70	115
July 15	145	120	105	90	73	59	48	46	41	35	55	55	70	117
1886—Mar. 1	145	120	105	90	73	59	48	46	41	35	55	55	70	*46
1888—Jan. 23	135	114	100	87	73	58	47	44	40	35	53	55	70	*44
Sept. 30	135	114	100	87	73	58	47	44	35	30	53	55	60	*44
1889—Oct. 14	135	114	100	87	73	58	47	47	40	36	53	55	72	*47
1890—Mar. 1	135	114	100	87	73	58	47	47	42	38	53	55	76	*47
1891—Oct. 15	135	114	100	87	73	58	47	47	37	33	53	55	66	*47

*Cents per 100 pounds.

TABLE 86.—FREIGHT RATES CHARGED FOR THE TRANSPORTATION OF CLASSIFIED TRAFFIC AND IMPORTANT COMMODITIES VIA ALL-RAIL, CHICAGO, ILL., TO JACKSONVILLE, FLA., FROM APRIL 1, 1879.

Date.	Rates (in cents per 100 pounds).												Rates (in cents per barrel).	
	1.	2.	3.	4.	5.	6.	Bagging and cotton ties.	Lard, meats, bacon, pork, and packed and loose meats (carloads).	Flour in sacks.	Grain.	Ale and beer in wood.	Whisky in wood.	Flour in barrels.	Beef and pork in barrels.
1879—Apr. 1	193	152	119	75	73	67	67	73	70	63	73	85	126	247
Sept. 19	162	127	100	70	56	47	44	47	47	42	52	57	79	162
Nov. 15	162	127	100	70	56	47	54	57	57	52	52	57	99	192
1880—Sept. 1	162	122	97	82	67	57	50	57	54	52	75	75	100	200
Sept. 8	162	122	97	82	67	57	55	57	52	47	62	67	89	195
1881—May 5	172	131	105	89	73	62	63	60	54	54	75	80	103	203
Oct. 1	152	126	105	89	73	62	51	55	49	46	72	83	96	175
Nov. 25	152	126	105	89	73	62	52	52	47	47	75	80	94	166
1882—Apr. 20	155	134	113	92	78	65	59	54	50	46	60	60	92	154
July 10	155	134	113	92	78	65	59	54	50	46	60	60	92	162
Sept. 1	155	129	113	97	81	66	59	58	53	51	73	73	102	174
1883—May 1	155	129	113	97	81	66	59	51	46	45	60	60	88	153
June 15	155	129	113	97	81	66	55	51	46	45	60	60	88	149
1884—Feb. 17	155	129	113	97	81	66	55	51	46	40	60	60	86	149
Apr. 10	145	120	105	90	75	61	50	46	41	35	55	55	70	134
1885—Feb. 18	145	120	105	90	73	59	48	46	41	35	55	55	70	115
July 15	145	120	105	90	73	59	48	46	41	35	55	55	70	117
1886—Mar. 1	145	120	105	90	73	59	48	46	41	35	55	55	70	*46
1888—Jan. 23	135	114	100	87	73	58	47	44	40	35	53	55	70	*44
1889—Oct. 14	135	114	100	87	73	58	47	47	40	36	53	55	72	*47
1890—Mar. 1	135	114	100	87	73	58	47	47	42	38	53	55	76	*47
1891—Oct. 15	135	114	100	87	73	58	47	47	37	33	53	55	68	*47

* Cents per 100 pounds.

TABLE 87.—FREIGHT RATES CHARGED FOR THE TRANSPORTATION OF CLASSIFIED TRAFFIC AND IMPORTANT COMMODITIES VIA ALL-RAIL, CINCINNATI, OHIO, TO CHATTANOOGA, TENN., FROM APRIL 1, 1879.

Date.	Rates (in cents per 100 pounds).												Rates (in cents per barrel).	
	1.	2.	3.	4.	5.	6.	Bagging and cotton ties.	Lard, meats, bacon, pork, and packed and loose meats (carloads).	Flour in sacks.	Grain.	Ale and beer in wood.	Whisky in wood.	Flour in barrels.	Beef and pork in barrels.
1879—Apr. 1	95	83	72	46	41	39	37	42	41	38	42	46	76	115
Sept. 19	95	83	72	53	45	39	38	34	32	28	38	53	56	119
Nov. 15	95	83	72	53	45	39	43	39	37	33	38	53	66	134
1880—Apr. 8	78	67	57	45	58	28	26	33	31	27	39	46	55	128
Sept. 1	84	74	63	54	43	33	20	33	31	27	37	50	58	98
1881—May 5	84	74	63	54	43	33	24	33	31	27	37	50	58	98
Sept. 1	67	60	53	46	39	32	24	27	24	22	37	43	47	82
Oct. 1	67	60	53	46	39	32	20	28	25	23	38	45	48	84
Nov. 25	67	60	53	46	39	32	24	33	30	28	43	50	58	100
1882—Jan. 1	67	60	53	46	39	32	24	33	30	28	38	45	58	100
Apr. 12	67	60	53	46	39	32	20	28	26	23	31	39	47	83
July 10	67	60	53	46	39	32	20	23	21	18	31	39	37	69
1883—May 1	84	72	62	52	42	33	20	32	24	23	37	44	47	96
1884—Feb. 17	84	72	62	52	42	33	20	27	23	22	36	44	44	81
Mar. 3	84	72	62	52	42	33	20	27	23	22	36	43	44	81
Apr. 10	76	65	57	48	40	33	20	26	22	19	34	38	38	77
1885—Feb. 18	76	65	57	48	40	33	20	26	22	19	34	38	38	62
1886—Mar. 1	76	65	57	48	40	33	20	26	22	19	34	38	38	*26
1887—July 15	76	65	57	48	40	33	20	26	23	19	34	38	38	*26
1888—Sept. 30	76	65	57	48	40	33	20	26	23	19	34	37	38	*26
1889—Oct. 14	76	65	57	48	40	30	20	26	23	19	34	33	38	*26
1890—Mar. 1	76	65	57	47	40	30	20	26	25	21	34	33	42	*26
1891—Mar. 31	76	65	57	47	40	30	20	26	23	19	34	33	38	*26

*Cents per 100 pounds.

TABLE 88.—FREIGHT RATES CHARGED FOR THE TRANSPORTATION OF CLASSIFIED TRAFFIC AND IMPORTANT COMMODITIES VIA ALL-RAIL, CINCINNATI, OHIO, TO ATLANTA, GA., FROM SEPTEMBER 19, 1879.

Date.	(Rates (in cents per 100 pounds).												Rates (in cents per barrel).	
	1.	2.	3.	4.	5.	6.	Bagging and cotton ties.	Lard, meats, bacon pork, and packed and loose meats (carloads).	Flour in sacks.	Grain.	Ale and beer in wood.	Whisky in wood.	Flour in barrels.	Beef and pork in barrels.
1879—Sept. 19	130	112	94	76	63	49	46	50	51	46	55	76	92	170
Nov. 15	130	112	94	76	63	49	51	55	56	51	55	76	102	188
1880—Apr. 8	110	95	80	64	53	40	37	47	43	38	54	65	77	180
Sept. 1	119	104	89	76	61	46	28	47	43	38	52	71	81	130
1881—May 5	119	104	89	76	61	46	36	50	46	40	55	75	86	146
Sept. 1	95	85	75	65	55	45	34	38	34	31	52	61	66	115
Oct. 1	95	85	75	65	55	45	28	38	34	31	52	61	66	115
Nov. 25	95	85	75	65	55	45	34	43	39	36	57	66	76	131
1882—Jan. 1	95	85	75	65	55	45	36	44	40	37	53	62	78	134
Apr. 12	95	85	75	65	55	45	30	41	38	35	50	57	70	127
July 10	95	85	75	65	55	45	28	34	31	28	48	55	56	102
Sept. 1	118	102	88	73	59	46	28	47	34	33	52	62	66	141
1883—May 1	118	102	88	73	59	46	28	40	34	33	52	62	66	120
July 15	118	102	88	73	59	46	28	38	32	31	50	60	62	114
1885—Feb. 18	107	92	81	68	56	46	28	36	31	27	48	53	54	86
1891—Oct. 15	107	92	81	68	56	46	28	35	28	24	48	53	48	*35

*Cents per 100 pounds.

TABLE 89.—FREIGHT RATES CHARGED FOR THE TRANSPORTATION OF CLASSIFIED TRAFFIC AND IMPORTANT COMMODITIES VIA ALL-RAIL, CINCINNATI, OHIO, TO CHARLESTON, S. C., AND SAVANNAH, GA., FROM APRIL 1, 1879.

Date.	Rates (in cents per 100 pounds).												Rates (in cents per barrel).	
	1.	2.	3.	4.	5.	6.	Bagging and cotton ties.	Lard, meats, bacon, pork, and packed and loose meats (carloads).	Flour in sacks.	Grain.	Ale and beer in wood.	Whisky in wood.	Flour in barrels.	Beef and pork in barrels.
1879—Apr. 1	142	112	88	56	55	45	53	60	58	52	60	66	104	202
Sept. 19	154	121	94	68	54	45	52	55	55	50	60	65	95	187
Nov. 15	154	121	94	68	54	45	62	65	65	60	60	65	115	217
1880—Feb. 1	154	121	94	68	54	45	57	60	60	55	55	60	105	201
Sept. 1	146	110	88	74	60	51	45	47	43	43	61	......	81	157
Sept. 8	142	105	85	70	57	48	53	54	50	45	59	60	85	189
1881—Apr. 15	146	110	88	74	60	51	53	50	40	40	64	69	75	173
May 5	146	110	88	74	60	51	53	50	45	45	64	69	85	173
Sept. 1	129	107	88	74	60	51	36	40	36	33	55	65	70	122
Nov. 25	112	93	78	66	53	44	38	38	35	35	58	62	69	124
1882—Jan. 1	112	93	78	66	53	44	38	38	35	35	58	69	69	124
Apr. 20	95	85	75	65	55	45	35	35	33	30	40	40	60	100
July 10	95	85	75	65	55	45	35	30	28	25	40	40	50	90
Sept. 1	95	80	75	70	58	46	35	39	36	35	52	52	70	117
1883—May 1	95	80	75	70	58	46	35	32	29	29	40	40	56	96
1884—Feb. 17	95	80	75	70	58	46	35	32	29	25	40	40	56	96
1885—Feb. 17	95	80	75	70	58	46	35	32	29	25	40	40	50	77
1886—Mar. 1	95	80	75	70	58	46	35	32	29	25	40	40	50	*32
1888—Sept. 30	95	80	75	70	58	46	35	52	24	20	40	40	40	*32
1889—Oct. 14	95	80	75	70	58	46	35	35	30	26	40	40	52	*35
1890—Mar. 1	95	80	75	70	58	46	35	35	32	28	40	40	56	*35
1891—Oct. 15	95	80	75	70	58	46	35	35	27	23	40	40	46	*35

*Cents per 100 pounds.

TABLE 90.—FREIGHT RATES CHARGED FOR THE TRANSPORTATION OF CLASSIFIED TRAFFIC AND IMPORTANT COMMODITIES VIA ALL-RAIL, CINCINNATI, OHIO, TO JACKSONVILLE, FLA., FROM APRIL 1, 1879.

Date.	Rates (in cents per 100 pounds).												Rates (in cents per barrel).	
	1.	2.	3.	4.	5.	6.	Bagging and cotton ties.	Lard, meats, bacon, pork, and packed and loose meats (carloads).	Flour in sacks.	Grain.	Ale and beer in wood.	Whisky in wood.	Flour in barrels.	Beef and pork in barrels.
1879—Apr. 1	173	137	107	68	67	60	61	71	68	61	71	78	122	239
Sept. 19	154	121	94	68	54	45	42	45	45	40	50	55	75	155
Nov. 15	154	121	94	68	54	45	52	55	55	50	50	55	95	185
1880—Feb. 1	154	121	94	68	54	45	52	55	55	50	50	55	95	185
Apr. 8	142	105	83	70	57	48	48	49	45	40	54	55	75	173
Sept. 1	146	110	88	74	60	51	45	52	50	48	69	69	92	186
1881—May 5	156	119	96	81	66	56	58	55	50	50	69	74	95	189
Sept. 1	139	116	96	81	67	56	41	45	41	38	60	70	80	138
Nov. 25	122	102	86	73	59	49	43	43	40	40	63	67	79	140
1882—Apr. 20	105	94	83	72	61	50	44	40	38	35	45	45	70	116
July 10	105	94	83	72	61	50	44	40	38	35	45	45	70	120
Sept. 1	105	89	83	77	64	51	40	44	41	40	57	57	80	132
1883—May 1	105	89	83	77	64	51	40	37	34	34	40	45	66	111
June 15	105	89	83	77	64	51	40	37	34	34	45	45	66	111
1884—Feb. 17	105	89	83	77	64	51	40	37	34	30	45	45	66	111
Apr. 10	95	80	75	70	58	46	35	32	29	25	40	40	50	96
1885—Feb. 18	95	80	75	70	58	46	35	32	29	25	40	40	50	77
1886—Mar. 1	95	80	75	70	58	46	35	32	29	25	40	40	50	*32
1888—Oct. 14	95	80	75	70	58	46	35	35	30	26	40	40	52	*35
1890—Mar. 1	95	80	75	70	58	46	35	35	32	28	40	40	56	*35
1891—Oct. 15	95	80	75	70	58	46	35	35	27	23	40	40	46	*35

* Cents per 100 pounds.

TABLE 91.—FREIGHT RATES CHARGED FOR THE TRANSPORTATION OF CLASSIFIED TRAFFIC AND IMPORTANT COMMODITIES VIA ALL-RAIL, LOUISVILLE, KY., TO CHATTANOOGA, TENN., FROM AUGUST 27, 1878.

Date.	Rates (in cents per 100 pounds).												Rates (in cents per barrel).	
	1.	2.	3.	4.	5.	6.	Bagging and cotton ties.	Lard, meats, bacon, pork, and packed and loose meats (carloads).	Flour in sacks.	Grain.	Ale and beer in wood.	Whisky in wood.	Flour in barrels.	Beef and pork in barrels.
1878--Aug. 27	100	95	80	55	45	....	38	38	34	35	......	......	70	110
1879--Jan. 15	75	66	58	34	31	30	25	34	34	31	34	......	62	93
Apr. 1	75	66	58	34	31	30	30	34	34	31	34	34	62	93
Sept. 19	75	66	58	41	35	30	31	26	25	21	30	41	42	97
Nov. 15	75	66	58	41	35	30	36	31	30	26	30	41	52	112
1880--Apr. 8	78	67	57	45	38	28	26	33	31	27	39	46	55	128
Sept. 1	84	74	63	54	43	33	20	33	31	27	37	50	58	98
1881--May 5	84	74	63	54	43	33	24	33	31	27	37	50	58	98
Sept. 1	67	60	53	46	39	32	24	37	24	22	37	43	47	82
Oct. 1	67	60	53	46	39	32	20	28	25	23	38	45	48	84
Oct. 5	67	60	53	46	39	32	24	33	30	28	43	50	58	100
1882--Jan. 1	67	60	53	46	39	32	24	33	30	28	38	45	58	100
Apr. 12	67	60	53	46	39	32	20	28	26	23	31	39	47	83
July 10	67	60	53	46	39	32	20	23	21	18	31	39	37	69
1883--May 1	84	72	62	52	42	33	20	32	24	23	37	44	47	96
1884--Feb. 17	84	72	62	52	42	33	20	27	23	22	36	43	44	81
Apr. 10	76	65	57	48	40	33	20	26	22	19	34	38	38	77
1885—Feb. 18	76	65	57	48	40	33	20	26	22	19	34	38	38	62
Mar. 1	76	65	57	48	40	33	20	26	22	19	34	38	38	*26
1887—July 15	76	65	57	48	40	33	20	26	23	19	34	38	37	*26
1888—Sept. 30	76	65	57	48	40	33	20	26	23	19	34	37	38	*26
1889—Oct. 14	76	65	57	48	40	30	20	26	23	19	34	33	38	*26
1890—Mar. 1	76	65	57	47	40	30	20	26	25	21	34	33	42	*26
1891—Mar. 31	76	65	57	47	40	30	20	26	23	19	34	33	38	*26

* Cents per 100 pounds.

TABLE 92.—FREIGHT RATES CHARGED FOR THE TRANSPORTATION OF CLASSIFIED TRAFFIC AND IMPORTANT COMMODITIES VIA ALL-RAIL, LOUISVILLE, KY., TO ATLANTA, GA., FROM JULY 15, 1870.

Date.	Rates (in cents per 100 pounds).												Rates (in cents per barrel).	
	1.	2.	3.	4.	5.	6.	Bagging and cotton ties.	Lard, meats, bacon, pork, and packed and loose meats (carloads).	Flour in sacks.	Grain.	Ale and beer in wood.	Whisky in wood.	Flour in barrels.	Beef and pork in barrels.
1870—July 15	161	134	114	84	64	....	......	84	87	57	......	......	......	153
1871—Feb. 25	150	125	100	85	58	....	......	85	73	......	......	......	......	132
1878—Jan. 7	106	94	82	48	44	....	......	48	45	44	......	......	......	82
July 1	....	....	....	....	....	....	......	33	33	30	......	......	......	60
1879—Jan. 15	119	104	79	71	56	41	......	48	49	44	......	......	......	88
Sept. 19	110	95	80	64	53	40	39	42	44	39	47	64	78	151
Nov. 15	110	95	80	64	53	40	44	47	49	44	47	64	88	166
1880—Sept. 1	119	104	89	76	61	46	28	47	43	38	52	71	81	138
Sept. 8	110	95	80	64	53	40	37	47	43	38	54	65	77	180
1881—May 5	119	104	89	76	61	46	36	50	46	40	50	75	86	146
Sept. 1	95	85	75	65	55	45	34	38	34	31	52	61	66	115
Oct. 1	95	85	75	65	55	45	28	38	34	31	52	61	66	115
Nov. 25	95	85	75	65	55	45	36	44	40	37	58	67	78	134
1882—Jan. 1	95	85	75	65	55	45	36	44	40	37	53	62	78	134
Apr. 12	95	85	75	65	55	45	30	41	38	35	50	57	70	127
July 10	95	85	75	65	55	45	28	34	31	28	48	55	56	102
Sept. 1	118	102	88	73	59	46	28	47	34	33	52	62	66	141
1883—May 1	118	102	88	73	59	46	28	40	34	33	52	62	66	120
July 15	118	102	88	73	59	46	28	38	32	31	50	60	62	114
1884—Mar. 3	118	102	88	73	59	46	28	38	32	31	50	60	62	114
Apr. 10	107	92	81	68	56	46	28	36	31	27	48	53	54	108
1885—Feb. 18	107	92	81	68	56	46	28	36	31	27	48	53	54	86
1891—Oct. 15	107	92	81	68	56	46	28	35	28	24	48	53	48	*35

* Cents per 100 pounds.

TABLE 93.—FREIGHT RATES CHARGED FOR THE TRANSPORTATION OF CLASSIFIED TRAFFIC AND IMPORTANT COMMODITIES VIA ALL-RAIL, LOUISVILLE, KY., TO CHARLESTON, S. C., AND SAVANNAH, GA., FROM JANUARY 15, 1879.

Date.	Rates (in cents per 100 pounds).												Rates (in cents per barrel).	
	1.	2.	3.	4.	5.	6.	Bagging and cotton ties.	Lard, meats, bacon, pork, and packed and loose meats (carloads).	Flour in sacks.	Grain.	Ale and beer in wood.	Whisky in wood.	Flour in barrels.	Beef and pork in barrels.
1879—Jan. 15......	156	123	97	61	61	50	42	54	52	46	54	......	92	188
Apr. 1......	142	110	86	51	51	43	52	54	53	47	54	61	94	188
Sept. 19......	142	110	86	58	46	38	47	49	50	45	54	55	85	172
Nov. 15......	142	110	86	58	46	38	56	59	60	55	54	66	105	202
1880—Feb. 1......	142	110	86	58	46	38	52	54	55	50	49	50	95	186
Apr. 8......	142	105	83	70	57	48	53	54	50	45	59	60	85	189
Sept. 1......	146	110	88	74	60	51	45	47	43	43	61	66	81	157
1881—Apr. 15......	146	110	88	74	60	51	53	50	45	45	64	69	85	173
May 5......	146	110	88	74	60	51	53	50	45	45	64	69	85	173
Sept. 1......	129	107	88	74	60	51	36	40	36	33	55	65	70	122
Nov. 25......	112	93	78	66	53	44	38	38	35	35	58	62	69	124
1882—Apr. 20......	95	85	75	65	55	45	35	35	33	30	40	40	60	100
July 10......	95	85	75	65	55	45	35	30	28	25	40	40	50	90
Sept. 1......	95	80	75	70	58	46	35	39	36	35	52	52	70	117
1883—May 1......	95	80	75	70	58	46	35	32	29	29	40	40	56	96
1884—Feb. 17......	95	80	75	70	58	46	35	32	29	25	40	40	56	96
Apr. 10......	95	80	75	70	58	46	35	32	29	25	40	40	50	96
1885—Feb. 18......	95	80	75	70	58	46	35	32	29	25	40	40	50	77
1886—Mar. 1......	95	80	75	70	58	46	35	32	29	25	40	40	50	*32
1888—Sept. 30......	95	80	75	70	58	46	35	32	24	20	40	40	40	*32
1889—Oct. 14......	95	80	75	70	58	46	35	35	30	26	40	40	52	*35
1890—Mar. 1......	95	80	75	70	58	46	35	35	32	28	40	40	56	*35
1891—Oct. 15......	95	80	75	70	58	46	35	35	27	23	40	40	46	*35

* Cents per 100 pounds.

TABLE 94.—FREIGHT RATES CHARGED FOR THE TRANSPORTATION OF CLASSIFIED TRAFFIC AND IMPORTANT COMMODITIES VIA ALL-RAIL, LOUISVILLE, KY., TO JACKSONVILLE, FLA., FROM JANUARY 15, 1879.

Date.	Rates (in cents per 100 pounds).												Rates (in cents per barrel).	
	1.	2.	3.	4.	5.	6.	Bagging and cotton ties.	Lard, meats, bacon, pork, and packed and loose meats (carloads).	Flour in sacks.	Grain.	Ale and beer in wood.	Whisky in wood.	Flour in barrels.	Beef and pork in barrels.
1879—Jan. 15	187	148	116	73	73	65	50	65	62	55	65	......	110	225
Apr. 1	173	135	105	63	63	58	60	65	63	56	65	73	112	225
Sept. 19	142	110	86	58	46	38	37	39	40	35	44	45	65	140
Nov. 15	142	110	86	58	46	38	47	49	50	45	44	45	85	170
1880—Sept. 8	142	105	83	70	57	48	48	49	45	40	54	55	75	173
Sept. 1	146	110	88	74	60	51	45	52	50	48	69	69	92	186
1881—Sept. 1	139	116	96	81	67	56	41	45	41	38	60	70	80	138
Nov. 25	122	102	86	73	59	49	43	43	40	40	63	67	79	140
1882—Apr. 20	105	94	83	72	61	50	44	40	38	35	45	45	70	116
July 10	105	94	83	72	61	50	44	40	38	35	45	45	70	120
Sept. 1	105	89	83	77	64	51	40	44	41	40	57	57	80	132
1883—May 1	105	89	83	77	64	51	40	37	34	34	45	45	66	111
1884—Feb. 17	105	89	83	77	64	51	40	37	34	30	45	45	66	111
Apr. 10	95	80	75	70	58	46	35	32	29	25	40	40	50	96
1885—Feb. 18	95	80	75	70	58	46	35	32	29	25	40	40	50	77
1886—Mar. 1	95	80	75	70	58	46	35	32	29	25	40	40	50	*32
1889—Oct. 14	95	80	75	70	58	46	35	35	30	26	40	40	52	*35
1890—Mar. 1	95	80	75	70	58	46	35	35	32	28	40	40	56	*35
1891—Oct. 15	95	80	75	70	58	46	35	35	27	23	40	40	46	*35

*Cents per 100 pounds.

TABLE 95.—FREIGHT RATES CHARGED FOR THE TRANSPORTATION OF CLASSIFIED TRAFFIC AND IMPORTANT COMMODITIES VIA ALL-RAIL, NASHVILLE TO CHATTANOOGA, TENN., FROM APRIL 1, 1879.

Date.	Rates (in cents per 100 pounds).												Rates (in cents. per barrel).	
	1.	2.	3.	4.	5.	6.	Bagging and cotton ties.	Lard, meats, bacon, pork, and packed and loose meats (carloads).	Flour in sacks.	Grain.	Ale and beer in wood.	Whisky in wood.	Flour in barrels.	Beef and pork in barrels.
1879—Apr. 1	63	49	44	22	21	21	23	26	27	24	26	22	48	71
Sept. 19	55	49	44	29	25	21	24	18	18	14	22	29	28	75
Nov. 15	55	49	44	29	25	21	29	23	23	19	22	29	38	90
1880—Apr. 8	58	50	43	33	28	19	19	25	24	20	31	34	41	106
Sept. 1	44	39	33	29	24	17	10	18	16	14	19	26	30	51
1881—May 5	44	39	33	29	24	17	12	18	16	14	19	26	30	51
Sept. 1	47	43	39	34	29	23	17	19	17	15	29	31	33	60
Oct. 1	43	39	34	30	25	21	12	19	17	15	25	30	32	55
Nov. 25	43	39	34	30	25	21	12	24	22	20	30	35	42	71
1882—Jan. 1	43	39	34	30	25	21	12	24	22	20	25	30	42	71
Apr. 12	32	30	28	24	21	19	12	20	18	16	17	18	33	43
July 10	32	30	28	24	21	19	12	15	13	11	17	18	23	45
1883—May 1	49	42	37	30	24	20	12	24	16	16	23	25	33	72
June 15	49	42	37	30	24	20	12	24	16	16	22	23	33	72
1884—Feb. 17	49	42	37	30	24	20	12	19	15	15	21	22	30	57
Apr. 10	41	35	32	26	22	20	12	18	14	12	19	17	24	53
1885—Feb. 18	41	35	32	26	22	20	12	18	15	14	19	17	28	43
1886—Mar. 1	41	35	32	26	22	20	12	18	15	14	19	17	28	*18
1887—July 15	41	35	32	26	22	20	12	18	18	14	19	17	28	*18
1889—Oct. 14	41	35	32	26	22	17	12	18	18	14	19	15	28	*18
1890—Mar. 1	41	35	32	25	22	17	12	18	20	16	19	15	32	*18
1891—Mar. 31	41	35	32	25	22	17	12	18	18	14	19	15	28	*18

* Rate per 100 pounds.

TABLE 96.—FREIGHT RATES CHARGED FOR THE TRANSPORTATION OF CLASSIFIED TRAFFIC AND IMPORTANT COMMODITIES VIA ALL-RAIL, NASHVILLE, TENN., TO ATLANTA, GA., FROM SEPTEMBER 19, 1879.

Date.	Rates (in cents per 100 pounds).												Rates (in cents per barrel).	
	1.	2.	3.	4.	5.	6.	Bagging and cotton ties.	Lard, meats, bacon, pork, and packed and loose meats (carloads).	Flour in sacks.	Grain.	Ale and beer in wood.	Whisky in wood.	Flour in barrels.	Beef and pork in barrels.
1879—Sept. 19	90	78	66	52	43	31	32	34	37	32	39	52	64	121
Nov. 15	90	78	66	52	43	31	37	39	42	37	39	52	74	144
1880—Apr. 8	90	78	66	52	43	31	30	39	36	31	46	53	63	158
Sept. 1	84	74	63	54	43	33	20	34	31	27	37	50	58	98
1881—May 5	84	74	63	54	43	33	26	37	34	26	40	54	63	106
Sept. 1	75	68	61	53	45	36	27	30	27	24	44	49	52	93
Oct. 1	71	64	56	49	41	34	20	29	26	23	39	46	50	86
Nov. 25	71	64	56	49	41	34	24	34	31	28	44	51	60	102
1882—Jan. 1	71	64	56	49	41	34	24	34	31	28	39	46	60	102
Apr. 12	68	61	54	46	39	32	22	33	30	28	26	41	56	90
July 10	68	61	54	46	39	32	22	28	25	23	36	34	46	84
Sept. 1	93	72	63	51	41	33	20	39	26	26	37	41	52	17
1883—May 1	83	72	63	51	41	33	20	32	26	26	37	41	52	96
June 15	83	72	63	51	41	33	20	30	24	24	35	32	48	90
1884—Apr. 10	72	62	56	46	38	33	20	28	23	20	33	32	40	84
1885—Feb. 18	72	62	56	46	38	33	20	28	23	20	33	32	40	*67
1887—July 1	72	62	56	46	38	33	20	28	24	20	33	32	40	*28
1891—Oct. 15	72	62	56	46	38	33	20	27	21	17	33	32	34	*27

* Cents per 100 pounds.

TABLE 97.—FREIGHT RATES CHARGED FOR THE TRANSPORTATION OF CLASSIFIED TRAFFIC AND IMPORTANT COMMODITIES VIA ALL-RAIL, NASHVILLE, TENN., TO CHARLESTON, S. C., AND SAVANNAH, GA., FROM APRIL 1, 1879.

Date.	Rates (in cents per 100 pounds).												Rates (in cents per barrel).	
	1.	2.	3.	4.	5.	6.	Bagging and cotton ties.	Lard, meats, bacon, pork, and packed and loose meats (carloads).	Flour in sacks.	Grain.	Ale and beer in wood.	Whisky in wood.	Flour in barrels.	Beef and pork in barrels.
1879—Apr. 1	122	93	72	39	39	34	45	46	46	40	46	49	80	166
Sept. 19	122	93	72	46	36	29	40	41	43	38	46	43	71	150
Nov. 15	122	93	72	46	36	29	40	41	43	38	37	33	71	148
1880—Feb. 1	122	93	72	46	36	29	45	46	48	43	41	38	81	164
Apr. 8	122	88	67	58	47	39	46	46	43	38	51	48	71	167
Sept. 1	126	93	74	62	50	42	38	39	36	36	53	54	67	135
1881—Apr. 15	126	93	74	62	50	42	46	42	33	33	56	57	61	151
May 5	126	93	74	62	50	42	46	42	38	38	56	57	71	151
Sept. 1	109	90	74	62	50	42	29	32	29	26	47	53	56	100
Nov. 25	92	76	64	54	43	35	31	30	28	28	50	50	55	102
1882—Apr. 20	72	65	57	50	42	34	27	27	25	23	31	31	46	76
July 10	72	65	57	50	42	34	27	22	20	18	31	31	36	66
Sept. 1	72	60	57	55	45	35	27	31	28	28	43	43	56	93
1883—May 1	72	60	57	55	45	35	27	24	22	22	31	31	42	72
1884—Mar. 3	72	60	57	55	45	35	27	24	22	19	31	31	42	73
Apr. 10	72	60	57	55	45	35	27	24	22	19	31	31	38	73
1885—Feb. 18	72	60	57	55	45	35	27	24	22	19	31	31	38	58
1886—Mar. 1	72	60	57	55	45	35	27	24	22	19	31	31	38	*24
1888—Sept. 30	72	60	57	55	45	35	27	24	19	15	31	31	30	*24
1889—Oct. 14	72	60	57	55	45	35	27	23	20	31	31	39	21	*23
1890—Mar. 1	72	60	57	55	45	35	27	27	25	21	31	31	42	*27
1891—Oct. 15	72	60	57	55	45	35	27	27	21	17	31	31	34	*27

* In cents per 100 pounds.

TABLE 98.—FREIGHT RATES CHARGED FOR THE TRANSPORTATION OF CLASSIFIED TRAFFIC AND IMPORTANT COMMODITIES VIA ALL-RAIL, NASHVILLE, TENN., TO JACKSONVILLE, FLA., FROM SEPTEMBER 19, 1879.

Date.	Rates (in cents per 100 pounds).												Rates (in cents per barrel).	
	1.	2.	3.	4.	5.	6.	Bagging and cotton ties.	Lard, meats, bacon, pork, and packed and loose meats (carloads).	Flour in sacks.	Grain.	Ale and beer in wood.	Whisky in wood.	Flour in barrels.	Beef and pork in barrels.
1879—Sept. 19	122	93	72	46	36	29	30	31	41	28	37	33	51	118
Nov. 15	122	93	72	46	36	29	40	41	43	38	37	33	71	148
1880—Apr. 8	122	88	67	58	47	39	41	41	38	33	46	43	61	151
Sept. 1	126	93	74	62	50	42	38	44	43	41	61	57	78	164
1881—May 5	136	102	82	69	56	47	51	47	43	43	61	62	81	167
Sept. 1	119	99	82	69	57	47	34	37	34	31	52	58	66	116
Nov. 25	102	85	72	61	49	40	36	35	33	33	55	55	65	118
1882—Apr. 20	82	74	65	57	48	39	32	32	30	28	36	36	56	92
July 10	82	74	65	57	48	39	32	32	30	28	36	36	56	96
Sept. 1	82	69	65	62	51	40	32	36	33	33	48	48	66	108
1883—May 1	82	69	65	62	51	40	32	29	27	27	36	36	52	87
1884—Feb. 17	82	69	65	62	51	40	32	29	27	23	36	36	52	87
Mar. 3	84	71	66	62	51	41	32	30	27	24	36	36	53	88
Apr. 10	72	60	57	55	45	35	27	24	22	19	31	31	38	73
1885—Feb. 18	72	60	57	55	45	35	27	24	22	19	31	31	38	58
1886—Mar. 1	72	60	57	55	45	35	27	24	22	19	31	31	38	*24
1887—July 15	72	60	57	55	45	35	27	24	23	19	31	31	38	*24
1889—Oct. 14	72	60	57	55	45	35	27	27	23	20	31	31	39	*27
1890—Mar. 1	72	60	57	55	45	35	27	27	25	21	31	31	42	*27
1891—Oct. 15	72	60	57	55	45	35	27	27	21	17	31	31	34	*27

* Rate per 100 pounds.

TABLE 99.—FREIGHT RATES CHARGED FOR THE TRANSPORTATION OF CLASSIFIED TRAFFIC AND IMPORTANT COMMODITIES VIA ALL-RAIL, MEMPHIS TO CHATTANOOGA, TENN., FROM APRIL 1, 1879.

Date.	Rates (in cents per 100 pounds).												Rates (in cents per barrel).	
	1.	2.	3.	4.	5.	6.	Bagging and cotton ties.	Lard, meats, bacon, pork, and packed and loose meats (carloads).	Flour in sacks.	Grain.	Ale and beer in wood.	Whisky in wood.	Flour in barrels.	Beef and pork in barrels.
1879—Apr. 1......	73	64	56	32	29	28	28	32	32	29	32	32	58	86
Sept. 19......	70	61	53	36	30	25	26	21	20	16	25	36	32	80
Nov. 15......	70	61	53	36	30	25	31	26	25	21	25	42	42	95
1880—Apr. 8......	73	62	52	40	33	23	21	28	26	22	47	41	45	111
1880—Sept. 1......	79	69	58	49	38	28	15	28	26	22	32	45	48	81
1881—May 5......	79	69	58	49	38	28	18	28	26	22	32	45	48	81
Sept. 1......	62	55	48	41	34	27	19	22	19	17	32	38	37	65
Oct. 1......	62	55	48	41	34	27	15	23	20	18	33	40	38	67
Nov. 25......	62	55	48	41	34	27	18	28	25	23	38	45	48	83
1882—Jan. 1......	62	55	48	41	34	27	18	28	25	23	33	40	48	83
Apr. 12......	62	55	48	41	34	27	15	23	21	18	26	34	37	66
July 10......	62	55	48	41	34	27	15	18	16	13	26	34	27	54
1883—May 1......	79	67	57	47	37	28	15	27	19	18	32	39	37	81
1884—Feb. 17......	79	67	57	47	37	28	15	22	18	17	31	38	34	66
Apr. 10......	71	60	52	43	35	28	15	21	17	14	29	33	28	62
1885—Feb. 18......	73	62	54	45	37	30	17	23	19	16	31	35	32	55
1887—July 15......	72	61	53	44	36	29	16	22	19	15	30	34	30	*22
1889—Oct. 14......	72	61	53	44	36	26	16	22	19	15	30	29	30	*22
1890—Mar. 1......	72	61	53	43	36	26	16	22	21	17	30	29	34	*22
1891—Mar. 31......	72	61	53	43	36	26	16	22	19	15	30	29	30	*22

* Cents per 100 pounds.

TABLE 100.—FREIGHT RATES CHARGED FOR THE TRANSPORTATION OF CLASSIFIED TRAFFIC AND IMPORTANT COMMODITIES VIA ALL-RAIL, MEMPHIS, TENN., TO ATLANTA, GA., FROM SEPTEMBER 19, 1879.

Date.	Rates (in cents per 100 pounds).												Rates (in cents per barrel).	
	1.	2.	3.	4.	5.	6.	Bagging and cotton ties.	Lard, meats, bacon, pork, and packed and loose meats (carloads).	Flour in sacks.	Grain.	Ale and beer in wood.	Whisky in wood.	Flour in barrels.	Beef and pork in barrels.
1879—Sept. 19	105	90	75	59	48	35	34	37	39	34	42	59	68	134
Nov. 15	105	90	75	59	48	35	39	42	44	39	42	59	78	149
1880—Apr. 8	105	90	75	59	48	35	32	42	38	33	49	60	67	164
Sept. 1	114	100	85	73	59	44	27	45	41	36	50	68	78	132
1881—May 5	114	100	85	73	59	44	35	48	44	38	53	72	83	140
Sept. 1	90	80	70	60	50	40	29	33	29	26	47	55	56	98
Oct. 1	90	80	70	60	50	40	23	33	29	26	47	56	56	98
Nov. 25	90	80	70	60	50	40	31	39	35	32	53	62	68	111
1882—Jan. 1	90	80	70	60	50	40	29	38	34	31	47	56	66	114
Apr. 12	90	80	70	60	50	40	31	36	33	30	45	52	60	110
July 10	90	80	70	60	50	40	25	31	28	25	45	50	50	93
Sept. 1	113	97	83	68	54	41	23	42	29	28	47	57	56	126
1883—May 1	113	97	83	68	54	41	23	35	29	28	47	57	56	105
July 15	113	97	83	68	54	41	23	33	27	26	45	55	52	99
1884—Mar. 3	113	97	83	68	54	41	23	35	29	28	47	57	56	105
Apr. 10	102	87	76	63	51	41	23	31	26	22	43	48	44	93
1885—Feb. 18	104	89	78	65	53	43	25	33	28	24	45	50	48	79
1887—July 15	103	88	77	64	52	42	24	32	27	23	44	49	46	*32
1891—Oct. 15	103	88	77	64	52	42	24	31	24	20	44	49	40	*31

* Cents per 100 pounds.

TABLE 101.—FREIGHT RATES CHARGED FOR THE TRANSPORTATION OF CLASSIFIED TRAFFIC AND IMPORTANT COMMODITIES VIA ALL-RAIL, MEMPHIS, TENN., TO CHARLESTON, S. C., AND SAVANNAH, GA., FROM APRIL 1, 1879.

Date.	Rates (in cents per 100 pounds).												Rates (in cents per barrel).	
	1.	2.	3.	4.	5.	6.	Bagging and cotton ties.	Lard, meats, bacon, pork, and packed and loose meats (carloads).	Flour in sacks.	Grain.	Ale and beer in wood.	Whisky in wood.	Flour in barrels.	Beef and pork in barrels.
1879—Apr. 1	140	108	84	49	49	41	50	52	51	45	52	59	90	181
Sept. 19	137	105	81	53	41	33	42	44	45	40	49	......	75	155
Nov. 15	137	105	81	53	41	33	52	54	55	50	49	50	95	185
1880—Feb. 1	137	105	81	53	41	33	47	49	50	45	44	45	85	169
Sept. 1	141	105	83	69	55	46	40	42	38	38	56	61	71	140
1881—Apr. 5	141	105	83	69	55	46	48	45	40	40	59	64	75	156
Apr. 8	137	100	78	65	52	43	48	49	45	43	54	75	75	172
May 5	141	105	83	69	55	46	48	45	40	40	59	64	75	156
Sept. 1	124	102	83	69	55	46	31	35	31	28	50	60	60	105
Oct. 1	124	102	83	69	55	46	31	35	31	28	50	60	60	105
Nov. 25	107	88	73	61	48	39	33	33	30	30	53	57	59	107
1882—Jan. 1	107	88	73	61	48	39	33	33	30	30	53	57	59	107
Apr. 20	90	80	70	60	50	40	30	30	28	25	35	35	50	85
July 10	90	80	70	60	50	40	30	25	23	20	35	35	40	75
Sept. 1	90	75	70	65	53	41	30	34	31	30	47	47	60	102
1883—May 1	90	75	70	65	53	41	30	27	24	24	35	35	46	81
1884—Mar. 3	90	75	70	65	53	41	30	27	24	20	35	35	46	81
1885—Feb. 18	92	77	72	67	55	43	32	29	26	22	37	37	44	70
1887—July 15	91	76	71	66	54	42	31	28	25	21	36	36	42	*28
1888—Sept. 30	91	76	71	66	54	42	31	28	20	16	36	36	32	*28
1889—Oct. 14	91	76	71	66	54	42	31	31	26	22	36	36	44	*31
1890—Mar. 1	91	76	71	66	54	42	31	31	28	24	36	36	44	*31
1891—Oct. 15	91	76	71	66	54	42	31	31	23	19	36	36	38	*31

* Cents per 100 pounds.

TABLE 102.—FREIGHT RATES CHARGED FOR THE TRANSPORTATION OF CLASSIFIED TRAFFIC AND IMPORTANT COMMODITIES VIA ALL-RAIL, MEMPHIS, TENN., TO JACKSONVILLE, FLA., FROM SEPTEMBER, 19, 1879.

Date.	Rates (in cents per 100 pounds).												Rates (in cents per barrel).	
	1.	2.	3.	4.	5.	6.	Bagging and cotton ties.	Lard, meats, bacon, pork, and packed and loose meats (carloads).	Flour in sacks.	Grain.	Ale and beer in wood.	Whisky in wood.	Flour in barrels.	Beef and pork in barrels.
1879—Sept. 19	137	105	81	53	41	33	32	34	35	30	39	40	58	123
Nov. 15	137	105	81	53	41	33	42	44	45	40	39	40	78	153
1880—Feb. 1	139	105	81	53	41	33	42	44	45	40	39	40	78	153
Apr. 1	137	100	78	65	52	43	43	44	40	35	49	50	67	156
Sept. 1	141	105	83	69	55	46	40	47	45	43	64	64	82	169
1881—May 5	151	114	91	76	61	51	53	50	45	45	64	69	85	172
Sept. 1	134	111	91	76	62	51	36	40	36	33	55	65	70	121
Oct. 1	134	111	91	76	62	51	36	40	36	33	55	65	70	121
Nov. 20	117	97	81	68	54	44	38	38	35	35	58	62	69	123
1882—Jan. 1	117	97	81	68	54	44	38	38	35	35	58	62	69	123
Apr. 20	100	89	78	67	56	45	39	35	33	30	40	40	60	100
July 10	100	89	78	67	56	45	39	35	33	30	40	40	60	105
Sept 1	100	84	78	72	59	46	35	39	36	35	52	52	70	117
1883—May 1	100	84	78	72	59	46	35	32	29	29	40	40	56	96
1884—Feb. 17	100	84	78	72	59	46	35	32	29	25	40	56	56	96
Mar. 3	100	84	78	72	59	46	35	32	29	25	40	40	56	96
Apr. 10	90	75	70	65	53	41	30	27	24	20	35	35	40	81
1885—Feb. 18	92	77	72	67	55	43	32	29	26	22	37	37	44	70
July 15	92	77	72	67	55	43	32	29	26	22	37	44	44	70
1886—Mar. 1	92	77	72	67	55	43	32	29	26	22	37	37	44	*29
1887—July 15	91	76	71	66	54	42	31	28	25	21	36	36	42	*28
1889—Oct. 14	91	76	71	66	54	42	31	31	26	22	36	36	44	*31
1890—Mar. 1	91	76	71	66	54	42	31	31	28	24	36	36	48	*31
1891—Oct. 15	91	76	71	66	54	42	31	31	23	19	36	36	38	*31

* Cents per 100 pounds.

COTTON RATES.

Four tables here follow showing the changes in cotton rates between various Southern and Eastern points.

TABLE 103.—FREIGHT RATES CHARGED FOR THE TRANSPORTATION OF COMPRESSED COTTON FROM MEMPHIS, TENN., TO NEW YORK AND BOSTON VIA ALL RAIL FROM SEPTEMBER 1, 1880.

[Rates in cents per 100 pounds.]

From Memphis, Tenn., to......	New York, N. Y.	Boston, Mass.	From Memphis, Tenn., to.......	New York, N. Y.	Boston, Mass.	From Memphis, Tenn., to.......	New York, N. Y.	Boston, Mass.
1880—Sept. 1.....	74	79	1884—Feb. 2....	50	55	1888—Oct. 1....	50½	55½
1881—Apr. 20.....	68	73	Apr. 5....	(*)	(*)			
July 20.....	65	70	Sept. 17....	62	67			
Sept. 9.....	52	57	1885—May 21....	45	50			
Sept. 27.....	65	70	Sept. 25....	62	57			
Nov. 14.....	52	57	Dec. 22....	53	58			
Dec. 12.....	57	62	1886—Sept. 18....	(*)	(*)			
1882—Apr. 8.....	47	52	Oct. 1....	53	58			
May 5.....	57	62	1887—Sept. 29....	(*)	(*)			
Sept. 16.....	72	77	Nov. 4....	50½	55½			
1883—Dec. 27.....	62	67	1888—Feb. 27....	45	50			
1884—Jan. 17.....	55	60						

* Nominal.

TABLE 104.—FREIGHT RATES CHARGED FOR THE TRANSPORTATION OF COMPRESSED COTTON FROM NEW ORLEANS, LA., TO BOSTON, NEW YORK, PHILADELPHIA, AND BALTIMORE, VIA ALL RAIL LINES FROM DECEMBER 10, 1880.

Date.	Rates (in cents, per 100 pounds).			
	To Boston, Mass.	To New York, N. Y.	To Philadelphia, Pa.	To Baltimore, Md.
1880—Dec. 10	60	55	55	55
1881—Nov. 4	50	45	50	50
1882—Sept. 20	60	55	53	52
1886—Mar. 13	50	45	43	42
1887—July 5	50	45	43	42
1888—June 12	45	40	38	37
Sept. 24	60	55	53	52
Nov. 10	50	45	43	42
1889—Sept. 25	60	55	53	52
Oct. 29	55	50	50	50
1890—Mar. 6	55	50	50	50
1892—Apr. 7	55	50	50	50

TABLE 105.—FREIGHT RATES CHARGED FOR THE TRANSPORTATION OF COMPRESSED COTTON FROM NEW ORLEANS, LA., TO NEW YORK AND BOSTON BY STEAMER FROM SEPTEMBER, 1875.

[There being no regular steamers from New Orleans to Boston, cotton for the latter point is shipped via steamer to New York, and thence via rail or water to destination.]

[Rates in cents, per 100 pounds.]

Date.	To New York.	To Boston.
1875—Sept. 1	62½	....
Sept. 13	30	....
Sept. 15	50	68¾
Sept. 29	......	75
Oct. 22	......	68¾
Oct. 27	62½	....
Oct. 28	75	100
Nov. 22	......	87½
Dec. 9	87½	100
1876—Jan. 6	75	....
Jan. 14	......	87½
Jan. 27	62½	75
Feb. 24	56¼	62½
Mar. 11	50	....
Oct. 7	62½	75
Nov. 29	75	87½
1877—Jan. 5	62½	75
Jan. 11	50	62½
Mar. 3	47¼	....
May 19	31¼	....
June 5	47¼	....
June 11	50	....
Nov. 14	62½	75
Nov. 21	75	....
Nov. 22	......	87½
Dec. 21	62½	75
1878—Jan. 3	50	62½
1879—Feb. 10	37½	50
Oct. 7	50	....
Nov. 29	......	75
Dec. 1	62½	....
1880—Jan. 3	......	62½
Feb. 18	50	....
Mar. 10	37½	50
Sept. 2	50	....
Sept. 4	......	62½
Oct. 27	......	55
Nov. 10	40	....
1881—Nov. 9	35	....
Nov. 10	......	50
1882—Mar. 15	30	....
Sept. 30	42	....
Oct. 17	......	54–60
1883—Jan. 2	50	....
Jan. 5	......	60
Jan. 12	40	52
Jan. 25	35	50
June 22	30	....
Nov. 7	40	55
1884—Jan. 11	25	40
Mar. 22	30	....
Apr. 3	......	45
Apr. 5	......	43–45
May 1	25	....
May 2	......	38–40
Sept. 16	30	....
Nov. 24	40	53–55
1885—Jan. 8	30	43–45
May 14	25	38–40
Sept. 25	35	....
Sept. 26	......	46–48
1886—Feb. 18	25	....
1886—Feb. 24	......	36–38
Sept. 9	35	46–50
1887—Mar. 24	25	36–40
Sept. 2	40	50
1888—Feb. 28	......	40–43
June 29	25	38
Aug. 30	40	48–50
Sept. 27	51	48–56
Oct. 15	......	48–56
Dec. 18	41	....
Dec. 19	......	56
1889—Aug. 20	40	....
Oct. 8	51	56
Oct. 29	46	51
1890—Feb. 15	33	38
Sept. 15	46	51
1891—Feb. 9	35	40
Sept. 21	46	51
1892—Feb. 11	32	40
Sept. 14	32	45
1893—Jan. 14	30	40

TABLE 106.—RATES IN CENTS PER 100 POUNDS CHARGED FOR THE TRANSPORTATION OF COMPRESSED COTTON VIA RAIL FROM POINTS IN GEORGIA AND ALABAMA TO THE VARIOUS ATLANTIC SEABOARD CITIES DURING 1886, 1890, AND 1893.

[Rates in cents per 100 pounds.]

To—	From—																	
	Atlanta, Ga.			Augusta, Ga			Chattanooga, Tenn., Dalton, Ga.			Macon, Ga.			Rome, Ga.			Montgomery, Ala., Selma, Ala.		
	1886	1890	1893	1886	1890	1893	1886	1890	1893	1886	1890	1893	1886	1890	1893	1886	1890	1893
Brunswick, Ga	45	43	43	....	....	....	45	45	51	40	34	34	45	45	51	....	45	45
Savannah, Ga	45	43	43	27	25	25	45	45	51	40	34	34	45	45	51	45	45	45
Port Royal, S. C.; Charleston, S. C.	45	43	43	27	25	25	45	45	51	40	34	34	45	45	51	45	45	45
Wilmington, N. C	45	43	43	27	25	25	45	45	51	40	34	34	45	45	51	45	45	45
Richmond, Va; West Point, Va	56	54	54	40	36	36	56	56	62	53	45	45	56	56	62	56	56	56
Petersburg, Va	56	54	54	40	36	36	56	56	62	53	45	45	56	56	62	56	56	56
Portsmouth, Va.; Norfolk, Va	56	54	54	40	36	36	56	56	62	53	45	45	56	56	62	56	56	56
Baltimore, Md	67	59	59	51	41	41	67	61	67	64	50	50	67	61	67	67	61	61
New York, N. Y; Philadelphia, Pa	75	64	64	57	46	46	75	66	72	70	55	55	75	66	72	75	66	66
Providence, R. I; Boston, Mass	85	69	69	67	51	51	85	71	77	80	60	60	85	71	77	85	71	71

RATES ON ORANGES FROM SOUTHERN POINTS TO EASTERN CITIES.

Three tables are next presented showing the changes in the rates on oranges from Jacksonville, Fla., to Eastern cities. Three principal routes are employed for the carriage of this traffic, one via all rail, the second via rail to Norfolk and Portsmouth, Va., and thence via water, and the third via rail to Savannah, Ga., and thence via water. The charges by each vary, the water lines charging lower rates than via all rail. Each table shows the changes which have taken place in these rates so far as the data have been obtainable.

TABLE 107.—RATES ON ORANGES FROM JACKSONVILLE, FLA., TO POINTS NAMED, VIA SAVANNAH, ALL RAIL, FROM DECEMBER 6, 1887.

Taking effect—	Rates in cents.							
	To Baltimore, Md.		To Philadelphia, Pa.		To New York, N. Y.		To Boston, Mass.	
	Ber box.	Per barrel.	Per box.	Per barrel.	Per box.	Per barrel.	Per box.	Per barrel.
1887—Dec. 6	40	80	40	80	40	80	40	80
1888—Oct. 8	40	80	41	81	43	85	49	98
1889—Sept. 21	40	80	41	81	43	85	49	98
1890—Nov. 23	50	100	51	102	53	106	59	118
1892—Jan. 2	50	100	51	102	53	106	61	122
Nov. 1	50	100	51	102	53	106	61	122

TABLE 108.—RATES ON ORANGES FROM JACKSONVILLE, FLA., TO POINTS NAMED, VIA SAVANNAH, RAIL TO NORFOLK OR PORTSMOUTH, AND THENCE VIA WATER, FROM OCTOBER 15, 1883.

Taking effect—	Rates in cents.							
	To Baltimore, Md.		To Philadelphia, Pa.		To New York, N. Y.		To Boston, Mass.	
	Per box.	Per barrel.	Per box.	Per barrel.	Per box.	Per barrel.	Per box.	Per barrel.
1883—Oct. 15	60	120	60	120	60	120	65	130
Dec. 7	50	100	50	100	50	100	60	120
1884—Oct. 15	30	60	30	60	30	60	45	80
1885—Jan. 12	40	80	40	80	40	80	54	96
1886—Nov. 1	.....	.....	.....	.....	.....	.....	40	60
Nov. 30	35	70	35	70	35	70	35	70
1888—Oct. 1	.....	.....	.....	.....	.....	.....	38	76
1889—Oct. 15	37½	75	37½	75	37½	75	40½	81
1890—Nov. 23	47½	95	47½	95	47½	95	50½	101
1892—Jan. 2	47½	95	47½	95	47½	95	50½	101
Nov. 1	47½	95	47½	95	47½	95	50½	101

TABLE 109.—RATES ON ORANGES FROM JACKSONVILLE, FLA., TO POINTS NAMED, VIA SAVANNAH AND STEAMSHIP, FROM OCTOBER 3, 1881.

Taking effect—	Rates in cents.							
	To Baltimore, Md.		To Philadelphia, Pa.		To New York, N. Y.		To Boston, Mass.	
	Per box.	Per barrel.	Per box.	Per barrel.	Per box.	Per barrel.	Per box.	Per barrel.
1881—Oct. 3	50	100	50	100	50	100	50	100
1883—Oct. 15	50	100	50	100	50	100	50	100
Nov. 15	50	100	50	100	50	100	50	100
1884—Oct. 6	30	60	30	60	30	60	30	60
1885—Jan. 12	40	80	40	80	40	80	40	80
Sept. 7	40	80	40	80	40	80	40	80
1886—Sept. 15	40	80	40	80	40	80	40	80
Nov. 18	30	60	30	60	30	60	30	60
1887—Sept. 1	30	60	30	60	30	60	30	60
Sept. 15	30	60	30	60	30	60	30	60
1889—Sept. 20	30	60	30	60	30	60	35	70
1890—Nov. 23	40	80	40	80	40	80	45	90
1892—Jan. 2	40	80	40	80	40	80	45	90
Nov. 1	40	80	40	80	40	80	45	90

TABLE 110.—FREIGHT RATES CHARGED FOR THE TRANSPORTATION OF CLASSIFIED TRAFFIC AND IMPORTANT COMMODITIES VIA ALL-RAIL, SAVANNAH TO ATLANTA, GA., FROM AUGUST 27, 1878.

Date.	Rates (in cents per 100 pounds).												Rates (in cents per barrel).	
	1.	2.	3.	4.	5.	6.	Bagging and cotton ties.	Lard, meats, bacon, pork, and packed and loose meats (carloads).	Flour in sacks.	Grain.	Ale and beer in wood.	Whisky in wood.	Flour in barrels.	Beef and pork in barrels.
1878—Aug. 27	100	85	70	55	40	....	40	40	35	25	*60	......	100	......
Sept. 11	85	75	60	45	35	....	30	30	30	20	......	......	85	......
1881—May 5	86	75	64	55	44	33	20	36	33	29	40	55	62	106
Nov. 25	68	61	54	47	40	32	20	34	31	29	45	52	60	104
1882—Jan. 1	68	61	54	47	40	32	20	34	31	29	40	47	60	104
Apr. 12	68	61	54	47	40	32	20	30	20	19	37	42	40	89
July 20	68	61	54	47	40	32	20	26	20	19	37	42	40	78
Sept. 1	80	73	58	48	38	33	20	33	20	19	38	48	40	99
1883—May 1	78	72	57	47	36	32	20	27	19	18	36	47	38	81
1884—Apr. 10	69	63	51	43	35	33	20	28	19	18	38	48	38	84
1885—Feb. 18	69	63	51	43	35	33	20	28	19	18	38	48	38	67
July 15	69	63	51	43	35	33	20	28	21	20	38	48	42	67
1886—Mar. 1	69	63	51	43	35	33	20	28	21	20	38	48	42	†28

* Rate per barrel. † Rate per 100 pounds.

TABLE 111.—FREIGHT RATES CHARGED FOR THE TRANSPORTATION OF CLASSIFIED TRAFFIC AND IMPORTANT COMMODITIES VIA ALL-RAIL, SAVANNAH, GA., TO CHATTANOOGA, TENN., FROM AUGUST 27, 1878.

Date.	Rates (in cents per 100 pounds).												Rates (in cents per barrel).	
	1.	2.	3.	4.	5.	6.	Bagging and cotton ties.	Lard, meats, bacon, pork, and packed and loose meats (carloads).	Flour in sacks.	Grain.	Ale and beer in wood.	Whisky in wood.	Flour in barrels.	Beef and pork in barrels.
1878—Aug. 27	100	85	70	55	45	....	40	40	35	25	*60	......	100	......
Sept. 11	85	75	60	45	35	....	30	30	30	20	*60	......	85	......
1879—Jan. 15	110	90	75	60	50	40	30	40	44	40	50	......	80	175
1881—Nov. 25	68	61	54	47	40	32	20	34	31	29	45	52	60	104
1882—Jan. 1	68	61	54	47	40	32	20	34	31	29	40	47	60	104
Apr. 12	68	61	54	47	40	32	20	30	20	19	37	42	40	89
July 10	68	61	54	47	40	32	20	26	20	19	37	42	40	78
1883—May 1	80	73	58	48	38	33	20	33	20	19	38	48	40	99
1884—Apr. 10	69	63	51	43	35	33	20	28	20	19	38	48	40	84
1885—Feb. 18	69	63	51	43	35	33	20	28	20	19	38	48	40	67
July 15	69	63	51	43	35	33	20	28	22	21	38	48	44	67
1886—Mar. 1	69	63	51	43	35	33	20	28	22	21	38	48	44	†128

* Rate per barrel. † Rate per 100 pounds.

TABLE 112.—FREIGHT RATES CHARGED FOR THE TRANSPORTATION OF CLASSIFIED TRAFFIC AND IMPORTANT COMMODITIES VIA ALL-RAIL FROM SAVANNAH, GA., TO MONTGOMERY, ALA., FROM JANUARY 15, 1879.

Date.	Rates (in cents per 100 pounnds).												Rates (in cents per barrel).	
	1.	2.	3.	4.	5.	6.	Bagging and cotton ties.	Lard, meats, bacon, pork, and packed and loose meats (carloads).	Flour in sacks.	Grain.	Ale and beer in wood.	Whisky in wood.	Flour in barrels.	Beef and pork in barrels.
1879—Jan. 15	105	90	75	60	50	35	30	35	38	35	50	......	70	150
1880—Sept. 1	86	75	64	55	44	33	20	36	33	29	40	......	62	106
1881—Sept. 1	68	61	54	47	40	32	24	29	26	24	40	47	50	88
Oct. 1	68	61	54	47	40	32	20	29	26	24	40	47	50	88
Nov. 25	68	61	54	47	40	32	20	34	31	29	45	52	60	104
1882—Jan. 1	68	61	54	47	40	32	20	34	31	29	40	47	60	104
Apr. 12	68	61	54	47	40	32	20	30	20	20	31	42	40	90
July 10	68	61	54	47	40	32	20	26	20	20	31	42	40	78
Sept. 1	80	73	58	48	38	33	20	33	20	19	38	48	40	99
1884—Apr. 10	69	63	51	43	35	33	20	28	20	19	38	48	40	84
1885—Feb. 18	69	63	51	43	35	33	20	28	20	19	38	48	40	67
July 15	69	63	51	43	35	33	20	28	22	21	38	48	44	67
1886—Mar. 1	69	63	51	43	35	33	20	28	22	21	38	48	44	*28

* Rate per 100 pounds.

TABLE 113.—FREIGHT RATES IN DOLLARS PER TON OF 2,000 POUNDS CHARGED FOR THE TRANSPORTATION OF FERTILIZERS IN CARLOAD QUANTITIES FROM CHARLESTON, S. C., TO VARIOUS POINTS NAMED FROM OCTOBER 1, 1884.

From Charleston, S. C., to—	Oct. 1, 1884.	Dec. 10, 1884.	Nov. 5, 1885.	Nov. 28, 1885.	Feb. 8, 1886.	Dec. 1, 1886.	Jan. 20, 1887.	Oct. 20, 1887.	Dec. 20, 1887.	Dec. 1, 1888.	Jan. 5, 1889.	Nov. 18, 1889.	Jan. 1, 1890.	Dec. 7, 1891.	Jan. 20, 1892.	Nov. 16, 1892.
Albany, Ga....	$4.30	$4.30	$4.15	$4.15	$4.00	$4.00	$4.00	$3.45	$3.45	$3.00	$3.00	$3.00	$3.00	$2.75	$2.75	$2.59
Americus, Ga..	4.48	4.48	4.33	4.33	4.33	4.33	4.33	4.33	4.18	3.00	3.00	3.00	3.00	3.00	3.00	2.75
Anniston, Ala.	3.65	3.65	3.65	3.78	3.78	3.50	3.50	3.50	3.50	3.50	3.50	3.50	3.50	3.50	3.50	3.50
Athens, Ga....	3.42	3.42	3.42	3.42	3.42	3.42	3.42	3.42	3.42	3.42	3.42	3.42	3.42	3.25	3.25	3.25
Atlanta, Ga....	3.42	3.42	3.42	3.42	3.42	3.42	3.42	3.42	3.42	3.42	3.42	3.42	3.42	3.14	3.14	3.14
Augusta, Ga...	2.00	2.00	2.00	2.00	2.00	2.00	2.00	2.00	2.00	2.00	2.00	2.00	2.00	2.00	2.00	2.00
Birmingham, Ala..........	4.00	4.00	4.00	4.00	4.00	3.25	3.25	3.25	3.25	3.25	3.25	3.25	3.25	3.50	3.50	3.50
Brandon, Miss.	5.60	5.60	5.60	5.25	5.00	4.50	4.50	4.50	4.50	4.50	4.50	4.50	4.50	4.50	4.50	4.50
Buford, Ga.....	4.50	4.50	4.50	4.50	4.50	4.50	4.50	4.50	4.46	4.46	4.46	4.46	4.46	3.74	3.95	3.95
Calera, Ala....	5.20	5.20	4.80	4.80	4.60	3.25	3.25	3.25	4.45	4.45	4.45	4.45	4.45	4.45	3.50	3.50
Carrollton, Ga.	4.84	4.84	4.69	4.69	4.69	4.69	4.69	4.69	4.54	3.66	3.67	3.66	3.66	3.36	3.36	3.36
Charlotte, N. C.	3.60	3.60	3.60	3.60	3.60	3.60	3.60	3.60	3.20	3.66	3.20	3.20	3.20	3.20	3.20	3.20
Chattanooga, Tenn........	4.00	4.00	4.00	4.00	4.00	3.50	3.50	3.50	3.50	3.50	3.50	3.50	3.50	3.50	3.50	3.50
Cincinnati, Ohio........	4.25	4.25	4.25	4.25	4.25	4.25	4.25	4.25	4.25	4.25	4.25	4.25	4.50	4.25	4.25	4.80
Columbus, Ga.	4.30	4.30	4.00	4.00	3.50	4.00	4.00	3.00	3.00	3.00	3.00	3.00	3.00	3.00	3.00	3.00
Columbus, Miss	5.60	5.60	5.60	5.25	5.00	4.60	4.60	4.00	4.00	4.00	4.00	4.00	4.00	4.00	4.00	4.00
Corinth, Miss..	4.60	4.60	4.25	4.25	4.25	4.25	4.25	4.25	4.15	4.15	4.15	4.15	4.15	4.15	4.00	4.00
Dalton, Ga.....	3.65	3.65	3.65	3.78	3.78	3.50	3.50	3.50	3.50	3.50	3.50	3.50	3.50	3.50	3.50	3.50
Gadsden, Ala..	4.60	4.60	4.60	4.60	4.60	4.20	4.20	4.20	4.20	3.50	3.50	3.50	3.50	3.50	3.50	3.50
Grenada, Miss.	6.00	5.75	5.75	5.75	5.75	5.75	5.75	5.75	5.00	5.10	5.10	5.10	4.75	5.10	5.10	5.00
Greenville, Tenn........	5.80	5.80	5.20	5.20	5.20	5.00	5.00	4.55	4.55	4.55	4.55	4.55	4.55	4.55	4.55	4.55
Hawkinsville, Ga...........	3.44	3.44	3.44	3.44	3.32	3.32	3.16	3.16	3.16	3.16	3.16	3.16	3.16	3.08	3.08	3.08
Henderson, Tenn........	5.40	5.40	5.40	5.05	4.80	4.15	4.15	4.15	4.40	4.90	4.90	4.90	4.90	4.75	4.75	5.00
Hernando, Miss	5.75	5.50	5.50	5.50	5.50	5.50	5.50	5.50	5.50	5.50	5.50	5.50	5.50	5.50	5.50	.....
Humboldt, Tenn........	5.60	5.60	5.60	5.25	5.00	4.45	4.45	4.45	4.70	5.20	5.20	5.20	5.20	5.20	5.20	5.20
Jackson, Miss.	5.60	5.60	5.60	5.25	5.00	4.50	4.50	4.50	4.50	4.50	4.50	4.50	4.50	4.00	4.00	4.50
Lauderdale, Miss.........	4.60	4.60	4.60	4.60	4.60	4.00	4.00	4.00	4.10	4.10	4.10	4.10	4.10	4.10	3.50	3.50
Louisville, Ky.	4.25	4.25	4.25	4.25	4.25	4.25	4.25	4.25	4.25	4.25	4.25	4.25	4.25	4.25	4.25	4.80
Macon, Ga.....	2.88	2.88	2.88	2.88	2.88	2.88	2.88	2.88	2.88	2.88	2.88	2.88	2.88	2.64	2.64	2.64
Marietta, Ga...	4.50	4.50	4.50	4.50	4.50	4.50	4.50	4.50	4.31	4.31	3.66	3.66	3.66	3.64	3.64	3.64
Memphis, Tenn	4.50	4.25	4.25	4.25	4.25	4.00	4.00	4.00	4.00	4.00	4.00	4.00	4.00	4.00	4.00	4.00
Milledgeville, Ga...........	2.88	2.88	2.88	2.88	2.88	2.88	2.88	2.88	2.88	2.88	2.88	2.88	2.88	2.64	2.64	2.64
Mobile, Ala....	4.50	4.50	4.50	4.50	4.00	3.50	3.50	3.50	3.50	3.50	3.50	3.50	3.50	3.50	3.50	3.50
Montgomery, Ala..........	4.00	4.00	4.00	3.00	3.00	3.00	3.00	3.00	3.00	3.00	3.00	3.00	3.00	3.00	3.00	3.00
Nashville, Tenn	4.00	4.00	4.00	4.00	4.00	3.75	3.75	3.75	3.75	3.75	3.75	3.75	3.75	3.75	3.75	3.80
Newnan, Ga...	3.54	3.54	3.54	3.54	3.54	3.54	3.54	3.54	3.54	3.54	3.54	3.54	3.54	3.25	3.25	3.25
Opelika, Ala...	4.40	4.40	3.60	3.60	3.60	3.60	3.60	3.60	3.60	3.00	3.00	3.00	3.00	3.00	3.00	3.00
Pensacola, Fla.	4.50	4.50	4.50	4.50	4.00	3.50	3.50	3.50	3.50	3.50	3.50	3.50	3.50	3.50	3.50	3.50
Pulaski, Tenn.	5.80	5.30	5.30	5.30	5.30	5.30	5.30	5.30	5.30	5.30	5.30	5.30	5.30	5.30	5.30	.....
Raleigh, N. C..	5.00	5.00	5.00	5.00	4.50	4.75	4.75	4.50	4.40	4.40	4.40	4.40	4.40	4.20	4.20	4.20
Rives, Tenn...	5.80	5.80	5.80	5.45	5.20	4.70	4.70	4.70	4.85	5.40	5.40	5.40	.....	.....	5.40	5.40
Rome, Ga......	3.65	3.65	3.65	3.78	3.78	3.50	3.50	3.50	3.50	3.50	3.50	3.50	3.50	3.50	3.50	3.50
Selma, Ala.....	4.00	4.00	4.00	4.00	3.00	3.00	3.00	3.00	3.00	3.00	3.00	3.00	3.00	3.00	3.00	3.00
Spartanburg, S. C............	4.69	4.69	2.29	2.29	3.89	4.00	4.00	4.21	4.21	4.21	4.21	4.21	4.21	3.60	3.60	3.60
Statesville, N. C	4.40	4.40	5.45	5.45	5.45	5.45	4.40	4.40	4.40	4.40	4.40	4.40	4.40	4.40	4.40	4.40
Tecumseh, Ala	4.20	4.20	4.20	4.20	4.20	4.20	4.20	4.20	4.20	4.20	4.20	4.20	4.20	4.20	4.20	4.20
Toomsuba, Miss	5.30	5.20	4.95	4.95	4.95	4.20	4.20	4.20	4.20	4.20	4.20	4.20	4.20	4.20	4.20	4.20
Tupelo, Miss...	5.40	5.40	5.40	5.05	4.80	4.20	4.20	4.20	4.20	4.50	4.50	4.50	4.50	4.50	4.50	4.50
Vicksburg, Miss.........	5.00	5.00	5.00	4.50	4.50	4.00	4.00	4.00	4.00	4.00	4.00	4.00	4.00	4.00	4.00	4.00
Washington, Ga...........	3.42	3.42	3.42	3.42	3.42	3.42	3.42	3.42	3.80	3.42	3.42	3.42	3.42	3.42	3.25	3.25

RATES ON CLASSIFIED TRAFFIC FROM NEW YORK TO ATLANTA, GA.

The following table shows the rates on various classes between the above-named points from 1869 to the present time.

Important reductions appear in the rates of each class, and similar changes have occurred from the other Eastern seaboard cities, and also to points other than Atlanta the rates to which are upon a basis similar to the Atlanta rates. The Southern Railway and Steamship Association classification governs these rates, in which it has been shown that many articles are now classified lower than formerly.

TABLE 114.—FREIGHT RATES CHARGED FOR THE TRANSPORTATION OF CLASSIFIED TRAFFIC FROM NEW YORK, TO ATLANTA, GA., DURING THE PERIOD FROM MAY, 1869.

Date.	Classes. (Rates in cents per 100 pounds.)					
	1.	2.	3.	4.	5.	6.
1869—May 1	198	168	130	115	100	.....
1873—May 12	170	140	110	90	80	70
1877—July 1	145	125	100	80	60	50
1879—Jan. 15	125	110	85	75	60	45
1881—Sept. 1	100	90	80	70	58	48
1884—Apr. 10	114	98	86	73	60	49
1889—Sept. 3	108	90	80	66	55	49
Oct. 14	114	98	86	73	60	49

TABLE 115.—FREIGHT RATES CHARGED FOR THE TRANSPORTATION OF CLASSIFIED TRAFFIC AND IMPORTANT COMMODITIES VIA ALL-RAIL, NEW YORK TO SELMA, ALA., FROM JUNE 29, 1877.

Date.	Rates (in cents per 100 pounds).												Rates (in cents per barrel).	
	1.	2.	3.	4.	5.	6.	Bagging and cotton ties.	Lard, meats, bacon, pork, and packed and loose meats (carloads).	Flour in sacks.	Grain.	Ale and beer in wood.	Whisky in wood.	Flour in barrels.	Beef and pork in barrels.
1877—June 29	145	130	105	85	70	60	......	......	......	......	......	......	......	......
1879—Jan. 15	125	110	85	75	60	45	30	45	45	45	60	......	85	150
Apr. 1	125	110	85	75	60	45	45	45	45	45	50	75	85	150
Sept. 19	125	110	85	75	60	45	34	45	45	45	50	75	85	150
1880—Sept. 1	126	110	94	81	65	49	30	53	49	43	58	81	91	156
1881—May 5	126	110	94	81	65	49	36	53	49	43	58	81	91	156
Sept. 1	100	90	80	70	58	48	36	42	38	35	58	69	74	129
Oct. 1	100	90	80	70	58	48	30	42	38	35	58	69	74	129
Nov. 25	100	90	80	70	58	48	36	47	43	40	63	74	84	145
1882—Jan. 1	100	90	80	70	58	48	36	47	43	40	58	69	84	145
Apr. 12	100	90	80	70	58	48	30	43	38	35	54	62	73	131
July 10	100	90	80	70	58	48	30	38	35	32	54	62	64	114
Sept. 1	125	108	93	78	63	49	36	53	40	39	58	68	78	159
1884—Apr. 10	114	98	86	73	60	49	36	48	40	39	58	68	78	144
1885—Feb. 18	114	98	86	73	60	49	36	48	40	39	58	68	78	115
1886—Mar. 1	114	98	86	73	60	49	36	48	40	39	58	68	78	*48

* Cents per 100 pounds.

TABLE 116.—FREIGHT RATES CHARGED FOR THE TRANSPORTATION OF CLASSIFIED TRAFFIC AND IMPORTANT COMMODITIES VIA ALL-RAIL, NEW YORK TO MONTGOMERY, ALA., VIA ALL-RAIL, FROM JUNE 29, 1877.

Date.	Rates (in cents per 100 pounds).												Rates (in cents per barrel).	
	1.	2.	3.	4.	5.	6.	Bagging and cotton ties.	Lard, meats, bacon, pork, and packed and loose meats (carloads).	Flour in sacks.	Grain.	Ale and beer in wood.	Whisky in wood.	Flour in barrels.	Beef and pork in barrels.
1877—June 29	145	130	105	85	70	60	......	......	......	......	......	......	......	......
1879—June 15	125	110	85	75	60	45	30	45	45	45	60	......	85	150
Sept. 19	125	110	85	75	60	45	34	45	45	45	50	75	85	150
1880—Sept. 1	126	110	94	81	65	49	30	53	49	43	58	81	91	156
1881—May 5	126	110	94	81	65	49	36	53	49	43	58	81	91	156
Sept. 1	100	90	80	70	58	48	36	42	38	35	58	69	74	129
Oct. 1	100	90	80	70	58	48	30	42	38	35	58	69	74	129
Nov. 25	100	90	80	70	58	48	36	47	43	40	63	74	84	145
1882—Jan. 1	100	90	80	70	58	48	36	47	43	40	58	69	84	145
Apr. 12	100	90	80	70	58	48	30	43	38	35	54	62	73	131
July 10	100	90	80	70	58	48	30	38	35	32	54	62	64	114
Sept. 1	125	108	93	78	63	49	36	53	40	39	58	68	78	159
1884—Apr. 10	114	98	86	73	60	49	36	48	40	39	58	68	78	144
1885—Feb. 18	114	98	86	73	60	49	36	48	40	39	58	68	78	115
1886—Mar. 1	114	98	86	73	60	49	36	48	40	39	58	68	78	*48

* In cents per 100 pounds.

TRANSCONTINENTAL TRAFFIC—WESTWARD BOUND.

Traffic originating at points east of the Missouri River and destined to the Pacific coast is known as transcontinental traffic. The rates on such traffic are established from various grouped points east of the Missouri River, beginning at the Atlantic seaboard. The tables following have been arranged to show the changes in important commodities carried to the Pacific coast from a principal point in each of the groups from which through rates are published.

TABLE 117.—RATES OF FREIGHT, ALL RAIL, FROM NEW YORK, N. Y., TO SAN FRANCISCO, PORTLAND, LOS ANGELES, AND OTHER PACIFIC COAST TERMINAL POINTS.

[NOTE.—Where the rates shown are not specifically described as applying on less than carload or carload quantities they apply on shipments regardless of quantity.]

Date.	Commodities (rates in cents per 100 pounds).																					
	Dry goods.	Cotton piece goods.	Furniture.		Stoves.		Canned goods.		Glassware.		Starch.		Drugs.	Crockery and earthenware.		Nails.		Hardware.	Agricultural implements.		Beer.	
			Less than carloads.	Carloads.	Less than carloads.	Carloads.	Less than carloads.	Carloads.	Less than carloads.	Carloads.	Less than carloads.	Carloads.		Less than carloads.	Carloads.	Less than carloads.	Carloads.		Less than carloads.	Carloads.	Less than carloads.	Carloads.
1870—Feb. 10	650	550	......	......	420	420	420	420	650	650	420	420	......	......	......	......	......	......	......	400	420	420
1876—Nov. 1	600	550	......	200	200	200	150	150	250	250	150	150	300	250	250	150	150	300	......	250	300	300
1880—Jan. 1	600	500	......	300	200	200	150	150	250	250	150	150	400	250	250	150	150	400	......	250	400	400
1882—Oct. 1	600	500	......	300	200	200	150	150	250	250	150	150	400	250	250	150	150	400	......	250	400	250
1885—Jan. 1	500	250	......	200	250	125	150	125	150	150	125	125	300	150	150	125	125	250	......	175	200	250
1887—Apr. 27	300	150	......	130	150	100	150	100	110	110	110	100	200	110	110	110	100	150	......	120	200	120
June 16	300	150	......	175	150	100	110	100	110	110	110	100	200	110	110	110	100	150	......	120	130	120
1888—Mar. 6	400	180	180	180	180	180	180	180	140	140	120	110	250	130	110	120	110	180	180	130	140	130
Sept. 1	400	180	180	140	200	200	200	200	140	140	140	100	300	140	120	140	100	180	300	115	160	100
1889—Jan. 1	420	215	170	170	200	120	200	120	150	150	170	120	330*	170	120	170	170	215	300	130	160	120
1891—Jan. 15	420	235	235	145	200	150	200	130	165	165	185	130	365*	185	120	185	185	235	300	145	160	120
1892—July 18	420	235	235	145	200	150	190	130	165	165	185	130	365*	185	120	185	185	235	300	145	160	120

* Lower rates for carloads.

TABLE 118.—RATES OF FREIGHT, ALL RAIL, FROM PITTSBURG, PA., TO SAN FRANCISCO, PORTLAND, LOS ANGELES, AND OTHER PACIFIC COAST TERMINAL POINTS.

Date.	Commodities (rates in cents per 100 pounds).																						
	Dry goods.	Cotton piece goods.	Furniture.		Stoves.		Canned goods.		Glassware.		Starch.		Drugs.	Crockery and earthenware.		Nails.		Hardware.	Agricultural implements.		Beer.	
			Less than car-loads.	Car-loads.	Less than car-loads.	Car-loads.	Less than car-loads.	Car-loads.	Less than car-loads.	Car-loads.	Less than car-loads.	Car-loads.		Less than car-loads.	Car-loads.	Less than car-loads.	Car-loads.		Less than car-loads.	Car-loads.	Less than car-loads.	Car-loads.
1876—Nov. 1	600	......	......	200	200	200	150	150	250	250	150	150	300	250	250	150	150	300	......	250	300	......
1880—Jan. 1	543	453	......	271	200	200	150	150	250	250	150	150	362	250	250	150	150	362	......	250	362	250
1885—Jan. 1	475	230	......	200	230	115	135	115	135	135	115	115	285	135	135	115	100	230	......	160	185	150
1887—July 18	270	135	......	158	135	90	99	90	99	99	99	90	180	99	99	99	90	135	......	108	117	108
1888—Mar. 6	360	162	162	162	162	162	162	162	126	126	108	99	225	117	99	108	99	162	162	117	126	117
Sept. 1	360	162	180	100	200	100	200	200	140	140	108	99	225	140	120	140	100	162	140	115	126	117
1889—Jan. 1	400	205	160	160	200	115	200	115	143	143	160	115	*310	160	115	160	160	205	140	125	126	115
1891—Jan. 15	400	220	220	138	200	143	200	125	155	155	175	125	*345	175	115	175	175	220	140	138	126	115
1892—July 18	400	220	220	138	200	143	180	125	155	155	175	125	*345	175	115	175	175	220	140	138	126	115

* Lower rates for carloads.

TABLE 119.—RATES OF FREIGHT, ALL RAIL, FROM CINCINNATI, OHIO, TO SAN FRANCISCO, PORTLAND, LOS ANGELES, AND OTHER PACIFIC COAST TERMINAL POINTS.

Date.	Commodities (rates in cents per 100 pounds).																				
	Dry goods.	Cotton piece goods.	Furniture.		Stoves.		Canned goods.		Glassware.		Starch.		Drugs.	Crockery and earthenware.		Nails.		Hardware.	Agricultural implements.		Beer.	
			Less than carloads.	Carloads.	Less than carloads.	Carloads.	Less than carloads.	Carloads.	Less than carloads.	Carloads.	Less than carloads.	Carloads.		Less than carloads.	Carloads.	Less than carloads.	Carloads.		Less than carloads.	Carloads.	Less than carloads.	Carloads.
1876—Nov. 1	531	......	......	212	212	212	159	159	239	239	159	159	265	239	239	159	159	265	......	239	265	......
1880—Jan. 1	531	425	......	265	212	200	150	150	239	239	150	150	345	239	239	150	150	345	......	239	345	239
1885—Jan. 1	450	225	......	200	225	115	135	115	135	135	115	115	275	135	135	115	115	225	......	155	180	155
1887—July 18	255	128	......	149	128	85	94	85	94	94	94	85	170	94	94	94	85	128	......	102	111	102
1888—Sept. 1	255	128	180	100	150	100	200	200	140	140	140	100	170	94	94	140	100	128	......	115	160	100
1889—Jan. 1	395	200	155	155	150	115	200	115	140	140	155	115	*365	155	115	155	155	200	......	124	160	115
1891—Jan. 15	395	215	215	135	150	140	200	124	150	150	170	124	*340	170	115	170	170	215	......	135	160	115
1892—July 18	395	215	215	135	150	140	175	124	150	150	170	124	*340	170	115	170	170	215	......	135	160	115

* Lower rate for carloads.

TABLE 120.—RATES OF FREIGHT, ALL RAIL, FROM CHICAGO, ILL., TO SAN FRANCISCO, PORTLAND, LOS ANGELES, AND OTHER PACIFIC COAST TERMINAL POINTS.

Commodities (rates in cents per 100 pounds).

Date.	Dry goods.	Cotton piece goods.	Furniture.		Stoves.		Canned goods.		Glassware.		Starch.	
			Less than car-loads.	Car-loads.	Less than car-loads.	Car-loads.	Less than car-loads.	Car-loads.	Less than car-loads.	Car-loads.	Less than car-loads.	Car-loads.
1870—Feb. 10	750	650	......	325	420	420	420	420	620	620	420	420
1876—Nov. 1	500	......	......	200	200	200	150	150	225	225	150	150
1880—Jan. 1	500	400	......	250	200	200	150	150	225	225	150	150
1885—Jan. 1	430	215	......	200	215	110	130	110	130	130	110	110
Mar. 16	400	200	......	160	200	100	120	100	120	120	100	100
1886—Apr. 26	200	100	......	80	100	50	60	50	60	60	50	50
1887—Apr. 5	470	470	......	275	335	245	275	245	335	335	335	275
Apr. 27	240	120	......	104	120	80	275	80	88	88	88	80
June 16	240	120	......	140	120	80	88	80	88	88	88	80
1888—Mar. 6	325	145	145	145	145	145	145	145	112	112	96	88
Sept. 1	325	145	160	140	200	100	200	200	140	140	140	100
1889—Jan. 1	390	195	150	150	200	110	200	110	130	130	150	110
1891—Jan 15	390	210	210	125	200	130	200	119	145	145	165	119
1892—July 18	390	210	210	125	200	130	170	119	145	145	165	119

Date.	Drugs.	Crockery and earthen ware.		Nails.		Hardware.	Agricultural implements.		Beer.	
		Less than car-loads.	Car-loads.	Less than car-loads.	Car-loads.		Less than car-loads.	Car-loads.	Less than car-loads.	Car-loads.
1870—Feb. 10	......	......	......	......	......	420	......	325	420	420
1876—Nov. 1	250	225	225	150	150	250	......	225	250	250
1880—Jan. 1	325	225	225	150	150	325	......	225	325	225
1885—Jan. 1	260	130	130	110	110	215	......	150	170	150
Mar. 16	240	120	120	100	100	200	......	140	160	140
1886—Apr. 26	120	60	60	100	50	100	......	70	160	50
1887—Apr. 5	470	275	275	275	245	400	......	230	......	220
Apr. 27	160	88	88	88	80	120	......	96	......	96
June 16	160	88	88	88	80	120	......	96	104	96
1888—Mar. 6	200	105	88	96	88	145	145	105	112	105
Sept. 1	200	140	100	140	100	145	145	115	160	100
1889—Jan. 1	*300	150	110	150	150	195	145	119	160	110
1891—Jan 15	*335	165	110	165	165	210	145	125	160	110
1892—July 18	*335	165	110	165	165	210	145	125	160	110

*Lower rates for carloads.

TABLE 121.—RATES OF FREIGHT, ALL RAIL, FROM ST. LOUIS, MO., TO SAN FRANCISCO, PORTLAND, LOS ANGELES, AND OTHER PACIFIC COAST TERMINAL POINTS.

Date.	Commodities (rates in cents per 100 pounds).																					
	Dry goods.	Cotton piece goods.	Furniture.		Stoves.		Canned goods.		Glassware.		Starch.		Drugs.	Crockery and earthenware.		Nails.		Hardware.	Agricultural implements.		Beer.	
			Less than car-loads.	Car-loads.	Less than car-loads.	Car-loads.	Less than car-loads.	Car-loads.	Less than car-loads.	Car-loads.	Less than car-loads.	Car-loads.		Less than car-loads.	Car-loads.	Less than car-loads.	Car-loads.		Less than car-loads.	Car-loads.	Less than car-loads.	Car-loads.
1870—Feb. 10	750	620	......	......	420	......	420	420	620	620	420	420	......	225	225	......	......	420	......	325	420	420
1876—Nov. 1	500	620	......	200	200	......	150	150	225	225	150	150	250	225	225	150	150	250	......	225	250	250
1880—Jan. 1	500	400	......	250	200	200	150	150	225	225	150	150	325	225	225	150	150	325	......	225	325	225
1882—Oct. 1	486	389	......	242	200	192	142	142	217	217	142	142	315	217	217	142	142	315	......	217	315	217
1885—Jan. 1	410	210	......	200	210	105	125	105	125	125	105	105	250	125	125	105	105	210	......	145	165	145
Mar. 16	382	192	......	153	192	96	115	96	115	115	96	96	230	115	115	96	96	192	......	134	153	134
1886—Apr. 26	191½	96	......	76½	96	50	57½	50	57½	57½	50	50	115	57½	57½	96	50	96	......	64	153	50
1887—Apr. 5	450	450	......	265	320	235	265	235	320	320	320	265	450	265	265	265	235	385	......	220	153	212
Apr. 27	230	115	......	100	115	77	265	77	84	84	84	77	154	84	84	84	77	115	......	92	153	92
June 16	230	115	......	134	115	77	84	77	84	84	84	77	154	84	84	84	77	115	......	92	100	92
1888—Mar. 6	312	140	140	140	140	140	140	140	108	108	92	85	190	100	85	92	85	140	140	100	108	100
Sept. 1	312	140	160	140	200	100	200	200	140	140	140	100	190	100	85	140	100	......	140	115	160	100
1889—Jan. 1	374	187	144	144	200	106	200	106	125	125	144	106	*288	144	106	144	144	187	140	114	160	106
1891—Jan. 15	370	205	202	120	200	125	200	114	139	139	158	114	*322	158	106	158	158	202	140	120	160	106
1892—July 18	370	205	202	120	200	125	163	114	139	139	158	114	*322	158	106	158	158	202	140	120	160	106

* Lower rate for carloads.

TABLE 122.—RATES OF FREIGHT, ALL RAIL, FROM MISSOURI RIVER POINTS TO SAN FRANCISCO, PORTLAND, LOS ANGELES, AND OTHER PACIFIC COAST TERMINAL POINTS.

Date.	Commodities (rates in cents per 100 pounds).																					
	Dry goods.	Cotton piece goods.	Furniture.		Stoves.		Canned goods.		Glassware.		Starch.		Drugs.	Crockery and earthenware.		Nails.		Hardware.	Agricultural implements.		Beer.	
			Less than car-loads.	Car-loads.	Less than car-loads.	Car-loads.	Less than car loads.	Car-loads.	Less than car-loads.	Car-loads.	Less than car-loads.	Car-loads.		Less than car-loads.	Car-loads.	Less than car-loads.	Car-loads.		Less than car-loads.	Car-loads.	Less than car-loads.	Car-loads.
1870—Feb. 10	625	625	......	......	......	......	550	550	625	625	625	625	......	......	......	......	500	550	......	285	550	550
1876—Nov. 1	450	625	......	185	185	185	150	150	200	200	150	150	225	200	200	150	150	225	......	200	225	225
1880—Jan. 1	450	375	......	225	185	185	145	145	200	200	145	145	300	200	200	145	145	300	......	200	300	200
1882—Oct. 2	455	375	......	235	185	185	135	135	210	210	135	135	300	210	210	135	135	300	......	210	300	210
1885—Jan. 1	375	185	......	185	185	100	110	100	110	110	100	100	220	110	110	100	100	185	......	130	160	140
Mar. 16	350	175	......	140	175	88	105	88	105	105	88	88	210	105	105	88	88	175	......	123	140	123
1886—Apr. 26	175	87½	......	70	87½	50	52½	50	52½	52½	50	50	105	52½	52½	88	50	87½	......	61½	140	50
1887—Apr. 5	400	400	......	250	300	225	250	225	300	300	300	255	400	250	250	250	225	350	......	210	140	200
Apr. 27	210	105	......	91	105	70	250	70	77	77	77	70	140	77	77	77	70	105	......	84	140	84
June 16	210	105	......	123	105	70	77	70	77	77	77	70	140	77	77	77	70	105	......	84	91	84
1888—Mar. 6	280	125	125	125	125	125	125	125	100	100	85	80	175	95	80	85	80	125	125	95	100	95
Sept. 1	280	125	180	140	125	125	125	125	100	100	85	80	175	95	80	85	80	125	300	300	160	100
1889—Jan. 1	351	176	135	135	125	99	125	99	117	117	135	99	*270	135	99	135	135	176	300	107	166	99
1891—Jan. 15	350	189	189	113	125	117	125	107	131	131	149	107	*302	149	99	149	149	189	300	113	160	99
1892—July 18	350	189	189	113	125	117	153	107	131	131	149	107	*302	149	99	149	149	189	300	113	160	99

* Lower rates for carloads.

TRANSCONTINENTAL TRAFFIC EASTWARD BOUND.

Through rates from the Pacific coast are established by transcontinental lines on traffic destined to the Missouri River and grouped territory east thereof. Traffic carried thereunder is known as "eastward bound transcontinental traffic."

Important reductions have taken place in these rates during the last twenty years. The tables following show such changes from the several Pacific coast points to a representative point in each of the groups to which through rates are published.

TABLE 123.—FREIGHT RATES, ALL RAIL, FROM SAN FRANCISCO AND LOS ANGELES, CAL., PORTLAND, OREGON, TACOMA AND SEATTLE, WASH., AND VANCOUVER, BRITISH COLUMBIA, TO OMAHA, NEBR.

Date.	Rates (in cents per 100 pounds).																					
	Canned goods.		Coffee, green.		Fruit, dried.		Hides, compressed.		Leather, in rolls.		Nuts.		Beans.		Raisins.		Vegetables.		Wine, in wood.		Hops.	
	Less than carloads.	Carloads.	Less than carloads.	Carloads.	Less than carloads.	Carloads.	Less than carloads.	Carloads.	Less than carloads.	Carloads.	Less than carloads.	Carloads.	Less than carloads.	Carloads.	Less than carloads.	Carloads.	Less than carloads.	Carloads.	Less than carloads.	Carloads.	Less than carloads.	Carloads.
1870—Feb. 10	550	550	500	500	550	550	625	625	500	500	625	625	500	500	625	625	......	......	400	400	550	550
1876—July 17	550	550	500	500	550	550	625	625	500	500	625	625	500	500	625	625	......	212½	400	400	550	550
1878—June 15	550	550	500	500	550	550	625	625	500	500	625	625	500	500	625	625	......	185	400	400	550	550
1881—May 21	150	150	185	150	200	185	185	150	200	185	275	185	170	125	200	150	......	185	170	150	225	225
July 25	150	140	190	150	205	190	190	150	205	190	280	190	175	125	205	150	......	185	175	150	230	230
Oct. 6	140	140	180	140	200	140	180	140	200	180	285	180	160	140	200	140	......	135	160	140	220	220
1884—Aug. 25	140	125	180	140	200	180	180	140	200	180	285	180	160	140	200	140	......	135	160	140	220	220
1885—Feb. 9	140	125	180	140	200	180	180	140	200	180	285	180	160	116⅔	200	140	......	135	160	140	220	220
Mar. 15	140	125	180	140	200	180	180	140	200	180	285	180	160	116⅔	200	140	......	140	160	140	220	220
Dec. 1	130	125	150	115	180	130	180	130	200	180	210	180	150	115	190	130	......	140	150	130	210	210
1886—Apr. 26	65	62½	75	57½	90	65	90	65	200	90	105	90	75	57½	95	65	75	65	150	130	210	210
Aug. 16	130	90	150	115	180	130	180	130	200	180	210	180	150	60	190	130	75	65	75	62	210	210
1887—Apr. 5	250	140	250	225	300	250	180	350	350	350	400	300	300	140	350	300	......	110	......	300	175	175
Apr. 27	130	125	150	115	180	130	180	130	......	180	210	180	150	115	......	......	......	90	180	115	175	175
May 25	130	125	123	88	140	105	140	105	......	140	175	140	123	88	151	105	......	90	123	88	140	140
June 16	130	88	123	88	140	105	140	70	......	140	175	140	123	88	......	......	......	90	......	26	140	140
July 18	105	75	123	88	140	105	70	70	......	140	175	140	123	88	150	105	......	90	123	88	140	126
Oct. 10	105	75	123	88	140	105	88	88	......	70	175	140	123	75	150	105	......	90	123	80	126	126
1888—Jan. 16	165	75	140	110	155	125	88	88	240	70	190	190	123	75	165	125	300	90	123	80	126	126
Mar. 10	165	125	140	110	155	125	110	110	125	125	190	190	140	100	165	125	300	90	155	110	155	155
July 5	165	110	140	110	155	125	110	110	125	125	190	190	140	100	165	125	300	90	155	110	155	155
Sept. 1	200	110	200	175	180	140	300	300	300	300	300	160	200	100	300	250	350	100	350	350	200	200
1889—Jan. 1	200	110	200	175	200	140	300	135	300	300	300	160	200	100	300	250	350	100	350	350	200	200
Jan. 10	200	110	200	175	200	140	300	135	300	300	300	160	200	100	300	250	350	100	350	350	200	200
Mar. 1	200	120	200	175	200	140	300	135	300	300	300	160	200	100	300	250	350	100	350	350	200	200
May 23	200	100	200	175	200	120	300	135	300	300	300	160	200	100	300	250	350	100	350	350	200	200
Aug. 20	200	100	200	175	200	120	300	135	300	300	300	160	200	100	300	250	350	100	350	100	200	200
Aug. 24	200	100	200	175	200	120	300	135	300	300	300	160	200	100	300	250	350	100	350	100	200	200
Sept. 1	200	100	200	175	200	140	300	135	300	300	300	160	200	100	300	250	350	100	350	100	200	200
Oct. 1	200	100	200	175	200	140	300	135	300	300	300	160	200	100	300	250	350	100	350	350	200	200
Nov. 1	200	100	200	175	200	140	300	135	300	300	300	160	200	100	300	250	350	100	205	100	200	200

1890—June 18	200	100	200	80	200	140	300	135	300	200	300	160	200	100	300	250	350	100	205	100	200	200
1891—Jan. 22	200	100	200	80	220	155	300	135	300	200	300	175	200	110	300	250	350	100	225	100	220	200
Sept. 21	200	110	200	80	220	150	300	135	300	200	200	175	200	110	300	250	350	100	225	100	220	200
1892—Mar. 5	200	110	200	80	220	150	300	135	300	200	200	175	200	110	300	250	350	200	225	100	220	200
Mar. 18	200	100	200	80	220	140	300	135	300	200	200	175	200	110	300	250	350	100	225	100	220	200
Nov. 21	200	100	200	80	220	140	300	135	300	200	200	175	200	110	300	250	350	100	225	100	220	200

TABLE 124.—FREIGHT RATES, ALL RAIL, FROM SAN FRANCISCO AND LOS ANGELES, CAL., PORTLAND, OREGON, TACOMA AND SEATTLE, WASH., AND VANCOUVER, BRITISH COLUMBIA, TO ST. LOUIS, MO.

Date.	Rates (in cents per 100 pounds).																					
	Canned goods.		Coffee, green.		Fruit, dried.		Hides, compressed.		Leather, in rolls.		Nuts.		Beans.		Raisins.		Vegetables.		Wine, in wood.		Hops.	
	Less than carloads.	Carloads.	Less than carloads.	Carloads.	Less than carloads.	Carloads.	Less than carloads.	Carloads.	Less than carloads.	Carloads.	Less than carloads.	Carloads.	Less than carloads.	Carloads.	Less than carloads.	Carloads.	Less than carloads.	Carloads.	Less than carloads.	Carloads.	Less than carloads.	Carloads.
1870—Feb. 10	420	420	......	......	420	420	520	520	520	520	520	520	......	......	420	420	......	......	420	420	420	420
1876—Feb. 17	420	420	......	......	420	420	520	520	520	520	520	520	......	......	420	420	......	250	420	420	420	420
1877—Feb. 16	420	420	......	......	420	420	520	520	520	520	520	520	......	......	420	420	......	250	420	420	420	420
1878—June 15	420	420	......	......	420	420	520	520	520	520	520	520	......	......	420	420	......	200	420	420	420	420
1881—May 21	150	150	200	150	225	200	200	150	225	200	300	200	175	125	225	150	......	200	175	150	250	250
Oct. 6	142	142	192	142	217	142	192	142	217	192	315	192	168	142	217	142	......	142	168	142	242	242
1884—Aug. 25	142	125	192	142	217	192	192	142	217	192	315	192	168	142	217	142	......	142	168	142	242	242
1885—Feb. 9	142	125	192	142	217	192	192	142	217	192	315	192	168	118⅓	217	142	......	142	168	142	242	242
Mar. 15	142	125	192	142	217	192	192	142	217	192	315	192	168	118⅓	217	142	......	145	168	142	242	242
Dec. 1	140	125	165	120	190	140	190	140	......	190	240	190	165	120	205	140	......	......	165	140	240	240
1886—Apr. 26	70	62½	82½	60	95	70	95	70	......	95	120	95	82½	60	120	60	102½	70	82½	70	240	240
Aug. 16	140	90	165	120	190	140	190	140	......	190	240	190	165	60	205	140	......	......	82½	70	240	240
Sept. 27	140	90	165	120	190	140	190	140	......	190	240	190	165	60	205	140	......	......	82½	70	240	100
1887—Apr. 5	265	150	265	235	320	265	......	385	385	......	450	320	320	150	385	320	......	120	......	320	185	185
Apr. 27	140	125	165	120	190	140	190	140	......	190	240	190	165	120	......	......	......	96	190	120	185	185
May 25	140	125	134	96	154	115	154	115	......	154	192	154	134	96	165	115	......	......	134	96	154	154
June 16	140	96	134	96	154	115	154	77	......	154	192	154	134	96	......	......	......	96	......	138	154	154
July 18	115	75	134	96	154	115	77	77	......	154	192	150	124	96	165	115	......	......	134	96	......	138
Oct. 10	115	75	134	96	154	115	96	96	......	77	192	154	134	83	165	115	......	96	134	80	138	138
1888—Jan. 16	170	75	145	110	160	125	96	96	245	77	195	195	170	83	170	125	315	96	315	80	138	138
Mar. 10	170	125	145	110	160	125	110	110	245	245	195	195	145	100	170	125	315	96	160	110	160	160
July 5	170	110	145	110	160	125	110	110	245	245	195	195	145	100	170	125	315	96	160	110	160	160
Sept 1	205	110	205	180	180	140	320	320	320	320	300	160	205	100	320	260	370	100	370	370	200	200
Sept. 20	205	110	205	110	180	140	320	320	320	320	300	160	205	100	320	260	370	100	370	370	200	200
1889—Jan. 1	205	110	205	110	200	140	320	135	320	320	300	160	205	100	320	260	370	100	370	370	200	200
Jan. 10	205	110	205	180	200	140	320	135	320	320	300	160	205	100	320	260	370	100	370	370	200	200
Mar. 1	205	120	205	180	200	140	320	135	320	320	300	160	205	100	320	260	370	100	370	370	320	320
Apr. 10	205	120	205	180	200	140	320	135	320	320	300	160	205	100	320	260	370	240	370	370	320	320
May 23	205	100	205	180	200	120	320	135	320	320	300	160	205	100	320	260	370	240	370	370	320	320
Aug. 20	205	100	205	180	200	120	320	135	320	320	300	160	205	100	320	260	370	240	370	100	320	320
Aug. 24	205	100	205	180	200	120	320	135	320	320	300	160	205	100	320	260	370	240	370	100	320	320
Sept. 1	205	100	205	180	200	140	320	135	320	320	300	160	205	100	320	260	370	240	370	100	320	320
Oct. 1	205	100	205	180	200	140	320	135	320	320	300	160	205	100	320	260	370	100	370	100	200	200
Nov. 1	205	100	205	180	200	140	320	135	320	320	300	160	205	100	320	260	370	100	205	100	200	200

1890—June 18	205	100	205	80	200	140	320	135	320	205	300	160	205	100	320	260	370	100	205	100	200	200
1891—Jan. 22	205	110	205	80	220	155	320	135	320	205	320	175	205	110	320	260	370	100	225	100	220	200
Sept. 21	205	110	205	80	220	150	320	135	320	205	320	175	205	110	320	260	370	100	225	100	220	200
1892—Mar. 5	205	110	205	80	220	150	320	135	320	205	320	175	205	110	320	260	370	200	225	100	220	200
July 18	205	100	205	80	220	140	320	135	320	205	320	175	205	110	320	260	370	100	225	100	220	200
Nov. 21	205	100	205	80	220	140	320	135	320	205	320	175	206	110	320	260	370	100	225	100	220	200

TABLE 125.—FREIGHT RATES, ALL RAIL, FROM SAN FRANCISCO AND LOS ANGELES, CAL., PORTLAND, OREGON, TACOMA AND SEATTLE, WASH., AND VANCOUVER, BRITISH COLUMBIA, TO CHICAGO, ILL.

Date.	Rates (in cents per 100 pounds).																					
	Canned goods.		Coffee, green.		Fruit, dried.		Hides, compressed.		Leather in rolls.		Nuts.		Beans.		Raisins.		Vegetables.		Wine, in wood.		Hops.	
	Less than carloads.	Carloads.	Less than carloads.	Carloads.	Less than carloads.	Carloads.	Less than carloads.	Carloads.	Less than carloads.	Carloads.	Less than carloads.	Carloads.	Less than carloads.	Carloads.	Less than carloads.	Carloads.	Less than carloads.	Carloads.	Less than carloads.	Carloads.	Less than carloads.	Carloads.
1870—Feb. 10	420	420	......	......	420	420	520	520	520	520	520	520	......	......	420	420	......	......	420	420	420	420
1876—July 17	420	420	......	......	420	420	520	520	520	520	520	520	......	......	420	420	......	250	420	420	420	420
1877—July 16	420	420	......	......	420	420	520	520	520	520	520	520	......	......	420	420	......	250	420	420	420	420
1878—June 15	420	420	......	......	420	420	520	520	520	520	520	520	......	......	420	420	......	200	420	420	420	420
1881—May 21	150	150	200	150	225	200	200	150	225	200	300	200	175	125	225	150	......	200	175	150	420	250
July 25	150	150	200	150	225	200	200	150	225	200	300	200	175	125	225	150	......	200	175	150	250	250
Oct. 6	150	150	200	150	225	150	200	150	225	150	325	200	175	150	225	150	......	150	175	150	250	250
1884—Aug. 25	150	125	200	150	225	200	325	200	225	200	325	200	175	150	225	150	......	150	175	150	250	250
1885—Feb. 9	150	125	200	150	225	200	325	200	225	200	325	200	175	125	225	150	......	150	175	150	250	250
Mar. 15	150	125	200	150	225	200	325	200	225	200	325	200	175	125	225	150	......	150	175	150	250	250
Dec. 1	150	125	175	125	200	150	200	150	225	200	250	200	175	125	215	150	......	150	175	150	250	250
1886—Mar. 4	37½	37½	37½	37½	37½	37½	37½	37½	37½	37½	37½	37½	37½	37½	37½	37½	......	37½	37½	37½	37½	37½
Mar. 10	30	30	30	30	30	30	30	30	30	30	30	30	30	30	30	30	......	30	30	30	30	30
Apr. 26	75	62½	87½	62½	100	75	100	75	......	100	125	100	87½	62½	107½	75	87½	75	......	......	......	......
Aug. 16	150	90	175	125	200	150	200	150	......	200	250	200	175	60	215	150	......	......	87½	75	250	250
Nov. 24	150	90	175	125	200	150	200	150	......	200	250	200	175	60	215	150	......	......	87½	75	250	105
1887—Apr. 5	275	155	275	245	335	275	......	400	400	400	470	335	335	155	400	335	......	125	......	335	195	195
Apr. 27	150	125	175	125	200	150	200	150	......	200	250	200	175	125	......	......	......	100	200	125	195	195
May 25	......	125	140	100	160	120	160	120	......	160	200	160	140	100	172	120	......	......	140	100	160	160
June 16	......	100	140	100	160	120	160	80	......	160	200	160	140	100	......	......	......	100	......	144	160	160
July 18	120	75	140	100	160	120	80	80	......	160	200	160	140	100	172	120	......	......	140	100	160	144
Oct. 10	120	75	140	100	160	120	100	100	......	80	200	160	140	86	172	120	......	100	140	80	144	144
1888—Jan. 16	175	75	150	115	165	130	100	100	255	80	200	200	175	86	175	130	325	100	325	80	144	144
Mar. 10	175	125	150	115	165	130	115	115	130	130	200	200	150	100	175	130	325	100	165	115	165	165
July 5	175	110	150	115	165	130	115	115	130	130	200	200	150	100	175	130	325	100	165	115	165	165
Sept. 1	175	110	210	185	180	140	340	340	340	340	300	160	210	100	340	270	390	105	390	390	200	200
Sept. 20	175	110	210	115	180	140	340	340	340	340	300	160	......	100	340	270		105	390	390	200	200
1889—Jan. 1	210	110	210	115	200	140	340	135	340	340	300	160	210	100	340	270	390	105	390	390	200	200
Jan. 10	210	110	210	185	200	140	340	340	340	340	300	160	210	100	340	270	390	105	390	390	200	200
Mar. 1	210	120	210	185	200	140	340	340	340	340	300	160	210	100	340	270	390	105	390	390	200	200
Apr. 10	210	120	210	185	200	140	340	340	340	340	300	160	210	100	340	270	390	250	390	390	200	200
May 23	210	100	210	185	200	120	340	340	340	340	300	160	210	100	340	270	390	250	390	390	200	200
Aug. 20	210	100	210	185	200	120	340	340	340	340	300	160	210	100	340	270	390	250	390	100	200	200
Aug. 24	210	100	210	185	200	120	340	340	340	340	300	160	210	100	340	270	390	250	390	100	200	200

Sept. 1	210	100	210	185	200	140	340	340	340	340	300	160	210	100	340	270	390	250	390	100	200	200
Oct. 1	210	100	210	185	200	140	340	135	340	340	300	160	210	100	340	270	390	100	390	390	200	200
Nov. 1	210	100	210	185	200	140	340	135	340	340	300	160	210	100	340	270	390	100	205	100	200	200
1890—June 18	210	100	210	80	200	140	340	135	340	340	300	160	210	100	340	270	390	105	205	100	200	200
1891—Jan. 22	210	110	210	80	220	155	340	135	340	340	340	175	210	110	340	270	390	105	225	100	220	200
Sept. 21	210	110	210	80	220	150	340	135	340	340	340	175	210	110	340	270	390	105	225	100	220	200
1892—Mar. 5	210	110	210	80	220	150	340	135	340	340	340	175	210	110	340	270	390	210	225	100	220	200
July 18	210	100	210	80	220	140	340	135	340	340	340	175	210	110	340	270	390	105	255	100	220	200
Nov. 21	210	100	210	80	220	140	340	135	340	340	340	175	210	110	340	270	390	105	225	100	220	200

TABLE 126.—FREIGHT RATES, ALL RAIL, FROM SAN FRANCISCO AND LOS ANGELES, CAL., PORTLAND, OREGON, TACOMA AND SEATTLE, WASH., AND VANCOUVER, BRITISH COLUMBIA, TO CINCINNATI, OHIO.

Date.	Rates (in cents per 100 pounds.)																					
	Canned goods.		Coffee, green.		Fruit, dried.		Hides, compressed.		Leather, in rolls.		Nuts.		Beans.		Raisins.		Vegetables.		Wine, in wood.		Hops.	
	Less than carloads.	Carloads.	Less than carloads.	Carloads.	Less than carloads.	Carloads.	Less than carloads.	Carloads.	Less than carloads.	Carloads.	Less than carloads.	Carloads.	Less than carloads.	Carloads.	Less than carloads.	Carloads.	Less than carloads.	Carloads.	Less than carloads.	Carloads.	Less than carloads.	Carloads.
1881—May 21	150	150	200	150	240	200	200	150	240	200	320	200	175	125	240	150	175	150	265	265	......	......
July 25	150	150	200	150	225	200	200	150	240	200	320	200	175	125	225	150	175	150	175	150	265	265
Oct. 6	150	150	200	150	239	150	200	150	239	200	345	200	175	150	239	150	175	150	175	150	265	265
1884—Aug. 25	150	125	200	150	239	200	200	150	239	200	345	200	175	150	239	150	175	150	175	150	265	265
1885—Feb. 9	150	125	200	150	239	200	200	150	239	200	345	200	175	125	239	150	175	150	175	150	265	265
Dec. 1	150	125	175	125	200	150	200	150	......	200	255	200	175	125	220	150	......	......	175	150	255	......
1886—Mar. 5	44	44	44	44	44	44	44	44	44	44	44	44	44	44	44	44	44	44	44	44	44	44
Apr. 26	84	70	98	70	112	84	112	84	......	112	142½	112	98	70	123	84	98	84	44	44	44	44
Aug. 16	150	90	175	125	200	150	200	150	......	200	255	200	175	75	220	150	98	84	87½	75	253	253
Nov. 24	150	90	175	125	200	150	200	150	......	200	255	200	175	75	220	150	98	84	87½	75	253	115
1887—July 18	128	85	149	106	170	128	85	85	......	170	213	170	149	106	183	128	......	......	149	106	......	153
Oct. 10	128	85	149	106	170	128	106	106	......	85	213	170	149	91	183	128	......	106	149	80	163	163
1888—Sept. 20	128	85	149	122	170	128	106	106	......	85	213	170	149	91	183	128	......	106	149	80	163	163
1889—Jan. 1	215	110	215	122	200	140	345	135	345	215	300	160	215	100	345	275	395	140	395	395	200	200
Jan. 10	215	110	215	190	200	140	345	135	345	215	300	160	215	100	345	275	395	140	395	395	200	200
Mar. 1	215	120	215	190	200	140	345	135	345	215	300	160	215	100	345	275	395	140	395	395	200	200
May 23	215	100	215	190	200	120	345	135	345	215	300	160	215	100	345	275	395	140	395	395	200	200
Aug. 20	215	100	215	190	200	120	345	135	345	215	300	160	215	100	345	275	395	140	395	100	200	200
Aug. 24	215	100	215	190	200	120	345	135	345	215	300	160	215	100	345	275	395	140	395	100	200	200
Sept. 1	215	100	215	190	200	140	345	135	345	215	300	160	215	100	345	275	395	140	395	100	200	200
Oct. 1	215	100	215	190	200	140	345	135	345	215	300	160	215	100	345	275	395	140	205	100	200	200
Nov. 1	215	100	215	190	200	140	345	135	345	215	300	160	215	100	345	275	395	140	205	100	200	200
1890—June 18	215	100	215	190	200	140	345	135	345	215	300	160	215	100	345	275	395	140	205	100	200	200
1891—Jan. 22	215	110	215	190	220	155	345	135	345	215	345	175	215	110	345	275	395	140	225	100	220	200
Sept. 21	215	110	215	190	220	150	345	135	345	215	345	175	215	110	345	275	395	140	225	100	220	200
1892—July 18	215	100	215	190	220	140	345	135	345	215	345	175	215	110	345	275	395	140	225	100	220	200
Nov. 21	215	100	215	190	220	140	345	135	345	215	345	175	215	110	345	275	395	140	225	100	220	200

TABLE 127.—FREIGHT RATES, ALL RAIL, FROM SAN FRANCISCO AND LOS ANGELES, CAL., PORTLAND, OREGON, TACOMA AND SEATTLE, WASH., AND VANCOUVER, BRITISH COLUMBIA, TO PITTSBURG, PA.

Date.	Rates (in cents per 100 pounds).																					
	Canned goods.		Coffee, green.		Fruit, dried.		Hides, compressed.		Leather, in rolls.		Nuts.		Beans.		Raisins.		Vegetables.		Wine, in wood.		Hops.	
	Less than carloads.	Carloads.	Less than carloads.	Carloads.	Less than carloads.	Carloads.	Less than carloads.	Carloads.	Less than carloads.	Carloads.	Less than carloads.	Carloads.	Less than carloads.	Carloads.	Less than carloads.	Carloads.	Less than carloads.	Carloads.	Less than carloads.	Carloads.	Less than carloads.	Carloads.
1881—May 21	150	150	200	150	250	200	200	150	250	200	345	200	175	125	250	150	......	......	175	150	280	280
July 25	150	150	200	150	250	200	200	150	250	200	345	200	175	125	240	150	......	......	175	150	280	280
Oct. 6	150	150	200	150	250	200	200	150	250	200	362	200	175	150	250	150	......	......	175	150	271	271
1884—Aug. 25	150	125	200	150	250	200	200	150	250	200	362	200	175	150	250	150	......	......	......	......	......	......
1885—Dec. 1	150	125	175	125	200	150	200	150	......	200	270	200	175	125	225	150	......	......	175	150	270	270
1886—Apr. 26	89	74½	104	74½	104	89	119	89	......	119	160	119	104	74½	133½	89	104	89	......	......	......	......
Aug. 16	150	90	175	125	200	150	200	150	......	200	270	200	175	67	225	150	104	89	87½	75	270	270
Sept. 27	150	90	175	125	200	150	200	150	......	200	270	200	175	62½	225	150	104	89	87½	75	270	270
Nov. 24	150	90	175	125	200	150	200	150	......	200	270	200	175	62½	225	150	104	89	87½	75	270	125
1887—Feb. 2	150	90	175	125	200	150	200	150	......	200	270	200	175	57½	225	150	104	89	87½	75	270	125
July 18	135	90	158	113	180	135	90	90	......	180	225	180	158	113	194	135	......	......	158	113	......	162
Oct. 10	135	90	158	113	180	135	113	113	......	90	225	180	158	96	194	135	......	113	158	85	162	......
1888—Jan. 16	198	90	160	120	180	140	113	113	288	90	225	225	198	96	198	140	360	113	360	90	162	162
Mar. 10	198	125	160	120	180	140	120	120	140	140	225	225	160	105	198	140	360	113	180	120	180	......
July 5	198	110	160	120	180	140	120	120	140	140	225	225	160	105	198	140	360	113	180	120	200	200
Sept. 1	220	110	220	195	180	140	350	350	350	350	300	160	220	100	350	280	400	140	400	400	350	350
1889—Jan. 1	220	110	220	195	200	140	350	135	350	350	300	160	220	100	350	280	400	140	400	400	350	200
Jan. 10	220	110	220	195	200	140	350	350	350	350	300	160	220	100	350	280	400	140	400	400	350	200
Mar. 1	220	120	220	195	200	140	350	350	350	350	300	160	220	100	350	280	400	140	400	400	350	200
May 23	220	100	220	195	200	120	350	350	350	350	300	160	220	100	350	280	400	140	400	400	350	200
Aug. 20	220	100	220	195	200	120	350	350	350	350	300	160	220	100	350	280	400	140	400	100	350	200
Aug. 24	220	100	220	195	200	120	350	350	350	350	300	160	220	100	350	280	400	140	400	100	350	200
Sept. 1	220	100	220	195	200	140	350	350	350	350	300	160	220	100	350	280	400	140	400	100	350	200
Oct. 1	220	100	220	195	200	140	350	135	250	350	300	160	220	100	350	280	400	100	400	400	200	200
Nov. 1	220	100	220	195	200	140	350	135	350	350	300	160	220	100	350	280	400	100	205	100	200	200
1890—June 18	220	100	220	195	200	140	350	135	350	220	300	160	220	100	350	280	400	140	205	100	200	200
1891—Jan. 22	220	110	220	195	220	155	350	135	350	220	350	175	220	110	350	280	400	140	225	100	220	200
Sept. 21	220	110	220	195	220	150	350	135	350	220	350	175	220	110	350	280	400	140	225	100	220	200
1892—July 18	220	100	220	195	220	140	350	135	350	220	350	175	220	110	350	280	400	140	225	100	220	200
Nov. 21	220	100	220	195	220	140	350	135	350	220	350	175	220	110	350	280	400	140	225	100	220	200

TABLE 128.—FREIGHT RATES, ALL RAIL, FROM SAN FRANCISCO AND LOS ANGELES, CAL., PORTLAND, OREGON, TACOMA AND SEATTLE, WASH., AND VANCOUVER, BRITISH COLUMBIA, TO NEW YORK, N. Y.

Date.	Rates (in cents, per 100 pounds).																					
	Canned goods.		Coffee, green.		Fruit, dried.		Hides, compressed.		Leather, in rolls.		Nuts.		Beans.		Raisins.		Vegetables.		Wine in, wood.		Hops.	
	Less than carloads.	Carloads.	Less than carloads.	Carloads.	Less than carloads.	Carloads.	Less than carloads.	Carloads.	Less than carloads.	Carloads.	Less than carloads.	Carloads.	Less than carloads.	Carloads.	Less than carloads.	Carloads.	Less than carloads.	Carloads.	Less than carloads.	Carloads.	Less than carloads.	Carloads.
1870—Feb. 10	420	420	......	......	420	420	550	550	550	550	550	550	......	......	420	420	......	......	550	550	420	420
1877—July 16	420	420	......	......	420	420	550	550	550	550	550	550	......	......	420	420	......	320	550	550	420	420
1878—June 15	420	420	......	......	420	420	550	550	550	550	550	550	......	......	420	420	......	257	550	550	420	420
1881—May 21	150	150	200	150	250	200	200	150	250	200	400	200	175	125	250	150	......	257	175	150	300	300
July 25	150	150	200	150	250	200	200	150	250	200	400	200	175	125	250	150	......	......	175	150	300	300
Oct. 6	150	150	200	150	250	150	200	150	250	200	400	200	175	150	250	150	......	150	175	150	300	300
1884—Aug. 25	150	125	200	150	250	200	200	150	250	200	400	200	175	150	250	150	......	150	175	150	300	300
1885—Feb. 9	150	125	200	150	250	200	200	150	250	200	400	200	175	125	250	150	......	150	175	150	300	300
Mar. 15	150	125	200	150	250	200	200	150	250	200	400	200	175	125	250	150	......	200	175	150	300	300
Dec. 1	150	125	175	125	200	150	200	150	250	200	300	200	175	125	250	150	......	......	175	150	300	300
1886—Feb. 28	50	50	50	50	50	50	50	50	50	50	50	50	50	50	50	50	50	50	50	50	50	50
Apr. 26	96½	81½	112½	81	128½	96½	128	90½	......	128	191	128	112½	81	159½	96½	112½	81	50	50	50	50
Aug. 16	150	127	175	125	200	150	200	150	......	200	300	200	175	97	250	150	......	......	87½	75	300	300
Nov. 24	......	......	......	......	......	......	......	......	......	......	......	......	......	......	......	......	......	......	......	......	......	135
1887—Apr. 5	......	180	305	260	380	295	......	445	425	425	......	360	......	180	435	435	......	160	......	370	245	245
Apr. 27	......	155	......	145	......	170	......	200	......	205	......	230	......	150	435	435	......	136	......	160	235	235
May 25	......	125	175	125	200	150	200	150	......	200	250	200	175	125	215	150	......	......	175	125	200	200
June 16	......	125	175	125	200	150	200	100	......	200	250	200	175	125	......	......	......	......	......	180	......	......
July 18	160	100	175	125	200	150	100	100	......	200	250	200	175	125	215	150	......	......	175	125	......	180
Oct. 10	160	100	175	125	200	150	125	125	......	100	250	200	175	107	215	150	......	125	175	90	180	180
1888—Jan. 16	160	100	175	125	200	150	125	125	320	100	250	250	220	107	220	150	400	125	400	100	180	180
Mar. 10	220	125	175	125	200	150	125	125	150	150	250	250	175	110	220	150	400	125	200	125	200	200
July 5	220	110	175	125	200	150	125	125	150	150	250	250	175	110	220	150	400	125	200	125	200	200
Sept 1	160	110	......	......	180	140	140	140	200	200	300	200	180	100	180	140	300	300	180	100	200	200
Sept. 26	160	110	......	......	180	140	180	100	200	200	300	200	180	100	180	140	300	300	180	100	200	200
1889—Jan. 1	230	110	230	200	200	140	370	135	370	370	300	160	230	100	370	295	420	145	420	420	200	200
Jan. 10	230	110	230	200	200	140	370	370	370	370	300	160	230	100	370	295	420	145	420	420	200	200
Mar. 1	230	120	230	200	200	140	370	370	370	370	300	160	230	100	370	295	420	145	420	420	200	200
May 23	230	100	230	200	200	120	370	370	370	370	300	160	230	100	370	295	420	145	420	420	200	200
Aug. 20	230	100	230	200	200	120	370	370	370	370	300	160	230	100	370	295	420	145	420	100	200	200
Aug. 24	230	100	230	200	200	120	370	370	370	370	300	160	230	100	370	295	420	145	420	100	200	200
Sept. 1	230	100	230	200	200	140	370	370	370	370	300	160	230	100	370	295	420	145	420	100	200	200

Oct. 1	230	100	230	200	200	140	370	135	370	370	300	160	230	100	370	295	420	145	420	420	200	200
Nov. 1	230	100	230	200	200	140	370	135	370	370	300	160	230	100	370	295	420	145	205	100	200	200
1890—June 18	230	100	230	200	200	140	370	135	370	370	300	160	230	100	370	295	420	145	205	100	200	200
1891—Jan. 22	230	110	230	200	220	155	370	135	370	370	370	175	230	110	370	295	420	145	225	100	220	220
Sept. 21	230	110	230	200	230	150	370	135	370	370	370	175	230	110	370	295	420	145	225	100	220	220
1892—July 18	230	100	230	200	220	140	370	135	370	370	370	175	230	110	370	295	420	145	225	100	220	220
Nov. 21	230	100	230	200	220	140	370	135	370	370	370	175	230	110	370	295	420	145	225	100	220	220

MISCELLANEOUS DATA—OCEAN RATES—MILEAGE RATES—TONNAGE MOVEMENT.

OCEAN RATES FROM NEW YORK TO LIVERPOOL, ENGLAND.

Data have been collected showing the rates charged on wheat and provisions from New York to Liverpool, England, via steamers, and the same are below given, showing the changes as reported from 1866 up to the present time.

TABLE 129.—FREIGHT RATES CHARGED FOR THE TRANSPORTATION OF WHEAT AND PROVISIONS FROM NEW YORK TO LIVERPOOL VIA STEAMERS FROM JANUARY 3, 1866.

Date.	Wheat per bushel.	Provisions per ton.	Date.	Wheat per bushel.	Provisions per ton.	Date.	Wheat per bushel.	Provisions per ton.
	Cents.	*Dolls.*		*Cents.*	*Dolls.*		*Cents.*	*Dolls.*
1866—Jan. 3	9	....	1868—Feb. 1	21	....	1870—Mar. 2	4	....
Jan. 17	9	....	Feb. 15	21	....	Mar. 16	9	....
Feb. 3	12	....	Mar. 4	20	....	Apr. 2	6	....
Feb. 17	13	....	Mar. 14	16	....	Apr. 16	6½	....
Mar. 3	11	....	Apr. 1	16	....	May 4	8	....
Mar. 17	11½	....	Apr. 15	13	....	May 18	8	....
Apr. 4	8	....	May 2	13	....	June 1	9½	....
Apr. 18	4	....	May 16	11½	....	June 15	11	....
May 2	6½	....	June 3	11	....	July 2	8	....
May 16	7½	....	June 17	9	....	July 16	14	....
June 2	7½	....	July 1	11	....	Aug. 3	24	....
June 16	8	....	July 15	12	....	Aug. 17	11	....
July 4	10½	....	Aug. 1	13	....	Sept. 3	14	....
July 18	9½	....	Aug. 15	9	....	Sept. 17	17	....
Aug. 1	9	....	Sept. 2	9	....	Oct. 1	12	....
Aug. 15	10	....	Sept. 16	8	....	Oct. 15	17½	....
Sept. 1	9½	....	Oct. 3	16	....	Nov. 2	20	....
Sept. 15	10½	....	Oct. 17	16	....	Nov. 16	19	....
Oct. 3	10½	....	Nov. 4	15	....	Dec. 3	16½	....
Oct. 17	10	....	Nov. 18	16	....	Dec. 17	15	....
Nov. 3	9	....	Dec. 2	13	....	1871—Jan. 4	16	....
Nov. 14	8	....	Dec. 16	12½	....	Jan. 18	12½	....
Dec. 1	12	....	1869—Jan. 2	19	....	Feb. 1	14	....
Dec. 15	11	....	Jan. 16	16½	....	Feb. 15	15	....
1867—Jan. 5	5½	....	Feb. 3	15	....	Mar. 1	14	....
Jan. 16	8	....	Feb. 17	10½	....	Mar. 15	12	....
Feb. 2	13	....	Mar. 3	8½	....	Apr. 1	12½	....
Feb. 16	13	....	Mar. 17	7	....	Apr. 15	16½	....
Mar. 2	13	....	Apr. 3	5	....	May 3	11	....
Mar. 16	10	....	Apr. 17	4	....	May 17	16½	....
Apr. 3	6½	....	May 1	2	....	June 3	17	....
Apr. 17	7	....	May 15	7	....	June 17	12	....
May 1	8	....	June 2	15	....	July 1	17½	....
May 15	6	....	June 16	13	....	July 15	16	....
June 1	5	....	July 3	16	....	Aug. 2	10½	....
June 15	8	....	July 18	18	....	Aug. 16	17½	....
July 3	8	....	Aug. 4	7½	....	Sept. 2	21	....
July 17	8	....	Aug. 18	21	....	Sept. 16	24	....
Aug. 3	7	....	Sept. 1	18½	....	Oct. 4	22	....
Aug. 17	7	....	Sept. 15	21	....	Oct. 18	23	....
Sept. 4	4	....	Oct. 2	20	....	Nov. 1	19	....
Sept. 18	11	....	Oct. 16	14½	....	Nov. 15	15	....
Oct. 2	12	....	Nov. 3	17	....	Dec. 2	15	....
Oct. 16	22	....	Nov. 17	15½	....	Dec. 16	15	....
Nov. 2	19	....	Dec. 1	10	....	1872—Jan. 3	12	....
Nov. 16	17	....	Dec. 15	10	....	Jan. 17	15	....
Dec. 4	18	....	1870—Jan. 5	8	....	Feb. 3	13	....
Dec. 18	12	....	Jan. 15	10	....	Feb. 17	13	....
1868—Jan. 1	11½	....	Feb. 2	8½	....	Mar. 2	13½	....
Jan. 15	15	....	Feb. 16	6	....	Mar. 16	12	....

TABLE 129.—FREIGHT RATES CHARGED FOR THE TRANSPORTATION OF WHEAT AND PROVISIONS FROM NEW YORK TO LIVERPOOL, ETC.—Continued.

Date.	Wheat per bushel.	Provisions per ton.	Date.	Wheat per bushel.	Provisions per ton.	Date.	Wheat per bushel.	Provisions per ton.
	Cents.	*Dolls.*		*Cents.*	*Dolls.*		*Cents.*	*Dolls.*
1872—Apr. 3	8	....	1875—May 7	13	6.00	1877—Mar. 9	11	6.00
Apr. 17	8½	....	May 11	13	6.00	Mar. 16	9	4.80
May 1	8	....	May 14	12½	6.00	Mar. 23	8	4.20
May 15	9½	....	May 18	12	6.60	Mar. 30	8	3.60
June 1	14	....	May 21	13	6.60	Apr. 6	8	3.60
June 15	17	....	May 25	18	8.40	Apr. 13	12	4.80
July 3	15½	....	May 28	18	8.40	Apr. 20	11	4.80
July 17	18½	....	June 1	18	8.40	Apr. 27	16	9.60
Aug. 3	16	....	June 4	16	9.60	May 4	12	9.60
Aug. 17	17½	....	June 8	16	9.60	May 11	11	9.60
Sept. 4	20	....	June 11	17	9.60	May 18	12	9.60
Sept. 18	22	....	June 15	15	8.40	May 25	14	9.60
Oct. 2	24	....	June 18	15	8.40	June 1	13½	8.40
Oct. 16	20	....	June 22	15	8.40	June 8	11	9.60
Nov. 2	18	....	June 25	16	8.40	June 15	8	6.00
Nov. 16	18½	....	June 29	16	8.40	June 22	8½	6.00
Dec. 4	18½	....	1876—Jan. 7	18	9.60	June 29	10	6.00
Dec. 18	16	....	Jan. 14	17½	9.00	July 6	9	4.80
1873—Jan. 1	17	....	Jan. 21	16	7.80	July 13	10	4.80
Jan. 15	15½	....	Jan. 28	16	7.20	July 20	12	4.80
Feb. 1	14½	....	Feb. 4	16½	8.40	July 27	11	6.00
Feb. 15	14	....	Feb. 11	16	7.80	Aug. 3	12	6.00
Mar. 1	14	....	Feb. 18	16	7.20	Aug. 10	17	9.60
Mar. 15	14	....	Feb. 25	15	7.20	Aug. 17	16	9.60
Apr. 2	16	....	Mar. 3	15	7.20	Aug. 24	22	9.60
Apr. 16	17	....	Mar. 10	15	7.20	Aug. 31	23	9.60
May 3	11	....	Mar. 17	16	7.20	Sept. 7	20	10.80
May 17	17	....	Mar. 24	17	7.20	Sept. 14	21	9.60
June 4	22	....	Mar. 31	15	7.20	Sept. 21	18	8.40
June 18	24	....	Apr. 7	10	6.00	Sept. 28	18	8.40
July 2	24	....	Apr. 14	8	6.00	Oct. 5	17	8.40
July 16	25	....	Apr. 21	9	4.80	Oct. 12	18½	8.40
Aug. 2	27	....	Apr. 28	13	6.00	Oct. 19	20	8.40
Aug. 16	25	....	May 5	16	7.20	Oct. 26	20½	8.94
Sept. 3	26	....	May 12	17	8.40	Nov. 2	18½	8.40
Sept. 17	27	....	May 19	17	9.60	Nov. 9	17	7.68
Oct. 1	27	....	May 26	16	9.60	Nov. 16	16	7.68
Oct. 15	26	....	June 2	19	9.60	Nov. 23	16½	7.80
Nov. 1	27	....	June 9	18	9.60	Nov. 30	16	7.20
Nov. 15	28	....	June 20	17	9.60	Dec. 7	15	7.20
Dec. 3	24½	....	June 23	16½	9.60	Dec. 14	16	8.40
Dec. 17	24½	....	June 30	14	9.60	Dec. 21	17	9.60
1875—Jan. 5	23	$12.00	July 7	17	9.60	Dec. 28	19	9.60
Jan. 8	24	12.00	July 14	19	9.60	1878—Jan. 4	19	9.60
Jan. 12	21½	12.00	July 21	20	9.60	Jan. 11	20	9.60
Jan. 15	22	12.00	July 28	18½	9.60	Jan. 18	19	9.60
Jan. 19	21	12.00	Aug. 4	16	9.60	Jan. 25	19	9.60
Jan. 22	21	10.80	Aug. 11	17	9.60	Feb. 1	19	9.60
Jan. 26	21	9.60	Aug. 18	14	8.40	Feb. 8	19	9.60
Jan. 29	22	9.60	Aug. 25	15	8.40	Feb. 15	20	9.60
Feb. 2	21½	9.60	Sept. 1	16	8.40	Feb. 22	18	9.60
Feb. 5	21½	9.60	Sept. 8	17	9.00	Mar. 1	16	9.00
Feb. 9	22	9.60	Sept. 15	17	8.40	Mar. 8	15	7.80
Feb. 12	21	9.60	Sept. 22	15½	7.80	Mar. 15	13½	6.60
Feb. 16	15	7.20	Sept. 29	16	7.20	Mar. 22	13½	6.00
Feb. 19	16	7.20	Oct. 6	17½	7.20	Mar. 29	14	6.00
Feb. 23	17½	7.20	Oct. 13	16	7.80	Apr. 5	16½	7.20
Feb. 26	16	7.20	Oct. 20	18	8.40	Apr. 12	16	7.20
Mar. 2	14	7.20	Oct. 27	15	8.40	Apr. 23	14	6.60
Mar. 5	15½	7.20	Nov. 3	15½	8.40	Apr. 26	15	6.60
Mar. 9	15½	7.20	Nov. 10	15	8.40	May 3	17	6.60
Mar. 12	14	7.20	Nov. 17	16	10.80	May 10	16	7.20
Mar. 16	13½	6.60	Nov. 24	18	11.40	May 17	17	7.20
Mar. 19	15	7.20	Dec. 1	18	11.40	May 24	15½	7.20
Mar. 23	15	7.20	Dec. 8	18	11.28	May 31	16	7.20
Mar. 26	14½	7.20	Dec. 15	17	10.80	June 7	16½	7.20
Mar. 30	14	7.20	Dec. 22	16	10.80	June 14	16½	7.20
Apr. 2	14	6.60	Dec. 29	17	10.80	June 21	16½	7.20
Apr. 6	12	6.00	1877—Jan. 5	14	9.60	June 28	15½	7.80
Apr. 9	12	6.00	Jan. 12	14	9.60	July 9	14	7.80
Apr. 13	12	6.00	Jan. 19	13	9.60	July 12	14	7.20
Apr. 16	13	6.00	Jan. 26	12	8.40	July 19	13½	7.20
Apr. 20	13	6.00	Feb. 2	9½	7.20	July 26	12	7.20
Apr. 23	10	6.00	Feb. 9	11	7.20	Aug. 2	15½	7.20
Apr. 27	12	6.00	Feb. 16	10	7.20	Aug. 9	16	7.20
Apr. 30	13	6.00	Feb. 23	9½	6.60	Aug. 16	16	7.20
May 4	12	6.00	Mar. 2	9	6.00	Aug. 23	15	7.20

TABLE 129.—FREIGHT RATES CHARGED FOR THE TRANSPORTATION OF WHEAT AND PROVISIONS FROM NEW YORK TO LIVERPOOL, ETC.—Continued.

Date.	Wheat per bushel.	Provisions per ton.	Date.	Wheat per bushel.	Provisions per ton.	Date.	Wheat per bushel.	Provisions per ton.
	Cents.	*Dolls.*		*Cents.*	*Dolls.*		*Cents.*	*Dolls.*
1878—Aug. 30 ..	14	7.20	1880—Feb. 27 ..	11	7.20½	1881—Sept. 2 ..	8½	5.40
Sept. 6 ..	12½	7.20	Mar. 5 ..	10	6.60	Sept. 9 ..	6	4.80
Sept. 13 ..	11	6.60	Mar, 12 ..	10½	7.20	Sept. 16 ..	7	4.80
Sept. 20 ..	11	6.00	Mar. 19 ..	12½	7.20	Sept. 23 ..	5¼	4.80
Sept. 27 ..	12½	6.60	Mar. 30 ..	15	7.20	Sept. 30 ..	6	3.60
Oct. 4 ..	13	8.40	Apr. 2 ..	15	7.20	Oct. 7 ..	6	3.60
Oct. 11 ..	13	9.00	Apr. 9 ..	13½	7.20	Oct. 14 ..	6	3.00
Oct. 18 ..	15	9.00	Apr. 16 ..	13	7.20	Oct. 21 ..	5	2.40
Oct. 25 ..	15	9.00	Apr. 23 ..	9	7.20	Oct. 28 ..	6	2.40
Nov. 1 ..	16	9.00	Apr. 30 ..	9	6.00	Nov. 4 ..	7½	2.40
Nov. 8 ..	15½	9.00	May 7 ..	9	6.00	Nov. 11 ..	9	2.40
Nov. 15 ..	15	9.00	May 14 ..	9	6.00	Nov. 18 ..	8¾	3.00
Nov. 22 ..	15½	9.60	May 21 ..	10	6.00	Nov. 25 ..	8	3.00
Nov. 29 ..	15½	9.60	May 28 ..	8	6.00	Dec. 2 ..	7	3.00
Dec. 6 ..	14½	8.40	June 4 ..	8	6.00	Dec. 9 ..	6½	3.00
Dec. 13 ..	12	7.20	June 11 ..	9½	6.00	Dec. 16 ..	6	3.00
Dec. 20 ..	11	6.00	June 18 ..	11	6.00	Dec. 27 ..	5	3.00
Dec. 27 ..	11½	6.00	June 25 ..	12	6.00	Dec. 30 ..	5½	3.00
1879—Jan. 3 ..	10½	....	July 2 ..	12	6.00	1882—Jan. 6 ..	6½	4.20
Jan. 10 ..	12	....	July 9 ..	13	6.00	Jan. 13 ..	6½	4.80
Jan. 17 ..	11½	....	July 16 ..	13	6.60	Jan. 20 ..	7½	4.80
Jan. 25 ..	12½	....	July 23 ..	16½	6.60	Jan. 27 ..	7½	5.40
Jan. 31 ..	11½	....	July 30 ..	18½	7.20	Feb. 3 ..	7½	5.40
Feb. 7 ..	11½	....	Aug. 6 ..	17	8.40	Feb. 10 ..	7	5.40
Feb. 14 ..	12	....	Aug. 13 ..	14½	8.40	Feb, 17 ..	8½	4.80
Feb. 21 ..	12	....	Aug. 20 ..	13½	7.20	Feb. 24 ..	8½	4.80
Feb. 28 ..	12	....	Aug. 27 ..	14	7.20	Mar. 3 ..	7	4.20
Mar. 7 ..	12½	....	Sept. 3 ..	12½	7.20	Mar. 10 ..	7	4.20
Mar. 14 ..	13	....	Sept. 10 ..	11	7.20	Mar. 17 ..	5¾	3.00
Mar. 25 ..	12	....	Sept. 17 ..	11	7.20	Mar. 24 ..	4	2.40
Mar. 28 ..	11½	....	Sept. 24 ..	11	7.20	Mar. 31 ..	4	2.40
Apr. 4 ..	11½	....	Oct. 1 ..	11	7.20	Apr. 11 ..	1	1.80
Apr. 15 ..	12	....	Oct. 8 ..	13	7.20	Apr. 14 ..	½	1.80
Apr. 18 ..	12	....	Oct. 15 ..	12½	7.20	Apr. 21 ..	2	1.20
Apr. 25 ..	12½	....	Oct. 22 ..	12	7.20	Apr. 28 ..	3	1.20
May 2 ..	11	....	Oct. 29 ..	13	7.20	May 5 ..	2	1.20
May 9 ..	10½	....	Nov. 5 ..	14½	8.40	May 12 ..	½	1.20
May 16 ..	10½	....	Nov. 12 ..	15	9.60	May 19 ..	1	1.20
May 23 ..	10¼	....	Nov. 19 ..	15½	10.80	May 26 ..	....	1.20
May 27 ..	10½	....	Nov. 26 ..	15½	10.20	June 2	....	.60
June 6 ..	10½	....	Dec. 3 ..	15	10.20	June 9 ..	4	1.20
June 13 ..	10	....	Dec. 10 ..	15	9.60	June 16 ..	7	3.60
June 20 ..	9½	....	Dec. 17 ..	15	8.40	June 23 ..	8	4.80
June 27 ..	8½	....	Dec. 29 ..	13½	8.40	June 30 ..	6	4.80
July 8 ..	8	....	1881—Jan. 7 ..	13	7.20	July 7 ..	8	4.20
July 11 ..	10	....	Jan. 14 ..	14½	7.20	July 14 ..	8	3.60
July 18 ..	13	....	Jan. 21 ..	14	7.68	July 21 ..	10	4.80
July 25 ..	15	....	Jan. 28 ..	12	7.20	July 28 ..	12	6.00
Aug. 1 ..	15½	....	Feb. 4 ..	10½	7.20	Aug. 4 ..	10½	4.80
Aug. 8 ..	17	....	Feb. 11 ..	10½	7.20	Aug. 11 ..	8	4.80
Aug. 15 ..	15	....	Feb. 18 ..	11	7.80	Aug. 18 ..	9	4.20
Aug. 22 ..	15½	....	Feb. 25 ..	11	7.80	Aug. 25 ..	9	4.20
Aug. 29 ..	15½	....	Mar. 4 ..	....	7.80	Sept. 1 ..	10½	4.20
Sept. 5 ..	14	....	Mar. 11 ..	10	7.20	Sept. 8 ..	10	6.00
Sept. 12 ..	13	....	Mar. 18 ..	9	6.00	Sept. 15 ..	10	4.80
Sept. 19 ..	15½	....	Mar. 25 ..	9	5.40	Sept. 22 ..	8	4.20
Sept. 26 ..	15½	....	Apr. 1 ..	9	4.80	Sept. 29 ..	7	4.20
Oct. 3 ..	18	....	Apr. 8 ..	9½	4.80	Oct. 6 ..	9	6.00
Oct. 10 ..	18	....	Apr. 19 ..	8½	4.80	Oct. 13 ..	9	7.20
Oct. 17 ..	17	....	Apr. 22 ..	8	4.80	Oct. 20 ..	7½	7.20
Oct. 24 ..	15½	....	Apr. 29 ..	5½	4.20	Oct. 27 ..	7½	6.00
Oct. 30 ..	13½	....	May 6 ..	4	3.60	Nov. 3 ..	10	6.00
Nov. 7 ..	16	....	May 13 ..	4	3.00	Nov. 10 ..	10	6.60
Nov. 14 ..	13	....	May 20 ..	7	3.00	Nov. 17 ..	10½	6.00
Nov. 21 ..	12½	....	May 27 ..	5	2.40	Nov. 24 ..	13	4.80
Nov. 28 ..	12½	....	June 3 ..	6½	2.40	Dec. 1 ..	14	7.20
Dec. 5 ..	10½	....	June 10 ..	7	2.40	Dec. 8 ..	17	9.60
Dec. 12 ..	8	....	June 17 ..	7	3.00	Dec. 15 ..	13½	9.60
Dec. 19 ..	8	....	June 24 ..	6	3.00	Dec. 22 ..	13	9.60
Dec. 30 ..	6	....	July 5 ..	7½	3.00	Dec. 29 ..	14	8.40
1880—Jan. 6 ..	6	3.60	July 15 ..	9	3.60	1883—Jan.. 5 ..	15	7.80
Jan. 16 ..	8	4.80	July 22 ..	9¼	3.60	Jan. 12 ..	15	8.40
Jan. 23 ..	8	4.80	July 29 ..	11	5.40	Jan. 19 ..	14	8.40
Jan. 30 ..	6	4.80	Aug. 5 ..	10¼	5.40	Jan. 26 ..	13	8.40
Feb. 6 ..	5½	4.20	Aug. 12 ..	12	5.40	Feb. 2 ..	14	7.80
Feb. 13 ..	6	4.20	Aug. 19 ..	9	5.40	Feb 9 ..	14½	8.40
Feb. 20 ..	5½	4.20	Aug. 26 ..	9	5.40	Feb. 16 ..	12½	8.40

TABLE 129.—FREIGHT RATES CHARGED FOR THE TRANSPORTATION OF WHEAT AND PROVISIONS FROM NEW YORK TO LIVERPOOL, ETC.—Continued.

Date.	Wheat per bushel.	Provisions per ton.
	Cents.	*Dolls.*
1883—Feb. 23 ..	12	7.74
Mar. 2 ..	11	5.40
Mar. 9 ..	9	5.40
Mar. 16 ..	8	4.80
Mar. 20 ..	6½	3.60
Mar. 27 ..	4½	2.70
Apr. 6 ..	5	3.60
Apr. 13 ..	6½	4.80
Apr. 20 ..	5½	3.72
Apr. 27 ..	2½	2.40
May 4 ..	5	2.40
May 11 ..	7	3.00
May 18 ..	6	3.00
May 25 ..	6½	3.00
June 1 ..	7	3.00
June 8 ..	5	3.00
June 15 ..	4	3.00
June 22 ..	6	3.00
June 29 ..	6	3.00
July 6 ..	7	3.00
July 13 ..	7¼	3.00
July 20 ..	10	3.60
July 27 ..	10	3.60
Aug. 3 ..	9	3.60
Aug. 10 ..	8	4.20
Aug. 17 ..	7½	4.20
Aug. 24 ..	5½	3.60
Aug. 31 ..	5½	3.60
Sept. 7 ..	7¼	3.00
Sept. 14 ..	7	3.00
Sept. 21 ..	7½	3.00
Sept. 28 ..	8	4.20
Oct. 5 ..	8½	3.60
Oct. 12 ..	9	4.80
Oct. 19 ..	10	6.00
Oct. 26 ..	10	6.00
Nov. 3 ..	10	6.60
Nov. 10 ..	8	6.60
Nov. 17 ..	9½	5.28
Nov. 24 ..	9	6.00
Dec. 1 ..	8	6.00
Dec. 8 ..	8	5.40
Dec. 15 ..	6	4.20
Dec. 22 ..	6	4.20
Dec. 29 ..	3	2.00
1884—Jan. 4 ..	4	4.80
Jan. 11 ..	7½	4.80
Jan. 18 ..	6	6.00
Jan. 25 ..	8	6.00
Feb. 1 ..	6½	4.80
Feb. 8 ..	6	4.80
Feb. 15 ..	5	4.80
Feb. 22 ..	5	4.80
Feb. 29 ..	3½	3.00
Mar. 7 ..	4	3.00
Mar. 14 ..	2	3.00
Mar. 21 ..	2	3.00
Mar. 28 ..	4	2.40
Apr. 4 ..	4	3.00
Apr. 15 ..	4	2.40
Apr. 22 ..	4½	2.40
Apr. 29 ..	4½	2.40
May 9 ..	2	2.10
May 16 ..	2	2.40
1884—May 23 ..	5½	3.60
May 30 ..	5½	4.20
June 6 ..	6	4.20
June 13 ..	6	4.20
June 20 ..	6½	4.20
June 27 ..	6½	3.60
July 4 ..	6½	4.20
July 11 ..	9¼	4.80
July 18 ..	10	4.80
July 25 ..	9½	5.40
Aug. 1 ..	10	5.40
Aug. 8 ..	11	6.00
Aug. 15 ..	9	6.00
Aug. 22 ..	8	6.00
Aug. 29 ..	9	4.80
Sept. 5 ..	5	3.60
Sept. 12 ..	5	3.60
Sept. 19 ..	6	3.60
Sept. 26 ..	7	4.20
Oct. 3 ..	7½	6.00
Oct. 10 ..	7	6.00
Oct. 17 ..	7	6.00
Oct. 24 ..	7	6.00
Oct. 31 ..	7½	6.00
Nov. 7 ..	10	6.60
Nov. 14 ..	12	8.40
Nov. 21 ..	12	7.20
Nov. 28 ..	12	7.20
Dec. 5 ..	12	8.40
Dec. 12 ..	12	7.20
Dec. 19 ..	12	7.20
Dec. 26 ..	13	6.60
1887—Jan.......	9	5.47½
Feb.......	7¼	5.10
Mar	3⅝	3.12
Apr	2	2.25
May......	4	2.10
June	4	2.10
July	6	3.60
Aug......	4⅛	3.97½
Sept	2⅞	2.66½
Oct.......	5⅝	3.60
Nov	6½	4.50
Dec	5½	4.26
1888—Jan.......	4⅛	3.52
Feb	2½	2.85
Mar	1¼	1.85
Apr	¾	1.65
May......	1¾	1.68
June	2½	2.14
July......	3⅞	2.34
Aug	7	3.41
Sept	9¾	6.00
Oct	7¾	6.00
Nov	11	6.96
Dec	10	7.08
1889—Jan.......	9½	3.96
Feb.......	9⅜	3.15
Mar	5⅞	2.55
Apr	4⅞	2.40
May......	6 4/11	2.22
June	5¾	2.25
July......	6⅞	2.58
Aug	4¼	3.75
1889—Sept	9⅞	3.48
Oct	9½	3.80
Nov	9¼	3.82½
Dec	9⅞	4.05
1890—Jan.......	11⅛	7.50
Feb.......	10¾	7.35
Mar	8	5.77½
Apr	4	4.47
May......	4⅛	3.18¾
June......	3¾	3.00
July	4¼	3.30
Aug	2	2.70
Sept	1⅜	2.40
Oct.	⅜	1.86½
Nov.	4½	3.30
Dec	5	4.35
1891—Jan	7¼	4.87
Feb.......	4¾	4.65
Mar	3	3.41¼
Apr	3	3.00
May......	3¼	2.24½
June	4	2.85
July	4	3.30
Aug	6	3.30
Sept	8⅝	4.42½
Oct	11⅛	6.18
Nov	11½	6.90
Dec.......	8¾	6.36
1892—Jan.......	9	......
Feb.......	6⅜	......
Mar	7½	......
Apr	3¾	......
May......	4⅞	......
June	4	......
July	5½	......
Aug	4¼	......
Sept	4	......
Oct	6	......
Nov	4⅞	......

NOTE.—For years 1887 to 1892, figures shown are monthly averages.

AVERAGE FREIGHT RATES PER TON PER MILE.

No presentation of the tendency toward lower charges for freight transportation by railways is at once so comprehensive, accurate, and readily understood as a statement of the average charges per ton per mile prevailing during successive periods. Such a statement has the advantage over all others that no portion of traffic is excluded, but that all business, whether through or local, of relatively great or inconsiderable importance, is represented in the final average.

Table No. 130 following is arranged to show the average freight rates per ton per mile charged by a number of important railways which have been selected with a view to the presentation of fairly representative data covering each of the physical divisions of the railway system. It has been found practicable to include in this table the average rates for several roads from 1852; many others are given for periods covering their entire existence, and it may be said that the table as here presented is much more complete than any heretofore published.

The full significance of these data cannot be appreciated by a merely superficial examination; they should be considered in connection with tables Nos. 131, 132, and 133, showing, respectively, the number of millions of tons of freight carried 1 mile, the number of tons carried regardless of distance, and the gross freight earnings of the same railways. Selecting as an individual example the Fitchburg Railroad, it is observed that its gross revenue from freight in 1852 was 3.12 cents for each ton carried 1 mile, or more than three times the amount received in 1892 for the same service, which was 0.925 cent.

The earliest years for which it is possible to present statistics of the amount of traffic for this road is 1860. During that year the average rate per ton per mile was 4.10 cents, the aggregate transportation of freight was equivalent to the carriage of 9,000,000 tons 1 mile, and the actual number of tons carried was 395,003. During 1892 the tonnage carried was 4,570,377, and the ton mileage 496,000,000. The average distance carried (and it should be remembered that this is a most important factor in the tendency toward cheaper transportation) increased from 22.7 miles in 1860 to 108.5 miles in 1892.

Had the tonnage of 1892 been carried at the rates of 1860, the gross freight earnings would have amounted to more than twenty-one millions, or over sixteen millions more than was actually received. Conversely, had the rates of 1892 been charged upon the business of 1860, the gross freight revenue, which was $369,000, would have been only about $84,000, a sum probably wholly insufficient to have paid the expenses of operation.

Such speculation, however interesting, can have little practical value. The intimate connection between the rates charged and the quantity of traffic is so thoroughly understood at the present time as to require little or no comment. That an increase in traffic from 395,000 to 4,570,377 tons carried, and from 9,000,000 to 496,000,000 ton miles, could not have taken place without a substantial reduction in charges, is as evident as that such an increase in quantity of traffic itself makes the required reduction in charges practicable.

The New York, Lake Erie and Western road presents a curious contrast to the Fitchburg Railroad in that, while the average distance freight is transported on the latter has increased to nearly four times that of 1860, the former carried traffic an average distance of only 153 miles in 1892 against 222 miles in 1852. Thus, whatever may be said in the case of the Fitchburg Railroad as to the apparent reduction being largely the result of the present preponderance of long-distance traffic, which is naturally taken at lower rates, it must be said that the reduction made by the Erie from 1.95 cents per ton per mile in 1852 to 0.614 cent in 1892 is probably the result of more economical methods and the greater volume of traffic.

The student of this table will undoubtedly find it practicable to carry on similar comparisons almost indefinitely, and will find that each of the roads shown presents some interesting and valuable contribution to the subject of reductions in railway freight charges.

TABLE 130.—AVERAGE FREIGHT RATES PER TON PER MILE CHARGED BY IMPORTANT RAILWAYS NAMED DURING EACH YEAR FROM 1852, FOR WHICH SUCH DATA CAN BE OBTAINED.

[Average rates for the years 1888 to 1892 are from reports made by the railways to the Interstate Commerce Commission; those for previous years have been compiled from sources believed to be reliable, and, with few exceptions, have been verified by officials of the roads. Figures for 1892 are as reported and have not been verified by the statistician.]

Years.	Boston and Albany R. R.	Boston and Worcester R. R.*	Western R. R.*	Fitchburg R. R.	Central Vermont R. R.	New York and New England R. R.	New York, New Haven and Hartford R. R.†	Canadian Pacific Rwy.	Delaware, Lackawanna and Western R. R.	New York, Ontario and Western Rwy.	Lehigh Valley R. R.	New York Central R. R.‡	Lake Shore and Michigan Southern Rwy.§	Michigan Central R. R.	New York, Chicago and St. Louis R. R.	Cleveland, Cincinnati, Chicago and St. Louis Rwy.
	Cts.	*Cts.*	*Cts.*	*Cts.*	*Cts.*	*Cts.*	*Cts.*	*Cts.*	*Cts.*	*Cts.*	*Cts.*	*Cts.*	*Cts.*	*Cts.*	*Cts.*	*Cts.*
1852	....	....	....	3.12	....	....	....	....	....	....	....	....	....	....	....	....
1853	....	....	....	2.77	....	....	....	....	....	....	....	....	....	....	....	3.03
1854	....	3.36	2.86	3.29	....	....	....	....	....	....	....	....	3.51	....	....	2.66
1855	....	3.68	2.83	3.66	....	....	....	....	....	....	....	3.02	3.21	....	....	2.60
1856	....	4.14	3.13	4.24	....	....	3.80	....	....	....	....	2.95	2.96	....	....	2.55
1857	....	4.25	3.22	3.93	....	....	4.44	....	....	....	....	3.12	2.74	....	....	2.52
1858	....	3.64	2.93	3.78	....	....	4.18	....	....	....	....	2.59	2.38	....	....	2.26
1859	....	3.87	2.96	3.88	....	....	4.20	....	....	....	....	2.13	2.29	....	....	1.97
1860	....	3.58	2.54	4.10	....	....	4.04	....	....	....	....	2.05	2.16	2.18	....	2.12
1861	....	3.09	2.43	3.94	....	....	4.54	....	....	....	....	1.96	2.09	1.96	....	1.86
1862	....	....	2.60	3.75	....	....	4.50	....	....	....	....	2.22	2.10	1.91	....	1.98
1863	....	....	2.75	3.26	....	....	4.09	....	....	....	....	2.38	2.30	1.99	....	2.13
1864	....	....	3.01	3.51	....	....	4.21	....	....	....	....	2.70	2.83	2.26	....	2.64
1865	....	3,88	3.55	4.09	....	....	4.76	....	....	....	....	3.26	2.90	3.06	....	2.65
1866	....	3.63	3.16	4.33	2.85	....	5.52	....	....	....	....	2.87	2.48	2.60	....	2.37
1867	....	3.36	2.98	4.21	2.75	....	4.94	....	....	....	....	2.46	2.43	2.49	....	2.16
1868	2.81	....	....	4.08	2.53	6.40	5.12	....	....	....	2.13	2.59	2.34	2.45	....	1.94
1869	2.43	....	....	4.35	2.35	5.53	5.69	....	....	....	2.40	2.20	1.71	2.09	....	1.80
1870	2.19	....	....	4.31	1.86	4.46	6.23	....	....	5.87	2.27	1.88	1.50	1.98	....	1.52
1871	2.09	....	....	....	1.75	4.54	5.69	....	....	2.60	2.25	1.62	1.39	1 61	....	1.36
1872	2.02	....	....	3.92	....	4.27	3.74	....	....	2.50	2.01	1.59	1.37	1.56	....	1.34
1873	1.96	....	....	3.77	1.83	4.42	3.78	....	....	2.47	2.11	1.57	1.34	1.57	....	1.36
1874	1.82	....	....	4.32	1.83	4.80	3.70	....	....	2.28	2.13	1.46	1.18	1.29	....	1.19
1875	1.53	....	....	4.13	....	4.81	4.10	....	....	2.61	2.06	1.27	1.01	1.16	....	1.01
1876	1.28	....	....	2.51	....	4.72	3.54	....	....	2.73	1.72	1.05	.82	1.03	....	.81
1877	1.21	....	....	2.08	1.41	4.22	3.34	....	....	2.75	1.40	1.01	.86	.98	....	.89
1878	1.13	....	....	1.60	1.24	2.60	2.87	....	....	2.93	1.36	.93	.73	.85	....	.75
1879	1.10	....	....	1.30	1.08	2.86	2.36	....	....	2.81	1.06	.78	.64	.69	....	.70
1880	1.21	....	....	1.36	1.13	2.86	2.09	....	1.30	2.87	1.34	.87	.75	.84	....	.79
1881	1.04	....	....	1.26	1.03	2.20	1.63	....	1.28	2.40	1.27	.78	.62	.72	....	.67
1882	1.07	....	....	1.17	1.02	1.77	1.76	....	1.19	1.97	1.33	.73	.63	.77	....	.71
1883	1.19	....	....	1.19	1.09	1.38	1.89	....	1.06	1.93	1.33	.91	.73	.83	.60	.75
1884	1.09	....	....	1.09	1.11	1.41	1.96	1.45	.97	1.55	1.26	.83	.65	.65	.48	.63
1885	.94	....	....	1.06	1.00	1.81	1.96	1.20	.94	1.20	1.07	.68	.55	.56	.44	.58
1886	1.10	....	....	1.07	.91	1.67	2.00	1.10	.93	1.53	1.11	.76	.64	.69	.54	.68
1887	1.10	....	....	1.13	.91	1.63	1.95	1.01	.96	1.65	1.12	.78	.67	.69	.55	.70
1888	1.099	....	....	1.116	.914	1.192	1.752	1.007	1.070	1.395	1.069	.753	.673	.702	.577	.685
1889	1.030	....	....	1.015	.869	1.344	1.830	.949	.983	1.400	.942	.712	.632	.702	.506	.675
1890	1.105	....	....	.995	.777	1.220	1.810	.885	.948	1.271	.855	.730	.664	.701	.524	.674
1891	1.089	....	....	.991	....	1.140	1.793	.871	.896	1.033	.774	.740	.630	.723	.519	.683
1892	1.060	....	....	.925	....	1.155	1.756	.869	.903	.939	....	.700	.602	.687	.537	.710

* Consolidated during 1867, forming Boston and Albany R. R.

† Formed by consolidation, in 1872, of New York and New Haven and Hartford and New Haven Railroads. Figures prior to 1872 are for New York and New Haven only.

‡ Figures prior to 1870 do not include Hudson River R. R.

§ Figures prior to 1865 show Michigan Southern and Northern Indiana Rwy.

TABLE 130.—AVERAGE FREIGHT RATES PER TON PER MILE CHARGED BY IMPORTANT RAILWAYS NAMED, ETC.—Continued.

Years.	New York, Lake Erie and Western R. R.	New York, Pensylvania and Ohio R. R.	Chicago and Erie R. R.	Pennsylvania R. R.	Pittsburg, Fort Wayne and Chicago Rwy.	Pittsburg, Cincinnati and St. Louis Rwy.	Chicago, St. Louis and Pittsburg R. R.	Pittsburg, Cincinnati, Chicago and St. Louis Rwy.	Baltimore and Ohio R. R.	Baltimore and Ohio Southwestern R. R.	Ohio and Mississippi Rwy.	Cincinnati, Hamilton and Dayton R. R.	Wabash R. R.	Louisville, New Albany and Chicago Rwy.	Chicago and Grand Trunk Rwy.	Chicago, Milwaukee and St. Paul Rwy.
	Cts.	Cts.	Cts.	Cts.	Cts.	Cts.	Cts.	Cts.	Cts.	Cts.	Cts.	Cts.	Cts.	Cts.	Cts.	Cts.
1852	1.95	.....	.....	5.42	.....	.....	.....	.....	.....	.....	.....	.....	.....	.....	.....	.....
1853	2.50	.....	.....	3.76	.....	.....	.....	.....	.....	.....	.....	.....	.....	.....	.....	.....
1854	2.58	.....	.....	3.29	.....	.....	.....	.....	.....	.....	.....	.....	.....	.....	.....	.....
1855	2.42	.....	.....	2.75	.....	.....	.....	.....	.....	.....	.....	.....	.....	.....	.....	.....
1856	2.48	.....	.....	2.71	.....	.....	.....	.....	.....	.....	.....	.....	.....	.....	.....	.....
1857	2.46	.....	.....	2.41	2.27	.....	.....	.....	.....	.....	.....	.....	.....	.....	.....	.....
1858	2.32	.....	.....	2.18	1.90	.....	.....	.....	.....	.....	3.25	.....	.....	.....	.....	.....
1859	1.62	.....	.....	2.03	1.65	.....	.....	.....	.....	.....	2.75	.....	.....	.....	.....	.....
1860	1.81	.....	.....	1.96	1.67	.....	.....	.....	.....	.....	2.38	.....	.....	.....	.....	.....
1861	1.77	.....	.....	1.93	1.71	.....	.....	.....	.....	.....	2.20	.....	.....	.....	.....	.....
1862	1.89	.....	.....	2.04	1.90	.....	.....	.....	.....	.....	2.35	.....	.....	.....	.....	.....
1863	2.09	.....	.....	2.19	2.01	.....	.....	.....	.....	.....	2.81	.....	.....	.....	.....	3.34
1864	2.34	.....	.....	2.50	2.38	.....	.....	.....	.....	.....	.....	.....	.....	.....	.....	3.82
1865	2.76	.....	.....	2.72	2.44	.....	.....	.....	.....	.....	3.43	.....	.....	.....	.....	4.11
1866	2.43	.....	.....	2.32	2.02	.....	.....	.....	.....	.....	.....	.....	.....	.....	.....	3.76
1867	2.04	.....	.....	2.08	1.95	.....	.....	.....	.....	.....	.....	.....	.....	.....	.....	3.94
1868	1.81	.....	.....	1.86	1.70	.....	.....	.....	.....	.....	.....	.....	.....	.....	.....	3.49
1869	1.54	1.26	.....	1.66	1.62	1.81	5.60	.....	.....	.....	2.24	.....	.....	.....	.....	3.10
1870	1.33	1.43	.....	1.50	1.45	.....	.....	.....	.....	.....	2.03	.....	.....	.....	.....	2.82
1871	1.43	1.34	.....	1.35	1.43	.....	.....	.....	.....	.....	2.14	.....	.....	.....	.....	2.54
1872	1.53	1.50	.....	1.46	1.40	1.41	1.27	.....	.....	.....	1.71	2.71	1.49	.....	.....	2.43
1873	1.45	1.45	.....	1.44	1.40	1.40	1.18	.....	.....	.....	1.81	.....	1.41	.....	.....	2.50
1874	1.31	1.19	.....	1.29	1.26	1.30	1.09	.....	.....	1.24	1.59	.....	1.26	.....	.....	2.38
1875	1.21	.98	.....	1.13	1.11	1.12	1.05	.....	.....	1.19	1.54	2.31	1.11	.....	.....	2.10
1876	1.10	.91	.....	.95	.93	.88	.85	.....	.....	1.03	1.27	2.04	.....	.....	.....	2.04
1877	.96	.91	.....	1.01	1.09	.93	.90	.....	.....	.85	1.04	1.54	.83	.....	.....	2.08
1878	.97	.84	.....	.93	.87	.79	.78	.....	.....	.....	1.14	1.56	.....	.....	.....	1.80
1879	.78	.70	.....	.82	.76	.72	.70	.....	.....	.....	.99	1.40	.....	.....	.....	1.72
1880	.84	.83	.....	.92	.92	.84	.80	.....	.....	.....	1.09	1.31	.86	.....	.62	1.76
1881	.81	.67	.....	.86	.75	.72	.67	.....	.....	.....	1.04	1.26	.93	.....	.52	1.70
1882	.75	.....	.....	.87	.75	.73	.66	.....	.....	.....	1.17	1.18	.95	.99	.58	1.48
1883	.79	.....	.....	.88	.79	.76	.72	.....	.....	.....	1.00	1.15	.95	.95	.66	1.39
1884	.72	.....	.52	.80	.67	.63	.60	.....	.....	.95	1.05	1.07	.86	.98	.57	1.29
1885	.66	.....	.44	.70	.58	.53	.52	.....	.....	.95	.82	.98	.80	.83	.52	1.28
1886	.66	.....	.42	.75	.69	.62	.59	.....	.....	.93	.70	.98	.82	.82	.62	1.17
1887	.69	.....	.46	.73	.72	.66	.63	.....	.....	.84	.72	.91	.86	.80	.59	1.09
1888	.716	.....	.511	.723	.66	.727	.646	.....	.655	.84	.763	.869	.744	.855	.590	1.020
1889	.644	.....	.525	.685	.69	.646	.594	.....	.637	.757	.813	.865	.709	.853	.582	1.067
1890	.665	.....	.541	.661	.69	.669	.626	.....	.636	.791	.854	.873	.647	.917	.600	.995
1891	.658	.....	.532	.656	.....	.657	.627	.736	.643	.839	.937	.858	.733	.863	.569	1.003
1892	.614	.....	.525	.647	.....	.....	.....	.706	.651	.765	.911	.828	.705	.868	.593	1.026

TABLE 130.—AVERAGE FREIGHT RATES PER TON PER MILE CHARGED BY IMPORTANT RAILWAYS NAMED, ETC.—Continued.

Years.	Chicago and Northwestern Rwy.	Chicago, Burlington and Quincy R. R., east of Missouri River.	Chicago, Rock Island and Pacific Rwy.	Chicago and Alton R. R.	Illinois Central R. R.	Wisconsin Central Lines.	Northern Pacific R. R.	Union Pacific Rwy.	Atchison, Topeka and Santa Fe R. R.	Denver and Rio Grande R. R.	Texas and Pacific Rwy.	Chesapeake and Ohio Rwy.	Louisville and Nashville R. R.	Richmond and Danville R. R.	Mobile and Ohio Rwy.	Chicago, Burlington and Quincy, west of Missouri River.
	Cts.	Cts.	Cts.	Cts.	Cts.	Cts.	Cts.	Cts.	Cts.	Cts.	Cts.	Cts.	Cts.	Cts.	Cts.	Cts.
1852	....	....	....	....	....	....	....	....	....	....	....	....	....	....	....	....
1853	....	....	....	....	....	....	....	....	....	....	....	....	....	....	....	....
1854	....	....	....	....	....	....	....	....	....	....	....	....	....	....	....	....
1855	....	....	....	....	....	....	....	....	....	....	....	....	....	....	....	....
1856	....	....	....	....	....	....	....	....	....	....	....	....	....	....	....	....
1857	....	....	....	....	....	....	....	....	....	....	....	....	....	....	....	....
1858	....	....	....	....	....	....	....	....	....	....	....	6.04	....	....	....	....
1859	....	....	....	....	2.14	....	....	....	....	....	....	6.61	....	....	....	....
1860	....	....	....	....	2.04	....	....	....	....	....	....	6.41	....	....	....	....
1861	....	....	....	....	1.91	....	....	....	....	....	....	5.82	....	....	....	....
1862	....	....	....	....	1.96	....	....	....	....	....	....	7.57	....	....	....	....
1863	....	2.35	2.68	....	1.95	....	....	....	....	....	....	9.86	....	....	....	....
1864	....	2.55	2.56	....	2.51	....	....	....	....	....	....	24.55	....	....	....	....
1865	....	3.64	3.51	....	3.10	....	....	....	....	....	....	....	....	....	....	....
1866	....	3.70	3.45	....	3.19	....	....	....	....	....	....	6.61	5.37	....	....	....
1867	....	....	3.05	....	2.90	....	....	....	....	....	....	5.22	4.13	....	....	....
1868	3.13	3.18	3.35	....	2.46	....	....	....	....	....	....	4.47	4.14	....	....	....
1869	....	3.25	2.98	....	2.49	....	....	....	....	....	....	5.08	3.31	5.99	....	....
1870	3.09	3.06	2.74	....	2.31	....	....	....	....	....	....	4.86	3.01	5.37	4.48	....
1871	2.87	2.39	2.64	....	2.32	....	....	....	....	....	....	4.97	2.57	5.43	4.16	....
1872	2.61	2.20	2.49	....	2.16	....	....	2.34	....	6.14	....	4.08	2.30	4.96	3.77	....
1873	2.35	1.92	2.29	....	2.20	....	....	2.17	3.10	5.38	....	2.19	2.21	4.83	3.83	....
1874	2.28	1.90	2.07	2.12	2.09	....	....	1.84	3.04	4.85	....	1.50	2.15	4.01	3.53	....
1875	2.10	1.95	1.92	1.89	1.93	2.57	....	2.07	2.41	4.49	5.13	1.48	1.92	3.49	3.07	....
1876	1.95	....	1.91	1.63	1.80	2.17	....	2.04	2.73	3.37	3.97	1.20	1.85	3.46	2.85	....
1877	1.86	....	1.71	1.45	1.82	2.02	....	1.92	2.55	3.09	3.34	1.10	1.76	2.92	2.63	....
1878	1.72	....	1.56	1.30	1.64	2.13	....	1.96	2.42	....	3.26	.98	1.71	2.87	2.29	....
1879	1.56	1.11	1.43	1.05	1.52	1.93	2.59	1.70	2.51	....	3.12	.86	1.56	2.43	2.48	....
1880	1.49	1.08	1.21	1.21	1.54	1.96	1.96	....	2.38	....	3.09	.87	1.60	2.16	2.20	3.15
1881	1.47	1.15	1.22	1.24	1.52	2.01	2.16	2.23	2.28	3.62	3.36	.89	1.50	2.07	2.06	3.20
1882	1.47	1.09	1.28	1.26	1.42	2.11	2.01	2.21	2.29	3.65	2.28	.79	1.35	1.95	2.15	3.04
1883	1.42	1.03	1.17	1.13	1.43	2.36	2.07	2.05	1.99	2.89	1.76	.72	1.32	2.06	2.28	2.71
1884	1.31	.97	1.10	1.01	1.37	2.11	1.90	1.80	1.93	2.90	1.64	.67	1.24	2.09	1.97	2.46
1885	1.19	.95	1.04	1.01	1.31	1.77	1.78	1.72	1.75	2.72	1.56	.55	1.16	1.95	1.70	2.24
1886	1.19	.94	1.07	.96	1.16	1.44	1.67	1.58	1.60	2.60	1.67	.54	1.10	1.93	1.51	2.04
1887	1.10	.87	1.01	.95	1.09	1.30	1.63	1.42	1.35	2.39	1.46	.54	1.02	1.92	1.32	1.81
1888	.983	.78	.964	.973	1.069	....	1.437	1.170	1.289	2.346	1.314	.54	1.049	1.710	1.018	1.42
1889	1.013	.88	.971	1.002	.839	.971	1.429	1.166	1.289	2.212	1.435	.538	.998	1.476	.958	1.60
1890	.977	.79	.995	.898	.942	.936	1.430	1.138	1.129	2.054	1.249	.561	.972	1.310	.924	1.49
1891	1.028	.88	1.039	.980	.934	.988	1.382	1.131	1.175	2.006	1.279	.525	.968	1.416	.867	1.41
1892	1.013	.987	1.055	.973	.908	.868	1.402	1.081	1.130	1.863	1.226	....	.948	1.355	.845	....

FREIGHT TONNAGE AND EARNINGS OF THE PRINCIPAL RAILWAYS IN THE UNITED STATES.

For the purpose of showing the increase which has taken place in the freight traffic of the United States data have been collected which are shown in the following tables.

The first table shows the number of tons of freight carried one mile by the more important railways of the United States, which, for convenience of expression, has been reduced to millions of tons. The growth of the business of each line is shown from as early a date as the data were available. The carriers selected are the important roads in different sections of the country, and represent about 60 per cent of the total railway mileage of the United States.

The second table shows the aggregate tonnage carried by various important roads in different sections of the country. The data of this table is shown, for a majority of the roads, for a period of thirty years.

The third table shows for the same carriers the gross freight earnings for as many years as such data could be obtained. The data included in these tables for years prior to 1888 have been collected from what are believed to be the most reliable sources available, while for the years from 1888 to 1892, inclusive, the figures shown are those given in the reports of the several railways to the Interstate Commerce Commission.

TABLE 131.—NUMBER OF MILLIONS OF TONS OF FREIGHT CARRIED ONE MILE BY THE MORE IMPORTANT RAILWAYS OF THE UNITED STATES DURING EACH YEAR FROM 1852, FOR WHICH SUCH DATA CAN BE OBTAINED.

[Compiled from reports to Interstate Commerce Commission and various numbers of Poor's Manual.]

Years.	Boston and Albany R. R.	Fitchburg R. R.	Central Vermont R. R.	New York and New England R. R.	New York, New Haven and Hartford R. R.	Canadian Pacific Rwy.	Delaware, Lackawanna and Western Rwy.	New York, Ontario and Western R. R.	Philadelphia and Reading R. R.	Lehigh Valley R. R.	New York Central and Hudson River R. R.	Lake Shore and Michigan Southern Rwy.	Michigan Central R. R.	New York, Chicago and St. Louis Rwy.	Cleveland, Cincinnati, Chicago and St. Louis Rwy.	New York, Lake Erie and Western R. R.
1852																97
1853																102
1854											99					1g1
1855											115					151
1856											166					183
1857											166					165
1858											161					166
1859	53										187					147
1860	56	9									239					214
1861	61	8									280					251
1862	67	9			3						358		82			351
1863	69	13			4					2	387		100			404
1864	76	14			6					2	387		92			422
1865	70	14			6					2	319		73			389
1866	96	14			7					3	389		85			478
1867	107	14		3	7					3	4[illegible]5		92			550
1868	121	16	47	9	21					4	455		101		95	596
1869	159	17	54	6	25					4	58[illegible]		132		116	818
1870	149	16	66	6	29			3		5	769	574	133		149	899
1871	227			8	29			8		4	888	731	191		211	897
1872	290	20	*164	9	39			24		6	1, 021	925	217		256	951
1873	318	21		9	39			39			1, 247	1, 054	246		274	1, 033
1874	291	22	*244	9	36		212	34	694		1, 392	999	313		264	1, 047
1875	282	22		9	35		229	15	605		1, 404	943	318		262	1, 017
1876	302	42		9	37		175	13	606		1, 674	1, 134	396		312	1, 040
1877	314	53	128	11	40		169	14	779		1, 620	1, 080	†474		276	1, 115
1878	330	68	123	19	46		188	13	666		2, 043	1, 340	{‡252 548		346	1, 225
1879	325	93	148	37	63		308	13	889		2, 296	1, 733	§721		401	1, 569
1880	375	109	176	44	78		317	14	861		2, 525	1, 851	736		420	1, 721
1881	417	117	170	65	117		676	20	957		2, 647	2, 022	790		481	1, 984
1882	374	129	177	104	117		712	31	1, 032		2, 395	1, 893	703	12	447	1, 954
1883	374	136		153	131		1, 080	39	1, 499		2, 201	1, 690	1, 141	334	408	2, 307
1884	374	144		139	126		1, 149	69	1, 695		1, 970	1, 411	1, 179	604	398	2, 499
1885	398	162		108	124	407	1, 163	94	1, 902		2, 138	1, 603	1, 232	668	429	2, 382
1886	390	195		135	139	555	1, 315	61	2, 098		2, 414	1, 592	1, 157	659	424	2, 882
1887	406	239	269	153	150	688	1, 476	55	1, 380		2, 705	1, 844	1, 341	811	453	3, 022
1888	405	283	289	188	168	757	1, 551	87	1, 347	712	2, 688	1, 840	1, 333	825	209	2, 990
1889	423	346	302	237	225	853	1, 526	92	1, 366	1, 220	2, 781	1, 782	1, 214	849	223	3, 109
1890	402	390	390	282	249	1, 057	1, 612	115	1, 562	1, 517	2, 956	2, 087	1, 328	978	1, 087	3, 515
1891	401	437		322	255	1, 337	1, 762	195	1, 631	1, 804	2, 890	2, 061	1, 298	1, 067	1, 222	3, 496
1892	447	496		311		1, 524	1, 817	264			3, 830	2, 430	1, 548	1, 085	1, 286	‖4, 048

*Two years ending July 1, 1872 and 1874. † Year ending May 31. ‡ Eight months, June 1 to December 31. § Year ending December 31. ‖ Figures as reported, not verified in this office.

TABLE 131.—NUMBER OF MILLIONS OF TONS OF FREIGHT CARRIED ONE MILE BY THE MORE IMPORTANT RAILWAYS OF THE UNITED STATES, ETC.—Continued.

Years	New York, Pennsylvania and Ohio R. R.	Chicago and Erie R. R.	Pennsylvania R. R.	Pittsburg, Fort Wayne and Chicago Rwy.	Pittsburg, Cincinnati and St. Louis Rwy.	Chicago, St. Louis and Pittsburg Rwy.	Pittsburg, Cincinnati, Chicago and St. Louis Rwy.	Baltimore and Ohio R. R.	Baltimore and Ohio Southwestern R. R.	Ohio and Mississippi Rwy.	Cincinnati, Hamilton and Dayton R. R.	Wabash R. R.	Louisville, New Albany and Chicago Rwy.	Chicago and Grand Trunk Rwy.	Chicago, Milwaukee and St. Paul Rwy.	Chicago and Northwestern Rwy.
1852	.....	.....	.....	.....	.....	.....	.....	.....	.....	.....	.....	.....	.....	.....	.....	.....
1853	.....	.....	.....	.....	.....	.....	.....	.....	.....	.....	.....	.....	.....	.....	.....	.....
1854	.....	.....	.....	.....	.....	.....	.....	.....	.....	.....	.....	.....	.....	.....	.....	.....
1855	.....	.....	102	.....	.....	.....	.....	.....	.....	.....	.....	.....	.....	.....	.....	.....
1856	.....	.....	120	.....	.....	.....	.....	.....	.....	.....	.....	.....	.....	.....	.....	.....
1857	.....	.....	140	29	.....	.....	.....	.....	.....	.....	.....	.....	.....	.....	.....	.....
1858	.....	.....	162	35	.....	.....	.....	.....	.....	.....	.....	.....	.....	.....	.....	.....
1859	.....	.....	180	58	.....	.....	.....	.....	.....	.....	.....	.....	.....	.....	.....	.....
1860	.....	.....	214	78	.....	.....	.....	.....	.....	.....	.....	.....	.....	.....	.....	.....
1861	.....	.....	280	111	.....	.....	.....	.....	.....	.....	.....	.....	.....	.....	.....	.....
1862	.....	.....	376	128	.....	.....	.....	.....	.....	.....	.....	.....	.....	.....	.....	.....
1863	.....	.....	394	167	.....	.....	.....	.....	.....	.....	.....	.....	.....	.....	.....	.....
1864	.....	.....	421	175	.....	.....	.....	.....	.....	.....	.....	.....	.....	.....	.....	.....
1865	.....	.....	420	194	.....	.....	.....	.....	.....	.....	.....	.....	.....	.....	41	.....
1866	.....	.....	513	233	.....	.....	.....	.....	.....	.....	.....	.....	.....	.....	44	.....
1867	.....	.....	566	229	.....	.....	.....	.....	.....	.....	.....	.....	.....	.....	96	.....
1868	.....	.....	676	307	.....	.....	.....	.....	.....	.....	.....	.....	.....	.....	120	.....
1869	320	.....	753	310	94	41	.....	.....	.....	58	.....	.....	.....	.....	158	.....
1870	232	.....	826	336	.....	.....	.....	.....	.....	70	.....	.....	.....	.....	181	365
1871	261	.....	1,012	391	.....	.....	.....	.....	.....	88	.....	.....	.....	.....	174	268
1872	228	.....	1,190	488	197	.....	.....	.....	.....	108	22	289	.....	.....	187	288
1873	311	.....	1,385	480	206	280	.....	.....	.....	143	21	307	.....	.....	258	366
1874	319	.....	1,373	465	204	247	.....	.....	112	147	22	278	.....	.....	259	461
1875	283	.....	1,479	491	208	240	.....	.....	101	145	22	214	.....	.....	273	455
1876	293	.....	1,630	563	250	275	.....	.....	108	173	.....	.....	.....	.....	265	503
1877	329	.....	2,180	440	237	254	.....	.....	111	.....	93	381	.....	.....	272	485
1878	331	.....	2,432	637	288	305	.....	.....	.....	167	.....	502	.....	.....	322	624
1879	436	.....	3,061	803	367	403	.....	.....	.....	209	.....	.....	39	.....	402	682
1880	474	.....	3,293	806	385	441	.....	.....	.....	247	.....	1,106	.....	160	505	866
1881	610	.....	3,701	1,044	401	542	.....	.....	.....	283	139	1,150	.....	229	697	981
1882	695	.....	3,977	992	415	548	.....	.....	.....	179	.....	1,248	103	244	945	1,192
1883	.....	.....	4,127	945	428	*401	.....	.....	.....	261	.....	1,264	120	301	1,177	1,184
1884	.....	196	4,192	908	432	485	.....	.....	.....	225	166	1,374	116	376	1,247	1,350
1885	.....	209	4,501	954	523	613	.....	.....	.....	253	169	1,184	.....	373	1,338	1,417
1886	.....	212	4,635	903	561	588	.....	.....	.....	319	170	1,102	164	354	1,487	1,467
1887	.....	320	5,261	1,107	657	684	.....	2,048	176	334	.....	1,075	202	416	1,629	1,755
1888	.....	339	5,413	1,005	744	642	.....	2,192	.....	297	237	610	184	401	1,660	1,954
1889	.....	299	5,834	1,087	767	657	.....	2,248	150	273	235	635	189	386	1,621	1,778
1890	.....	371	6,908	1,226	879	782	.....	2,645	83	285	250	1,430	187	477	1,843	2,034
1891	.....	310	6,870	1,122	233	208	1,151	2,562	164	249	270	1,209	217	456	1,896	1,945
1892	.....	420	7,362	.....	.....	.....	1,746	2,723	220	271	323	1,391	246	464	2,266	2,302

* Nine months, ending December 31.

TABLE 131.—NUMBER OF MILLIONS OF TONS OF FREIGHT CARRIED ONE MILE BY THE MORE IMPORTANT RAILWAYS OF THE UNITED STATES, ETC.—Continued.

Years.	Chicago, Burlington and Quincy.	Chicago, Rock Island and Pacific.	Chicago and Alton R. R.	Illinois Central R. R.	Wisconsin Central R. R.	Northern Pacific R. R.	Union Pacific Rwy.	Atchison, Topeka and Santa Fe R. R.	Denver and Rio Grande R. R.	Texas and Pacific Rwy.	Chesapeake and Ohio Rwy.	Louisville and Nashville R. R.	Richmond and Danville R. R.	Mobile and Ohio R. R.
1852	....	....	....	....	....	....	....	....	....	....	....	....	....	....
1853	....	....	....	....	....	....	....	....	....	....	....	....	....	....
1854	....	....	....	....	....	....	....	....	....	....	....	....	....	....
1855	....	....	....	....	....	....	....	....	....	....	....	....	....	....
1856	....	....	....	....	....	....	....	....	....	....	....	....	....	....
1857	....	....	....	....	....	....	....	....	....	....	....	....	....	....
1858	....	....	....	....	....	....	....	....	....	....	....	....	....	....
1859	....	....	....	....	....	....	....	....	....	....	....	....	....	....
1860	....	....	....	....	....	....	....	....	....	....	....	....	....	....
1861	....	....	....	....	....	....	....	....	....	....	....	....	....	....
1862	....	....	....	....	....	....	....	....	....	....	....	....	....	....
1863	108	39	....	....	....	....	....	....	....	....	....	....	....	....
1864	117	57	....	....	....	....	....	....	....	....	....	....	....	....
1865	108	63	....	136	....	....	....	....	....	....	....	....	....	....
1866	114	59	....	135	....	....	....	....	....	....	....	....	4	....
1867	138	80	....	171	....	....	....	....	....	....	5	....	6	....
1868	132	88	....	226	....	....	....	....	....	....	7	29	6	....
1869	146	120	....	253	....	....	....	....	....	....	....	41	6	....
1870	147	131	....	265	....	....	72	....	....	....	7	72	8	36
1871	207	152	....	262	....	....	134	....	....	....	8	....	9	47
1872	241	169	....	272	....	....	178	....	3	....	9	....	10	57
1873	418	219	....	275	....	....	223	25	4	....	32	142	13	54
1874	446	250	162	274	15	....	262	27	4	7	60	147	14	52
1875	436	288	169	285	19	....	269	46	5	14	66	136	16	46
1876	477	268	218	264	22	....	292	62	....	28	98	....	17	53
1877	655	337	212	249	23	....	335	73	14	43	117	202	22	61
1878	952	370	248	306	23	....	366	133	....	51	153	225	24	71
1879	1,139	511	402	335	31	....	436	....	....	51	168	237	33	58
1880	1,248	686	481	381	42	81	....	267	....	66	*230	320	41	80
1881	1,275	712	447	386	48	96	783	396	120	102	298	493	70	87
1882	1,222	788	475	418	....	193	733	461	121	208	345	597	119	75
1883	1,552	702	549	605	39	244	746	521	193	259	426	664	126	75
1884	1,580	735	603	578	43	400	922	635	152	245	406	687	120	87
1885	1,813	781	529	623	56	391	1,110	608	169	125	480	751	....	90
1886	1,852	720	561	720	70	482	1,261	687	193	257	613	802	....	98
1887	2,126	794	642	831	105	537	1,490	909	242	287	653	954	....	133
1888	1,581	931	582	771	152	705	1,171	817	239	333	655	1,104	315	192
1889	1,727	903	494	1,061	123	875	1,102	755	48	305	612	773	428	218
1890	1,998	1,235	595	1,063	367	1,096	1,281	1,330	280	406	1,006	884	555	256
1891	1,646	1,082	477	1,302	379	1,258	1,209	1,456	309	380	1,136	902	473	306
1892	†2,173	1,188	562	1,411	459	†1,228	1,318	1,691	323	387	....	†1,051	468	302

* For fifteen months, termination of year being changed from September 30 to December 31.
† Figures as reported, not verified in this office.

TABLE 132.—AGGREGATE TONNAGE CARRIED BETWEEN ALL POINTS BY VARIOUS IMPORTANT RAILWAYS DURING EACH YEAR FROM 1852, FOR WHICH SUCH DATA CAN BE PROCURED.

Year.	Freight (tons carried).							
	Boston and Albany R. R.	Fitchburg R. R.	Central Vermont R. R.	New York, and New England R. R.	New York, New Haven and Hartford R.R	Canadian Pacific Rwy.	Delaware, Lackawanna and Western R. R.	New York, Ontario and Western R. R.
1859....	775, 695	....	....	....	....	....	....	....
1860....	858, 546	395, 003	....	....	....	....	....	....
1861....	853, 353	325, 500	....	....	....	....	....	....
1862....	969, 998	345, 254	....	....	245, 712	....	1, 316, 892	....
1863....	1, 077, 658	419, 314	....	....	307, 346	....	1, 510, 495	....
1864....	1, 174, 892	466, 530	....	....	375, 333	....	1, 621, 360	....
1865....	1, 121, 158	486, 015	....	....	406, 622	....	1, 200, 097	....
1866....	1, 433, 883	512, 874	....	....	472, 663	....	1, 920, 874	....
1867....	1, 532, 005	511, 488	....	102, 314	482. 005	....	2, 140, 134	....
1868....	1, 319, 059	559, 368	477, 608	370, 191	489, 148	....	2, 128, 512	....
1869....	1, 613, 940	670, 439	650, 146	233, 271	588, 271	....	1, 993, 946	....
1870....	[1]1, 531, 149	634, 615	675, 884	214, 191	695, 579	....	3, 398, 004	50, 006
1871....	....		[2]1, 833, 660	294, 177	755, 740	....	2, 363, 568	137, 151
1872....	2, 732, 907	740, 123		345, 662	892, 579	....	3, 347, 671	370, 418
1873....	2, 884, 520	777, 268	[3]2, 766, 154	363, 734	895, 985	....	4, 448, 769	490, 706
1874....	2, 668, 403	965, 796		362, 513	815, 379	....	3, 653, 763	455, 372
1875....	2, 439, 472	726, 766	....	344, 508	827, 832	....	3, 898, 344	235, 042
1876....	2, 541, 274	887, 859	....	330, 667	836, 019	....	2, 923, 089	228, 103
1877....	2, 601, 657	955, 771	1, 069, 822	350, 005	886, 476	....	2, 922, 803	222, 507
1878....	2, 642, 555	1, 115, 771	1, 006, 162	435, 367	898, 799	....	3, 193, 531	212, 541
1879....	2, 738, 096	1, 313, 289	1, 204, 637	871, 187	1, 209, 630	....	5, 283, 442	216. 100
1880....	3, 310, 539	1, 546, 950	1, 811, 228	968, 549	1, 348, 678	....	5, 269, 359	255, 410
1881....	3, 593, 923	1, 776, 960	1, 465, 712	1, 176, 795	1, 655, 513	....	7, 115, 065	348, 513
1882....	3, 415, 329	1, 822, 262	1, 661, 887	1, 572, 374	1, 908, 322	....	7, 452, 757	469, 526
1883....	3, 411, 324	2, 031, 122	1, 612, 352	1, 801, 360	2, 160, 023	....	8, 159, 299	562, 836
1884....	3, 325, 517	2, 112, 155	1, 544, 871	1, 786, 531	2, 181, 250	....	8, 411. 216	1, 004, 248
1885....	3, 446, 413	2, 158, 283	1, 600, 266	1, 715, 661	2, 148, 463	1, 996, 355	8, 203, 714	1, 470, 808
1886....	3, 506, 476	2, 509, 131	1, 802, 966	2, 099, 339	2, 376, 195	2, 046, 195	9, 318, 773	807, 441
1887....	3, 674, 589	2, 919, 629	2, 659, 031	2, 225, 141	2, 602, 157	2, 144, 327	10, 558, 055	661, 825
1888....	3, 719, 992	3, 117, 152	2, 586, 334	2, 526, 937	2, 336, 224	2, 321, 957	11, 070, 369	1, 277, 519
1889....	3, 859, 516	3, 448, 160	2, 715, 251	2, 705, 332	3, 246, 833	2, 636, 121	10, 793, 278	1, 353, 885
1890....	3, 883, 115	3, 971, 318	3, 273, 143	2, 973, 813	3, 563, 873	3, 095, 784	10, 936, 685	1, 473, 788
1891....	3, 913, 873	4, 215, 024	....	3, 299, 876	3, 802, 012	3, 675, 113	12, 199, 053	1, 737, 059
1892....	4, 256, 575	4, 570, 377	....	3, 272, 110	....	4, 058, 575	12, 910, 744	2, 085, 769

[1] Ten months only. [2] Two years ending July 1, 1872. [3] Two years ending July 1, 1874.

TABLE 132.—AGGREGATE TONNAGE CARRIED BETWEEN ALL POINTS BY VARIOUS IMPORTANT RAILWAYS DURING EACH YEAR, ETC.—Continued.

Year.	Freight (tons carried).							
	Philadelphia and Reading R.R.	Lehigh Valley R. R.	New York Central and Hudson River R.R.	Lake Shore and Michigan Southern Rwy.	Michigan Central R. R.	New York, Chicago and Saint Louis R. R.	Cleveland, Cincinnati, Chicago and Saint Louis Rwy.	New York, Lake Erie and Western R. R.
1852	....	....	....	....	....	....	....	436, 460
1853	....	....	....	....	....	....	....	631, 039
1854	....	....	549, 805	....	....	....	....	743, 250
1855	....	....	670, 073	....	....	....	....	842, 055
1856	....	....	932, 844	....	....	....	....	983, 221
1857	....	....	1, 075, 589	....	....	....	....	978, 067
1858	....	....	925, 604	....	....	....	....	816, 964
1859	....	....	1, 093, 284	....	....	....	....	869, 072
1860	....	....	1, 366, 035	....	....	....	....	1, 139, 554
1861	....	....	1, 537, 400	....	....	....	....	1, 253, 419
1862	....	....	1, 905, 173	....	463, 812	....	....	1, 632, 955
1863	....	....	2, 106, 571	....	564, 827	....	....	1, 815, 096
1864	....	....	2, 158, 972	....	542, 410	....	....	2, 170, 798
1865	....	....	1, 767, 149	....	485, 275	....	....	2, 234, 350
1866	....	....	2, 099, 504	....	533, 451	....	....	3, 242, 972
1867	....	....	2, 249, 363	....	578, 177	....	....	3, 484, 546
1868	....	....	2, 562, 862	....	638, 586	....	628, 356	3, 908, 209
1869	....	....	3, 190, 840	....	802, 835	....	825, 465	4, 312, 209
1870	....	....	4, 122, 000	2, 978, 725	823, 770	....	935, 840	4, 852, 505
1871	....	....	4, 532, 056	3, 784, 525	1, 105, 875	....	1, 777, 657	4, 844, 208
1872	....	....	4, 393, 965	4, 443, 092	1, 708, 964	....	1, 444, 354	5, 564, 274
1873	10, 663, 333	6, 901, 905	5, 522, 724	5, 176, 661	1, 999, 671	....	1, 680, 588	6, 312, 702
1874	10, 209, 500	6, 606, 555	6, 114, 678	5, 221, 267	2, 186, 786	....	1, 531, 952	6, 364, 276
1875	8, 886, 317	5, 402, 271	6, 001, 954	5, 022, 490	2, 375, 496	....	1, 611, 174	6, 239, 943
1876	8, 759, 908	6, 148, 583	6, 803, 680	5, 635, 167	2, 686, 248	....	1, 745, 367	5, 972, 818
1877	10, 963, 604	7, 424, 969	6, 351, 356	5, 513, 398	[1]4, 764, 611	....	1, 624, 200	6, 182, 456
1878	9, 376, 075	6, 127, 093	7, 695, 413	6, 098, 445	3, 564, 731	....	1, 949, 484	6, 150, 468
1879	13, 303, 265	7, 616, 523	9, 015, 753	7, 541, 294	3, 513, 819	....	2, 299, 711	8, 212, 641
1880	13, 184, 982	8, 807, 246	10, 533, 038	8, 350, 336	3, 797, 137	....	2, 441, 643	8, 715, 892
1881	14, 384, 710	10, 761, 795	11, 591, 379	9, 164, 508	4, 196, 896	....	2, 880, 923	11, 086, 823
1882	15, 212, 320	10, 693, 454	11, 330, 393	9, 195, 538	3, 913, 869	45, 758	2, 755, 867	11, 895, 238
1883	19, 118, 517	10, 434, 508	10, 892, 440	8, 478, 605	5, 197, 278	981, 830	2, 527, 993	13, 610, 623
1884	19, 781, 705	9, 336, 906	10, 212, 418	7, 365, 688	5, 141, 597	1, 762, 778	2, 347, 792	11, 071, 938
1885	20, 208, 932	10, 179, 171	10, 802, 957	8, 023, 093	5, 236, 276	1, 984, 364	2, 513, 780	10, 253, 498
1886	22, 669, 394	11, 295, 044	12, 718, 101	8. 305, 597	5, 345, 570	2, 056, 148	2, 644, 021	12, 806, 918
1887	18, 195, 990	11, 247, 513	14, 626, 954	9, 326, 852	6, 014, 233	2, 468, 796	2, 808, 149	13, 949, 260
1888	17, 747, 615	9, 670, 987	14, 939, 255	9, 262, 397	6, 076, 936	2, 582, 308	1, 705, 293	20, 629, 840
1889	18, 438, 707	14, 371, 247	14, 988, 281	9, 304, 575	6, 194, 473	2, 732, 102	1, 778, 372	21, 287, 751
1890	19, 401, 123	13, 550, 147	16, 108, 441	10, 975, 241	6, 798, 467	3, 084, 590	6, 591, 610	23, 926, 198
1891	21, 084, 490	14, 394, 933	16, 621, 567	11, 259, 811	6, 947, 945	3, 304, 425	7, 801, 377	24, 304, 597
1892	....	....	20, 721, 752	13, 332, 519	7, 731, 061	3, 445, 947	8, 524, 986	[2]26, 531, 799

[1] Twenty months.

[2] Figures as reported, not verified in this office.

TABLE 132.—AGGREGATE TONNAGE CARRIED BETWEEN ALL POINTS BY VARIOUS IMPORTANT RAILWAYS DURING EACH YEAR, ETC.—Continued.

Year.	Freight (tons carried).							
	New York, Pennsylvania and Ohio R. R.[1]	Chicago and Erie R. R.	Pennsylvania R. R.[2]	Pittsburg, Fort Wayne, and Chicago Rwy.	Pittsburg, Cincinnati and St. Louis Rwy.	Chicago, St. Louis and Pittsburg Rwy.	Pittsburg, Cincinnati, Chicago and St. Louis Rwy.	Baltimore and Ohio R. R.
1857	....	....	826, 518	304, 769	....	....	....	....
1858	....	....	1, 046, 899	285, 663	....	....	....	....
1859	....	....	1, 170, 240	362, 606	....	....	....	....
1860	....	....	1, 346, 525	465, 204	....	....	....	....
1861	....	....	1, 482, 087	526, 379	....	....	....	....
1862	....	....	2, 058, 548	643, 107	....	....	....	....
1863	....	....	2, 265, 413	805, 525	....	....	....	....
1864	....	....	2, 585, 379	858, 928	....	....	....	....
1865	....	....	2, 555, 709	832, 615	....	....	....	....
1866	....	....	3, 186, 356	1, 025, 978	....	....	....	....
1867	....	....	3, 709, 224	1, 154, 351	....	....	....	....
1868	....	....	4, 427, 884	1, 509, 052	....	....	....	....
1869	....	....	4, 991, 995	1, 665, 190	....	516, 815	....	....
1870	....	....	5, 427, 401	1, 740, 585	....	....	....	....
1871	....	....	6, 575, 843	2, 047, 114	....	....	....	....
1872	....	....	7, 844, 778	2, 407, 018	....	1, 390, 597	....	....
1873	....	....	9, 211, 234	2, 292, 644	....	1, 473, 623	....	....
1874	2, 709, 134	....	16, 420, 321	2, 309, 128	1, 471, 207	1, 390, 483	....	....
1875	2, 429, 421	....	15, 772, 722	2, 496, 148	1, 536, 261	1, 370, 069	....	....
1876	2, 507, 195	....	16, 333, 353	2, 604, 767	1, 808, 761	1, 617, 133	....	....
1877	2, 761, 493	....	16, 382, 268	2, 690, 735	1, 722, 386	1, 521, 141	....	....
1878	2, 653, 839	....	17, 600, 447	3, 026, 250	2, 142, 155	1, 791, 981	....	....
1879	3, 259, 843	....	22, 867, 162	3, 679, 382	2, 726, 847	2, 310, 053	....	....
1880	4, 125, 979	....	26, 051, 091	3, 865, 675	3, 099, 994	2, 484, 321	....	....
1881	....	....	32, 606, 264	4, 753, 220	3, 297, 844	2, 967, 149	....	....
1882	....	....	35, 840, 060	4, 837, 236	3, 125, 645	3, 001, 619	....	....
1883	....	....	37, 379, 546	5, 076, 311	3, 466, 544	2, 135, 148	....	....
1884	....	831, 761	38, 106, 544	4, 696, 583	3, 630, 919	2, 517, 062	....	....
1885	....	900, 209	40, 880, 100	4, 711, 888	4, 066, 386	3, 031, 595	....	....
1886	....	955, 334	44, 121, 327	5, 413, 597	4, 864, 889	3, 075, 385	....	....
1887	....	1, 274, 204	51, 215, 785	6, 315, 075	5, 560, 539	3, 546, 260	....	....
1888	....	1, 582, 324	51, 782, 247	6, 210, 816	7, 717, 282	3, 374, 433	....	11, 438, 320
1889	....	1, 445, 143	54, 686, 113	7, 113, 671	7, 909, 760	3, 997, 634	....	12, 236, 223
1890	....	1, 792, 782	65, 173, 118	7, 942, 888	8, 936, 566	4, 772, 290	....	14, 245, 975
1891	....	1, 491, 301	50, 013, 674	....	[3]2, 375, 841	[3]1, 254, 398	[4]10, 231, 022	15, 097, 632
1892	....	1, 992, 932	54, 769, 382	....	....	....	13, 725, 857	15, 738, 858

[1] Years subsequent to 1880 included in New York, Lake Erie and Western R. R.
[2] Figures for 1873 and previous years cover Pennsylvania R. R. division only.
[3] Three months. [4] Nine months.

TABLE 132.—AGGREGATE TONNAGE CARRIED BETWEEN ALL POINTS BY VARIOUS IMPORTANT RAILWAYS DURING EACH YEAR, ETC.—Continued.

Year.	Freight (tons carried).							
	Baltimore and Ohio Southwestern R. R.	Ohio and Mississippi Rwy.	Cincinnati, Hamilton, and Dayton R. R.[1]	Wabash R. R.	Louisville, New Albany and Chicago Rwy.	Chicago and Grand Trunk Rwy.	Chicago, Milwaukee and St. Paul Rwy.	Chicago and Northwestern Rwy.
1861			276, 193					
1862			249, 540					
1865								956, 484
1866			412, 847					1, 370, 516
1867								1, 726, 919
1868			497, 466				1, 134, 565	1, 982, 429
1869			508, 692				1, 344, 358	2, 211, 826
1870			395, 432				1, 522, 753	2, 222, 978
1871			486, 030				1, 463, 156	2, 298, 170
1872			551, 936	1, 349, 052			1, 687, 826	2, 510, 016
1873			564, 542	1, 442, 963			1, 791, 504	2, 958, 390
1874			616, 830	1, 277, 356			1, 735, 535	3, 591, 090
1875			617, 860	1, 092, 219			1, 832, 527	3, 153, 315
1876			711, 230				1, 765, 801	3, 471, 927
1877			744, 723	1, 403, 866			1, 687, 057	3, 413, 398
1878			759, 569	1, 952, 003			1, 955, 699	3, 911, 261
1879			815, 963		415, 998	135, 644	2, 559, 734	4, 265, 937
1880			823, 272	4, 533, 187		702, 153	3, 260, 553	5, 574, 635
1881			2, 187, 632	5, 393, 917		878, 325	4, 276, 088	6, 662, 112
1882				5, 911, 012	764, 661	978, 812	5, 127, 767	8, 190, 893
1883				5, 859, 566	830, 318	1, 131, 251	5, 661, 667	7, 874, 665
1884			2, 681, 861	6, 358, 761	902, 246	1, 370, 530	6, 023, 016	8, 453, 994
1885			2, 753, 999	5, 558, 571		1, 380, 958	6, 482, 869	8, 235, 127
1886			2, 827, 048	5, 486, 067	1, 179, 736	1, 375, 851	7, 085, 072	8, 494, 239
1887				3, 337, 678	1, 462, 205	1, 584, 720	7, 573, 795	9, 737, 312
1888		1, 630, 477	3, 724, 865	3, 358, 988	1, 259, 491	1, 540, 659	7, 675, 934	11, 059, 616
1889	1, 375, 570	1, 652, 548	3, 556, 831	3, 580, 366	1, 250, 190	1, 562, 480	7, 769, 875	11, 084, 841
1890	757, 747	1, 787, 058	3, 803, 251	6, 832, 358	1, 251, 978	1, 896, 325	9, 292, 992	13, 450, 324
1891	1, 730, 357	1, 866, 836	2, 786, 592	6, 256, 064	1, 354, 174	1, 860, 752	10, 397, 035	13, 547, 496
1892	1, 966, 471	2, 096, 789	3, 611, 175	6, 928, 051	1, 594, 801	1, 874, 615	11, 568, 930	15, 768, 548

[1] Figures for years prior to 1880 show Cincinnati, Hamilton and Dayton R. R. main line only.

Year.	Freight (tons carried).							
	Chicago, Burlington and Quincy R. R.	Chicago, Rock Island and Pacific Rwy.	Chicago and Alton R. R.	Illinois Central R. R.	Wisconsin Central R. R.	Northern Pacific R. R.	Union Pacific Rwy.	Atchison, Topeka and Santa Fe R. R.
1862				806, 685				
1863	777, 736	879, 879		952, 814				
1864	809, 674	441, 570	386, 197	1, 022, 024				
1865	737, 511	472, 557	511, 012	1, 034, 946				
1866	821, 883	459, 986	636, 360	1, 153, 175				
1867	978, 583	598, 914	750, 657	1, 300, 835				
1868	937, 489	654, 435	915, 682	1, 439, 675				
1869	1, 029, 746	846, 787	1, 076, 878	1, 601, 972				
1870	1, 052, 754	856, 668	1, 261, 032	1, 623, 944				98, 917
1871	1, 382, 515	914, 345	1, 501, 496	1, 831, 944				87, 571
1872	[1]3, 031, 314	1, 014, 348	1, 601, 799	2, 039, 321			378, 650	
1873	2, 221, 744	1, 286, 966	1, 642, 443	2, 057, 360	40, 652		487, 484	156, 033
1874	2, 420, 628	1, 399, 384	1, 421, 158	2, 069, 935	189, 492	39, 111	482, 806	186, 312
1875	2, 396, 933	1, 717, 727	1, 545, 842	2, 016, 424	202, 383	21, 540	501, 410	252, 383
1876	2, 892, 614	1, 640, 000	1, 818, 235	1, 899, 627	215, 463	36, 759	629, 947	325, 629
1877	3, 249, 625	1, 651, 409	1, 560, 188	1, 803, 044	221, 835	47, 985	716, 112	372, 084
1878	3, 975, 010	1, 768, 118	1, 967, 306	2, 067, 832	244, 976	104, 941	844, 019	611, 086
1879	4, 686, 520	2, 236, 270	2, 634, 177	2, 324, 485	325, 078	145, 268	992, 886	802, 121
1880	6, 636, 186	2, 966, 764	3, 071, 788	2. 703, 582	405, 785	365, 743		953. 701
1881	6, 710, 750	3, 376, 260	3, 275, 004	2, 875, 833	469, 198	449, 087	2, 065, 030	1, 166, 483
1882	6, 346, 259	3, 754, 531	3, 522, 840	2, 909, 578		787, 471	2, 101, 635	1, 475, 149
1883	7, 645, 701	3, 454, 888	3, 488, 496	3, 538, 562	426, 448	1, 093, 336	2, 583, 287	1, 754, 385
1884	7, 525, 997	3, 618, 142	3, 598, 284	3, 454, 085	444, 849	1, 442, 800	2, 663, 016	2, 725, 191
1885	8, 431, 808	3, 980, 502	3, 631, 108	3, 587, 270		1, 256, 880	3, 183, 770	2, 602, 056
1886	8, 534, 708	3, 873, 605	3, 651, 100	4, 051, 823	689, 378	1, 547, 626	3, 561, 572	2, 938, 364
1887	9, 752, 325	4, 180, 109	4, 123, 120	4, 910, 248	1, 172, 549	2, 128, 166	3, 894, 250	3, 839, 578
1888	8, 667, 567	4, 381, 257	3, 962, 264	4, 899, 030	1, 039, 314	2, 597, 897	4, 372, 580	3, 464, 051
1889	9, 472, 578	4, 656, 261	3, 485, 536	5, 422, 967	1, 380, 632	2, 877, 978	4, 389, 291	2, 933, 104
1890	11, 201, 874	5, 540, 795	3, 675, 179	6, 063, 586	2, 623, 732	3, 569, 969	5, 057, 825	5, 158, 689
1891	10, 272, 274	5, 198, 365	3, 271, 387	6, 948, 867	2, 653, 764	4, 388, 819	4, 529, 887	5, 754, 545
1892	[2]12, 418, 634	6, 033, 943	3, 548, 052	7, 519, 192	2, 889, 115	[2]3, 936, 977	4, 787, 388	6, 224, 294

[1] 20 months.

[2] Figures as reported, not verified in this office.

TABLE 132.—AGGREGATE TONNAGE CARRIED BETWEEN ALL POINTS BY VARIOUS IMPORTANT RAILWAYS DURING EACH YEAR, ETC.—Continued.

Year.	Freight (tons carried).					
	Denver and Rio Grande R. R.	Texas and Pacific Rwy.	Chesapeake and Ohio Rwy.	Louisville and Nashville R. R.	Richmond and Danville R. R.	Mobile and Ohio Rwy.
1866	....	....	....	....	68, 121	....
1867	....	....	63, 537	222, 937	81, 638	....
1868	....	....	82, 544	243, 918	88, 679	....
1869	....	....	....	317, 208	99, 323	....
1870	....	....	86, 585	438, 413	120, 959	258, 409
1871	....	....	99, 596	535, 711	161, 122	333, 659
1872	46, 212	....	115, 473	716, 753	174, 919	437, 307
1873	59, 229	....	248, 226	947, 468	225, 446	347, 488
1874	55, 436	88, 343	306, 465	1, 348, 214	197, 920	343, 488
1875	57, 969	138, 596	359, 569	1, 212, 160	221, 017	305, 243
1876	78, 794	254, 288	415, 452	....	227, 650	223, 106
1877	132, 838	355, 789	471, 660	1, 995, 044	241, 081	251, 427
1878	....	388, 967	588, 066	2, 644, 007	235, 962	275, 017
1879	....	379, 125	686, 526	2, 282, 180	308, 060	246, 898
1880	651, 833	525, 093	941, 123	2, 139, 153	372, 226	333, 553
1881	1, 136, 311	715, 204	1, 435, 597	3, 286, 000	710, 706	364, 431
1882	1, 151, 330	1, 049, 262	1, 367, 469	6, 533, 317	1, 210, 267	345, 755
1883	1, 416, 426	946, 219	1, 748, 676	7, 302, 145	1, 311, 624	357, 493
1884	1, 093, 841	1, 056, 726	1, 579, 106	7, 969, 776	1, 319, 585	408, 889
1885	1, 207, 897	952, 017	1, 849, 938	8, 365, 521	1, 451, 646	429, 141
1886	1, 352, 252	1, 099, 304	2, 174, 523	8, 942, 102	1, 500, 164	484, 549
1887	1, 694, 207	1, 152, 858	2, 414, 303	11, 257, 812	1, 671, 687	777, 298
1888	1, 662, 118	1, 192, 727	2, 485, 322	13, 675, 170	1, 764, 283	1, 205, 279
1889	353, 469	1, 263, 895	2, 663, 350	9, 212, 322	2, 675, 690	1, 051, 335
1890	1, 833, 874	1, 617, 201	3, 760, 577	10, 306, 013	3, 617, 723	1, 142, 708
1891	2, 093, 660	1, 554, 857	4, 166, 102	10, 367, 379	2, 766, 530	1, 230, 029
1892	1, 904, 255	1, 545, 328	....	[1]12, 149, 938	5, 359, 408	1, 193, 641

[1] Figures as reported, not verified in this office.

TABLE 133.—GROSS FREIGHT EARNINGS EXCLUSIVE OF RECEIPTS FROM ELEVATORS, WHARVES, STOCK YARDS, ETC., OF VARIOUS IMPORTANT RAILWAYS, DURING EACH YEAR FROM 1852 FOR WHICH SUCH DATA CAN BE PROCURED.

Year.	Freight (gross earnings).							
	Boston and Albany R. R.	Fitchburg R. R.	Central Vermont R. R.	New York and New England R. R.	New York, New Haven and Hartford R. R.	Canadian Pacific Rwy.	Delaware, Lackawanna and Western R. R.	New York Ontario and Western R. R.
1862	....	....	....	....	$125, 092	....	$1, 417, 196	....
1863	....	....	....	....	166, 614	....	1, 614, 813	....
1864	....	....	....	....	214, 354	....	1, 788, 658	....
1865	....	....	....	....	263, 904	....	1, 485, 832	....
1866	....	....	....	....	340, 017	....	2, 466, 797	....
1867	....	....	....	....	333, 381	....	2, 476, 010	....
1868	$3, 410, 893	$639, 592	$1, 209, 857	$557, 761	953, 965	....	3, 414, 644	....
1869	3, 861, 052	736, 796	1, 319, 934	332, 926	1, 138, 311	....	2, 201, 115	....
1870	3, 265, 481	[2]584, 360	1, 439, 288	[2]264, 823	[3]1, 475, 956	....	[4]3, 826, 002	$166, 470
1871	4, 747, 180	755, 837	1, 529, 111	364, 488	[2]1, 176, 772	....	3, 095, 573	216, 989
1872	5, 846, 768	769, 936	....	....	1, 445, 952	....	4, 266, 081	600, 826
1873	6, 221, 183	788, 554	....	404, 473	1, 468, 578	....	5, 507, 388	971, 275
1874	5, 283, 599	932, 030	[1]4, 471, 489	449, 108	1, 331, 527	....	4, 629, 862	781, 911
1875	4, 328, 131	909, 629	....	447, 261	1, 431, 498	....	5, 422, 850	393, 355
1876	3, 886, 132	1, 045, 780	....	447, 385	1, 317, 646	....	3, 418, 245	354, 207
1877	3, 790, 781	1, 106, 161	1, 858, 064	477, 400	1, 326, 707	....	2, 954, 636	371, 991
1878	3, 721, 436	1, 091, 516	1, 531, 486	505, 809	1, 309, 778	....	3, 128, 974	371, 850
1879	3, 588, 839	1, 205, 954	1, 599, 364	1, 058, 722	1, 492, 261	....	4, 695, 694	353, 530
1880	4, 530, 913	1, 496, 459	1, 993, 378	1, 250, 527	1, 634, 092	....	8, 871, 475	377, 926
1881	4, 328, 906	1, 658, 139	1, 752, 740	1, 420, 758	1, 903, 703	$231, 378	10, 426, 756	469, 156
1882	3, 984, 133	1, 521, 576	1, 806, 826	1, 837, 890	2, 065, 856	890, 385	9, 634, 910	605, 479
1883	4, 472, 180	1, 835, 422	1, 885, 526	2, 114, 524	2, 507, 623	3, 112, 932	12, 638, 812	754, 279
1884	4, 090, 302	1, 775, 248	1, 664, 753	1, 955, 686	2, 440, 919	3, 410, 365	12, 382, 015	1, 067, 808
1885	3, 765, 929	1, 712, 162	1, 643, 503	1, 850, 266	2, 423, 594	4, 881, 865	12, 149, 082	1, 125, 063
1886	4, 299, 083	2, 078, 446	1, 663, 380	2, 262, 479	2, 795, 241	6, 112, 379	14, 647, 355	938, 285
1887	4, 493, 588	2, 707, 544	2, 354, 355	2, 485, 913	2, 928, 001	6, 924, 130	18, 317, 758	907, 247
1888	4, 458, 688	3, 164, 311	2, 644, 267	3, 033, 397	2, 953, 645	7, 619, 758	16, 608, 146	1, 218, 326
1889	4, 350, 172	3, 508, 281	2, 621, 988	3, 189, 904	4, 109, 128	8, 095, 114	15, 004, 531	1, 291, 097
1890	4, 446, 586	3, 880, 252	3, 032, 887	3, 445, 385	4, 489, 611	9, 354, 480	15, 293, 486	1, 455, 994
1891	4, 369, 007	4, 330, 784	....	3, 666, 545	4, 557, 071	11, 643, 641	15, 790, 589	2, 013, 685
1892	4, 722, 856	4, 591, 008	....	3, 601, 462	4, 900, 936	13, 249, 454	16, 418, 334	2, 456, 048

[1] 2 years ending July 1, 1874. [2] 10 months. [3] 15 months. [4] 14 months.

TABLE 133.—GROSS FREIGHT EARNINGS EXCLUSIVE OF RECEIPTS FROM ELEVATORS, WHARVES, STOCK YARDS, ETC.—Continued.

Year.	Freight (gross earnings).							
	Philadelphia and Reading R. R.	Lehigh Valley R. R.	New York Central and Hudson River R. R.	Lake Shore and Michigan Southern Rwy.	Michigan Central R. R.	New York, Chicago and St. Louis Rwy.	Cleveland, Cincinnati, Chicago and St. Louis Rwy.	New York, Lake Erie and Western R. R.
1852....	$2,289,641	....	....	....	....	....	....	$1,883,198
1853....	2,435,306	....	....	....	....	....	....	2,537,215
1854....	3,485,449	....	$2,943,966	....	....	....	....	3,659,590
1855....	3,989,946	....	3,755,320	....	....	....	....	3,655,002
1856....	3,591,157	....	5,052,059	....	....	....	....	4,545,722
1857....	2,742,909	....	5,275,876	....	....	....	....	4,097,610
1858....	2,201,608	....	4,244,639	....	....	....	....	3,843,310
1859....	2,358,573	....	4,049,530	....	....	....	....	3,195,869
1860....	2,927,778	....	4,943,638	....	....	....	....	3,884,343
1861....	2,517,344	....	5,557,019	....	....	....	....	4,351,464
1862....	3,402,836	....	7,972,304	....	$1,559,661	....	....	6,642,915
1863....	5,570,343	....	9,449,554	....	1,983,757	....	....	8,432,234
1864....	8,157,551	....	10,685,672	....	2,073,275	....	....	9,855,088
1865....	9,792,569	....	11,000,058	....	2,233,529	....	....	10,726,264
1866....	9,667,236	....	12,017,532	....	2,208,592	....	....	11,611,023
1867....	7,970,429	....	11,993,008	....	2,285,522	....	....	11,204,689
1868....	7,667,947	$4,270,650	12,479,950	....	2,480,974	....	$1,813,130	10,780,976
1869....	9,925,863	4,482,033	14,066,386	....	2,755,200	....	2,090,544	12,583,794
1870....	8,189,315	5,462,607	14,489,217	$8,746,126	2,634,439	....	2,269,038	11,983,547
1871....	10,593,936	4,825,667	14,470,402	10,341,218	3,072,558	....	2,873,536	12,861,999
1872....	10,201,145	5,513,439	16,259,647	12,824,862	3,398,346	....	3,439,999	14,509,745
1873....	12,707,271	6,202,892	19,616,018	14,192,399	3,852,933	....	3,735,895	15,015,807
1874....	12,301,215	6,224,927	20,348,725	11,918,350	4,447,839	....	3,148,197	13,740,042
1875....	10,662,707	5,526,366	17,899,702	9,639,038	4,417,276	....	2,647,225	12,287,399
1876....	9,658,183	6,221,740	17,593,265	9,405,629	4,158,887	....	2,537,009	11,429,929
1877....	10,418,795	6,035,697	16,424,317	9,476,608	2,516,686	....	2,453,804	10,647,807
1878....	9,897,718	5,117,053	19,045,830	10,048,952	4,646,248	....	2,601,385	11,914,489
1879....	11,013,718	5,500,023	18,270,250	11,288,261	4,986,988	....	2,796,405	12,233,481
1880....	13,415,957	7,232,178	22,190,966	14,077,294	6,195,971	....	3,328,209	14,391,115
1881....	14,756,547	8,805,347	20,736,750	12,659,987	5,675,731	....	3,225,356	15,979,576
1882....	16,062,379	9,427,765	17,672,252	12,022,577	5,426,455	....	3,159,417	14,642,128
1883....	21,675,654	9,387,201	20,142,433	12,480,094	9,472,365	2,000,562	3,068,717	17,212,621
1884....	22,308,523	8,058,711	16,434,983	9,358,816	7,620,887	2,879,309	2,518,873	15,773,005
1885....	20,971,666	7,696,778	14,702,538	9,031,417	6,906,207	2,909,246	2,471,863	13,813,249
1886....	22,103,555	7,775,705	18,476,532	10,329,625	7,938,572	3,522,548	2,877,157	16,894,908
1887....	15,967,363	8,596,172	21,143,098	12,547,923	9,309,987	4,471,697	3,170,563	18,466,701
1888....	15,099,105	7,615,665	20,259,352	12,197,661	9,365,073	4,767,223	3,150,474	20,359,293
1889....	14,717,172	11,498,017	19,821,550	11,270,451	8,519,068	4,292,586	2,971,110	20,023,148
1890....	16,328,628	12,981,104	21,515,907	13,433,192	9,307,029	5,122,149	7,319,921	22,507,184
1891....	16,714,855	13,971,815	21,392,168	12,988,400	9,389,985	5,534,574	8,337,130	22,233,916
1892....	....	....	26,777,687	14,617,655	10,628,916	5,823,882	9,129,417	24,859,494

TABLE 133.—GROSS FREIGHT EARNINGS EXCLUSIVE OF RECEIPTS FROM ELEVATORS, WHARVES, STOCK YARDS, ETC.—Continued.

Year.	Freight (gross earnings).							
	New York, Pennsylvania and Ohio R. R.	Chicago and Erie R. R.	Pennsylvania R. R.	Pittsburg Fort Wayne and Chicago Rwy.	Pittsburg, Cincinnati and St. Louis Rwy.	Chicago, St. Louis and Pittsburg Rwy.	Pittsburg, Cincinnati, Chicago and St. Louis Rwy.	Baltimore and Ohio R. R.
1855	....	....	$2,805,306	....	....	....	....	....
1856	....	....	3,244,292	....	....	....	....	....
1857	....	....	3,374,041	$657,686	....	....	....	....
1858	....	....	3,536,206	667,296	....	....	....	....
1859	....	....	3,656,111	964,133	....	....	....	....
1860	....	....	4,191,784	1,309,714	....	....	....	....
1861	....	....	5,398,026	1,905,707	....	....	....	$2,324,367
1862	....	....	7,668,420	2,401,630	....	....	....	2,712,362
1863	....	....	8,602,262	3,341,034	....	....	....	4,177,139
1864	....	....	10,361,999	4,148,504	....	....	....	5,963,110
1865	....	....	11,193,565	4,739,068	....	....	....	6,704,337
1866	....	....	11,709,294	4,707,582	....	....	....	6,516,261
1867	....	....	11,832,300	4,483,616	....	....	....	6,224,376
1868	$3,702,860	....	12,882,165	5,231,857	$1,483,454	....	....	6,619,864
1869	4,022,915	....	12,932,657	5,020,874	1,690,382	$2,299,595	....	7,999,011
1870	3,318,902	....	12,793,160	4,892,326	1,880,024	....	....	7,471,007
1871	....	....	14,052,305	5,581,051	2,320,076	2,852,014	....	9,133,518
1872	4,126,479	....	16,856,891	6,909,306	6,863,733	3,201,585	....	9,758,885
1873	4,134,844	....	19,608,555	6,716,399	2,725,024	3,298,011	....	10,658,999
1874	3,738,243	....	17,227,504	5,841,961	2,653,317	2,691,990	....	10,175,432
1875	2,913,581	....	15,651,741	5,430,511	2,317,645	2,522,593	....	8,900,940
1876	2,729,627	....	14,539,785	5,266,172	2,193,116	2,328,911	....	7,957,885
1877	2,911,543	....	14,642,109	4,790,424	2,191,782	2,293,411	....	6,897,241
1878	2,764,781	....	15,904,501	5,600,557	2,270,836	2,379,661	....	7,363,110
1879	3,084,716	....	17,016,989	6,066,593	2,643,714	2,815,910	....	7,693,794
1880	3,945,494	....	20,234,046	7,395,452	3,217,078	3,521,559	....	9,819,891
1881	4,057,264	....	32,572,448	7,785,730	2,884,041	3,625,508	....	9,407,337
1882	4,315,028	....	34,829,240	7,464,057	2,927,998	3,636,670	....	8,634,169
1883	....	....	36,400,551	7,432,479	3,243,607	3,781,107	....	9,559,555
1884	....	$1,028,730	30,366,227	6,111,247	2,706,212	2,902,433	....	9,424,494
1885	....	927,004	30,895,748	5,500,653	2,793,620	3,159,887	....	8,003,037
1886	....	896,689	34,623,877	6,249,610	3,504,742	3,448,447	....	7,895,976
1887	....	1,497,819	38,080,823	7,940,113	4,327,355	4,314,563	....	15,780,460
1888	....	1,731,648	39,147,056	6,671,751	5,414,648	4,086,640	....	14,382,285
1889	....	1,570,293	39,935,701	7,443,913	4,961,085	3,895,286	....	14,311,052
1890	....	2,003,954	45,632,959	8,434,588	5,877,749	4,895,496	....	16,820,156
1891	....	1,646,426	45,085,147	....	....	....	$11,300,325	16,475,903
1892	....	2,202,798	47,019,280	....	....	....	12,328,023	17,742,040

Year.	Freight (gross earnings).							
	Baltimore and Ohio Southwestern R. R.	Ohio and Mississippi Rwy.	Cincinnati, Hamilton, and Dayton R. R.	Wabash R. R.	Louisville, New Albany and Chicago Rwy.	Chicago and Grand Trunk Rwy.	Chicago, Milwaukee and St. Paul Rwy.	Chicago and Northwestern Rwy.
1865	....	....	....	....	....	....	....	$4,448,599
1866	....	....	....	....	....	....	....	5,393,191
1867	....	....	....	....	....	....	....	6,649,590
1868	....	$1,586,819	$727,276	....	....	....	$4,266,284	8,266,809
1869	....	1,567,498	696,692	....	....	....	4,909,525	9,291,478
1870	....	1,789,140	493,342	....	....	....	5,148,356	8,187,597
1871	....	1,883,780	544,150	....	....	....	4,444,568	7,700,808
1872	....	2,164,499	592,215	....	....	....	4,566,991	7,521,275
1873	....	2,589,361	590,161	....	....	....	6,421,369	8,614,260
1874	....	2,329,745	574,847	....	....	....	6,137,152	10,270,519
1875	....	1,949,519	531,980	....	....	....	5,690,568	8,837,828
1876	....	....	509,696	....	....	....	5,384,231	9,001,178
1877	....	[1]1,295,832	521,954	....	....	....	5,627,906	8,415,599
1878	....	1,908,809	492,643	$3,514,999	....	....	5,750,497	10,016,921
1879	....	2,522,338	505,161	....	....	....	6,850,755	9,924,030
1880	....	2,686,608	1,493,977	....	$618,778	1,086,849	8,884,227	11,995,975
1881	....	2,949,350	1,721,790	....	710,490	1,182,106	11,844,796	14,414,151
1882	....	2,099,345	1,748,872	....	1,022,292	1,419,726	14,002,335	17,525,134
1883	....	2,631,748	1,855,381	....	1,142,329	1,989,757	16,365,354	16,894,352
1884	....	2,379,626	1,772,569	....	1,087,240	2,155,807	16,128,964	17,677,866
1885	....	2,063,548	1,657,670	....	1,185,286	1,944,598	17,101,742	16,917,394
1886	....	2,227,255	1,668,424	....	1,343,564	2,900,990	17,358,294	17,503,244
1887	....	2,407,825	2,030,879	....	1,627,217	2,444,932	17,742,142	19,329,484
1888	....	2,268,672	2,062,668	4,537,282	1,570,822	2,382,385	16,933,042	19,208,436
1889	$1,135,195	2,218,962	2,036,071	4,502,257	1,612,300	2,244,049	17,297,317	18,018,182
1890	657,433	2,433,555	2,183,089	9,258,053	1,718,962	2,848,656	18,337,010	19,864,152
1891	1,375,221	2,332,248	2,317,739	8,860,819	1,871,460	2,591,371	19,012,159	19,980,910
1892	1,678,800	2,467,779	2,676,120	9,800,969	2,139,357	2,749,298	23,241,421	23,320,914

[1] 8 months.

TABLE 133.—GROSS FREIGHT EARNINGS EXCLUSIVE OF RECEIPTS FROM ELEVATORS, WHARVES, STOCK YARDS, ETC.—Continued.

Year.	Freight (gross earnings).							
	Chicago, Burlington and Quincy R. R.	Chicago, Rock Island and Pacific Rwy.	Chicago and Alton R. R.	Illinois Central R. R.	Wisconsin Central R. R.	Northern Pacific R. R.	Union Pacific Rwy.	Atchison, Topeka and Santa Fe R. R.
1862	....	....	[1]$215,467	$1,893,998	....	....	....	....
1863	$2,542,827	$1,034,850	1,120,448	2,500,960	....	....	....	....
1864	2,979,016	1,448,965	1,479,659	3,706,633	....	....	....	....
1865	3,919,860	2,222,309	2,155,152	4,010,587	....	....	....	....
1866	4,204,741	2,016,306	2,309,499	3,945,865	....	....	....	....
1867	4,124,693	2,428,824	2,430,008	4,490,521	....	....	....	....
1868	4,216,911	2,934,504	2,953,629	4,172,841	....	....	$3,458,104	....
1869	4,758,864	3,575,916	3,066,144	4,602,817	....	....	....	....
1870	4,514,629	3,587,002	3,312,068	4,609,890	....	....	3,058,515	$110,754
1871	4,949,684	4,023,272	3,740,203	4,737,975	....	....	3,629,489	256,187
1872	5,299,874	4,213,372	3,607,643	4,305,617	$68,214	....	4,768,419	....
1873	8,035,349	4,597,983	3,897,462	4,148,901	98,864	$237,154	5,516,908	805,557
1874	8,445,910	5,003,001	3,446,881	3,986,691	378,998	251,325	5,664,731	836,197
1875	8,502,617	5,292,412	3,173,531	3,619,239	420,038	259,318	6,641,512	1,116,749
1876	....	5,121,557	3,541,346	3,190,448	....	....	7,304,123	1,688,107
1877	9,554,544	5,253,779	3,067,769	3,032,337	483,996	563,780	7,597,681	1,853,248
1878	11,152,179	5,575,733	3,409,510	3,174,160	496,018	779,616	8,295,878	2,826,483
1879	11,650,623	6,920,926	4,242,791	3,262,526	596,544	701,696	8,692,414	4,883,435
1880	16,054,197	8,045,165	5,808,484	3,671,373	815,417	1,585,514	15,218,507	6,499,981
1881	16,595,819	8,690,480	5,546,870	5,875,649	960,045	2,207,299	17,063,127	9,051,623
1882	15,711,510	9,687,097	5,948,123	5,918,152	937,132	3,909,423	15,402,167	10,537,201
1883	19,514,161	7,928,237	6,197,681	8,664,959	924,699	5,409,080	14,268,292	10,374,012
1884	18,514,431	8,056,316	6,073,675	7,902,043	916,262	7,865,367	11,660,311	11,946,453
1885	19,565,853	8,144,142	5,482,633	8,145,920	990,258	7,446,266	12,070,749	10,873,621
1886	19,367,935	7,713,659	5,392,059	8,332,151	1,012,369	8,189,615	12,230,271	11,100,967
1887	18,675,655	8,037,452	6,070,639	9,034,863	1,358,246	8,730,547	13,436,495	12,248,344
1888	15,660,444	8,975,020	5,672,808	8,246,163	1,419,176	10,127,461	13,700,499	10,538,462
1889	17,222,739	8,773,829	4,952,952	8,910,464	2,642,711	12,671,095	12,849,983	9,731,075
1890	19,698,608	12,293,176	5,345,620	10,004,754	3,437,206	15,447,885	14,575,124	15,017,156
1891	16,495,602	11,240,988	4,672,880	12,160,600	3,743,347	17,388,955	13,679,227	17,114,821
1892	21,444,246	12,525,794	5,472,271	[2]12,809,973	[2]3,987,833	[2]17,220,705	14,251,969	19,114,978

[1] 2½ months. [2] As reported; not verified in this office.

Year.	Freight (gross earnings).					
	Denver and Rio Grande R. R.	Texas and Pacific Rwy.	Chesapeake and Ohio Rwy.	Louisville and Nashville R. R.	Richmond and Danville R. R.	Mobile and Ohio R. R.
1862	....	....	....	$403,231	....	....
1863	....	....	....	831,659	....	....
1864	....	....	....	1,110,106	....	....
1865	....	....	....	1,311,342	....	[3]$894,541
1866	....	....	....	1,426,890	$381,773	1,433,491
1867	....	....	....	1,152,477	399,500	1,400,815
1868	....	....	$316,985	1,215,703	363,001	1,179,182
1869	....	....	....	1,353,795	375,192	1,384,402
1870	....	....	360,481	1,723,644	405,701	1,760,072
1871	....	....	421,904	1,847,089	476,535	....
1872	....	....	[1]393,201	2,015,266	514,648	2,089,681
1873	$200,129	$231,557	710,385	3,135,798	613,872	2,074,795
1874	200,846	572,473	950,312	3,172,550	602,130	1,838,924
1875	213,631	729,866	993,862	2,615,936	608,793	1,423,998
1876	....	1,113,044	1,177,942	....	589,518	1,493,421
1877	520,259	1,449,988	1,285,184	3,455,704	612,637	1,614,240
1878	....	1,660,645	1,527,151	3,723,643	669,713	1,625,071
1879	....	1,582,926	1,444,768	3,627,925	801,247	1,444,737
1880	2,411,457	2,053,018	1,993,812	5,134,225	1,275,889	1,772,984
1881	4,332,150	2,408,083	2,658,361	7,407,403	1,437,016	1,791,503
1882	4,412,186	3,806,944	2,600,539	8,050,339	2,318,122	1,617,932
1883	5,351,912	4,567,043	3,081,032	8,786,574	2,606,225	1,716,339
1884	4,232,447	4,057,484	2,728,468	9,233,671	2,511,760	1,712,923
1885	4,580,491	3,868,716	2,639,569	8,703,795	2,660,755	1,526,494
1886	5,003,160	4,282,448	3,319,371	8,655,860	2,646,434	1,471,097
1887	5,772,172	4,186,782	3,504,421	10,254,483	2,716,699	1,762,181
1888	5,621,209	4,384,699	3,515,909	11,594,266	5,385,859	1,957,347
1889	5,243,879	4,365,922	3,296,801	7,715,865	6,323,713	2,090,797
1890	5,743,750	5,065,557	5,285,402	8,599,267	7,311,908	2,333,020
1891	6,189,360	4,857,269	5,963,516	8,750,893	6,696,386	2,653,444
1892	6,017,044	4,748,077	....	[2]9,965,266	[2]6,334,433	[2]2,554,407

[1] Eastern division. [2] As reported; not verified in this office. [3] 7½ months.

CHANGES IN LOCAL RATES.

Rates charged between points located upon the same road are designated as "local rates." Numerous causes have operated to reduce the charges upon traffic carried at such rates; principal among these have been the reductions in freight classifications and the operation of the act to regulate commerce. Prior to April, 1887, local rates were in many instances upon a higher basis than those charged between terminals, the latter, in the majority of cases, being competitive points and having the benefit of competitive rates. When the act referred to became effective it was found that the majority of these rates were at variance with the fourth section, known as the long and short haul clause of the act. A very general revision of the tariffs covering the local traffic therefore became necessary, which has resulted in large reductions to local points.

Aside from these causes there has been a gradual downward tendency of rates of this character, and there are few roads throughout the United States which within the last ten or fifteen years have not reduced their local rates from 10 to 50 per cent. Considerable data have been collected for the purpose of showing the extent of these changes upon roads in various sections of the United States, and will here follow. The most satisfactory form of presenting these changes would be to show the rates upon the principal commodities carried by the different roads for which tables are given. It has been, however, impossible to do this through failure to obtain the classifications applying exclusively to local traffic, and the comparisons are, therefore, necessarily confined to the rates of the respective classes.

TABLE 134.—COMPARISON OF LOCAL MILEAGE RATES CHARGED BY MAINE CENTRAL RAILROAD DURING 1872 AND 1893.

Distances.	Classes (rates in cents per 100 pounds).							
	1.		2.		3.		4.	
	1872.	1893.	1872.	1893.	1872.	1893.	1872.	1893.
For 50 miles	33	26	22	18	12½	12½	9	9
For 100 miles	42	34	32	26	18	18	15	15
For 150 miles	49	40	39	31	22	22	19	19
For 200 miles	54	45	44	35	25	25	22	22

TABLE 135.—COMPARISON OF FREIGHT RATES CHARGED FOR THE TRANSPORTATION OF THE ARTICLES NAMED FROM BOSTON, MASS., TO LOCAL STATIONS IN MASSACHUSETTS DURING 1868, 1874, 1881, 1887, AND 1893.

[Compiled from tariffs of Boston and Albany Railroad.]

[Cents per 100 pounds.]

Articles.	From Boston, Mass., to—																										
	South Framingham, Mass.									Westboro, Mass.									Worcester, Mass.								
		1874.		1881.		1887.		1893.			1874.		1881.		1887.		1893.			1874.		1881.		1887.		1893.	
	1868.	C. L.	L. C. L.	C. L.	L. C. L.	C. L.	L. C. L.	C. L.	L. C. L.	1868.	C. L.	L. C. L.	C. L.	L. C. L.	C. L.	L. C. L.	C. L.	L. C. L.	1868.	C. L.	L. C. L.	C. L.	L. C. L.	C. L.	L. C. L.	C. L.	L. C. L.
Bacon	12	11	11	8	8	5	5	5	5	14	12	12	9	9	6	6	6	6	15	15	15	11	11	7	7	7	7
Boots and shoes	12	11	11	9	9	9	9	9	9	14	12	12	10	10	10	10	10	10	15	15	15	12	12	12	12	12	12
Coffee	12	11	11	6	6	5	5	5	5	14	12	12	8	8	6	6	6	6	15	15	15	9	9	7	7	7	7
Cutlery	12	11	11	9	9	8	8	8	8	14	12	12	10	10	9	9	9	9	15	15	15	12	12	11	11	11	11
Dry goods	12	11	11	9	9	9	9	9	9	14	12	12	10	10	10	10	10	10	15	15	15	12	12	12	12	12	12
Glassware	12	11	11	9	9	8	8	6	8	14	12	12	10	10	9	9	8	9	15	15	15	12	12	11	11	9	11
Starch	12	11	11	6	6	5	5	5	5	14	12	12	8	8	6	6	6	6	15	15	15	9	9	7	7	7	7
Twine	12	11	11	9	9	9	9	5	9	14	12	12	10	10	10	10	6	10	15	15	15	12	12	12	12	7	12
Crockery, in hogsheads or casks	9	8	8	6	6	5	5	5	5	11	9	9	8	8	6	6	6	6	12	10	10	9	9	7	7	7	7
Flour	9	8	8	5	6	5	5	5	5	11	9	9	6	8	6	6	6	6	12	10	10	7	9	7	7	7	7
Rice	9	9	9	6	6	5	5	5	5	11	11	11	8	8	6	6	6	6	12	12	12	9	9	7	7	7	7
Soap	9	9	9	8	8	5	5	5	5	11	11	11	9	9	6	6	6	6	12	12	12	11	11	7	7	7	7
Vinegar	9	9	9	6	6	5	6	5	6	11	11	11	8	8	6	8	6	8	12	12	12	9	9	7	9	7	9
Axle grease	8	8	8	6	6	5	5	5	5	9	9	9	8	8	6	6	6	6	10	10	10	9	9	7	7	7	7
Cement	8	6	8	5	6	5	5	5	5	9	7	9	6	8	6	6	6	6	10	9	10	7	9	7	7	7	7
Lard	8	8	8	6	6	5	5	5	5	9	9	9	8	8	6	6	6	6	10	10	10	9	9	7	7	7	7
Nails	8	8	8	6	6	5	5	5	5	9	9	9	8	8	6	6	6	6	10	10	10	9	9	7	7	7	7
Sugar, in hogsheads	8	8	9	6	8	5	5	5	5	9	9	11	8	9	6	6	6	6	10	10	12	9	11	7	7	7	7
Coal	7	6	9	5	8	5	9	5	9	8	7	11	6	9	6	10	6	10	9	9	12	7	11	7	12	7	12
Plaster	7	6	8	5	6	5	5	5	5	8	7	9	6	8	6	6	6	6	9	9	10	7	9	7	7	7	7

Articles.	From Boston, Mass, to—																										
	Springfield, Mass.									North Adams, Mass.									Brookfield, Mass.								
		1874.		1881.		1887.		1893.			1874.		1881.		1887.		1893.			1874.		1881.		1887.		1893.	
	1868.	C. L.	L. C. L.	C. L.	L. C. L.	C. L.	L. C. L.	C. L.	L. C. L.	1868.	C. L.	L. C. L.	C. L.	L. C. L.	C. L.	L. C. L.	C. L.	L. C. L.	1868.	C. L.	L. C. L.	C. L.	L. C. L.	C. L.	L. C. L.	C. L.	L. C. L.
Bacon	25	24	24	17	17	12	12	12	12	38	38	38	27	27	15	15	15	15	21	18	18	13	13	9	9	9	9
Boots and shoes	25	24	24	20	20	20	20	20	20	38	38	38	31	31	30	30	30	30	21	18	18	15	15	15	15	15	15
Coffee	25	24	24	14	14	12	12	12	12	38	38	38	23	23	15	15	15	15	21	18	18	11	11	9	9	9	9
Cutlery	25	24	24	20	20	17	17	17	17	38	38	38	31	31	27	27	27	27	21	18	18	15	15	13	13	13	13
Dry goods	25	24	24	20	20	20	20	20	20	38	38	38	31	31	30	30	30	30	21	18	18	15	15	15	15	15	15
Glassware	25	24	24	20	20	17	17	14	17	38	38	38	31	31	27	27	22	27	21	18	18	15	15	13	13	11	13
Starch	25	24	24	14	14	12	12	12	12	38	38	38	23	23	15	15	15	15	21	18	18	11	11	9	9	9	9
Twine	25	24	24	20	20	20	20	12	20	38	38	38	31	31	30	30	15	30	21	18	18	15	15	15	15	9	15
Crockery, in hogsheads or casks	21	17	17	14	14	12	12	12	12	32	25	25	23	23	15	15	15	15	17	13	13	11	11	9	9	9	9
Flour	21	17	17	12	14	12	12	12	12	32	25	25	19	23	15	15	15	15	17	13	13	9	11	9	9	9	9
Rice	21	21	21	14	14	12	12	12	12	32	32	32	23	23	15	15	15	15	17	16	16	11	11	9	9	9	9
Soap	21	21	21	17	17	12	12	12	12	32	32	32	27	27	15	15	15	15	17	16	16	13	13	9	9	9	9
Vinegar	21	21	21	14	14	12	14	12	14	32	32	32	23	23	15	22	15	22	17	16	16	11	11	9	11	9	11
Axle grease	18	21	21	14	14	12	12	12	12	25	25	25	23	23	15	15	15	15	14	13	13	11	11	9	9	9	9
Cement	18	14	17	12	14	12	12	12	12	25	21	25	19	23	15	15	15	15	14	11	13	9	11	9	9	9	9
Lard	18	17	17	14	14	12	12	12	12	25	25	25	23	23	15	15	15	15	14	13	13	11	11	9	9	9	9
Nails	18	17	17	14	14	12	12	12	12	25	25	25	23	23	15	15	15	15	14	13	13	11	11	9	9	9	9
Sugar	18	17	21	14	17	12	12	12	12	25	25	32	23	27	15	15	15	15	14	13	16	11	13	9	9	9	9
Coal	15	14	21	12	17	12	20	12	20	21	21	32	19	27	15	30	15	30	12	11	16	9	13	9	15	9	15
Plaster	15	14	17	12	14	12	12	12	12	21	21	25	19	23	15	15	15	15	12	11	13	9	11	9	9	9	9

TABLE 135.—COMPARISON OF FREIGHT RATES CHARGED FOR THE TRANSPORTATION OF THE ARTICLES NAMED FROM BOSTON, MASS., ETC.—Continued.

Articles.	From Boston, Mass., to—																										
	Pittsfield, Mass.									Chatham, N. Y.									East Albany, N. Y.								
		1874.		1881.		1887.		1893.			1874.		1881.		1887.		1893.			1874.		1881.		1887.		1893.	
	1868.	C. L.	L. C. L.	C. L.	L. C. L.	C. L.	L. C. L.	C. L.	L. C. L.	1868.	C. L.	L. C. L.	C. L.	L. C. L.	C. L.	L. C. L.	C. L.	L. C. L.	1868.	C. L.	L. C. L.	C. L.	L. C. L.	C. L.	L. C. L.	C. L.	L. C. L.
Bacon	35	33	33	24	24	15	15	15	15	42	38	38	27	27	15	15	15	15	45	42	42	30	30	15	15	15	15
Boots and shoes	35	33	33	28	28	28	28	28	28	42	38	38	32	32	30	30	30	30	45	42	42	35	35	30	30	30	30
Coffee	35	33	33	20	20	15	15	15	15	42	38	38	23	23	15	15	15	15	45	42	42	25	25	15	15	15	15
Cutlery	35	33	33	28	28	24	24	24	24	42	38	38	32	32	27	27	27	27	45	42	42	35	35	27	27	27	27
Dry goods	35	33	33	28	28	28	28	28	28	42	38	38	32	32	30	30	30	30	45	42	42	35	35	30	30	30	30
Glassware	35	33	33	28	28	24	24	20	24	42	38	38	32	32	27	27	22	27	45	42	42	35	35	27	27	22	27
Starch	35	33	33	20	20	15	15	15	15	42	38	38	23	23	15	15	15	15	45	42	42	25	25	15	15	15	15
Twine	35	33	33	28	28	28	28	15	28	42	38	38	32	32	30	30	15	30	45	42	42	35	35	30	30	15	30
Crockery, in hogsheads or casks	29	23	23	20	20	15	15	15	15	35	27	27	23	23	15	15	15	15	37	30	30	25	25	15	15	15	15
Flour	29	23	23	16	20	15	15	15	15	35	27	27	18	23	15	15	15	15	37	30	30	20	25	15	15	15	15
Rice	29	29	29	20	20	15	15	15	15	35	33	33	23	23	15	15	15	15	37	36	36	25	25	15	15	15	15
Soap	29	29	29	24	24	15	15	15	15	35	33	33	27	27	15	15	15	15	37	36	36	30	30	15	15	15	15
Vinegar	29	29	29	20	20	15	20	15	20	35	33	33	23	23	15	22	15	22	37	36	36	25	25	15	22	15	22
Axle grease	23	23	23	20	20	15	15	15	15	29	27	27	23	23	15	15	15	15	30	30	30	25	25	15	15	15	15
Cement	23	19	23	16	20	15	15	15	15	29	22	27	18	23	15	15	15	15	30	24	30	20	25	15	15	15	15
Lard	23	23	23	20	20	15	15	15	15	29	27	27	23	23	15	15	15	15	30	30	30	25	25	15	15	15	15
Nails	23	23	23	20	20	15	15	15	15	29	27	27	23	23	15	15	15	15	30	30	30	25	25	15	15	15	15
Sugar	23	23	29	20	24	15	15	15	15	29	27	33	23	27	15	15	15	15	30	30	36	25	30	15	15	15	15
Coal	19	19	29	16	24	15	28	15	28	23	22	33	18	27	15	30	15	30	25	24	36	20	30	15	30	15	30
Plaster	19	19	23	16	20	15	15	15	15	23	22	27	18	23	15	15	15	15	25	24	30	20	25	15	15	15	15

TABLE 136.—COMPARISON OF LOCAL FREIGHT RATES CHARGED BY THE NEW YORK AND NEW ENGLAND RAILROAD FROM BOSTON TO STATIONS NAMED DURING 1886 AND 1893.

[1886, Local classification; 1893, Official classification.]

Distance.	From Boston, Mass., to—	Classes (rates in cents per 100 pounds).									
		1.		2.		3.		4.		5.	6.
		1886.	1893.	1886.	1893.	1886.	1893.	1886.	1893.	1893.	1893.
Miles.											
57	Thompson, Conn	18	18	15	15	12	12	10	10	9	8
74	Hampton, Conn	19	18	16	16	14	13	12	11	10	9
86	Willimantic Conn	21	20	19	18	15	15	13	13	11	9
95	Andover, Conn	23	22	19	19	15	16	13	14	12	10
101	Bolton, Conn	25	22	21	19	17	16	15	14	12	10
109	Rockville, Conn	26	24	22	21	18	17	16	15	13	11
109	Manchester, Conn	25	22	21	19	17	16	15	14	12	10
117	Hartford, Conn	25	22	21	19	17	16	15	14	12	10
126	New Britain, Conn	25	22	21	19	17	16	15	14	12	10
131	Plainville, Conn	28	22	24	19	19	16	16	14	12	10
133	Forestville, Conn	30	26	25	23	20	19	17	15	13	12
135	Bristol, Conn	30	26	25	23	21	19	17	15	13	12
150	Waterbury, Conn	30	27	25	24	21	20	17	15	14	13
174	Hawleyville, Conn	38	30	33	25	28	20	23	15	15	14
180	Danbury, Conn	38	30	33	25	28	20	23	15	15	14
185	Mill Plain, N. Y	40	30	35	25	29	20	24	15	15	14
190	Brewster, N. Y	40	30	35	25	29	20	24	15	15	14
196	Towners, N. Y	40	30	35	25	29	20	24	15	15	15
198	West Patterson, N. Y	40	30	35	25	29	20	24	15	15	15
207	Poughquag, N. Y	42	30	37	25	31	20	26	15	15	15
211	Stormville, N. Y	42	30	37	25	31	20	26	15	15	15
215	Hopewell, N. Y	42	30	37	25	31	20	26	15	15	15
228	Fishkill Landing, N. Y	45	30	40	25	34	20	28	15	15	15
229	Newburg, N. Y	49	30	43	25	36	20	30	15	15	15

TABLE 137.—COMPARISON OF LOCAL FREIGHT RATES CHARGED BY THE NEW YORK, LAKE ERIE AND WESTERN RAILROAD BETWEEN ELMIRA, N. Y., AND STATIONS NAMED DURING 1886 AND 1893.

Distance.	Between Elmira, N. Y., and—	Classes (rates in cents per 100 pounds).												
		1.		2.		3.		4.		A.	5.	B.	6.	C.
		1886.	1893.	1886.	1893.	1886.	1893.	1886.	1893.	1886.	1893.	1886.	1893.	1886.
Miles.														
73	Great Bend, Pa	21	21	17	18	13	15	10	10	8½	8½	7½	7½	6¼
81	Susquehanna, Pa	21	22	18	19	14	16	11	11	8½	9	7½	8	6½
97	Deposit, N. Y	24	24	19	21	15	17	12	12	9	10	8	9	7
110	Hancock, N. Y	26	26	20	22	16	18	13	13	10	11	9	10	7½
138	Callicoon, N. Y	28	28	22	24	17	20	15	15	11¼	12½	10	11½	8½
151	Narrowsburg, N. Y	28	28	22	25	17	21	15	15	11¾	13	10½	12	9¼
157	Mast Hope, Pa	30	30	23	26	18	21	16	16	12	13½	10½	12½	9¼
163	Lackawaxen, Pa	30	30	23	26	18	21	16	16	12¼	13½	10¾	12½	9¾
167	Shohola, Pa	31	31	24	27	19	22	17	17	12½	13½	10¾	12½	9¾
186	Port Jervis, N. Y	33	33	27	28	20	23	17	17	13	14	11½	13	10½
198	Otisville, N. Y	34	34	27	29	21	24	18	18	13¼	14	11¾	13	10¾
203	Howells, N. Y	35	35	28	30	22	25	18	18	13¾	15	12½	13	11¼
207	Middletown, N. Y	35	35	28	30	22	25	18	18	13¾	15	12½	13	11¼
210	Hampton, N. Y	35	35	28	30	22	25	18	18	13¾	15	12½	13	11¼
214	Goshen, N. Y	35	35	28	30	22	25	18	18	13¾	15	12½	13	11¼
220	Greycourt, N. Y	37	35	29	30	23	25	18	18	14	15	13	13	11¾
224	Monroe, N. Y	37	35	29	30	23	25	18	18	14	15	13	13	11¾
226	Turners, N. Y	37	35	29	30	23	25	18	18	14	15	13	13	11¾
239	Sterlington, N. Y	38	35	30	30	23	25	18	18	14½	15	13½	13	12¼
246	Ramseys, N. J	39	35	31	30	23	25	18	18	15	15	14	13	12½
250	Hohokus, N. J	40	35	32	30	23	25	18	18	15½	15	14½	13	12¾
252	Ridgewood, N. J	40	35	32	30	23	25	18	18	15½	15	14½	13	12¾
257	Paterson, N. J	40	35	32	30	23	25	18	18	15½	15	14½	13	12¾
262	Passaic, N. J	40	35	32	30	23	25	18	18	15¾	15	15	13	13
264	Rutherford, N. J	40	35	32	30	23	25	18	18	15¾	15	15	13	13
273	Jersey City, N. J	41	35	33	30	24	25	19	18	16	15	15	13	13¼
274	New York, N. Y	41	35	33	30	24	25	19	18	.....	15	.....	13	.....

NOTE.—Rates given for 1886 were subject to Joint Merchandise classification; those for 1893 to Official classification.

TABLE 138.—COMPARISON OF LOCAL FREIGHT RATES CHARGED BY THE NEW YORK, LAKE ERIE, AND WESTERN RAILROAD BETWEEN PATERSON, N. J., AND STATIONS NAMED DURING 1886 AND 1893.

[1886, Joint Merchandise classification; 1893, Official classification.]

Distance.	Between Paterson, N. J., and—	Classes (rates in cents per 100 pounds).												
		1.		2.		3.		4.		A.	5.	B.	6.	C.
		1886.	1893.	1886.	1893.	1886.	1893.	1886.	1893.	1886.	1893.	1886.	1893.	1886.
Miles.														
5	Ridgewood, N. J	8	8	7	7	6	6	4	5	3	3	2¾	2½	2½
7	Hohokus, N. J	8	10	7	8	6	7	4	5	3¼	3½	2¾	3	2½
11	Ramseys, N. J	8	11	7	9	6	7	5	5	3½	4	3	3½	2¾
15	Suffern, N. Y	10	12	8	10	7	8	5	6	4	4½	3½	4	3
18	Sterlington, N. Y	10	13	8	10	7	9	5	7	4	5	3½	4½	3
31	Turners, N. Y	14	14	11	11	10	10	7	7	4¾	5½	4¼	5	3¾
37	Greycourt, N. Y	15	15	12	12	10	10	7	7	5½	6	4½	5	4
43	Goshen, N. Y	16	16	13	13	11	11	8	8	6¼	6½	5¼	5½	4½
47	Hampton, N. Y	17	17	13	14	11	12	8	8	6½	6½	5½	5½	4¾
50	Middletown, N. Y	18	18	14	15	12	13	9	9	6¾	7	5¾	6	5¼
71	Port Jervis, N. Y	21	21	17	18	13	15	10	10	8½	8½	7½	7½	6¼
94	Lackawaxen, Pa	24	24	19	21	15	17	12	12	9	10	8	9	6¾
160	Deposit, N. Y	30	30	23	26	18	21	16	16	12¼	13½	10¾	12	9¾
176	Susquehanna, Pa	33	33	26	28	20	23	17	17	12½	14	11	13	10
184	Great Bend, Pa	33	33	27	28	20	23	17	17	13	14	11½	13	10½
198	Binghamton, N. Y	34	34	27	29	21	24	18	18	13¼	14	11¾	13	10¾
220	Owego, N. Y	37	35	29	30	23	25	18	18	14	15	13	13	11¾
239	Waverly, N. Y	38	35	30	30	23	25	18	18	14½	15	13½	13	12¼
244	Chemung, N. Y	39	35	31	30	23	25	18	18	15	15	14	13	12½
257	Elmira, N. Y	40	35	32	30	23	25	18	18	15½	15	14½	13	12½
274	Corning, N. Y	41	35	33	30	24	25	19	18	16	15	15	13	13¼
285	Addison, N. Y	42	35	34	30	25	25	20	18	16¼	15	15¼	13	13½
311	Canisteo, N. Y	45	35	36	30	27	25	21	18	16¾	15	15¾	13	13¾
327	Canaserago, N. Y	45	35	36	30	27	25	21	18	16¾	15	15¾	13	13¾
332	Swains, N. Y	45	35	37	30	27	25	22	18	17	15	16	13	14¼
339	Dalton, N. Y	45	35	37	30	27	25	22	18	17	15	16	13	14¼
345	Portage, N. Y	45	35	37	30	27	25	22	18	17	15	16	13	14¼
351	Silver Springs, N. Y	46	35	38	30	28	25	23	18	17	15	16	13	14½
358	Warsaw, N. Y	46	35	38	30	28	25	23	18	17	15	16	13	14½
364	Date, N. Y	46	39	38	33	28	28	23	19	17	16	16	13	14½
368	Linden, N. Y	46	39	38	33	28	28	23	19	17	16	16	13	14½
375	Attica, N. Y	47	39	38	33	29	28	24	19	17¼	16	16¼	13	14¾
396	Lancaster, N. Y	49	39	40	33	30	28	24	19	17¼	16	16¼	13	14¾
406	Buffalo, N. Y	50	39	40	33	30	28	25	19	17¼	16	16¼	13	14¾

TABLE 139.—COMPARISON OF RATES CHARGED FOR THE TRANSPORTATION OF CLASSIFIED TRAFFIC BY THE LEHIGH VALLEY RAILROAD FROM NEW YORK TO POINTS NAMED DURING 1876, 1886, AND 1893.

[1876 and 1886, Joint Merchandise classification; 1893, Official classification.]

Distance.	From New York, N. Y., to—	Classes (rates in cents per 100 pounds).																		
		1876.						1886.							1893.					
		1.	2.	3.	4.	*A.	*B.	1.	2.	3.	4.	*A.	*B.	*C.	1.	2.	3.	4.	5.	6.
Miles.																				
78	Easton, Pa	33	28	22	15	200	160	25	22	18	15	200	160	140	22	18	15	12	10½	9½
90	Bethlehem, Pa	37	30	22	19	240	220	25	22	18	15	200	165	150	24	21	17	14	12	11
94	Allentown, Pa	38	31	23	20	250	225	31	22	18	16	210	190	170	26	22	18	15	13	11
110	Slatington, Pa	41	34	26	22	300	260	35	27	20	16	250	225	200	30	26	20	16	14	11
123	Mauch Chunk, Pa	44	37	28	23	340	280	35	27	20	17	250	225	200	33	27	21	16	14	11
155	Hazelton, Pa	51	43	33	25	400	340	35	30	25	17	280	250	225	35	30	23	17	15	12
159	Mahanoy City, Pa	45	35	27	22	310	310	40	32	25	18	260	235	210	35	30	23	17	15	12
177	Wilkesbarre, Pa	53	43	33	23	390	360	35	30	25	17	280	250	225	35	30	23	17	15	12
208	Tunkhannock, Pa	58	46	35	26	440	370	41	32	26	19	310	270	250	35	30	23	17	15	12
255	TowandaPa	60	48	37	26	450	380	46	36	29	21	340	300	270	35	30	25	18	15	13
308	Ithaca, N. Y	60	48	37	26	450	400	50	39	30	22	360	320	290	35	30	25	18	15	13
346	Geneva, N. Y	62	50	39	28	450	400	50	40	30	23	380	340	300	35	30	25	18	15	13

* Rates per ton.

TABLE 140.—COMPARISON OF LOCAL FREIGHT RATES UPON A MILEAGE BASIS CHARGED BY THE LEHIGH VALLEY RAILROAD FROM 1876 TO THE PRESENT TIME.

Distance.	Classes (rates in cents per 100 pounds).														Classes (rates in cents per ton).				
	1.			2.[1]			3.			4.			5.	6.	A.		B.		C.
	1876–1881.	1882–1886.	1887–1893.	1876–1881.	1882–1886.	1887–1893.	1876–1881.	1882–1886.	1887–1893.	1876–1881.	1882–1886.	1887–1893.	1887–1893.	1887–1893.	1876–1881.	1882–1886.	1876–1881.	1882–1886.	1882–1886.
25 miles	16	15	14	13	12	11	10	9	9	8	7	7	5½	4½	120	110	95	100	90
50 miles	23	21	20	19	17	16	15	13	13	12	10	10	8	7	180	170	150	140	130
75 miles	31	25	24	24	19	19	19	15	15	15	12	12	9	8	250	190	180	170	150
100 miles	36	29	27	28	22	22	23	18	18	17	14	14	10	9	300	220	225	190	170
125 miles	42	32	30	32	24	24	25	20	19	19	15	15	11	10	340	240	260	210	190
150 miles	46	34	32	36	26	26	29	21	21	21	17	16	12	11	380	260	300	230	200
175 miles	52	37	34	41	29	28	32	23	23	24	18	17	14	12	410	280	330	250	220
200 miles	58	40	35	46	31	30	35	25	25	26	19	18	15	13	450	300	360	270	240

NOTE.—Rates 1876 to 1886, inclusive, were governed by a local classification; 1887 to 1893, by successive issues of Official classification.

TABLE 141.—COMPARISON OF FREIGHT RATES CHARGED BY THE PENNSYLVANIA RAILROAD FOR THE TRANSPORTATION OF CLASSIFIED TRAFFIC FROM NEW YORK, PHILADELPHIA, AND BALTIMORE TO POINTS NAMED DURING THE YEARS, 1876, 1886, AND 1893.

[1876 and 1886, Joint Merchandise classification; 1893, Official classification.]

To—	Year.	Classes (rates in cents per 100 pounds).																	
		From New York, N. Y.						From Philadelphia, Pa.						From Baltimore, Md.					
		1.	2.	3.	4.	5.	6.	1.	2.	3.	4.	5.	6.	1.	2.	3.	4.	5.	6.
Trenton, N. J	1876	20	17	15	12	...	...	14	12	11	11	...	...	...	...	...	...	...	...
	1886	17	17	14	12	...	...	10	10	9	8	...	...	35	30	25	18	...	...
	1893	20	16	13	9	8	7	13	11	10	7½	6½	6	29	24	20	14½	12½	10½
Harrisburg, Pa	1876	45	30	25	20	...	...	30	25	20	15	...	...	30	25	20	15	18	...
	1886	35	30	23	17	...	...	30	25	20	15	...	...	35	25	20	15	...	...
	1893	33	28	22	17	15	12	27	22	18	13½	11½	10	27	22	18	13½	11½	10
Altoona, Pa	1876	45	30	25	20	...	...	36	32	28	20	...	...	...	...	...	...	...	...
	1886	43	35	26	20	...	...	37	29	24	18	...	...	35	27	23	17	...	...
	1893	45	39	30	21	18	15	39	33	28	19	16	13	39	33	28	19	16	13
Pittsburg, Pa	1876	45	30	25	29	...	...	36	32	28	20	...	...	...	...	...	...	...	...
	1886	43	35	26	20	...	...	37	29	24	18	...	...	35	27	23	17	...	...
	1893	45	39	30	21	18	15	39	33	28	19	16	33	39	33	28	19	16	13
Williamsport, Pa	1876	40	35	30	25	...	...	36	32	27	23	...	...	43	38	33	25	...	...
	1886	40	32	23	18	...	...	37	29	23	18	...	...	35	27	23	17	...	...
	1893	35	30	23	17	15	12	35	30	23	17	15	12	35	30	23	17	15	12
Erie, Pa	1876	40	35	30	25	...	...	36	32	27	23	...	...	43	38	32	28	...	...
	1886	43	35	26	20	...	...	37	29	24	18	...	...	35	27	23	17	...	...
	1893	45	39	30	21	18	15	39	33	28	19	16	13	39	33	28	19	16	13

TABLE 142.—COMPARISON OF LOCAL FREIGHT RATES CHARGED BY THE BUFFALO, ROCHESTER AND PITTSBURG RAILWAY BETWEEN ROCHESTER, N. Y., AND STATIONS NAMED DURING 1886 AND 1893.

[1886, Joint Merchandise classification; 1893, Official classification.]

Distance.	From Rochester, N. Y., to—	Classes (rates in cents per 100 pounds.)												
		1.		2.		3.		4.		A.	5.	B.	6.	C.
		1886	1893	1886	1893	1886	1893	1886	1893	1886	1893	1886	1893	1886
Miles.														
2	Lincoln Park, N. Y	10	8	8	7	6	6	5	5	4	3	3½	2½	3
12	Scottsville, N. Y	12	10	10	8	8	7	6	5	5	3½	4	3	3½
18	Mumford, N. Y	14	13	12	10	9	9	7	7	6	5	5	4	4
26	Le Roy, N. Y	15	13	12	11	10	9	7	7	6	5	5	4	4
34	Pavilion, N. Y	17	15	13	12	11	10	8	7	7	6	6	5	5
51	Silver Springs, N. Y	18	17	14	13	12	11	9	8	8	6½	7	5½	6
84	Machias, N. Y	20	18	15	15	13	13	9	9	8	7	7	6	6
94	Ashford, N. Y	20	18	15	15	13	13	9	9	8	7	7	6	6
109	Salamanca, N. Y	19	19	15	16	12	14	9	9	8	7½	7	6½	6
109	Kilbuck, N. Y	20	19	16	16	13	14	10	9	9	7½	8	6½	7
118	Limestone, N. Y	27	21	21	18	17	15	13	10	9	8½	8	7½	7
123	Kendall, Pa	27	22	21	19	17	16	13	11	10	9	9	8	8
124	Bradford, Pa	27	22	21	19	17	16	13	11	10	9	9	8	8
131	Big Shanty, Pa	27	23	21	20	17	16	13	11	10	9½	9	8½	8
138	Riderville, Pa	35	24	28	21	21	17	18	12	.....	10	.....	9	.....
144	Mt. Jewett, Pa	35	24	28	21	21	17	18	12	.....	10	.....	9	.....
156	Rasselas, Pa	35	26	28	22	21	18	18	13	.....	11	.....	10	.....
166	Johnsburg, Pa	35	27	28	23	21	19	18	14	.....	11½	.....	10	.....
174	Ridgeway, Pa	27	28	22	24	18	20	15	14	12	12	11	10	10
192	Brockwayville, Pa	27	29	22	24	18	21	15	14	12	12	11	10	10
206	Du Bois, Pa	27	30	22	24	18	21	15	14	12	12	11	10	10
214	Sykes, Pa	35	31	30	27	25	22	20	17	17	13½	16	12½	15
228	Punxsutawney, Pa	35	31	30	27	25	22	20	17	17	13½	16	12½	15
231	Walston, Pa	35	31	30	27	25	22	20	17	17	13½	16	12½	15

TABLE 143.—COMPARISON OF LOCAL FREIGHT RATES FROM BUFFALO, N. Y., TO STATIONS NAMED CHARGED BY THE LAKE SHORE AND MICHIGAN SOUTHERN RAILWAY DURING 1886 AND 1893.

[1886, Middle and Western States classification; 1893, Official classification.]

Distance.	From Buffalo, N. Y., to —	Classes (rates in cents per 100 pounds).											
		1.		2.		3.		4.		5.		6.	
		1886.	1893.	1886.	1893.	1886.	1893.	1886.	1893.	1886.	1893.	1886.	1893.
Miles.													
129	Ashtabula, Ohio	28	21	23	18½	18	13½	13	10	10	8½	7½	7½
183	Cleveland, Ohio	30	22	24	19½	18	14	13	10½	10	9½	8	8
239	Norwalk, Ohio	35	27½	28	24	22	17½	16	13	12	11½	10	10
296	Toledo, Ohio	35	27½	28	24	22	17½	16	13	12	11½	10	10
329	Adrian, Mich	45	36½	35	32	25	23½	19	17	15	15	12	12
368	Butler, Ind	45	37	35	34	25	25	19	17	15	15	12	12
381	Homer, Mich	47	40½	37	35½	27	26	21	19	16	16½	14	14
385	Coldwater, Mich	47	41	37	36½	27	26½	21	19	16	17	14	14
388	Kendallville, Ind	45	37	35	34	25	25	19	17	15	15	12	12
410	Eaton Rapids, Mich	47	40½	37	35½	27	26	21	19	16	16½	14	14
455	South Bend, Ind	50	41	40	36½	30	26½	22½	19	17½	17	15	14
470	Plainwell, Mich	50	41	40	37	30	27	22½	19	17½	17	15	14
540	Chicago, Ill	50	42½	40	37½	30	27½	22½	20	17½	17½	15	15

TABLE 144.—COMPARISON OF LOCAL FREIGHT RATES CHARGED BY THE LAKE SHORE AND MICHIGAN SOUTHERN RAILWAY FROM TOLEDO, OHIO, TO STATIONS NAMED DURING 1886 AND 1893.

[1886, Middle and Western States classification; 1893, Official classification.]

Distance.	From Toledo, Ohio, to—	Year.	Classes (rates in cents per 100 pounds).					
			1.	2.	3.	4.	5.	6.
Miles.								
33	Adrian, Mich	1886	13	11	10	8	6	5
		1893	9	8½	8	7½	6	4½
71	Jackson, Mich	1886	22	19	15	12	7	6
		1893	15½	14	11½	9½	7½	6
85	Homer, Mich	1886	23	21	17	12	9	8
		1893	17	15½	12½	9½	8	7
89	Coldwater, Mich	1886	26	21	17	13	10	8
		1893	19	17	15	11	9	7½
113	Cleveland, Ohio	1886	25	20	15	10	8	6
		1893	20	18	14	10	8	6
114	Eaton Rapids, Mich	1886	30	25	20	15	11	8
		1893	17	15½	12½	9½	8	7
136	Three Rivers, Mich	1886	33	26	20	15	12	9
		1893	24	21½	16½	12	10	8½
159	South Bend, Ind	1886	37	29	20	15	12	10
		1893	26½	24	18	13	11	9
174	Plainwell, Mich	1886	38	30	20	15	12	10
		1893	25	22½	17	12½	10½	9
187	Allegan, Mich	1886	40	30	20	15	12	10
		1893	26½	24	18	13	11	9
244	Chicago, Ill	1886	40	30	20	15	12	10
		1893	33	30	23	15	13	9

TABLE 145.—COMPARISON OF LOCAL FREIGHT RATES CHARGED BY THE LAKE SHORE AND MICHIGAN SOUTHERN RAILWAY FROM CHICAGO, ILL., TO STATIONS NAMED DURING 1886 AND 1893.

[1886, Middle and Western States classification; 1893, Official classification.]

Distance.	From Chicago, Ill., to—	Year.	Class (rates in cents per 100 pounds).					
			1.	2.	3.	4.	5.	6.
Miles.								
49	Otis, Ind	1886	16	14	13	11	8	6
		1893	11½	10½	9½	8	6½	5
89	Mishawaka, Ind	1886	25	22	18	13	10	7½
		1893	18	16	13	10	8	7
130	Three Rivers, Mich	1886	35	26	23	16	13	10
		1893	24	21½	16½	12	10	8
155	Coldwater, Mich	1886	37	30	25	18	13	10
		1893	26	23½	17½	13	11	9
162	Butler, Ind	1886	35	28	22	13	12	10
		1893	27	24	18½	13	10	8½
168	Plainwell, Mich	1886	40	30	20	15	12	10
		1893	28	24½	18½	13½	11½	9
187	Homer, Mich	1886	40	34	27	20	15	12
		1893	29½	26½	20	14	12	9
198	Jackson, Mich	1886	40	34	27	20	15	12
		1893	30½	27	20½	14½	12½	9
211	Adrian, Mich	1886	40	30	23	16	12½	10
		1893	32	28½	21	15	13	9
244	Toledo, Ohio	1886	40	30	23	16	12½	10
		1893	33	30	23	15	13	9
357	Cleveland, Ohio	1886	50	40	30	20	15	12
		1893	37	34	25	17	15	12

TABLE 146.—COMPARISON OF FREIGHT RATES CHARGED FOR THE TRANSPORTATION OF CLASSIFIED TRAFFIC BY THE MICHIGAN CENTRAL RAILROAD FROM DETROIT, MICH., KALAMAZOO, MICH., AND CHICAGO, ILL., TO POINTS NAMED DURING YEARS 1884 AND 1893.

Distance.		Classes (rates in cents per 100 pounds).											
		1.		2.		3.		4.		5.		6.	
		1884.	1893.	1884.	1893.	1884.	1893.	1884.	1893.	1884.	1893.	1884.	1893.
Miles.	From Detroit, Mich., to—												
37½	Ann Arbor, Mich	19	9½	15	9	11	8½	8	7½	7	6	6	5
29	Ypsilanti, Mich	19	7½	15	7½	11	7½	8	7	6	5½	5	4½
76	Jackson, Mich	22	15½	19	14	15	11½	12	9½	7	7½	6	6
108	Bay City, Mich	25	25	20	20	15	15	12	12	10	10	8	8
108	East Saginaw, Mich	25	25	20	20	15	15	12	12	10	10	8	8
96	Albion, Mich	26	17	23	15½	20	12½	14	9½	9	8	8	7
121	Battle Creek, Mich	30	21½	25	19	19	15	14	11	10	9½	9	8
113	Lansing, Mich	30	19	25	16	20	13½	15	11	11	9	9	7
108	Marshall, Mich	30	19½	25	17½	19	13½	14	10½	10	9	9	7½
140	Owosso, Mich	32	19	25	16	20	13½	16	11	12	9	10	7
144	Kalamazoo, Mich	35	25	28	22½	20	17	15	12½	12	10½	9½	9
285	Chicago, Ill	40	33	30	30	20	23	15	15	12	13	10	10
170	Grand Rapids, Mich	40	26½	30	24	20	18	15	13	12	11	10	9
179	Niles, Mich	40	26½	30	24	20	18	15	13	12	11	10	9
228	Michigan City, Ind	40	33	30	30	20	23	15	15	12	13	10	10
	From Kalamazoo, Mich., to—												
107	Ann Arbor, Mich	35	20½	28	18½	20	14½	15	11	12½	9	9½	8
115	Ypsilanti, Mich	35	21½	28	19	20	15	15	11	12½	9½	9½	8
68	Jackson, Mich	24	14½	20	13½	16	11	12	9	8	7½	7	6
182	Bay City, Mich	40	30	30	26	25	19½	18	14	14	12	12	10
169	East Saginaw, Mich	40	30	30	26	25	19½	18	14	14	12	12	10
48	Albion, Mich	24	11½	18	10½	14	9½	12	8	8	6½	7	5½
23	Battle Creek, Mich	22	7½	18	7½	14	7½	10	7	7	5½	5	4
105	Lansing, Mich	33	20	26	18	20	14	15	10½	12	9	9	7½
36	Marshall, Mich	24	9½	18	9	14	8½	12	7½	8	6	7	5
132	Owosso, Mich	40	24	30	21½	25	16½	18	12	15	10	12	8½
144	Detroit, Mich	35	25	28	22½	20	17	15	12½	12½	10½	9½	9
141	Chicago, Ill	35	26½	28	24	20	18	15	13	12	11	9½	8½
162	Grand Rapids, Mich	23	.....	18	.....	15	.....	10	.....	6	.....	5	.....
47	Niles, Mich	30	11½	22	10½	18	9½	14	8	10	6½	7½	5½
84	Michigan City, Ind	35	26½	28	24	20	18	15	13	12	11	9½	8½
	From Chicago, Ill., to—												
248	Ann Arbor, Mich	45	33	35	30	30	22	20	15	15	13	12½	9
256	Ypsilanti, Mich	45	33	35	30	30	22	20	15	15	13	12½	9
209	Jackson, Mich	40	30½	34	27	27	20½	20	14½	15	12½	12	9
323	Bay City, Mich	50	33	40	30	30	23	20	15	12½	13	10	10
309	East Saginaw, Mich	50	33	40	30	30	23	20	15	12½	13	10	10
189	Albion, Mich	40	30½	34	27	27	20½	20	14½	15	12½	12	9
164	Battle Creek, Mich	38	27	30	24	25	18	18	13	15	11	10	8½
246	Lansing, Mich	40	32	35	29	28	22	20	15	15	13	12	9
177	Marshall, Mich	40	29	34	25½	27	19	20	13½	15	12	12	9
273	Owosso, Mich	45	33	35	30	28	23	18	15	14	13	12	9
68	Kalamazoo, Mich	35	26½	28	24	23	18	16	13	13	11	10	8½
285	Detroit, Mich	40	33	30	30	23	23	16	15	12½	13	10	9
303	Grand Rapids, Mich	25	29½	20	26	15	19½	12	14	10	12	9	9
94	Niles, Mich	25	18	22	16	18	13	13	10	10	8	7½	7
57	Michigan City, Ind	18	13	16	12	13	10½	11	8½	10	7½	7½	6

NOTE.—During 1884 rates were subject to Middle and Western States classification; 1893 rates are governed by Official classification.

TABLE 147.—COMPARISON OF LOCAL FREIGHT RATES CHARGED BY THE CINCINNATI, JACKSON AND MACKINAW RAILROAD BETWEEN TOLEDO, OHIO, AND STATIONS NAMED DURING 1886 AND 1893.

[1886 Local classification; 1893 Official classification.]

Distance.	Between Toledo, Ohio, and—	Year.	Classes (rates in cents per 100 pounds).					
			1.	2.	3.	4.	5.	6.
Miles.								
60	Addison, Mich	1886	36	27	21	17	.....	.....
		1893	13	12	10½	8½	7	6
114	Battle Creek, Mich	1886	47	38	29	22	.....	.....
		1893	21½	19	15	11	9½	8
156	Allegan, Mich	1886	53	43	33	27	.....	.....
		1893	26½	24	18	13	11	9

TABLE 148.—COMPARISON OF LOCAL FREIGHT RATES CHARGED BY THE GRAND RAPIDS AND INDIANA RAILROAD DURING 1886 AND 1893.

[1886, Middle and Western States classification; 1892, Official classification.]

Distance.	Classes (rates in cents per 100 pounds).													
	1.		2.		3.		4.		A.	5.	Lumber.	6.	Coal.	6.
	1886.	1893.	1886.	1893.	1886.	1893.	1886.	1893.	1886.	1893.	1886.	1893.	1886.	1893.
Miles.														
5	10	8	8	7	7	6	6	5	5	4	3	3	3½	3
20	17	11	15	10	12	8	10	7	7	6	7	5	5	5
40	25	12½	20	11	16	9	14	7	11	6	8	5	6½	5
60	28	18	23	14	19	11	16	9	12½	7	9	6	7½	6
80	35	22	28	18	23	13	18	11	14½	8	10	7	8	7
100	38	25	31	20	24	15	20	11	17	9	10	7	10	7
200	52	35	42	30	32	22	24	16	22	13	17	12	14	12
250	58	40	48	34	38	26	28	18	24	16	17	14	16	14
300	63	45	53	38	43	28	35	19	30	18	18	16	17½	16
400	67	50	57	40	47	30	38	22	32	20	21	20	19	20
500	70	50	60	40	50	30	40	25	34	23	23	20	21½	20

TABLE 149.—COMPARISON OF LOCAL FREIGHT RATES CHARGED BY THE DETROIT, LANSING AND NORTHERN RAILROAD FROM DETROIT, MICH., TO STATIONS NAMED DURING THE YEARS 1887 AND 1893.

Distance.	From Detroit, Mich., to—	Date.	Classes (rates in cents per 100 pounds)					
			1.	2.	3.	4.	5.	6.
Miles.								
52	Howell, Mich	1887—Prior to Apr. 4	22	19	15	12	10	8
		After Apr. 4	20	16	13	10	8	6½
		1893	14½	12½	10½	9½	7½	6
85	Lansing, Mich	1887—Prior to Apr. 4	30	25	20	15	11	9
		After Apr. 4	23½	21	16	11½	10	8
		1893	19	16	13½	11	9	7
123	Ionia, Mich	1887—Prior to Apr. 4	40	30	20	15	12	10
		After Apr. 4	32	29	20	15	12	9
		1893	25	21	17	13	10½	8½
161	Howard City, Mich	1887—Prior to Apr. 4	42	33	24	17	12½	10
		After Apr. 4	35	29	22	16	12½	10
		1893	31	27	21	15	12½	10
191	Big Rapids, Mich	1887—Prior to Apr. 4	42	33	24	17	12½	10
		After Apr. 4	40	32	24	17	12½	10
		1893	35	30	23	16	12½	10

NOTE.—Rates prior to April 4, 1887, were governed by Middle and Western States classification; subsequent rates, by Official classification.

TABLE 150.—COMPARISON OF LOCAL FREIGHT RATES CHARGED BY THE CHICAGO AND GRAND TRUNK RAILWAY FROM FLINT, MICH., TO POINTS NAMED DURING 1882, 1887, AND 1893.

[During 1882 rates were governed by a local classification; during 1887 by the Middle and Western States classification, and during 1893 by Official classification.]

Distance.	From Flint, Mich., to—	Classes (rates in cents per 100 pounds).																	
		1.			2.			3.			4.			5.			6.		
		1882.	1887.	1893.	1882.	1887.	1893.	1882.	1887.	1893.	1882.	1887.	1893.	1882.	1887.	1893.	1882.*	1887.	1893.
Miles.																			
224	Ainsworth, Ind	59	40	33	49	30	29	39	20	21½	32	15	15	...	12	12	23	10	10
194	Kingsbury, Ind	57	40	30	47	30	27	37	20	20	30	15	14½	...	12	12	22	10	10
156	Edwardsburg, Mich	53	40	26½	43	30	24	33	20	18	27	15	13	...	12	11	20	10	9
138	Wakelee, Mich	51	40	24½	41	30	22	31	20	16½	25	15	12	...	15	10½	19	12	9
104	Climax, Mich	45	40	20	36	30	18	28	20	14	21	15	10½	...	12	9	17	10	7½
21	Bancroft, Mich	22	22	7½	18	18	7½	14	14	7½	10	10	7	...	8	5½	9	6	4
6	Otterburn, Mich	13	13	7	12	12	7	11	11	7	7	7	6	...	5	4½	6	4	3½
48	Emmet, Mich	34	25	11½	25	20	10½	19	15	9½	15	12	8	...	10	6½	12	8	5½

* Rates under head of 6th class for 1882 applied on grain and flour in carloads.

TABLE 151.—COMPARISON OF LOCAL FREIGHT RATES CHARGED BY THE CHICAGO AND GRAND TRUNK RAILWAY FROM CHICAGO, ILL., TO STATIONS NAMED DURING 1882, 1887, AND 1893.

[Rates prior to April 5, 1887, were subject to Middle and Western States classification, and subsequently to Official classification.]

Distance.	From Chicago, Ill., to—	Classes (rates in cents per 100 pounds).																	
		1.			2.			3.			4.			5.			6.		
		1882.	1887.	1893.	1882.	1887.	1893.	1882.	1887.	1893.	1882.	1887.	1893.	1882.	1887.	1893.	1882.	1887.	1893.
Miles.																			
55	Ainsworth, Ind	10	10	9½	9	9	9	8	8	8½	7	7	7½	7	6	6	7	5	5
75	Kingsbury, Ind	23	18	16	22	16	13	18	13	12	13	9	10	12	7	8	10	6	6
113	Edwardsburg, Mich	29	29	20	25	25	18	20	20	14	14	14	10½	13	13	9	10	10	7
131	Wakelee, Mich	35	35	24	28	28	21½	23	23	16½	16	16	12	14	13	10	13	9½	8
165	Climax, Mich	38	38	27	30	30	24	25	25	18	18	18	13	15	15	11	12½	10	8½
248	Bancroft, Mich	45	45	33	35	30	30	30	28	22	20	18	15	18	14	13	15	11	9
263	Otterburn, Mich........	42	40	33	40	35	30	30	28	23	25	18	15	15	12	13	12½	10	9
317	Emmet, Mich...........	50	45	33	40	35	30	30	30	23	20	20	15	18	15	13	15	12½	9

TABLE 152.—COMPARISON OF LOCAL FREIGHT RATES CHARGED BY THE CHICAGO AND GRAND TRUNK RAILWAY FROM CHARLOTTE, MICH., TO STATIONS NAMED DURING 1882, 1886, AND 1893.

[During 1882 rates were governed by a local classification; during 1886 by the Middle and Western States classification, and during 1893 by Official classification.]

Distance.	From Charlotte, Mich., to—	Classes (rates in cents per 100 pounds).																	
		1.			2.			3.			4.			5.			6.		
		1882.	1886.	1893.	1882.	1886.	1893.	1882.	1886.	1893.	1882.	1886.	1893.	1882.	1886.	1893.	1882.*	1886.	1893.
Miles.																			
156	Ainsworth, Ind	53	40	26½	43	30	24	33	20	18	27	15	13	...	12	11	20	10	8
126	Kingsbury, Ind	50	40	23½	40	30	21	30	20	16	24	15	11½	...	12	10	18	10	8
83	Edwardsburg, Mich....	42	36	18	33	28	16	26	20	13	20	15	10	...	12	8½	16	10	7
70	Wakelee, Mich.........	39	36	15½	30	28	14	24	20	11½	18	15	9½	...	12	7½	14	10	6½
36	Climax, Mich	30	30	9½	23	23	9	17	17	8	13	13	7½	...	10	6	11	7	5
47	Bancroft, Mich.........	34	34	11½	25	25	10½	19	19	9½	15	15	8	...	12	6½	12	10	5½
62	Otterburn, Mich	37	35	14	28	28	12½	22	20	10½	17	15	8½	...	12	7	13	10	6
116	Emmet, Mich	47	35	21½	38	30	19	29	20	15	22	15	11	...	12	9½	17	10	8

*Rates under head of 6th class for 1882 applied on grain and flour in car loads.

TABLE 153.—COMPARISON OF LOCAL FREIGHT RATES CHARGED BY THE CHICAGO AND GRAND TRUNK RAILWAY FROM PORT HURON, MICH., TO STATIONS NAMED DURING 1881, 1887, AND 1893.

[Rates prior to April 5, 1887, were subject to Middle and Western States classification, and subsequently to Official classification.]

Distance.	From Port Huron, Mich., to—	Classes (rates in cents per 100 pounds).																	
		1.			2.			3.			4.			5.			6.		
		1881.	1887.	1893.	1881.	1887.	1893.	1881.	1887.	1893.	1881.	1887.	1893.	1881.	1887.	1893.	1881.	1887.	1893.
Miles.																			
290	Ainsworth, Ind	52	40	33	42	30	30	36	20	23	25	15	15	21	12	12	19	10	10
260	Kingsbury, Ind	45	40	33	35	30	30	25	20	23	18	15	15	15	12	12	12½	10	10
222	Edwardsburg, Mich....	40	40	26½	30	30	24	20	20	18	15	15	13	12½	12	11	10	10	9
204	Wakelee, Mich..........	41	40	26½	32	30	24	25	23	18	20	18	13	17	15	11	15	12	9
170	Climax, Mich	40	35	25	31	28	22½	25	22	17	20	16	12½	14	12	10½	12	10	9
87	Bancroft, Mich.........	30	30	18	22	22	16	17	17	13	14	14	10	12	12	8½	10	10	7
72	Otterburn, Mich........	26	26	15½	21	21	14	16	16	11½	13	13	9½	11	11	7½	8	8	6½
18	Emmet, Mich...........	18	18	7½	15	15	7½	12	12	7½	10	10	7	8	8	5	6	6	4

TABLE 154.—LOCAL FREIGHT RATES CHARGED FOR VARIOUS DISTANCES BY THE LAKE ERIE AND WESTERN RAILROAD DURING 1886 AND 1893.

[1886, Local classification; 1893, Official classification.]

Distance.	Classes (rates in cents per 100 pounds).											
	1.		2.		3.		4.		5.		6.	
	1886.	1893.	1886.	1893.	1886.	1893.	1886.	1893.	1886.	1893.	1886.	1893.
10 miles	16	10	14	9	12	7	9	5½	7	4	2½	3½
25 miles	19	13	17	12	15	8	11	6	7	5	5	4½
50 miles	27	16½	22	14½	18	10½	15	8	9	6½	7	5½
100 miles	36	21	31	19	26	15	20	11	14	9	9	7½
200 miles	54	31	44	29	36	23	28	15	21	12½	13½	9
300 miles	65	36	55	33	45	24	35	17	26	14	18½	11
400 miles	77	40	67	36	53	25½	41	18	31	15	22	12

TABLE 155.—COMPARISON OF LOCAL FREIGHT RATES CHARGED BY THE CLEVELAND, CINCINNATI, CHICAGO AND ST. LOUIS RAILWAY FROM CINCINNATI TO STATIONS NAMED DURING 1886 AND 1893.

Distance.	From Cincinnati, Ohio, to—	Classes (rates in cents per 100 pounds).											
		1.		2.		3.		4.		5.		6.	
		1886.	1893.	1886.	1893.	1886.	1893.	1886.	1893.	1886.	1893.	1886.	1893.
Miles.													
22.3	Mands, Ohio	15	7½	12	7½	9	7½	8	7	7	5½	5	4½
48.8	Carrollton, Ohio	20	12	17	11½	12	11	10	9	8	7½	6	6
87.3	Moorefield, Ohio	29	25	24	22	17	20	14	13	11	9	8	8
113.2	Marysfield, Ohio	40	25	30	22	20	20	15	13	12	9	8	8
	White Sulphur, Ohio	41	25	31	22	21	20	16	13	13	9	8	8
146.7	Cardington, Ohio	44	28	35	24	25	21	18	13½	15	10	9	8½
158.5	St. James, Ohio (Iberia)	45	28	36	24	25	21	18	13½	16	10	9	8½

TABLE 156.—COMPARISON OF LOCAL FREIGHT RATES CHARGED BY THE CLEVELAND, CINCINNATI, CHICAGO, AND ST. LOUIS RAILWAY FROM CLEVELAND, OHIO, TO STATIONS NAMED DURING 1886 AND 1893.

Distance.	From Cleveland, Ohio, to—	Classes (rates in cents per 100 pounds).											
		1.		2.		3.		4.		5.		6.	
		1886.	1893.	1886.	1893.	1886.	1893.	1886.	1893.	1886.	1893.	1886.	1893.
Miles.													
	North Eaton, Ohio	15	7½	11	7½	8	7	7	6½	7	6	5	5
	Rochester, Ohio	19	15½	16	14	11	13	10	10	7	7½	6	6
	Shiloh, Ohio	24	16½	20	14	15	13	13	10	9	7½	7	6
110.6	Agosta, Ohio	38	25	29	22	20	17	15	13	11	9	8	8
150.0	De Graff, Ohio	44	31	35	26	25	22	18	14	15	11	9	9
	Houston, Ohio	45	31	36	26	26	22	19	14	18	11	9	9
215.6	Farmland, Ind	48	33	38	30	30	23	22	15	19	13	11	10
255.0	Pendleton, Ind	50	35	40	32	33	24	24	16	20	13	11	11

TABLE 157.—COMPARISON OF LOCAL FREIGHT RATES CHARGED BY THE OHIO AND MISSISSIPPI RAILWAY FROM CINCINNATI, OHIO, TO STATIONS NAMED DURING YEARS 1876, 1887, AND 1893.

[Governed by Official classification.]

Distance.	From Cincinnati, Ohio, to—	Classes (rates in cents per 100 pounds).																	
		1.			2.			3.			4.			5.			6.		
		1876.	1887.	1893.	1876.	1887.	1893.	1876.	1887.	1893.	1876.	1887.	1893.	1876.	1887.	1893.	1876.	1887.	1893.
Miles.																			
52	Osgood, Ind	20	24	24	18	22	22	15	19	19	13	12½	12⅓	...	9	9	...	8	8
73	North Vernon, Ind	20	24	24	16	22	22	13	19	19	9	12½	12½	7	9	9	6	8	8
98	Lexington, Ind	43	24	21	35	22	22	30	19	19	25	12½	12½	...	9	9	...	8	8
130	Louisville, Ky	25	25	25	20	22	20	15	20	15	10	13	10	8	9	8	8	8	8
106	Medora, Ind	44	25	25	36	22	22	31	20	20	25	13	13	...	9	9	...	8	8
127	Mitchell, Ind	32	25	25	25	22	22	18	20	20	13	13	13	10	9	9	9	8	8
158	Loogootee, Ind	45	31	31	40	26	26	30	22	22	25	14	14	...	11	11	...	9	9
173	Washington, Ind	55	31	31	45	26	26	37	22	22	28	14	14	22	11	11	18	9	9
192	Vincennes, Ind	40	31	31	30	26	26	20	22	22	15	14	14	13	11	11	10	9	9
223	Olney, Ill	50	33	33	40	30	30	27	23	23	18	15	15	15	13	13	12	10	10
245	Flora, Ill	70	40	40	55	34	34	45	25	25	33	17	17	...	15	15	...	12	12
270	Salem, Ill	73	40	40	58	34	34	48	25	25	34	17	17	...	15	15	...	12	12
293	Carlyle, Ill	74	40	40	59	34	34	49	25	25	35	17	17	...	15	15	...	12	12
316	Lebanon, Ill	75	40	40	60	34	34	50	25	25	35	17	17	...	15	15	...	12	12
341	East St. Louis, Ill	50	40	40	40	34	34	27	25	25	18	17	17	15	15	15	12	12	12

TABLE 158.—COMPARISON OF LOCAL FREIGHT RATES CHARGED BY THE OHIO AND MISSISSIPPI RAILWAY FROM EAST ST. LOUIS, ILL., TO STATIONS NAMED DURING YEARS 1876, 1887, AND 1893.

[Governed by Official classification.]

Distance.	From East St. Louis, Ill., to—	Classes (rates in cents per 100 pounds).																	
		1.			2.			3.			4.			5.			6.		
		1876.	1887.	1893.	1876.	1887.	1893.	1876.	1887.	1893.	1876.	1887.	1893.	1876.	1887.	1893.	1876.	1887.	1893.
Miles.																			
48	Carlyle, Ill	31	21	21	25	19	19	21	17	17	15	11½	11½	12	8	8	...	7	7
96	Flora, Ill	40	24	24	32	22	22	26	19	19	19	12½	12½	16	9	9	...	8	8
118	Olney, Ill	45	25	25	35	22	22	28	20	20	22	13	13	17	9	9	...	8	8
149	Vincennes, Ind	40	31	31	30	26	26	20	22	22	15	14	14	11	11	11	9	9	9
191	Shoals, Ind	59	31	31	49	26	26	40	22	22	30	14	14	...	11	11	...	9	9
214	Mitchell, Ind	50	33	33	40	30	30	30	23	23	20	15	15	15	13	13	13	10	10
268	North Vernon, Ind	50	40	40	40	34	34	30	25	25	20	17	17	15	15	15	13	12	12
289	Osgood, Ind	74	40	40	59	34	34	49	25	25	35	17	17	...	15	15	...	12	12
341	Cincinnati, Ohio	50	40	40	40	34	34	30	25	25	20	17	17	15	15	15	13	12	12
293	Lexington, Ind	74	40	40	59	34	34	49	25	25	35	17	17	...	15	15	...	12	12
325	Louisville, Ky	53	40	40	43	34	34	33	25	25	23	17	17	17	15	15	15	12	12

TABLE 159.—COMPARISON OF LOCAL FREIGHT RATES CHARGED BY WABASH RAILROAD FROM CHICAGO TO STATIONS NAMED DURING YEARS 1882, 1887, AND 1893.

[Subject to Western classification.]

Distance.	From Chicago, Ill., to—	Year.	Classes (rates in cents per 100 pounds).								
			1.	2.	3.	4.	5.	A.	B.	C.	D.
Miles.											
549	Belknap, Ia	1882	70	60	50	40	......	34	29	26	23
		1887	75	60	50	35	30	35	30	25	20
		1893	40	30	22	17	12.5	17	15	12	10
544	Bloomfield, Ia	1882	70	60	50	40	30	34	29	26	23
		1887	75	60	50	35	30	35	30	25	20
		1893	40	30	22	17	12.5	17	15	12	10
617	Burlington Junction, Mo	1882	101	83	65	40	......	38	38	29	27
		1887	102	85	70	45	40	45	40	35	30
		1895	60	50	35	25	18	25	20	15	14
497	Carrollton, Mo	1882	82	67	50	32	29	32	29	24	22
		1887	85	70	50	35	30	35	30	25	20
		1893	60	50	35	25	18	25	20	15	14
410	Centralia, Mo	1882	73	61	49	26	24	26.5	23.5	21	17.5
		1887	73	61	49	26	26	26.5	23.5	21	17.5
		1893	60	50	35	25	18	24	20	15	12.5
511	Chillicothe, Mo	1882	75	66	48	30	......	35	29	19	19
		1887	75	65	48	30	30	35	29	19	19
		1893	60	50	35	25	18	25	20	15	14
636	Cain, Ia	1882	102	85	70	45	40	45	40	35	30
		1887	102	85	70	45	40	45	40	35	30
		1893	60	50	35	25	18	25	20	15	14
490	Cunningham, Mo	1882	80	65	50	31	......	31	28	23	21
		1887	85	70	50	35	30	35	30	25	20
		1893	60	50	35	25	18	25	20	15	14
572	Darlington, Mo	1882	90	75	55	35	30	35	30	25	20
		1887	90	75	55	35	30	32.5	29.5	23	23
		1893	60	50	35	25	18	25	20	15	14
537	Gallatin, Mo	1882	85	70	45	30	30	35	30	25	......
		1887	90	75	50	35	30	32.5	29.5	23	23
		1893	60	50	35	25	18	25	20	15	14
	Glasgow, Mo	1882	75	62	50	30	30	30	27	24.5	21
		1887	75	62	50	30	30	30	27	24.5	21
		1893	60	50	35	25	18	25	20	15	14
516	Glenwood and Glenwood J	1882	73	58	48	33	28	33	28	23	20
		1887	75	60	50	35	30	35	30	25	20
		1892	40	30	22	17	12.5	17	15	12	10
491	Kirksville, Mo	1882	75	60	50	35	30	25	30	25	20
		1887	75	60	50	35	30	35	30	25	20
		1893	60	50	35	25	18	24	20	15	13
	Lathrop, Mo	1882	85	70	45	30	......	37.5	30	20	......
		1887	90	75	50	35	30	32.5	29.5	23	23
		1893	60	50	35	25	18	25	20	15	14
456	Macon, Mo	1882	60	54	38	25	......	27.5	22.5	15	......
		1887	60	54	38	25	25	27.5	22.5	15.5	15.5
		1893	60	50	35	25	18	24	20	15	13
671	Malvern, Iowa	1882	104	84	60	45	......	40	36	31	28
		1887	102	85	70	45	40	45	40	35	30
		1893	60	50	35	25	18	25	20	15	14
604	Maryville, Mo	1882	94	81	65	32	......	33	33	30	25.75
		1887	102	85	70	45	40	45	40	35	30
		1893	60	50	35	25	18	25	20	15	14
396	Mexico, Mo	1882	70	60	46	25	......	25	22	19.5	17
		1887	70	60	46	25	25	25	22	19.5	17
		1893	60	50	35	25	18	24	20	15	12.5
434	Moberly, Mo	1882	75	60	50	35	......	35	30	20	......
		1887	75	60	45	30	27	30	25	20	18
		1893	60	50	35	25	18	24	20	15	12.5
530	Moulton, Iowa	1882	70	60	50	40	......	34	29	26	23
		1887	75	60	50	35	30	35	30	25	20
		1893	40	30	22	17	12.5	17	15	12	10
565	Ottumwa, Iowa	1882	70	60	50	29	......	34	29	24	24
		1887	68	55	40	27.5	22.5	27.5	22.5	20	15
		1893	40	30	22	17	12.5	17	15	12	10
	Plattsburg, Mo	1882	85	70	45	30	......	35	30	25	......
		1887	90	75	50	35	30	32.5	29.5	23	23
		1893	60	50	35	25	18	25	20	15	14
616	Roseberry, Mo	1882	101	83	58	44	......	47	42	35	30
		1887	102	85	70	45	40	45	40	35	30
		1893	60	50	35	25	18	25	20	15	14
318	St. Peters, Mo	1882	62	50	39	25	23	25	22	20	15
		1887	60	50	40	25	20	25	20	17	15
		1893	60	50	35	25	18	24	20	15	12.5
649	Shenandoah, Iowa	1882	102	83	59	44	......	40	35	30	27
		1887	102	85	70	45	40	45	40	35	30
		1893	60	50	35	25	18	25	20	15	14
537	West Grove, Iowa	1882	70	60	50	40	......	34	29	26	23
		1887	75	60	50	35	30	35	30	25	20
		1893	40	30	22	17	12.5	17	15	12	10

TABLE 160.—COMPARISON OF LOCAL FREIGHT RATES CHARGED BY THE WABASH RAILROAD FROM TOLEDO, OHIO, TO STATIONS NAMED DURING 1876, 1882, 1887, AND 1893.

[Rates in effect prior to April, 1887, were governed by Middle and Western States classification; subsequent rates by Official classification.]

Distance.	From Toledo, Ohio, to—	Classes (rates in cents per 100 pounds).																					
		1.				2.				3.				4.				5.			6.			A.	B.
		1876.	1882.	1887.	1893.	1876.	1882.	1887.	1893.	1876.	1882.	1887.	1893.	1876.	1882.	1887.	1893.	1882.	1887.	1893.	1882.	1887.	1893.	1876.	1876.
Miles.																									
50	Defiance, Ohio	24	16	16	12	20	13	13	11	16	10	10	10	12	7	7	8	6	6	7½	5	5	6	11¼	9¼
94	Fort Wayne, Ind	32	20	20	20½	27	15	16	18½	25	12	12	14½	17	10	10	11	8	8	9	7	6	7	15	12½
118	Huntington, Ind	37	24	24	25	32	20	20	22	24	15	15	19	19	11	11	12	9	9	10	8	6	7½	16¾	14
137	Wabash, Ind	40	28	28	27	34	23	23	24	27	18	18	19	21	13	13	13	11	10	10	9	9	7½	17¾	15¼
166	Logansport, Ind	45	28	30	30	38	23	24	27	30	18	17	21	24	13	13	14	11	9	10	9	6	8½	19¾	17¼
249	Danville, Ill	55	40	59	37	48	30	45	32	28	25	35	25	30	20	25	16	16	18	12½	13	14	12	25	22½
287	Champaign, Ill	..	50	69	38	..	40	47	33	..	30	35	26	..	25	25	18	22	21	14	20	17	13	...	...
285	Tolono, Ill	61	50	63	38	53	40	47	33	41	30	35	26	33	25	25	18	20	18	14	16	15	13	26¼	23¾
323	Decatur, Ill	66	55	63	39	57	45	47	34	45	35	35	26	36	30	25	18	22	19	15	19	15	13	27½	25
361	Springfield, Ill	71	60	63	40	62	50	47	36	49	40	35	26	40	28	25	18	22½	19	15	20½	15	13	30¼	27¾
395	Jacksonville, Ill	75	60	63	40	66	50	47	36	52	40	35	27	42	30	25	19	23	19	15	21	15	13	32½	30
461	East Hannibal, Ill	85	..	46	47½	74	..	35	42½	59	..	25	31	48	..	17	22½	...	13	20	...	10	16½	36½	34
433	East St. Louis, Ill	80	50	46	41	70	45	35	37	55	35	25	27	45	23	17	19	19	13	17	17	10	14	35	32½

TABLE 161.—COMPARISON OF LOCAL FREIGHT RATES CHARGED BY THE TERRE HAUTE AND INDIANAPOLIS RAILROAD FROM INDIANAPOLIS TO STATIONS NAMED DURING 1883 AND 1893.

Distance.	From Indianapolis, Ind., to—	Commodities (rates in cents per 100 pounds).											
		Alcohol.				Apples, dried.				Fertilizers.			
		Less than carloads.		Carloads.		Less than carloads.		Carloads.		Less than carloads.		Carloads.	
		1883.	1893.	1883.	1893.	1883.	1893.	1883.	1893.	1883.	1893.	1883.	1893.
Miles.													
38	Greencastle, Ind	19	18	11.2	9.5	19	15	11.2	9.5	14	9.5	5.65	6.5
72	Terre Haute, Ind	25	22	14.4	11.5	25	18	14	11.5	17.5	11.5	7	7
80	Farrington, Ill	25.3	23	14.4	11.5	25.3	19.5	14.4	11.5	18	11.5	7.2	7.5
90	Marshall, Ill	25.9	23	15.2	11.5	25.9	19.5	15.2	11.5	19	11.5	7.55	7.5
108	Casey, Ill	27.1	24	16.64	12	27.1	20	16.64	12	20.8	12	8.2	8
117	Greenup, Ill	27.7	26	17.28	12.5	27.7	21	17.28	12.5	21.6	12.5	8.55	8.5
140	Effingham, Ill	28.9	26	18.56	13	28.9	22	18.56	13	23.2	13	9.2	9
152	Altamont, Ill	29.8	28	19.36	14	29.8	22	19.36	14	24.2	14	9.6	9
171	Vandalia, Ill	31	28.5	20	14	31	22.5	20	14	25	14	10	9.5
185	Smithboro, Ill	31.6	30	20.32	14	31.6	23	20.32	14	25.4	14	10.2	9.5
238	East St. Louis, Ill	34.5	32	22.08	15	34.5	24	22.08	15	27.6	15	11.55	10

Distance.	From Indianapolis, Ind., to—	Commodities (rates in cents per 100 pounds).															
		Glassware.				Horse and mule shoes.				Iron fencing.				Oranges and lemons.			
		Less than carloads.		Carloads.		Less than carloads.		Carloads.		Less than carloads.		Carloads.		Less than carloads.		Carloads.	
		1883	1893	1883	1893	1883	1893	1883	1893	1883	1893	1883	1893	1883	1893	1883	1893
Miles.																	
38	Greencastle, Ind	23	18	14	15	14	9.5	7.35	7.5	23	15	9.45	7.5	28	18	19	15
72	Terre Haute, Ind	30	22	17.5	18	17.5	11.5	8.8	9	30	18	11.75	9	36	22	25	18
80	Farrington, Ill	31	23	18	19.5	18	11.5	9	9	31	19.5	12	9	37	23	25.3	19.5
90	Marshall, Ill	32	23	19	19.5	19	11.5	9.4	9	32	19.5	12.4	9	39	23	25.9	19.5
108	Casey, Ill	34	24	20.8	20	20.8	12	10.25	10	34	20	13.2	10	43	24	27.1	20
117	Greenup, Ill	35	26	21.6	21	21.6	12.5	10.7	10.5	35	21	13.6	10.5	45	26	27.7	21
140	Effingham, Ill	37	26	23.2	22	23.2	13	11.55	11	37	22	14.4	11	47	26	28.9	22
152	Altamont, Ill	38.4	28	24.2	22	24.2	14	12	11	38.4	22	14.8	11	48.5	28	29.8	22
171	Vandalia, Ill	40	28.5	25	22.5	25	14	12.6	11.5	40	22.5	15.2	11.5	50.2	28.5	31	22.5
185	Smithboro, Ill	40.8	30	25.4	23	25.4	14	12.9	11.5	40.8	23	15.4	11.5	51	30	31.6	23
238	East St. Louis, Ill	44.4	32	27.6	24	27.6	15	14.5	12	44.4	24	16.6	12	54.8	32	34.5	24

TABLE 161.—COMPARISON OF LOCAL FREIGHT RATES CHARGED BY THE TERRE HAUTE AND INDIANAPOLIS RAILROAD, ETC.—Continued.

Distance.	From Indianapolis, Ind., to—	Commodities (rates in cents per 100 pounds).															
		Poultry, dressed.				Seeds, garden.				Binding twine.				Zinc, pigs and slabs.			
		Less than car-loads.		Car-loads.		Less than car-loads.		Car-loads.		Less than car-loads.		Car-loads.		Less than car-loads.		Carloads.	
		1883	1893	1883	1893	1883	1893	1883	1893	1883	1893	1883	1893	1883	1893	1883	1893
Miles.																	
38	Greencastle, Ind	28	20	14	20	28	18	14	7.5	23	15	14	9.5	14	9.5	11.2	6.5
72	Terre Haute, Ind	36	24.5	17.5	24.5	36	22	17.5	9	30	18	17.5	11.5	17.5	11.5	14	7
80	Farrington, Ill	37	25	18	25	37	23	18	9	31	19.5	18	11.5	18	11.5	14.4	7.5
90	Marshall, Ill	39	25	19	25	39	23	19	9	32	19.5	19	11.5	19	11.5	15.2	7.5
108	Casey, Ill	43	26	20.8	26	43	24	20.8	10	34	20	20.8	12	20.8	12	16.64	8
117	Greenup, Ill	45	29	21.6	29	45	26	21.6	10.5	35	21	21.6	12.5	21.6	12.5	17.28	8.5
140	Effingham, Ill	47	29	23.2	29	47	26	23.2	11	37	22	23.2	13	23.2	13	18.56	9
152	Altamont, Ill	48.5	31	24.2	31	48.5	28	24.2	11	38.4	22	24.2	14	24.2	14	19.36	9
171	Vandalia, Ill	50.2	31	25	31	50.2	28.5	25	11.5	40	22.5	25	14	25	14	20	9.5
185	Smithboro, Ill	51	33	25.4	33	51	30	25.4	11.5	40.8	23	25.4	14	25.4	14	20.32	9.5
238	East St. Louis, Ill	54.8	35	27.6	35	54.8	32	27.6	12	44.4	24	27.6	15	27.6	15	22.08	10

TABLE 162.—COMPARISON OF LOCAL FREIGHT RATES CHARGED BY THE CENTRAL IOWA RAILWAY FROM PEORIA, ILL., TO POINTS NAMED DURING YEARS 1886 AND 1893.

[Governed by Western classification.]

Distance.	From Peoria, Ill., to—	Classes (rates in cents per 100 pounds).																			
		1.		2.		3.		4.		5.		A.		B.		C.		D.		E.	
		1886.	1893.	1886.	1893.	1886.	1893.	1886.	1893.	1886.	1893.	1886.	1893.	1886.	1893.	1886.	1893.	1886.	1893.	1886.	1893.
Miles.																					
335	Mason City, Iowa	73	50	63	40	50	35	36	22	27½	17	31	21	28	16	21	14½	18	11½	...	11
247	Marshalltown, Iowa	66	50	53	40	40	33	26	22	23½	17	26	21	23½	16	21	13½	16	11½	...	10
190	Oskaloosa, Iowa	61	50	48	40	35	33	23½	22	21	17	23½	21	21	16	16	13½	11	11½	...	10
109	Morning Sun, Iowa	44	37	37	28	31	24	23	17	21	12	22½	11	18½	10	15	9½	11	8½	...	7

TABLE 163.—COMPARISON OF LOCAL FREIGHT RATES CHARGED BY THE BURLINGTON, CEDAR RAPIDS AND NORTHERN RAILROAD BETWEEN CHICAGO, ILL. AND STATIONS NAMED, DURING 1886 AND 1893.

[Subject to Western classification.]

Distance.	From Chicago, Ill., to—	Year.	Classes (rates in cents per 100 pounds).									
			1.	2.	3.	4.	5.	A.	B.	C.	D.	E.
Miles.												
215	Latty, Iowa	1886	50	40	34	25	24	24	20	17	15	....
		1893	47	38	29	20	15	15	14	12	11	9
229	Morning Sun, Iowa	1886	53	44	36	27	25	26	22	19	15	....
		1893	47	38	29	20	15	15	14	12	11	9
261	Nichols, Iowa	1886	65	54	44	29	26	27	23	20	16	....
		1893	53	44	32	22	16	19	16	13	12	10
281	Elmira, Iowa	1886	73	58	48	36	27	32	27	23	20	....
		1893	55	45	33	23	16	20	16	14	13	11
295	Ely, Iowa	1886	74	60	50	37	27	32	27	25	20	....
		1893	55	45	33	23	18	23	18	15	13	11
327	Vinton, Iowa	1886	68	57	45	32	26	31	27	21	20	....
		1893	57	47	35	24	18	24	18	15	13	11
357	Waterloo, Iowa	1886	72	59	48	33	28	32	28	22	20	....
		1893	60	50	38	25	20	25	20	16	14	12
362	Cedar Falls, Iowa	1886	73	60	48	33	28	33	28	22	20	....
		1893	60	50	38	25	20	25	20	16	14	12
385	Clarksville, Iowa	1886	76	62	49	35	29	34	29	23	20	....
		1893	60	50	38	25	20	25	20	16	14	12
417	Nora Junction, Iowa	1886	82	68	55	40	31½	38	32	25	23	....
		1893	60	50	40	25	20	25	20	17	14	13
431	Manly Junction, Iowa	1886	84	72	57	41	31½	40	32	25	23	....
		1893	60	50	40	25	20	25	20	17	14	13
447	Gordonsville, Minn	1886	93	78	64	44	34	40	33	25	23	....
		1893	60	50	40	25	20	25	20	17	14	13
459	Albert Lea, Minn	1886	95	80	65	44	35	38	33	25	22½	....
		1893	60	50	40	25	20	25	20	17	14	13

TABLE 164.—COMPARISON OF LOCAL FREIGHT RATES CHARGED FOR THE TRANSPORTATION OF CLASSIFIED TRAFFIC BY THE CHICAGO, MILWAUKEE AND ST. PAUL RAILWAY FROM CHICAGO, ILL., TO STATIONS NAMED DURING YEARS 1883 AND 1893.

[Governed by Western classification.]

Distance.	From Chicago, Ill., to—	Year.	Classes (rates in cents per 100 pounds).									
			1.	2.	3.	4.	5.	A.	B.	C.	D.	E.
Miles.												
228	Marion, Iowa	1883	70	55	45	35	27½	32½	27½	25	20	....
		1893	55	45	33	23	18	23	18	15	13	11
282	Tama, Iowa	1883	75	60	45	35	30	35	30	25	20	....
		1893	58	48	37	24	19	24	18	15	13	12
309	Melbourne, Iowa	1883	75	60	45	35	30	35	30	25	20	....
		1893	62	52	38	26	21	26	21	17	15	13
365	Perry, Iowa	1883	77	62	47	37	32	37	32	26	20	....
		1893	66	53	39	28	23	23	23	19	16	14
417	Manning, Iowa	1883	87	70	56	40	35	40	35	30	24	....
		1893	75	60	42	30	25	30	25	20	17½	16
487	Council Bluffs, Iowa	1883	90	75	50	32	28	37½	32	23	23	....
		1893	75	60	42	30	25	30	25	20	17½	16

TABLE 165.—COMPARISON OF LOCAL FREIGHT RATES CHARGED BY THE CHICAGO AND GREAT WESTERN RAILWAY BETWEEN CHICAGO, ILL., AND POINTS NAMED DURING 1886 AND 1893.

[1886 Joint Western classification, 1893 Western classification.]

Distance.	Between Chicago, Ill., and—	Year.	Classes (rates in cents per 100 pounds).									
			1.	2.	3.	4.	5.	A.	B.	C.	D.	E.
Miles.												
345	Hayfield, Minn	1886	75	60	45	33	25	30	25	22	18	....
		1893	60	50	40	25	20	25	20	17	14	13
354	Dodge City, Minn	1886	70	55	40	30	23	28	24	21	17½	....
		1893	60	50	40	25	20	35	20	17	14	13
363	West Concord, Minn	1886	70	55	40	30	23	27	23	20	17½	....
		1893	60	50	40	25	20	25	20	17	14	13
373	Kenyon, Minn	1886	70	55	40	30	23	27	23	20	17½	....
		1893	60	50	40	25	20	25	20	17	14	13
379	Nerstrand, Minn	1886	70	55	40	30	23	27	23	20	17½	....
		1893	60	50	40	25	20	25	20	17	14	13
393	Randolph, Minn	1886	70	55	40	30	23	27	23	20	17½	....
		1893	60	50	40	25	20	25	20	17	14	13
399	Hampton, Minn	1886	71	53	36	29	23	27	23	20	16	....
		1893	60	50	40	25	20	25	20	17	14	13
403	Empire, Minn	1886	71	53	36	29	23	27	23	20	16	....
		1893	60	50	40	25	20	25	20	17	14	13
410	Rich Valley, Minn	1886	67	50	33	26	21	25	20	18	15	....
		1893	60	50	40	25	20	25	20	17	14	13
418	Invergrove, Minn	1886	64	46	30	24	20	25	20	18	15	....
		1893	60	50	40	25	20	25	20	17	14	13
373	Lyle, Minn	1886	82	70	54	40	31	36	30	26	20	....
		1893	60	50	40	25	20	25	20	17	14	13
368	Varco, Minn	1886	82	75	54	40	30	36	30	25	20	....
		1893	60	50	40	25	20	25	20	17	14	13
362	Austin, Minn	1886	80	65	50	35	27	30	28	25	20	....
		1893	60	50	40	25	20	25	20	17	14	13
355	Red Rock, Minn	1886	80	65	50	35	27	30	28	25	20	....
		1893	60	50	40	25	20	25	20	17	14	13
350	Waltham, Minn	1886	75	60	45	33	25	30	25	22	18	....
		1893	60	50	40	25	20	25	20	17	14	13

TABLE 166.—COMPARISON OF LOCAL FREIGHT RATES CHARGED BY THE WISCONSIN CENTRAL RAILROAD BETWEEN CHICAGO AND POINTS NAMED DURING 1886 AND 1893.

[Subject to Western classification.]

Distance.	Between Chicago, Ill., and—	Classes (rates in cents per 100 pounds).																									
		1.		2.		3.		4.		5.		A.		B.		C.		Salt.		Cement, stucco, and plaster.		Lumber, lath, and shingles.		Cattle.		Hogs and sheep.	
		1886.	1893.	1886.	1893	1886.	1893.	1886.	1893.	1886.	1893.	1886.	1893.	1886.	1893.	1886.	1893.	1886.	1893.	1886.	1893.	1886.	1893.	1886.	1893.	1886.	1893.
Miles.																											
86	Mukwonago, Wis.	28	25	24	20	18	15	14	12	10	8	10	10	8½	7	7½	6	8⅔	5	8⅔	5	7	5	8½	7	8½	10
221	Waupaca, Wis	59	50	51	42	43	33	32	23	25	18	23½	23	19	18	18	15	13⅓	10	13⅓	10	15¾	12	16½	14½	16½	19
250	Stevens Point, Wis	63	50	55	42	44	33	34	23	25	18	26½	23	21½	18	19	15	15	10	15	10	16	12	20	14½	20	20
281	Marshfield, Wis	72	58	62	48	54	37	41	23	30	18	31½	23	24½	18	22	16	18	10	18	10	20¼	12	24	23	24	27[illegible]
317	Medford, Wis	79	60	67	50	58	40	45	25	33	20	35½	25	28	20	23½	17	20⅓	12⅔	20⅓	12½	22½	13	27½	25	27½	32½
358	Phillips, Wis	86	62	74	52	63	42	50	26	40	20	38	26	31½	20	25½	17	23⅔	15	23⅔	12½	24¼	13½	31	27½	31	34½
402	Glenwood, Wis	80	60	70	50	60	40	45	25	30	20	35	25	30	20	25	17	23⅓	12⅓	23⅓	10	24	14	30	25	30	27

TABLE 167.—COMPARISON OF CLASS RATES FROM MILWAUKEE, WIS., TO LOCAL STATIONS ON THE MILWAUKEE AND NORTHERN RAILROAD DURING 1882 AND 1893.

[Subject to Western classification.]

Distance.	From Milwaukee, Wis., to—	Classes (rates in cents per 100 pounds).																			
		1.		2.		3.		4.		5.		A.		B.		C.		D.		E.	
		1882.	1893.	1882.	1893.	1882.	1893.	1882.	1893.	1882.	1893.	1882.	1893.	1882.	1893.	1882.	1893.	1882.	1893.	1882.	1893.
Miles.																					
18	Thiensville, Wis	12	12	11	10	9	9	8	8	6	6	5	5	3½	4	3	3½	...	3	...	3
25	Grafton, Wis	15	15	13	13	11	11	9	9	7	7	6	6	5	5	4½	4½	...	4	...	3
36	Fredonia, Wis	18	18	13	16	13	13	11	11	9	9	7½	7½	6	6	5	5	...	4½	...	4
55	Plymouth, Wis	22	22	20	17½	17	15	13	13	11	10	10	10	8	8	7	7	...	6	...	5
68	Kiel, Wis	28	28	25	22½	20	20	15	16	12	11½	11	11½	9	9	8	8	...	7	...	6
77	Hayton, Wis	32	32	27	27	22	22	17	16	14	12½	12½	14½	10	10	9½	9½	...	8	...	6
86	Hilbert, Wis	32	33	27	28	22	23	17	16	14	12½	14	14	11	11	9½	9½	...	8	...	6
106	Apppleton, Wis	35	35	30	30	24	24	20	16	16	12½	16	14	12	12	10	9½	...	8	...	6
99	Greenleaf, Wis	35	35	30	30	24	24	20	16	16	12½	16	14	12	12	10	9½	...	8	...	6
124	Tremble, Wis	45	37	37	32	30	25	26	18	21	13½	21	15	16	14	14½	12	...	9	...	7
139	Stiles, Wis	53	40	43	33	35	25	29	20	23	15	25	17½	18	15	16	12½	...	10	...	8

TABLE 168.—COMPARISON OF CLASS RATES FROM CHICAGO, ILL., TO LOCAL STATIONS ON THE MILWAUKEE AND NORTHERN RAILROAD DURING 1882 AND 1893.

[Subject to Western classification.]

Distance.	From Chicago, Ill., to—	Classes (rates in cents per 100 pounds).																			
		1.		2.		3.		4.		5.		A.		B.		C.		D.		E.	
		1882.	1893.	1882.	1893.	1882.	1893.	1882.	1893.	1882.	1893.	1882.	1893.	1882.	1893.	1882.	1893.	1882.	1893.	1882.	1893.
Miles.																					
103	Thiensville, Wis	27	27	23	23	19	19	15	15	12	12	10	11	8½	8½	8	8	...	7½	...	6
110	Grafton, Wis	30	30	25	25	21	21	16	16	13	12½	11	12	9½	9½	9	9	...	8	...	6
121	Fredonia, Wis	33	33	28	27	23	23	18	18	15	12½	12½	12½	11	11	10	10	...	9	...	7
140	Plymouth, Wis	37	37	30	30	25	25	20	20	16	12½	14	14	12	12	11	11	...	10	...	8
153	Kiel, Wis	40	40	32	32	27	27	22	20	18	13	15½	16	13	13	12½	12½	...	10	...	8
162	Hayton, Wis	43	43	36	36	29	29	24	20	19	14	17	17½	14	14	13½	12½	...	10	...	8
171	Hilbert, Wis	43	43	36	36	29	29	24	20	19	15	18	17½	15	15	13½	12½	...	10	...	8
191	Appleton, Wis	43	43	36	36	29	29	24	20	19	15	20	17½	16	15	14	12½	...	10	...	8
184	Greenleaf, Wis	43	43	36	36	29	29	24	20	19	15	20	17½	16	15	14	12½	...	10	...	8
209	Tremble, Wis	48	43	39	36	33	29	27	22	22	15	23½	18	19½	15½	17	14	...	11	...	8½
224	Stiles, Wis	53	43	43	36	35	29	29	23	23	17	26	20	21½	17	19	15	...	12	...	11½

TABLE 169.—COMPARISON OF LOCAL FREIGHT RATES CHARGED BY THE MINNEAPOLIS, ST. PAUL AND SAULT STE. MARIE RAILWAY DURING 1886 AND 1893.

[1886, Local classification. 1893, Western classification.]

Miles.		Classes (rates in cents per 100 pounds).																			
		1.		2.		3.		4.		5.		A.		B.		C.		D.		E.	
		1886.	1893.	1886.	1893.	1886.	1893.	1886.	1893.	1886.	1893.	1886.	1893.	1886.	1893.	1886.	1893.	1886.	1893.	1886.	1893.
	From Minneapolis, Minn., to—																				
82.5	Paynesville, Minn	58	45	47	38	37	29	30	23	...	18	...	18	...	16	...	14	...	11	...	9
120.4	Glenwood, Minn	62	52	54	44	44	34	36	26	...	21	...	21	...	18	...	16	...	13	...	10
	From St. Paul, Minn., to—																				
217	Rhinelander, Wis	77	52	66	43	55	33	45	21	35	15	...	21	...	15	...	13	...	11	...	10

TABLE 170.—RATES CHARGED FOR THE TRANSPORTATION OF WHEAT, FLOUR, MILLSTUFFS, CORN, AND OATS FROM POINTS ON THE NORTHERN PACIFIC RAILROAD TO ST. PAUL, AND DULUTH, MINN., FROM AUGUST 5, 1881, TO THE PRESENT TIME.

Distance to St. Paul.	To St. Paul and Duluth from—	Rates in cents per 100 pounds, carloads.													
		Aug. 5, 1881.	Sept. 1, 1882.	Aug. 25, 1883.	Aug. 15, 1884.	Aug. 5, 1885.	Apr. 1, 1886.	Aug. 1, 1886.	Jany. 15, 1887.	Apr. 5, 1887.	Aug. 25, 1887.	Sept. 20, 1888.	Oct. 22, 1888.	Aug. 25, 1890.	Sept. 15, 1892.
Miles.															
	Fergus Falls, Minn	25	23	23	21	21	20	17	17	16½	15	15	15	15	15
251	Fargo, N. Dak	25	25	25	23	23	23	20	20	20	18	18	16	16	15½
344	Jamestown, N. Dak	30	30	30	28	27	25	24	24	24	22	22	22	22	20
445	Bismarck, N. Dak	33	33	33	30	30	30	30	30	30	27	27	27	27	24
95	Grand Forks, N. Dak	....	....	....	....	....	....	....	21	21	19	19	18	18	17
189	Pembina, N. Dak	....	....	....	....	....	....	....	....	....	....	21	19	19	18

TABLE 171.—COMPARISON OF LOCAL FREIGHT RATES CHARGED BY THE NORTHERN PACIFIC RAILROAD BETWEEN THE POINTS NAMED DURING 1886 AND 1893.

Distance from St. Paul.	Between St. Paul, Minneapolis, or Duluth and—	Classes (rates in cents per 100 pounds).																			
		1886, Northern classification.										1893, Western classification.									
		1.	2.	3.	4.	S. 1.	S. 2.	S. 3.	S. 4.	S. 6.	S. 7.	1.	2.	3.	4.	5.	A.	B.	C.	D.	E.
Miles.																					
138	Brainerd, Minn	70	60	50	40	18	36	54	16	30	15	49	42	32	25	20	20	17	15	12	10
204	Detroit, Minn	95	80	65	56	23	46	69	21	38	21	69	59	45	35	28	28	24	21	17	14
251	Fargo, N. Dak	100	85	70	60	23	46	69	22	42	25	80	68	52	40	32	22	28	24	20	16
344	Jamestown, N. Dak	130	115	100	80	28	56	84	30	50	40	95	81	62	48	38	38	33	29	24	19
445	Bismarck, N. Dak	160	145	130	100	40	80	120	41	65	50	120	102	84	72	60	48	42	36	30	24
560	Dickinson, N. Dak	206	180	159	133	58	116	174	52	84	61	142	115	96	85	74	64	55	50	44	36
666	Glendive, Mont	250	220	185	160	80	160	240	60	100	70	155	126	106	94	83	73	63	57	52	42
891	Billings, Mont	295	245	195	170	100	200	300	80	130	95	225	195	158	135	115	100	85	75	65	55

TABLE 172.—COMPARISON OF LOCAL FREIGHT RATES CHARGED BY THE NORTHERN PACIFIC RAILROAD BETWEEN ST. PAUL, MINNEAPOLIS, AND DULUTH, MINN., AND STATIONS NAMED DURING 1887 AND 1893.

[Subject to Western classification.]

Distance from St. Paul.	Between St. Paul, Minneapolis, or Duluth, Minn., and—	Classes (rates in cents per 100 pounds).																		
		1.		2.		3.		4.		5.		A.		B.		C.		D.		E.
		1887.	1893.	1887.	1893.	1887.	1893.	1887.	1893.	1887.	1893.	1887.	1893.	1887.	1893.	1887.	1893.	1887.	1893.	1893.
Miles.																				
1,032	Bozeman, Mont	300	250	250	215	200	175	175	145	160	125	150	110	135	92	125	82	100	72	62
1,130	Helena, Mont	300	250	250	215	200	175	175	145	160	125	150	110	135	92	125	82	100	72	62
1,254	Missoula, Mont	325	260	275	225	225	185	200	155	180	135	170	120	155	102	135	87	110	77	67
1,356	Thompson Falls, Mont	380	295	319	253	253	208	220	172	200	152	185	141	168	134	145	114	118	92	79
1,427	Hope, Idaho	430	322	362	275	286	230	228	186	212	166	197	163	178	146	155	123	125	102	84

TABLE 173.—COMPARISON OF LOCAL FREIGHT RATES CHARGED BY THE UNION PACIFIC RAILWAY BETWEEN OMAHA AND KANSAS CITY AND POINTS NAMED DURING 1883, 1887, AND 1893.

[Subject to Western classification.]

Miles.		Classes (rates in cents per 100 pounds).														
		1.			2.			3.			4.			5.		
		1883.	1887.	1893.	1883.	1887.	1893.	1883.	1887.	1893.	1883.	1887.	1893.	1883.	1887.	1893.
Miles.	Between Omaha, Nebr., and—															
91	Columbus, Nebr	41	41	35	37	37	30	32	32	27	30	30	21	30	30	16
153	Grand Island, Nebr	67	62	51	59	54	45½	51	46	38	45	40	30	45	40	26
196	Kearney, Nebr	72	72	60	64	64	56	56	56	47	50	50	40	50	50	34
569	Denver, Colo	240	210	125	200	170	95	175	140	80	135	115	65	125	100	50
720	Leadville, Colo	395	350	235	345	245	190	310	255	160	255	215	140	225	185	110
1,428	Butte, Mont	300	300	250	250	250	215	200	200	175	175	175	145	....	160	125
1,165	Pocatello, Idaho	340	317	250	305	264	215	265	211	175	225	164	145	220	158	125
	Between Kansas City, Mo., and—															
139	Junction City, Kans	55	55	50	50	49	45½	45	43	37	40	36	28	35	32	24
186	Salina, Kans	65	65	56	58	55	50	50	50	42½	45	43	34	42	38	29
420	Wallace, Kans	126	92	89	114	84	80	101	77	72	86	71	60	84	66	54
639	Denver, Colo	240	210	125	200	170	95	175	140	80	135	115	65	125	100	50
790	Leadville, Colo	395	350	235	345	245	190	310	255	160	255	215	140	225	185	110
746	Cheyenne, Wyo	200	210	125	170	170	95	155	140	80	135	115	65	125	100	50
938	Rawlins, Wyo	263	257	220	228	218	180	210	200	154	160	155	129	160	150	104
1,656	Butte, Mont	300	300	250	250	250	215	200	200	175	175	175	145	....	160	125
1,259	Ogden, Utah	315	300	250	265	250	215	210	200	175	160	155	145	....	150	125
1,393	Pocatello, Idaho	340	317	250	305	264	215	265	211	175	225	164	145	220	158	125

Distance.		Classes (rates in cents per 100 pounds).														
		Class A.			Class B.			Class C.			Class D.			Class E.		
		1883.	1887.	1893.	1883.	1887.	1893.	1883.	1887.	1893.	1883.	1887.	1893.	1883.	1887.	1893.
Miles.	Between Omaha, Nebr., and—															
91	Columbus, Nebr	22½	22½	14	19½	19½	13	15	15	12	15	15	8	....	....	5½
153	Grand Island, Nebr	35	29½	25	25	20	18	22½	17½	15½	....	17½	11	....	....	7½
196	Kearney, Nebr	32½	32½	27½	22½	22½	19½	20	20	18	20	20	13	....	....	9
569	Denver, Colo	100	100	55	75	75	45	65	65	40	50	50	35	....	....	30
720	Leadville, Colo	195	180	115	160	145	100	118	115	90	103	95	70	....	....	65
1,428	Butte, Mont	150	150	110	135	135	92	125	125	82	125	100	72	....	....	62
1,165	Pocatello, Idaho	245	158	110	175	142	92	150	116	82	125	84	72	....	....	62
	Between Kansas City, Mo., and—															
139	Junction City, Kans	30	28	23	20	19	18	15	15	14	15	15	11	....	....	7½
186	Salina, Kans	35	33	27	22	22	21	18	18	17	18	18	13	....	....	10
420	Wallace, Kans	62	51	47	47	41	39	40	32	30	35	32	23	....	....	19
639	Denver, Colo	100	100	55	75	75	45	65	65	40	50	50	35	....	....	30
790	Leadville, Colo	195	180	115	160	145	100	118	115	90	103	95	70	....	....	65
746	Cheyenne, Wyo	100	100	55	75	75	45	75	65	40	50	50	35	....	....	30
938	Rawlings, Wyo	136	131	104	123	118	84	99	92	69	99	80	60	....	....	48
1,656	Butte, Mont	150	150	110	135	135	92	125	125	82	125	100	72	....	....	62
1,259	Ogden, Utah	180	150	110	145	135	92	115	110	82	83	80	72	....	....	62
1,393	Pocatello, Idaho	245	158	110	175	142	92	150	116	82	125	84	72	....	....	62

TABLE 174.—COMPARISON OF LOCAL FREIGHT RATES CHARGED BY THE FREMONT, ELKHORN AND MISSOURI VALLEY RAILROAD BETWEEN OMAHA, NEBR., AND STATIONS NAMED DURING 1886 AND 1893.

[Subject to Western classification.]

Distance.	Between Omaha, Nebr., and—	Year.	Classes (rates in cents per 100 pounds).									
			1.	2.	3.	4.	5.	A.	B.	C.	D.	E.
Miles.												
46	Kennard, Nebr	1886	28	26	23	20	20	15	14	13	11	.....
		1893	26	22	19	17	14	12	10	8	6	4
73	Nickerson, Nebr	1886	34	27	25	23	20	18	15	13	12	.....
		1893	29	26	22	17	13	13	11	9	7	4
100	West Point, Nebr	1886	55	48	41	36	36	28	24	22	19	.....
		1893	37	32	27	23	17	17	14	12	8	5
133	Stanton, Nebr	1886	65	55	48	40	38	28	25	22	19	.....
		1893	45	39	31	23	18	19	15	13	9	7½
155	Battle Creek, Nebr	1886	65	55	48	40	38	29	26	23	19	.....
		1893	48	42	32	24	19	20	15	13	10	7
219	O'Neill, Nebr	1886	84	71	55	50	46	43	38	32	26	.....
		1893	63	53	44	36	28	32	25	20	15	10½
277	Long Pine, Nebr	1886	100	80	70	60	55	51	42	37	29	.....
		1893	76	65	58	48	43	39	31	25	18	12½
333	Valentine, Nebr	1886	124	104	86	67	62	59	49	40	33	.....
		1893	84	76	66	55	51	44	36	28	22	15
438	Rushville, Nebr	1886	148	136	114	94	89	74	64	50	42	.....
		1893	99	91	81	69	63	56	43	36	28	20
470	Chadron, Nebr	1886	158	145	126	103	98	80	71	58	48	.....
		1893	110	99	89	75	69	61	46	38	30	21½

TABLE 175.—COMPARISON OF LOCAL FREIGHT RATES CHARGED BY THE ATCHISON, TOPEKA AND SANTA FE RAILROAD FROM KANSAS CITY, ST. LOUIS, AND CHICAGO TO STATIONS NAMED DURING 1886 AND 1893.

[Subject to Western classification.]

To—	From—	Distance.	Classes (rates in cents per 100 pounds). 1.		2.		3.		4.		5.		A.		B.		C.		D.		E.	
			1886.	1893.	1886.	1893.	1886.	1893.	1886.	1893.	1886.	1893.	1886.	1893.	1886.	1893.	1886.	1893.	1886.	1893.	1886.	1893.
		Miles.																				
Topeka, Kans	Kansas City, Mo	66	30	29	25	24	20	19	15	15	12	12	12	12	11	10	9	8	9	7	.....	5½
	St. Louis, Mo	349	100	84	80	64	60	51	45	40	37	32	37	34½	33	27½	27	23	27	19½	.....	16½
	Chicago, Ill	524	120	104	100	84	70	61	50	45	42	37	44½	42	40½	35	32	28	32	24½	.....	21½
Strong City, Kans	Kansas City, Mo	134	58	51	48	43	43	36	35	28	32	24	28	23	19½	18	15	15	15	11	.....	7½
	St. Louis, Mo	417	128	106	103	83	83	68	65	53	57	44	53	45½	41½	35½	33	30	33	23½	.....	18½
	Chicago, Ill	592	148	126	123	103	93	78	70	58	62	49	60½	53	49	43	38	35	38	28½	.....	23
Florence, Kans	Kansas City, Mo	159	61	52	51	47	46	40	39	32	35	27½	31	26	21	19	17	16	17	12	.....	8½
	St. Louis, Mo	442	131	107	106	87	86	72	69	57	60	47½	56	48½	43	36½	35	31	35	24½	.....	19½
	Chicago, Ill	617	151	127	126	107	96	82	74	62	65	52½	63½	56	50½	44	40	36	40	29½	.....	24½
Newton, Kans	Kansas City, Mo	187	65	58	55	52	50	45	43	36	38	31	33	30	23	22	18	18	18	14	.....	10½
	St. Louis, Mo	470	135	113	110	92	90	77	73	61	63	51	58	52	45	39½	36	33	36	26½	.....	21½
	Chicago, Ill	645	155	133	130	112	100	87	78	66	68	56	65½	59½	52½	47	41	38	41	31½	.....	26½
Wichita, Kans	Kansas City, Mo	214	73	66	64	58	58	50	49	41	43	36	38	32½	25	24	21	20	21	16	.....	12
	St. Louis, Mo	497	143	115	119	93	98	78	79	62½	68	53	63	52	47	39½	39	33	39	27	.....	22
	Chicago, Ill	672	163	135	139	113	108	88	84	67½	73	58	70½	59½	54½	47	44	38	44	32	.....	27
Hutchinson, Kans	Kansas City, Mo	220	73	66	64	58	58	50	49	41	43	36	37	32½	24½	24	21	20	21	16	.....	12
	St. Louis, Mo	503	143	115	119	93	98	78	79	62½	68	53	62	52	46½	39½	39	33	39	27	.....	22
	Chicago, Ill	678	163	135	139	113	108	88	84	67½	73	58	69½	59½	54	47	44	38	44	32	.....	27
Great Bend, Kans	Kansas City, Mo	269	80	66	70	58	62	50	55	41	48	36	40	32½	25½	24	22	21	22	16	.....	12
	St. Louis, Mo	552	150	121	125	98	102	82	85	66	73	56	65	55	47½	41½	40	36	40	28½	.....	23
	Chicago, Ill	727	170	141	145	118	112	92	90	71	78	61	72½	62½	55	49	45	41	45	33½	.....	28
Kinsley, Kans	Kansas City, Mo	304	88	78	78	71	70	63	63	55	55	48	46	40	31	28	26	23	26	20	.....	16
	St. Louis, Mo	587	158	133	133	111	110	95	93	80	80	68	71	62½	53	45½	44	38	44	32½	.....	27
	Chicago, Ill	762	178	153	153	131	120	105	98	85	85	73	78½	70	60½	53	49	43	49	37½	.....	32
Dodge City, Kans	Kansas City, Mo	341	92	87	82	78	74	71	67	60	62	55	49	46	36	32	30	27	30	23	.....	18
	St. Louis, Mo	624	162	142	137	118	114	103	97	85	87	70	72	68½	58	49½	48	42	48	35½	.....	29
	Chicago, Ill	799	182	162	157	138	124	113	102	90	92	75	81½	76	65½	57	53	47	53	40½	.....	34
Garden City, Kans	Kansas City, Mo	390	100	94	90	84	80	76	75	65	70	59	55	51	43	37	33	30	33	26	.....	19
	St. Louis, Mo	673	170	149	145	124	120	108	105	90	95	70	80	73½	65	54½	51	45	51	38½	.....	30
	Chicago, Ill	848	190	169	165	144	130	118	110	95	100	75	87½	81	72½	62	56	50	56	43½	.....	35
Coolidge, Kans	Kansas City, Mo	457	131	94	115	84	98	77	85	65	78	59	66	51	52	41	41	32	41	26	.....	19
	St. Louis, Mo	740	201	149	170	124	138	109	115	90	103	70	91	73½	74	58½	59	47	59	38½	.....	30
	Chicago, Ill	915	221	169	190	144	148	119	120	95	108	75	98½	81	81½	66	64	52	64	43½	.....	35
Las Animas, Kans	Kansas City, Mo	524	172	145	149	117	126	104	103	83	93	73	85	71	63	59	52	44	52	36	.....	29
	St. Louis, Mo	807	242	180	204	135	166	112	133	90	118	70	110	77½	85	62½	70	55	70	47½	.....	40
	Chicago, Ill	982	262	200	224	155	176	122	138	95	123	75	117½	85	92½	70	75	60	75	52½	.....	45

TABLE 175.—COMPARISON OF LOCAL FREIGHT RATES CHARGED BY THE ATCHISON, TOPEKA AND SANTA FE RAILROAD, ETC.—Continued.

To—	From—	Distance.	Classes (rates in cents per 100 pounds). 1.		2.		3.		4.		5.		A.		B.		C.		D.		E.	
			1886.	1893.	1886.	1893.	1886.	1893.	1886.	1893.	1886.	1893.	1886.	1893.	1886.	1893.	1886.	1893.	1886.	1893.	1886.	1893.
		Miles.																				
Colorado common points.	Kansas City, Mo	....	210	125	170	95	140	80	115	65	100	50	100	55	75	45	65	40	50	35	.....	30
	St. Louis, Mo	....	280	180	225	135	180	112	145	90	125	70	125	77½	97	62½	83	55	68	47½	.....	41
	Chicago, Ill	....	300	200	245	155	190	122	150	95	130	75	132½	85	104½	70	88	60	73	52½	.....	46
Utah common points	Kansas City, Mo	....	300	250	250	215	200	175	155	145	150	125	150	110	135	92	110	82	80	72	.....	62
	St. Louis, Mo	....	370	305	305	255	240	207	185	170	175	145	175	132½	157	109½	128	97	98	84½	.....	73
	Chicago, Ill	....	390	325	325	275	250	217	190	175	180	150	182½	140	164½	117	133	102	103	89½	.....	78
Raton, N. Mex	Kansas City, Mo	647	235	180	195	140	165	120	135	95	120	81	115	85	90	70	70	54	65	49	.....	44
	St. Louis, Mo	930	305	212	250	180	205	152	165	120	145	101	140	107½	108	87½	88	69	83	61½	.....	55
	Chicago, Ill	1,105	325	232	270	200	215	162	170	125	150	106	147½	115	115½	95	93	74	88	66½	.....	60
Dorsey, N. Mex	Kansas City, Mo	664	243	188	205	148	175	127	143	102	127	87	121	92	95	75	73	59	68	50	.....	45
	St. Louis, Mo	947	313	212	260	188	215	159	173	127	152	107	146	114½	113	92½	91	74	86	62½	.....	56
	Chicago, Ill	1,122	333	232	287	208	225	169	178	132	157	112	153½	122	120½	100	96	79	91	67½	.....	61
Springer, N. Mex	Kansas City, Mo	688	248	193	210	154	179	131	148	107	131	90	125	94	98	80	75	62	70	53	.....	46
	St. Louis, Mo	971	318	212	265	194	219	163	178	132	156	110	150	116½	116	97½	93	77	88	65½	.....	57
	Chicago, Ill	1,146	338	232	285	210	229	173	183	137	161	115	157½	124	123½	105	98	82	93	70½	.....	62
Wagon Mound, N. Mex.	Kansas City, Mo	713	254	193	217	167	185	143	154	115	138	98	129	101	102	85	78	68	73	58	.....	50
	St. Louis, Mo	996	324	212	272	194	225	175	184	140	163	118	154	123½	120	102½	96	83	91	70½	.....	61
	Chicago, Ill	1,171	344	232	292	210	235	185	189	145	168	123	161½	131	127½	110	101	88	96	75½	.....	66
Watrous, N. Mex	Kansas City, Mo	738	261	193	224	171	192	153	161	123	145	105	134	108	107	89	81	72	76	62	.....	53
	St. Louis, Mo	1,021	331	212	279	194	232	182	191	148	170	125	159	130½	125	106½	99	87	94	74½	.....	64
	Chicago, Ill	1,196	351	232	299	210	242	194	196	153	175	130	166½	138	132½	114	104	92	99	79½	.....	69
Las Vegas, N. Mex	Kansas City, Mo	758	265	193	229	171	197	153	165	130	150	108	137	113	110	93	83	73	78	63	.....	55
	St. Louis, Mo	1,041	335	212	284	194	237	182	195	155	175	128	162	135½	128	110½	101	88	96	75½	.....	66
	Chicago, Ill	1,216	355	232	304	210	247	194	200	160	180	133	169½	143	135½	118	106	93	101	80½	.....	71
Bernal, N. Mex	Kansas City, Mo	777	269	193	234	171	202	153	169	137	154	110	139	117	113	95	85	78	80	70	.....	56
	St. Louis, Mo	1,060	339	212	289	194	242	182	199	162	179	130	164	139½	131	112½	103	93	98	82½	.....	67
	Chicago, Ill	1,235	359	232	309	210	252	194	204	167	184	135	171½	147	138½	120	108	98	103	87½	.....	72
Glorieta, N. Mex	Kansas City, Mo	813	277	193	243	171	210	153	177	137	161	110	144	117	118	99	89	84	84	70	.....	59
	St. Louis, Mo	1,096	347	212	298	194	250	182	207	162	186	130	169	139½	136	116½	107	99	102	82½	.....	70
	Chicago, Ill	1,271	367	232	318	210	260	194	212	167	191	135	176½	147	143½	124	112	104	107	87½	.....	75
Santa Fe, N. Mex	Kansas City, Mo	841	285	193	248	171	216	153	184	137	166	110	150	117	121	102	93	86	88	70	.....	60
	St. Louis, Mo	1,124	355	212	303	194	256	182	214	162	191	130	175	139½	139	119½	111	100	106	82½	.....	71
	Chicago, Ill	1,299	375	232	323	210	266	194	219	167	196	135	182½	147	146½	127	116	106	111	87½	.....	76
Wallace, N. Mex	Kansas City, Mo	854	287	193	254	171	220	153	187	137	169	110	151	117	124	103	95	87	90	70	.....	60
	St. Louis, Mo	1,137	357	212	309	194	260	182	217	162	194	130	176	139½	142	120	113	100	108	82½	.....	71
	Chicago, Ill	1,312	377	232	329	210	270	194	222	167	199	135	183½	147	149½	128	118	107	113	87½	.....	76
Albuquerque, N. Mex.	Kansas City, Mo	890	295	193	264	171	228	153	194	137	175	110	155	117	130	105	99	90	94	70	.....	60
	St. Louis, Mo	1,173	365	212	319	194	268	182	224	162	200	130	180	139½	148	120	117	100	112	82½	.....	71
	Chicago, Ill	1,348	385	232	339	210	278	194	229	167	205	135	187½	147	155½	128	122	107	117	87½	.....	76

San Antonia, N. Mex.	Kansas City, Mo	976	295	193	270	171	235	153	200	137	175	110	155	117	130	105	105	90	100	70	.....	60
	St. Louis, Mo	1,259	365	212	325	194	275	182	230	162	200	130	180	139½	148	120	123	100	118	82½	.....	71
	Chicago, Ill	1,434	385	232	345	210	285	194	235	167	205	135	187½	147	155½	128	128	107	123	87½	.....	76
Deming, N. Mex	Kansas City, Mo	1,121	295	110	270	104	235	102	200	96	175	86	155	89	130	84	105	76	100	65	.....	57
	St. Louis, Mo	1,404	365	129	325	127	275	124	230	116	200	99	180	106½	148	96½	123	86	118	74	.....	65
	Chicago, Ill	1,579	385	149	345	143	285	136	235	121	205	104	187½	114	155½	104	128	91	123	79	.....	70
El Paso, Tex	Kansas City, Mo	1,144	270	145	250	130	220	120	185	112	160	83	145	86	115	78	95	62	85	51	.....	44
	St. Louis, Mo	1,427	315	145	290	130	250	120	210	112	185	83	165	86	135	78	110	62	100	51	.....	44
	Chicago, Ill	1,602	335	165	310	146	260	132	215	122	190	90	172½	95	142½	86	115	69	105	57	.....	49

TABLE 176.—COMPARISON OF LOCAL FREIGHT RATES CHARGED BY THE DENVER AND RIO GRANDE RAILROAD FROM DENVER, COLO., TO STATIONS NAMED DURING 1887 AND 1893.

[Governed by Western classification.]

Distance.	From Denver Colo., to—	Classes (rates in cents per 100 pounds).																			
		1.		2.		3.		4.		5.		A.		B.		C.		D.		E.	
		1887.	1893.	1887.	1893.	1887.	1893.	1887.	1893.	1887.	1893.	1887.	1893.	1887.	1893.	1887.	1893.	1887.	1893.	1887.	1893.
Miles.																					
277	Leadville, Colo	140	125	125	115	115	105	100	95	85	80	80	75	70	65	50	60	45	40	45	40
456	Grand Junction, Colo	260	200	245	175	225	140	195	109	165	105	130	105	125	90	82	77	72	50	72	50
502	Durango, Colo	265	185	245	170	230	145	200	120	170	105	130	105	125	75	85	65	75	55	75	55
547	Silverton, Colo	300	215	280	195	265	170	230	145	200	130	150	130	145	95	100	70	90	60	90	60

TABLE 177.—COMPARISON OF LOCAL FREIGHT RATES CHARGED BY THE ATLANTIC AND PACIFIC RAILROAD BETWEEN ALBUQUERQUE, N. MEX., AND STATIONS NAMED, DURING 1887 AND 1893.

[1887, Local classification; 1893, Western classification.]

Distance.	From Albuquerque N. M., to—	Year.	Classes (rates in cents per 100 pounds).									
			1.	2.	3.	4.	5.	A.	B.	C.	D.	E.
Miles.												
286	Winslow, Ariz	1887	195	177	153	138	123	115	90	80	.....	....
		1893	157	143	127	106	93	88	63	49	47	44
344	Flagstaff, Ariz	1887	220	200	173	157	138	131	100	89	.....	....
		1893	168	153	131	109	96	95	66	53	50	47
401	Ash Fork, Ariz	1887	242	219	189	168	147	141	107	97	.....	....
		1893	175	159	136	112	98	100	72	58	53	49
575	The Needles, Cal	1887	312	277	241	201	172	169	126	112	.....	....
		1893	205	182	157	127	106	114	86	70	63	58
735	Daggett, Cal	1887	338	302	262	221	191	187	138	124	.....	....
		1893	258	237	181	149	123	130	104	84	74	73
744	Barstow, Cal	1887	340	303	263	222	192	188	139	125	.....	....
		1893	260	240	182	150	124	130	105	85	75	74
815	Mojave, Cal	1887	352	312	272	232	201	195	144	130	.....	....
		1893	294	254	190	155	130	140	120	95	85	80

TABLE 178.—COMPARISON OF LOCAL FREIGHT RATES CHARGED BY THE ATLANTIC AND PACIFIC RAILROAD BETWEEN MOJAVE, CAL., AND STATIONS NAMED, DURING 1887 AND 1893.

Distance.	From Mojave, Cal., to—	Year.	Classes (rates in cents per 100 pounds.									
			1.	2.	3.	4.	5.	A.	B.	C.	D.	E.
Miles.												
71	Barstow, Cal	1887	54	52	50	49	47	47	35	31	.....	....
		1893	54	52	50	49	47	47	35	31	31	24
80	Daggett, Cal	1887	60	58	56	54	52	52	38	34	.....	....
		1893	60	58	56	54	52	52	38	34	34	26
240	The Needles, Cal	1887	163	154	132	120	106	101	75	69	.....	....
		1893	163	143	113	95	85	85	75	57	52	46
414	Ash Fork, Ariz	1887	255	230	199	173	151	146	107	96	.....	....
		1893	210	180	151	113	102	107	92	77	65	53
471	Flagstaff, Ariz	1887	280	251	217	184	160	154	114	100	.....	....
		1893	225	215	170	120	106	113	97	81	68	58
657	Gallup, N. Mex	1887	327	292	254	214	182	177	132	118	.....	....
		1893	268	235	184	142	120	128	110	92	79	71
815	Albuquerque, N. Mex	1887	352	313	272	232	201	195	144	130	.....	....
		1893	294	254	190	155	130	140	120	95	85	80

TABLE 179.—COMPARISON OF FREIGHT RATES CHARGED FOR THE TRANSPORTATION OF CLASSIFIED TRAFFIC FROM GALVESTON, TEX., TO STATIONS NAMED, VIA INTERNATIONAL AND GREAT NORTHERN RAILROAD AND TEXAS AND PACIFIC RAILWAY DURING 1893 WITH THOSE IN EFFECT DURING 1887.

1887, Joint Texas classification; 1893, Western classification.

Distance.	From Galveston, Tex., to—	Year.	Classes (rates in cents per 100 pounds).									
			1.	2.	3.	4.	5.	A.	B.	C.	D.	E.
Miles.												
594	Sweetwater, Tex	1887	115	105	91	82	.....	65	59	51	42	30
		1893	110	102	88	76	60	66	57	48	38	29
613	Lorraine, Tex	1887	115	105	91	82	.....	65	59	51	42	30
		1893	110	102	88	76	60	66	57	48	38	29
660	Big Springs, Tex	1887	135	123	101	92	.....	75	69	56	46	35
		1893	135	120	110	97	77	79	72	56	45	37
720	Odessa, Tex	1887	167	153	131	122	.....	100	92	75	59	45
		1893	135	120	110	103	77	79	72	56	45	38
793	Pecos City, Tex	1887	197	180	156	133	.....	111	100	81	67	48
		1893	135	120	110	103	77	79	72	56	45	38
811	Toyah, Tex	1887	202	185	160	136	.....	113	102	84	70	51
		1893	135	120	110	103	77	79	72	56	45	38
832	San Martine, Tex	1887	206	189	163	139	.....	116	104	90	72	55
		1893	135	120	110	103	77	79	72	56	45	38
881	Van Horn, Tex	1887	219	199	173	149	.....	126	109	94	75	60
		1893	135	120	110	103	77	79	72	56	45	38
908	Arispe, Tex	1887	230	208	182	157	.....	133	113	94	75	62
		1893	135	120	110	103	77	79	72	56	45	38

TABLE 180.—COMPARISON OF FREIGHT RATES CHARGED BY THE TEXAS AND PACIFIC RAILWAY FROM NEW ORLEANS TO STATIONS NAMED, DURING 1887 AND 1893.

[1887, Joint Texas classification; 1893, Western classification.]

Distance.	From New Orleans, La., to—	Year.	Classes (rates in cents per 100 pounds).									
			1.	2.	3.	4.	5.	A.	B.	C.	D.	E.
Miles.												
562	Iona, Tex	1887	128	112	96	85	.....	71	64	59	49	44
		1893	123	107	92	83	66	69	61	51	40	33
565	Aledo, Tex	1887	128	112	96	85	.....	71	64	59	49	44
		1893	123	107	92	83	66	69	61	51	40	33
578	Weatherford, Tex	1887	130	114	98	87	.....	72	65	60	50	45
		1893	123	107	92	83	66	69	61	51	40	33
602	Brazos, Tex	1887	140	124	108	92	.....	77	70	65	55	47
		1893	123	107	92	83	66	69	61	51	40	33
628	Strawn, Tex	1887	150	132	115	102	.....	82	75	70	60	47
		1893	123	107	92	83	66	69	61	51	40	33
662	Cisco, Tex	1887	150	132	115	102	.....	82	75	70	60	47
		1893	123	107	92	83	66	69	61	51	40	33
682	Vigo, Texas	1887	150	132	115	102	.....	82	75	70	60	47
		1893	123	107	92	83	66	69	61	51	40	33
708	Abilene, Tex	1887	150	132	115	102	.....	82	75	70	60	47
		1893	123	107	92	83	66	69	61	51	40	33
749	Sweetwater, Tex	1887	175	153	133	112	.....	92	85	80	65	49
		1893	135	119	102	87	70	76	67	61	50	40
767	Lorraine, Tex	1887	183	158	137	116	.....	96	89	82	67	50
		1893	135	119	102	87	70	76	67	61	50	40
816	Big Springs, Tex	1887	200	174	148	127	.....	107	100	88	71	55
		1893	160	137	123	108	85	88	82	69	57	48
837	Marionfeld, Tex	1887	210	184	158	137	.....	117	105	90	73	58
		1893	160	137	123	112	85	88	82	69	57	49
876	Odessa, Tex	1887	226	200	174	146	.....	126	112	94	77	62
		1893	160	137	123	112	85	88	82	69	57	49
948	Pecos City, Tex	1887	250	224	193	162	.....	142	125	100	85	65
		1893	160	137	123	112	85	88	82	69	57	49
968	Toyah, Tex	1887	255	229	198	167	.....	147	130	103	88	68
		1893	160	137	123	112	85	88	82	69	57	49
988	San Martine, Tex	1887	260	239	206	175	.....	153	136	109	93	72
		1893	160	137	123	112	85	88	82	69	57	49
1,042	Van Horn, Tex	1887	260	240	215	180	.....	158	143	113	93	79
		1893	160	137	123	112	85	88	82	69	57	49
1,066	Arispe, Tex	1887	265	245	215	180	.....	158	143	113	93	82
		1893	160	137	123	112	85	88	82	69	57	49

TABLE 181.—COMPARISON OF LOCAL FREIGHT RATES CHARGED BETWEEN NEW ORLEANS AND STATIONS NAMED, BY THE SOUTHERN PACIFIC COMPANY DURING 1887 AND 1893.

[Subject to Western classification.]

Distance.	Between New Orleans, La., and—	Year.	Classes (rates in cents per 100 pounds).									
			1.	2.	3.	4.	5.	A.	B.	C.	D.	E.
Miles.												
1,217	Rogers, N. Mex	1887	290	265	230	195	170	150	120	95	85	85
		1893	139	124	113	105	79	82	76	63	51	43
1,239	Lanark, N. Mex	1887	290	265	230	195	170	150	120	95	85	85
		1893	155	140	129	121	93	96	87	72	60	52
1,274	Cambray, N. Mex	1887	290	265	230	195	170	150	120	95	85	85
		1893	182	165	152	143	116	119	103	87	75	62
1,300	Deming, N. Mex	1887	290	265	230	195	170	150	120	95	85	85
		1893	202	184	171	151	120	130½	114	94	75	64
1,360	Lordsburg, N. Mex	1887	304	278	242	205	179	158	126	100	90	90
		1893	228	205	185	169	144	150	124	102	90	81
1,394	San Simon, Ariz	1887	313	286	249	211	183	162	130	103	92	92
		1893	254	229	209	192	164	161	128	105	92	92
1,434	Willcox, Ariz	1887	322	295	256	217	189	167	134	106	95	95
		1893	282	257	235	196	174	166	132	108	95	95
1,474	Benson, Ariz	1887	332	304	264	224	195	173	138	110	98	98
		1893	312	283	250	196	174	172	136	112	98	98
1,491	Pantano, Ariz	1887	336	308	268	227	197	175	140	111	100	100
		1893	325	283	250	196	174	174	138	113	100	99
1,519	Tucson, Ariz	1887	343	314	273	231	202	179	143	114	102	102
		1893	325	283	250	196	174	175	141	116	102	99
1,585	Casa Grande, Ariz	1887	359	329	286	242	211	187	149	119	107	107
		1893	325	283	250	196	174	175	147	121	107	99
1,611	Maricopa, Ariz	1887	365	335	291	247	215	190	152	121	109	109
		1893	325	283	250	196	174	175	150	124	109	99

TABLE 182.—COMPARISON OF LOCAL FREIGHT RATES CHARGED BY THE KANSAS CITY, FORT SCOTT AND MEMPHIS RAILROAD BETWEEN MEMPHIS, TENN., AND STATIONS NAMED DURING 1886 AND 1893.

[Subject to Western classification.]

Distance.	Between Memphis, Tenn., and—	Year.	Classes (rates in cents per 100 pounds).													
			1.	2.	3.	4.	5.	6.	A.	B.	C.	D.	E.	Packing house products.	Wheat.	Corn.
Miles.																
66	Jonesboro, Ark	1886	55	45	35	30	25	25	20	15	12	12	....	....	....	....
		1893	51	44	34	27	22	....	21	17	13	10	6	10	10	10
172	West Plains, Mo	1886	70	60	50	40	35	35	30	25	20	20	....	....	....	....
		1893	70	60	50	40	30	....	30	24	20	16	11	25	16	15
285	Springfield, Mo	1886	80	70	60	45	40	40	31	26	22	22	....	....	....	....
		1893	70	60	50	40	30	....	30	25	20	17	14	25	16	16
348	Lamar, Mo	1886	100	80	60	45	40	40	37	32	25	25	....	....	....	....
		1893	85	65	50	40	30	....	33	28	22	18	17	25	22	20
388	Fort Scott, Kans	1886	100	80	60	45	40	40	40	35	27	27	....	....	....	....
		1893	85	65	50	40	30	....	33	28	22	18	17	25	22	20
444	Paola, Kans	1886	105	85	65	55	45	45	45	40	27	27	....	....	....	....
		1893	85	65	50	40	30	....	33	28	22	18	17	25	22	20

TABLE 183.—COMPARISON OF RATES CHARGED FOR THE TRANSPORTATION OF CLASSIFIED FREIGHT FROM ST. LOUIS TO POINTS NAMED BY THE MISSOURI PACIFIC RAILWAY DURING 1883 AND 1893.

[Governed by Western classification.]

Distance.	From St. Louis, Mo., to—	1883. / 1893.	Classes (rates in cents per 100 pounds).															
			1. / 1.	2. / 2.	3. / 3.	4. / 4.	5. / 5.	6. / A.	A. / B.	B. / C.	C. / D.	D. / E.	Wheat, carloads.	Corn, carloads.	Horses and mules.	Cattle.	Hogs.	Sheep.
Miles.																		
188	Sedalia, Mo ...	1883.	70	55	40	27	25	20	25	22	18	18	18	15	*$37.00	*$35.00	*$30.00	*$28.00
		1893.	50	40	29	22	17	19½	16	13½	11	10	14	11½	*39.00	13¾	15	15½
283	Kansas C'y, Mo	1883.	70	55	40	27	23	...	25	22	18	18	....	....	......	......	......	......
		1893.	55	40	32	25	20	22½	17½	15	12½	11	18	14	*50.00	20	15	21½
463	Wichita, Kans	1883.	152	127	102	78	68	65	65	49	41	41	41	29	*75.00	*70.00	*67.50	*60.00
		1893.	115	93	78	62½	53	52	39½	33	27	22	25	20	*65.00	28¾	35	34
485	Concordia, Ks.	1883.	125	105	85	65	63	60	51½	43	33	33	36.4	27.2	*82.00	*75.00	*61.50	*54.50
		1893.	106	85½	70	55	46	47½	35½	30½	23½	18½	23	18	*60.00	27¼	32	32½
414	Auburn, Nebr	1883.	86	67	50	36	31	28	34½	29	24	24	....	....	*67.50	*57.50	*62.00	*45.00
		1893.	55	40	32	25	20	22½	17½	15	12½	11	14	14	*50.00	20	20	22¼

* Per car.

TABLE 184.—COMPARISON OF LOCAL FREIGHT RATES CHARGED BY THE LOUISVILLE AND NASHVILLE RAILROAD FROM CINCINNATI TO STATIONS NAMED UPON CLASSES 1, 2, 3, AND 4, AND ALSO UPON FLOUR AND BACON DURING 1886 AND 1893.

[1886 Local classification. 1893 Southern Railway and Steamship Association classification.]

Distance.	From Cincinnati, Ohio, to—	Classes (rates in cents per 100 pounds).								Rates in cents per barrel.				Rates in cents per 100 pounds.	
		1.		2.		3.		4.		Flour, less than car loads.		Flour, car loads		Bacon, any quantity.	
		1886	1893	1886	1893	1886	1893	1886	1893	1886	1893	1886	1893	1886	1893
Miles.															
1	Newport, Ky	5	5	5	5	5	5	5	5	8	6	6	6	5	5
5	Milldale, Ky	9	9	8	8	7	7	6	6	10	8	8	8	6	6
17	Bank Lick, Ky	12	12	11	11	10	10	8	8	14	12	12	12	8	8
40	Glencoe, Ky	25	29	20	25	18	22	15	19	24	22	20	22	15	17
52	Eagle, Ky	30	32	26	27	24	24	20	21	32	24	26	24	20	19
56	Worthville, Ky	30	24	26	20	24	19	20	18	32	24	26	24	20	16
69	Campbellsburg, Ky	35	37	30	32	25	28	22	25	36	28	30	28	22	22
77	Pendleton, Ky	35	41	30	35	25	31	22	28	36	32	30	32	22	24
83	La Grange, Ky	40	41	35	35	30	31	25	28	40	32	34	32	25	24
98	Anchorage, Ky	40	38	35	33	30	29	25	26	40	30	34	30	25	22
106	Crescent Hill, Ky	40	35	35	30	30	26	25	23	40	28	34	28	25	19
110	Louisville, Ky	....	25	....	20	....	15	....	10	....	10	....	8	....	....
116	Strawberry, Ky	37	35	30	30	24	26	17	23	28	28	26	28	17	19
123	Brooks, Ky	40	38	33	33	27	29	19	26	32	30	30	30	19	22
135	Belmont, Ky	47	46	39	40	31	34	23	30	40	36	38	36	23	26
144	Colesburg, Ky	55	52	45	45	36	39	28	34	48	40	44	40	28	30
149	Tunnel Hill, Ky	57	55	48	47	40	41	30	36	50	42	46	42	30	32
152	Elizabethtown, Ky	57	55	48	46	40	37	30	30	50	38	46	32	30	18
160	Glendale, Ky	60	58	50	50	42	44	31	38	52	44	48	44	31	34
183	Munfordville, Ky	72	70	61	61	51	53	37	47	62	48	58	48	37	40
191	Horse Cave, Ky	72	72	63	62	52	54	38	48	62	48	58	48	38	40
200	Glasgow Junction Ky	74	74	64	64	55	55	40	50	64	50	60	50	40	41
210	Smiths Grove, Ky	76	76	65	65	56	56	40	51	66	50	62	50	40	42
219	Bristow, Ky	78	78	65	67	57	57	40	52	66	52	62	52	40	43
224	Bowling Green, Ky	80	78	65	67	57	58	40	52	66	52	62	52	40	43
232	Rich Pond, Ky	80	78	65	67	57	58	40	52	66	52	62	52	40	43
269	Gallatin, Tenn	80	78	65	67	57	58	40	48	66	52	62	52	40	38
274	Pilot Knob, Tenn	80	76	65	67	57	56	40	46	66	52	62	52	40	36
280	Hendersonville, Tenn	80	68	65	61	57	51	40	42	66	46	62	46	40	32
290	Maplewood, Tenn	80	65	65	58	57	48	40	39	66	44	62	44	40	29
295	Nashville, Tenn	53	53	48	48	39	39	31	31	35	34	35	34	27	23
306	Brentwood Tenn	72	65	58	58	48	48	36	39	58	44	56	44	36	29
315	Franklin, Tenn	80	67	64	61	53	51	40	42	66	48	64	48	40	32

TABLE 184.—COMPARISON OF LOCAL FREIGHT RATES CHARGED BY THE LOUISVILLE AND NASHVILLE RAILROAD, ETC.—Continued.

Distance.	From Cincinnati, Ohio, to—	Classes (rates in cents per 100 pounds).								Rates in cents per barrel.				Rates in cents per 100 pounds.	
		1.		2.		3.		4.		Flour, less than car-loads.		Flour, car-loads.		Bacon, any quantity.	
		1886	1893	1886	1893	1886	1893	1886	1893	1886	1893	1886	1893	1886	1893
Miles.															
342	Columbia, Tenn	97	78	80	68	68	57	50	48	84	58	76	58	40	38
382	Aspen Hill, Tenn	106	99	88	83	70	65	56	60	90	60	84	60	56	45
395	Elkmont, Ala	106	99	88	83	70	65	56	60	90	60	84	60	56	37
414	Harris, Ala	106	97	88	82	70	65	56	60	90	53	84	53	56	30
417	Decatur, Ala	92	85	80	72	72	65	58	54	72	43	72	43	44	24
440	Wilhite, Ala	118	106	95	87	76	68	62	63	96	61	90	61	62	37
470	Blount Springs, Ala	125	108	100	88	80	69	65	64	100	66	100	66	65	47
480	Warrior, Ala	125	108	100	88	80	69	65	64	100	62	100	62	65	46
504	Birmingham, Ala	108	89	102	79	88	68	71	55	56	40	56	40	33	33
510	Oxmoor, Ala	117	89	105	79	85	68	70	55	110	40	106	40	70	33
521	Helena, Ala	125	109	110	90	85	70	70	65	110	58	106	58	70	44
537	Calera, Ala	108	110	102	90	88	70	71	65	56	68	56	68	40	49
548	Jemison, Ala	135	110	110	90	85	70	70	65	110	70	106	70	70	54
568	Verbena, Ala	138	113	120	92	90	72	75	67	116	66	116	66	75	50
588	Elmore, Ala	123	113	115	92	90	72	75	67	116	56	116	56	75	42
600	Montgomery, Ala	108	108	102	102	88	88	71	71	56	40	56	40	33	33
616	Morganville, Ala	128	113	118	102	90	88	75	71	120	58	120	58	75	44
633	Fort Deposit, Ala	138	113	120	102	90	88	75	71	120	66	120	66	75	50
681	Evergreen, Ala	155	116	130	102	100	88	85	71	130	82	130	82	85	57
719	Flomaton, Ala	160	120	135	102	105	88	85	71	134	83	132	83	85	52
755	Bay Minnette, Ala	160	120	135	102	105	88	85	71	134	69	132	69	85	42
775	Magazine Point, Ala	160	110	135	93	105	82	85	62	134	59	132	59	85	33
780	Mobile, Ala	83	98	73	83	63	73	44	54	56	49	56	49	31	27
820	Scranton, Miss	165	124	140	106	110	88	91	71	138	69	138	69	91	42
841	Biloxi, Miss	165	124	140	106	110	88	91	71	138	69	138	69	91	42
862	Pass Christian, Miss	165	124	140	106	110	88	91	71	138	69	138	69	91	42
901	Chef Menteur, Miss	170	118	145	100	115	88	94	67	142	63	142	63	94	38
912	Lee, Miss	170	110	145	93	115	82	94	62	142	59	142	59	94	33
921	New Orleans, La	83	98	73	83	63	73	44	54	44	49	44	49	26	27

TABLE 185.—COMPARISON OF LOCAL FREIGHT RATES CHARGED BY THE SAVANNAH, FLORIDA AND WESTERN RAILWAY BETWEEN SAVANNAH AND STATIONS NAMED DURING 1886 AND 1893.

[Subject to Southern Railway and Steamship Association classification.]

Distance.	From Savannah, Ga., to—	Classes (rates in cents per 100 pounds).																								Rates in cents per barrel.	
		1.		2.		3.		4.		5.		6.		A.		B.		C.		D.		E.		H.		F.	
		1886.	1893.	1886.	1893.	1886.	1893.	1886.	1893.	1886.	1893.	1886.	1893.	1886.	1893.	1886.	1893.	1886.	1803.	1886.	1893.	1886.	1893.	1886.	1893.	1886.	1893.
Miles.																											
86	Blackshear, Ga	59	45	53	41	46	35	41	32	31	24	24	19	24	19	17	19	11	11	10	10	31	24	40	32	21½	21½
122	Homerville, Ga	70	59	60	57	53	45	43	36	34	29	27	23	27	23	21	23	12½	12½	12	12	34	29	43	36	25½	25½
130	Dupont, Ga	70	63	60	53	53	47	43	37	34	30	27	24	27	24	21	24	12½	13	12	12½	34	30	43	37	25½	26½
166	Ousley, Ga	80	70	67	59	59	52	46	41	38	33	31	28	31	28	25	28	15½	15½	14½	14½	38	33	46	41	31	31
210	Quitman, Ga	83	73	70	62	60	53	48	42	39	34	33	29	33	29	26	29	15½	15½	14½	14½	39	34	48	42	31	31
224	Boston, Ga	85	75	73	64	61	54	49	43	39	35	34	30	34	30	27	30	16½	16½	15½	15½	39	35	49	43	33	33
236	Thomasville, Ga	85	78	74	68	61	56	49	45	39	36	34	31	34	31	27	31	16½	17	15½	16	39	36	49	45	33	33½
279	Faceville, Ga	90	83	84	77	66	61	54	50	42	39	36	33	36	33	30	33	19	19	18	18	42	39	54	50	38	38
294	Chattahoochee, Fla	75	75	60	60	50	50	45	45	40	39	35	33	20	20	30	30	20	19	18	18	40	39	45	45	40	38

www.ingramcontent.com/pod-product-compliance
Lightning Source LLC
LaVergne TN
LVHW010552110826
845149LV00003B/636

* 9 7 8 1 4 1 8 1 8 7 6 6 8 *